TITLE TO TERRITORY IN AFRICA

TITLE TO TERRITORY IN AFRICA

International Legal Issues

MALCOLM SHAW

CLARENDON PRESS · OXFORD

This book has been printed digitally and produced in a standard specification in order to ensure its continuing availability

OXFORD
UNIVERSITY PRESS

Great Clarendon Street, Oxford OX2 6DP

Oxford University Press is a department of the University of Oxford.
It furthers the University's objective of excellence in research, scholarship,
and education by publishing worldwide in

Oxford New York

Auckland Cape Town Dar es Salaam Hong Kong Karachi
Kuala Lumpur Madrid Melbourne Mexico City Nairobi
New Delhi Shanghai Taipei Toronto
With offices in
Argentina Austria Brazil Chile Czech Republic France Greece
Guatemala Hungary Italy Japan South Korea Poland Portugal
Singapore Switzerland Thailand Turkey Ukraine Vietnam

Oxford is a registered trade mark of Oxford University Press
in the UK and in certain other countries

Published in the United States
by Oxford University Press Inc., New York

Reprinted 2011

ISBN 978-0-19-825379-2

Printed and bound in Great Britain by CPI Antony Rowe,
Chippenham and Eastbourne

For my Parents

PAULETTE AND BEN SHAW

Preface

THIS work is a revised, updated, and reduced version of my Ph.D thesis on 'International Law and Title to Territory in Africa'. It was undertaken under the supervision of Dr Michael Akehurst of Keele University and to him go my deep thanks for his patience, encouragement, and helpful comments. I am very grateful for our many stimulating conversations. My thanks also go to Professor Ian Brownlie who was the external examiner for the thesis and whose suggestions subsequently were most gratefully received.

A work of this sort relies very heavily on library and other sources for primary materials. I could not have obtained the range of materials that I did without the help of the libraries of Liverpool Polytechnic, Keele University, and Essex University. The help of Mr Peter Luther at the latter institution is particularly acknowledged. In addition, of course, the operations of the inter-library loan service proved invaluable. I am very grateful to many colleagues and friends with whom I have discussed the project over the last few years. Their help was most welcome.

I am also very grateful to Miss V Jennings, Mrs G Primrose, and Mrs C Benner for their indispensable secretarial assistance. The ability to transfer rough handwriting to polished typescript can only be justly appreciated by those who have been through the mill. A debt of gratitude is also owed to Miss D. Gomien who with her customary flair and dedication has prepared the Index and Table of Cases. My thanks are also due to the Editors of the *British Year Book of International Law*, the *Year Book of World Affairs*, the *Liverpool Law Review*, and the *Netherlands Year Book of International Law* for their permission to reproduce material that first appeared in those journals.

Lastly, but most importantly, I owe a very deep debt to my family. My children, Talia, Ilan, and Daniella, had to put up with a father forever disappearing into studies or libraries, while my wife Judith provided indispensable encouragement, support, and enthusiasm. Without her assistance it is doubtful that this work would have been completed.

The work has taken account of material available as at spring 1984.

March 1984 MALCOLM SHAW

Contents

Abbreviations

AD	*Annual Digest of Public International Law Cases*
AFDI	*Annuaire français de droit international*
AJIL	*American Journal of International Law*
ARB	*Africa Research Bulletin*
BFSP	*British and Foreign State Papers*
BYBIL	*British Year Book of International Law*
CLJ	*Cambridge Law Journal*
ECOSOC OR	*Economic and Social Council Official Records*
GAOR	*General Assembly Official Records*
HR	*Recueil des cours de l'académie de droit international, The Hague*
ICJ Reports	*Reports of the International Court of Justice*
ICLQ	*International Law and Comparative Law Quarterly*
IJIL	*Indian Journal of International Law*
ILA	*International Law Association*
ILM	*International Legal Materials*
ILR	*International Law Reports*
JMAS	*Journal of Modern African Studies*
KCA	*Keeting's Contemporary Archives*
LNOJ	*League of Nations Official Journal*
LNTS	*League of Nations Treaty Series*
LQR	*Law Quarterly Review*
MLR	*Modern Law Review*
PASIL	*Proceedings of the American Society of International Law*
PCIJ	*Permanent Court of International Justice*
RIAA	*Reports of International Arbitral Awards*
SCOR	*Security Council Official Records*
UNC	*United Nations Chronicle*
UNMC	*United Nations Monthly Chronicle*
UNTS	*United Nations Treaty Series*
YBWA	*Year Book of World Affairs*
Yearbook of the ILC	*Yearbook of the International Law Commission*
Yearbook of the UN	*Yearbook of the United Nations*

INTRODUCTION
Territory in International Law

THE international community is formed first and foremost by States, which are defined by Vattel as 'political bodies, societies of men who have united together and combined their forces in order to procure their mutual welfare and security'.[1] The element missing from this definition relates to the need for a territorial basis for such political bodies. This necessity, however, is self-evident. As Oppenheim has noted, 'a State without a territory is not possible'.[2] This does not mean that territoriality is a criterion of personality in international law, but statehood is inconceivable in the absence of a reasonably defined geographical base. The frontiers of such an entity need not be established beyond dispute, nor is there any prescribed minimum of territory for the existence of a State, but some piece of land is essential before one can accept the establishment and continuation of a State.

Territory is, of course, itself a geographical conception relating to physical areas of the globe, but its centrality in law and international law in particular derives from the fact that it constitutes the tangible framework for the manifestation of power by the accepted authorities of the State in question. The principle whereby such a State is deemed to exercise exclusive power over its territory can be seen as a fundamental axiom of classical international law.[3] More than this, Hill declares that 'international relations in their more vital aspects revolve about the possession of territory'.[4] This crucial role, thus played by territory and its attendant legal concepts, has been evident in all stages of the development of international law and changes in the nature and structure of international law cannot but be expressed in the light of this fact.

1. *The Role of Territory*

The notion of territory as an essential element in the sovereignty of a particular society geographically located was known to the ancient Greeks.[5] The Roman attitude was predicated upon the creation and defence of a large empire, with relatively fluid borders, and subsisted in the light of a belief in the universality of its domination, but the post-Roman era saw for many reasons, including religion, the rise of the concept of society as based primarily upon personal allegiance rather than territory. As Gottmann puts it, 'for a millennium the significance of territory in Europe was to be reduced to a very little indeed, even on the local scale'.[6] Political and social life revolved around individual and tribal allegiance to a sovereign and to the Church. From about the fourteenth century communities began to be seen in terms of territorial entities and the notion of a State as understood in contemporary thought began to develop.[7] It was, however, the Peace of Westphalia of 1648 that marked a crucial point in the creation of modern international law, based as it has been upon defined territorial units.[8] The Treaties of Westphalia taken as a whole may be regarded as the first sustained attempt to establish a world order 'on the basis of States exercising untrammelled sovereignty over certain territories and subordinated to no earthly authority'.[9] This order involved the recognition of all independent States as having equal rights of sovereign jurisdiction over a determined territory. This sovereign equality of States was founded upon the exclusivity of action of each State within its defined territory and the right of all States to participate within the sphere of international relations. Since such States were territorially delineated, the introduction of the Westphalia system marked the demise of the concept of personal allegiance as the foundation of political society. But the break between the two was not clean. The concept of sovereignty drew to some extent upon the ideas associated with feudalism, since the latter defined power in terms of territory,[10] while the state developed into the framework and symbol of national identity to which citizens owed a form of personal allegiance. Nevertheless, the development of international law upon the basis of the exclusive authority of the State within an accepted territorial framework meant that territory became, as O'Connell has suggested, 'perhaps the fundamental concept of international law'.[11] From this Westphalian view it follows logically that 'this problem of the legal ordering of territorial stability and territorial change lies at the heart of the whole problem of the legal ordering of international society'.[12] The Westphalian concept of the territorial sovereign State, therefore, has remained the basis of most analyses of international law, although not without challenge. Before the territorial basis of international society is further considered, however, a few comments will be made regarding the functions of territory.

Gottmann specifies two main functions, viz. the need for a shelter for security, and the possibility of acting as a springboard for opportunity. Both these functions require an internal organization of the territory and a subsequent organization of its external relations.[13] They are complementary in that once a community feels secure in its land, it will seek to develop relations with other communities, but both processes are closely linked. One influences and sometimes determines the other. The nature of a community's success in achieving a measure of stable tenure over its territory will often have a profound impact upon neighbouring societies, both in a positive sense as an example and in a negative sense as an area for satisfaction of acquisitive instincts. On the other hand, the search for security may conflict with the desire for developing horizons of opportunity. Self-sufficiency and international intercourse do not always complement each other. The concept of territory will not only express the power balance between coexisting or competing entities, it also reflects the relationship between the people and the geographical space they inhabit. The mystical nature of territory is not a new phenomenon. It was known and manifested in religious terms in the civilizations of Egypt, Greece, ancient Israel, and Rome.[14] Modern nationalism in the vast majority of cases points a deep, almost spiritual, connection between land and people. This can be related to the basic psychological needs of mankind, in terms of the need for security and a sense of group identity, for instance. Scelle has written that 'the concern for the preservation of habitat exists as a passionate psychological reflex in all human communities'.[15] Gottmann declares that territory is a 'psychosomatic phenomenon of the community',[16] since it is intimately involved in the purposes and aims of the particular society in question, as perceived by its inhabitants. Territory is the physical aspect of the life of the community as an entity and therefore reflects and conditions the identity of that community. It has also been the prime means by which in modern international relations peoples have conducted their external affairs.

Territory therefore plays not only a definitional role, but a constitutive one historically as well. It is the link between a people, its identity as a State, and its international role. It has thus been of crucial importance in Westphalian international law, and even more so since the American and French revolutions in the eighteenth century inaugurated the era of that people–territory nexus recognized as nationalism.

If the notion of territory in international law has evolved in response to the needs of peoples and individuals and as a result of historical developments affecting the world order, and if, as will be seen, fundamental principles of international law reflect and reinforce this, the question arises as to the functions of territory today. As far as security is concerned, modern developments have shown that the mere possession of territory cannot of itself guarantee the protection of its inhabitants. The era of aviation, missiles, and various devices of mass destruction has meant that no State can provide absolute security for its people. Therefore, States have sought to establish their security by other means, such as mutual deterrence, international agreements, international organizations, and so on. Boundaries as the geographical barriers protecting the inhabitants of a territory now play a much more humble role. Modern technology has also meant that the function of territory as a means of excluding the activities of other entities has been much diminished. Pollution and the after-effects of other industrial and scientific advances cannot always be confined within the territorial limits of the State wherein the process takes place. The problem of nuclear fall-out affecting third States is just one further example of this.[17] The growth of multinational industry and the development of international economic institutions has meant that in this sphere also, the power and influence of States within their own territories is much circumscribed. Ball has been quoted as saying that the multinational corporation 'not only promises the most efficient use of world resources, but as an institution it poses the greatest challenge to the power of the nation-State since the temporal position of the Roman Church began to decline in the 15th century'.[18]

These factors have led a number of writers to postulate the decline of the Westphalian system of international law based fundamentally on sovereign territorial States. De Visscher noted that territory, which since the end of the Middle Ages has provided the firmest base for international relations and ensured their stability, no longer possessed the same significance.[19] Gottmann has stressed that the movement toward statehood and national sovereignty based upon exclusive territorial jurisdiction seems to have reached its apogee and that 'by 1970 sovereignty has been by-passed, and a new fluidity has infiltrated the recently shaped map of multiple national States'.[20] Dembinski writes that new technological developments have minimized the importance of the territorial factor,[21] while international law specialists have not really appreciated the changes that have occurred that impinge upon the theory of the supremacy of the territorial State.[22] Indeed, one of the reasons for the failure of international law to adapt to the problem of contemporary international relations is seen as its concentration upon territory as the fundamental concept of international law.[23] This theme has been particularly developed by Falk, who has declared that 'the State system is being superseded by a series of interlocking social, economic, political, technological and ecological tendencies'.[24] The world-order system is moving away from the dominant statist conception enshrined in the

Westphalian model towards one based upon 'an augmented capacity for central guidance and an increased role for non-territorial actors'.[25] In other words, structural changes in the political, economic, social, and cultural environments are altering the fundamental basis upon which the exclusivity of the territorial State developed. As a result of this, the State-centred framework of international law is in the process of being modified to accommodate these changes in the world system. One may add to this the influence of the revival of natural law thinking[26] and the consequent growth of an international co-operation approach as the hallmark of developing functional interdependence.[27] A further consequence has been the growing emphasis upon human rights in international law and the legal protection of individuals and non-State groups.[28] One may note Article 1(2) of the Charter of the United Nations which declared that one of the purposes of the organization was the development of friendly relations among nations based on respect for the principle of equal rights and self-determination of peoples, while Article 1(3) referred to international co-operation in solving international problems of an economic, social, cultural, or humanitarian character and to the promotion and encouragement of respect for human rights and fundamental freedoms for all, without distinction as to race, sex, language, or religion.[29] Such principles are primarily applicable to non-State entities and are therefore illustrative of the move away from the dominance of the territorial concept. The principle of self-determination, which, it is submitted, is now of vital importance with regard to the international law of territory, is specifically stated to be the right of 'all peoples'[30] and is thus not restricted to established sovereign States. The rise and growth of the increasing number of international organizations also underlines the need felt in the world community for co-operation and co-ordination beyond that provided within the strict confines of a rigidly territorially based State system. The range and universality of such institutions bears witness to the defects of the territorial State system.[31] It has also been accepted that the Westphalian State concept of international relations is inadequate for the exploration and exploitation of areas of relative inaccessibility requiring highly advanced technology, the two examples being outer space and the sea-bed and ocean floor of the high seas. In both cases, the international community has declared that the territorial concept is invalid. The Treaty on Principles Governing the Activities of States in the Exploration and Use of Outer Space, 1967,[32] declared that outer space, including the moon and other celestial bodies, was not subject to national appropriation by claim of sovereignty and that its exploration and use was to be for the benefit of mankind as a whole. Celestial bodies were to be used solely for peaceful purposes and no weapons of mass destruction were to be placed in outer space or in orbit around the Earth.[33] As far as the deep sea-bed is concerned, the Declaration of Principles governing the Sea-Bed and the Ocean Floor and the Subsoil thereof, Beyond the Limits of National Jurisdiction, 1970,[34] stated that the area in question, as well as its resources, were the 'common heritage of mankind' and were not subject to appropriation by States or persons and that no State could claim or exercise sovereignty or sovereign rights over any part thereof.[35] The recourse to a collectivist doctrine of use in the one case and ownership and use in the other reveals the perceived limitations of the territorial doctrine. Certain interests were deemed common to all mankind and a territorial solution deemed inappropriate, impossible, and inequitable.

2. *The Territorial Exclusivity of the State*

It thus appears that trends are emerging in international relations challenging or at least restraining the dominant territorial conception of world affairs. It remains to be seen how far such trends have become enshrined in contemporary international law. But first one must note the extent of State territory. It clearly includes its land areas, subterranean areas, waters, rivers, lakes, the airspace above the land, etc., and the territorial sea. The exclusive economic zone concept would not, it appears, fall within the territory of a State.[36]

Oppenheim declares that in addition to the 'real parts' of State territory, there exist also certain 'fictional parts'. As examples, he cites the cases of the official residence of foreign diplomatic envoys, public vessels on the high seas and in territorial waters of foreign States, and merchant vessels on the high seas.[37] However, this would appear to involve a confusion between territory and jurisdiction. A State may exercise its jurisdiction perfectly legitimately in situations that are not to be classified as territorial. There is no requirement in international law for State territory to be geographically indivisible and contiguous. Pakistan prior to 1971 was divided into two widely separated geographical parts.[38]

Many of the most fundamental principles of international law are predicated upon the concept of the territorial exclusivity of the State, and are aimed at protecting it. The sovereignty and equality of States, the 'basic constitutional doctrine of the law of nations' in Brownlie's words,[39] involves a number of crucial propositions. These were expressed in the

1970 Declaration on Principles of International Law in the following terms:

> All States enjoy sovereign equality. They have equal rights and duties and are equal members of the international community, notwithstanding differences of an economic, social, political or other nature. In particular, sovereign equality includes the following elements: (*a*) States are juridically equal; (*b*) Each State enjoys the rights inherent in full sovereignty; (*c*) Each State has the duty to respect the personality of other States; (*d*) The territorial integrity and political independence of the States are inviolable; (*e*) Each State has the right freely to choose and develop its political, social, economic and cultural systems; (*f*) Each State has the duty to comply fully and in good faith with its international obligations and to live in peace with other States.[40]

The rules relating to the use of force are similarly based on and intended to protect the territorial concept. Article 2(4) of the UN Charter declares that 'all Members shall refrain in their international relations from the threat or use of force against the territorial integrity or political independence of any State'.[41] Article 1 of the Consensus Definition of Aggression adopted in 1974[42] stated that 'aggression is the use of armed force by a State against the sovereignty, territorial integrity or political independence of another State, or in any other manner inconsistent with the Charter of the United Nations, as set out in this definition'.[43] In the sphere of State responsibility for internationally unlawful acts, the International Court of Justice[44] emphasized 'every State's obligation not to allow knowingly its territory to be used for acts contrary to the rights of other States'.[45]

The *Lotus* case emphasized that the exercise of jurisdiction was primarily territorially based,[46] while within its territory, the laws of a State apply to all except where treaty provisions otherwise stipulate.[47] The supremacy of the authority of the territorial law was further noted in the *Diplomatic Asylum* case, in which the court held that 'derogation from territorial sovereignty cannot be recognised unless its legal basis is established in each case', and asylum was such a derogation.[48] The right of passage between Portuguese enclaves over Indian territory was recognized by the International Court as 'subject to full recognition and exercise of Indian sovereignty over the intervening territory and without any immunity in favour of Portugal'.[49] The rules governing recognition and State succession are also closely bound up with the territorial conception of international relations.

Thus, it can be seen that many of the fundamental principles of international law are aimed at the protection and preservation of the dominant statist order founded upon territorial exclusivity. Such a system is by its very nature static, with the use of force constituting one of the most dynamic elements regarding the modification of the existing distribution of territory.[50] The room left for the development and growth of non-State entities within the dominant order was consequently rather limited. Even the League of Nations was primarily aimed at the preservation of international security and thus the freezing of the territorial status quo in the light of the concept of collective security. Members of the League agreed to respect and preserve the territorial integrity and existing political independence of all members against external aggression.[51] However, in this it failed, as the events of the 1930s clearly demonstrated. The Charter of the United Nations marks a change since, as noted above, the concepts of self-determination, human rights, and international social, economic, and cultural co-operation were firmly inserted and further developed via later resolutions, declarations, conferences, etc. However, the United Nations itself is founded upon the sovereign equality of members, the protection of States' territorial integrity, and political independence from the threat or use of force, and maintenance of international peace and security and the provision in Article 2(7) preventing the organization from intervening in matters essentially within the domestic jurisdiction of any State.[52] In the expansion of State jurisdiction and sovereignty this century, it is instructive to note that territorialist conceptions have on the whole prevailed. This is so with regard to the recognition of the sovereignty of States over airspace above their land territory,[53] and with respect to the development of the notions of the contiguous zone, continental shelf, and exclusive economic zone. In the case of the latter concepts, the principle used has not been that of the extension of territory to comprise such areas but rather the recognition of coastal States' 'sovereign rights' with regard to such areas.[54] While this distinction is a very important one, the point to be made is that the concept of *res communis* as applied to the high seas and the deep sea-bed and ocean floor has been progressively whittled away in favour of the extension of State authority and control.[55]

Perhaps the major principle of international law that would appear to have challenged the dominant territorial doctrine with success has been that of self-determination. This principle, deemed applicable to all peoples, has been the legal weapon in the process of decolonizing the European empires.[56] In the process, it ensured that the territory of a colony or other non-self-governing territory was accepted as having under the Charter 'a status separate and distinct from the territory of the State administering it' until such time as the people in question had exercised the right of self-determination.[57] The exercise of the right resulted in the disruption of the recognized territorial sphere of the administering Stage and to that extent proved an exception to the principle of the territorial integrity of existing States. Although Article 2(7) of the UN Charter was pleaded as a way of forestalling UN debates and resolutions on decolonization issues, it came to be accepted that such matters did not fall 'essentially within the domestic jurisdiction' of States.[58] The range of concern of international law had moved beyond, it seemed, territorial exclusivity. Such a view, which may be related to the proposition stated by the Permanent Court of International Justice that the question whether a certain matter is or is not solely within the jurisdiction of a State was an essentially relative question which depended upon the development of international relations,[59] was reflected also in the institution of the mandate and trusteeship systems, for these were predicated upon the creation of a special status for particular territories. This special status involved the division of sovereignty into three distinct entities with varying degrees of powers, viz., the people of the territory, the administering power, and the League of Nations or United Nations.[60] Despite the different categories of mandates and the different formulations of mandate and trust responsibilities,[61] and the reference to non-self-governing territories in the UN Charter,[62] as the International Court of Justice noted, 'the subsequent development of international law ... made the principle of self-determination applicable to all of them'.[63] Therefore, in a sense, the principle of self-determination superseded prior obligations. This does not mean that such obligations ceased to exist, but rather that one could subsume them within the more general category of self-determination. However, self-determination as a legal principle under international law has been restricted to the colonial situation, although it does have greater potential in the light of its meaning in political theory. Where a non-self-governing territory has attained independence, the principle of self-determination coupled with that of territorial integrity will operate to protect the territorial unity and framework of the new State. Indeed, a basic presumption of the application of self-determination is that it will be exercised by the people in question within the territorial framework of the entity as administered by the colonial power before independence. In the light of this, it is to be wondered how far indeed the principle of self-determination has affected the territorial basis of international law. The answer, it appears, is 'not to a substantial extent'. The territorial framework of the non-self-governing entity has been, with only a few exceptions,[64] substantially accepted as the identification pattern for the exercise of the right to self-determination. Once a State has obtained independence, international law imposes a duty upon other States[65] to respect and preserve this territorial arrangement.

It is clear that in a number of areas patterns of functional co-operation have modified the statist-centred conception of international law, while further inroads have been made with regard to the international protection of human rights and self-determination, although in the latter instances, potential for change far exceeds actual change. However, the territorially-based view of international law still retains its position as the fundamental paradigm. It is instructive to note that Third World States are vitally concerned with the maintenance of their independence, and the concept of the sovereign equality of States within a defined territorial sphere is being continually re-emphasized. The first three principles of the Organization of African Unity, as enshrined in Article 3 of the Charter, emphasize the sovereign equality of States, non-interference in the internal affairs of States, and respect for the sovereignty and territorial integrity of each State and for its inalienable right to independent existence. In the field of economic development, which together with decolonization has constituted a prime concern of African as well as other Third World States, the notion of State sovereignty has been declared to be the fundamental principle. In the Charter of Economic Rights and Duties of States,[66] for example, this emerges quite clearly. Article 1 proclaims that States have the sovereign and inalienable right to choose their own economic as well as political, social, and cultural systems without outside interference. Article 2 declares that every State possesses full permanent sovereignty over all its wealth, natural resources, and economic activities and provides that States may regulate foreign investment in their jurisdiction, transnational corporation activities, and nationalizations of foreign property according to their own domestic laws (and therefore not in accordance with international law principles necessarily).[67] While this Charter is not to be taken as part of customary law, and it is not an international convention, it does illustrate how the vast majority of States in the world community see the international legal order in the light of the concept of territorial exclusiveness. The demise of the Westphalian dogma is not therefore imminent. On the contrary, in a number of areas it has been fervently adopted by the newly independent States and other countries of the Third World, in a quite specific manner.

The global, or inter-territorial, approach is, however, of developing importance in certain fields, but not to the extent envisaged by some writers.[68] The two approaches are not exclusive, it should be noted, but may exist side by side as dual tendencies in international life.[69] But it is submitted that the territorial pattern of international law remains the dominant one even if its predominance has been modified.

3. *Territorial Sovereignty*

The concept of territorial sovereignty is concerned with the nature of the authority exercised by the State over its territory. The ideas of territory and sovereignty are closely linked in international law, since the concept of territory itself is concerned with those geographical areas over which sovereignty or sovereign rights may be exercised. Territorial sovereignty is, therefore, centred upon the rights and powers coincident upon territory in the geographical sense. As such it has provided the basis for modern international law.[70] Territorial sovereignty is essential before one can talk of a State. Huber noted in the *Island of Palmas* case, the leading case on the subject, that 'sovereignty in relation to a portion of the surface of the globe is the legal condition necessary for the inclusion of such portion in the territory of any particular State'.[71] Jennings referred to the 'mission and purpose of traditional international law' as being the delimitation of the exercise of sovereign power on a territorial basis,[72] while Judge Huber regarded the principle of the exclusive competence of the State in regard to its own territory as the point of departure in settling most questions that concern international relations.[73] What then is the nature of sovereignty[74] over territory? Brierly emphasized that it refers not to a relation of persons to persons, nor to the independence of the State itself, but to the characteristics of rights over territory and is a convenient way of contrasting 'the fullest rights over territory known to the law' with certain minor territorial rights, for example leases and servitudes.[75] Territorial sovereignty has a positive and a negative aspect. The former relates to the exclusive competence of the State with respect to its own territory, and in Huber's words 'sovereignty in the relation between States signifies independence. Independence in regard to a portion of the globe is the right to exercise therein, to the exclusion of any other State, the functions of a State.'[76] The negative aspect of the notion relates to the obligation to protect within the territory the rights of other States, for instance, regarding their right to integrity and inviolability.[77] Thus territorial sovereignty in fact marks a link between a particular people and a particular territory, so that within that area that people may exercise through the medium of the State its jurisdiction while being distinguished from other peoples exercising jurisdiction over other areas. It consists of a coherent body of rights and duties imposed upon States in relation to specific pieces of territory.[78]

It is important to distinguish the two notions of sovereignty and property here. They may be related to the distinction made in Roman law between *imperium* and *dominium*,[79] which appear to have been subsequently confused with the rise of feudalism.[80] O'Connell believes that as a result of the foundation of common law theories of land in feudal law 'sovereignty and property are indistinguishable conceptions to the Anglo-American lawyer' and held this capable of having repercussions with regard, for example, to the developing law of the sea-bed.[81] International law, however, was built upon the Roman law distinction of *imperium* and *dominium*. Vattel noted that there existed two elements relating to the connection between a nation and the territory it inhabits. The first was ownership, by virtue of which the nation could use the territory for its needs, benefit from it, and dispose of it, and the second was sovereignty or 'the right of supreme jurisdiction by which the nation regulates and controls at will whatever goes on in the territory'.[82] The entire space over which a nation extended its sovereignty and which formed the sphere of its jurisdiction was termed its domain.[83] The distinction between sovereignty and property, or ownership, is an important one and may be related to a variety of needs in international law. As defined, it could help one appreciate the nature of mandated and trusteeship situations, as well as other cases where absolute sovereignty is not in the hands of one State alone. Whether it could be used to solve problems relating to the use of *res communia*, such as the sea-bed, is more doubtful.

The *Western Sahara* case clearly demonstrates that the concept of territorial sovereignty involved far more than personal ties of allegiance between a people and a ruler and certain rights relating to the land in question. While the court accepted that there did exist at the relevant time (the period of Spanish colonization) 'legal ties of allegiance' between the Sultan of Morocco and some of the tribes living in the territory of Western Sahara and 'some rights relating to the land, which constituted legal ties between the Mauritanian entity, as understood by the court, and the territory of Western Sahara', no ties of territorial sovereignty were involved.[84] The differentiating factor in Morocco's case appeared to be the absence of the exercise of effective internal sovereignty over Western Sahara,[85] and in Mauritania's case the fact that the 'Mauritanian entity' did not have the 'character of a personality or corporate entity distinct from the several emirates and tribes which composed it'.[86] Judge Ammoun, however, regarded such personal ties as equivalent to State ties and therefore transmuted, as it were, into ties of territorial sovereignty merely by virtue of the existence of a particular territory relative to the accepted personal ties.[87] This cannot be accepted, for the notion of territory in the context of territorial sovereignty denotes more than the existence of a defined geographical space. It refers additionally to a particular kind of relationship between people and space, as characterized by the existence of an effective governmental authority. As the Commission of Jurists noted in the *Aaland Islands* case,

> if the essential basis of . . . territorial sovereignty is lacking, either because the State is not yet fully formed or because it is undergoing transformation or dissolution, the situation is obscure and uncertain from a legal point of view, and will not become clear until the period of development is completed and a definite new situation, which is normal in respect to territorial sovereignty, has been established.[88]

Thus, the link between territorial sovereignty and statehood becomes manifest. Judge de Castro, on the other hand, took the view that such personal ties as were involved in the Saharan situation as regards both the Sultan of Morocco and the 'Mauritanian entity' could not be regarded as binding ties.[89] Whether such ties could be regarded as legal or not—and it is a complex and difficult issue—they could not affect the decolonization process or the principle of self-determination. This was the court's view, correctly expressed, it is suggested.[90] Such ties, however, could have an influence upon the various procedures concerned in the decolonization process,[91] although what this might amount to was not explored by the court. Presumably, it might affect the nature of any questions that might be asked in a plebiscite seeking the views of the population of the territory on the future political status of the territory in question. As such, these personal ties, etc., cannot be regarded as being of significant importance within the general context of territorial sovereignty.

A number of theories have been elaborated to explain the nature of the relationship between State and territory. The patrimonial theory appears to be the oldest of such theories. According to this approach, territory is regarded as a piece of property pertaining to the ruler. Based upon feudal ideas of land tenure, it confused the concepts of sovereignty and property, or *imperium* and *dominium*. In this form, the theory lasted for a number of centuries,[92] and evolved into the so-called object theory (or property theory or *Eigentumstheorie*). This continued the notion of territorial sovereignty as concerning a real right, within the context of property. In other words, the State was regarded as exercising its power over its territory much as in private law an owner would treat his possessions.[93] While this theory explains the juridical fact that States may dispose of parts of their territory, it faces problems in dealing with the notion of federal states[94] and it does not appear to answer the question of why a State disappears upon the disposal of all of its territory. In spite of this, the theory is of significance in Anglo-American jurisprudence.[95] The approach that such an abstract distinction exists between State and territory can be compared with the subjectivist doctrine[96] or space or quality theory (or *Eigenschaftstheorie* or *Raumstheorie*),[97] according to which the territory of a state is regarded not as something separate but as an integral part of the personality of the State itself. An attack on the territory of a State is seen therefore not as affecting the property or possession of the State but as a violation of the personality of the victim State. The emphasis is thus upon *imperium* rather than *dominium*. However, there are a number of drawbacks with regard to this view. It appears to suggest that any change in territorial extent, whether by cession or by acquisition, seriously affects the personality of the State itself. It is difficult to assimilate with regard to federal States and condominiums, and there are problems in explaining the existence of leases. By way of contrast, the objectivist[98] or competence theory (*Kompetenztheorie*),[99] linked with the Austrian 'pure theory of law' school,[100] sees the territory of a State as the area of State jurisdiction or the space in which the State exercises its competence. Kelsen wrote that 'the unity of the State territory, and therefore the territorial unity of the State, is a juristic and not a geographical unity, for the territory of a State is legally nothing but the territorial space of validity of the national legal order called a State'.[101] In other words, the notion of territory is minimized and seen merely as a limiting factor as regards the exercise of the power of the State. Thus, Kelsen defines State territory as 'that space within which a State is authorised by general international law to perform all acts provided for by its national law or . . . the space within which according to general international law the organs determined by a national legal order are authorised to execute this order'.[102] This theory has attracted support.[103] Oppenheim declares that 'the importance of State territory lies in the fact that it is the space within which the State exercises its supreme authority'.[104] Lauterpacht has attempted to combine this approach, which is sophisticated and can readily account for situations of split sovereignty, with the advantages of the object theory. He has written that if one accepts a State as the totality of individuals organized in a State, rather than as an absolute and mystical entity, there is then no objection or artificiality in regarding the State as the owner of territory. Indeed, the objects theory is the most attractive theory to account for the cession of territory. However, territory is also the basis on which and the area in which a State exercises jurisdiction in conformity with international and municipal law. Thus, 'territory is both the object of the State's right and the space within which its sovereignty and jurisdiction are exercised'.[105] In addition, territorial sovereignty is not an absolute element; it may be divided,[106] and property 'is a bundle of rights capable of modification, division and adjustment'.[107] This composite approach appears the most acceptable one, not only because most proponents in fact have sought to synthesize the various elements involved rather than adhere strictly to one or other of the three major doctrines,[108] but because a highly flexible view of the concept of territorial sovereignty appears the most satisfactory. Territorial sovereignty should be examined on the basis of its provision of opportunities for co-operation and development rather than in a rigid strait-jacket.

If territorial sovereignty is to be seen in terms of a particular relationship between State, people, and territory and the concomitant possession by the State of a collection of powers, rights, duties, etc. as regards the territory in question, the problem arises as to the source of such powers, etc. There are two possibilities: either they emerge as a consequence or an attribute of sovereignty itself, or they are granted to the State by the rules of international law. The sovereignty[109] argument leans against the latter view since it 'has against it the conviction of States to which nothing is more distasteful than the idea that the power they yield is granted them by the international order.'[110] The sovereignty approach, in De Visscher's view, is derived from the psychological ties that exist between a nation and its territory and is founded upon the notion of power as delineating that territory.[111] Yet the sovereignty approach in the true sense is valid only if one posits the supremacy of municipal law. It is believed that the better view is to accept the primacy of international law, at least as far as the relative distribution of competence. It was stated in the *Lotus* case that 'all that can be required of a State is that it should not overstep the limits which international law places upon its jurisdiction; without these limits its title to exercise jurisdiction rests in its sovereignty'.[112] This same minimal approach is adopted by Waldock, who wrote that international law limits the competence of States but beyond that is the domain of free action, i.e. domestic jurisdiction; 'The reserved domain begins where international law ends'.[113] But it is clear that the delineation of the area of domestic jurisdiction is within the competence of international law.[114] As Kelsen wrote, 'the international legal order determines how the validity of the national legal order is restricted to a certain space and what are the boundaries of this space'.[115] Both the reason for and the sphere of the validity of national law are determined by the principle of efficacy, which is a notion of international law.[116] It would therefore follow that States' rights would flow from the norms of international law rather than from the fact of statehood itself.[117] Thus the collection of competences associated with the concept of territorial sovereignty may be seen as derived ultimately from the norms of the international legal order itself. But this should not be understood so as to detract from the important social and psychological role played by the State in the life of a community. Sovereignty in international law reflects the need for security and stability, but it also constitutes, in Alvarez's words, 'an institution, an international social function of a psychological character'.[118] Territorial sovereignty is the answer provided by international law as regards the needs for security, stability, and identity felt by a particular group within a certain area. It also constitutes the method by which a community may enter upon the international scene and by virtue of sovereign equality of States play a particular role in the development of the international system. It is submitted that, as regards these two functions, the concept of territory and the sovereignty of States associated with it has been enthusiastically adopted by Third World States, although without forgoing the advantages of the global approach.

4. *Title to Territory*

The concept of title involves in essence a description of those legal and factual elements which by virtue of the norms of international law must be present before territorial sovereignty may be validly acquired or maintained. It also expresses the fullest extent of competence that may be exercised by a State over its territory, and in this sense reflects a theoretical rather than an actual position, since States continually consent to the limitation of their competences by agreements with other subjects of international law. Jennings regards the primary meaning of title as 'the vestitive facts which the law recognises as creating a right'.[119] Title may be relative,[120] although it will operate *erga omnes*, and it is closely linked with the notion of effective control,[121] although not inevitably so.[122]

5. *The Acquisition of Territorial Sovereignty*

In classical international law, five modes of acquisition exist, viz. occupation of *terra nullius*, prescription, cession, accretion, and subjugation (or conquest),[123] and these are further divided into original or derivative modes.[124] There are, however, a number of problems associated with the traditional method of classification, based as it is on Roman law principles.[125] The neat doctrinal categories are often extremely difficult to apply in practice. A set of facts may have applicability to more than one of the modes of acquisition. This is particularly so with regard to the modes of occupation and prescription. Theoretically, the distinction is marked. Occupation relates to the acquisition of *terra nullius* by a State in an effective manner, while prescription (or more accurately acquisitive prescription) refers to the acquisition of territory not *terra nullius* by effective control. However, in many cases the status of the territory at the relevant time may be unsure. International tribunals have often not applied the classic criteria,[126] thus leading to the suspicion that such classifications are not of great significance although their underlying principles will be. In addition, the status of acquisitive prescription is itself controversial.[127] As far as the other modes are concerned, accretion (or accession)[128] and cession, being the transfer of sovereignty over territory from one State to another,[129] are relatively straightforward, but the status of conquest as a mode of acquisition is now highly questionable. It is submitted that the acquisition of territory by force alone is now accepted as illegal in international law,[130] while a treaty providing for the transfer of territory may be void for duress.[131] It is thus clear that a new framework for the elucidation of the relevant rules is required.[132] Another serious defect of the classic modes that should be noted relates to the acquisition of title by newly emerged States. This situation cannot be satisfactorily analysed in terms of the traditional modes.[133] The absence of any reference to the principle of self-determination merely compounds the problems.

It is believed that in such a situation recourse must be made to the fundamental rules underlying the international order and the interests that are manifest therein. Such interests revolve around the need for stability, and territorial stability in particular, in international relations, the desire to prevent illegal acts and situations from generating rights and thus consciously subverting international justice and equity, and the need to accept the realities of State sovereignty. In addition, the positive seeking of just ends, such as the preservation and establishment of human rights and the right to self-determination, must also be brought into account. These interests may be expressed through the media of a number of legal doctrines,[134] which are of broader scope than the exposition of the classic modes and thus eliminate unnecessary distinctions at certain levels.

The doctrine of sovereignty in international law relates to the collection of rights, powers, and duties adhering to each particular State. By virtue of this doctrine, a State may limit its powers and dispose of parts of its territory.[135] Thus, the cession of regions may be seen as a logical consequence of the possession of sovereignty under international law. Title passes by virtue of an act of sovereignty,[136] so that the cessionary state can only receive those rights, etc., ceded by the former sovereign.[137] Similarly, territory acquired by accretion, such as additions of land to the seashore by operation of nature, is really acquired as a direct consequence of the sovereignty of the State over the appurtenant land. As Schwarzenberger has noted, 'the title to newly created land rests primarily on the unilateral assumption of jurisdiction in situations in which, for all practical purposes, the territorial sovereign has a monopoly of changes'.[138] In a sense, this relatively minor mode of acquisition reflects geographical reality and is attendant upon sovereignty. Coupled with this concept is that of effectiveness, but this principle is of far wider application and permeates the whole of the law of territory. Its importance is a consequence of the structure of international law, with its fundamentally horizontal nature and emphasis upon the State as both the creator and subject and object of international law. In many ways, the principle of effectiveness underlies much of international law, for it stands as a test for the existence of particular facts which may have particular legal consequences. All legal systems possess mechanisms for the determination of those facts and situations to which it is provided legal consequences will attach. International law, however, because of its decentralized and horizontal structure, attached more importance to the criterion of effectiveness as a creator of legal results.[139] In no sphere of international law is this more apparent than with regard to the law relating to the acquisition of territorial sovereignty. To such an extent is this so, that one may regard the principle of effectiveness as the basic applicable doctrine regarding the acquisition of territory, although in particular cases it will operate in conjunction with other relevant rules, such as sovereignty and recognition. Within the category of effective control, delineated as it is by the international community, one may find those situations previously classified as those of occupation or prescription. Apart from the fact that occupation in the traditional exposition of the acquisition of territory relates only to *terra nullius*, of which there is virtually none today, the tests for both it and prescription revolve around the notion of effective control. It would seem, therefore, unnecessary so to distinguish the modes since the guiding principle is identical.[140] The fact that international tribunals have in general not analysed territorial acquisitions in terms of these two categories reinforces this conclusion. De Visscher's discussion of the concept of consolidation by historic title stresses that

> proven long use, which is its foundation, merely represents a complex of interests and relations which in themselves have the effect of attaching a territory or an expanse of sea to a given State. It is these interests and relations, varying from one case to another, and not the passage of a fixed term, unknown in any event to international law, that are taken into direct account by the judge to decide *in concreto* on the existence or non existence of a consolidation by historic titles.[141]

Thus, the crucial test is that of effective control, rather than passage of time, and it matters not what the status of the territory was prior to the start of the control.[142] As Johnson has written, De Visscher has simplified the problem considerably for one can now include under one heading 'straightforward possession' and 'adverse possession'.[143] As Jennings notes, this analysis is 'a penetrating and illuminating observation of the way courts actually tackle questions of title to territorial sovereignty'.[144] But one should mention that the passage in the *Anglo-Norwegian Fisheries* case relied on by De Visscher[145] was really concerned with general acquiescence with regard to a maritime area,[146] while the criticism has been made that De Visscher has overemphasized the aspect of the 'complex of interests and relations which *in themselves* have the effect of attaching a territory or an expanse of sea to a given State'.[147] These defects may be remedied, it is suggested, by reliance upon effectiveness rather than consolidation as the appropriate term. The fact that the original possession was contrary to law rather than in pursuance of it is certainly relevant within the context of effective control, but it is not felt that this in itself displaces the contention submitted.[148] Both occupation and prescription are primarily based upon the acquiring of title by virtue of effective possession and control. Although the time element has been seen as important for prescription, as distinct from occupation, it really is concerned with the effectiveness of such possession.

The principle of effective control applies in different ways to different situations, but the essence is that 'the continuous and peaceful display of territorial sovereignty . . . is as good as title'.[149] Such control has to be exercised by the State with the intention of seeking control, although the latter aspect may only be evident after a certain lapse of time. What amounts to effective control will vary with regard to the circumstances of the case, for example the geographical nature of the region and the existence or not of competing claims. This was expressed by Huber in the *Island of Palmas* case,[150] and reiterated in the *Eastern Greenland*,[151] *Clipperton Island*,[152] and *Minquiers and Ecrehos*[153] cases. Nor is it necessary for the control to be effective equally throughout the region.[154] The doctrine of effectiveness has displaced the earlier doctrines of discovery and symbolic annexation as in themselves sufficient to generate title,[155] as well as the validity of geographical contiguity alone as the basis of title,[156] while the so-called hinterland theory as regards territory in Africa in the nineteenth century never became established as a viable doctrine.[157] It should also be noted that Article 35 of the General Act of the Congress of Berlin, 1885, laid down that the signatories recognized the obligation to 'insure the establishment of authority in the regions occupied by them on the coast of the African continent'.[158]

Effectiveness may also, depending on the circumstances of the particular case, have a temporal as well as a spatial dimension. This was most forcefully expressed by Judge Huber with regard to the doctrine of inter-temporal law. He noted that 'the growing insistence with which international law . . . has demanded that the occupation shall be effective would be inconceivable if effectiveness were required only for the act of acquisition and not equally for the maintenance of the right',[159] although it was conceded that this stringent test would not be posed regarding territories with an 'established order of things'.[160] Nevertheless, the requirement that the existence of a right as distinct from its creation has to be justified in terms of the evolving rules of international law is highly controversial.[161] The better view would be to see this as only one element in the bundle of factors relevant to the determination of effective control. Its value would clearly be greatly reduced in the absence of a serious competitor to title.[162] It is also suggested that further relevant factors with regard to the ascertainment of effective control are the public or open nature of the control alleged (a clandestine occupation could not really be considered to be effective with regard to the international community)[163] and any consent or acquiescence on the part of a party directly concerned.[164] The latter element, a requirement of prescription, would appear to be rather of evidential value concerning effective control (if of crucial value) than a substantive requirement for title. Thus, the dominant principle regarding the acquisition of territory would seem to be that of effectiveness for reasons relating to stability and the nature of the international system. It follows, of course, from this that effectiveness as the base principle is far more comprehensive than mere possession by force, even if at the particular time no other State has the power to eject the possessor from the territory. The rules relating to the concept of belligerent occupation, affording such a possessor certain rights and duties under international law but most clearly not territorial sovereignty *per se*, witness this.[165] Force of itself is not a source of title nor may it validate by possession a territorial claim based on controversial elements, although incidents have occurred that have appeared to challenge this. In the Goan episode, India forcibly took over the Portuguese colony and annexed it. The basis of the Indian case as argued before the Security Council was that Goa constituted an integral part of India that had been illegally occupied for some 45 years of the colonial power and that accordingly force could be used to remedy the wrong.[166] Clearly, as a matter of international law, such contentions cannot be regarded as a valid mechanism for the transfer of territorial sovereignty. The colonial status of Goa, its existence as an enclave totally surrounded on the landward side by India, and its population of overwhelmingly Indian inhabitants may be factors of relevance in the sense of conditioning the ultimate destination of the territory,[167] but are in themselves insufficient to legitimate the use of force as a means of acquiring title to territory. The debate on the issue in the Security Council reached an inconclusive end in the light of the exercise of the Soviet veto.[168]

The dispute concerning East Timor is also of interest in this context.[169] Following the Portuguese coup of 1979, steps were taken with regard to the ultimate decolonization of the territory. The two leading parties, UDT and Fretilin, formed a coalition, but this broke down amid civil war. An Indonesian invasion occurred in December 1975 following the success of Fretilin and its declaration of East Timor independence. The UN General Assembly in resolution 3485 (xxx) called upon all States to respect the inalienable right of the people of Portuguese Timor to self-determination and for the withdrawal of Indonesian forces. The Security Council adopted resolution 384 deploring Indonesia's intervention and calling for the withdrawal of its forces and respect for the territorial integrity of East Timor.[170] In May 1976 a 'People's Assembly' of East Timor was constituted and formally requested Indonesia to integrate the territory. This was accomplished in July of that year.[171]

The General Assembly rejected the claim that East Timor had been integrated properly into Indonesia in resolution 31/51 of December

1976, since the people of the territory had not been able to exercise fully their right to self-determination and independence. This stand was repeated in subsequent years and the Assembly has called upon all interested parties, namely Portugal as the administering power and the representatives of the East Timor people as well as Indonesia, to co-operate fully with the United Nations with a view to guaranteeing the full exercise of the right to self-determination by the people of East Timor.[172] The Indonesian view remains that the people of the territory have already exercised self-determination by integration with Indonesia.[173] The United Nations has thus clearly held to the principle that mere effective control is not of itself sufficient to generate title to territory, certainly if allied to claim to territory of dubious weight.

Contentions as to contiguity, historic claims, and colonial title had also been advanced by Indonesia with regard to West Irian, which it regarded as falling within the territorial integrity of the Indonesian republic.[174] The 1962 agreement between Indonesia and the colonial power, the Netherlands, stipulated that the territory concerned was to be transferred to the former via a United Nations Temporary Executive Authority, to be followed by an 'act of free choice' by the inhabitants.[175] Several of the provisions of the 1962 agreement appear not to have been satisfactorily carried out, particularly those relating to rights of free speech, freedom of movement, and assembly, and the 'act of free choice' was implemented by means of consultations with 'representative councils' alone.[176]

Several African States in particular were unhappy about the carrying out of this act of free choice, while other States asserted that the issue really concerned not self-determination but the affirmation of the national unity and territorial integrity of Indonesia. India emphasized that West Irian was a special case and the methods employed there could not be regarded as a precedent with regard to self-determination in colonial territories.[177] Nevertheless, and within the particular context of the 1962 bilateral agreement, States in the international community were prepared to accept Indonesia's title.

The principle of effectiveness comprises a series of elements, and clearly the more such elements are satisfied the stronger and more certain will the title be. But this principle, which relies upon acts performed or assimilated by a State authority,[178] must be seen in conjunction with the important principle of recognition.

With regard to this principle, one must distinguish between international recognition and bilateral recognition. In the former case, one is concerned with the acceptance by the international community as a whole of a particular situation as a valid one despite any ambiguous or illegal origin, while in the latter case one or more States recognize a particular situation and may therefore be estopped from denying the validity of the same in the future; that is, the situation is opposable to such States but not necessarily to others. The two may shade into one another, but it is believed that a fundamental distinction lies between the two. Bilateral recognition is important as regards evidence of effective control and should therefore be treated as an element within that principle.[179] International recognition not only involves the development of rules of international law,[180] but may validate situations of dubious origin. A series of recognitions may validate an unlawful acquisition of territory,[181] for example, while the principle may be regarded as an exception to the proposition *nemo dat quod non habet*. A further instance of what might be termed international recognition acting in a constitutive fashion is the doctrine of *uti possidetis*, for this creates a legally obligatory situation with regard to all or a defined section of the international community. Similarly, the doctrine may prevent effective control from founding title, as for example in the Namibia situation,[182] and may form an exception to the general rule that a State is free to dispose of its own territory.[183] The impact of a series of UN General Assembly resolutions—and this will particularly be relevant with regard to self-determination issues—cannot be regarded as of no value in the field of title to territory.[184] The use of the right of self-determination can be important as regards title. As a manifestation through international recognition of a legal rule it is important as a constituent of statehood. As such it may deny title in situations of effective control[185] and it imposes a duty in particular circumstances to transfer territorial sovereignty. It has been suggested that the consent of the people of any area to be ceded is required to be demonstrated by a plebiscite,[186] but State practice does not really support this argument.[187]

Thus it can be seen that the acquisition of territorial sovereignty in international law rests upon an interplay of several crucial principles, the most important of which would appear to be that of effectiveness. The question of the balance between these relevance principles, in particular sovereignty, the territorial integrity of States, effectiveness, recognition, and self-determination, is a difficult one and one that has changed in the last few decades. The role of effectiveness as the base principle remains valid, but is limited by consideration of, for example, self-determination and the rules relating to non-acquisition of territory by force. Recognition is the primary way in which the international community has sought to reconcile illegality or doubt with political reality and the need for certainty. As the international community evolves, so some of its fundamental values undergo a transformation and the various interacting elements relating to territory are reordered.

6. *The Extent of Territory—Some Further Issues*

The extent of a State's territory in international law has already been alluded to in section 2 and the distinction between territorial sovereignty and jurisdiction noted.

A State will have full sovereignty over its land areas, rivers, and airspace, although such sovereignty is limited in the case of the territorial sea by the right of innocent passage.[188] A State will possess certain sovereign rights for exploration, exploitation, conservation, and management matters within its exclusive economic zone and jurisdiction with regard to, in particular, the establishment and use of artificial islands, installations, and structures in this zone, although the zone itself is subject to a specific legal regime under the 1982 Convention. Similarly, a coastal State will possess certain sovereign rights over the continental shelf for exploration and exploitation purposes.[189] Although the word 'sovereignty' is deliberately not employed, since one is not dealing with territorial title, it is interesting to note that the definition of the continental shelf refers explicitly to the 'natural prolongation' of the land territory of the coastal State as the basic principle.[190] This projection of the territorial concept has clear implications in the realm of States' rights, but not necessarily in the context of sovereignty as such.

Also of interest are artificial islands and installations constructed on the continental shelf and in the exclusive economic zone. These are subject to the exclusive jurisdiction of the coastal state, but do not constitute part of the territorial sovereignty of that State. They do not generate any territorial sea of their own nor does their presence affect the delimitation of the territorial sea, exclusive economic zone, or continental shelf.[191] The difference between territory and jurisdiction is thus underlined, with the prime distinction revolving around the extent of the collection of rights, powers, and duties possessed by the State.

States will possess title to their various colonies (although the question of sovereignty is controversial with regard to mandated and trusteeship territories), but this will be constrained by the application of the principle of self-determination. The Declaration on Principles of International Law Concerning Friendly Relations, adopted by the General Assembly in resolution 2625 (XXV) on 24 October 1970 and which can be seen as an authoritative interpretation of the UN Charter, notes that the territory of a colony or other non-self-governing territory has, under the Charter, a status separate and distinct from the territory of the State administering it. Such separate and distinct status is to exist until the right of self-determination has been exercised by the people of the territory concerned. Accordingly, it would be inaccurate to regard such a colony or non-self-governing territory as part of the territory of the State itself, although subject to the title of that State.

The question of the extent of State territory was touched upon in discussions leading to the final adoption of the Vienna Convention on the Law of Treaties. In Article 58 of Waldcock's Third Report to the International Law Commission in 1964 it was noted that 'a treaty applies with respect to all the territory for which the parties are internationally responsible', unless a contrary intention existed. Waldock expressly referred to the view that State practice did not justify the conclusion that a treaty applied to overseas territories only if specifically mentioned in a treaty. On the contrary, a treaty automatically embraced all the territories of the contracting parties unless a contrary intention had been expressly stated or could be inferred. The British practice from about 1880 of seeking the insertion of a 'colonial clause' in certain treaties, whereby the treaty was not to apply to overseas territories unless and until notification to that effect had been given, demonstrated the desire to negative by implication the automatic application of the treaty to non-metropolitan territories.[192] The issue raised in this draft article covered not only non-self-governing territories, but also federal States and States that consisted of separate geographical units.

In the discussions in the Commission on this draft, a certain amount of criticism was evident, particularly with regard to colonial territories within the sphere of applicability of treaties. Elias, for example, noted that if the general rule posited were to apply to territories that were not contiguous to the metropolitan territory, account would have to be taken of the tendency for third parties to insist on some evidence of consent by the non-metropolitan territory to be bound.[193] Others pointed to the problem that the colonial clause might appear as a means of perpetuating colonial dependence by keeping large areas of the world outside the province of international regulation.[194] In the redrafting of the clause, the phrase 'all the territory or territories for which the parties are internationally responsible' was dropped in favour of the statement that the scope of application of a treaty extended 'to the entire territory of each party' unless the contrary intention appeared from the treaty, and in the event this phrase appeared in the Commission's draft articles.[195]

The redrafting reduced the confrontation aspects as perceived but left in essence the problem as to the extent of State territory. Was it to include non-metropolitan territory or not? Of course, the argument could be put in terms of examining the particular treaty in question to see which conclusion could be inferred, but in many ways this merely side-steps the issue. While non-self-governing territories do have a special status in international law, it is important that within the context of treaties, especially humanitarian treaties, as wide a sphere of operation as possible is ensured.[196]

Article 29 of the Vienna Convention on the Law of Treaties, 1969, follows in essence closely upon the Commission's draft. The prime difference between the two consists of the change in phraseology from 'the application of a treaty extends to the entire territory of each party' to 'a treaty is binding upon each party in respect of its entire territory'. This was designed to avoid the problem that the original phrasing might be taken to mean that it was required that under municipal law a treaty automatically applied internally, and this, of course, was by no means the case.[197] To the same end, the title of the article was altered from 'application of treaties to territory' to 'territorial scope of treaties'.[198]

I

The Colonization of Africa

1. AFRICA AND TERRITORY

Pre-colonial Africa did not consist of a series of European-style States existing within fixed borders. On the other hand, identifiable empires and States were evident in certain areas of the continent.[1] The notion of the boundary line, however, was not known in Africa, while the use of frontier zones was widespread. Reasons for this include the lack of demographic constraint and the existence of a large number of natural separation zones, such as deserts and forests.

Anene has identified three types of frontier in existence in the nineteenth century. The frontiers of contact involved situations where political and cultural groups lived and worked together, for example as occurred in the West African States of the Yorubas and Dahomey and in the East African State of Buganda and its neighbours. Frontiers of separation consisted of geographical buffer zones physically dividing communities and not claimed by any authority, as for instance in the central Sudanic belt around States such as Bornu and the Fulani empire. The third type of frontier is to be explained rather in terms of enclaves or considerable overlapping of various groups than as conventional borders, and the examples cited are the migrating tribes of the Tuareg and the Masai.[2]

Thus, frontiers possessed at this time a highly dynamic and fluid character.[3] In such a situation, the nation-State with a stable territorial base was very much the exception even in pre-colonial Africa.[4] This is not to say that the notion of a State or territorially based centralized political entity did not exist in Africa. Around the turn of the first millennium, for instance, a series of States existed in the Sudanic belt stretching across north-central Africa from the Red Sea to the mouth of the Senegal River, and other examples may be seen at other times and places in Africa.[5] Not all African communities formed States, of course. Fortes and Evans-Pritchard note that in addition to societies with some form of centralized authority, administrative machinery, and judicial institutions, in which cleavages of wealth, privilege, and status correspond to the distribution of power and authority, societies existed without such governmental machinery and with no sharp divisions of rank, status, or wealth.[6] Accordingly, the territorial aspect regarding the respective political organizations differed. In the former case, the administrative unit was a territorial unit and political rights and obligations were territorially delimited, while in the latter case the unit was not a territorial one defined by an administrative system but was instead a local community defined in terms of lineage ties.[7] However, it does appear as if the concept of territory was viewed rather differently from how it was in Europe. Bozeman writes with regard to ancient African and later Muslim communities that 'territorial consolidation was nowhere a major concern'.[8] In addition, land was traditionally seen as 'the spatial expression of social relations rather than of strategic, material or ideological functions', and migrations were continually taking place.[9] The great African societies were neither territorial States nor nation-States in the Western sense of the terms and the personality of the king or paramount chief was the crucial factor in such organizations. Such African States were marked 'by the absence either of regionally shared conceptions about the territorial and national configuration of political entities or of traditionally fixed or reliable rules for the conduct of statecraft and intertribal relations'.[10]

The Islamic conception of territory differed also from the modern European paradigm. Flory has pointed out how territory in Islamic law was not connected with the State, but rather with the socio-religious concept of the Umma, or community founded upon the Muslim religion, which, unlike Christianity, did not develop a dichotomy between spiritual and temporal spheres of existence.[11] Territory was defined, therefore, not with regard to political power wielded within a delimited space as in Europe, but in terms of religious manifestions. The Dar el-Islam was the dynamic framework within which the community of believers lived and worked and was not to be identified with State territorial sovereignty developed in European thought.[12] The Dar el-Islam extended as far as the Muslim community and was thus not a static structure but a very flexible one, developing as the community developed.[13]

To some extent this was recognized by the International court in the *Western Sahara* case.[14] Morocco asked the court to take account of the special structure of the Sherifian State, founded as it was upon the common religious bond of Islam existing among the peoples and on the allegiance of various tribes to the Sultan of Morocco through their caids or sheikhs rather than on the notion of territory.[15] The court accepted this and noted that international law did not specify the type of structure a State had to adopt, but at the same time the allegiance offered to the authority of the State, if it was to be referrable to the sovereignty of the ruler, 'must clearly be real and manifested in acts evidencing acceptance of his political authority, otherwise there will be no genuine display or exercise of State authority'.[16] Although authority was in pre-colonial Africa often defined in personal rather than territorial terms, communities were accepted as having rights over the land they inhabited and utilized and the role of territory was indispensable in the existence of such communities.[17] In the colonial period, the territories as colonially defined acquired a personality and integrity of their own,[18] and upon independence formed the framework of the new nations for the purpose of identity and sovereignty.

Until the latter half of the nineteenth century, the impact of Europe upon Africa in general terms was relatively slight. Except for certain areas, African communities retained considerable freedom for independent development.[19] In fact, the late eighteenth and nineteenth centuries marked in Africa a significant stage in the development of indigenous States as well as witnessing population movements in southern Africa and the rise of commercialism in West Africa.[20] As far as European trade with Africa was concerned, prior to 1880 it constituted only a small part of the total foreign commerce of Europe. Hargreaves notes that the share of trade with West Africa in Europe's overseas trade was under one per cent.[21] By the late 1870s, however, the increasing activity in Africa by explorers, merchants, missionaries, engineers, and soldiers led both to a greater impact upon indigenous societies and to a growing awareness in Europe's political capitals of the advantages to be derived from a more forward policy with respect to the African continent. No longer were the European States primarily interested in trading advantages and coastal forts: the radically new phase inaugurated in the late 1870s demonstrated a concern with territorial acquisition and the extension of the national sovereignties of an expanding Europe. The reasons for this change are many and complex and beyond the scope of this work, but in addition to religious, scientific, economic, and ideological motivations one may note the role played by territorial acquisition in Africa in the process of maintaining the uneasy balance of power in Europe.[22] To some extent because of this, the whole episode of the 'scramble for Africa' was cloaked with the aura of legality, and the care taken in preserving legal form and conforming with the principles of international negotiation and treaty-making.[23] However, where such alleged titles went without contradiction by other European States, various mistakes and inadequacies went unnoticed,[24] but where the claim was disputed a close examination of the 'title deeds' was to be expected and any weaknesses discovered caused acute embarrassment and occasionally led to an abandonment of the claim.[25]

The modes of acquisition of territory used by the European States with regard to African lands ranged from treaties of cession to conquest and the gradual transformation of the colonial protectorates, while the notion of spheres of influence proved of some relevance in the process. An analysis of the methods then in operation and the way in which territory was acquired is of more than purely historical interest, since the vast majority of African borders today were in the first instance delimited by treaties between the European powers. Had the new African States decided upon independence to embark upon a general rearrangement of territorial borders, as at one time seemed not improbable, the question of the nature of the colonial acquisitions would be of little actual value. However, the colonially defined frontiers were reaffirmed and upheld. Therefore, the process of colonial delimitation and title remains relevant, particularly with respect to the large number of boundary disputes existing in modern Africa. The parties to such conflicts invariably base their claims upon European treaties and the validity and extent of such treaties can have important repercussions today.[26]

The charge that the colonial partition of Africa divided tribes and united antagonists in an uneasy relationship is easily sustained, but it is important to note that the nation-State in the European sense did not really develop in Africa. Fluid frontiers characterized the continent and where identifiable States arose they invariably contained a variety of tribal groups. On the other hand, defined communities such as the Ibos of West Africa or the Kikuyu of East Africa did not create an administratively centralized structure, but lived politically disorganized though culturally united.[27] The disruptive effect, thus, of European colonization, though certainly a significant factor in African history, should not be treated in isolation and exaggerated.

II. THE MODES OF ACQUISITION OF TERRITORY IN AFRICA IN COLONIAL TIMES

The methods of acquiring title adopted by the European powers in nineteenth-century Africa demonstrate not only the way in which the international law modes of territorial acquisition were interpreted in a large-scale operation, but also the views of the European powers as to the status in international law of the heads of the African communities encountered and, of course, of those communities themselves.

(a) Effective Occupation and the Concept of terra nullius

The concept of *terra nullius* has developed in the light of the acquisition of territory by occupation, i.e. the peaceable acquisition of sovereignty over territory otherwise than by cession or succession.[28] In order for this to occur, the territory had to be *terra nullius*, or a *territoire sans maître* in the French phrase. Thus, a determination of what entity could constitute a *maître* was called for. Salomon noted that virtually all international controversies dealing with the notion of the occupation of territory have been based upon the different ways in which the *res nullius* has been defined.[29]

While it is clear that certain types of territory are without doubt *terra nullius*, for example uninhabited areas, abandoned territories (*res derelicta*)[30] and areas inhabited by relatively few persons totally lacking in any kind of social or political organization, there has been considerable ambiguity concerning the situation where the territory is inhabited by recognizable entities. In such cases, a number of different theses have been presented.[31] The view that peoples possessed sovereign rights, thus precluding the acquisition of their territory by means of occupation under international law, was put forward by a number of the founding fathers of the law of nations. These included Vitoria, Soto, La Casas, Ayala, Gentilis, Selden, and Grotius.[32] The essence of this attitude was that the acquisition of sovereignty over the lands of such peoples depended upon the concept of conquest not occupation, and accordingly discussion centred around the notion of just war and the legality of hostilities against non-Christians. The second theory concerning the relationship between a people and its land under international law recognized that such peoples could exercise sovereign rights in certain circumstances only. Vattel, for example, declared that where the occupying State was in need of more land, it could acquire by occupation that part of the territory of indigenous wandering tribes which could be deemed to be in excess of the latter's requirements. This followed from the obligation to cultivate the earth, which meant that tribes could not take for themselves more land than they had need of.[33]

The third approach that can be identified is the one that appeared to dominate throughout the later nineteenth century when Africa was being divided amongst the competing European powers. This thesis propounded the view that the organized tribes of peoples of non-European lands had no sovereign rights over their territories and thus no sovereign title by means of effective occupation. The inhabitants, therefore, were merely factually and not legally in occupation of the territory, which could be treated as *terra nullius* and acquired by any State in accordance with the requirements of international law. Foremost among such theorists was Westlake, who took the view that government was the international test of civilization[34] and that those communities unable to furnish a government readily recognizable as such to Western eyes could not hold territorial title.[35] This marked the high point of the exclusivity concept of the State in international law as fostered by nineteenth-century positivism.[36] Oppenheim noted that 'only such territory can be the object of occupation as belongs to no State, whether it is entirely uninhabited, for instance an island, or inhabited by natives whose community is not to be considered a State'.[37] Jennings has written that occupation was accepted as 'the appropriation by a State of a territory which is not at the time subject to the sovereignty of any State . . . Natives living under a tribal organization were not regarded as a State for this purpose.'[38]

The problem of *terra nullius* was examined in the oral pleadings in the *Western Sahara* case and in the opinion of the International Court.[39] The court had been requested to answer two questions, of which the first stated, 'Was Western Sahara (Rio de Oro and Sakiet El Hamra) at the time of colonization by Spain a territory belonging to no one (*terra nullius*)?'[40] In the pleadings, Ambassador Bedjaoui on behalf of the Algerian government particularly carefully analysed the concept of *terra nullius*, and emphasized that the concept, linked with the acquisition of territory by occupation alone, constituted a basis for all the imperialisms and all the phenomena of oppression in the history of civilization. It was a device which involved the 'thingification' of numerous peoples since it divorced them from the process of territorial sovereignty.[41] The original function of the concept and its most valuable success concerned the regulation of international relationships with respect to the peaceful extension of State sovereignty to uninhabited areas, such as polar regions, deserts, and new islands, but it became perverted by application to inhabited territories. In Roman Antiquity, any territory which was not Roman was *terra nullius*. In the fifteenth and sixteenth centuries any territory which did not belong to a Christian sovereign was *terra nullius*, and in the nineteenth century any territory which did not belong to a civilized State was *terra nullius*.[42] Such a historical survey is used to demonstrate how law has followed on meekly from power, while the development of the concept in the nineteenth century saw it primarily as a method of adjusting relationships between the colonizing powers themselves, rather than as between the colonizer and the colonized.

It was utilized to emphasize that might was right.[43] In the course of time, European rivalries precipitated what Bedjaoui termed the overheating of the concept of *terra nullius* and led to the development of effective occupation as a method of acquiring territory not under the sovereignty of a civilized State.[44] The endogenous function of the concept, that is in its regulation of the distribution of territories between imperial powers, was reflected in the attitudes of the Berlin Conference of 1884–5 convened to regulate the 'scramble for Africa'. These were characterized by the Algerian agent in the statement that 'a territory owned by no one, and thus open to occupation by any European colonizing State, was any territory which that same State decided to regard as such, with the agreement of the other States of the European club'.[45] In accordance with this approach, it was claimed that in the late nineteenth century the distinctions between occupations of *terra nullius* and conquest, cession, and acquisitive prescription of other territories were 'ruthlessly set aside by the practice of States and appeared ridiculously unreal'.[46] The practice of entering into agreements with indigenous groups had the sole purpose of being opposable to the other European States, which could not then claim the particular territory as *terra nullius*.[47]

This critique of the use of the concept of *terra nullius* as the legal spearhead of European colonization in the last century is a valuable one and is a reminder of the intimate relationship between law, power, and territory, as well as demonstrating one aspect of the manner in which European international law began to achieve an almost universal application in practice. However, the degree of its accuracy can be seriously questioned. In fact, a perusal of State practice of the period reveals that Africa was not regarded as *terra nullius* and that occupation was not therefore available as a mode of acquiring legal title to territory. Territory was acquired on the continent primarily by means of agreements of cession with local leaders.[48] It seems that Bedjaoui, by concentrating upon the European scramble aspect, or the endogenous aspect, has minimized the exogenous aspect, or the relationship between the European power and the colonized territory, to such an extent that the doctrine of occupation of *terra nullius* under international law has become confused with the political occupation (in the sense of colonization) of Africa. To this extent, he has apparently misunderstood the scope of the Berlin Conference of 1884–5 which did not establish that the method of acquiring territory in Africa was by way of occupation (in the legal sense) but rather used the term 'occupation' as a general expression comprising all modes of acquisition, to be interpreted synonymously with acquisition or appropriation.[49]

In fact, the International Court made the same point. It declared that although 'occupation' was used often in a non-technical sense to mean acquisition of sovereignty, this did not necessarily, or always, signify that sovereignty was actually acquired by way of an occupation of *terra nullius* in the legal sense of these expressions.[50]

As regards Western Sahara, the Algerian argument could in fact lead only to one result, namely, that under the international law of the period, the territory was indeed *terra nullius*. This made the conclusion inevitable that 'it is enough for Western Sahara to have been colonized for one to be obliged . . . to infer inevitably that Spain and Europe had considered it to be *terra nullius*, totally disregarding the owner of the territory'.[51] Algeria, however, was unhappy at this conclusion, which would appear to have rendered the request to the International Court redundant since it required a positive response to the first question and thus no consideration of the second question.[52] Accordingly, it suggested two alternative lines of proceeding, both of them of significance. On the one hand, it was proposed that colonialist law be disregarded and reference made to the legal system operative in the area at the relevant time, while on the other it was postulated that the application of inter-temporal law with consequent recourse to the principles developed by international law might provide a satisfactory answer to the problems of the situation. Both of these solutions were methods of getting around the problem posed by the view that Western Sahara was *terra nullius* at the time of Spanish colonization and bringing to the fore the crucial role to be played by the wishes of the population regarding its political role.[53]

The other States involved in the *Sahara* case appear to be unanimous in their conclusion that the territory was not at the relevant time *terra nullius*,[54] but their reasons for this were not identical. Spain had declared before the UN General Assembly that it had never regarded the territory as *terra nullius*.[55] In its written statement, it noted that an area was *terra nullius* if not under the sovereignty of a State authority,[56] while the issue was not discussed in the Spanish submissions in the oral pleadings.[57] In view of the fact that Spain denied that either Morocco or the Mauritanian entity possessed sovereign rights over the Saharan territory at the time in question, or that the tribes of the area constituted a State, it should logically have accepted that the territory was *terra nullius*. This it did not do[58] and thus its position remained to that extent confused and ambiguous.

Morocco and Mauritania both criticized the Algerian approach as equating *terra nullius* with colonized territories or territories that were being colonized. Morocco declared that the Algerian argument was 'a real piece of intellectual conjuring',[59] while Mauritania held that the international law of the period should not be represented as worse than it was. A humanistic stand did exist, it was averred, which ensured the consent of populations in the process of territorial acquisition in order to render the cession of sovereignty valid.[60] Despite the Moroccan–Mauritanian view that Algeria had over-extended the concept of *terra nullius* and dismissed the importance of the numerous agreements made between the colonizing powers and the inhabitants of the territories concerned, they appeared to differ slightly as to why Western Sahara was not *terra nullius* during the period in question. Morocco declared that the territory was not *terra nullius* since Morocco was at the time a recognized State and its presence in the territory was thus in the nature of State sovereignty, and that this automatically disposed of the problem.[61] At a later stage, this attitude was carefully modified to take account of Mauritania's claims in the light of the accord reached between the two.[62] Mauritania all along maintained that the territory was not *terra nullius* since international law at the time recognized the legal personality of tribes and therefore did not regard their lands as *terra nullius*, and the part of Western Sahara linked with the so-called Mauritanian entity clearly fell into this category.[63] Morocco, therefore, appeared to adopt a slightly ambiguous median position between the statist approach of Spain on the one hand and the wide approach preferred by Mauritania on the other.

A number of judges of the International Court in the *Sahara* case were a little unhappy as regards the nature of the question posed on *terra nullius*. Judge Gros maintained that the question as to whether the territory was *terra nullius* at the time of Spanish colonization was not a legal one, but purely academic, and served no useful purpose. This was because none of the States interested in the territory's status at the time of colonization had relied upon the concept of *terra nullius*.[64] It was, therefore, a sterile exercise to ask the court to discuss a hypothetical situation.[65] Judge Petren declared that the question was without object in the context of the *Western Sahara* case, and it was pointless and inappropriate for the court to answer it.[66] Judge Dillard emphasized that Spain's original title was not in question nor had any State in fact asserted that Western Sahara was at the relevant time *terra nullius*.[67] However, the question was of some legal relevance in the case since it served as an introduction to the second question dealing with the alleged Moroccan and Mauritanian ties with the territory. A determination that the territory was *terra nullius* would automatically dispose of the Moroccan and Mauritanian claims. To this extent, the first question was of interest. As Judge Dillard pointed out, it 'helped clear the decks for question II'.[68] It helped establish the requisite framework for the examination of the Moroccan and Mauritanian contentions. This, incidentally, raises the problem as to why there were two questions, since one question dealing with the legal status of the territory at the date of colonization would appear to have been adequate.[69] The answer to this is to be sought in the political processes leading up to the adoption of resolution 3292 (XXIX) and the contending pressures from the various parties, which created the guide-lines for the court's advisory opinion. In any case, the opportunity it provided for an analysis of the nature of *terra nullius* was fortunately grasped.

In its functional examination of the concept of *terra nullius*, the court ignored any reference to the processes of colonization and declared that the concept was a legal term of art used in connection with the mode of acquiring sovereignty over territory known as occupation.[70] It was also clearly emphasized that the question had to be understood in the light of the law in force at the time of colonization.[71] The court noted the differences of opinion between jurists regarding the concept, which have been briefly noted above, and then proceeded to place full emphasis upon the State practice of the era in question. The court unambiguously asserted that 'the State practice of the relevant period indicates that territories inhabited by tribes or peoples having a social and political organization were not regarded as *terra nullius*'.[72] This posthumous rehabilitation of the classic authors of international law and side-stepping of those late nineteenth-century theorists denying any form of international legal personality inherent in non-European-style State entities, places considerable stress upon the numerous agreements concluded between the European colonizing powers and the local communities. It elevated them from the status of mere methods by which European powers demonstrated their occupation of a particular territory as against each other[73] to documents of a central character in the acquisition of sovereignty over territory.[74]

Agreements dismissed as 'trinket treaties' [75] or 'glass-bead' treaties[76] therefore did have legal significance.[77] The unanimity of the court's opinion reinforces this determination of the situation. As far as Western Sahara was concerned, the court declared that the territory was not *terra nullius* on the grounds that the inhabitants, although nomadic, were socially and politically organized with chiefs competent to represent them and that Spain recognized this. Spain had all along treated its acquisition of the territory as achieved by virtue of a series of agreements with the independent tribes of the area. In fact, its decree of 26 December 1884, treated by the court as the starting date of the time of colonization, proclaimed the establishment of a protectorate based upon local agreements, and, as Judge Dillard noted, one cannot protect a *terra nullius*.[78] For this judge, it was the nature of the Spanish presence as expressed through numerous treaties of protection that constituted a controlling factor. What might have been the case and the court's attitude had Spain not signed such agreements remains open to speculation, and it is not clear from the opinion whether the court felt that the general rule regarding the existence of organized tribes would have sufficed.

In any event, it does seem that the conclusion of treaties of protection constitutes a recognition of personality both of the ruler and of the people concerned and therefore eliminates the possibility of the area in question being considered a *terra nullius*. The suggestion by Judge Huber in the *Island of Palmas* case that agreements with rules of peoples 'not recognized as members of the community of nations', while not amounting to titles in international law, 'are nonetheless facts of which that law must in certain circumstances take account',[79] can be seen as too tentative. Indeed, such agreements can be seen as constituting recognition of membership of the community of nations. They most certainly mark acceptance of the contracting party as representing an organized tribe or people by the relevant European power and thus negating the possibility of a *terra nullius* situation.

Occupation as a method of obtaining title to territory was thus only open as regards uninhabited territories or territories inhabited only by a number of individuals not constituting a social or political aggregation.[80]

Where, in Lindley's words, 'the inhabitants exhibit collective political activity',[81] the acquisition could only have been achieved by way of cession or conquest or prescription.

(b) Cession

It thus appears that the prime method of acquiring territory in Africa in the period of colonization was by way of cession. This raises the questions as regards the status of both contracting parties and with respect to the legal quality of the agreement concerned. Since the existence of sovereignty and of political organization excluded the possibility of treating Africa as *terra nullius*, the European powers had resort to bilateral treaties as a means of acquiring territory from the local sovereign.[82]

The General Act of the Berlin Conference of 1884–5 itself recognized implicitly the existence of African sovereign entities. Article 1 noted that the principle of freedom of trade and navigation in the 'conventional basin of the Congo' would only operate in the territories of an independent sovereign State if approved by such State.[83] The core of the General Act revolved around the principles enunciated in Articles 34 and 35. The former declared that any power taking possession of land on the coasts of Africa, or establishing a protectorate there, may notify the other signatory powers, while the latter provision stipulated that the signatory powers 'recognize the obligation to ensure the establishment of authority in the regions occupied by them on the coasts of the African continent sufficient to protect existing rights and, as the case may be, freedom of trade and of transit under the conditions agreed upon.'[84] These provisions were, it should be emphasized, concerned with the relations of the European powers *inter se* and not with the direct acquisition of territory from the African sovereign. They denoted that in any territory acquired on the African coastline, the European powers agreed amongst themselves that effective occupation was to be the norm. O'Connell has written that this indicated also what was involved in the notion of effective occupation, viz. the display of sufficient authority to protect acquired rights.[85] While this would be of use in cases of occupation of *terra nullius*, it cannot be taken to specify the declaration of Africa as *terra nullius*. The Berlin Conference[86] can be seen as a turning-point in European–African relations.[87] Although the conference did not itself partition Africa, but rather was intended to 'limit the effects of the scrambling on European relationships',[88] it did involve an institutionalization of the process of acquiring territory in the African continent. And this process, as Alexandrowicz has correctly stated, 'was in the first instance not a race for the occupation of land by original title, but a race for obtaining derivative title deeds which the European powers had to acquire according to the rule of international law relating to negotiation and conclusion of treaties.'[89] In the case of the Cameroons territory, for example, Britain had intended to acquire the region but before it had acted Germany signed a treaty with the local chief placing the territory under its protection. The title acquired by Germany, in late 1883, was not disputed by Britain. Had the area been regarded as *terra nullius*, the mere signing of a document would not have been sufficient and there would therefore have been scope for Britain to recoup the situation.[90] Similar races took place between Britain, France, and Germany on the Niger and in each case the aim was to obtain treaties with local chiefs, which would give title. None of this vast area of West-Central Africa was acquired by occupation alone.[91] Lindley declares that 'the territorial rights of the European powers in Africa were in general those which they had obtained by cession from the native chiefs'.[92]

Since in the case of a cession the cessionary State receives such title as is possessed by the ceding party, the nature and status of the latter is of great importance to the former. No serious problem will in general arise where the cessionary party is accepted as a subject of international law or, in Lindley's words, is 'an advanced sovereign'.[93] An example of such a transaction affecting colonized territory would be the sale of the Danish West Indies to the United States in 1916.[94] In addition, in 1907 and 1908 treaties, King Leopold as the 'Roi-Souverain du Congo' ceded to Belgium 'la souveraineté des territoires composant l'État Indépendant du Congo avec tous les droits et obligations qui y sont attachés'.[95] However, where the chiefs or leaders of indigenous communities are involved, issues as to capacity may arise. In a number of treaties, African rulers specifically declared the powers they possessed. For example, in an 1840 treaty with Britain, it was stipulated that 'all sovereignty of the before specified territory is now vested in the said King of Congo and has descended to him from his ancestors'.[96] In a treaty of 1861, the ruler of Lagos was deemed to be 'King in the usual African signification'.[97] In the general form of treaties used by African companies in dealing with local rulers, cessions were to be 'with all sovereign rights'.[98] Problems arose in certain cases because of uncertainty as to the precise status of the ruler with whom the European State (or company) was making the particular agreement. In the *Bulama* arbitration, Britain claimed that certain territories in West Africa had been ceded to it in 1792, but the arbitrator held that those purporting to cede were in fact under Portuguese sovereignty and that therefore the cession was invalid.[99] A similar situation occurred in the *Delagoa Bay* award of 1875, as certain chiefs had purported to cede land on the eastern coast of southern Africa to Britain in 1823. The cession was declared to be invalid, since the chiefs were under Portuguese sovereignty.[100]

An attempt to analyse the various types of rules or chiefs from the point of view of external sovereignty was attempted in the *Barotse* arbitral award of 1905 concerning the western boundary of the Barotse Kingdom. It was noted that 'a Paramount Ruler is he who exercises governmental authority according to [customary law], that is, by appointing the subordinate chiefs or by granting them investiture, by deciding disputes between these chiefs, by deposing them when circumstances call for it and by obliging them to recognize him as their Paramount Ruler.'[101] The arbitrator examined the facts regarding the payment of tribute, the submission of tribal disputes, and the exercise of authority in general, but eventually decided to stipulate an arbitrary boundary in view of the constant intermingling of tribes making it impossible to establish a precise delimitation. The question of capacity was also at issue regarding a treaty made by Britain with the ruler of Boussa over territory to be ceded on the Niger. France established that that chief was in fact subordinate to another at Nikki, and a race ensued to gain the superior chief's signature on a treaty of cession.[102] Similar situations arose respecting the cession of land at Assab Bay to Italy in 1880–1 and the following year in Madagascar over the cession of land to France.[103]

In a number of treaties, the ceding party expressly stated that he was in no way dependent upon an external power. In a treaty of 1888 between the United Kingdom and the Kingdom of Igbessa, it was proclaimed that the latter was 'perfectly independent and pays tribute to no other power'.[104] In the same year, the chiefs of Kita stated that their kingdom was also perfectly independent and paid tribute to no other power.[105] In a treaty of 1880 between France and the country of Kita, the chiefs, notables, and inhabitants of Kita expressly declared that they were independent of any foreign power and this was repeated with respect to the chiefs of Benito in 1883.[106]

In order to transfer title in strict accordance with the international rules of cession, the treaty has to be entered into with such persons or institutions as, according to the law of the community, possessed the capacity to make the cession. In the *Delagoa Bay* case, Portugal objected to one of the treaties relied upon by Britain on the grounds that the chief concerned lacked capacity according to the law and custom of Tembe.[107]

In certain cases, the agreement itself specified that the necessary constitutional requirements of the community with regard to the cession of land had been complied with.[108] In legal form, at least, the cessionary power had to be able to demonstrate that the person making the cession had the capacity so to act. The greater the rivalry between the European powers in the particular region concerned, the greater this need appeared. One may note that in the Report on the Insurrection in the Sierra Leone Protectorate, it was stated that 'in [all] treaties from the foundation of the Colony . . . to the latest treaty made in 1895, the character of the chiefs as the owners and sovereigns and as independent contracting powers is unequivocally and universally recognised'.[109]

Since such agreements were intended to constitute binding obligations on the parties, it was generally necessary to show that the local ruler appreciated the nature of the transaction, otherwise the treaty might be invalid. This was clearly demonstrated in the *Lamu* arbitration of 1889. The arbitrator rejected a German claim to the territory on the ground that the agreement purporting to cede the island of Lamu was not in writing and was therefore inadequate. He declared that 'the adoption of the written form is particularly necessary in dealings with the governments of but little-civilized nations, which often only attach binding force to promises made in a solemn form or in writing'.[110] This would appear to be going a little too far and it is suggested that Lindley's rider that 'any solemn form which is recognized by the laws and traditions of the native society should be equally effective'[111] is preferable. That African communities were capable of understanding the binding nature of agreements with other communities is quite clear. Lugard, for example, believed he had found the equivalent of the European concept of a treaty as a binding arrangement in the ceremony of blood brotherhood.[112] The more significant question that followed was whether in practice such communities had consented to the particular treaties involving the cession of territory or the creation of a protectorate, or whether indeed such consent was seen as necessary. To take the latter point first, it does seem as if it was established that the contracting African party had clearly to comprehend the nature of the transaction. Lord Salisbury in 1889, discussing the distribution of Portuguese flags to chiefs who appeared in ignorance of the possible interpretation of vassalage involved in the acceptance of such gifts, stated that 'Her Majesty's Government cannot recognize any claims which may be hereafter advanced on the part of Portugal to sovereignty over territories in the Nyasa districts, based upon the distribution of flags to the *ignorant* native chiefs'.[113] The 1893

Convention between the United Kingdom and the South African Republic stated that the United Kingdom would not recognize any agreement between the latter and the Swazis relating to South African protection unless it could be shown that the Swazi Queen Regent and Council understood the nature, terms and conditions of such an agreement.[114] In fact, a large number of treaties expressly stipulated that the particular African rulers had understood the terms and effects of the agreement in question. In the treaty between Britain and the chiefs and headmen of the Congo River of 1854, the latter stated that they understood the agreement and considered it binding.[115] The many agreements entered into by the Royal Niger Company contained a stipulation, one form of which declared that, 'We, the undersigned, are witnesses to the marks of the [chiefs] and also vouch for their understanding what they have signed . . . [and] do hereby declare that the foregoing agreement was duly and correctly explained to [them] and that they fully understood it.'[116] Some of the agreements made by this company also included a declaration that the chiefs had entered into the particular arrangements 'of their own free will and consent'.[117] However, knowledge does not automatically or always indicate free consent, and one interesting indication of the true situation is provided by the declaration of the US delegate to the Berlin Conference of 1884–5 which was sought to be added to the protocol of the final Act. It was stated that 'modern international law steadily follows the road which leads to the recognition of the right of native races to dispose freely of themselves and of their hereditary soil. Conformably to this principle, my Government would willingly support the more extended rule which one should apply to the said occupation [of territory] in Africa, a principle looking to the voluntary consent of the natives of whose country possession is taken [by treaty] in all cases where they may not have provoked the act of aggression.'[118] The fact that this view did not receive support at the Conference, and bearing in mind that the US did not ultimately ratify the final Act of the Conference, would seem to point to an ambiguous approach to the question of consent by the various African chiefs. In a number of cases, it is probable that what appeared to be free consent would, upon examination, turn out to be something rather less. Alexandrowicz, perhaps a little optimistically, concluded that 'it must be assumed that the principle of voluntary consent was at least tacitly accepted by the Conference'.[119]

While duress would in modern international law vitiate a treaty,[120] the issue was less certain with regard to nineteenth-century practice regarding the colonization of Africa. In fact, State practice tends to show that treaties imposed by force upon indigenous communities were still regarded as valid. In 1881, for example, a French army invaded Tunisia and a French general with an armed escort surrounded the palace of the Bey, giving him four hours to sign a treaty placing Tunisia under French protection. The Bey signed under protest and in the presence of French power.[121] Lindley notes that there seemed to be no case in which a treaty made by 'a member of the International Family' with 'a backward people' was objected to on the ground that its conclusion was obtained by force.[122]

The approach that the treaties of cession with local rulers were purely private arrangements having regard to the status, or rather lack of it, of those rulers under international law, cannot really be maintained in view of the large amount of practice on this point. To emphasize this, one may refer to the situation regarding colonial protectorates. Lindley has pointed out that 'it is difficult to see how, having regard to the universality of the practice grounding a colonial protectorate upon an agreement with the local authority, and of the importance attached by the European powers to these agreements in their relations *inter se*, the requirement for such an agreement can be regarded otherwise than as a rule of law.'[123] It can be argued that such instances took place against a background of greater legal personality, but it is submitted that treaties of cession made with local rulers were the main method whereby the European powers acquired territory in Africa.[124] Thus, the question of the status in international law of African communities in the nineteenth century is clearly raised. Nineteenth-century views of the universality of international law were distinctly limited.[125] Westlake, for example, stated that the international society which developed international law was composed of all the States of European blood plus, as a late addition, Japan. International law also applied to the three Christian States of Africa, viz. Abyssinia (Ethiopia), Liberia, and the Congo State (regarded as Christian since its sovereign was the king of the Belgians), although it could hardly be said that such States contributed to the development of international law. In addition to this, international society could admit States to parts of its law only and examples of this would include Turkey, Morocco, Muscat, Siam, Persia and China.[126] One may draw from this two conclusions. Firstly, that basically only States within the European circle were or could be members of the 'International Family' and full subjects of international law, and secondly, that only *States* were involved in any event.

As for the first contention, the nineteenth-century test was that of 'civilization'. Smith noted that one important requirement of statehood was that a State should be 'under a system of law which gives strangers and natives a reasonable approach to equality of treatment. The assimilation of European ideas, the growth of humane habits, the frank attempt to break down the barriers of exclusion, all these will insensibly prepare the way.'[127] Oppenheim wrote that 'the Law of Nations, as a law between States based on the common consent of the members of the Family of Nations, naturally does not contain any rules concerning intercourse with and treatment of such States as are outside the circle. That this intercourse and treatment ought to be regulated by the principles of Christian morality is obvious.'[128] Rivier excluded from international law 'a horde of nomadic tribe, the negro tribes of Africa and the native races of Australia, the North American Indians, and chance communities, organized temporarily, such as bands of brigands and associations of pirates'.[129] However, such statements were never an accurate reflection of the evolution of international law. European powers had treaty relations with the Ottoman empire, and with Algiers, Tunis, Tripoli, and Morocco for a number of centuries.[130] Scott noted in 1801 in *The Helena* that although African States such as Algiers had once been considered as pirates, 'they have long acquired the character of established governments, with whom we have regular treaties, acknowledging and confirming to them the relations of legal States'.[131] However, in another case, he emphasized that with regard to African (i.e. north African) States, the 'European law of nations is not to be applied in its full vigour to the transactions of persons . . . residing in that part of the world'.[132]

International law was thus the law governing civilized States. The British law officers wrote of it in 1859, 'as it has been hitherto recognized and now subsists by the common consent of Christian nations.'[133] However, this requirement of 'civilization' is perhaps best seen as referrable to entry into the European family of nations, rather than as a condition of statehood itself. In the *Western Sahara* case, the International Court emphasized that 'no rule of international law . . . requires the structure of a State to follow any particular pattern, as is evident from the diversity of the forms of State found in the world today'.[134] Thus, Morocco was at the time of the Spanish colonization of Western Sahara a State, although of a special character, as being founded upon the common religious bond of Islam and personal allegiance to the Sultan rather than upon the notion of territory.[135]

From this it may be deduced that international law in the nineteenth century, and as transformed by positivism and European colonization, operated a dual system of States, those within and those without the European family of nations. This also affected the applicability of international law. However, where non-State entities were concerned a further level of the international society was involved. It has been seen that practice demonstrates that the European colonization of Africa was achieved in law not by virtue of the occupation of *terra nullius* but by cession from local rulers. This means that such rulers were accepted as being capable in international law not only of holding title to territory, but of transferring it to other parties. Accordingly, one may postulate a three-level structure of international law during this period as it related to the issue of international personality. States within the European-defined 'family of nations' were full and complete subjects of international law, States outside this 'family' had only a limited impact upon the development of the law and not all of it applied to them, while certain non-State entities or communities possessed only a limited personality in international law, although this certainly included the capacity to hold title to territory and territorial sovereignty.

(c) Conquest

This involves the taking of possession of enemy territory through military force in time of war.[136] Of dubious legality today,[137] it was historically important and certainly operative in the nineteenth century as a method of acquiring territory.[138] It was noted in the case of *In Re Southern Rhodesia*[139] that conquest as a way of obtaining title to territory assumed the absence of any formal transfer on the part of the previous sovereign and required the taking possession of the territory by force, together with the intention and ability to hold the territory as its sovereign.[140] The title by conquest was completed when the intention to annex was signalled and the territory involved was effectively occupied.[141] It was not necessary apparently for all of the territory and all opposition to be totally subjugated, as the British proclamations of May and September 1900, annexing the Orange Free State and the Transvaal while some Boer forces were still fighting, demonstrate.[142] The Italian annexation of Libya in 1911 was clearly premature. Serious if sporadic fighting continued until and during the First World War and it was only in 1923 that Turkey recognized Italy's sovereignty over the Libyan provinces.[143] It is therefore doubtful whether title by conquest was involved in this case.

Title by conquest was rare in Africa in the nineteenth century. The Judicial Committee of the Privy Council noted that the territory of

Matabeleland and Mashonaland had been acquired by conquest,[144] while Britain claimed that upon the defeat of the Khalifa's army at Omdurman in 1818, 'all the territories which were subject to the Khalifa passed by right of conquest to the British and Egyptian governments'.[145] By a French law of 6 August 1896, Madagascar with the dependent islands was declared to be a French colony, with title being based upon conquest.[146]

Conquest involves, it would seem, an implicit recognition of the international personality of the opposing party. In the case of Southern Rhodesia, the British had concluded a treaty with Lobengula in 1888 and a year later had informed the Portuguese that Lobengula was the independent ruler of Matabeleland and Mashonaland,[147] while in the case of Madagascar, the other main example of title by conquest in Africa, the conquest was preceded by treaties of protection.[148] In Africa, however, title by conquest was the exception.[149]

III. COLONIAL PROTECTORATES

The establishment of protectorates was so widespread during the period of colonization in Africa that O'Connell has stated that it became in the nineteenth century almost a mode of acquisition.[150] However, the assumption by a comparatively powerful State of the duty of protecting a weaker State was an institution of some antiquity. One example of such a relationship was to be found in the protectorate exercised by Britain over the Ionian Islands between 1815 and 1864. This was set up by treaties with Russia, Austria, and Prussia, which stipulated that the islands were to be a free and independent State under the immediate and exclusive protection of the king of Great Britain. In 1864 they were ceded to Greece at the request of the islanders with the consent of the guaranteeing powers.[151] In the *Tunis and Morocco Nationality Decrees* case, the Permanent Court declared that protectorates had 'individual legal characteristics resulting from the special conditions under which they were created, and the stage of their development'.[152] As regards the creation of the French protectorate over Morocco by the treaty of Fez in 1912, the International Court noted that Morocco remained a sovereign State, and had granted certain sovereign powers to France.[153] Thus, much depends upon the particular circumstances of the case. In this classic conception of the institution of the protectorate, should the protecting power exceed its authority as derived from the relevant agreement, the protected party could treat this agreement as broken.[154] In *R.* v. *Crewe*, it was stated that the concept of a protectorate excludes, in contradistinction to the idea of annexation, 'that absolute ownership which was signified by the word dominion in Roman Law and which though perhaps not quite satisfactory is sometimes described as territorial sovereignty. The protected country remains in regard to the protecting State a foreign country.'[155] The concept of the protectorate was founded, initially at least, upon a divison made between external and internal sovereignty, with the former being delegated to the protecting power. But the concept was developed in the case of the colonial protectorate so that the institution became one more method of acquiring territory rather than the model of the classic approach.

Lindley observed that 'an essential feature of the colonial protectorate is that it is recognised by the other members of the international family as giving to the protecting power the right as against themselves to take steps in the direction of annexing the protected territory as its dominions'.[156] The Berlin Conference of 1884–5 appears to have marked the turning-point. Prior to that date, a number of treaties of protection were signed consistent with traditional practice, i.e. granting the protecting State powers in the external field and quite often determining that the local ruler was restricted in his external relations by the consent of the protecting power.[157] After 1885, 'State practice . . . revealed a tendency to deform the original classic concept of the protectorate and to convert it into an instrument of colonialism'.[158] This can be seen with regard to Bechuanaland, where internal as well as external sovereignty gradually passed to the protecting power. In 1884, a number of treaties were signed with local rulers and the following year a British protectorate was made a Crown Colony and its governor exercised jurisdiction over the protectorate as well. In effect, Britain acquired both internal and external sovereignty over the territory.[159] Kennedy LJ emphasized in *R.* v. *Crewe* that in the protectorate 'every branch of such government as exists—administrative, executive and judicial—has been created and is maintained by Great Britain'.[160] Nevertheless, the theoretical distinction was maintained. Vaughan-Williams LJ noted that 'the Bechuanaland protectorate is under His Majesty's dominion in the sense of power and jurisdiction, but is not under his dominion in the sense of territorial dominion'.[161]

This revisionist approach to the nature of protectorates in essence treated them as hardly distinguishable from colonial possessions.[162] Other examples of protectorates established in Africa by the European powers included Tunisia in 1881,[163] Madagascar in 1885, Zanzibar in 1890, Uganda in 1895, Egypt in 1889, and Morocco in 1912. Basutoland and Swaziland also became protectorates, but Italian efforts to enforce a protectorate over Ethiopia rapidly collapsed.[164] Under the Act of the Berlin Conference, only Article 34 relating to notification applied to protectorates and not the requirement under Article 35 relating to effective occupation. However, in subsequent interpretations, it was declared that protectorates had also to be effectively occupied by the European State concerned.[165] This meant in effect that little practical distinction was made between ordinary colonies and protectorates and it marked the development of the colonial protectorate with its substantial differences from the traditional protectorate.[166]

IV. SPHERES OF INFLUENCE AND THE HINTERLAND DOCTRINE

In a large number of cases, before the European powers established colonial protectorates, they agreed among themselves as to the division of areas of the African continent into spheres of influence, or spheres of action.[167] Such agreements merely amounted to an acceptance by the parties that certain territories would be subject to the attentions of one of their number and that the others were to abstain.[168] Westlake sees the reason for their development in the haste for the provisional appropriation of territories in advance of anything resembling occupation that characterized the latter part of the nineteenth century. This 'more shadowy form of earmarking' was especially needed since colonial protectorates differed so little in practice from annexations.[169] A sphere of influence could arise as a result of a unilateral declaration of one power, which would become a reality if uncontested, or, more usually, from an agreement between two or more powers not to interfere in the 'spheres' of the other(s). By distinguishing between exercising 'influence' and exercising 'sovereign rights' in Articles 6 and 9, the Final Act of the Berlin Conference formally inaugurated the prolific era of spheres of influence in the partition of Africa.[170] The first such arrangement was the Anglo-German agreement of May 1885, which defined the spheres of interest of the parties and provided for non-interference by each party in the sphere of interest of the other.[171] Other such agreements followed rapidly between France and Germany, Britain and Germany, France and Portugal, and Germany and Portugal.[172] In effect, these agreements, binding upon the parties, marked a transitional stage on the road to colonial acquisition. Agreements with the local chiefs invariably followed, to be succeeded by the establishment of protectorates. Thus, while the spheres-of-interest agreements were of no legal effect as regards the African populations,[173] they tended to inaugurate the acquisition of title to the territories concerned. In any event the process re-emphasizes the predominant inter-European aspect of the partition of Africa.

The principles established by the General Act of the Berlin Conference relating to the creation of European colonies and protectorates in Africa were solely related to territories on the African coasts and were not applicable in the interior of the continent. This was due not only to the fact that such interiors had not by then been seriously explored by Europeans to any great extent, but also to the difficulty of establishing effective occupation in such areas. Accordingly, various doctrines were utilized aiming at the acquisition of title and its recognition by all the European powers in a way which would obviate the need to establish effective occupation. Prominent among these were the notions of contiguity and hinterland.

Such expansive geographical doctrines, originally formulated, it seems, with regard to the occupation of the American continent,[174] were transferred to Africa, with the idea that possession of a coastal strip in some way placed the occupier in a privileged position (at least) with regard to the interior of the country bounded by that coastal strip. France used the argument with regard to Senegal and the British with regard to Nigeria.[175] Britain, however, objected to Portuguese claims to a belt running across Africa from Angola to Mozambique on the grounds that no doctrine of constructive acquisition existed in the absence of bona fide occupation and *de facto* jurisdiction.[176] The hinterland doctrine, according to the arbitrator in the *Walfisch Bay* award, required for its application 'the existence or assertion of political influence over certain territory or a treaty in which is concretely formulated'.[177] However, the doctrine, replete with geographical uncertainty, ambiguity, and possibilities for confusion, was never really accepted. Britain, for example, abandoned its claim of 1883 to large areas of land outside its acquired territory of Walfish (or Walvis) Bay in south-west Africa on the grounds of contiguity or hinterland, once Germany had made territorial acquisitions in that region.[178] Lord Salisbury declared in 1896 that 'the modern doctrine of hinterland, with its inevitable contradictions, indicates the unformed and unstable condition of international law as applied to territorial claims resting on constructive occupation or control',[179] while the US Secretary of State declared in the same year that 'spheres of influence and the theory or practice of the "hinterland" idea are things unknown to international law and do not as yet rest upon any recognized principles of either international or municipal law'.[180] These notions were political expressions of the colonizing spirit, not legal concepts. They soon gave way to cessions and effective occupation as the guiding juridical principles.

V. CONSIDERATION OF GEOGRAPHICAL AND ETHNIC FACTORS DURING COLONIZATION

In the process of the European colonization of Africa, ethnic considerations were, in general, ignored and the colonies and protectorates included within their borders, with few exceptions, large numbers of different, often antagonistic tribes, while dividing others between different jurisdictions.[181] However, this should not be taken to mean that no account was taken of local conditions in the delimitation of colonial frontiers in Africa. While some 30 per cent of the total length of African borders follows geometrical lines and thus would appear to have been established irrespective of local conditions, the majority of the borders were delimited, partly at least, in the light of some indigenous factors.[182]

Geographical factors were sometimes relevant, as in the delimitation of Gabon's frontiers,[183] while on a number of occasions ethnic considerations were taken into account as well as the structure of African political entities. By the mandate agreements of 1922, the former German East Africa was divided into Belgian and British mandated territories. Soon after the mandates came into force, the Permanent Mandates Commission was petitioned to rectify the border delimitation, since the district of Kissaka has been separated from Ruanda and placed in Tanganyika.[184] The Commission deplored the territorial transfer and referred to the protests of the local population, and after Belgian–British talks, the boundary was altered and the district returned to Ruanda.[185] On similar grounds, the Council of the League of Nations suggested in 1924 that certain readjustments be made to the frontier between the French and British mandated areas in the Cameroons.[186]

In a series of treaties, provisions were incorporated stipulating that account be taken of tribal groupings and African entities in the drawing of boundaries. In the Anglo-French treaty of 1890, for example, Article 2 declared that the northern border of what was later to become Nigeria should be drawn 'in such a manner as to comprise in the sphere of action of the Niger Company all that fairly belongs to the Kingdom of Sokoto'.[187] The frontier between Nigeria and Dahomey as delimited by the Anglo-French agreement of 1898 contained alterations to take account of treaties made by Britain with local rulers,[188] while a treaty between Britain and Portugal in 1891 provided that part of the border between their central African territories would follow the western boundary of the Barotse Kingdom.[189] A comprehensive agreement regarding colonial delimitations was made between the UK and France in 1904 and this provided that the line separating Niger from Nigeria (as they are now) should be changed to place three particular sultanates with whom France had made treaties within the French sphere and that in determining the frontier regard should be had to the political divisions of the territories.[190]

The treaties between France and Liberia in 1907, and Italy and Ethiopia in 1908, also provided that close regard was to be had to existing tribal divisions so as to avoid splitting tribes.[191] In a number of instances, treaties provided for the problem of tribes divided by borders, not by amending the borders, but by some other form of recognition of the situation. For example, the Anglo-French treaty of 1904 provided for the transfer of the Îles de Los and a part of Gambia to France and stipulated that the populations of the areas concerned could opt for British citizenship if they wished.[192] The Anglo-Belgian treaty of 1915 regarding the Uganda–Congo border and the Anglo-Italian agreement of 1927 regarding the Kenyan–Italian Somaliland border also included similar provisions.[193]

However, such considerations must be seen against the background of European power politics, which had much to do with the siting of borders and the influence of administrative convenience. In 1910, for instance, an area know as the Lado enclave was transferred from the Congo to Sudan and for ease of administration its southern part became a part of Uganda,[194] while the inclusion within German south-west Africa of the Caprivi Strip was due to poor geographical knowledge, since the intention had been to secure access to the Zambezi for the German colony, in the belief that an important communications route was involved.[195] As an example of the vagaries of colonial boundary-making, one may cite the instance of a part of French West Africa. In 1890 the Sudan was created as an administrative entity, but nine years later was dismembered and distributed amongst its neighbours. In 1902 the territory of Sénégambie and Niger was established. Two years later, the western part was renamed the French Sudan. In 1935 Upper Volta was abolished and parts of it were incorporated into the French Sudan, but fifteen years later it was reconstituted, while in 1944 parts of the Sudan were given to Mauritania.[196]

VI. LEGAL TIES

The second question put to the International Court in the *Western Sahara* case asked 'what were the legal ties between this territory and the Kingdom of Morocco and the Mauritanian entity?'[197] and in the discussion of this point a number of interesting matters were raised that highlighted the relationship between people, territory, and sovereignty so crucial in the law of territory.

Morocco argued that it possessed sovereignty over Western Sahara by virtue of immemorial possession founded upon 'the public display of sovereignty, uninterrupted and uncontested for centuries'[198] as 'evidenced by the general acquiescence of the international community which it was accorded for several hundred years'.[199] These internal and international aspects had to be understood, however, in the light of the special nature of the Moroccan State based upon personal allegiance to and the religious significance of the Sultan.[200] Moroccan sovereignty extended also, it was claimed, to the Bled Siba, the area not in fact submissive under the complete power of the Sultan, since it acknowledged the spiritual authority of the Sultan.[201] Morocco pleaded that a number of religious and tax documents demonstrated political allegiance, to which could be added various military activities,[202] while a series of international agreements were invoked which purportedly constituted international recognition of its title to Western Sahara.[203]

Mauritania was in a different position, since it clearly had not existed as a State during the colonization period. It therefore emphasized that the problem centred around the re-unification of its people.[204] In order to substantiate this, reference was made to the 'Mauritanian entity', or Bilad Shinguitti. This was a distinct, cultural entity inhabiting a certain area.[205] This entity, with its own language and social structure, was not a State, nor even a federation or confederation. The concept of a league as it had existed in ancient Greece was the nearest analogy presented to the court,[206] and this entity, consisting of a number of different, even warring, tribes was reinforced by a unified Saharan law.[207] Although it was acknowledged that the constituent parts of the entity were sovereign and independent,[208] the entity lived as a distinct unit in complete independence from neighbouring States.[209] The concept of nomadism was used to express this method of linking people and territory in a legal relationship.[210] The nature of the relationship between the individual parts and the entity was described as co-sovereignty. This meant that, despite its political diversity, the entity could be regarded as an independent nation, in which all the people jointly exercised sovereignty over the Mauritanian entity.[211] Included in this entity were the inhabitants of Western Sahara, who therefore partook of the co-sovereignty.

Both Moroccan and Mauritanian contentions were rejected by Spain, who emphasized that Morocco had never exercised State functions over Western Sahara[212] while the Mauritanian entity was simply a sociological phenomenon with no legal implications whatsoever.[213] On the contrary, the population of the Western Sahara itself constituted a distinct people with its own characteristics.[214]

In its analysis of the Moroccan claim, the International Court laid emphasis upon the actual manifestation of sovereignty by Morocco with regard to Western Sahara during the time of Spanish colonization. What was of decisive importance was not indirect inferences drawn from history, but 'evidence directly relating to effective display of authority in Western Sahara'.[215] The court firmly resisted the temptation to accord historical and geographical factors other than peripheral value.[216] This meant that Morocco's claim was to be analysed in the light both of 'the intention and will to act as sovereign, and some actual exercise or display of such authority'.[217] While the court accepted that the Moroccan State of this period was based on personal and religious bonds rather than territorial ones, such allegiance had to be manifested clearly in acts evidencing acceptance of the ruler's political authority.[218] The court, thus, was not willing to project the internal characteristics of Morocco on to the international scene so as to obviate the need to comply with recognized rules of international law.[219] The court concluded that the material submitted[220] did not show that Morocco had displayed 'effective and exclusive State activity inWestern Sahara' and that, therefore, there was no tie of territorial sovereignty between the two.[221]

The court, however, went further to state that legal ties of allegiance had existed between the Sultan of Morocco and some of the nomadic tribes of the territory.[222] However, there is a qualitative difference between personal influence exercised by the Sultan over tribes inhabiting areas adjacent to the frontiers of his State and legal ties of allegiance between the two parties. Quite why the court recognized legal ties of allegiance here is difficult to appreciate. It may be that the special local conditions required such an unusual conclusion, but it must be regarded as misguided, especially since, unlike ties of sovereignty which might influence the process of decolonization of the territory, legal ties of allegiance with part of the population did not. It is also doubtful whether the material available could support the existence of such ties of allegiance and it is hard to avoid the conclusion that the court was trying to present Morocco with a consolation prize.[223] In the event, Morocco later misinterpreted and misused this part of the court's opinion.[224]

In discussing the nature of the Mauritanian entity, the court took into account that subjects of law varied in their nature and the exercise of their rights, and gave full weight to the special characteristics of the Sahara region, but the essential test of legal personality was that such an entity be in 'such a position that it possesses in regard to its members, rights which it is entitled to ask them to respect' and be 'an entity capable of availing itself of obligations incumbent upon its members'.[225] As a matter of fact, the Mauritanian entity did not constitute such an entity and could therefore have exercised no sovereignty in Western Sahara.[226] However, certain legal ties could still have existed, based on the facts of nomadism. Such rights included those relating to the lands comprised on the nomadic routes. This appears correct, for nomadic tribes should be regarded as possessing legal rights respecting the land over which they have customarily migrated. The special nature of Saharan life at the time demanded a more flexible view of the manifestation and creation of legal ties.[227] However, the court went beyond the assertion of legal rights between the nomadic peoples concerned and the lands which they traversed, to declare that such rights 'constituted legal ties between the territory of Western Sahara and the "Mauritanian entity" '.[228] It is felt that this conclusion is far too generalized. What the correct analysis would have led to was that there were some legal ties between some of the tribes of the alleged entity relating to *some* of the territory of the Sahara. To transmute nomadic rights over part of a territory to rights possessed by the 'Mauritanian entity' over the whole of the territory in question must be seen as mistaken.[229]

The court's acceptance of such non-territorial legal ties provides a legal loophole through which States with irredentist claims may seek recognition of pre-colonial legal ties and then declare that such ties should be accepted as having an influence upon the decolonization process and after. The question is then raised of the effects of the legal ties discussed in the *Sahara* case. As far as ties of territorial sovereignty are concerned, it seems clear that their existence would have been of relevance not in superseding the principle of self-determination,[230] but in providing guide-lines for its application,[231] such as with regard to the framing of questions for a plebiscite in the territory.[232] As regards the other legal ties recognized by the court, they could not affect the application of resolution 1514 (XI) and the principle of self-determination to the inhabitants of the territory, but some uncertainty now exists as to their function in other such situations.

It may be concluded, therefore, that while international law will take into account any special characteristics there may be in attempting to identify legal personality, particularly statehood, with regard to non-European entities, the ultimate test of sovereignty is the classic one of objectively determined exercise of authority coupled with the intention to act as sovereign. As far as non-sovereign legal ties are concerned, these may be demonstrated in the light of the special characteristics of the region and people in question and may be founded on religious or tribal practices. While such ties will not be relevant in the field of sovereignty, it seems, they may be of relevance to the various procedures involved in the decolonization process, although in what form and to what extent is open to question.

VII. THE PROBLEM OF LEGAL PARTICULARISM

The circumstances of the *Sahara* case, which required an analysis of the legal situation in that area during the 1880s, raised the issue of particularism and the validity of competing international legal orders. A number of different approaches were propounded during the case.

Algeria declared that one of the ways in which one could get around the conclusion that European international law regarded colonies as *terra nullius* was to reject colonialist law and recognize that there existed an Arab–Islamic civilization at that time and place, with a developed public law dimension. Thus, it could be argued that Western Sahara was not *terra nullius* since it belonged to the Dar el-Islam, or Moslem *civitas*.[233] Mauritania claimed on rather similar lines that the entity, or Bilad Shinguitti, had since the seventeenth century an extremely precise meaning throughout the Moslem world and was within the Arab–Islamic community a clearly individualized entity. It was argued that there had been nothing in the nineteenth century to prevent international law coexisting with various special legal orders such as Latin American law, or the internal relations of the British Commonwealth, or indeed the law of the dar el-Islam.[234] Spain adopted a different approach and stressed instead the unity of international law. To accept that different legal frameworks were to apply on the one hand to the establishment of Spanish sovereignty, would mean the annihilation of international law. In addition, the parties concerned had not supplied proof of the existence and applicability of such rules.[235] Spain stressed that departure from the idea that there is only one legal order, a general international law governing relationships between independent States, would have grave consequences, the most serious of which being that legal reasoning would be incapable of producing a minimum of agreement since different basic categories would be used.[236]

Morocco adopted a median position. It pleaded the special character of its State structure in the nineteenth century, while declaring that its ties of territorial sovereignty with Western Sahara were valid under general international law. In the nineteenth century, Morocco could only be understood as an Islamic State with its mixture of temporal and spiritual elements.[237] To judge the nature of its ties with Sahara, 'it was essential to abandon the constitutional pattern of the European State of the nineteenth century'.[238] But Morocco claimed that international law did recognize such diversity of State systems and that, therefore, its approach was within the framework of general international law.[239]

Faced with such contentions, the court was prepared to move some way towards the acceptance of legal particularism, but not with regard to the question of *terra nullius*, which was treated purely in the light of the (European) State practice of the period. This side-stepped the possibility raised by Algeria of Sahara not being *terra nullius* because it was part of the Dar el-Islam. The court declared that 'the legal regime of Western Sahara, including its legal relations with neighbouring territories, cannot properly be appreciated without references to [the territory's] special charcteristics',[240] viz. the desert nature of the land and the nomadism of its population. The question of legal ties had to be examined 'in the context of such a territory and such a social and political organisation of the population'.[241] In discussing the nature of the Moroccan State and the Mauritanian entity at the relevant time, the court was prepared to reach its conclusion in the light of the local particularism. However, the general framework was firmly established as that of the general international law of the period. The court recognized the special nature of the Moroccan State and noted that 'the particular structure of a State may be a relevant element in appreciating the reality or otherwise of a display of State activity adduced as evidence of that sovereignty'.[242] Nevertheless, the key factor was whether Morocco had effectively exercised sovereignty in Sahara at the relevant time. Religious ties had existed in other parts of the world and did not necessarily amount to legal ties of sovereignty, while ties of allegiance had to be 'real and manifested in acts evidencing acceptance of . . . political authority'[243] for one to talk of the display of State sovereignty. The real analysis had to be concerned with proof of effective sovereignty.[244] As far as Mauritania was concerned, the court noted that it had given full weight to the 'special charactersitics of the Saharan region and peoples'.[245] However, whether the entity did enjoy sovereignty in the area was to be determined in the light of the general international law test revolving around the existence of an identity separate from its constituent parts and involving the sense of obligation.[246]

The court, however, accepted the existence of legal ties of allegiance between the Sultan of Morocco and some of the people of Sahara, based on the exercise of the former's influence over certain tribes and, therefore, upon the specific nature of the Sherifian State. In the case of Mauritania, the court recognized that the nomadism of the people of the area at the time of colonization 'gave rise to certain ties of a legal character . . . [and] . . . those ties neither had nor could have any other source than the usages of the tribes themselves or Koranic law'.[247] In other words, the court emphasized the existence of valid rights under international law at the time of colonization founded upon the particularism of the region, even though these had no effect upon the decolonization process. However, the fact that the court concluded that certain rights over nomadic routes amounted to legal ties between Western Sahara and the tribes of the entity in question can only raise questions as to the parameters of particular juridical systems within international law. The court's overall treatment of the function of particularism and the problems of coinciding legal orders, therefore, does leave something to be desired.

Morocco also raised the attendant problem of the validity of the pre-colonial legal system. Since that had been replaced by the colonial order consistent with inter-temporal law,[248] could it be revived upon the demise of colonization by virtue of inter-temporal law? It was declared that 'logic would require that the new law which reopens the question of the title acquired by Spain at the time of colonization should also reopen the question of Morocco's loss of title at the same period.'[249] This was, however, based upon a twofold misconception. The new law did not reopen the question of the title acquired at the date of colonization, but rather demanded its cessation. Secondly, the new law patently did not operate on the basis of re-examining old titles, but based itself on the right of the inhabitants of the colonially defined territory to self-determination. As Bedjaoui noted on behalf of Algeria, the function of inter-temporal law was not 'to confer fresh legal life on a title prior to the title which today has become obsolete or is obsolescent'.[250] The court did not discuss this problem, but its attitude may be appreciated in view of its support of the right of self-determination as the vital operative principle.[251] Judge de Castro noted that colonization had created rights and ties, just as General Assembly resolutions calling for decolonization had created new facts, so that by the date of resolution 3292 (XXIX) it could be stated that the law then in force was based upon self-determination.[252] The continuation or re-emergence of historic rights, thus, had to be judged in the light of the right to self-determination, which posited the supremacy of the will of the inhabitants of the colonially defined territory. It was unfortunate that the court itself did not discuss such issues. The question as to which legal ties of the 1880s may be relevant to decolonization in the 1970s raises all sorts of problems that were only peripherally considered.

2

The Establishment of the Legal Right to Self-Determination[1]

I. HISTORICAL INTRODUCTION

Verzijl has remarked that 'seldom has there been advanced as a legal right a claim so obviously of a political nature and of such a sloganlike quality as the so-called "right of self-determination".'[2] Despite this phraseology self-determination has clearly proved to be a principle of the utmost importance in international relations since 1945.

The history of the principle can be traced to the French revolution at the close of the eighteenth century with its twin proclamations of human rights and popular sovereignty. Its peculiar blend of nationalism and democracy profoundly influenced the political development of Europe[3] and ultimately produced the concept of self-determination. This was interpreted as the capacity of the nation to decide for itself its own political structure, for nationalism appeared as a framework for the operation of the new theory of sovereignty called democracy.[4] Although this 'principle of nationalities', as it was sometimes known, was not recognized as an integral part of European law,[5] it has a profound effect, particularly upon the nations of central and eastern Europe.

However, the three constituent elements of this concept, i.e. people, the nation, and the State, did not always coalesce in the same fashion and the role of the democratic factor often fluctuated. In many instances in central Europe it re-emerged as a form of national determinism, whereby the fact of birth alone determined the issue and the idea of subjectivity was rejected as irrelevant. The individual could not operate in a manner inconsistent with the mystical concept of the nation.[6] On the other hand, western European liberal thought emphasized the subjective element and the element of choice over the pull of the nation.[7] But self-determination was in no sense thought of as legally binding.[8]

It was the events and views precipitated by the outbreak of the First

World War[9] that thrust the principle on to the centre of the stage. President Wilson of the United States declared before Congress in 1916 that 'every people has a right to choose the sovereignty under which they shall live',[10] and this idea was developed in the following years. In 1918 he promised that 'all well-defined national aspirations shall be accorded the utmost satisfaction that can be accorded them without introducing new or perpetuating old demands of discord and antagonism'.[11]

In spite of such protestations, it was clear that the 1919 Peace Conference did not treat national self-determination as an overwhelmingly important principle. It did not appear in the final draft of the Covenant of the League of Nations,[12] and it was treated 'as a purely political factor and not as a legal principle applicable to all peoples whose fate has to be determined'.[13]

Nevertheless, its impact upon the legal constitution of the world community can be detected in the various provisions for minority protection,[14] which can be regarded as a restricted application of self-determination in its creation of protective norms for certain cultural and language groups. It was even conceivable that minority rights could rise to secession, but this was considered an 'altogether exceptional situation, a last resort where the State lacks the will or the power to enact and apply just and effective guarantees'.[15]

Self-determination also made its mark in the institution of the mandate system[16] which replaced the annexation of territories belonging to the defeated States outside Europe and was founded on the proposition that 'the well-being and development of such non-independent peoples form a sacred trust of civilisation'.[17]

In the inter-war years there was relatively little practice dealing with the application of self-determination.[18] In the leading discussion of its juridical character that did take place it was emphasized that 'the recognition of this principle in a certain number of international treaties cannot be considered as sufficient to put it upon the same footing as a positive rule of the Law of Nations' and stated that international law 'does not recognise the right of national groups as such to separate themselves from the State of which they form part by the simple expression of a wish'.[19]

Verzijl regarded the decision in the Aaland Islands question as based upon the acceptance by the Commission of Jurists that positive international law did not know of the asserted 'right' of self-determination.[20] Although the idea of self-determination probably helped encourage the growing nationalist movements in the Arab and Asian worlds, Brownlie points out that this had 'no immediate counterpart on the legal plane'.[21]

The Second World War stimulated further consideration of this concept. The Atlantic Charter, 1941, declared 'the right of all peoples to choose the form of government under which they will live' and the desire to see no 'territorial changes that do not accord with the freely expressed wishes of the people concerned.'[22]

Self-determination was not mentioned in the Dumbarton Oaks proposals of 1944, but it came into prominence at the San Francisco Conference at the instigation of the Soviet Union[23] and was incorporated into Article 1(2) of the Charter of the United Nations. This noted that one of the purpose of the Organization was the development of friendly relations among nations 'based on respect for the principle of human rights and self-determination of peoples' and was echoed in Article 55.

Although widely accepted before 1945 as a political moral principle entailing no legal obligation,[24] its inclusion in the UN Charter raised questions as to its juridical character.[25] However, the Charter only refers to self-determination as a 'principle' and not a 'right' and this induced the Australian delegate to the Commission on Human Rights to point out that 'where the Charter laid down a principle, it did not necessarily signify a right, and it must be left to the authority responsible for the administration of a given dependent territory to determine the extent to which the principle of self-determination could be applied to it'.[26]

The view is reinforced by a consideration of the context in which the principle is proclaimed, that is, as a basis for friendly relations among States. Article 1(2) comes within the section dealing with the purposes of the UN and not the more important section concerned with the principles of the Organization and appears merely as a guidance framework for UN activities rather than prescribing legal norms.[27]

A further factor is the absence of definition or clarification of the concept in the Charter, and this leaves one to question its legal validity as proclaimed in the Charter.[28] This is reinforced by the coupling of self-determination of peoples with equal rights. Not every expression of a political concept in the Charter can be taken as creating legal obligations, notwithstanding the character of the Charter as a multilateral treaty, since the Charter is not only the constitution of the UN but a document of political faith.

The majority of writers have taken the view that the combined effect of Articles 1(2) and 55 is not such as to create binding legal obligations upon States to grant self-determination to nonindependent peoples. Bentwich and Martin regard Article 1(2) merely as 'a declaration of goodwill towards peoples who have not yet achieved self-determination',[29] while Fawcett considers self-determination as formulated in the Charter as a 'directive principle' similar in essence to Part IV, Article 37 of the Indian Constitution which lays down principles fundamental to the government of the country but nevertheless unenforceable by the courts.[30] In other words, the Charter provisions could not provide the legal basis for claims to self-determination by non-independent peoples.[31]

Kelsen adopted a different approach and took self-determination as expressed in the Charter as simply emphasizing the concept of the sovereignty of States. Since 'self-determination of the people usually designated a principle of internal policy, the principle of democratic government' and Article 1(2) referred to relations among States, and since 'the terms "peoples" too . . . in connection with "equal rights" means probably States since only States have "equal rights" according to general international law . . . then the self-determination of peoples in Article 1(2) can mean only sovereignty of the States'.[32]

This conservative interpretation, strongly influenced by traditional positivist philosophy, can no longer be accepted today in view of the wealth of State practice relating to the development of rights under international law for persons other than States. The view that the combination of equal rights and self-determination amounted only to a reinforcement of the sovereign equality of States can only be regarded as a misunderstanding of the basic trends in international law, while the idea that self-determination refers only to internal political situations has been contradicted by the evolution of the principle. However, there is a strong current of irony involved here, since Kelsen's conclusion that self-determination reinforces State sovereignty is not far off the mark in the light of the subsequent interpretation of the principle, although his reasoning is flawed. If one takes self-determination to be the right of non-independent peoples to sovereignty within accepted territorial limits (usually those defined by the administering power) and that alone, then the sanctity of the territorial sovereign is enhanced, the principle of territorial integrity underlined, and the right of minorities to secede from independent States eliminated.

Quincy Wright, however, has argued that the Charter did introduce binding duties for member States with respect to self-determination. He bases this opinion upon the proviso in Article 56 whereby all members 'pledge themselves to take . . . action for the purposes set forth in Article 55'. By ratifying the Charter, States have, according to Wright, undertaken such legal obligations.[33] But the point has to be made that the purposes in Article 55 are many and various, and it is by no means sure that the principle of the self-determination of peoples could be included as such a purpose.

In addition it is not certain that the expression 'pledge' alone can convert the humanitarian aims set out into binding legal obligations. For example, it would be difficult to say that the aim of 'full employment' is a legal duty on the State, indeed that it could be, merely by virtue of this provision in the UN Charter.

Although the discussion as to the legal status of the principle in the Charter has revolved around Articles 1(2) and 55, Bowett has noted that it is permissible 'to regard the entirety of Chapters XI and XII of the . . . Charter as reflections of the basic idea of self-determination'.[34] Chapter XI deals with non-self-governing territories, while Chapter XII deals with the trusteeship system. In neither is the concept expressly referred to, but those administering non-self-governing territories have by Article 73(b) to 'develop self-government, to take due account of the political aspirations of the peoples and to assist them in the progressive development of their free political institutions', and among the basic objectives of the trusteeship system in Article 76 is 'progressive development towards self-government or independence'. The freely expressed wishes of the people concerned have to be taken into account in fulfilling these objectives.

Van Asbeck has written that Chapter XI being in the form of a declaration imposes international duties,[35] but this was decidedly a minority viewpoint.[36]

The question as to the establishment of a legal right to self-determination has to be answered rather in the light of developments subsequent to the UN Charter. Practice since 1945 reveals certain trends towards regarding self-determination as a rule of international law. Declarations and resolutions adopted by the United Nations relating to the concept both in general theoretical terms and in specific cases have been numerous and have manifested a definite approach to the problem. But the issue as to whether such expressions have been sufficient to establish self-determination as a legal right lies at the heart of the matter and must be disentangled from the political aspects of the question.

It is generally accepted that its inclusion in the Charter did not *per se* transform it into a binding obligation as distinct from a non-legal guideline,[37] but the relevant provisons possessed considerable potential for development.[38]

The point should also be made that the fact that a particular purpose of the United Nations is not deemed to constitute a legally binding rule does not mean that it is devoid of effect within the sphere of law. It will be relevant as regards the interpretation of the Charter of the United Nations and may contribute towards the development of customary law.

There are basically two methods by which self-determination may have subsequently attained the status of law.[39]

The first derives from the character of the Charter as a multi-lateral treaty and the consequent capacity of the parties thereto to interpret its provisions. Could it be stated that subsequent practice has revealed the interpretation of the relevant Charter provisions in terms of self-determination as a legal right? The second manner in which State conduct could construe self-determination as a binding rule is by virtue of its development as a rule of customary law. Both methods utilize to some extent the same material, namely UN declarations and resolutions, but comprehend their role slightly differently.[40]

II. CHARTER INTERPRETATION

(a) General

The development of International legal rules through the medium of the United Nations has been one of the most striking and controversial aspects of post-1945 norm creation. The problem has already been considered at length,[41] but what we need to note here is a difficulty that has arisen as regards the relevance and application of the traditional sources of law to this phenomenon. The international community has recognized as law-creating mechanisms conventions, custom, and general principles of law recognized by civilized nations,[42] but it is clear that many of the activities connected with the UN Organization may be implicitly or explicitly creative of law in a manner which straddles the traditional classifications, and this is particularly so with regard to the political organs of the United Nations.[43] This has led Higgins to refer to the blurring in the United Nations of the historically separate sources of law and to emphasize the twilight zone between custom and treaty in the development of international law in the Charter and in the Organization as a whole.[44]

This arises primarily because of the tremendous amount of State practice generated through the UN Organization and produced by virtually all the independent States of the international community in an ever-increasing variety of situations, ranging from debates on colonialism in plenary session to discussion in committees such as the Commission of Human Rights and the International Law Commission. This vast array of State behaviour pattern has inevitably led to an increased awareness and emphasis upon such practice as norm-creative in given circumstances. One result of this has been the faster emergence of rules of customary law, while another has been the enhanced potentialities of Charter interpretation by State practice.

However, since the Charter as a multilateral treaty may be amended or interpreted by treaty action (i.e. by following the prescribed methods of amendment stipulated by Chapter XVIII), by custom, and (it is suggested) by State practice not amounting to custom, it is hardly surprising that the precise boundaries between the different processes are frequently difficult to clarify. Similarly, it is often hard to pin-point the exact legal manner in which a rule has emerged in the United Nations, since it could conceivably arise by virtue of Charter interpretations or amendment or customary international law or even as a general principle of law. In addition, an emerging proposition may be a legal norm or a principle by reference to which existing rules are to be interpreted.

This apparent flexibility in the methods of international law creation in the framework of the international organization has contributed to the relative decline of the consent theory of law and the rise of the consensus approach,[45] and this has some bearing upon the issue of the emergence of self-determination as a legal right through the process of General Assembly resolutions and declarations. The blurring of the division between the sources of law has led to great confusion as to whether or not a particular proposition is or is not law and to greater difficulties in identifying the criteria of norm-creation. It has also meant the comparative neglect of Charter interpretation as a separate category distinct from customary law. A number of writers, in fact, have discussed the role of UN resolutions as interpretations of the Charter in terms of the development of customary law,[46] and this had led to insufficient attention being paid to this process in the development of legal rules.

The parties to a treaty may subsequently interpret its provisions and could possibly be legally bound by such interpretations.[47] This proposition is illustrative of the principles of consent and good faith and reflects an old-established concept of international law. Article 31 of the

Vienna Convention on the Law of Treaties, 1969, notes that 'a treaty shall be interpreted in good faith in accordance with the ordinary meaning to be given to the terms of the treaty in their context and in the light of its object and purposes', while 'any subsequent practice in the application of the treaty which establishes the agreement of the parties regarding its interpretation' should be taken into account (Article 31(3)b).

It is this concept of subsequent practice interpreting the treaty which marks, as it were, the frontier between treaty and custom in the emergence of new international legal norms. It may be valid as a straightforward act of treaty interpretation or it may constitute State practice evidencing or leading to a new customary rule.

By Article 5, the Vienna Convention is deemed applicable to any treaty which is the constituent instrument of an international organization.[48] Such multilateral treaties are clearly in a special category since they create international entities with defined powers and purposes and go beyond the bounds of ordinary treaties. They invariably operate on a higher level of complexity as they specify not only the rights and duties of the signatories but also the function and aspirations of the newly created organization, and the intended pattern of its relationships with the member States. Nevertheless, in form such instruments are treaties and as such as subject *mutatis mutandis* to the law of treaties.[49]

Such treaty-charters incorporate a dynamic element which increases the likelihood of interpretation by subsequent practice, since the operations of the organizations of which they are the constitutional instruments invariably provide evidence and examples of the understanding of their charters by the member States.[50] Invariably the activities of international organizations emphasize the role and importance of interpretation by subsequent practice even if this is not always expressly recognized.

Higgins has pointed out that the notion of subsequent practice is ambiguous since it may refer either to treaty interpretation or to developing custom, but she appears to adopt the prevalent attitude by stressing that 'it seems to me that the repeated practice here of the organ interpreting the treaty establishes a *practice* and ultimately *custom*'.[51]

The Charter of the United Nations is a multilateral treaty and has been subjected to over thirty-five years of discussion, interpretation, and judicial opinion. It is unique in its universality of membership and function, and the wide range of subsequent practice relating to its role and powers places it in a category of its own. The question of the interpretation of the UN Charter, therefore, must be prefaced with a few words illustrating the general approach adopted.

It appears clear that, in the light of the special nature of the treaty-charters, the ordinary rules of interpretation of treaties may not suffice. This is primarily because of the powers and purposes ascribed to the organization, which have the effect of altering the emphasis of interpretation from the intention of the original parties to the intention of member States on the contemporary plane as manifested by practice and in the light of a collective appreciation of the purposes of the organization. This point was clearly put by Judge De Visscher, who noted that 'one must bear in mind that in the interpretation of a great international constitutional instrument like the UN Charter, the individualistic concepts which are generally adequate in the interpretation of ordinary treaties do not suffice.'[52]

Thus, a shift in the time-frame of reference from the past, i.e. the date of the treaty, to the present, coupled with an added emphasis upon a consensus perception of the purposes of the organization, constitute the main differentiating factors regarding the interpretation of treaty-charters as distinct from ordinary treaties.[53]

The intentions of the original contracting parties remain important[54] but as the amount of subsequent practice increases and the membership grows, the need for a wider base for interpreting the Charter becomes more apparent.[55] This process inevitably emphasizes the teleological approach to treaty interpretation, by which the treaty is comprehended in the light of its aims and objects[56] as against the textual and 'founding fathers' methods.[57] This approach has found favour with most of the representatives in UN debates,[58] and been propounded by a number of Judges of the International Court.[59] Such an approach means that 'an international instrument has to be interpreted and applied within the framework of the entire legal system prevailing at the time of the interpretation'.[60] This phrase, together with the statement that the concepts embodied in Article 22 of the Covenant of the League of Nations were 'by definition evolutionary',[61] appeared to mark the demise of the school emphasizing the predominant role to be played by the intentions of the original parties in treaty-charter interpretations.[62]

Judge De Castro declared that 'the teaching of the court is, in fact, that for the interpretation of the Charter, account must be taken of its fundamental purposes and it must be recognized that it has the powers which are necessary to achieve them "by necessary implication".'[63] This must be accepted as correct and the teleological approach to charter interpretation as the most important by far of the various schools and the one most productive of viable development. As De Castro pointed out

> it should not be forgotten that the General Assembly and the Security Council have the responsibility for promoting the purposes laid down in the Charter. They cannot remain bound by the possible intentions of the draftsmen, not only because it is difficult to know what those intentions were . . . but also because interpretation necessarily undergoes a process of development and as in municipal law must adapt itself to the circumstances of the time and to the requirements so far as they are foreseeable of the future. The text breaks away from its authors and lives a life of its own.[64]

The nature of the United Nations as an active political structure has reinforced these tendencies, particularly since the balance of membership has moved drastically since 1945.[65] International organizations are competent to interpret their own constitutions, but this is not an unrestricted capacity. They must have regard to the terms of the instrument and the aims and powers of the organisation. As far as the United Nations is concerned, the prime-facie scope for interpretation by subsequent practice is extensive in view of the essential characteristics and purpose of the Organization. Committee IV/2 of the San Francisco Conference reported that 'in the course of operations of the various organs of the organization, it is inevitable that each organ will interpret such parts of the Charter as are applicable to its particular functions . . . Accordingly it is not necessary to include in the Charter a provision authorising or approving the normal operation of this principle'.[66]

One question which is of particular concern is whether any special procedure is necessary to bring about a binding interpretation. Vallat, for example, takes the view that authoritative interpretations can only be by way of amendment,[67] while others consider that General Assembly resolutions on their own are quite sufficient.[68] Yet other jurists declare that where resolutions purporting to be interpretations are rejected by some other member States amendments would then be required.[69]

In any event, it appears to be accepted by most writers that at the very least, as noted by Judge Nervo, 'the General Assembly has competence in respect of the interpretation of the Charter'.[70]

The teleological approach has permitted a certain amount of flexibility within the basic structure of the UN Organization and its constitution and has been supported by judicial opinion. In the *Expenses* case, the International Court discussed the meaning of the word 'action' as it appeared in Article 11(2) of the Charter,[71] and came to the conclusion that it referred not to any kind of action, which would effectively reduce the General Assembly's function to simple recommendation, but to coercive or enforcement action alone.[72] In other words, 'action' meant only 'such action as is solely within the province of the Security Council',[73] and in deciding whether the actual expenses authorized were within the meaning of Article 17(2),[74] one had to test them by their relationship to the purposes of the United Nations. Such purposes, though broad, are not unlimited, 'but when the Organization takes action which warrants the assertion that it was appropriate for the fulfilment of one of the stated purposes of the United Nations, the presumption is that such action was not ultra vires the Organization'.[75] Thus the General Assembly was able to establish peace-keeping forces.[76]

The recognition by the ICJ of the competence of the General Assembly to make determinations as to the meaning and scope of Charter provisions, albeit not unlimited with regard to the stated purposes of the Organization, is valuable, but a few guidelines are proposed. The issue basically relates to the political structure and interrelationships of the United Nations and, as the court pointed out,

> in the legal system of States there is often some procedure for determining the validity of even a legislative or governmental act, but no analogous procedure is to be found in the structure of the United Nations. Proposals made during the drafting of the Charter to place the ultimate authority to interpret the Charter in the International Court of Justice were not accepted . . . therefore each organ must, in the first place at least, determine its own jurisdiction.[77]

Accordingly, therefore, one must examine the practice of the organ in question in order to see how it has tackled the problem of interpreting the various provisions of the Charter.

The problem is also raised that it is the UN's organs themselves that will usually constitute the fora for the determination of the constitutionality of their own acts.[78] As the court itself remarked in the statement quoted above, attempts to make the ICJ a final authority regarding the interpretation of the Charter were rejected. Recourse to the court will depend upon a positive decision by the particular organ, and the opinions of the International Court are only advisory in this field, though in practice usually adopted by resolution.[79]

This means that in practice a very high proportion of questions relating to the constitutionality of, for example, General Assembly resolutions will be considered only by the Assembly itself, and this has had a blurring effect on the subject of Charter interpretation and its limits.[80] There are indeed dangers inherent in the situation where organs are deemed to be the final authority as regards the constitutionality of their own acts, since majority voting could validate, as it were, provisions manifestly contrary to the stipulations enshrined in the Charter. Some safeguards therefore are necessary to prevent the process from degenerating into licence. These will take the form of determining the requirement of authoritativeness surrounding Charter interpretations in such a way as to protect the interests of the minority as well as to preserve some elements of continuity and stability in evolution of international legal principles.[81]

There have been varying views expressed as to the way in which the Charter may be amended, altered, and interpreted, and such views range widely. At this point we shall take a brief look at some of them in order to clarify the role and potentialities of Charter interpretation, particularly with regard to self-determination.

Chapter XVIII of the Charter prescribes two ways in which the Charter may be changed. The first (Article 108) is by way of amendments, which are to come into force for all UN members when adopted by a vote of two-thirds of the members of the General Assembly and ratified by at least two-thirds of UN members including all the permanent members of the Security Council. The second (Article 109) is by way of alteration, which is to follow upon a general conference for the review of the Charter and a recommendation by a two-thirds vote of the conference ratified by two-thirds of the members of the United Nations, including all the permanent members of the Security Council. These methods are the declared constitutional procedures enshrined in the constituent document of the UN Organization and there is a minority view to the effect that they are the sole means available for the modification of the Charter.[82]

However, despite this view it is possible to achieve some measure of change in the Charter. An instrument may be amended by the subsequent practice of the States parties to it. It is clear that custom may modify a previous treaty norm just as a treaty may alter a previous customary rule,[83] but practice not amounting to custom may accomplish the same objective. As Fitzmaurice has written, 'the way in which the parties have actually conducted themselves in relation to the treaty affords legitimate evidence as to its correct interpretation',[84] and the International Court has on a number of occasions had recourse to subsequent practice in order to aid in the process of treaty interpretation.[85] However, subsequent practice may not only clear up doubts and ambiguities in the text of the treaty, that is, act as an extraneous means of elucidation in the absence of clarity in the ordinary meaning of the words, but may also result in actual revision of the treaty itself.[86] This, as we have already noted, is particularly evident in the case of the international organizations where changing conditions and a wealth of day-to-day practice cannot but result in some modification of the original constituent documents.[87]

The question then arises as to the conditions under which this procedure might operate. It is generally accepted that the conduct involved will have to encompass a large number of the parties to the treaty[88] though conduct by one party might be relevant as regards the doctrines of acquiescence and estoppel. One cannot go so far, however, as to insist upon universal compliance since this could result in one State out of about 150 frustrating an agreement reached by all the others.[89]

Tunkin emphasizes that a further element must be that the practice in question is evidence of an agreement by the relevant parties to the intended modification.[90] This follows from his well-known views of custom as a form of tacit agreement and his emphasis upon the importance of the concordance of States' wills in the formation of rules of international law.[91] To the extent that the subsequent practice must clearly relate to a particular provision or set of provisons in the relevant treaty and that the States involved in the practice clearly wish to amend the treaty, Tunkin's opinion is valid. However, it is felt that the requirement that the practice should evidence the existence among the parties of an agreement respecting the attempted amendments is going too far and fails to recognize the point that the conduct need not amount to a custom before achieving a modification in the terms of the treaty.[92] Of course, a customary norm may alter a previous treaty provision if the necessary conditions apply, but conduct not amounting to custom may operate to alter treaty norms so long as it is clearly aimed as modifying such norms.[93]

General Assembly resolutions are in this instance particularly suited in form for this purpose. They constitute State practice and they are inherently linked to the UN Organization and its Charter. This does not mean that other practice is irrelevant but by the very nature of things Charter modification, by way of amendment or interpretation, may be more readily accomplished by General Assembly resolutions than by other methods.[94]

Judge Spender declared that although members of international organizations have the right to interpret the constituent instruments in good faith, 'their right to interpret . . . gives them no power to alter'.[95] This strict positivist viewpoint is predicated upon the need to preserve the consensual aspect of international law creation and lays excessive emphasis upon the actual wording of the text of the particular instrument. It ignores the fact that to interpret is to create and that the line to be drawn between interpretation *stricto sensu* and actual alteration is hazy and incapable of precise definition.[96]

Fitzmaurice appears to be moving towards this, and tentatively suggests that where subsequent practice has brought about a change or development in the meaning of a treaty through a revision of its terms by conduct, 'it is permissible to give effect to this change or development as an agreed revision but not as an interpretation of its original terms'.[97] Although this may seem confusing in introducing a concept of agreed revision and treating interpretations as equivalent (it would appear) to amendment, it is a recognition that subsequent conduct may reinterpret a treaty, particularly the UN Charter, within certain limits. But the problem still remains; that is, where to draw the line between interpretation and alteration (or, in Fitzmaurice's phrase, agreed revision), if indeed a line has to be drawn.

Tunkin takes the view that custom may amend treaties but not change the basic provisions of the treaty[98] and he gives as an example the modification of Article 27 of the UN Charter,[99] but he criticizes the Uniting for Peace resolution of 1950 as a violation of the Charter since it purported to amend basic provisions of the Charter.[100] In practice this distinction could prove elusive since perceptions as to such basic provisions may well alter with the passage of time and lead to complex problems of determination, while in theory it creates difficulties since it is arguable that even rules of *jus cogens* may be changed by virtue of the tacit consent of the vast majority of the members of a universal organization.[101]

However, one distinction does remain, and that is between amendments by subsequent practice and interpretations. It is a distinction that is in practice extremely difficult to define precisely, since the mechanics of change will be the same and States will rarely specify whether they feel that by a series of, for example, resolutions, they are amending or interpreting the Charter. Nevertheless, it is possible for a Charter provision to be interpreted by a majority of UN members in circumstances that might not amount to an amendment, for example, with respect to the members voting for it. In such cases, the persuasiveness of the interpretation would depend upon the number and identity of the States voting for it. Schachter, however, regards virtual unanimity as the true test of interpretation,[102] and this demonstrates again the process of merging amendment and interpretation in Charter modification.[103] This raises the question of the authoritativeness of such interpretations. Whereas an amendment by subsequent practice will be binding, whether a particular interpretation of a Charter provision contained in one or more resolutions of the General Assembly possesses a persuasive quality, and to what extent, will be determined on the basis of the numbers and identity of States voting for the proposed interpretation. Thus, Charter interpretation in this narrow sense constitutes one element of Charter modification by practice and is subsumed under the generally recognized heading of Charter interpretation. The advantage of this latter process is that it enables the majority of States to modify the Charter to accord with contemporary conditions, while imposing certain limitations as to the quantity of States proposing the change, and thus providing some protection to minorities. It is also necessary for the proposed modification to be directly referable to a particular provision of the Charter.

Such changes may be, and generally will be, accomplished by Assembly resolutions, which may either be related to a specific situation or be more generally framed. Thus, Charter interpretations may occur other than as responses to particular disputes. Not all such resolutions will be of the same persuasive nature and a series of resolutions over a period of time will usually be required.

(b) Self-Determination

1. *General Approach*

At this point we shall turn to examine the question of whether the right of self-determination can be regarded as established through the medium of Charter interpretation as a result of practice subsequent to the creation of the UN Organization. As an introduction, one should note the Universal Declaration of Human Rights. This was adopted on 10 December 1948, in the form of an Assembly resolution by 48 votes to 0, with 8 abstentions. It built upon Charter provisions regarding human rights (for example, Articles 1, 55, 56, 62, and 76) and enumerated a list of human rights and fundamental freedoms 'as a common standard of achievement for all peoples and all nations'.[104] Although the principle of self-determination was not referred to in this Declaration, which concentrated upon the elucidation of individual rights, its path forward was cleared in the same way in that democratic rights seemed to lead inevitably in international society to consideration of the rights of peoples to define their own cultural and national status.[105]

The Declaration was not legally binding as such in view of the terms in which it is expressed and the circumstances surrounding its adoption,[106] but has come to have a significant effect within the international community. Some of its provisions might be taken as reflecting general principles of law, others as relatively new international stipulations. However, it can be regarded in essence as an influential interpretation by the General Assembly of the relevant Charter provisions upon human rights and fundamental freedoms, and as such of legal value as part of the law of the United Nations.[107]

There have been a number of resolutions dealing with self-determination both generally and with regard to particular situations, and it is possible to point here to what appears to be a significant distinction. Resolutions and declarations that posit principles of law may be regarded as valid interpretations of the Charter if the necessary requirements of unanimity (or near-unanimity) and referral have been met. However, resolutions and other UN and State practice referable to the specific situations are often limited by two factors. Firstly, such practice in concentrating upon a particular situation is of restrictive value since it deals only with one aspect of the principle under discussion which may be modified or even distorted by virtue of other principles, deemed relevant in that particular situation,[108] and secondly by the greater likelihood of opposing votes and behaviour that will rob the practice of its claim to universality.[109] However, it is possible for such defects to be remedied by a consideration of the temporal element. In other words, a series of resolutions, for example calling for self-determination in different colonial territories, may be regarded as subsequent practice relevant to the interpretation of the particular Charter provisions in question. Examples of such practice will be noted in the following section,[110] but it will be useful in this context to recall the views of the ICJ regarding Article 27 of the Charter. The court declared that 'the proceedings of the Security Council extending over a long period supply abundant evidence that presidential rulings and the position taken by members of the Council . . . have consistently and uniformly interpreted the practice of voluntary abstention by a permanent member as not constituting a bar to the adoption of resolutions . . . . This procedure followed by the Security Council . . . has been generally accepted by members of the United Nations and evidences a general practice of that Organization.'[111]

A similar process can be seen with regard to Article 2(7) of the Charter, concerning domestic jurisdiction, which has over the years been increasingly restrictively interpreted[112] while the General Assembly has progressively widened the scope of its jurisdiction under Chapter XI of the Charter by asserting its competence both to request political information on non-self-governing territories under Article 73(e) and to decide which territories may be regarded as non-self-governing.[113] The Assembly has also proclaimed its authority to decide between competing aspirations of the right to self-determination and to declare whether territories have exercised or should exercise the right to self-determination.[114]

In all of these instances State practice over a period of time has been consolidated into Charter interpretation. Whether such practice can be treated as a valid interpretation will depend on all the circumstances of the case, but the presumption would be that the larger the number of resolutions, for instance applying the principle of self-determination to different territories, and the longer the period during which such practice has been operating, the greater would be the likelihood that a persuasive or even binding view of the Charter term has been expressed.

Resolution 421 (V) of 4 December 1950 embodied the request of the General Assembly for a study of the ways and means 'which would ensure the right of peoples and nations to self-determination', and this was taken further by resolution 545 (VI), which stated that the proposed article on self-determination in the International Covenants on Human Rights should be expressed in the terms that all peoples have the right to self-determination. It also noted that the article should stipulate that all States should promote the realization of the right in conformity with the principles and purposes of the United Nations. Resolution 637 (VII) proclaimed that self-determination was a fundamental human right.[115] This resolution also declared that UN member States 'shall recognise and promote the realization of the right' with regard to the peoples of trust and non-self-governing territories under their administration 'according to the principles and spirit of the Charter of the United Nations'.[116] The Commission on Human Rights considered the concept of self-determination over a number of sessions[117] and submitted recommendations to the UN Economic and Social Council, including a suggestion for the establishment of a Special Commission to examine situations resulting from alleged denials or inadequate realizations of the right to self-determination in certain circumstances.[118] This was, however, opposed and the matter was referred back to the Commission on Human Rights for reconsideration.[119] During the reconsideration a number of representatives pointed out that self-determination was only a principle and not a right. It was declared that the Charter had not granted the General Assembly competence to implement self-determination, although by way of contrast, implementation of Article 1(1) was provided for by Article 11 and that of Article 1(3) by Article 13.

Such objections were overridden, as was the view that the realization of self-determination fell essentially within the domestic jurisdiction of States, and the Commission reaffirmed its previous recommendation which was sent to the General Assembly.[120] The General Assembly at its eighth session asked the Commission to give priority to recommendations regarding international respect for the right of self-determination,[121] and by the next session the Assembly already had before it the draft International Covenants on Human Rights prepared by the Commission and transmitted by the Economic and Social Council.[122]

The Commission suggested that both International Covenants should have an identical first article[123] and this article, according to the draft of the Third Committee of the Assembly, read as follows:

> 1. All peoples have the right to self-determination. By virtue of the right they freely determine their political status and freely pursue their economic, social and cultural development . . . .
>
> 3. All States parties to the Covenant including those having responsibilities for the administration of non-self-governing and trust territories shall promote the realization of the right of self-determination and shall respect that right in conformity with the provisions of the UN Charter.[124]

At the Twelfth Session, the Assembly declared in resolution 1188 (XII) that member States were to give due respect to the right of self-determination. From this point, the proposed Covenants became enmeshed in UN discussions from which they were only to emerge nine years later.

At this point we shall turn to two General Assembly declarations that might be treated as authoritative interpretations of the Charter.[125]

The Declaration on the Granting of Independence to Colonial Countries and Peoples (the Colonial Declaration) was adopted by the General Assembly of 14 December 1960 in resolution 1514 (XI) by 89 votes to 0 with 9 abstentions. This has had a profound impact upon international affairs and has been treated with particular reverence by the States of the Third World. It has been regarded by many as the 'second Charter' of the United Nations drawn up for the subjugated peoples of Africa and Asia.[126] Indeed, Parry has written that the Declaration by itself has had the effect of modifying that part of international law that deals with territorial sovereignty.[127]

The Declaration emerged after a debate in the Assembly initiated by the Soviet premier[128] and was drafted by forty-three States.[129] The preamble noted that 'all peoples have an inalienable right to complete freedom, the exercise of their sovereignty and the integrity of their national territory' and proclaimed the necessity of 'bringing to a speedy and unconditional end colonialism in all its forms and manifestations'. The Declaration laid down seven principles, stressing that 'all peoples have the right to self-determination; by virtue of that right they freely determine their political status and freely pursue their economic, social and cultural development'. Inadequacy of political, economic, social, or educational preparedness was not to serve as a pretext for delaying independence. Immediate steps were to be taken to transfer power to the peoples of non-independent countries, but attempts aimed at the partial or total disruption of the national unit and territorial integrity of a country were deemed incompatible with the purposes and principles of the UN Charter.

The Declaration has been treated by a number of countries as constituting a binding interpretation of the Charter, or a restatement of principles enshrined in the Charter,[130] and it has been similarly regarded by some writers.[131] However, there are others who dispute this. One view already discussed is that any action by the General Assembly could only be recommendatory in such circumstances and that therefore the Declaration could be nothing more than a general statement of objectives.[132]

But the most significant criticism of the Declaration as an authoritative interpretation of the Charter is concerned with the inconsistencies that are noticeable between the two instruments. Paragraph 1 of the Declaration proclaimed that 'the subjection of peoples to alien subjugation, domination and exploitation constitutes a denial of fundamental human rights [and] is contrary to the Charter of the United Nations'. However, this is not too clear in the Charter itself, for Chapters XI and XII legitimize certain relationships of dependence regarding non-self-governing and trust territories,[133] subject to defined conditions.

The Declaration in paragraph 3 notes that 'inadequacy of political, economic, social or educational preparedness should never serve as a pretext for delaying independence', while Article 73(b) declares that States administering non-self-governing territories must 'assist them in the progressive development of their free political institutions, according to the particular circumstances of each territory and its peoples and their varying stages of advancement' and Article 76(b) underlines that among the basic objectives of the trusteeship system is the 'progressive development towards self-government or independence as may be appropriate to the particular circumstances of each territory and its peoples'.

Paragraph 5 of the Declaration emphasizes that 'immediate steps' should be taken in all non-independent territories to transfer power to the people, and this seems inconsistent with Articles 73 and 76. However, the call by the USSR, in particular, for immediate independence or the proclamation of a date at the end of 1961 for this to be achieved was not accepted[134] and this provision should perhaps be regarded rather as a change of pace than as a change of essence. The Declaration also blurs the distinction between trust and non-self-governing territories by positing the same provisions for all territories that have not yet attained independence. In addition, the Declaration in paragraph 5 appears to regard independence as the only legitimate goal of the whole process. This latter provision runs counter to a number of UN resolutions, for example those recognizing the exercise of self-determination involved in the relationship of dependence between the USA and the Commonwealth of Puerto Rico,[135] and between New Zealand and The Cook Islands[136] and Niue[137] after elections had been held in the respective dependent territories. In fact, the UN Secretary-General noted in 1963 that 'the emergence of dependent territories by a process of self-determination to the status of self-government either as independent sovereign States or as autonomous components of larger units has always been one of the purposes of the Charter and one of the objectives of the United Nations'.[138]

Such inconsistencies have led Bokor-Szego[139] and Martine,[140] for example, to deny that the Colonial Declaration is an authoritative interpretation since it appears actually to amend the Charter, the argument turning on where the line between interpretation and amendment should be drawn. Fifteen years of State practice in the process of decolonization formed the background to the Colonial Declaration and enabled it to bring up to date the relevant Charter provisions in a way marking contemporary consensus views as to, for example, the effect of inadequacy of political, social, economic, or educational preparedness. All interpretations refine and develop the concept under consideration, in a manner acceptable to those concerned, and may be no less influential or binding because of that.[141]

However, it does not follow that everything contained in the Declaration (or in similar resolutions, for that matter) constitutes a binding obligation. Some elements would remain upon a purely hortatory level, for example the solemn proclamation in the preamble to the Declaration stressing 'the necessity of bringing to a speedy and unconditional end colonialism in all its forms and manifestations'. On the other hand, there may be statements which are inconsistent with instruments interpreting the Charter—for instance, the apparent acceptance in the Declaration that independence is the sole object of self-determination. This contrasts with UN practice, as noted above, recognizing other relationships, and with the 1970 Declaration on Principles of International Law Concerning Friendly Relations and Co-operation among States in Accordance with the Charter of the United Nations (resolution 2625 (XXV)), which noted that 'the establishment of a sovereign and independent State, the free association or integration with an independent State or the emergence into any other political status freely determined by a people constitute modes of implementing the right of self-determination by that people'.[142]

It would therefore seem that where one is faced by conflicting interpretations of equal standing, resort must be had to the intentions of the members of the United Nations, as revealed in their practice, and upon this basis it would seem that the stipulation in the 1960 Declaration restricting self-determination to the attainment of independence must be regarded as only a suggestion and not an authoritative interpretation of the Charter. Nevertheless the core of the Declaration does constitute an interpretation of the Charter and one that has underpinned the end of colonialism.[143]

Higgins has noted that it 'must be taken to represent the wishes and beliefs of the full membership of the United Nations'.[144] As to the juridical character of the Declaration, Higgins stresses that in it the right of self-determination is regarded 'as a legal right enforceable here and now'.[145]

This approach is underlined by the action taken by the United Nations to implement the Declaration. On 27 November 1961 the General Assembly created a subsidiary organ entitled the Special Committee on the Situation with regard to the Implementation of the Declaration on the Granting of Independence,[146] which was enlarged from seventeen to twenty-four member States the following year.[147] It has gradually widened its sphere of activity so that, apart from the Trusteeship Council (which is only concerned now with the trust territory of the Pacific Islands), it is the only organ responsible for issues dealing with dependent territories. The Committee has been very active and has done much to pressure the colonial powers and the administering powers.[148] It has also stressed the position that the United Nations intended the Colonial Declaration to act as a juridical signpost to complete decolonization and not merely as a solely hortatory pronouncement.

Virtually all UN resolutions proclaiming the right to self-determination of particular peoples expressly refer to the 1960 Declaration.[149] Judge De Castro particularly noted in the *Western Sahara* case how the African group at the United Nations that prepared a draft resolution on the Sahara problems for discussion in the Fourth Committee was at pains to refer four times to resolution 1514 (XV) in reaffirming the right of the people of Western Sahara to self-determination.[150] The International Court has specifically referred to the Colonial Declaration as an 'important stage' in the development of international law regarding non-self-governing territories,[151] and as 'the basis for the process of decolonization'.[152]

On 16 December 1966 the General Assembly adopted the International Covenants on Human Rights, which consisted of the International Covenant on Economic, Social and Cultural Rights, the International Covenant on Civil and Political Rights, and the Optional Protocol to the latter. Both Covenants have an identical first article which declares *inter alia* that 'all peoples have the right to self-determination. By virtue of that right they freely determine their political status and freely pursue their economic, social and cultural development' and that 'the States parties to the present Convention including those having responsibility for the administration of non-self-governing and trust territories shall promote the realization of the right of self-determination and shall respect that right in conformity with the provisions of the Charter of the United Nations'.

The inclusion of the right to self-determination in the International Covenants occurred because the General Assembly in resolution 545 (VII) recommended that the proposed Covenants should incorporate such a provision and in resolution 637 (VII) declared that the right to self-determination was a 'fundamental human right'. It is to be noted that the preambles to both the Covenants refer to the 'obligation of states under the Charter of the United Nations to promote universal respect for and observance of human rights and freedom'.[153]

The International Covenants came into force in 1976[154] and are thus binding as between the parties, but it would seem that they are of legal value over and above that, not only as practice leading to or reflecting a customary rule, but also as a persuasive interpretation of the notion of human rights as embodied in the Charter.[155]

This appears so in view of the drafting history of the Covenants through the various organs of the United Nations, culminating in the adoption of resolution 2200 (XXI), and the emphasis in the many discussions and resolutions and in the Covenants themselves upon the actual provisions of the Charter.[156] The preambles to the Covenants specifically recall various Charter provisions (particularly Articles 1, 55, and 56) and the Universal Declaration of Human Rights.

The Declaration on Principles of International Law Concerning Friendly Relations and Co-operation among States in accordance with the Charter of the United Nations was unanimously adopted without a vote on 24 October 1970 and is contained in the annexe to General Assembly resolution 2625 (XXV). It proclaims seven principles, including the principle of equal rights and self-determination of peoples. And the question that is raised at this stage is whether this Declaration may be regarded as a binding interpretation of the Charter. The Declaration was specifically stated to deal with certain international legal principles 'in accordance with the Charter of the United Nations' and the preamble includes the phrase 'considering the provisions of the Charter as a whole and taking into account the role of relevant resolutions adopted by the competent organs of the United Nations relating to the content of the principles'. This suggests not only that such resolutions are relevant in a Declaration of principles 'in accordance with the Charter', thus impliedly reinforcing the importance of the interpretative role of such resolutions, but also that the Declaration itself constitutes an interpretation of the Charter provisions. The reason for the interpretation is emphasized in the preamble, which notes that 'the great political, economic and social changes and scientific progress which have taken place in the world since the adoption of the Charter of the United Nations give increased importance to these principles and to the need for their more effective application in the conduct of States wherever carried on'. The Declaration stresses that 'nothing in this Declaration shall be construed as prejudicing in any manner the provisions of the Charter or the rights and duties of member States under the Charter or the rights of peoples under the Charter, *taking into account the elaboration of these rights in this Declaration*'.[157]

The Declaration states that 'by virtue of the principle of equal rights and self-determination of peoples enshrined in the Charter of the United Nations, all peoples have the right freely to determine . . . their political status and to pursue their economic, social and cultural development', while 'every State has the duty to respect this right in accordance with the provisions of the Charter'. Arangio-Ruiz strongly asserts the non-legal status of the Declaration since it was effected at the merely organic or institutional level rather than on a formal, legally binding inter-State level[158] and concludes that 'there can hardly be any doubt . . . that the Declaration embodied in Resolution 2625 (xxv) . . . is to be considered from a legal point of view as an instrument of a purely hortatory value'.[159] This approach, however, cannot be supported. The Declaration was intended to act as an elucidation of certain important Charter provisions, although not as an actual amendment of the Charter, and was adopted by member States on that basis.[160]

State practice within and outside the United Nations also supports the view that the right to self-determination exists in international law. State practice, other than resolutions and declarations purporting to express principles of law, can be important in the process of Charter interpretation provided it is linked to particular Charter stipulations and provided over a period of time sufficient practice has accumulated for it to be treated as a valid and general interpretation rather than as strictly limited conduct specifically related to a particular situation.

It is realized that this formulation may fail to provide an adequate guide as to whether a proposition can be accepted as an authoritative Charter interpretation in a number of instances, but it is clearly impossible to lay down firm conditions as to the time that should be encompassed or the number of relevant resolutions that must be adopted. In each case much will depend upon acceptance and acquiescence by an increasing number of States regarding the propositions involved in particular situations constituting general principles interpreting the Charter.

One must be careful not to deny the members of an organization the capacity to harmonize its constitution with contemporary needs by means of their subsequent practice. After all, the aim of interpretation is to enable the overwhelming majority to determine the nature and extent of the obligations and rights they have agreed to in circumstances minimizing adverse effects upon dissentient members.[161]

State practice that does not fall within the categories mentioned may nevertheless be relevant in the process of Charter interpretation as evidence of recognized interpretations, and thus may be of value in emphasizing the form and content of a particular interpretation. It may also play a vital role in pointing out which interpretations are to be regarded as valid, binding ones, much as State practice may also constitute evidence of particular rules of customary law. State practice, of course, may also lead to a new customary law. One should note that those member States that abstain with regard to such interpreting resolutions as the 1960 and 1970 Declarations discussed above may well still be bound by them.[162]

2. *Specific Approach*

State practice, particularly as manifested in the United Nations, concerning the status and application of self-determination in specific situations exceeds the abstract, general expression of self-determination as a right, in terms of both frequency and diversity, and accordingly must be considered as a significant factor.

General Assembly resolutions proclaiming that specific territories should be entitled to the exercise of the right of self-determination are ultimately founded upon the established competence of the Assembly to determine which territories are non-self-governing. This is partly because self-determination has been deemed non-applicable to independent territories and partly to side-step the doctrine of domestic jurisdiction.

Article 2(7) of the Charter declares that 'nothing contained in the present Charter shall authorize the United Nations to intervene in matters which are essentially within the domestic jurisdiction of any State' and the history of the first decade and a half of the UN Organization largely centres around attempts to establish a balance between this provision and the perceived need to end colonialism. This latter aim was achieved, at least as far as the United Nations was concerned, through establishing a clear divison between the administering State and its administered territories, contrary to the wishes of a number of colonial powers, particularly France with regard to Algeria and Portugal with regard to its African possessions. Having instituted this division and provided an exception to Article 2(7), the Assembly proceeded to make recommendations regarding the future of these non-self-governing territories.[163] Based upon its recognized competence to decide which territories were non-self-governing territories, the General Assembly successfully asserted its competence to determine whether or not a non-self-governing territory had attained a full measure of self-government as referred to in Chapter XI of the Charter, and to this end a series of resolutions were adopted expressing the Assembly's views as regards specific cases.[164] Despite the objections of the colonial powers, the doctrine of domestic jurisdiction as declared in Article 2(7) has been interpreted by the subsequent practice of the UN Organization and its members so that the affairs of non-self-governing territories may be discussed within the Organization and rendered subject to UN resolutions and declarations as to their political status.

The competence of the Assembly was initially founded upon Chapter XI of the Charter, but later resolutions disregarded this Chapter and concentrated instead on the concept of self-determination as the basic relevant principle.

The large number of Assembly resolutions calling for self-determination in specific cases represents international practice regarding the existence and scope of a rule of self-determination in customary law. They also constitute subsequent practice relevant to the interpretation of particular Charter provisions. For example, resolutions proclaiming that an obligation exists under Article 73(e) of the Charter to transmit information in a particular case may be regarded as a binding interpretation of the Charter provision in that specific instance since the competence of the General Assembly to determine such matters has been clearly recognized.[165] The change from Chapter XI to self-determination with the Colonial Declaration as the juridical basis for the process marks the stronger line taken by the Assembly as a whole but the effect remains broadly similar—that is, the determination by the General Assembly of a factual situation within which the declared norm will be deemed to operate. By such methods, of course, the outlines of the norm itself will be elucidated, and to that extent factual determinations by the Assembly will be juridically relevant.

However, unlike Assembly resolutions of a general nature, they cannot themselves authoritatively interpret a principle as a legally binding norm; their function in this sphere rests rather upon delimitation,[166] though such determinations may also provide for the application of non-legal principles to a particular situation.

The Algerian problem[167] was first included on the agenda of the assembly in 1955, and it was claimed that France had broken the provisions of the Charter on self-determination.[168] The Assembly, however, decided not to pursue the matter[169] and the Security Council did not place it upon its agenda.[170] In succeeding sessions, resolutions proclaiming the right of the Algerian people to self-determination failed to be adopted although support for the proposition was growing.[171] In fact, it was only in 1960 that a resolution was adopted which referred to the right of the Algerian people to self-determination.[172] Despite this hesitant start, and in view of the changed climate of opinion in France itself, the Assembly passed without opposition in the following session resolution 1724 (XVI) which called for the implementation of 'the right of the Algerian people to self-determination and independence respecting the unity and territorial integrity of Algeria'.

This resolution, which significantly referred to the Colonial Declaration of 1960, also asserted that the United Nations had a part to play in the fulfilment of this right.

A large role has been performed in this process by the Special Committee established after the adoption of the Colonial Declaration.[173] For example, the Special Committee was requested to study the situation in Southern Rhodesia by General Assembly resolution 1745 (XVI) and its report formed the basis of an Assembly resolution criticizing the failure of the United Kingdom to carry out the Colonial Declaration, and affirming that Southern Rhodesia was a non-self-governing territory.[174] The Assembly adopted resolution 1755 (XVII) proclaiming the right of the people of Southern Rhodesia to self-determination, and the problem has been discussed at the United Nations at great length.[175] The claim of the United Kingdom that the problem was an internal matter and that therefore the United Nations could not consider it, was clearly rejected, and resolution 1747 (XVI) affirmed that 'the territory of Southern Rhodesia is a non-self-governing territory within the meaning of Chapter XI of the Charter of the United Nations'.[176] This situation was altered, at least as far as the United Kingdom was concerned, by the unilateral declaration of independence by the government of Southern Rhodesia, but the General Assembly vigorously attacked 'any agreement reached between the administering power and the illegal racist minority regime which will not recognise the inalienable rights of the people of Zimbabwe to self-determination and independence in accordance with General Assembly resolution 1514 (XV)'[177]

In its first six years, the Special Committee considered some seventy territories,[178] and in 1974, for example, it discussed thirty-nine territories, the majority being Pacific or Atlantic islands.[179] In virtually all cases the Special Committee has recommended that the territory become independent in the light of its right to self-determination, although in some instances association with another State was accepted, for example, Niue and the Cook Islands.

Throughout the years of the existence of the UN Organization a great number of resolutions have been adopted calling for self-determination in particular situations and these constitute State practice and international practice of overwhelming importance. The majority of such resolutions have referred specifically to the 1960 Colonial Declaration, thus strengthening its claim to be the fount of legality as far as the right to self-determination is concerned. It has been noted that 'if this right [of self-determination] is still not recognized as a juridical norm in the practice of a few rare States or the writings of certain even rarer theoreticians, the attitude of the former is explained by their concern for their traditional interests, and that of the latter by a kind of extreme respect for certain long-entrenched postulates of classical international law'.[180]

It is submitted in conclusion that the right to self-determination has been accepted by the United Nations by virtue of the process of Charter interpretation as a basic principle in the law of the United Nations, and that from this proposition certain legal effects flow with regard to, for example, the definition of the determining unit, the capacity of the people of the territory in question to decide its political, economic and social status, the role of force in the process, and the *locus standi* of the colonial power.[181] Some of these notions will be examined in later chapters.[182]

III. CUSTOMARY INTERNATIONAL LAW

The practice supporting the right of self-determination as emanating from Charter interpretation may also be of relevance in establishing the existence of a right to self-determination as a rule of customary law. Custom differs from treaty interpretation in a number of vital ways. It is founded on State practice, whereas treaty interpretation relates to practice construed with reference to a treaty provision, and it is dependent upon the *opinio juris*, the belief or expression of an accepted legal obligation. This, as we have seen, is not necessarily the case with respect to the interpretation of treaty-charters, for practice not amounting to custom may have the effect of interpreting a particular stipulation.

The International Court of Justice is directed by Article 38(1) of its statute to apply 'international custom as evidence of a general practice accepted as law' and Brierly emphasized this in terms of a 'usage felt by those who follow it to be an obligatory one'.[183] Oppenheim notes that 'whenever and as soon as a line of international conduct frequently adopted by States is considered legally obligatory or legally right, the rule which may be abstracted from such conduct is a rule of customary international law'.[184]

Precisely how one is to interpret and balance the two factors of State practice and *opinio juris* is subject to conflicting analyses,[185] but it is commonly recognized that both elements are required. Usage is needed as the source material delineating the content and scope of the proposed rule, while the *opinio juris* is essential in differentiating norms of customary international law from State behaviour embarked upon for reasons of courtesy, morality, or expediency alone, since the latter forms of conduct are clearly intended to have no legal effect at all.

As far as self-determination is concerned, practice is extensive both within and outside the United Nations. Tied to the issue of colonialism as it has been virtually since the adoption of the Charter, it has constituted one of the major concerns of the Organization as any analysis of debates, resolutions, and declarations will attest. Kay notes that between 1960 and 1967 the number of speeches by representatives of the new nations devoted to decolonization outweighed those relating to any other topic in plenary and main committee meetings, with the exception of the Assembly's Twentieth Session when the issue of economic aid received marginally more attention.[186]

If one includes the topic of South Africa, which has been treated by many nations as an aspect of the general problem of decolonization, the emphasis becomes even more evident. It is clear that the interest of the Third World nations of Africa and Asia has focused primarily upon the decolonization issue, with the problems of economic aid and development coming more to the fore as the number of countries still under colonial rule rapidly declines. This issue has been broadly defined and extended so that it has assumed the status of a general category incorporating a number of specific questions. The Ghanaian representative to the Sixteenth Session of the General Assembly declared that 'in our view, colonialism is the greatest evil of the modern world, the source of all the troubles which presently afflict mankind. It is the root-cause of the arms race and the problem of disarmament. Colonialism and neo-colonialism are a perpetual threat to the peace and sovereignty of the world. Colonialism is the cause of war and conflict among nations and is, therefore, the greatest danger to world peace.'[187]

The number of resolutions directly concerned with self-determination is high and forms a vital part of the UN attitude to the decolonization process. Of necessity, therefore, one must consider whether such resolutions can be regarded as constituting State practice for the purposes of customary law formation.

Resolutions may be relevant in the context of norm creation or determination in a number of differing ways. They may constitute binding or persuasive interpretations of the UN Charter. They may evidence and reflect recognized rules of international law whether created through the medium of treaty or custom or as general principles of law recognized by civilized nations.[188] In this case, resolutions merely underline the accepted position and have no norm-creating functions to fulfil. More crucial is the role played by resolutions within the process of customary law formation. This may take the form either of a stimulus to State practice[189] or of actual State practice or indeed of manifesting the *opinio juris*.

In the first case, that of a resolution encouraging the growth of usage, what is involved is clearly an extra-legal factor and one which does not need to be considered further, since many activities may perform such an encouraging role, ranging from resolutions of private bodies to opinions of legal writers. But the second and third possibilities must be considered briefly. Whether a usage is solely a practice or also incorporates within itself the expression of *opinio juris* is often difficult to decide. A State which makes a claim asserted as a legal right is not only exhibiting a practice but is also evidencing the *opinio juris*, thus the borderline between the material and psychological requirements of customary law created is blurred. This is particularly true with respect to Assembly resolutions, since they are often assertions of rights under international law. An example of this would be the Declaration of Legal Principles Governing the Activities of States in the Exploration and Use of Outer Space, adopted unanimously on 13 December 1963.[190] It was regarded as a declaration of existing law by many States, including the most important in the field,[191] as well as by a number of writers.[192]

The expression of State support for a particular declaration or resolution, however, whether by statement or voting, constitutes State practice,[193] while the assertion of the legality of the principles outlined therein is clear evidence of the *opinio juris*.[194] Thirlway has emphasized the need to maintain a clear distinction between usage and *opinio juris* in order to prevent alleged rules lacking both components from becoming part of customary law,[195] but the fact remains that the two are closely intertwined, particularly with regard to UN practice. The difficulty of unravelling the two with respect to Assembly resolutions is one more aspect of the changes brought about by the institution and operations of the United Nations within the sphere of international law.[196] Self-determination was clearly not a rule of customary law prior to the Charter[197] and the overwhelming bulk of practice regarding the concept has clearly occurred in connection with the United Nations.[198] Thus one must focus on this aspect.

The concern of the United Nations with regard to self-determination has been two-pronged. On the one hand, the Organization has affirmed the right to self-determination of all peoples in general terms and consistently since 1952. This has been included not only in a number of

Assembly resolutions and declarations but also in the International Covenants on Human Rights adopted in 1966. On the other hand, the right has been declared in a number of specific situations and disputes. This had tended to increase the plausibility of the entry of self-determination into the panoply of international customary rules, since the greater the practice relating to a particular proposition, the greater the likelihood that it has been accepted as a custom. This also applies to the length of time during which the principle has been affirmed as a right. The longer the process has taken the greater the chances that it has hardened into a rule. In any event, it is clear that more practice affords more opportunity from which to infer the *opinio juris*. It is interesting to note that Judge Dillard has stated that 'even if a particular resolution of the General Assembly is not binding, the accumulative impact of many resolutions when similar in content, voted for by overwhelming majorities and frequently repeated over a period of time, may give rise to a general *opinio juris* and thus constitute a norm of customary international law'.[199]

IV. CONCLUSIONS

It is thus concluded that the right to self-determination is a legal right as a result of Charter interpretation and that the possibility, additionally, is raised of the right constituting also a customary right, although UN practice appears to have strongly favoured the former approach.

Recent judicial pronouncements on self-determination are surprisingly rare and centre around the *Namibia* case of 1971 and the *Western Sahara* case of 1975.[200] The court, in the former case, noted that 'the subsequent development of international law in regard to non-self-governing territories as enshrined in the Charter of the United Nations made the principle of self-determination applicable to all of them'[201] without really specifying how this has occurred or what possibly is involved,[202] and proceeded to refer to the Colonial Declaration as 'a further important stage in this development'[203] without further clarification. In interpreting the mandate, therefore, the court had to consider 'the changes which have occurred in the supervening half-century . . . by the subsequent development of law, through the Charter of the UN and by way of customary law'.[204] However, the court failed to confirm whether or not self-determination was a binding legal principle in its own right.

The court's observations of self-determination in the *Namibia* case were quoted extensively in the *Western Sahara* case, where the court similarly refrained from a clear declaration. The Colonial Declaration was referred to as 'the basis for the process of decolonization',[205] and the essence of self-determination was discussed in relation to resolution 1541 (xv) and the 1970 Declaration on Principles of International Law.[206] Such instruments constituted the 'basic principles governing the decolonization policy of the General Assembly'.[207] Judge Dillard regarded the opinion as forthright in proclaiming the existence of the rights as far as the proceedings were concerned, but he went further and declared that 'the pronouncements of the Organization thus indicate . . . that a norm of international law has emerged applicable to the decolonization of those non-self-governing territories which are under the aegis of the United Nations'.[208] Although he does not expressly bring out the process by which this has occurred, Judge Dillard draws attention to the long list of resolutions dealing with self-determination following in the wake of the Colonial Declaration.[209] The result, therefore, appears to be that the opinion recognizes that self-determination is a legal right[210] but is unclear as to how that has arisen exactly.[211]

A norm created as a result of Charter interpretation, it should be noted, will bind all members of the United Nations, while a customary rule will bind all States save those objecting *ab initio*. Thus, the former method would appear the more advantageous, particularly as regards, for example, South Africa. Indeed, the fact that self-determination applies virtually exclusively within the colonial sphere (although with some potential for development) is a further argument favouring the Charter interpretation approach, since the distinction between colonies and metropolitan territories is one made by the Charter.

One further point remains, and that is the possibility that self-determination constitutes a rule of *jus cogens*, and thus a peremptory norm of international law from which no derogation is permitted. The question of the existence and nature of *jus cogens* is one that has received much attention in recent years, being partly stimulated by discussions and debates leading up to the Vienna Convention on the Law of Treaties in 1969.[212] The basis of such rules, which cannot be changed save by contradictory rules of the same status, has been variously ascribed to natural law[213] and to international public policy.[214]

However, despite differences as to the origin of *jus cogens*, its essence is generally accepted.[215] The International Law Commission discussed the concept[216] and incorporated it into the final draft on the law of treaties in 1966.[217] Article 53 of the Vienna Convention specifies that a treaty is void if, at the time of its conclusion, it conflicts with a peremptory norm of general international law. For the purposes of the present Convention, a peremptory norm of general international law is a norm accepted and recognized by the international community of States as a whole as a norm from which no derogation is permitted and which can be modified only by a subsequent norm of general international law having the same character.

O'Connell has written that 'the inclusion of the concept of *jus cogens* in the Vienna Convention constitutes an important recognition of the fact that contemporary society is bound together by the acceptance of fundamental principles constituting the rule of law'.[218]

If the concept of *jus cogens* is generally accepted, no such agreement is manifested with regard to the creation of rules of *jus cogens* or their scope or, indeed, which rules can be included as rules of *jus cogens*. However, there is a body of juristic opinion which declares that the rules of *jus cogens* are formed in the same way as other norms of international law, that is, primarily by way of custom and treaty, and can be modified by such means,[219] thereby placing the concept firmly within the ambit of positive law and away from any variant of natural law thinking.[220]

The problem of the emergence of a new rule of *jus cogens* is centred upon the conduct of States as a whole and a new principle might arise by way of inference from State practice.[221] How one might decide whether a new rule appertains to *jus dispositivum* or to *jus cogens* is open to question and would depend to a large extent upon the intentions of the international community and the universality of the rule involved.

One may illustrate this point by noting some examples of *jus cogens*.[222] The most recognizable relate to the proscription of aggression[223] and the prohibition of crimes against humanity and peace,[224] while other possibilities include the banning of slavery, piracy, and genocide.[225] Some jurists regard the rule against racial discrimination as an aspect of *jus cogens*.[226]

It is arguable that the principle of self-determination also falls within the category of *jus cogens*[227] and a number of members of the International Law Commission appeared to be of this opinion.[228] It would indeed be difficult to conceive of a treaty providing for the continuation of a colonial relationship against the wishes of the inhabitants of the territory being upheld as valid. Self-determination is a basic principle of international law of universal application, while the weight of international opinion appears to suggest that the right may be part of *jus cogens*.

3
Self-Determination, Decolonization and Territory

ONE of the major factors in any consideration of international relations since 1945 has been the advent of decolonization, whereby scores of entities administered by European powers have emerged upon the world scene as sovereign and independent nations. This process has been of tremendous significance within international law. However, although decolonization has been extensively discussed in the United Nations, it has only really been considered by the judicial organs of the international community in the *Namibia*[1] and *Western Sahara*[2] cases, and then not in any great detail. Until these cases, and to some extent after them, the status in law of the principles relating to decolonization has been the subject of much debate. In particular, the definition of the entity seeking independence and the precise extent of its territorial and temporal delimitation remain open to conflicting interpretations. Clearly, much hinges upon an appreciation of the principle of self-determination and the definition of the 'self', but that notion as comprehended in moral or political terms is more extensive than is apparently the case with the legal concept, since it would permit any set of persons linked together by a sense of group-consciousness to determine its political status.[3] To permit such a wide proposition within the framework of international legal regulations, with consequent obligations, would be hazardous to the dominant State system in international relations. It would threaten the territorial basis of international law as it has developed, and it would pose particular dangers to the precarious stability of Third World States, the vast majority of which are not nation-States in the nineteenth-century European sense, but State-nations,[4] in that diverse ethnic, religious, linguistic, and cultural groupings have to be reconciled within the framework of one State. In other words, the State precedes the development of the territorial nation, but is faced with powerful loyalities generated by sub-State community ties. This creates a crisis of legitimacy, since the State is founded not upon a genuine sense of community, but upon the vagaries and power-ranking of nineteenth-century European colonial empires. Thus, the emphasis upon the necessity of maintaining colonial frontiers clearly demonstrated by the overwhelming majority of Afro-Asian and South American States[5] can be understood in terms of the necessity of establishing stable legitimacy factors. But this has meant a general freezing of territorial entities as at the eve of decolonization and a consequent disregard for ethnic and historical ties which cross the old colonial border, or at the least a minimization of their importance in territorial terms. Accordingly, the principle of self-determination has operated in practice to safeguard the colonial delimitations and overrule purely ethnic definitions of the 'self', so that the 'self' must be determined within the colonial territorial context. Despite some controversy, it is clear that the concept of self-determination has played a crucial role in the replacement of the colonial African (and Asian) empire by individual, sovereign States. The reference of the Western Sahara problem to the International Court of Justice was particularly advantageous, in that an opportunity was thus presented for clear judicial pronouncements on the relevance and hierarchy of the various principles involved.

I. SELF-DETERMINATION AND DECOLONIZATION: THE WESTERN SAHARA ANALYSIS

The principle of self-determination has been defined in very wide terms in international agreements. It has been propounded as the right of all peoples to determine their political status and pursue their own economic, social, and cultural development.[6] This broad approach incorporates a series of propositions. Firstly, that all 'peoples', however defined, have the right to establish their own sovereign, independent State. Secondly, that every people has the right freely to choose its own political system internally.[7] Thirdly, that upon the achievement of independence via self-determination as formulated in the first proposition the people (in the sense of the State) attains sovereignty free from the claims of other peoples (in the sense of resident minorities).[8] Fourthly, the right of the people (i.e. the State and maybe its inhabitants) to develop its own patterns of social, economic, and cultural behaviour, and fifthly, the right of peoples and nations to permanent sovereignty over their natural wealth and resources.[9] The second, fourth, and fifth propositions are beyond the scope of this work, but are mentioned to illustrate the range of this principle.

The nature of self-determination and its relationship with the process of decolonization was extensively discussed during the course of the *Western Sahara* case.[10] The questions posed by Assembly resolution 3292 (XXIX)[11] were firmly placed within the context of self-determination and decolonization. The resolution reaffirmed the right of the people of the territory to self-determination in accordance with resolution 1514 (XV), noted that the request to the court was made without prejudice to the principles embodied in that resolution, and specified that the court's opinion would be of value in the process of decolonization of Western Sahara. The court recognized that the principles of decolonization were an essential part of the framework of the questions contained in the request[12] and that the right of the people of the territory to self-determinaton constituted a basic assumption of the questions.[13] In the case of Western Sahara, both Morocco and Mauritania, the claimant States, had voted in favour of Assembly resolutions proclaiming the right of self-determination for the population of the territory,[14] as had Spain[15] and Algeria.[16] These States had also supported the right in express terms.[17] The problem was that the parties had different views both of the role of self-determination within the context of decolonization and the framework of international law in general, and of the actual content of the principle.

Morocco declared that the fundamental relevant rule was that of decolonization, characterized as a rule of *jus cogens* and an 'end-norm', towards the attainment of which a variety of techniques and principles were available as 'means-norms'.[18] As examples of such principles, one could cite self-determination and territorial integrity. Therefore, a wide range of possibilities lay before the Assembly in its task of decolonizing territories, in the light of the UN Charter and various resolutions, such as resolutions 1514 (XV), 1541 (XV) and 2625 (XXV). The right to self-determination was certainly relevant, but it had to coexist with other principles, such as that of territorial integrity, and in certain cases it was deemed subordinate to the latter concept. The Moroccan representative, Professor Dupuy, put forward a typology by which to reconcile the various factors in the light of State practice. It was accepted that the right of self-determination existed with regard to non-self-governing territories in areas where no State had been recognized by the international community in the nineteenth century. It was agreed that the right did not exist respecting independent States so as to destroy the unity of such countries. However, in the case of States which had enjoyed international recognition prior to colonization and had then been dismembered, such as Morocco, it was suggested that self-determination gave way to reunification and the re-establishment of the former State's territorial integrity. Thus, the pre-colonial State came back into existence with all of its dismembered parts recovered.[19]

Mauritania characterized the issue as 'quite simply that of our territorial integrity, the unity of our people'.[20] Although the principle of self-determination was accepted, it was emphasized that the Sahara was an integral part of Mauritania and that the latter had a right of reunification.[21] The principle of self-determination was connected with the principle of national unity and territorial integrity referred to *inter alia* in resolutions 1514 (XV) and 2625 (XXV), and in practice the General Assembly often gave priority to the latter principle, it was claimed, particularly where colonialism had taken lands from an existing State and artificially created a new territory.[22]

The attitude taken by Algeria and Spain was completely different. Algeria recognized the right of self-determination as 'one of the great principles of contemporary international law and decolonization . . . only one of its manifestations'.[23] It was an essential and primary legal principle from which the other principles governing the international community flowed, and therefore was a rule of *jus cogens*. It operated as a direct opposite to the concept of *terra nullius*[24] in reaffirming the rule of peoples and was a higher principle than those underlying territorial claims.[25] The territorial integrity of a non-self-governing territory was guaranteed under international law and its incorporation into a neighbouring State could only be justified by the wishes of the former's population, and not upon the basis of any alleged territorial integrity of the latter. Moroccan reliance upon paragraph 6 of resolution 1514 (XV)[26] was based upon a misinterpretation, since it did not aim at giving territorial claims priority over self-determination. The paragraph referred only to future attempts and not to disputes of the past.[27] Therefore, Algeria supported the right of the population of Western Sahara to self-determination as the fundamental principle to which all other factors were subordinate. A division of the territory would only be acceptable if the people freely expressed itself in favour of that solution.[28] The point was also made that the General Assembly had recognized the right of the people of Sahara to self-determination as had resolutions of the Organizations of African Unity and conferences of non-aligned countries and various meetings of Morocco, Mauritania, and Algeria.[29]

Spain took a similar line in emphasizing self-determination as the fundamental relevant principle. But whereas Algeria wished for a restatement by the court of the supremacy of that principle, Spain declared that the request to the court was without object since the General Assembly had already decided that the right of self-determination should apply and that a plebiscite should be held. Just as the title of the administering power has to cease on decolonization so the claims of third parties become legally without effect, for otherwise the rights of the Saharan people as recognized by the Assembly would be disregarded and imperilled.[30]

Since the court emphasized that the request lay within the framework of the consideration by the Assembly of the decolonization of Western Sahara, it decided to review the basic principles governing the decolonization policy of the Assembly. Article 1(2) of the UN Charter reinforced by Articles 55 and 56, referred to the development of friendly relations among States based upon respect for the principle of equal rights and self-determination. The principle was discussed in resolution 1514 (XV), which the court regarded as 'the basis for the process of decolonisation'[31] without specifying whether a legal or political basis was meant. This called for immediate steps to be taken in non-independent territories for the transfer of power in the light of the principle that all peoples had the right to self-determination. Resolution 1541 (XV) noted that self-determination could take the form of independence, free association with an independent State, or integration with an independent State.[32] In each case the essential feature was the free choice of the people.[33] Resolution 2625 (XXV), the Declaration on Principles of International Law, was noted, as was the court's view in the *Namibia* case that the principle of self-determination applied to all non-self-governing territories.[34] The court also pointed out that the General Assembly had reaffirmed the right of the inhabitants of Western Sahara to self-determination.[35]

The court emphasized that the right of the Saharan population to self-determination constituted 'a basic assumption of the questions put to the court'.[36] Judge Dillard declared that the opinion of the court had been forthright in proclaiming the existence of the right in the instant proceedings and presented his view that the pronouncement of the court indicated 'that a norm of international law has emerged applicable to the decolonization of those non-self-governing territories which are under the aegis of the United Nations'.[37] The court did not enter directly into the Moroccan-Algerian debate as to decolonization and self-determination. However, its attitude appeared to be to regard decolonization as the basic framework and self-determination as the most important relevant principle. In that sense, it sought implictly to reconcile the competing assertions. Judge Petren made the point that 'although its guiding principles have emerged, the law of decolonization does not yet constitute a complete body of doctrine and practice'.[38] The court, unfortunately, did not take this opportunity of further analysing the subject, but certain factors may be discerned.

The court concluded that no ties of territorial sovereignty could be established, thus 'the court has not found legal ties of such a nature as might affect the application of resolution 1514 (xv) in the decolonization of Western Sahara and, in particular, of the principle of self-determination'.[39] In other words, the implication is that only ties of territorial sovereignty could affect the application of the relevant decolonization principles. But if self-determination is one of the guiding principles of the decolonization of non-self-governing territories, may this be overridden by ties of sovereignty in the past, and if so, on which basis? The court here declared that the validity of the principle of self-determination had not been affected by the failure in certain cases to consult the population of a territory, since these cases were based either on the grounds that such a population 'did not constitute a "people" entitled to self-determination or on the conviction that a consultation was totally unnecessary, in view of special circumstances'.[40] Therefore, two avenues are open in the event of the recognition of past ties of sovereignty, it appears. Either the people involved are not a 'people' for the General Assembly, or special circumstances are involved. Precisely what 'special circumstances' might amount to for this purpose was not made clear. The ambiguity inherent in the conclusion of the court in this respect could well open the door to other claims of pre-colonial sovereignty rendering the application of self-determination redundant.[41] A far better approach would have been to state, as did Judge Boni,[42] that even a finding of ties of sovereignty would have entailed the obligatory consultation of the inhabitants of the territory, thus affirming the right of self-determination as the primary principle involved. The uncertainty in the court's opinion in this respect is to be regretted. In the light of the *Sahara* case and State practice,[43] the centrality and legal character of the principle of self-determination can hardly be denied, but one vital question which was raised by Morocco concerned the role of the principle of territorial integrity. Could this principle be employed to bring back into being the pre-colonial frontiers of a State recognized at that time? Morocco argued that it could, but was strenuously opposed by Algeria.[44] The court, however, did not discuss the issue at all, since by declaring that no ties of territorial sovereignty had existed, it avoided the necessity.[45] On the other hand, the tenor of the court's opinion appeared to favour the supremacy of self-determination and therefore the rejection of the Moroccan thesis concerning territorial integrity.[46]

The principle of self-determination itself was defined by the court as 'the need to pay regard to the freely expressed will of peoples'[47] and this was clearly accepted as the crucial point, although consultation could be dispensed with in limited instances.[48] Judge Nagendra Singh regarded consultation on the decolonization process as 'an inescapable imperative',[49] while Judge Dillard referred to the 'cardinal restraint which the legal right of self-determination imposes . . . it is for the people to determine the destiny of the territory and not the territory the destiny of the people'.[50]

II. THE NATURE OF THE 'SELF' AND TERRITORY

The relevant instruments of the United Nations have consistently referred to the application of self-determination to 'all peoples'. Accordingly, some discussion of a 'people' is merited. Sociological dicussions of the nature of a people centre around certain common characteristics, which are reinforced by an awareness of a distinct consciousness. Deutsch writes that by 'peoples' one means groups of individuals bound together by certain complementary habits and characteristics, including language, customs, and history.[51] Scelle noted that the term indicated that legal rights 'may be exercised collectively by any group of nationals of a State without further prerequisites as regards such group than that of the common wish of the individuals of which it is composed',[52] while Cobban held that 'any territorial community, the members of which are conscious of themselves *as* members of a community and wish to maintain the identity of their community, is a nation'.[53] Although this may be acceptable as a guide-line in socio-political theory, it does not necessarily follow that the same concepts should govern the legal definition of a people, since the additional perspective of an international community founded upon the basis of a finite number of territorially based entities called States is involved. This extra factor argues for certainty and stability in the process of State formation as in the protection of the integrity of existing States.

Part of the problem lies in the confusion for terminology apparent in Article 1(2) of the UN Charter. This called for 'friendly relations among nations based on . . . self-determination of peoples', and the question arose as to whether these terms were interchangeable. Certain delegates to the Commission on Human Rights replied in the affirmative,[54] but others emphasized that 'peoples' was wider than 'nations' since it could comprise all or part of the population of a State or indeed the inhabitants of several States.[55] However, by referring to 'nations' in Article 1(2), the Charter is in essence concerned with States, since this would provide the only likely explanation of Article 1(4), whereby the United Nations was to be 'a centre for harmonizing the actions of nations in the attainment of . . . common ends'.

A trend emerged in later discussions in favour of restricting the notion of 'peoples' to the inhabitants of a particular State or colony, that is, to clearly defined political units.[56] Johnson regarded the use of the term as signifying the desire to ensure that a narrow application of 'nations' would not prevent the extension of the principle of self-determination to peoples who might not yet qualify as nations.[57] However, such discussions failed to reach a clear conclusion and one must turn to State practice to determine the juridical definition of a people.

In Europe, the principle of self-determination centred around recognized nations such as the Magyars, Germans, Poles, and Italians, the aim being to create a sophisticated political structure upon the basis of the nation and thus to ensure the emergence of the national-State and the demise of the multinational empires. As Cobban noted, 'the history of self-determination is a history of the making of nations and the breaking of States'.[58] In actual fact, very few of the colonial borders in Africa coincided with ethnic lines. Each territory tended to contain a multitude of different tribal groupings and each border to split tribes amongst different administrative authorities. For example, the frontiers of Ghana cut through the areas of seventeen major tribes.[59] The Bakongo Kingdom was partitioned between the Belgian Congo, the French Congo, and Portuguese Angola, while the Ewes were to be found in the British Gold Coast, British Togoland, and French Togoland. On the other hand, Kenya included over 200 tribes and Nigeria comprised hundreds of separate groups.[60] All this has meant that in Africa, with few exceptions, one could not establish a newly independent State emerging from within colonially drawn frontiers upon the basis of a unified ethnic self.

Mazrui has attempted to get around this problem by stressing the notion of 'pigmentational self-determination' as the basis for sovereignty in Africa. He has written that 'the right to sovereignty was not merely for nation-States recognizable as such in a Western sense, but for "peoples" recognizable as such in a racial sense, particularly where differences of colour were manifest'.[61] This approach leads to the notion of 'racial sovereignty' rather than national sovereignty in discussions of self-determination problems in the States of Africa and Asia. However, it confuses more than it elucidates, for it appears to ignore questions of domination by one people over another of the same race and the dilemma of secession. It has also been contradicted in State practice, in cases of the alleged denial of self-determination to a minority racial group within an independent State, as for example in Southern Sudan.[62] Mazrui's thesis can also lead to severe definitional problems with respect to 'pigment' and 'race'. In any event, it is far too simplistic as a legal tool for analysing the nature of self-determination in Africa.

Umozurike defines the concept of 'people' for the purposes of self-determination in very wide terms indeed. He notes that 'the legitimate "self" . . . is a collection of individuals having a legitimate interest which is primarily political, but may also be economic, cultural or of any other kind'[63] and continues by stating that 'individuals, as peoples, are entitled to exercise rights and enjoy a commensurate share in determining their political, cultural and economic future'.[64] To reconcile this broad approach with reality, he is impelled on the one hand to extend the concept of self-determination to include self-government, local autonomy, merger, association and other forms of participation in government[65] and on the other to declare that the mere assertion of a right to self-determination does not *ipso facto* make the claim a question of self-determination in international law.[66] It is a matter of degree depending upon all the circumstances of the case, particularly the seriousness of the 'abuse of sovereign power, to the detriment of a section of the population'.[67] In other words, whether the claim is one of international law appears to be dependent upon a prior contravention of the principle by the government complained of, i.e. the legal right of self-determination arises upon the abuse of the political principle of self-determination. It is clear that this approach confuses the political and legal principles and appears also to misunderstand the nature of self-determination as developed through international practice. Part of the problem may have occurred because of the linking of self-determination of peoples with individual human rights in the world community, something which tended to downgrade the importance of human rights by the focus upon self-determination as a fundamental human right.

In determining the nature of the 'self' in self-determination, it must be realized that the relevant definition of 'peoples' is not the sociological one but the legal one. There is a difference, and upon that difference the legal concept of self-determination is predicated. The International Court has pointed to this by noting that the fact that the General Assembly has not consulted the inhabitants of a particular territory in relation to self-determination may be due to the consideration that 'a certain population did not constitute a "people" entitled to self-determination'.[68] International instruments have consistently maintained that any attempt aimed at the partial or total disruption of the national unity and territorial integrity of a country is incompatible with the UN Charter[69] and this would appear to rule out the right of secession from an independent State. In addition, practice reveals that not every 'people' is deemed to have the right in law of self-determination. The legal concept of self-determination is founded upon a particular definition of the 'self' that has emerged in doctrine and in practice this definition is centred upon the non-self-governing territories (and the mandated and trust territories as well). Whether or not the political concept has been infringed may be relevant in a broad political sense, but it has no bearing upon the legal issue. The concept of self-determination has been the legal instrument in the process of ending colonialism.[70]

An early attempt to extend the doctrine of self-determination in international law to all countries occurred in the so-called 'Belgian thesis'. This was a move spearheaded by the Belgians to widen the obligations under Chapter XI of the Charter to include 'colonial situations' within independent States. As was noted, many States oppress groups within their own frontiers by a variety of discriminatory measures, and there seemed to be no reason, it was argued, why such groups could not count as 'peoples [who] have not yet attained a full measure of self-government'.[71] However, this proposition was strongly rejected by the non-colonial powers, who argued that the term 'non-self-governing territories' clearly referred to entities distinct from the metropolitan State.[72]

The terms in which UN resolutions have been expressed have also manifested the rejection of the Belgian thesis. Resoluton 1514 (XV), the Colonial Declaration, emphasized the necessity to end colonialism and called for immediate steps to be taken in non-independent territories to transfer power to the people, while resolution 1541 (XV) noted that 'the authors of the Charter... had in mind that Chapter XI should be applicable to territories which were then known to be of colonial type'[73] and declared that 'prima facie' there is an obligation to transmit information in respect of a territory which is geographically separate and is distinct ethnically and/or culturally from the country administering it'. Once this has been established, then under Principle V other elements may be brought into consideration. These elements 'may be *inter alia* of an administrative, political, judicial, economic or historical nature. If they affect the relationship between the metropolitan State and the territory concerned in a manner which arbitrarily places the latter in a position or status of subordination, they support the presumption that there is an obligation to transmit information under article 73(e) of the Charter.' To make the point even clearer, the 1970 Declaration on Principles of International Law (resolution 2625 (XXV)) stipulated that 'the territory of a colony or other non-self-governing territory has, under the Charter, a status separate and distinct from the territory of the State administering it; and such separate and distinct status under the Charter shall exist until the people of the colony or non-self-governing territory have exercised their right of self-determination in accordance with the Charter.'[74]

The provisions of Article 1 of the International Covenants on Human Rights are, however, more problematic. It is noted that 'all peoples have the right of self-determination'. There exist here a number of possibilities. It may be argued indeed that every group that regards itself as a 'people' may be entitled under international law to 'freely determine their political status and freely pursue their economic, social and cultural development'. But in the sense of permitting such groups to secede from independent States, such an interpretation is not acceptable under international law. If it is understood to mean that such groups are entitled to play a part within the internal structures of States to resolve their own domestic status, this may be acceptable even if in practice grave doubts must exist as to the efficiency of such a principle, particularly where a number of groups exist within any one State. It could be argued that the phraseology of Article 1 is intended to relate only to non-self-governing territories in the sense that 'peoples' could only be interpreted in such a context. The Indonesian representative, for example, noted that it was perfectly clear that in a discussion of the right of self-determination 'the peoples concerned were the inhabitants of colonies administered by foreign peoples, absolutely different in race, culture and geographical habitat. Academic discussions of the definition of such peoples were therefore superfluous, since everyone, especially the administering Powers, knew perfectly well which peoples were aspiring towards self-government.'[75]

Within the context of his study on the historical and current development of self-determination for the Sub-Commission on Prevention of Discrimination and Protection of Minorities of the UN

Commission on Human Rights, Cristescu notes that it would be premature and even presumptuous to provide a definition that would be comprehensive. However, one could point to certain elements of a definition that have been emerging in UN discussions.

These elements are:

(1) that the term 'people' denotes a social entity possessing a clear identity and its own characteritics;

(2) the term implies a relationship with a territory, even if the people in question have been wrongfully expelled from it and artifically replaced, for example by another population;

(3) a people should not be confused with ethnic, religious, or linguistic minorities, whose existence and rights are recognized in Article 27 of the International Covenant on Civil and Political Rights.[76]

These elements, however, raise many questions. In particular, the lack of guide-lines by which to measure a 'social entity', a 'clear identity', and 'its own characteristics'; the lack of any kind of restriction of time or circumstances with regard to the wrongful expulsion of a people from a territory and artificial replacement, a factor which, if taken seriously, could have momentous consequences; and the lack of a proper analysis of the concept of minorities. With respect to the latter point, it may be pointed out that in some cases whether or not a 'people' is a 'minority' depends upon where one draws the territorial line and this is at the heart of many self-determination claims, for example the Somali situation. The problems associated with this may be illustrated by noting the definition given by Capotorti in his 1979 Study on the *Rights of Persons Belonging to Ethnic, Religious and Linguistic Minorities* for the UN Sub-Commission on Prevention of Discrimination and Protection of Minorities.[77] He analysed the issue in terms of groups

> numerically inferior to the rest of the population of a State, in a non-dominant position, whose members—being nationals of the State—possess ethnic, religious or linguistic characteristics differing from those of the rest of the population and show if only implicitly a sense of solidarity, directed towards preserving their culture, traditions, religion or language.

While the minority issue has been clearly differentiated from the self-determination issue in UN practice, the difficulty remains of drawing the line firmly between the two and in many cases it is not really possible. Certainly, many claims to self-determination are met with the response that the group in question constitutes only a minority and thus is entitled only to this lower-level right.

UN practice on a number of occasions has discussed the right to self-determination in the context of 'colonial domination', 'alien occupation', and 'racist regimes',[78] and it could be argued that the right itself is to be so qualified, but this again raises many definitional problems, particularly relating to the concepts of 'alien occupation' and 'racist regimes'. The confusion inherent here is taken a step further by Gros-Espiel's view in his Report that if 'beneath the guise of ostensible national unity, colonial and alien domination does in fact exist, whatever legal formulation may be used in an attempt to conceal it, the right of the subject people concerned cannot be disregarded without international law being violated'.[79]

This appears to require a probing behind the veil of State independence and sovereignty that would not appear to be acceptable in the current situation of international law.

The current situation would appear to be that, as a legal right, self-determination as leading to modifications in the international status of a territory applies only to an accepted non-self-governing territorial situation. All groups may be entitled to self-determination in the sense of fully participating within the internal constitutional structure of a particular State, but they will not thereby acquire a right under international law to self-determination in the former sense.[80] The possibility exists of developments in the interpretation of self-determination, both in the twilight areas of territories occupied by foreign powers where a basic sovereignty dispute exists and of States where a minority oppresses a majority of a different 'people', and generally with regard to all States, but certainly in the latter case one must pay heed to international practice and accept that that is clearly not the situation at the moment. The people–territory dialectic may open the way in the future for modifications of the basic principle, but that is yet to come.[81]

The problem of defining a 'people', which so engrossed UN delegates in the 1950's in particular, has currently resolved itself for legal purposes, therefore, in a territorial sense. A people in a sociological sense would only be accepted as a people in legal terms for the purposes of self-determination if it inhabited a particular type of territory. The distinction between trust and non-self-governing territories was fundamental in the UN Charter, with differing provisions for each and emphasis upon the former, but it has been of decreasing importance in practice. The call for self-determination has been made regarding both types of territory and the right has been accepted as being equally applicable to both. State practice reveals that the clarification of the 'self' has been made in clear territorial terms and within a particular temporal framework, i.e. in terms of pre-independent territories. The former proposition will be examined in the light of practice relating to Africa in the following section, and the latter in Chapter 5.

III. THE SPATIAL FACTOR—STATE PRACTICE

The determination of the self in terms of a defined territorial framework raises the question also as to inviolability of the territorial unit as colonially determined prior to independence, since the date at which the territorial 'self' crystallized is of crucial importance, and thus the relationship between self-determination and territorial integrity in the pre-independence situation.

(a) Namibia (South-West Africa)

South-West Africa was awarded to the Union of South Africa as a mandated territory after the First World War under the League of Nations system.[82] In 1946 the League adopted a resolution recommending the termination of its functions as regards mandated territories and noting that Chapters XI, XII, and XIII of the United Nations Charter corresponded to Article 22 of the Covenant of the League, which had dealt with the creation of the mandate system.[83] Following this recommendation and the dissolution of the League, the United Nations requested in resolution 61 (I) that South-West Africa be placed under the trusteeship system and rejected in resolution 65 (I) South African proposals to incorporate the territory into the Union of South Africa. The issue was eventually referred to the International Court which held that South Africa alone was not competent to modify the international status of the territory. That competence rested with South Africa acting with the consent of the United Nations.[84] Liberia and Ethiopia as the two black African member-States of the League sought a declaration from the court that South Africa had broken the terms of the mandate and was thus in breach of international law.[85] The Court decided in 1962 that it had jurisdiction to decide the case on its merits, but in 1966 it held that individual League members had no *locus standi* to sue the mandatory power in respect of its treatment of the inhabitants of the mandated territory and dismissed the case.[86] The problem then reverted to the political organs of the United Nations.

One of the primary objectives of the United Nations in this situation has been to preserve the territorial integrity of South-West Africa and prevent South Africa annexing or partitioning it. Assembly resolution 65 (I) firmly rejected any attempt at annexation and this was reinforced by the stand of the International Court in 1950, when the principle of non-annexation was declared to be of paramount importance. However, over the years, South Africa has sought to divide the territory on racial and tribal grounds on a number of occasions. In 1958 the Good Offices Committee, established by the Assembly the previous year in resolution 1143 (XII), issued its Report in which it suggested that some form of partition of the territory involving annexation of part by South Africa and the establishment of a trusteeship over the remainder might provide the basis for an agreement with South Africa.[87]

This was quickly rejected by the General Assembly, which called for full discussion for an agreement 'which would continue to accord to the mandated territory of South-West Africa *as a whole* an international status'.[88] In 1961 the Assembly proclaimed 'the inalienable right of the people of South-West Africa to independence and national sovereignty' and established a UN Special Committee for South-West Africa.[89] However, the government of South Africa proceeded with preparations to divide the territory. The report of the Odendaal Commission was tabled early in 1964 and advocated a series of ten separate homelands for the Africans, three coloured townships, and a white area. However, the bulk of the industrial and mineral wealth would be situated within the European areas.[90] In discussions before the UN Special Committee against Apartheid, it was reported that the objective of the plan 'was seen to be to divide the territory on tribal lines, create Bantustans with small populations and integrate the territory more closely with the Republic (of South Africa)'.[91] The South Africa government in a White Paper of April 1964 accepted the report and endorsed the view that 'it should be the aim as far as practicable to develop for each population group its own homeland in which it can attain self-determination and self-realisation'.[92]

This view was not accepted by the United Nations, which strove to emphasize the territorial integrity of South-West Africa. The Odendaal Report was criticized by the Special Committee on Decolonization as a device to prolong the control of the South African authorities[93] and condemned by the General Assembly in 1965.[94] In 1966, following the decision of the International Court, the Assembly adopted a resolution reaffirming the inalienable right of the people of South-West Africa to self-determination, freedom, and independence and proclaiming that the territory had an international status which it would retain until independence.[95] The resolution reaffirmed the applicability of resolution 1514 (XV) and terminated the mandate. The intention was that thenceforth South-West Africa would come under the direct responsiblity of the United Nations, and to this end an *ad hoc* Committee for South-West Africa was established.

In resolution 2248 (XXII) the Assembly re-emphasized the 'territorial integrity of South-West Africa' and the right of its people to freedom and independence in accordance with the UN Charter, resolution 1514 (XV), and all other resolutions concerning the territory. A UN Council for South-West Africa of eleven members was established to exercise various powers and functions.[96] The Assembly declared in resolution 2325 (XXII) that South Africa's continued presence in the territory was a 'flagrant violation of its territorial integrity and international status as determined by General Assembly resolution 2145 (XXI)'. However, in 1968 the South African parliament adopted the Development of Self-Government for Native Nations in South-West Africa Act, which was intended to implement the Odendaal Report,[97] and accordingly the Act established certain areas for the different nations and provided for various administrative machinery in each homeland. In pursuance of this policy, legislative and executive councils were created between 1969 and 1972 for the Ovambos, Kavangos, and the inhabitants of the Eastern Caprivi.[98] In April 1968 the Assembly resolved to change the name of the territory to Namibia and condemned the Pretoria government for consolidating its illegal control and destroying the unity of the people and the territorial integrity of the country. Following the Development of Self-Government Act, the Assembly adopted resolution 2403 (XXIII) attacking South Africa for destroying the territorial integrity of Namibia. At this point, the Security Council by resolution 264 (1969) recognized the termination of the mandate by the General Assembly and declared that the actions of the South African government 'designed to destroy the national unity and territorial integrity of Namibia through the establishment of Bantustans are contrary to the provisions of the United Nations Charter'. By resolution 269 (1969), the Council declared that the continued occupation of Namibia by South African authorities constituted an 'aggressive encroachment on the authority of the United Nations, a violation of the territorial integrity and a denial of the political sovereignty of the people of Namibia'. It also called upon South Africa to withdraw its administration from the territory immediately.[99] By resolution 284 (1970), the Council requested an advisory opinion from the International Court on the legal consequences for States of the continued presence of

South Africa in Namibia. In its opinion, the court emphasized that the principle of self-determination was applicable to all non-self-governing territories[100] by virtue of the 'subsequent development of international law', in particular resolution 1514 (XV), and the subsequent independence of all but two of the trust territories. The opinion of the court was that the continued presence of South Africa in the territory was illegal and should be terminated. UN members were obliged to recognize this illegality and refrain from actions and declarations implying recognition or lending support to such presence and administration.[101] The opinion was approved by the Security Council in resolution 301 (1971), which also reaffirmed the national unit and territorial integrity of Namibia and condemned all measures by the government of South Africa to destroy that unity and integrity, including the establishment of Bantustans.

South Africa, however, continued to maintain its policy of separate development with the proposed partition of the territory into separate black and white States.[102] In 1973 the South African Foreign Minister appeared to suggest that Namibia might beome independent in about ten years,[103] while the United Nations continued to adopt resolutions proclaiming the right of the people of the territory to self-determination and independence and reaffirming the national unity and territorial integrity of Namibia, as well as criticizing the Bantustan proposals.[104]

In 1975 a Constitutional Conference opened in Windhoek in Namibia with delegates from eleven ethnic groups, but without the participation of SWAPO, the UN-recognized national liberation movement.[105] The aim was to establish a multiracial government to run the territory until independence, which was intended to be the end of 1978, according to a committee of the conference.[106] The conference ended in the spring of 1977, with proposals for a draft constitution with a three-tier system based on ethnicity, not on separate Bantustans. The principle of the territorial integrity of Namibia was thus accepted by the South African-supported conference.[107] However, the ethnically based proposals were rejected by the UN Council for Namibia, which reiterated its support for the struggle of the people under SWAPO's leadership to achieve self-determination and independence and called upon the Security Council to take action.[108] In resolution 31/146, the General Assembly criticized the convening of the conference as an attempt by South Africa to 'perpetuate its colonial exploitation of the people' and impose upon the people a 'bogus constitutional structure aimed at subverting the territorial integrity and unity of Namibia'. This resolution also expressed support for the armed struggle of the people, led by SWAPO, to achieve self-determination, freedom, and independence in a united Namibia. The International Conference in Support of the Peoples of Zimbabwe and Namibia held in Maputo, Mozambique, in May 1977 rejected all attempts by South Africa to dismember the territory of Namibia.[109] The plan for an interim administration on multi-ethnic lines as envisaged by the Windhoek conference was, however, abandoned by South Africa, and Judge Steyn was appointed instead as Administrator-General for Namibia during the transition period.[110] Assembly resolution 32/9D reaffirmed the terms of resolution 31/146, in particular as regards the need for maintaining the territorial integrity of Namibia.[111]

In the spring of 1978 South Africa announced its acceptance of Western proposals[112] for a settlement in Namibia involving a UN peace-keeping force. However, concern for the territorial integrity of Namibia was evident in the Ninth Special Session of the General Assembly,[113] and in resolution S-9/2, containing the Declaration on Namibia and a Programme of Action, South Africa was urged to respect the integrity of the territory. Namibia was declared to be the direct responsibility of the United Nations until genuine self-determination and independence, and the mandate given to the Council for Namibia as the legal Administering Authority until independence was reaffirmed.

Since 1978 negotiations have continued between the five-nation Western contact group, South Africa, and SWAPO. A variety of proposals have been discussed, with some problems eliminated and other problems, for example the Cuban presence in Angola, appearing.[114] In April 1981 the security Council failed to adopt four draft resolutions which would have imposed comprehensive and mandatory sanctions against South Africa because of its actions regarding Namibia, on account of negative votes cast by the USA, United Kingdom and France.[115] The UN Council for Namibia, however, in June 1981 issued the Panama Declaration, condemning South Africa for its attempts to impose an 'internal settlement', reaffirming free support for SWAPO as the sole and authentic representative of the Namibian people, and stating that Namibia's accession to independence must be with its territorial integrity intact, including Walvis Bay and the offshore islands.[116].

It has been accepted by all parties that the territorial integrity of Namibia prior to independence is to be maintained and that the appropriate 'self' for the exercise of self-determination is to be defined in terms of a united territory of Namibia. It could be argued that Namibia as a mandated territory was a special case in this respect, but practice seems to show that the same principle operates with respect to other non-governing territories.

(b) Pre-Independent Kenya and Somali Claims for Self-Determination[117]

Any examination of the Kenya colony and protectorate in relation to its minority Somali population must centre on the strong desire to maintain the territorial integrity of the colony that was clearly manifested both by the British administration and by the colony's emerging African rulers.[118]

The Northern Frontier District (NFD) of Kenya consisted in 1962 of some 102,000 sq. miles in six administrative areas and a population of 388,000, including approximately 240,000 Somalis. These people had gradually migrated southwards over the years and displaced the majority of the Galla tribes, themselves representatives of an earlier Hamitic invasion. In the years preceding 1939 there were many disputes between those of Somali origin and the non-Muslim Gallas which necessitated much stricter military control than was exercised in southern Kenya. After the Second World War there were increasing signs of Somali nationalism, and with the creation of the Somali Republic in July 1960, the Somalis of the NFD began demanding the right to secede from the Kenyan colony and join their brethren.[119] The British Prime Minister, however, declared in April 1960 that 'Her Majesty's Government does not and will not encourage or support any claim affecting the territorial integrity of French Somaliland, Kenya or Ethiopia. This is a matter which could only be considered if that were the will of the Governments and peoples concerned.'[120] This clearly appeared to define such 'governments and peoples' in terms of the whole of the territories involved and not parts of them.

Nevertheless, a delegation from the NFD consisting of pro-secessionist members was invited to the Kenyan Constitutional Conference in London in 1962. They requested autonomous status for the area so that upon Kenya's independence it could join the Somali Republic.[121] A UN plebiscite in the area was suggested, but the idea was rejected. However, a commission was appointed to discover the views of the area's population to various constitutional proposals. This commission reported that the majority of the population supported the secessionist approach.[122] But at the same time, the Regional Boundaries Commission visited the area and a new system of regions was proposed for Kenya, which would split the NFD into three regions: the north-eastern region and parts of the eastern and coast regions. The commission declared that they would have preferred to see a separate Somali district, but had been precluded from suggesting this. This impelled Somalia to break off diplomatic relations with the United Kingdom in March 1963, and ultimately to pledge non-cooperation by Somali leaders in the NFD with Kenyan authorities.[123] It was also disclosed that the British Prime Minister's statement of April 1960 had been interpreted by the British authorities as 'precluding any cession of Kenyan territories so long as Her Majesty's Government is responsible for Kenya'.[124] This approach appeared to allow for secession upon independence, but that, of course, depended on the attitude of the Kenyan leaders, who were strongly opposed to any readjustment of its frontiers. In a memorandum on the Somali question submitted by the Kenyan delegation to the Addis Ababa summit conference of 1963 (prior to Kenyan independence), it was emphasized that 'the principle of self-determination has relevance where foreign domination is the issue. It has no relevance where the issue is territorial disintegration by dissident citizens.'[125]

This case demonstrates the supremacy of the principle of the unity of the colonially defined territories, even when faced with an accepted majority preference by a distinct group in a defined area for secession as the logical expression of self-determination. Ethnic identity was not to disturb the integrity of the colonially established territory. Kenya became independent on 12 December 1963, and in October 1964 it abolished the regions and became a unitary State.[126]

(c) *British Togoland*[127]

The situation in this case revolved around the division of the Ewe people amongst the British-administered Gold Coast and the British Togoland and French Togoland trust territories.[128] By the early 1950s the Ewe problem had become linked with the proposed unification of the two Togolands. The General Assembly unequivocally recognized this as an ethnic issue and declared, in resolution 652 (VII), that 'the unification of the two Togolands is the manifest aspiration of the majority of the population of both trust territories'. The complicating factor was that British Togoland was administered together with the Gold Coast and this impelled the British authorities to regard an all-Ewe solution with some disfavour. The General Assembly sent a Special Mission to the British Togoland which recommended the division of the area into four units for the purposes of a plebiscite. The United Kingdom opposed this as failing to accord with democratic practice which had to be manifested in terms of majority opinion throughout the country as a whole, and declared that if this were to be followed elsewhere the result could be 'none other than the break-up of viable political and economic units and the frustration of true constitutional progress'.[129] The argument was put that in view of the diversity of the people in the territory the only fair assessment would be by plebiscites by area[130] but this was overwhelmingly rejected.[131]

The Assembly decided in favour of treating British Togoland as a unit and by resolution 944 (x) called for a UN-sponsored plebiscite to ascertain the wishes of the majority of the population. The results of the plebiscite, held in May 1956, showed a majority in favour of union with the Gold Coast, although over half the votes in the southern part of the territory were against such a union. The result was endorsed by the Assembly, which subsequently approved of the union of British Togoland with the Gold Coast.[132] Subsequent elections held in July 1956 in the Gold Coast and Togoland revealed a large majority in favour of integration and this was clearly of importance as regards the correctness of the plebiscite decision. The UN Plebiscite Commissioner declared that 'the fate of the plebiscite was bound up with the results of the general election'[133] and stressed the point in his report.[134] The importance of these elections was underlined by the fact that when the General Assembly discussed the outcome of the plebiscite, the results of the elections were already known. The Gold Coast and British Togoland became independent in 1957 as the State of Ghana.[135] Thus the concept of pre-independent territorial integrity was emphasized and the relevant determination made by the majority of the inhabitants of the territory as a whole.

(d) British Cameroons[136]

This trust territory was administered by the United Kingdom in two parts, the northern part together with the northern region of Nigeria, and the southern part as a separate unit. This *de facto* partition was upheld as valid by a Trusteeship Council Visiting Mission, which noted that the inhabitants of the northern sector were closer to their northern Nigerian neighbours than to the population of the southern part of British Cameroons, who resembled the inhabitants of the French Cameroons.[137] Accordingly, separate determinations of the wishes of the population were recommended.[138] The General Assembly accepted this and requested separate plebiscites.[139] There was also a different choice to be made in each case. The north was to choose between joining Nigeria or deciding its political future at a later date, while the south was to choose between joining Nigeria or the independent republic of Cameroun.[140]

The result of the plebiscite in the north revealed a majority in favour of postponing the decision,[141] an outcome which was attributed by the UN Plebiscite Commissioner to protests against inadequate local administration policies.[142] In the south a large majority voted for joining the republic of Cameroun.[143] The General Assembly decided to hold a second plebiscite in the north, the choice being restricted to joining Nigeria or Cameroun, and the result this time favoured joining Nigeria.[144]

However, taking British Cameroons as a single unit, a majority had voted in favour of joining Cameroun[145] and this emphasizes the importance of ascertaining the necessary 'self' for the exercise of self-determination, as well as the importance of the questions asked in any plebiscite. The only valid factor differentiating the Cameroons from Togoland would appear to be the Visiting Mission's ethnic observations, coupled with the influence of the views of the administering power.[146] It is also to be noted that the British Cameroons was administered as two separate units. But in any event, this case does mark an exception to the general rule.

(e) Ruanda-Urundi

In 1959 the General Assembly in resolution 1413 (XIV) asked the Belgian authorities of this trust territory to put forward a timetable for its independence. This followed a series of disturbances between the rival Tutsi and Hutu tribes.[147] Within a couple of months, a UN Visiting Mission had arrived in the territory.[148] The question of independence for Ruanda-Urundi was discussed at the Twenty-Sixth Session of the Trusteeship Council, which recommended, in view of the essential community of interest and the facts of history and geography, the evolution of a single, united and composite State.[149] This approach was endorsed by the General Assembly, which established a UN Commission for Ruanda-Urundi consisting of delegates from Haiti, Togo, and Iran and proposed the introduction of such arrangements regarding internal autonomy for Ruanda and Urundi as would be agreed by the representatives of the area. This was in resolution 1579 (XV).

In early 1960 there was an upheaval in Ruanda which resulted in the establishment of a republic, but this did not affect the view of the General Assembly.[150] Resolution 1605 (XV) was adopted, which emphasized the conviction of the Assembly that 'the best future for Ruanda-Urundi lies in the accession of that territory to independence as a single, united and composite State'. More disturbances occurred in the area, and in

December 1961 Belgium signed Protocols separately with Rwanda and Burundi granting them a large measure of self-goverment.[151] The issue was discussed in the UN Fourth Committee and the delegates were overwhelmingly in favour of the creation of a single State. Belgium was severely criticized for fomenting distrust in the area.[152] As recommended by the Fourth Committee, the General Assembly reaffirmed the single-State idea.[153] A five-member Commission for Ruanda-Urundi was established to reconcile the rival factions, to aid the return of refugees, to help in the guarantee of human rights in the territory, and generally to assist in the maintenance of law and order. In addition, the Commission was to convene a conference at Addis Ababa to find an acceptable formula for the closest possible political, economic, and administrative union between the two areas. However, the conference was not a success and the Commission was forced to admit 'the regrettable fact that the territory was divided'.[154] Its report referred to the 'psychosis of mutual distrust which has prevented the two sides from taking a clearer view of their long-term prospects'. This report convinced the delegates of the UN Fourth Committee of the need to partition the territory.[155]

Accordingly, the Assembly adopted resolution 1746 (XV) noting that the efforts to maintain the unity of Ruanda-Urundi had not succeeded and taking account of the desires of Rwanda and Burundi to become separate, independent States on 1 July 1962. This decision by the United Nations reflected acceptance of the fact that the interests of peace and security were paramount and that this overrode the desirability of retaining the pre-independence territorial structure.[156] The wishes of the two units must also be accepted as an important element here. It is also to be presumed that the United Nations was concerned with the possibility of a repetition of events that had occurred in the neighbouring Belgian Congo and that this influenced the ultimate decision.

(f) Cabinda[157]

This enclave formed part of Portuguese Angola, although physically separated from it by the Zaïre river and some forty miles of Zaïre territory. The General Assembly in resolution 1542 (XV), which listed nine Portuguese territories deemed to fall within Chapter XI of the UN Charter, recognized its status as an enclave and as part of Angola.[158] In 1975 members of the Front for the Liberation of the Enclave of Cabinda (FLEC) declared the area independent and attempted to invade it from their bases in Zaïre and take control from the Angolan MPLA organization. They did not succeed, although the movement was recognized by Gabon and the Congo Republic.[159] No State, however, recognized the independence of Cabinda. Indeed, one of the few factors on which the three rival Angolan movements (MPLA, FNLA, and Unita) did agree was the territorial integrity of Angola, including Cabinda.[160] Cabinda was the only instance of a former Portuguese territory where the threat of a break-up of the colonially defined unit was acute.[161] Despite the MPLA victory in the Angolan civil war, unrest continued in Cabinda.[162]

(g) Equatorial Guinea

This territory was created by Spain in 1963 by merging the island of Fernando Po with mainland Rio Muni. The General Assembly noted the merger[163] in 1965 and the following year requested Spain to ensure that 'the territory accedes to independence as a single political and territorial unit and that no step is taken which would jeopardise the territorial integrity of Equatorial Guinea'.[164] The territory became independent in 1968 despite the fact that in a referendum in August of that year a majority of Fernando Po voted against independence.[165] Accordingly, the integrity of the colonial unit as it existed just before independence was maintained at the express request of the United Nations.

(h) Comoros

The attitude of the international community in general and of African States in particular to the independence of the four Comoro islands ruled until 1975 by France clearly reveals the acceptance of the territory as a whole as the relevant unit for self-determination. The General Assembly in January 1974 reaffirmed the right of the people of the archipelago to self-determination in accordance with resolution 1514 (XV) and stressed the unit and territorial integrity of the territory.[166] In December 1974 a referendum held by the French authorities on the islands revealed a 95 per cent vote for independence, but on Mayotte island a majority voted against independence and for continued ties with France.[167] The consequence of this result was that the French parliament passed a bill in June the following year which provided for Mayotte to remain linked with France after the independence of the Comoros.[168] This disturbed the representatives of the three other islands and on 6 July the Comoros parliament unilaterally declared independence notwithstanding the absence of the Mayotte deputies. In response to a plea for help from the latter, France, while recognizing the independence of the Comoros, reserved its position regarding Mayotte. Within a short time, eleven

African States had recognized the independence of the four islands of the Comoros, including Mayotte.[169] The African group at the United Nations issued a statement supporting the Comoros' membership of the Organization and calling on France to refrain from any action likely to compromise the independence and territorial integrity of the new State.[170] The French, however, claimed that the principle of self-determination was superior to the need to respect the territorial integrity of the colonial territory, but this implied a version of the 'self' of self-determination not consistent with international practice.[171] According to a bill later adopted by the French Council of Ministers in May 1975, Mayotte was to become the 102nd French *département*.[172] But in December the National Assembly adopted a bill, later confirmed by the Senate, declaring Mayotte to be a 'territorial collectivity' in the French Republic. This was attacked by the Organization of African Unity, which reaffirmed the view that Mayotte was part of the Comoros.[173] In resolution 31/4, the Assembly, by 102 votes to 1 (France), with 28 abstentions, condemned the French referenda and declared them void. The French occupation of Mayotte was a flagrant encroachment on the national unity of the Comoros and a violation of resolution 1514 (xv).[174] In resolution 32/7, the General Assembly called on the Comoros and France to settle the problem of Mayotte, respecting the political unity and territorial integrity of the Comoros, while the OAU Summit Conference on July 1978 at Khartoum condemned France's illegitimate occupation of Mayotte, which constituted a threat to the national unity and territorial integrity of the Comoros as well as an act of aggression.[175] In resolution 34/69, by a vote of 112 in favour to 1 against (France) and 23 abstentions, the General Assembly again called upon France to negotiate with the Comoros government with a view to implementing UN resolutions on Mayotte and reaffirmed again the sovereignty of the Comoros over the island of Mayotte. These points were rejected in subsequent sessions in resolutions 35/43, 36/105 and 37/65. Since 1980, France and the Comoros government had been holding discussions, although little progress on the central issue of sovereignty was reported. France continued to maintain that the Mayotte question was a matter within its own domestic jurisdiction.[176] However, following the Equatorial Guinea example, the claims of a territorially distinct part of the colonial unit were denied by the international community in the interests of the territory as a whole.[177]

(i) Eritrea, 1941–52[178]

The history of the colony of Eritrea from the defeat of the Italian occupation forces in 1941 until its eventual incorporation within the Ethiopian empire in 1952 affords an interesting example of the way in which the decolonization of the territory failed to lead to independence, while the integrity of the territory was maintained. The case emphasized the relevance of a series of factors ranging from the wishes of the population to the requirements of peace and security and the nature of the claims of other States. It is particularly instructive in that the decision was left in the hands of the United Nations.

Prior to the Italian conquest of Eritrea in the late nineteenth century, the territory had existed on the fringes of the Ethiopian empire, but not as any kind of distinct entity either in fact or in name.[179] The people in the colony were divided by race and religion. Eritrea was captured by British forces in 1941 and there were basically two interlinked objections to an ultimate grant of independence to the territory as a unit. The first was the claim maintained by neighbouring Ethiopia founded upon historical, ethnic, and economic grounds, and the second was the attitude adopted by the Eritrean Christians. The population of the territory of just over one million was virtually equally divided between Christians and Muslims,[180] with the former wishing to maintain ties with Ethiopia[181] and the latter objecting to annexation by Ethiopia. This rivalry resulted in intermittent violence in the 1940s. Ethiopia's claims were partly historical, although its sovereignty over the area prior to the Italian conquest had been tenuous, and partly ethnic and cultural in relation to the Eritrean Christians. There were also economic and strategic factors operating.

Impelled by these claims and by the communal friction, British opinion in the 1940s tended to support partition, with the Muslim tribes of the west being incorporated with Sudan and the Christians being merged into Ethiopia.[182] Such a solution was also proposed at meetings of the Big Four between 1945 and 1947.[183] In February 1947 the United Kingdom, France, USA, and USSR agreed on an Italian Peace Treaty, which provided *inter alia* that the future of the former Italian possessions in Africa (Libya, Somalia, and Eritrea) was to be decided by the Big Four in accordance with the wishes and welfare of the local populations and in the interests of peace and security. The opinions of other interested States were also to be taken into account. However, if the Big Four were unable to reach a decision within a year of the treaty entering into force, the problem was to be sent to the General Assembly for a recommendation, which the Powers agreed to accept and implement. Thus the Assembly was to be given the power to make a binding decision by virtue of the express agreement of the parties.[184] The four Powers sent a Commission of Enquiry to Eritrea, which confirmed that while the Christians were in favour of immediate union with Ethiopia, the Muslims favoured eventual independence after a period as a UN trust territory. Both parties appeared to reject partition.[185] In the event, the four Powers failed to agree and the matter was referred to the General Assembly in September 1948.

In the First Committee, the United Kingdom proposed a partition of the territory between Ethiopia and Sudan, and this was accepted.[186] However, following anti-Italian riots in Tripolitania, the General Assembly rejected the draft resolution dealing with the disposal of Italy's former possessions,[187] and the issue was postponed until the following session. During that session, a Commission was established to ascertain the wishes of the inhabitants. The Commission (comprising representatives of Norway, Guatemala, South Africa, Pakistan, and Burma) was to take account of

(*a*) the wishes and welfare of the inhabitants of Eritrea, including the views of the various racial, religious and political groups of the provinces of the territory and the capacity of the people for self-government; (*b*) the interests of peace and security in East Africa; (*c*) the rights and claims of Ethiopia based on geographical, historical, ethnic or economic reasons, including in particular Ethiopia's legitimate need for adequate access to the sea.[188]

This inquiry was less thorough than that of the four Powers and two separate reports and three sets of proposals emerged. The Norwegian representative called for the territory's union with Ethiopia, except for the western province, which was to continue under British administration and be allowed to choose at a later date between union with Ethiopia or Sudan. The South African and Burmese representatives suggested that Eritrea should become a self-governing unit federated with Ethiopia under the sovereignty of the Ethiopian Crown, while the Pakistani and Guatemalan representatives called for a ten-year trusteeship followed by independence. Both reports and all the representatives, apart from the Norwegian, emphasized the necessity of maintaining the unit of the territory.[189] The General Assembly also took this line and on 2 December 1950 recommended that Eritrea was to become an 'autonomous unit federated with Ethiopia under the sovereignty of the

Ethiopian crown'.[190] The territory was to have its own legislative, executive, and judicial powers in domestic affairs, while the federal government was to have control over defence, foreign affairs, finance, and inter-State and international commerce and communications. An Imperial Federal Council with equal representation was to be set up and a single nationality established throughout the federation.[191] This solution was deemed by the UN Commissioner to constitute a middle-of-the-road answer to the conflicting aspirations of the inhabitants of the territory.[192] In reaching its decision, the UN General Assembly considered the three points specified in resolution 289C (IV) and called for the fullest respect for the institutions and traditions of the Eritrean territory.[193]

The importance of the choice of the unit for self-determination is underlined in this case, since a separate consideration of the Christian and Muslim areas would have led to the partitioning of the territory. Both parties called for the unity of the territory and this was a factor of some significance, no matter what the ultimate intentions of the parties were.[194] In the event, the United Nations, given a determinative role by the Big Four Powers, decided to maintain the territorial integrity of the unit, partly because of the views of the parties involved and partly since the territory was administered as one unit. The ultimate solution of a self-governing federation with Ethiopia was deemed to comprise sufficient safeguards for the preservation of the Muslim traditions of half the inhabitants. It is also possible that the Assembly was influenced by its experiences over Libya, where proposals to divide the territory had been rejected.[195]

(j) *The French Territory of the Afars and Issas*[196]

This territory of some 23,000 sq. km. has a population of around 200,000 roughly equally split between Afars and Issas. The territory was at one time coveted both by Somalia on the grounds of the reunification of the Somali people and by Ethiopia for historic, economic, and ethnic reasons.[197] France transmitted information on the territory to the United Nations in accordance with Chapter XI of the Charter from 1946 until 1957. As from that year, France declared that French Somaliland had become a self-governing territory.[198] In 1967 the French authorities held a referendum to ascertain the views of the inhabitants as regards the future of the territory and a substantial majority voted in favour of continued French rule. However, there were objections that this had been achieved by deporting large numbers of sympathizers with the Somali cause and imprisoning thousands of others, as well as by altering electoral constituencies.[199] The French view was that the population had expressed its wishes to remain French and that this was to be respected.[200]

Neither Somalia nor Ethiopia had openly called for the annexation of the territory. They declared instead that French had to respect the principle of self-determination and proclaim the territory independent.[201] In 1966 the General Assembly affirmed the right of the people of the territory to self-determination and independence in accordance with resolution 1514 (XV).[202] Somalia proposed that France should grant immediate independence to the territory and that the United Nations should administer it for two years to enable the deportees to return and to permit the inhabitants to decide for themselves whether they favoured an independent status or some other solution to the problem.[203] The United Nations limited itself to a declaration of the right of the people to self-determination and independence. In resolution 2356 (XXII), the Assembly called on France to create the necessary political conditions for accelerating the implementation of the right, including the return of all refugees. Ethiopia's position seemed to be at one stage an acceptance of the status quo, but if the French were to leave, its claim to the territory might be revived.[204] In August 1975, however, the Ethiopian Head of State appeared to renounce Ethiopia's historic claim to the territory in favour of allowing a free choice to the population.[205] Somalia at the same time demanded the unconditional independence of the territory and the return of all expellees.[206] In January 1976 the General Assembly adopted resolution 3480 (XXX) calling on all States to refrain from any action that might alter the independence and territorial integrity of the territory, which should be granted immediate independence, and urged all States to renounce claims to the territory.[207] Round-table discussions on the territory opened in Paris in February 1977 and the following month a conference was held in Accra by the OAU. A referendum took place in May of that year and 77·2 percent of the votes were cast for independence, and at midnight of 26–7 June the territory became independent. Military and other agreements were signed with France and the new State of Djibouti was welcomed *inter alia* by Somalia, Ethiopia, and Sudan.[208]

(k) Mauritania

The issue of Mauritania was officially taken up by the Moroccan government in early 1958 and the territory claimed as part of Morocco.[209] The problem came before the General Assembly at its Fifteenth Session following a request from Morocco. This request was accompanied by a memorandum in which it was argued that the territory of Mauritania had always formed part of Morocco and that the the dismemberment of the latter's territory could not be accepted. The General Committee recommended that the item be included on the agenda of the General Assembly, and this was accepted by the Assembly, which allocated it to the First Committee.[210]

Morocco declared that prior to the French occupation, Mauritania had never constituted a distinct entity while 'the frontiers of Morocco had at all times been the Mediterranean to the north, the Atlantic Ocean to the west and the Senegal river to the south'.[211] In other words, until the French take-over the territory of Mauritania had been an integral part of Morocco. It was argued that until 1912 the currency of Mauritania was Moroccan and that the Moroccan central authority was responsible for public order and national defence. The Moroccan government emphasized that France had pledged in the General Act of the Algeciras Conference, 1906, to respect the sovereignty of the Sultan and the integrity of his domains, but that this promise had been broken by the occupation of increasingly large areas in the region by France. In addition, a French decree of 1904 was null and void since it wrongly defined what was termed the 'civil territory of Mauritania' in the light of the actual occupation by France of under 10 per cent of the area. French actions were also inconsistent with an exchange of notes between France and Germany in November 1911, wherein both parties argued that Morocco comprised all of North Africa between Algeria, French West Africa, and the Spanish territory of Rio de Oro. It was not until 1920 that Mauritania was declared a colony and partly merged with French West Africa. This led Morocco to the view that Mauritania had formed part of Morocco at least until 1906 and that France since its assumption of a protectorate over Morocco in 1912 had broken its obligations to respect Moroccan territorial rights.[212]

Morocco received some support from the 1958 Tangier Conference for the Unity of the Arab Maghreb, where the three North African delegations acknowledged Moroccan interest in Mauritania within the framework of Morocco's 'historic and ethnic unity', while at Conakry in 1960 representatives of African and Asian peoples condemned the existence of Mauritania.[213] However, Morocco lost support on this issue and it resulted in Morocco's absence from the important Addis Ababa Conference in 1963.[214]

France denied that Mauritania had constituted a single entity with

Morocco and emphasized that 'no Moroccan suzerainty or authority had existed either in fact or in law'.[215] Any suggestion of historical rights by Morocco was totally devoid of substance, while ethnic, linguistic, and religious claims were unconvincing. The Sultan's authority over Mauritania until the French occupation was of a 'fragmentary, uncertain and intermittent nature' only, while arguments regarding international agreements were incorrect and ignored treaties signed by Morocco, after it had become a protectorate, which showed that Mauritania was not part of its territory. It was also noted that in the referendum of September 1958, 94 per cent of the electorate in Mauritania had voted in favour of the French Community and thus impliedly against Morocco.[216]

The Moroccan argument centred on the significance of pre-colonial historical and religious ties and their continuing validity in terms of the definition of the subject of self-determination. It also involved minimizing the relevance of the colonial territorial unit in the decolonization process. The Moroccan view was criticized by many States, particularly African ones, both in the First Committee and later in the Security Council. Senegal declared that 'the independence of the African countries had rightly been established on the basis of the existing frontiers; if old political entities had to be reconstituted, independence would not have been achieved in the conditions of peace and harmony'.[217] The right of self-determination was the relevant principle and it was for the people of Mauritania to decide alone.[218] Gabon referred to the 'foolish course of revising frontiers' and emphasized the wisdom of retaining the status quo,[219] while Niger declared that the frontiers of Africa should be left undisturbed.[220] Ultimately no vote was taken in the First Committee.

Upon achieving independence in November 1969, Mauritania applied for UN membership. Its case received majority support, with only the USSR supporting Morocco's claims in the Security Council. Following the Soviet Union's veto in the Council, the issue came before the General Assembly and resolution 1602 (XV) was adopted. This noted that no recommendation had been made regarding membership because of the opposition of a permanent member and declared that, in the view of the General Assembly, 'the Islamic Republic of Mauritania is a peace-loving State within the meaning of Article 4 of the Charter, that it is able and willing to carry out the obligations of the Charter and that it should in consequence be admitted to membership in the United Nations'. Mauritania was admitted to the United Nations at the following session.

This case clearly demonstrated the supremacy of the territorial mode of self-determination in the face of closely argued historical, cultural, and religious affiliations with a neighbouring State. Ultimately, in June 1970, Morocco and Mauritania signed a treaty of co-operation and both agreed to respect each other's territorial integrity.[221]

(l) Spanish Sahara[222]

The question of Spanish Sahara first came before the United Nations at the end of 1963, while in 1964 the Special Committee on Decolonization called on Spain to implement resolution 1514 (XV) and liberate Spanish Sahara (and the enclave of Ifni) from colonial rule.[223] This was reaffirmed in Assembly resolution 2072 (XX), while in resolution 2229 (XXI) Spain was called on to determine at the earliest possible date the procedures for holding a referendum under UN auspices to enable the indigenous population to exercise freely its right to self-determination. This call was repeated annually (save for 1971) until 1974.[224]

Moroccan claims to the territory[225] were pursued consistently since independence in 1956. In 1958 King Mohammed V declared that Morocco would do everything possible to recover the Sahara. Moroccan claims were based on a number of factors. Historically, the continuity of the authority of the sovereigns of the dynasties which had ruled over Morocco was noted.[226] Morocco talked in terms of 'a permanent and peaceful Moroccan presence, an immemorial possession' extending over more than three centuries,[227] which was based on two elements, internal display of Moroccan authority[228] and 'certain international acts said to constitute recognition by other States of its sovereignty over the whole or part of the territory'.[229] The religious ties binding Western Sahara to Morocco, which Morocco contended also demonstrated political allegiance, were evidenced by documents dealing with the appointment of caids (or sheikhs), the allegiance of such caids renewed upon the accession of every sultan, and the imposition of Koranic taxes and levies.[230] To these could be added what were termed 'military decisions' or the dispatch of armed forces to drive out foreigners landing on the Sahara coasts and the sending of arms to various groups resisting foreign penetration, in particular Ma ul-'Aineen in the south.[231] Morocco thus claimed sovereignty over Western Sahara by virtue of immemorial possession founded upon 'the public display of sovereignty, uninterrupted and uncontested for centuries' as 'evidenced by the general acquiescence of the international community which it was accorded for several hundred years'.[232] This will to act as sovereign could additonally be determined, it was suggested, by the series of travels undertaken by sultans in the territory, the commercial policy of the sultans aimed at evicting foreign companies from the coasts, and the diplomatic protests addressed to the representatives of the European powers against attempts to occupy territory in Western Sahara.[233] Morocco laid great emphasis upon the geographical, historical, ethnological, and cultural ties linking it with the territory, 'because international law attaches decisive importance to these factors'.[234] These arguments had also to be understood in the light of the special nature of the Moroccan State at the time of the colonization of the Sahara, based upon personal allegiance and the religious significance of the Sultan. Accordingly, the territorial sovereignty of the Sultan extended as far as his religious authority reached.[235] Morocco also asserted that it was not possible for international law to condone the dismemberment of an independent State by colonial powers in the nineteenth century and thus the territorial integrity of Western Sahara was not a necessary prerequisite of self-determination.[236] The principle of the intangibility of frontiers in Africa could not affect changes made before independence.[237]

Mauritania was in a different position from Morocco since it clearly had not existed as a State during the time of colonization of Western Sahara and therefore it had to base its claim on something other than a modified form of recognized European State requirements for the acquisition of title to territory. Its claims to Western Sahara were based on ethnic, cultural, linguistic, and economic ties, and the need to 'reunify' its people.[238] This involved the description of 'the Mauritanian entity' as a distinct unit, with a unified Saharan law dealing *inter alia* with the use of water-holes, grazing areas, and agricultural lands, rules relating to war, and methods for the peaceful settlement of disputes. All the people, organized separately in tribes, confederations of tribes, and emirates, jointly exercised sovereignty over the 'Mauritanian entity',[239] and the Western Saharans were included in this.[240]

Both these claims were based therefore on the proposition that ethnic, historical, and other ties pre-dating colonization could operate to override the wishes of the people within the colonially established territorial framework, in other words, that the 'self' in question was not necessarily territorially defined but could be determined in the light of ethnic, historical, and other factors. Morocco, for example, noted that the problem of decolonization in this case was identical to the return of 'territories and populations torn away by colonial usurpation' to the Moroccan State. To put it another way, 'the decolonization of Western Sahara implied *ipso facto* its reintegration into the Moroccan State'.[241]

The discussions that took place prior to the adoption of resolution

3292 (XXIX), containing the reference to the International Court, revealed considerable emphasis upon the right to self-determination with regard to Western Sahara. Spain had agreed in 1966 to the application of the principle of self-determination while pointing out some of the difficulties involved because of the nature of the territory and its people.[242] But it was from 1973 that a new approach in Spanish policy took place. Spain gave an assurance to the Yemaᶜa, or general assembly of the people of the territory, that the population of Sahara would freely determine its future, and it guaranteed the territorial integrity of the territory.[243] In July 1974 Spain announced a new political statute for Sahara[244] and in August declared that it would hold a referendum under UN auspices during the first half of 1975.[245] This precipitated vigorous political activity in the area and Morocco suggested to Spain that the International Court should arbitrate the matter, but Spain refused.[246] At about this time the idea arose of seeking an advisory opinion from the court on aspects of the status of Sahara at the date of Spanish colonization. It seems that Morocco's intention was that a statement from the court accepting the existence of ties between the territory and the Moroccan State would support its claims upon the decolonization of Western Sahara. In the discussion in the Fourth Committee, a large number of countries underlined the importance of the principle of self-determination in the light of the terms of resolution 3292 (XXIX). These included the Ivory Coast, Cameroon, and Syria, Cuba, Grenada, Equatorial Guinea, Colombia, Costa Rica, Malaysia, Venezuela, Portugal, Libya, Ecuador,[247] and Algeria.[248] Such discussions clearly demonstrated the central role to be played in the decolonization of Spanish Sahara by the principle of self-determination. As noted above,[249] the court emphasized the principle of self-determination as the basic assumption of the questions put to it[250] and concluded that it had found no legal ties of such a nature as to affect the application of resolution 1514 (XV) in the decolonization of Western Sahara and in particular the principle of self-determination.[251] Self-determination was defined as 'the need to pay regard to the freely expressed will of peoples'[252] and in terms of 'the free and genuine expression of the will of the people of the territory'.[253] The UN Visiting Mission to the territory, reporting within a few days of the court's opinion, stated that 'there was an overwhelming consensus among Saharans within the territory in favour of independence and opposing integration with any neighbouring country'[254] and concluded 'after visiting the territory that the majority of the population within the Spanish Sahara was manifestly in favour of independence'.[255] The sanctity of the colonially defined territorial unit as the framework for the operation of the principle of self-determination appeared to be decisively established.

However, Morocco asserted incorrectly that

> the opinion of the court can only mean one thing: the so-called Western Sahara was part of Moroccan territory over which the sovereignty was exercised by the Kings of Morocco and that the population of this territory considered themselves and were considered to be Moroccans. . . . Today Moroccan claims have been recognized by the legal advisory organ of the United Nations.[256]

To underline their approach, the Moroccan authorities announced their intention to organize a mass march of civilians into the territory, 'to gain recognition of [the] right to national unity and territorial integrity'.[257] The march took place on 6 November 1975[258] despite requests by the Security Council to States to avoid any action which might further increase tension in the area.[259] Algeria remarked that 'not a single African country will fail to see consequences both immediate and long term of the success of such a solution if applied to the various boundaries and territorial problems which arise on the African continent'.[260] The Security Council in resolution 380 (1975) deplored the march and called on Morocco to withdraw from the territory and resume negotiations under the aegis of the UN Secretary-General. A few days later, Morocco ordered the marchers to leave and entered into negotiations with Mauritania and Spain over a solution to the problem. At the end of these talks, a joint communiqué was issued comprising a declaration of principles according to which a temporary tripartite administration over the territory was to be established, consisting of Morocco, Mauritania, and Spain, with the collaboration of the Saharan Yema^ca, and Spain agreed to terminate its presence by 28 February 1976 at the latest.[261] Additional terms in the agreement, which remained secret at the time, dealt with the partition of the territory between Morocco and Mauritania and various other issues.[262]

On 10 December 1975 the General Assembly adopted two resolutions dealing with the Sahara question. Resolution 3458A (xxx), adopted by 88 votes to 0, with 41 abstentions, reaffirmed the inalienable right of the people of the territory to self-determination in accordance with resolution 1514 (xv). It also emphasized 'its concern to see that principle applied to the territory of Spanish Sahara within a framework that guarantees and permits them the free and genuine expression of their will in accordance with the relevant resolutions of the United Nations'. Spain was called on to take all necessary measures 'in consultation with all the parties concerned and interested so that all Saharans . . . may exercise fully and freely, under United Nations supervision, their inalienable right to self-determination'.

However, the effect of this resolution was confused somewhat by the adoption of resolution 3458B (xxx) by 56 votes to 42, with 34 abstentions, which 'takes note of the tripartite agreement concluded at Madrid on 14 November 1975'. This resolution also reaffirmed the Saharan people's right to self-determination and called for its exercise 'through free consultations organized with the assistance of a representative of the United Nations appointed by the Secretary-General'. Although both resolutions refer to self-determination, they are inconsistent on a number of points. The former resolution called for UN supervision of the free and genuine expression of the will of the people, for instance, while the latter resolution accepted the partition agreement between Spain, Morocco, and Mauritania and called only for 'respect' for the aspirations of the population and merely 'free consultations' organized by a UN representative rather than UN supervision of the act of self-determination. Of the African States voting on these resolutions, 29 voted in favour of resolution 3458A (xxx) and 11 abstained, while 12 States (excluding Morocco and Mauritania) voted in favour of resolution 3458B (xxx), 21 opposed it, and 8 abstained. Fighting broke out in the territory during November 1975, leading to a clash between Algerian and Moroccan forces at Amghala.[263] In February 1976 the Polisario independence movement declared the sovereign Saharan Arab Democratic Republic.[264] In April 1976 Morocco and Mauritania formally agreed the division of Sahara between them. The border was to pass from the point where the western coast meets the 24th parallel near Dakhla (Villa Cisneros) eastwards to where the 23rd parallel cuts the 13th western meridian.[265] The UN Secretary-General announced that the UN would refuse to legitimate the actions of Morocco and Mauritania, which together with the fighting taking place rendered any genuine consultation under resolution 3458B (xxx) impossible.[266]

The partition solution, far from being accepted by the population as a whole, was based only on the most cursory consultations with the rump of the Yema^{c}a.[267] In the declaration of principles in the tripartite agreement, it was argued that 'the views of the Saharan population dissolved itself by a majority vote in November 1975'.[268] Morocco claimed that eighty of its members were present at a special meeting which unanimously accepted the partition, but this was contradicted by press reports which put the figure at sixty, i.e. less than the necessary two-thirds.[269] A number of the members of the Yema^{c}a joined Polisario and defected to Algeria.[270] In other words, not only did Morocco and Mauritania refuse to hold a plebiscite in the territory, they also failed to consult adequately the very organ they had declared would express the will of the population. In March 1976 the UN Secretary-General declared that he had been asked by Mauritania to send a UN representative to observe the proceedings of the Yema^{c}a and that he had replied that he would not do this as the necessary steps to ensure the exercise of the right to self-determination by the Saharan people had not been taken.[271]

The meeting of the OAU Council of Ministers in June 1976 adopted a resolution proposed by Benin with 29 votes in favour of unconditionally supporting the just struggle of the Saharan people and calling for respect for the territorial integrity of Western Sahara and the withdrawal of foreign and occupation forces. As a result of this, Morocco boycotted the subsequent OAU summit meeting and hinted that it and Mauritania might leave the OAU if the pro-Saharan resolution was supported.[272] In the event, discussion was postponed and OAU plans to hold a special session on the Saharan problem were put off on a number of occasions.[273] At the July 1978 OAU summit conference a resolution was adopted which reaffirmed the intention to hold a special session on the Saharan issue and a committee was set up 'to find a solution to this question compatible with the right of self-determination'.[274]

In July 1978 a coup took place in Mauritania, which led to the unilateral declaration of a cease-fire by the Polisario with respect to its southern opponent, and ultimately to an agreement whereby Mauritania renounced all claims to the southern part of Western Sahara under its control.[275]

The OAU Committee established in July 1978 (the so-called 'Committee of Wise Men') set up in December 1978 a subcommittee, consisting of the heads of State of Nigeria and Mali, to make an on-the-spot investigation of the dispute,[276] and in that month the UN General Assembly adopted two resolutions on the issue. The first, resolution 33/31A, stressed the inalienable right of the Saharan People to self-determination and independence as well as the responsibility of the UN in the matter. Resolution 33/31B took note of the decision of the OAU summit in July 1978 to establish an *ad hoc* committee and expressed support for its efforts. An increase in fighting in the area in 1979 between Morocco and the Algerian-supported Polisario occurred and a number of towns in the Western Sahara and in southern Morocco were attacked. In addition, a growing number of States recognized the Saharan Republic.[277]

The OAU Committee reported to the OAU summit in July 1979, calling for a referendum on self-determination for the Western Sahara, and this report was adopted by the necessary two-thirds majority, after a Moroccan walk-out. This was the first time that the OAU Assembly of Heads of State and Government had taken a clear stand on the issue and it reflected a continuing decline in Morocco's influence.[278]

The OAU 'Committee of Wise Men' dealing with the problem held a meeting in December 1979 at which Morocco was urged to withdraw from the territory, and a referendum on self-determination was called for.[279] The OAU summit in July 1980, however, postponed a decision on the question of the admission of the Saharan Arab Democratic Republic to the Organization, despite indications that a clear majority favoured this, in the light of threats to leave the OAU made by Morocco and its supporters.[280] The 'Committee of Wise Men' organized a meeting in Sierra Leone in September 1980 of all the parties involved, including Morocco, Mauritania, Algeria, and Polisario, at which a fair and general referendum was called for, to be organized by the UN and the OAU, together with a cease-fire which would be supervised by UN peace-keeping troops.[281] This did not materialize, however, until an apparent Libyan–Moroccan reconciliation at the June 1981 summit prompted by King Hassan of Morocco to accept the need for 'a controlled referendum' which would 'simultaneously respect the objectives of the latest recommendations of the "Committee of Wise Men" and the conviction which Morocco has of its legitimate rights'. In the light of this, the OAU established an implementation committee to oversee in essence the carrying out of the September 1980 proposals.[282]

However, a number of problems arose with regard to the referendum plan, including the nature of the consultation process and responsibility for its organization. Morocco also refused to engage in direct negotiations with Polisario. The committee proposed in February 1982 that a commissioner be appointed to head an interim administration in the territory at least one month before the cease-fire took effect and that a mixed UN/OAU commission be sent to supervise the arrangements for the poll. At the meeting of the OAU Council of Ministers in that month a major row was precipitated by the decision of the OAU Secretary-General to seat the delegation from the Saharan Arab Democractic Republic, on the grounds that twenty-six of the fifty OAU members had recognized the SADR and that this constituted admittance by virtue of simple majority. Nineteen States walked out of the conference and the stability of the OAU was gravely threatened.[283]

(m) The British Indian Ocean Territory

The issue of the territorial integrity of the colonial unit in the period prior to independence was also raised with regard to the creation of the British Indian Ocean Territory in 1965. The arrangements were introduced by Order in Council made on 8 November 1965. The territory was to consist of the Chagos archipelago, formerly administered by the government of Mauritius, and the islands of Aldabra, Farquhar, and Desroches, formerly governed by the Seychelles authorities. The aim of the creation of the new colony was the establishment of defence facilities by the UK and USA governments and an Exchange of Notes between the two governments on this subject occurred in December 1966.[284]

Compensation was to be paid to the Mauritius and Seychelles governments, and the figure mentioned with respect to the former was in the region of £3 million. The issue of the level of compensation and the problem of the deportation to Mauritius of the one thousand or so inhabitants of the Chagos archipelago caused considerable controversy, as did the construction of a large American base on the island of Diego Garcia in the archipelago,[285] but the problem to be considered here revolves around the territorial integrity of colonial units prior to independence.[286]

In 1965 the UN General Assembly considered the Mauritius situation and several States emphasized that the proposed arrangement with regard to the Chagos archipelago would be contrary to the 1960 Colonial Declaration and the principle of self-determination. The suggested creation of military bases in particularly aroused opposition. The UK representative denied that any question of splitting up national territorial units was involved since the islands concerned had been uninhabited when acquired and had been attached to the Mauritius and Seychelles administrations as a matter of administrative convenience.[287] However, this argument misses the point about the evolution of territorial units as colonially determined and the consequent right of the inhabitants of that entity as it has developed over time to concretize its existing political status and proceed to self-determination and independence.[288] To disrupt the territorial integrity of colonial units at the pre-independence stage on the basis of the haphazard nature of their original constitution would be to undermine the viability and meaning of the principles of territorial integrity and self-determination as they have developed. The General Assembly ultimately adopted resolution 2066 (xx), without opposition, in which it noted that 'any step taken by the administering power to detach certain islands from the territory of Mauritius for the purpose of establishing a military base' would contravene the Colonial Declaration and in particular paragraph 6 thereof. This provision stipulates that any attempt aimed at the partial or total disruption of the national unit and territorial integrity of a country is incompatible with the UN Charter.

The resolution also invited the United Kingdom not to dismember the territory of Mauritius and violate its territoral integrity. A number of succeeding General Assembly resolutions reiterated the proposition that any attempt aimed at the partial or total disruption of the national unit and territorial integrity of colonial territories and the establishment of military bases in such territories was incompatible with the UN Charter and the Colonial Declaration of 1960.[289]

The issue resurfaced in 1980 in response, it would seem, to the growth of the American military presence on the Chagos islands. On 26 June 1980, forty-eight of the seventy-member parliament of Mauritius called for the return of Diego Garcia and this prompted the Mauritius government to take up the issue.[290] At the OAU summit of July 1980 a resolution on the issue, unanimously adopted, declared that Diego Garcia 'had always been an integral part of Mauritius, a member State of the OAU' and that the island be unconditionally returned to Mauritius and its peaceful character be maintainted.[291] The British attitude has been that the Chagos islands were under British sovereignty and that once they were not required for defence purposes they should revert to Mauritius.[292]

On 7 July 1982 an agreement relating to compensation for families moved to Mauritius from the Chagos archipelago was signed by the United Kingdom and Mauritius, in which both sides maintained their respective positions on the sovereignty issue.[293]

The issue raised within the context of decolonization and self-determination is whether the colonial power may alter the territorial composition of the unit concerned prior to independence. It is clear that historically States have been regarded as having sovereignty over their colonial territories and that this would include the competence to modify the extent of the territory of a given unit. Many colonial rearrangements attest to this. However, the development of the right of self-determination clearly introduced constraints upon the authority and capacity of the colonial power. To permit the administering authority to alter the territorial composition of the colonial entity upon independence would be to undermine the concept of self-determination and would allow the colonial power to affect the choice to be made by a process of territorial severance, irrespective of the potential economic consequences of such a policy.

The Chagos case raises the temporal factor, since the episode took place some three years prior to independence. However, it is clear that the event was part of the process leading to Mauritian independence. Madeley claims that Mauritian independence was made conditional upon agreement to the Chagos archipelago removal from the territorial framework concerned.[294] It could, therefore, be argued that, in the light of the evolution and status of the principle of self-determination by the mid 1960s, the United Kingdom was under an obligation to maintain the existing territorial framework of the colonial unit until independence and that any defence arrangements with regard to Diego Garcia should have been made after Mauritian independence. The one mitigating factor in this case to be noted relates to the apparent acceptance of the arrangement by the Mauritian government from independence and until 1980. A map of Mauritius was prepared during 1980, with the help of an expert from the British Ministry of Defence, which excluded the Chagos archipelago, and an opposition amendment to include the islands was rejected in the Legislative Assembly. Indeed, the Minister for Foreign Affairs was reported as arguing that 'Diego is legally British. There is no getting away from it. This is a fact that cannot be denied.'[295] Following talks with the British Prime Minister on 17 July 1980, the Mauritian Prime Minister in a press conference acknowledged British sovereignty over Diego Garcia (and thus presumably over the whole of the Chagos archipelago) at present.[296]

These factors, coupled with the apparent lack of protest prior to 1980, weaken to some extent the Mauritian case, since they would suggest that they had adopted the 1965 arrangement and might therefore be stopped from subsequently denying the legality of the transaction. Although this would appear to lay a heavy burden upon a poor, newly independent State, it is an important factor to be considered.[297]

(n) *The Malagasy Islands*

Issues similar in essence to those involved in the Chagos archipelago dispute and in the same geographical region have been raised with regard to the Malagasy Islands of Glorieuses, Juan de Nova, Europa, and Bassas da India. These islands are situated in the Indian Ocean between Madagascar and Mozambique.[298]

The Glorieuses islands were acquired by France in 1892 and were administered at first in conjunction with the colony of Mayotte and then together with the Comoros archipelago (including Mayotte) as part of Madagascar. Ultimately the Comoros archipelago was removed from Madagascar in 1946, leaving the Glorieuses islands as a dependence of the latter.[299] The other islands constituting the Malagasy islands complex were acquired in 1897 and were regarded as dependencies of the colony of Madagascar from that time.[300]

On 14 October 1958 the overseas territory of Madagascar became an autonomous State within the French community and on 26 June 1960 it became a fully independent State. However, on 1 April 1960, during the course of independence negotiations, France issued a decree in which it placed the Malagasy Islands (and the island of Tromelin)[301] under the authority of the Minister dealing with overseas *départements* and territories and thereby revoked all earlier and contrary dispositions.[302] In other words, the territorial integrity of the colonial unit was altered and at a very late stage indeed. Since 1960, the islands have not comprised part of an overseas territory or *département* of France, although they have been administered by the Prefect of the Département of Reunion.[303]

France has argued in addition that Madagascar has, since 1960, acquiesced in French sovereignty over the islands, and particularly noted the transmission to it by Madagascar in 1962 of various administrative documents or 'dossiers domaniaux' relating to the islands, Bardonnet's opinion is that the transmission amounted to an implicit recognition of French sovereignty[304] and certainly such a presumption would appear to be raised, particularly since Madagascar did not raise the issue until after a change in government in 1972.

From the mid 1970s, Madagascar began to assert its claim and a telegram in such terms was sent to the UN Secretary-General on 10 February 1976. Recourse was had to both the OAU and the United Nations. In July 1979 the OAU Assembly discussed the issue and called for the return of the islands to Madagascar.[305] In December 1979 the General Assembly of the United Nations adopted resolution 34/91 inviting France to initiate negotiations with Madagascar without delay for the reintegration of the islands in question arbitrarily separated from Madagascar. The Assembly also called upon the French government to repeal the measures which infringed upon the sovereignty and territorial integrity of Madagascar. This resolution was adopted by 93 votes to 7, with 36 abstentions. The following year, resolution 35/123 was adopted, by 81 votes to 13, with 37 abstentions, calling upon France as a matter of urgency to initiate the negotiations envisaged in resolution 34/91. France refused to recognize the competence of the General Assembly in the matter, stating that the Assembly did not have the power to distribute territories or remodel existing boundaries. The islands had never had an indigenous population and had been acquired during the last century at a time when they were *res nullius*. For Madagascar, the issue was one of incomplete decolonization as well as one of sovereignty, national unity, and territorial integrity.[306]

Thus, a similar question to the Chagos archipelago matter is posed, although the time factor was more drastic in this case. Islands of relatively tiny populations were detached from the colonial units within which they had been administered in the period leading up to independence and after a short period of silence the independent state concerned asserted a claim based essentially on self-determination. As a rule, the need to maintain the colonial unit during the period leading up to independence is clearly a crucial element in the viability of the concept of self-determination, and the arguments based on separate acquisition in the colonial era cannot be permitted to override the territorial integrity of the entity as established in the practice of the colonial State. Further factors may be introduced to modify this and they will be considered briefly in the 'Conclusions' section of this Chapter.

IV. COLONIAL ENCLAVES

One important exception to the proposition that the inhabitants of a non-self-governing or trust territory should have the right to determine their own political structure and future within the colonially defined borders is afforded by that category of small territories known as colonial enclaves. The normal definition of an enclave refers to an area totally surrounded by the territory of other States or the territory of one other State.[307] However, in the case of colonial enclaves, the framework for discussion relates to a relatively small area totally surrounded on the landward side by the territory of one other State, thus allowing for a stretch of coast. This type of enclave is a territory detached by a colonial power from the surrounding territory and placed under the administration of a separate party from that governing the dismembered State. In such cases, the United Nations has adopted the doctrine that the country from which the enclave was originally taken should have the right to reacquire the territory. This approach, which is fundamentally a concession to geographical and political reality, is strictly limited, for UN practice demonstrates that smallness and paucity of resources are not to be regarded as a barrier to independence.[308] It is clearly aimed at preventing threats to international peace and security by the establishment of precariously independent small States or indeed the maintenance of colonial status of areas surrounded on the landward side by larger States with irredentist claims.[309] It also amounts to a recognition of the validity of historical claims in restricted situations.

The concept was utilized with regard to the Spanish enclave of Ifni, which was surrounded on its landward side by Moroccan territory. It covered an area of some fifteen hundred square kilometres, with a population estimated in 1966 of some 53,000 inhabitants, the majority of whom were nomads. The basis of Spanish title to Ifni was the treaty of Tetuan (1860) concluded with Morocco, and this title was confirmed in the Franco-Spanish conventions of 1904 and 1912. However, Spain did not actually administer the area until 1934. In 1957 Morocco sought to seize the enclave and succeeded in forcing a partial Spanish withdrawal.[310] The issue was first examined by the United Nations in the discussions of the Special Committee on Decolonization in 1963 and again in 1964.[311] In resolution 2072 (XX), the General Assembly called on Spain to enter into negotiations regarding the application of resolution 1514 (XV) to Ifni and the Spanish Sahara. The differences between Ifni and the Spanish Sahara were clearly recognized by the United Nations. In resolution 2229 (XXI), the Assembly declared that as far as Ifni was concerned Spain was 'to take immediately the necessary steps to accelerate the decolonization of Ifni and to determine with the government of Morocco, bearing in mind the aspirations of the indigenous population, procedures for the transfer of powers', while as far as Spanish Sahara was concerned, reference was made to the need for a referendum to enable the population to 'exercise freely its right to self-determination'. Resolution 2354 (XXII) was divided into distinct sections dealing separately with Ifni and Spanish Sahara, while resolution 2428 (XIII) noted in its preamble 'the difference in nature of the legal status of these two territories'. This resolution stressed the intention of Spain as administering power to sign a treaty with Morocco on the transfer of Ifni, while reaffirming with regard to Sahara the inalienable right of its people to self-determination and calling for a referendum to enable the people to exercise freely its right to self-determination. On 4 January 1969 the Treaty of Fez was signed between Spain and Morocco and in it the term 'retrocession' is used in transferring the enclave.[312] A number of points can thus be made with regard to the distinguishing characteristics of colonial enclaves. The surrounding State, or former possessor, is entitled to a special status during the process of decolonization; the choice open to the inhabitants of the enclave is strictly curtailed, although their views are to be considered; and no referendum is available, it seems, to ascertain such views. It appears, therefore, that once the status of colonial enclave is established, the surrounding State possesses prime-facie right to assimilate the territory in question. The right of self-determination, accordingly, is not exercisable by the population save in the sense of decolonization *simpliciter*. Rigo Sureda has argued that the special status accorded in UN resolutions to Morocco, Mauritania, and 'any other interested Party' (i.e. Algeria) with regard to self-determination for the territory of Western Sahara might be due to the status of Sahara as a colonial enclave.[313] However, this is not a satisfactory explanation for a number of reasons, including the size of the territory and the fact that it is bordered by three States, not one. UN practice has also clearly demonstrated that the Sahara was not to be treated as a colonial enclave, sharply differentiating the territory from the enclave of Ifni.[314]

The status of colonial enclave has also been suggested with respect to Gibraltar.[315] Assembly resolution 2352 (XXII) noted that 'any colonial situation which partially or completely destroys the national unity and territorial integrity of a country is incompatible with the purposes and principles of the Charter of the United Nations and specifically with paragraph 6 of General Assembly resolution 1514 (XV)'. This, however, seems to run contrary to the traditional interpretation of paragraph 6 of resolution 1514 (XV), which was intended to protect the territorial integrity of independent States and not that of former entities in the colonial era.[316] But if one interprets resolution 2353 (XXII) as referring to colonial enclaves alone, rather than all colonial situations, it is then possible to integrate the proposition within the framework of the law relating to decolonization. A wide interpretation would be inconsistent with international practice regarding self-determination. The Assembly has indeed recommended negotiations aimed at the transfer of power from the United Kingdom to Spain in the case of Gibraltar[317] in similar terms to those used in the Ifni case.

The status of a territory as a colonial enclave would at the very least afford the surrounding State a *locus standi* in discussions covering the disposition of a territory and where this has not happened the presumption must be that a colonial enclave is not involved, as for example in the case of the French Territory of the Afars and Issas. However, the converse is not necessarily true and one may point to a number of territories where neighbouring States have been accepted as having a *locus standi* without the territory in question being regarded as a colonial enclave.[318]

In the context of Africa, the question has arisen as to the status of the enclave of Walvis Bay.[319] The enclave, some eleven hundred square kilometres in area with a seasonal fluctuating population of 27,000 or so, constitutes the fifth largest port of South Africa and the only deep-water port of Namibia. It is situated half-way down the Namibian coastline. The Penguin Islands are a number of small islands, islets, and rocks a few miles off the coast, stretching along the coast of Namibia. In 1878 the British authorities decided to annex Walvis Bay and the surrounding area as part of the Cape Colony. In 1884, after the Cape Colony Legislature had passed the appropriate measures, the Cape Governor officially proclaimed the annexation of Walvis Bay and surrounding area as part of the Colony of the Cape of Good Hope.[320] Between 1884 and 1890 a German protectorate was established over Namibia and its borders defined by agreements with Portugal and the United Kingdom. A dispute over the southern boundary of Walvis Bay was ultimately settled by arbitration in 1911.[321] Following the South African Act of 1909, the Union of South Africa came into being on 31 May 1910. The Union comprised the colonies of the Cape of Good Hope, Natal, the Transvaal, and the Orange River by section 2 of the Act, with the same boundaries as those of the colonies by section 6. Since the Penguin Islands were formally annexed to the Cape Colony in 1866 and Walvis Bay in 1884, these territories became in 1910 part of the territory of the Union of South Africa. In 1931 the Union gained sovereign status and in 1961 became a republic. In 1915 South-West Africa was captured from Germany, and in 1920 'the territory which formerly constituted the German protectorate of South-West Africa' was given to South Africa to administer as a 'C' mandate.[322] By section 1 of the South African South-West Africa Affairs Act, Act No. 24 of 1922, Walvis Bay was to be administered as part of the mandated territory. This was basically for reasons of administrative convenience.[323]

With the moves towards a constitutional settlement in Namibia, the issue of Walvis Bay began to assume some importance. In April 1976 the South African Prime Minister stated that whatever happened with regard to Namibia, Walvis Bay remained South African territory.[324] This was repeated in June 1977 in the context of the discussions with the five-power Western nations contact group, and in the Walvis Bay Administration Proclamation of 1977 it was provided that as from 1 September 1977 'Walvis Bay shall cease to be administered as if it were part of the territory [of South-West Africa] . . . and shall again be administered as part of the province [of the Cape of Good Hope]'.[325] The International Conference in Support of the Peoples of Zimbabwe and Namibia, 1977, recognized Walvis Bay as part of Namibia and rejected South Africa's attempts to separate it from the rest of Namibia. All governments were called up to 'decisively reject all attempts to dismember the territory of Namibia and especially the design to annex Walvis Bay'.[326] In September 1977 the UN Council for Namibia issued a statement condemning 'this unilateral attempt by South Africa to destroy the territorial integrity and unity of Namibia. Walvis Bay has always been an integral part of Namibia and South Africa has no right to change its status or to appropriate it as a part of its own territory.'[327] The General Assembly adopted resolution 32/90 in which it declared that the South African decision to 'annex' Walvis Bay was an attempt to undermine the unity and territorial integrity of Namibia and was 'an act of colonial expansion in violation of the purposes and principles of the Charter of the United Nations and of General Assembly resolution 1514 (xv)'. Such annexation, it was stated, was illegal, null, and void.[328] The OAU Ministerial Council also condemned South Africa's 'illegal annexation' of Walvis Bay, which was an integral part of Namibia.[329] South Africa's action was also condemned by the Special Committee on Decolonization, which called on all States not to take any action which 'might give any semblance of legitimacy to South Africa's claim to Walvis Bay'.[330]

The General Assembly discussed the Namibia issue at its Ninth Special Session in spring 1978, and in resolution S-9/2, adopted by 119 votes to 0, with 21 abstentions, reiterated that Walvis Bay was an integral part of Namibia and strongly condemned South Africa's 'annexation' of the territory, which violated the principle of the territorial integrity of Namibia, embodied in Assembly and Security Council resolutions.[331] The South African action was held to be illegal, null, and void and an act of aggression against the Namibian people. All States were urged to do their utmost to compel South Africa to renounce its 'spurious claims' to Walvis Bay and respect the territorial integrity of Namibia. In the debates, a number of States emphasized that Walvis Bay was an integral part of Namibia, the territorial integrity of which had to be preserved.[332] The Western proposals, drawn up by the USA, United Kingdom, France,

Canada, and West Germany, submitted to the Security Council on 10 April 1978,[333] deliberately ignored the issue of Walvis Bay, since no way of settling the question could be found in the context of the negotiations held. It was stated that this question should be the subject of discussions between South Africa and the elected government of Namibia.[334] SWAPO accepted this while maintaining that Walvis Bay was part of Namibia,[335] while South Africa emphasized that Walvis Bay was a separate and distinct issue and should be treated by the United Nations as such.[336] The Security Council on 27 July 1978 adopted resolution 432 (1978) unanimously, in which it declared that 'the territorial integrity and unity of Namibia *must* be assured through the *integration* of Walvis Bay within its territory' (emphasis added) and decided to remain seized of the matter until such reintegration.

On the same day, a statement on behalf of the Western contact group reiterated the stand that a discussion of the legal status of Walvis Bay would not be useful, while its future should be determined in negotiations between the parties concerned. It was recognized that Walvis Bay was critical to the future of Namibia. It was further stated that there were arguments of a geographic, political, social, cultural, and administrative nature which supported the union of Walvis Bay with Namibia, and accordingly the Security Council resolution was appropriate. The resolution, it was noted, did not prejudice the legal position of any party.[337]

Since the United Nations has therefore quite clearly asserted that Walvis Bay is part of Namibia and that any attempt by South Africa to retain control of it is illegal and null and void, the question arises as to the legal justification for this approach. International law has accepted that titles to territory acquired in the colonial era retain their validity, subject only to a right of self-determination on the part of the people concerned. Therefore the acquisition of Walvis Bay by first the United Kingdom and then the Union of South Africa was perfectly legitimate. States, in particular African States, have repeatedly reaffirmed the sanctity and legitimacy of the former colonial borders. Thus, South Africa's title appears lawful. Neither the arguments of geographical contiguity nor those of historical continuity can be used to invalidate the primacy of the colonially established frontiers, while the fact of joint administration of Walvis Bay and Namibia is in itself insufficient to found title in the absence of South Africa's intention to dispose of it. There would, therefore, appear to be only one viable argument in the sphere of international law, as distinct from political considerations and factors, upon which one might found the legality of a claim for Walvis Bay's incorporation into Namibia, and that is based on the doctrine of colonial enclaves.

Walvis Bay fills the requirements of the doctrine in all but one respect. It is small, surrounded by one State from which it was originally taken, and the special status of Namibia in relation to the enclave has been clearly recognized. However, the State administering the enclave, while deriving its title through an act of colonization, is not itself a colonial power in the traditional sense, although it could be argued that South Africa's administration of Namibia renders it a colonial power in the broad sense. The question is whether the crucial economic importance of the enclave to Namibia plus the virtually unanimous view of the international community with respect to Walvis Bay's status as part of Namibia can overcome this problem.

The terms of the unanimously adopted Security Council resolution to the effect that the unit of Namibia *must* be assured through the *reintegration* of Walvis Bay suggest a recognition of the enclave as part of the territory of Namibia. The ambiguous stand of the five Western Powers on the legal issue can hardly affect this. The critical importance of Walvis Bay to an independent Namibia coupled with the extreme difficulty of maintaining South African control in such circumstances once Namibia becomes a sovereign State, especially in the light of the enclave's dependence on electricity and water supplies from Namibia, would appear to point to a colonial enclave status for Walvis Bay, which would involve a right of reincorporation into Namibia proper, but the question must be regarded as still open.

V. CONCLUSIONS

The application of the principle of self-determination to non-self-governing territories is indisputable, but the basis of the principle has been transformed from the personal concept implicit in the political definition of self-determination to the strict territorial concept of international practice. It is the territorial factor which is prescriptive and the personal element is secondary, usually being of little or no significance. The 'self' of self-determination is therefore to be understood in strict spatial terms so that the right accrues to a colonial people within the framework of the existing territorial unit as established by the colonial power. Pre-colonial and/or subsisting ethnic, religious, or cultural ties are not strictly relevant, for it is the people of the defined territory who alone have the competence to exercise the right of self-determination. Indeed, practice relating to Rhodesia demonstrates further that self-determination is the right of the majority of the people, certainly in racial minority situations, and cannot be understood to mean simply freedom from the control of the colonial power in all cases.[338] It can thus be stated that self-determination is to be exercised within the colonial territory treating that territory as a unit, and that therefore the principle of territorial integrity operates prior to independence in these situations as a guarantor of the territorial basis of self-determination.[339] This would appear to be overridden clearly where there are exceptional circumstances threatening peace and security, as in Ruanda-Urundi.

The question arises here as to whether there are any further accepted exceptions. The Cameroons situation may be partly explained by reference to the administrative division of the territory upon ethnic grounds (as noted by a UN mission) by the administering power, and the principle has been modified in the case of colonial enclaves. The OAU and UN reaction to the Chagos archipelago and Malagasy islands situation clearly manifests belief in the crucial centrality of the principle linking, as it does, self-determination and territorial integrity.

In the Chagos case, the argument from the United Kingdom's point of view would also take account to some extent of the consent of the major pre-independent Mauritius party to the arrangement and the greater length of time between the detaching of the islands and actual independence. In the Malagasy islands episode, the detaching took place a matter of weeks before independence. In the Chagos case, the numbers involved were relatively meaningful whereas in the Malagasy islands it would appear that virtually no inhabitants were affected. In both instances, however, the colonial power would seem to have regarded the arrangements concerned as manifestations of their sovereign power over the colonial territories. It is suggested that both were wrong. The sovereignty involved with regard to colonies is clearly limited, although not overridden, by the right of self-determination and it is believed that a crucial element in that right is the spatial factor. This is to be defined in terms of the territorial integrity of the colonial unit as administered by the colonial power in the period leading up to independence.

Both the cases here also involve the question as to whether the decolonized States acquiesced in these arrangements in the time between independence and the raising of the particular claims. In each case, the gap was at least twelve years. Acquiescence occurs in situations where protests might reasonably be regarded as necessary and have not in fact materialized. MacGibbon emphasizes that the

> formulation of a protest would appear to be almost an instinctive defence mechanism and this circumstance has led tribunals to scrutinize with a certain degree of scepticism the reasons advanced by a party to excuse its failure to protest in appropriate circumstances.[340]

In general, international tribunals have underlined the role of absence of protests within the context of acquiescence by the State losing sovereignty over an area in the title of the acquiring State.[341] There are many reasons for this, including the search for stability in territorial relations and the dominant prescriptive role of States within the international system. But the cases and learned articles really revolve around territorial disputes arising between two separate sovereign entities and not with regard to a dispute between the colonial power and its successor State over the extent of the territorial identity of the same piece of territory, where clearly no issue arises over competing administrative acts in a disputed area. In such a case, the colonial power is under a duty by virtue of the principle of self-determination to decolonize the whole unit as administered, and if it fails to do so in fact, then it is to that extent in breach of its obligations. It is, of course, possible for this situation to be regularized by the acquiescence or consent of the successor State, but the relevant criteria would have to take into account the consequences of newly independent statehood status. This would primarily affect the reasonable time requirement necessary for the validity of protests. Nevertheless, the period of twelve years or more before a protest is made does appear problematic, but one may legitimately also note in this context the views of most of the international community as manifested through the relevant UN General Assembly resolutions.

The basic proposition regarding territorial integrity and self-determination is upheld by the Saharan issue, although the inability of the international community to rectify the situation has tended to obscure this. One may also point in non-African practice to the Belize and Timor issues as reinforcing the accepting rules. In the case of Timor, the Security Council adopted unanimously resolution 384 (1975) which called for respect for the territorial integrity of the former Portuguese colony and the right of its people to self-determination and this was repeated in resolution 389 (1976).[342] Assembly resolution 3485 (XXX) deplored Indonesia's intervention and called for its withdrawal to enable the exercise of self-determination and this call was subsequently repeated a number of times.[343] In the case of Belize, a former British colony subject to Guatemalan claims, the United Nations has reaffirmed the right of its people to self-determination and stressed that the territorial integrity of the territory must be preserved.[344]

The essence of self-determination is the free choice open to the inhabitants of the particular territory as to their future political status.[345] By virtue of this, the application of the right of pre-emption was overruled. This right was a device whereby one colonial power declared that in the event of disposing of a particular territory, a second power would have first option over it.[346] In the Franco-Spanish Convention of June 1860, for instance, it was provided that if the Spanish government decided to cede its possessions in West Africa in whole or in part in favour of any party, the French government would have the right of pre-emption (or *droit de préférence*).[347] However, when the Spanish colonies in West Africa became independent no mention of the right was made. France had also a right of pre-emption over the territory of the Congo Free State after Belgium. It was stated that 'le gouvernement belge reconnaît à la France un droit de préférence sur ses possessions congolaises en cas d'aliénation de celles-ci à titre onéreux, en tout ou en partie'.[348] In this case, France did seek to enforce these rights. On 26 February 1960 the French Foreign Minister informed the Belgian government that it regarded the latter as bound by the agreements granting it a right of pre-emption over the Congo, but Belgium rejected the claim and maintained that territories and populations were no longer 'goods which could be the subject of international trade'.[349]

The factor of free choice may be rendered precarious when other parties are given a special status with regard to the determination of the future of a territory by its population. However, this practice is highly unusual in the process of decolonization. By resolution 2229 (XXI), Morocco, Mauritania, and 'any other interested party', i.e. Algeria,[350] were accorded a special status, and although one explanation, as noted, is based on the contention that Western Sahara was a colonial enclave, the true reason is to be sought rather in the general geopolitical situation in the area. The territorial claims by Morocco and Mauritania and the strong opposition to them by Algeria had created a delicate situation in that region and the Assembly clearly felt impelled to take account of this. Nevertheless, it is felt that the sole valid interpretation of such status is to be seen in the context of discussions and consultations rather than in the field of substantive solutions.[351]

Once the principle of free choice is accepted as the basis of the exercise of self-determination, the question is then posed of the method by which it may be demonstrated. This is important, since a free choice is invariably dependent upon its efficacious exercise. Such exercise may be accomplished by a variety of methods, ranging from plebiscites and elections to commissions of enquiry. It is in this field that the United Nations has often had a practical role to play. However, an examination of the cases in which such operations have occurred reveals no clear pattern.[352] Commissions of Enquiry were sent to Eritrea,[353] British Cameroons,[354] British Togoland,[355] and Western Sahara.[356] Plebiscites were held in British Cameroons, British Togoland, Ruanda-Urundi,[357] and Papua New Guinea, while ordinary elections sufficed in a number of cases. In the case of Eritrea[358] the commission was not followed by a plebiscite and its report was accepted, but the report of the Visiting Mission to British Cameroons was not accepted and the General Assembly decided that plebiscites should be held in the north and south of the territory.[359] The mission to British Togoland recommended that a plebiscite be held and this indeed took place.[360]

In a large number of colonies, neither plebiscites nor elections were held in a way directly related to the exercise of self-determination. This is because in the majority of cases no serious alternative to independence was proposed regarding the future of the territory. In other words, a deterministic view was taken of the territory–people nexus.[361] However, in the case of the trust territories, in the light of the special responsibility of the United Nations[362] and especially where a serious dispute existed as to the disposition of the territory, some method of determining the wishes of the population had to be applied. Thus, although plebiscites have been comparatively rare in non-self-governing territories, they occurred with some frequency in the case of trust territories.

4

Statehood, Territory, and Title

WITHIN the body of international law, the concept and consequences of statehood clearly play a crucial role.[1] The State is the primary, although not the sole, subject of international law and the law cannot therefore remain indifferent to the circumstances of its coming into existence. The creation of new States can only be accomplished as a result of the break-up of or secession from existing States, since *terrae nullius* no longer present themselves.[2] The consequent disruption on the international scene has of necessity to be carefully regulated. The struggle for statehood has constituted the prime objective of the decolonization movement and has led to a re-examination of the nature and relevance of the traditional criteria, while the phenomenon of the entity of controversial status had added to this process.[3]

The creation of new States and their entry into international life raise questions as to the relative balance between factual and legal criteria. Is the birth of a new State primarily an issue of fact or of law? If the former, then is effectiveness sufficient to guarantee membership of the international community within the framework of international law irrespective of the method by which the result was achieved? If the latter, the problem of enforcement is immediately raised. The relationship between effectiveness and various other principles of international law deemed of relevance is of crucial importance here. Of especial interest is the concept of self-determination and the extent to which it has or has not modified the traditional criteria of statehood embodying, as they do, the tests of effectiveness. Other factors may also be regarded as part of the concerns of actors on the international scene, such as the nature and status of dependent territories and the impact of international constitutional documents like the UN Charter.[4] Since statehood is but one method of participation in the international community, the question of legal personality is thus brought into focus.

I. STATEHOOD AND TERRITORY

A. THE CRITERIA

In any examination of the concept of statehood in international law, the role of territory is obviously indispensable. There can be no State without territory. The most widely accepted formulation of the criteria of statehood in international law is provided in Article 1 of the Montevideo Convention on Rights and duties of States, 1933. This stipulates that 'the State as a person of international law should possess the following qualifications: (*a*) a permanent population, (*b*) a defined territory, (*c*) government, and (*d*) capacity to enter into relations with the other States'. The definition of each of these elements is far from settled and these four elements are not to be seen as exhaustive.[5] It is apparent, however, that this framework is to a large extent concerned with territorial effectiveness. A permanent population is, of course, essential,[6] but the notions of government and capacity to enter into relations with other States, linked as they are with the concepts of sovereignty and independence, relate to factors of internal and external authority founded upon a determinate piece of territory.

1. A Defined Territory

The requirement of a defined territory is less stringent than would first appear. It is not necessary for the frontiers of the new State to be precisely delimited or demarcated, as long as an accepted core of territory is rendered subject to the authority of the new entity. It was stated in *Deutsche Continental Gas Gesellschaft* v. *Polish State* that in order to say that a State exists 'it is enough that this territory has a sufficient consistency even though its boundaries have not yet been accurately delimited and that the State actually exercises independent public authority over that territory'.[7] Jessup declared that 'one does not find in the general classic treatment of this subject any insistence that the territory of a State must be exactly fixed by definite frontiers . . . both reason and history demonstrate that the concept of territory does not necessarily include precise delimitation of the boundaries of that territory'.[8] Albania was recognized by a number of States prior to the fixing of its frontiers, while most of the new States that emerged after the First World War were recognized *de facto* or *de jure* before their frontiers were determined by treaties.[9] Despite arguments that Israel did not constitute a State since its boundaries were in dispute,[10] that country was admitted to the United

Nations on 11 May 1949.[11] The general rule was reaffirmed by the International Court of Justice in the *North Sea Continental Shelf* case.[12]

In certain cases the new State may be faced with a dispute not as regards its frontiers, but with respect to all of its territory. Where this happens, the rules relating to the effective control of a central core of territory may be augmented by other principles of international law, such as that of self-determination, which lays down in colonial cases the territorial framework of the self within which the choice as to political status may be made. The Moroccan objection to Mauritania's independence and admission to the United Nations is an example of this. Morocco claimed that the territory of Mauritania belonged to it and that its sovereignty had been interrupted by French occupation. Once the French left, it was alleged, the territory should revert to Moroccan sovereignty.[13] In the event, Morocco's contentions attracted little support and Mauritania was admitted to the United Nations.[14]

2. *Government*

Crucially linked with the availability of a coherent piece of territory is the exercise of effective control over it by the authorities of the entity claiming statehood. Lauterpacht defines this requirement in terms of 'a sufficient degree of internal stability as expressed in the functioning of a government enjoying the habitual obedience of the bulk of the population'.[15] If the community is internally so unstable 'as to be deprived of a representative and effective government' the result will be that the community 'will be lacking in a vital condition of Statehood'.[16] The Commission of Jurists reporting on the Aaland Islands dispute declared that it was difficult to say at what date the Finnish Republic actually became a definitely constituted sovereign State. It was asserted that 'this certainly did not take place until a stable political organization had been created and until the public authorities had become strong enough to assert themselves throughout the territories of the State without the assistance of foreign troops'.[17] Higgins has also emphasized how, prior to the admission of certain African States to the United Nations, a tendency had been manifest to interpret the government criterion of statehood to mean 'democratic rather than pure *effective* government'.[18]

3. *Independence*

The capacity to enter its relations with other States is not limited to States. Accordingly, this criterion is better examined in terms of the concept of independence.[19] In any analysis of statehood in international law, independence is clearly of fundamental importance. It is a manifestation of territorial effectiveness in relation to other entities of international law and to this extent it is an external aspect of government founded upon internal facts. It therefore amounts to a conclusion of law, in the light of international law, dependent upon particular circumstances. Judge Anzilotti in the classic formulation of the concept stated that 'independence is really no more than the normal condition of States according to international law; it may also be described as sovereignty (*suprema potestas*), or external sovereignty, by which is meant that the State has over it no other authority than that of international law'.[20] Independence was to be contrasted with the class of dependent States, thus demonstrating the requirement of formal independence.[21] A certain degree of 'actual' independence may also be necessary.[22] Independence in actuality is a relative phenomenon. In a world of increasing interdependence, absolute self-sufficiency is a rare phenomenon, but while a certain degree of real as distinct from formal dependence will not result in the extinction of statehood, there may come a point beyond which such dependence may be incompatible with statehood. An interesting instance of what may or may not prejudice independence in the legal as opposed to political sense is that afforded by defence agreements with the former colonial power.

It was argued that the treaty between the United Kingdom and Transjordan,[23] which provided for the latter's independence and permitted the stationing of British troops in the country, legally restricted the sovereignty of Transjordan on account of its military clauses.[24] Similar arguments were raised with regard to Ceylon's defence arrangements with the United Kingdom.[25] A mutual defence agreement was arranged between the United Kingdom and the government of Nigeria, but for political reasons was soon abrogated.[26] A number of former French colonies entered into defence arrangements with France,[27] and as of the late 1970s France was maintaining bases in Senegal, Ivory Coast, Gabon, and Djibouti and was involved in armed action in Chad and Mauritania.[28] It was never suggested, however, that these countries thereby lost the attribute of legal independence.[29]

Although the requirement of independence is primarily formal and does not necessitate an analysis of political and economic ties with other States, it may be that there is an irreducible minimum of real independence in factual terms below which an entity may not fall and be entitled to statehood.[30] The question has been raised with regard to the grant of independence by South Africa to its Bantustans. The OAU adopted resolution CM/Res.493 (XXVII) in which it referred to the 'so-called independence' and 'fraudulent pseudo-independence' of the Transkei, which was officially declared independent on 26 October 1976. General Assembly resolution 31/6A, adopted by 132 to 0, with 1 abstention (the USA), referred to the 'sham independence' of the Transkei. The Transkei is heavily dependent upon South Africa. Some 360,000 Transkeians work in South Africa each year, contributing about 70 per cent of the entity's budget.[31] However, it does possess a sea coast. Bophuthatswana, on the other hand, does not, and is in addition split into a series of areas divided by South African territory.[32] Over half of this entity's citizens as defined by South Africa live in South Africa itself. Bophuthatswana was declared independent on 6 December 1977 and the OAU in a press statement criticized the Bantustans as 'pseudo-States'.[33]

On 12 September 1979 South Africa declared the independence of the Republic of Venda. This new entity depends upon South Africa for some 50 per cent of its food and all of its fuel, while 67 per cent of the male work-force work in South Africa's urban areas. On 21 September the Security Council issued a statement condemning as totally invalid the establishment of Venda and calling upon all governments to deny it any form of recognition.[34] The fourth Bantustan to undergo the process was Ciskei on 3 December 1981.[35] The Security Council again issued a statement to deal with the matter, on 15 December 1981, declaring invalid the proposed independence of Ciskei and calling for non-recognition and a ban on any dealings with it.[36] The Status of these four entities, unrecognized by any State apart from South Africa, is clearly problematic. The fact that they are heavily dependent on South Africa economically is of relevance, but numerous States are equally dependent on other States' assistance and it is clear that even if they were to become economically more successful, the international community would not treat this as adequate to recognize them as States. Formally they would appear to be independent, since South Africa is able under international law to alienate parts of its sovereign territory. It is submitted that the answer to the question of their status lies elsewhere than in the traditional exposition of independence as a criterion of statehood.[37]

B SELF-DETERMINATION[38]

1. As Affecting the Sovereignty Issue

During discussions in the International Law Commission on State Responsibility in the particular context of insurrectional movements,

Bedjaoui emphasized that 'the territory of a colony was not, in law, the territory of the colonial State'. Indeed, he went on to state that insurrectional movements possessed an international status and a new 'legal order' distinct from that of the colonial State and were situated in territory 'which was now regarded as separate from that of the metropolitan country and in which the latter's presence was considered unlawful'.[39] This view was based on the provision in the 1970 Declaration on Principles of International Law affirming the separate and distinct status of the territory of a colony or other non-self-governing territory with respect to the territory of the administering State. However, the conclusion drawn from this regarding loss of sovereignty is not really tenable. The Declaration itself does not talk in such terms, nor does it present the sovereignty of the people in such a context. What is clearly meant and has been understood to be meant is that the developing right of self-determination renders the administering power in such a situation subject to the exercise of the right of the people in question. Sovereignty is thus limited, not terminated, and until such time as the right has been validly exercised title to the territory remains in the colonial power. Sovereignty may indeed be validly limited under international law without affecting its essence and existence.[40] The loss-of-sovereignty argument is further weakened by problems as to the repository of sovereignty until the new State becomes independent. If sovereignty is automatically lost, to whom does it pass? It could be argued that the people of the territory in question hold the title pending the formation of an independent State, but this poses severe problems in both theory and practice for international law. Sovereignty, for example, needs a mechanism by which it may be manifested, not dissipated, and basic concepts such as jurisdiction, non-intervention, and consent would in practical terms in such a situation be rendered meaningless. The argument could be put that title might vest in the relevant liberation movement, but in practice this has never been claimed. Liberation movements may claim to represent, and may be taken to represent, certain peoples in particular situations and before particular organs, but they have not been recognized as holding title to territory or being in any other way sovereign entities. With regard to Namibia, for example, it is instructive to note that the relevant administrative organ for UN purposes is the UN Council for Namibia, not SWAPO, the liberation movement. One must also point out that the legitimate exercise of self-determination may well lead to association or integration with an existing State and this further undermines the two suggestions noted. There is, however, another manifestation of the loss-of-sovereignty concept, and one that adopts an extreme approach. This states that colonial title is *ipso facto* void and thus never serves to pass sovereignty, which would presumably continue to reside in the initial pre-colonial holder. This view was put forward by India in the Goa debates of 1961. The Indian representative emphasized that

> Portugal has no sovereign right over this territory. There is no legal frontier—there can be no legal frontier—between India and Goa. And since the whole occupation is illegal as an issue—it started in an illegal manner, it continues to be illegal today, and is even more illegal in the light of resolution 1514 (XV)—there can be no question of aggression against your own frontier, or against your own people, whom you want to liberate.

The view that colonial powers have sovereign rights over territories conquered in Asia and Africa is no longer acceptable.[41] This extreme approach, impliedly positing a continuing sovereignty of pre-colonial entities despite colonization, raises many serious problems. It is clearly inconsistent with the accepted rules relating to inter-temporal law by which situations are analysed in the legal framework existing at the requisite time[42] and it brings to the fore questions relating to the identity and continuity of the pre-colonial States and combinations of territories that existed in the pre-colonial era, and any attempt to trace legal title on the basis of the earlier sovereignty would be virtually impossible. This approach, which has few supporters, appears in the claims made by Morocco with regard to territories supposedly forming part of its pre-colonial empire.[43] The inconsistencies between this approach and the concept of self-determination, which is temporally grounded in the closing phase of colonial rule and which indeed implicitly depends upon a recognition of the competence of the colonial power to grant independence, are manifestly apparent. It is also clear that the UN regime with regard to non-self-governing territories is founded upon the presumed legality of the colonial title, certainly until such time as the principle of self-determination comes into operation.

2. *As Modifying the Traditional Criteria of Statehood*

(a) Defined Territory

The principle of self-determination identifies the territorial unit within which the inhabitants determine their political status. It reinforces the notion of territorial integrity, in that the territory as colonially defined on the eve of self-determination is the recognized spatial frame for the exercise of the right. In this sense, the core of territory necessary for statehood is reinforced in colonial instances. This is demonstrated by the acceptance of Mauritania as an independent State despite Moroccan claims, and within its colonial borders.[44]

(b) Government

It is in this category that the principle of self-determination has most affected the application of the traditional criteria of statehood. The earlier formulations of the criteria had primarily emphasized the stability and effectiveness needed for this factor to be satisfied, while the representative and democratic nature of the government was also put forward as a requirement. The concept of self-determination has affected both.

The notion of government has, as Crawford pointed out,[45] two aspects. One is the right or title to exercise authority and the other is the actual exercise of authority. As far as the first is concerned, the principle of self-determination in those situations to which it has been accepted that it applies, will identify the people in question, while a grant of independence by the former sovereign will specify those entitled to exercise authority. As far as the actual exercise of authority is concerned, it is submitted that practice has demonstrated that in self-determination situations a lower level of effectiveness has now been accepted.

(i) *The Congo, 1960*. The Belgian administration of the colony had virtually excluded Africans from key posts, with the result that an educated élite scarcely existed. According to the UN Economic Commission for Africa, 80 per cent of commercialized production was in European hands.[46] By the date of independence on 30 June 1960, tribal fighting had broken out, with widespread clashes spreading to the capital.[47] On 5 July the Force Publique mutinied[48] and Belgian troops became involved again in the country.[49] On 11 July the province of Katanga announced its secession.[50] UN financial and military aid soon followed. Despite the virtual breakdown of government, the Congo was recognized by a large number of countries soon after independence and was admitted as a member state of the United Nations without opposition.[51] The UN Security Council resolved on 14 July to provide the Congolese government with the necessary military assistance[52] and ultimately took action to defeat the Katangan secession.[53]

(ii) *Rwanda-Urundi, 1962*[54] Tribal fighting broke out in the territory in 1959 and a UN mission was dispatched to discover the relevant facts. The United Nations hoped to establish one independent State, but it had to accept the independence of two States. A General Assembly Commission sent in 1962 referred to the 'psychosis of mutual distrust' in the territory,[55] and expressed doubts as to the nature and degree of governmental control in Burundi, while as far as Rwanda was concerned, the situation, it was stated, was 'not calculated to dispel the many misgivings which the General Assembly had always felt with regard to the conditions in which the people of Rwanda are approaching Statehood'.[56] In the event, Assembly resolution 1746 (XVI), in adopting the report of the Commission, permitted Belgian troops to remain in the two States for a short while after independence. Rwanda and Burundi were soon after admitted to the United Nations.[57]

(iii) *Guinea-Bissau, 1973*. After a number of years' fighting in the Portuguese colony, a UN Special Mission was sent to the 'liberated areas' of the territory pursuant to a decison of the Special Committee on Decolonization,[58] approved by the General Assembly.[59] The Mission concluded that Portugal had lost effective administrative control of large areas of the territory. The liberation movement, PAIGC, estimated that it controlled between two-thirds and three-quarters of the territory, and this was verified by many foreign observers. The Mission further reported that the population in those areas supported the PAIGC, which exercised *de facto* administrative control in such areas and effectively protected the inhabitants' interests.[60]

It was the Mission's belief that the Special Committee's recognition of the PAIGC as the *de facto* authority and the sole and authentic representative of the aspirations of the people of the territory should be taken into account by States and UN organs.[61]

The report of the Mission was endorsed by the Special Committee on 1 August 1972. It was felt that the effectiveness of the control of the PAIGC had been proved, and many States, including Bulgaria, Czechoslovakia, Guinea, India, Syria, Trinidad and Tobago, and Tanzania were of the opinion that Guinea-Bissau had achieved *de facto* independence and that the PAIGC administration should be recognized as the *de facto* government. The PAIGC was recognized as the only authentic representative of the people of the territory and the successful completion of its task by the Mission was declared to constitute a major contribution to the process of decolonization.[62]

On 24 September 1973 the PAIGC declared the independence of the Republic of Guinea-Bissau.[63] Within three days, the new State was recognized by Algeria, the Congo, Guinea, Upper Volta, Chad, Tanzania, Ghana, Somalia, Togo, Nigeria, Mauritania, Madagascar, Libya, Senegal, Syria, and Yugoslavia.[64] By the beginning of October, twenty-eight of the then forty-one members of the OAU had recognized Guinea-

Bissau, as well as a number of other States; including the USSR, Cuba, Iraq, and the German Democratic Republic.[65] During that month, Guinea-Bissau became the eighteenth member of the Liberation Committee of the OAU[66] and by the middle of the month sixty-two countries had recognized the new State.[67]

On 22 October an item was placed on the agenda of the General Assembly of the United Nations entitled 'the illegal occupation by Portuguese military forces of certain sectors of the Republic of Guinea-Bissau and acts of aggression committed by them against the people of the Republic'.[68]

The pattern of the Assembly debate had already been set by the discussions in the General Committee, which had called for the inscription of the item by 17 votes to 1, with 5 abstentions. A number of States, including Mauritius, Somalia, Pakistan, Guinea, Madagascar, and Ghana, affirmed the validity of the independence of Guinea-Bissau in international law.[69] France, Netherlands, the USA, and the United Kingdom declared that since Guinea-Bissau had not met the traditional statehood requirement of effective control it remained a non-self-governing territory.[70]

A number of different approaches were adopted in the debate in the General Assembly as regards the question of the statehood of Guinea-Bissau. Portugal noted that a State only became independent when a people in a well-defined territory had a sovereign capable of exercising supreme authority independent of any other entity.[71] A series of questions were posed regarding the territory of the 'phantom State', the exercise of effective control, the existence of a capital city, and the proposed siting of the diplomatic missions of the recognizing States.[72] The net effect of this was to emphasize that the PAIGC did not in any way fulfil the criteria for statehood.

Portugal maintained that the UN Mission had seen only 20 sq. km. of a territory with a total area of some 36,125 sq. km.[73] and that the territory and its population were subject to the sovereignty of the Lisbon government.[74] A number of Western and Latin American States opposed the 65-power draft resolution[75] on the grounds expressed by Portugal. Greece, for example, declared that the functional coexistence of the three indispensable elements of territory, sovereignty, and people was not fulfilled to the degree necessary to enable the new entity to assume the full rights and responsibilities of a State. The United Kingdom stated that Guinea-Bissau as an independent State was factually and objectively not a reality,[76] while the USA declared that since Portugal controlled the population centres, most of the rural areas, and the administration of the territory, it must be regarded as the sovereign under international law, otherwise facts would be disregarded.[77]

The majority of the thirty abstainers to resolution 3061 (XXVIII) also denied the status of Guinea-Bissau as an independent State, on the basis that effective control over the major portion of the territory in question was not proved, while at the same time condemning Portugal's colonialism.[78]

Ninety-three States, however, voted in favour of resolution 3061 (XVIII) which was accordingly adopted on 2 November 1973. This resolution welcomed 'the recent accession to independence of the people of Guinea-Bissau, thereby creating the sovereign State of the Republic of Guinea-Bissau'.[79]

Two themes may be discerned in the speeches of these States. One attitude was that Guinea-Bissau did indeed fulfil the criteria for statehood as classically expressed. This was based on the report of the UN Special Mission. Guinea noted that after ten years of struggle, over three-quarters of the territory had been liberated by the PAIGC, which had established a working administration comprising schools, health services, shops, etc.[80] Ghana stressed that, unlike the current situations in Mozambique and Angola, the people of Guinea-Bissau fulfilled the conditions for recognition of belligerency and that in addition the classical prerequisites for the recognition of a new State, viz. *de facto* control of territory and machinery of government, the assent of the bulk of the population, and willingness to comply with international obligations, were in existence in this case.[81] The second theme manifested in a number of speeches of delegates supporting the resolution was the importance of the concept of self-determination.

Senegal declared that the Western powers were applying the classical rules of international law with regard to recognition among European States to deny recognition to Guinea-Bissau, but colonial liberation called for the application of other rules of law. Such other rules were those enshrined in the Charter and resolutions of the United Nations.[82]

Madagascar emphasized that the agenda item under discussion resulted directly from the implementation of the principles of resolution 1514 (XV),[83], while Uganda stressed the importance of resolutions referring to the right of self-determination, such as General Assembly resolutions 1514 (XV) and 2918 (XXVII) and Security Council resolution 322, in interpreting Chapter XI of the Charter.[84]

(iv) *Angola, 1975–6.*[85] On 10 November the departing Portuguese

High Commissioner proclaimed the independence and full sovereignty of the State of Angola. Two governments of Angola were thereupon proclaimed, that of the MPLA and that of the FNLA–Unita coalition, both purporting to speak for the whole country.[86] Both of the rival movements controlled determinate areas of territory and both received increasing foreign support. A number of States recognized the MPLA regime, but OAU policy was to seek to set up a government of national unity. In the event, after the Soviet- and Cuban-backed MPLA victory over the South-African-, Zaïre-, and USA-supported forces of FNLA and Unita, a majority of African States recognized the MPLA government. On 11 February 1976 Angola was admitted as the forty-seventh member of the OAU.[87] A distinction, however, has to be drawn between the existence of Angola as an independent State and the recognition of the MPLA regime as the legitimate government of that State. Whereas a recognized government only emerged as regards the majority of African States, the OAU, and a large number of other States by January or February 1976, it is clear that an independent State of Angola was in existence as of 11 November 1975. The alternatives of a continuation of non-self-governing territory status until early 1976 or the existence of an intermediate status are not viable propositions.

(v) *Saharan Arab Democratic Republic.* In February 1976 the Polisario movement in Western Sahara proclaimed the sovereign, independent Saharan Arab Democratic Republic.[88] Over the years an increasing number of States recognized SADR and at the meeting of the OAU Council of Ministers in February 1982 an attempt was made by the OAU Secretary-General to seat a delegation from SADR on the grounds that twenty-six of the fifty OAU members had recognized the republic. Admittance by simple majority was deemed sufficient.[89] In the event a major constitutional crisis was caused within the OAU and nineteen States walked out of the conference, and as a direct result the scheduled meetings of both the Council of Ministers and the Assembly of Heads of State and Government over July–August 1982 failed to achieve the necessary quorum.[90] By the spring of 1982, it appeared that some fifty countries had recognized SADR.[91]

The question is thus raised as to the existence or not of an independent State called the Saharan Arab Democratic Republic. The Spanish decolonization process which resulted in the partition of the territory of Western Sahara between Morocco and Mauritania was clearly inconsistent with the accepted operation of self-determination, as subsequent UN and OAU practice affirms. Accordingly, the people of the territory are still entitled to exercise the right despite Moroccan denials to date. Although a large number of States have recognized SADR, including a majority of OAU members, it remains doubtful whether the requisite criterion of effectiveness has been demonstrated. Recognition on its own is insufficient; it must be coupled with some degree of effective control with regard to the territory in question. This element remains, although in self-determination situations it may have been modified. No UN resolution has been adopted recognizing SADR and admitting it to membership and this must remain a crucial evidential point. This is reinforced by the major crisis precipitated within the OAU on the issue of SADR membership.[91a] Accordingly, it must be seen that, at this stage at least, acceptance of SADR as a viable State in international law is premature.

It thus appears that practice, and primarily African practice at that, has succeeded in modifying the effective-government criterion of the existence of statehood. In the Congo, Rwanda and Burundi, and Angola, circumstances were such at the commencement of independence as to deny the existence of effective government. However, this did not result in a denial of statehood. On the contrary, the Congo, Rwanda, and Burundi, were admitted to the United Nations at the time of upheaval or relative instability. This weakening of the effective-government requirement is a result of the principle of self-determination, which stipulates that in colonial situations the people of the particular territory has the right to determine its own political status. This right is not qualified by any reference to the need for an effective government. Indeed, it is a question not of territorial control or efficacy but of status. The maintenance of the traditional approach with regard to government might well have resulted in the creation of entities with an intermediate status as territories decolonized, occasionally with weak or non-existent authorities. Such a situation, even were it remotely viable politically, would have led to serious problems as to the rights and duties of such entities. In the event, this has not proved to be the case, and the international community has accepted that in self-determination situations, the requirement of effective government for statehood has been substantially modified. The Guinea-Bissau type of situation, nevertheless, remains problematic. While the territory was non-self-governing and its people entitled to the exercise of self-determination, one was not faced with the position where, as for example in the cases discussed above, a colonial power granted independence to an indigenous government which could not be regarded as effective. It was a situation where the colonial power was maintaining its claims to sovereignty and denying the liberation movement control over the whole of the territory. Although the report of the Special Mission of the United Nations stated that the overwhelming bulk of the territory was under the effective control of the PAIGC administration, many Western and Latin American States denied that this was so, or at the least argued that a substantial degree of ambiguity existed as to the precise factual situation. In such circumstances, it is far from clear that the facts alone warranted a viable claim of statehood from the PAIGC, even in the light of the impact of self-determination.[92]

Similarly, the proclamation by Polisario of SADR would appear to be premature. This is especially so in the absence of clear evidence as to the extent and nature of effective control over the territory and in view of the situation in the United Nations and OAU.

Although the criterion of effective governmental control has been modified by the principle of self-determination,[93] it still exists as regards other situations. For example, it is submitted that the rule remains intact as far as secessionist attempts are concerned, and, indeed, with respect to divided States. Katanga and Biafra are both instances of entities that for a time exercised 'governmental' control over determinate areas of land, but such control could not be seen as effective until the factual situation had been clearly resolved. Where there is continued fighting, effective control in the sense of the international law criteria of statehood cannot be established. Okeke, however, has argued that Biafra satisfied the essential elements of statehood in international law for the time it lasted.[94] But it is suggested that in such circumstances, international law requires that the criteria of statehood be fully satisfied. The exception with regard to recognized self-determination situations is not applicable in other cases, and certainly not where secession is concerned, for that involves a violation of the territorial integrity of the existing State.[95] It is not in the interest of States in general to sanction the break-up of existing States by the lax application of the requirement of statehood. Although, once the factual position has been clearly resolved, international law will accept the result, there is a presumption against the status of statehood in secession situations.

(c) Independence

The concept of self-determination, once the people concerned has attained sovereignty, emphasizes the independence of the new State as against external interference. It maintains that the people as a whole and as previously defined[96] may freely determine its political status and freely pursue its economic, social, and cultural development. It reinforces the domestic jursidiction provisions of international law.

3. An Additional Requirement of Statehood

The principle of self-determination has clearly had an important effect in qualifying the traditional criteria of statehood in certain circumstances. Is it then possible to go further than this and state that it has become itself one of the criteria of statehood? If this were to be so, not only would statehood be concerned with the right of a colonial people to become independent but the nature of that people's progress to independence would also be at issue. In general, it would appear that international law is not interested in how a people exercises its right to determine its political status and pursue its economic, social, and cultural development. It imposes no restriction on the type of political structure chosen nor does it bar particular economic systems from consideration. But it seems as if there may be an important exception to this with regard to racial discrimination. The arguments would be that in situations of racial discrimination enshrined in the political system of a new entity, that entity may be denied that status of statehood in international law even though the criteria traditionally enumerated have been fully complied with. The issue is clearly a difficult one, but important State practice with respect to it has, however, been rather sparse. The Rhodesia case is the prime instance of material which is of relevance, and one may also add the case of the 'independent' South Africa Bantustans.

(a) Rhodesia

In October 1965 the General Assembly adopted resolution 2012 (XX) which called on the United Kingdom not to accept a unilateral declaration of independence by the authorities in that territory as it would be in the sole interest of the minority. Resolution 2022 (XX), adopted on 5 November, called on the United Kingdom to effect, if necessary by force, the release of political detainees and the repeal of all discriminatory legislation. The day after UDI, on 12 November the Assembly adopted resolution 2024 (XX) condemning the UDI 'made by the racialist minority' and requesting the United Kingdom to end the rebellion. Resolution 2151 (XXI) reaffirmed the inalienable right of the Africans to freedom and independence and condemned any arrangement for the transference of power unless based on self-determination. Security Council resolution 216 (1965) called on all States not to recognize 'this illegal racist minority regime' or assist it, while resolution 217 (1965) called the continuance in time of the rebellion a threat to international peace and security. The declaration of independence was deemed to be of 'no legal validity' and the regime in power an 'illegal authority'. The United Kingdom view was that UDI had no constitutional effect and that the only way the territory could become independent was by way of an Act of Parliament.[97] In international law, of course, this is not strictly correct. The test revolves around the criteria of statehood and the municipal law requirements of the metropolitan State are not critical. Lauterpacht has written that 'the refusal of the mother country to recognize such independence is not conclusive' and that once evidence has demonstrated the displacement of the mother country and that the 'effectiveness of its authority does not exceed a mere assertion of right . . . the illegality of origin, from the point of view of the constitutional law of the parent State, is of no consequence'.[98] Fawcett has written that the UK claim with regard to post-UDI Rhodesia is only a 'mere assertion of right'.[99] In factual terms, the undoubtedly effective control maintained by the Smith regime over the territory and population of the former Southern Rhodesia for some years after UDI meant that in this respect at least the entity seemed to fulfil the classical requirements of statehood. The British response could not be described as a vigorous attempt to end the rebellion by all possible means. However, no State recognized Rhodesia. The United Nations persisted in regarding it as a non-self-governing territory[100] and the legal responsibility of the United Kingdom,[101] and adopted a number of resolutions denying legal validity to the regime in power. One could nevertheless still regard Rhodesia as a State in the light of its satisfaction of the factual requirements of statehood in international law, but this seems a dubious proposition.[102] The fact that no State at all recognized it as a State, coupled with the strenuous denunciations of the validity of its declared independence, detract substantially from the viability of this alternative.[103] Adoption of the constitutive theory of recognition would solve the problem of the reason in law for its existence as a State, but there are strong objections to this theory.[104]

It would seem that the firmest legal foundations for denying the existence of Rhodesia as a State lies in the development of an additional criterion of statehood, viz. the principle of self-determination. According to this approach, if the requirement of consistency with the provisions of self-determination were not present, an entity claiming statehood would not fulfil the requisite conditions and its claim would therefore fail. However, the proposition cannot be as broadly stated as that, for the reasons that practice has demonstrated that States have emerged with regimes in control which have not acted in accordance with the postulates of self-determination. The application of this additional criterion of statehood is restricted at the moment, it is suggested, to those peoples regarded as having the right in international law of self-determination. It would therefore not apply in cases of secessions from existing States, for example. One may envisage a situation in which the international community might wish for this to happen, but practice to date is insufficient to substantiate this. The proposition does not operate in cases of already existing States so as to lead to the extinction of statehood.

However, in the case of an entity seeking to become a State and accepted by the international community as being entitled to exercise the right of self-determination, it may well be necessary to demonstrate that internally it is complying with the requirements of the principle of self-determination. In view of State practice to date, one cannot define this condition too severely, but institutionalized and systematic discrimination will *semble* invalidate a claim to statehood.[105]

It has been suggested that this additional requirement forms an appendage to the criterion of effective government.[106] However, while the concept of self-determination in this context is naturally concerned with the character of government of the territory in question, it does appear a confusion to link the two in this fashion. Government as an element in the creation of statehood refers primarily to the relationship between the authority of an entity and the territory involved, although clearly the notion of effectiveness is related to the degree of acceptability of that authority by the inhabitants concerned. It has been seen also how in self-determination situations, the requirement of effectiveness has been modified. The notion of self-determination as an additional requirement for statehood is essentially concerned with the relationship between the government and the people and centres around the absence of systematized discrimination within that entity.[107]

(b) The 'Independent' Bantustans

If an entity claiming statehood may be denied such a claim on the grounds that it is a territory recognized as within the self-determination context and it has enshrined a discriminatory system within its authority structures, the prime example being the Rhodesian situation, is it possible to go beyond this to deal with cases where the new entity is being established in pursuance of an illegal object such as the institutionalization of racial discrimination? This is one of the questions raised by the purported grant of independence by South Africa to its Bantustans. A sovereign State may legitimately dispose of part of its own territory should it so wish. This is one aspect of the sovereignty of States under international law and it has been regarded as being more or less without exception. What is therefore under consideration is a derogation from the general rule, such exception being based upon general principles of international law, including perhaps self-determination, since the creation of new States is posited.

The Status of the Transkei Act adopted in 1976 by South Africa declared the territory known as the Transkei to be a sovereign and independent State, free from any authority exercised by the Republic of South Africa.[108]

However, it was South Africa which determined the relevant citizenship conditions for the new entity. In particular, it covered a large number of Xhosas living in the Republic itself.[109] The Prime Minister of the Transkei took exception to this, stating that the Transkei was not responsible for the Xhosas living and working in South Africa.[110] As noted above,[111] the United Nations and the OAU have declared themselves firmly against recognizing any of the Bantustans as independent and no State apart from South Africa has recognized such independence. As reasons for such non-recognition, UN resolutions have cited the principles of territorial integrity and self-determination.[112] As far as the former is concerned it is to be doubted whether it may be understood to include the proposition that a State's territorial definition may never be altered. The principle of self-determination, however, may be relevant. This principle may well be applicable to South Africa here, as the one exception to date to the rule that the principle applies only to non-independent States,[113] in the light of the institutionalized and systematic racial discrimination established by the government of that country,[114] and in the context of the purported creation of new States. Accordingly the policy of creating the Bantustans and purporting to endow them with statehood in an attempt to further the policy of apartheid may be seen as not complying with the norms of self-determination as relevant in the creation of new States and thus as a violation of that principle. It would thus appear that where an entity is granted independence in order to further illegal policies in international law, and perhaps contrary thus to self-determination, such an entity may not be acceptable as a State.[115]

C. RECOGNITION

Recognition is one mechanism whereby the international community accepts certain factual situations and endows them with legal significance.[116] But the relationship between fact and law is a complex one and susceptible to many conflicting interpretations. The law may endorse the legality of a particular situation even though it is factually precarious and the extent of the interaction between effectiveness and the law is a constantly changing one. As far as statehood itself is concerned, two opposing doctrines have been preferred. The constitutive theory 'deduces the legal existence of new States from the will of those already established'[117] so that it is only through recognition that a State becomes an international person under international law;[118] the declaratory theory, on the other hand, maintains that once a State satisfies the criteria of statehood, it becomes a subject of international law and recognition is merely a political act of no legal significance in this context.[119] The problem with the former approach is that State practice appears to be inconsistent with it,[120] and it copes with difficulty with the question of the unrecognized State.[121] The problem with the declaratory approach is that it ignores or decries the effect upon a situation of its recognition by States of the international community. The constitutive position cannot be accepted as formulated, it is suggested, while the declaratory theory needs to be modified. Lauterpacht's view that, once the criteria of statehood are fulfilled, a legal duty to recognize arises[122] is not borne out in State practice,[123] but as Brownlie notes, 'if an entity bears the marks of Statehood, other States put themselves at risk legally if they ignore the basic obligations of State relations'.[124] Recognition can have a strong evidential effect as regards fulfilment of the various criteria of statehood. In those cases where there is dispute as to the satisfaction of the necessary factual requirements, recognition by States will tend to settle the issue. This may also be true with respect to non-recognition. African practice has provided examples of both.

The PAIGC movement in the Portuguese territory of Guinea (Bissau) declared itself independent on 26 September 1973 and within a short space of time was recognized by the majority of States in the international community.[125] This was despite the fact that Portugal controlled at least one-third of the territory by the PAIGC's admission and all of it by its own account. In addition to States' recognitions of the new Republic of Guinea-Bissau, ninety-three States voted in favour of resolution 3061 (XXVIII), which 'welcomes the recent accession to independence of the people of Guinea-Bissau, thereby creating the sovereign State of the Republic of Guinea-Bissau'. A number of questions thereby arise. Was such recognition (prior to Portugal's recognition on 10 September 1974)[126] premature? What is the effect of such recognitions? And, what was the effect of the General Assembly resolution?

Oppenheim states that an untimely and precipitate recognition not only violates the dignity of the mother State, but is an unlawful act and 'it is frequently maintained that such untimely recognition amounts to intervention'.[127] The test of whether an entity is sufficiently well established to be recognized (in the absence of the recognition of the mother State) may be found 'either in the fact that the revolutionary State has utterly defeated the mother State, or that the mother State has ceased to make efforts to subdue the revolutionary State, or even that the mother State, in spite of its efforts, is apparently incapable of bringing the revolutionary State back under its sway'.[128] None of these was the case with regard to the Republic of Guinea-Bissau at the time in question. Thus, the issue centres around whether the fact that the conflict was a self-determination one affects any change in the traditional position.

Portugal maintained during the General Assembly debate in October 1973 that since the PIAGC regime did not exercise effective control over the particular territory and population and did not alternatively possess control over a substantial part of the territory and population and was not in a position to displace the parent State's government, any recognition was premature and premature recognition was tantamount to intervention and participation in the conflict.[129] A couple of States invoked the French recognition of the United States in 1778 and the US and UK recognitions of the former Spanish colonies in the 1820s, as well as the American recognition of Panama immediately after its secession from Colombia in 1903, as valid precedents for recognizing Guinea-Bissau.[130] However, it is to be doubted whether such examples constitute a strong justification for the recognition of Guinea-Bissau prior to Portuguese recognition. French recognition of and military aid to the USA in 1778 has been accepted as 'precipitate'[131] and a 'breach of international law'.[132] The British and American recognition of the former Spanish South American colonies occurred over a decade after the initial declarations of independence in 1810, while the immediate American recognition of Panama was declared by Oppenheim to be an intervention.[133] These instances, therefore, illustrate the parameters of premature recognition and are of relevance with regard to secessionist attempts to break away from existing, independent States, but not necessarily in self-determination situations.

There was little attempt in the debates by those supporting the PAIGC to argue that the effect of the numerous recognitions was to endow Guinea-Bissau with statehood, but this is perhaps not surprising since the preponderant argument was that Guinea-Bissau did indeed fulfil the requisite criteria for statehood. Cameroon did state that the view that Guinea-Bissau was a fiction could not be maintained since a fiction recognized by over seventy UN members was a reality,[134] while Nigeria declared that the large number of UN members recognizing the new Republic was evidence that Guinea-Bissau was a reality.[135] Apart from this the effect of such recognitions was not discussed. This in itself argues against the constitutive position, but it should not be taken to mean that the question is peripheral. It has been seen that in self-determination cases, the requirements for statehood have been modified, so that the test for effectiveness of government is by no means as stringent as in other cases of claims for statehood. Recognition is one way in which a State may signal its belief that a particular entity has complied with the prerequisites of statehood. In the normal course of events, the impact of individual recognitions in terms of the generality of international law will be minimal. However, in difficult cases where the factual conditions have not been conclusively ascertained, recognition may constitute evidence of the fulfilment of the necessary requirements. The large number of recognitions of Guinea-Bissau,[136] therefore, demonstrates that a majority of States in the international community accepted that the new State satisfied the relevant conditions as modified by the doctrine of self-determination.

Recognition by one or two or a small number of States might have been regarded as premature,[137] but where some eighty to ninety States are involved, it is submitted, a significant statement with regard to the relevant factual situation has been made.[138]

The effect of such recognitions was reinforced by the admission of Guinea-Bissau as a member of the OAU[139] and by resolution 3061 (XXVIII).[140] Both mark further evidence of conformity with formal criteria on the part of Guinea-Bissau. The former is of interest not only as a forceful example of African State practice but also as providing for one of the possible consquences of statehood in Africa. The General Assembly resolution was not of itself binding, of course, but it is an instance of collective recognition, and as such of importance, though this importance is diminished by the fact that Guinea-Bissau[141] was not admitted to the United Nations as a member-State until 17 September 1974, i.e. one week after Portuguese recognition.[142]

The non-recognition of Rhodesia also illustrates this point, for it may be taken as evidence of the non-compliance of Rhodesia with the necessary requirements of statehood. The fact that this was also the result of UN direction makes it of added emphasis. The United Nations had implicitly called for the non-recognition of Katanga in 1960–1,[143] and with respect to South Africa's Bantustans the General Assembly explicitly called on all governments to deny any form of recognition to the 'so-called independent Transkei'.[144] According to the constitutive theory, such entities cannot be States in the absence of all recognition, while in the view of the adherents of the declaratory theory, the issue revolves around the possession or otherwise of the necessary requirements of statehood. It is suggested that Rhodesia and the two Bantustans[145] declared 'independent' by South Africa are not States in international law, not because they have not been recognized but because they have failed to confirm with the criteria for statehood as modified by the principle of self-determination, and the absence of recognition constitutes evidence of this. A further question arises at this stage, and that is whether there exists a duty not to recognize in such circumstances.

Recognition here may be deemed contrary to the principle of self-determination since it is aimed at the acceptance of a situation based upon its contravention. Non-recognition[146] may operate as a sanction of international society, but its use is sometimes controversial and not always efficacious. States may be obliged not to recognize territorial changes based upon the illegal use of force,[147] but recognition may sometimes be the means whereby the law accepts factual situations despite illegality of origin. As a policy weapon, non-recognition is clearly of value here, but it is felt that abuses of self-determination which prevent the attainment of statehood should not be endorsed by the use of recognition and that until the facts demonstrate compliance with the criterion of self-determination in statehood cases, a positive duty of non-recognition may arise.

The consequences of non-recognition were discussed by the International Court of Justice in the *Namibia* case,[148] in which it was stated that acts, treaties, etc. which implied recognition of governmental authority were illegal, although in cases of general conventions of a humanitarian character, the non-performance of which may adversely affect the people of the territory, the same rule would not apply. Non-recognition should not in general result in depriving the people involved of any advantages derived from international co-operation.[149]

In the cases of Rhodesia prior to 1980 and the Bantustans concerned, *de jure* title remained in the United Kingdom and remains with South Africa respectively, although *de facto* administration may be carried on by other regimes. This *sui generis* status will clearly cause some problems in municipal courts[150] but this should not detract from the importance of maintaining such status and refusing to accept the statehood of such entities. Denial of statehood in such cases cannot be taken to mean that the issue is removed from the jurisdiction of international law. Practice has shown that with regard to Rhodesia, the rules of international law regarding the use of force are applicable[151] and the same would be true if analogous situations arose with respect to the so-called independent Bantustans. It is clear that other relevant norms of international law would apply in such cases, since to deny such applicability would be to create a situation wherein such entities of dubious origin would be unrestricted by law in their activities and thus in an advantageous position *vis-à-vis* States and other subjects of international law. To conclude that international law covers such entities does not mean that such entities must be regarded as States, since international law regulates international activity in general and its scope is not confined to inter-State relations.[152]

D. CONCLUSIONS

The doctrine of statehood in international law has historically been an ambiguous amalgam of law and fact. The birth of a new State is a question of fact. That is clear. One cannot spirit a State out of a vacuum. On the other hand, it is a question to which the law is not indifferent. To put it another way, the criteria of statehood may be founded upon effectiveness, but not exclusively so. The traditional view of the requirements of statehood has, it is felt, concentrated heavily upon the notion of effectiveness as the basis of the creation of new States. Moushkely notes that in this context 'il s'agit d'un phénomène sociologique et historique indépendant de toute condition juridique'.[153] While effectiveness itself may well be a criterion or prerequisite established by law, it is in essence a political manifestation and not a legal one. Thus law followed demonstrated fact. Modern practice, however, has seen a modification of the exclusive reliance upon effectiveness, and such modification has arisen as a result of the principle of self-determination. In the case of Rhodesia,[154] effectiveness alone would have posited the existence of a State, and the same might apply as regards the 'independent' Bantustans. But their creation without fulfilling the criterion of self-determination, as evidenced by the lack of third-party recognition, has meant that such entities are not States, despite the factual situation. On the other hand, it is believed that the case of Guinea-Bissau demonstrates that the criterion of effectiveness is seriously weakened in self-determination situations, so that while a reliance upon effectiveness alone would have led to a denial of statehood, this must be qualified in the light of the principle of self-determination. The large number of recognitions made by States of the new entity as a State must suggest the conclusion that Guinea-Bissau, despite the factual situation, was, at that stage and prior to Portuguese recognition, a State.[155] In other situations, effectiveness remains the prime basis for statehood. It is only with regard to the scope and contents of self-determination that this criterion is qualified. It is believed that this is consistent with the classic formulation of Lauterpacht to the effect that 'international law acknowledges as a source of rights and obligations such facts and situations as are not the result of acts which it prohibits and stigmatizes as unlawful'.[156]

II. NEW STATES AND TITLE TO TERRITORY

Under traditional international law, a severe problem was posed concerning the acquisition by new States of title to their own territory since until the new State was created there was no legal person competent to hold the title. This demonstrated a gap in legal theory for title to territory is a fundamental requirement of statehood.[157] The classical modes of acquisition of territory are unhelpful in this respect since they are predicated upon activity by a particular type of subject of international law and in any event fail to explain the factual circumstances involved.

There are a number of ways in which the theoretical problems may be overcome, but first a brief survey of the means whereby an entity can obtain independence will be attempted. The most usual method is by the consent and agreement of the colonial power, whether it be signalled by internal legislation or by some form of agreement with the accepted representatives of the new entity.[158] In some cases, a plebiscite will be held putting various options to the population, including that of independence, as for example the Algerian plebiscite of July 1962. Independence may be achieved, on the other hand, as a result of a rebellion contrary to the wishes of the administering power. Although in most cases a successful war of secession from the colonial power has culminated in a grant of independence, as for example in Algeria, Angola, and Mozambique, the theoretical problem is posed since it is not invariably so. Title cannot be derived through the previous territorial sovereign where the latter has refused consent. It is also possible for such a rebellion against the administering power to be contrary to international law. The Rhodesian case is the prime example of this.

One factor which has constrained the development of the law in this field has been that the doctrine of domestic jurisdiction has historically hidden from international law those events taking place prior to the establishment of a new State, so that the way in which territory was acquired was not a matter of concern to the traditional law. This appeared to lead to either one of two conclusions. Either the factual possession by a State of territory was just accepted in law, or the constitutive theory of recognition extended to legitimize the acquisition by the State of its own territory. The classic approach to the problem was put by Oppenheim, who noted that the 'formation of a new State is . . . a matter of fact not law' and that the foundation of a new State must not be confused with the acquisition of territory by an existing State.[159] International law does not create States but recognizes their factual existence and gives legal effect to that situation. The declaratory view of recognition and statehood would *semble* leave the issue at this point, relying fundamentally upon the principle of effectiveness. However, this approach can no longer be strictly maintained. The right of peoples to self-determination in certain circumstances has imposed a corresponding duty upon administering States to permit the exercise of that right and international law has been vitally concerned with this process. This has led to a reassessment of the role of domestic jurisdiction in such cases and therefore the consideration of particular events and facts prior to the establishment of the new State. It also means that international law theory can no longer merely assume that States have acquired the right to their territory by virtue of the factual situation upon independence, but may have to delve further.

One approach to the problem is that of the constitutive theory of recognition. This view proposes that recognition not only constitutes the new State as an international legal person but also vests the title to its territory in that State.[160] By this method, a series of recognitions would establish a new legal personality complete with a good title to its territory. This has led Starke to refer to an 'international quasi-adjudication of territory'.[161] Jennings appears to be in favour of this approach, and notes that in such a situation 'recognition plays a primary and perhaps decisive role in the constitution of a territorial title'.[162] He continues by saying that in this case 'it is ordinarily impracticable to separate out from the process of the creation of the new State the simple element of title to sovereignty over its territory for each is a constituent of the other'.[163] In other words, the creation of a State of necessity involves the acquisition by it of title to its territory. This achieved, however, by recognition, or rather a series of recognitions, since international law has not developed any collective machinery in this respect. It is a process which may be termed non-historical consolidation since time is unimportant.[164] Many of the criticisms made with regard to the constitutive theory are applicable in this context, for example inconsistent States practice and the problem of the status in international law of an entity recognized by some States as a State, but not by others. Title to territory and statehood must march together, so that in this sense non-recognition by a large number of States can be a crucial problem.[165] The issue of the unrecognized entity may be disposed of by the constitutive theory, but it is to be queried whether the means whereby this is accomplished are truly satisfactory, particularly in view of the development of the doctrine of self-determination. The 'factual' approach to the problem of newly emerged States and title to territory suffers from the disadvantage that matters prior to the establishment of the new State upon the basis of the principle of effectiveness are clearly of relevance in the contemporary law of territory. Self-determination has undoubtedly effected an important change here and one that cannot be ignored. The problem with accepting the alternative 'recognition' thesis is that it is predicated upon an espousal of the constitutive doctrine of recognition and it is believed that the disadvantages of this theory make it unwise to found the solution to the question of tracing title to territory upon it.

There exist a number of other possibilities. Various writers have concentrated upon the vast majority of cases whereby non-independent territories have become independent with the consent of the adminstering power, and have characterized the situation as one of succession,[165] or quasi-cession,[167] or quasi-prescription.[168] Such cases are based on the proposition that in non-self-governing territories, sovereignty rests with the administering power which then transfers title to the people of representatives of the emerging State. But such approaches also appear to accept the legitimacy of looking beyond the fact of independence to establish title and in a way which centres upon the relationship between the administering power and the pre-State entity.

The approaches which concern themselves with the question of the nature of this pre-State entity will be examined, but first the distinction between self-determination and non-self-determination situations must be stressed. In the latter case—and the primary example of such a situation will be secession from an existing non-colonial State—the traditonal rules of statehood apply, so that the seceding State will establish its statehood by adhering to the relevant conditions and its title to territory will be based upon its successful acquisition of the same from the parent State. The element of effectiveness is thus crucial. Recognitions by third States and particularly by the parent State will constitute vital evidence of the compliance of the new State with the necessary criteria. In such cases, the fact of statehood will comprise also the transference of title.

In the case, however, of non-independent territories within the purview of the right to self-determination, the interposition of that right creates a different juridical situation. Where mandate and trust territories were concerned, of course, it was always accepted that sovereignty and title did not lie with the administering power; Judge McNair declared that a new legal institution was involved which did not fit the old conception of sovereignty and that indeed sovereignty was in abeyance until 'the inhabitants of the territory obtain recognition as an independent State'.[169] The International Court noted that the 'rights of the mandatory in relations to the mandated territory and the inhabitants have their foundation in the obligations of the mandatory and they are so to speak mere tools given to enable it to fulfil its obligations'.[170] These obligations related to the eventual self-determination of the population of the territory.[171]

Judge Nervo declared with regard to Namibia that 'the mandate did not confer ownership or sovereignty or permanent rights but consisted only of a conditional grant of powers for the achievement of a purpose—not for the benefit of the grantee but for the benefit of a third party, the people and territory of Namibia'.[172]

Sovereignty over colonies and other non-self-governing territories, on the other hand, lay with the administering power. But the development of the principle of self-determination as a legal concept appeared to render the situation with regard to such territories on a par with mandated and trust territories,[173] although there was apparently a difference as regards the immediate sovereign. With the acceptance of the right to self-determination it could no longer be said that the administering power possessed absolute sovereignty, since it was clearly subject to a duty with regard to the exercise of the right. As the 1970 Declaration on Principles of International Law stated, 'the territory of a colony or other non-self-governing territory has, under the Charter, a status separate and distinct from the territory of the State administering it . . . until the people of the colony or non-self-governing territory have exercised the right to self-determination'. The Declaration did not state that title rested with the people concerned, it should be noted. Indeed, a number of territorial adjustments were made by the colonial powers,[174] so that title was accepted as residing in the adminstering authority. However, contemporary international law has restricted the sovereignty of the administering State and made it subject to the right of the people to self-determination. Thus, while the administering State in such a situation still possesses the title to the territory in question, it is qualified by the right of the people of the territory to call for its transfer in the context of the exercise of self-determination. In cases where the administering power seeks by force to deprive the relevant population of this right, the people may take action in order to establish its own sovereignty and statehood, and consequently title to that territory. It is believed that the Guinea-Bissau episode, 1973–4, demonstrates this. But it is predicated upon a number of factors, viz. the active hampering by the use of force of the right of the people to self-determination, action taken by the people to counteract this, the achievement of a certain minimum of success expressed in terms of territorial control and effectiveness by the people, and the consequent formal declaration of independence which will implicitly include a claim to the title of the territory concerned. The point that differentiates this situation from an attempt to secede from a non-colonial independent State is the lower level of effectiveness that needs to be manifested as a result of the operation of the principle of self-determination. In addition, the territory with regard to which title is claimed will be all of that territory formerly administered by the colonial power, unless there are exceptional circumstances.[175]

This means that the veil of domestic jurisdiction, barring inquiry by international law before actual independence, has been clearly pierced in self-determination situations. It leads to the conclusion that events and facts prior to the claim to formal independence may be examined in order to test the legitimacy of the claim, as for example in the Rhodesia and Bantustan cases. Indeed, the test of self-determination may prevent a successful claim to title and statehood. In addition, it opens the way to a consideration of the proposition that territorial sovereignty may be transferred prior to the moment of independence, thus obviating the doctrinal problem relating to the tracing of title. This suggests that where a people is entitled in law to self-determination and demonstrates the intention to seek statehood and title, then, providing the minimum-effectiveness criterion is satisfied, title may be acquired pending or at the same time as statehood.

Since in the case of non-independent territories (not forming part of a non-colonial sovereign State) title remains in the administering power but subject to the right of the people to call for its transfer in conformity with the principle of self-determination, while in the case of mandated and trust territories the territorial sovereignty possessed by the administering power is further restricted, it is not possible to talk in terms of absolute title. Title in either case is to a certain degree subject to external constraint. This raises the further question of the identity of the transferee in such instances. Is it the people as a whole or the representatives of the people or some other entity? It is submitted that in general one should regard the people of the territory in question as a whole as the legal personality capable of receiving the transfer of title, then held by the authorities of the new State on its behalf. This is because the right of self-determination is vested in the people as an entity and not in some other body. The theoretical possibility of the disposal of part of the territory by the people prior to the actual emergence of the new State is thus presented, but for many reasons this is highly unlikely to take place in practice.

This leaves open the question of the status of national liberation movements in the process of acquiring title and statehood, and to this issue we shall now briefly turn.

III. THE STATUS OF NATIONAL LIBERATION MOVEMENTS

As Lauterpacht noted, 'the orthodox positivist doctrine has been explicit in the affirmation that only States are subjects of international law'.[176] However, this doctrine has been modified, particularly in the years since 1945. The International Court of Justice recognized the status of the United Nations as an international person and subject of international law in the *Reparations* case[177] while the characterization of individuals as subjects of international law has proceeded apace.[178] In addition, the development of the concept of self-determination has raised the question of peoples as subjects of international law. The issue of personality in the law is therefore complex and the required conditions needed to be satisfied rather ambiguous. In fact, it has to be left to international practice to determine whether an entity is accepted as a legal person and the consequences in international law of such personality as is presented. Although the UN Charter restricts membership to States, recent years have witnessed a proliferation of what have been variously termed non-territorial actors, non-governmental entities, and supranational functional communities.[179] Therefore, the question as to the status of national liberation movements has to be discussed in the light of the developing requirements of the international community as demonstrated through practice.

In the early years of the United Nations, the peoples of non-self-governing territories were regarded as within the jurisdiction of the administering power and not entitled to a separate status.[180] The next stage involved the characterization of what might be generally regarded as prototype national liberation movements as petitioners within the framework of the United Nations. It was originally part of the trusteeship system but was extended beyond this to relate to colonial territories in general. However, the hearing of such petitions was discretionary and the petitioners themselves participated as private individuals and not as representatives of organizations.[181] As a result of dissatisfaction with this approach, the General Assembly Fourth Committee (which deals with trusteeship and non-self-governing territories) decided to admit representatives of certain national liberation movements to take part in proceedings in an observer capacity. The request for observer status in order to enable representatives of national liberation movements to participate in discussions in the Fourth Committee on the questions of the Portuguese African territories, Southern Rhodesia, and Namibia emanated from a letter sent to that Committee from the chairman of the Special Committee on Decolonization. Significantly, the invitation was to be made in consultation with the OAU. This proposal was accepted by the Fourth Committee by a vote of 79 to 13, with 16 abstentions, on 27 September 1972.[182] In accordance with this decision, representatives of Frelimo and the PAIGC took part in the debates regarding Portugal's African territories. In 1973 representatives of those movements and those of the FNLA and MPLA took part as observers in the discussions in the Committee on Portugal's colonies in Africa,[183] and the pattern was established.

The interposition of the OAU requirement was intended as a screening process and also as a method of excluding in practice secessionist movements from such status and participation. In effect, only those movements recognized by the OAU[184] were to benefit from observer status in the United Nations. The OAU organ with the capacity to recognize such movements is the Liberation Committee. The main criteria for recognition centre upon the effectiveness of the struggle of the organization concerned and the degree of support it enjoys.[185] Although ideological and political considerations are supposed to be absent, in fact they are often crucial. The backing given to FNLA by Zaïre and to Unita by Zambia complicated the issue as regards Angola, and threats by

Morocco and Mauritania to leave the OAU if Polisario were given the status of an OAU liberation organization proved effective.[186] The importance awarded to OAU recognition in the context of the status of liberation movements was never actually debated by the United Nations, but arose naturally out of the conscious use by the African group at the United Nations of its power in order to further OAU objectives, such as decolonization.[187] One should note here in particular that by resolution 3151G (XXVII) the General Assembly authorized the Committee on Apartheid, in consultation with the OAU, to associate the African liberation movements recognized by the OAU with its work. In accordance with this, the ANC and PAC[188] joined the committee as observers in 1974.[189]

The General Assembly endorsed the Fourth Committee's decision regarding observer status for liberation movements recognized by the OAU, in resolution 2918 (XXVII). The process continued in resolution 3247 (XXIX), whereby liberation movements recognized by the OAU or the Arab League were to participate as observers in sessions of the General Assembly, in conferences held under the auspices of the Assembly as well as in meetings of specialized UN agencies and its various organs.[190] Attempts to persuade the Assembly to permit a declaration before it by one of the leaders of African liberation movements, Amilcar Cabral, failed[191] and further attempts were rendered pointless by the Portuguese coup of April 1974. However, the leader of the PLO was invited to deliver a speech at the Assembly.[192]

In recent resolutions on co-operation between the United Nations and the OAU, the General Assembly has resolved

> to invite as observers, on a regular basis and in accordance with earlier practice, representatives of the national liberation movements recognized by the Organization of African Unity to participate in the relevant work of the Main Committees of the General Assembly and its subsidiary organs concerned, as well as in conference, seminars and other meetings held under the auspices of the United Nations which relate to their countries and requests the Secretary-General, in consultation with the Organization of African Unity, to ensure that the necessary arrangements are made for their effective participation, including the requisite financial provisions.[193]

In an analogous, though more far-reaching move, the General Assembly in 1974 adopted resolution 3237 (XXIX) by 95 votes to 17, with 19 abstentions. This invited the PLO to participate in the sessions and work of the Assembly as an observer and in the same capacity to take part in all international conferences concerned under the auspices of the various organs of the United Nations.

The Economic and Social Council has, since 1969, mirrored the efforts of the General Assembly with respect to liberation movements, although with special emphasis upon technical co-operation and assistance programmes and on means by which these movements might participate in the internal affairs of the UN agencies. Under the Economic and Social Council's procedural rules, it may invite 'any national liberation movement recognized by or in accordance with resolutions of the General Assembly to participate, without the right to vote, in its deliberations on any matter of particular concern to that movement'[194] and one of its organs, the Human Rights Commission, recommended in 1973 that 'moral and material assistance to liberation movements and the liberated territories and their population should be extended on a full scale'.[195]

In a number of resolutions, the Assembly and Council have called upon the specialized agencies and other UN-related organizations to assist the peoples of the colonial territories and their national liberation movements, noting also that such assistance so far extended has been inadequate.[196] A number of agencies have, however, produced programmes entailing co-operation with liberation movements, particularly UNESCO, the Food and Agriculture Organization, the World Health Organization, and the International Labour Organization. The UN Development Programme, for instance, established a National Liberation Movement Trust Fund in 1975 of $1.5 million, which was being dispensed in close collaboration with the OAU and the host governments of the countries where the liberation movements were based, while part of the assistance to refugees from colonial territories granted by the UN High Commissioner for Refugees was being channelled through national liberation movements recognized by the OAU.[197]

National liberation movements have also been invited to attend a range of international conferences, for example the World Conferences on Population (held in Bucharest in 1974) and on Food (held in Rome in 1974). At the Caracus session of the Third UN Conference on the Law of the Sea, the internal rules of the conference were amended to permit national liberation movements recognized by the OAU or the Arab League to participate.[198] In the case of the Conference on International Humanitarian Law, the General Assembly had already adopted resolution 3102 (XXVIII) urging that the liberation movements recognized by the various regional intergovernmental agencies concerned be invited to participate in the conference as observers 'in accordance with the practice of the United Nations'. Accordingly, and despite opposition, the conference adopted by consensus a proposal permitting this, at its first session in 1974.[199]

In the same year, the Assembly adopted resolution 3247 (XXIX) on Participation in the UN Conference on the Representation of States in their Relations with International Organizations. The resolution invited 'all States' to participate, but also called for invitations as observers to 'the national liberation movements in their respective regions recognized by the OAU and/or by the League of Arab States'. Indeed, it should be noted that in connection with the convention that emerged from this conference, the General Assembly in resolution 35/167 of 15 December 1980 called on States to accord to the delegations of the national liberation movements recognized by the OAU and/or the Arab League and accorded observer status by international organizations 'the facilities, privileges and amenities necessary for the performance of their functions' in accordance with this convention. This marks a step towards a further assimilation of the attributes of liberation movements and States and is a development that needs to be carefully considered.

Participation in an international conference is one thing, signature upon the final document quite another. Objections to liberation movements signing the Final Act of the conference on International Humanitarian Law in 1977 were side-stepped by having the movements concerned, the PLO, the Pan-Africanist Congress of South Africa, and the South-West Africa People's Organization, sign on a separate page from that of the participating States. It was also footnoted that 'the signature by these movements is without prejudice to the positions of participating States on the question of a precedent'.[200]

It may, therefore, be stated that the question of observer status for liberation movements recognized by the appropriate regional intergovernmental organization has been affirmatively settled in international practice. The issue of the meaning in law of such status is consequently raised.

In general, the term 'observer' in such a context would seem to imply that the party concerned has been recognized as having an interest with regard to the matter being discussed in the particular forum and possibly that that party possesses some form of very restricted international personality. By itself, no more than this would seem to be implied. However, by relating this to the principle of self-determination something wider might seem to emerge. The link between the two is constituted by the recognition of the movements as the authentic representatives of the people as a whole of the territory. At the ninth summit of the OAU, liberation movements were given the status of representatives of their people at OAU sessions instead of their former status of observers,[201] while a number of UN General Assembly resolutions have commented on the nature of particular movements. Resolution 2918 (XXVII), for example, declared that 'the national liberation movements of Angola, Guinea (Bissau) and Cape Verde and Mozambique are the authentic representatives of the true aspirations of the peoples of those territories' and this was repeated in resolution 3113. (XXVIII).[202] By resolution 3295 (XXIX), SWAPO was recognized as the authentic representative of the Namibian people. What would seem to be suggested is that such movements represent the attempt of the people concerned to secure the exercise of the right to self-determination and thus may be seized of that right by virtue of a process of delegation. It is important to note, however, that recognition plays a vital role in this as well as effectiveness. The fact that a people is deemed in law to possess the right to self-determination has an effect upon the minimum of effectiveness necessary for the purpose of status and statehood; recognition plays here an evidential role. However, in deciding whether a movement can be taken to embody the rights of a people, what is at the least needed is recognition by the appropriate regional organization. In this sense and in this context, recognition can be stated to be playing a constitutive role. Effectiveness is, of course, an important determining factor in leading to recognition but it itself cannot create the necessary status for the movement in question. In the absence of such recognition, as in Rhodesia[203] or Angola for example, the full right to self-determination remains in the people as a whole and it is left to the principle of effectiveness to resolve the dilemma of the identity of the authority of the emerging State.

Ago has written that 'what, in fact, characterises the situation created by the emergence of an insurrectional movement as defined in international law is the very existence parallel with the State and in a portion of the territory under its sovereignty of a separate subject of international law'.[204] Such a movement is essentially a 'provisional' subject of international law[205] since it is on its way to statehood, or even an 'embryo State'.[206] Ago was writing of insurrectional movements in general in the light of a new State's retroactive responsibility for acts of the successful liberation movement, not specifically those operating within the context of self-determination, and related the question of personality solely, it seems, to the criterion of effectiveness,[207] but he was prepared to accept the possibility not only of international personality but also that 'the structures of the organization of the insurrectional movement then became those of the organization of the new State'.[208] This appears to be suggesting that such movements are potentially States, only requiring a particular level of effectiveness to be manifested before statehood is actually acquired. Accordingly, could one accept that such entities may hold title to territory pending actual statehood? It is recognized that for some legal purposes there may be continuity before and after statehood is firmly established.[209] National liberation movements[210] ultimately derive their personality from the right of the people of the territory in question to self-determination.[211] Such peoples are subjects of international law by virtue of this right, although this does not mean that they are thereby assimilated to States,[212] since 'the subjects of law in any legal system are not necessarily identical in their nature or in the extent of their rights, and their nature depends upon the needs of the community'.[213] The issue of personality in this context is particularly acute where there is armed conflict between the people and the administering power. Farer has characterized the status of 'rebellious non-self-governing territories' as 'inchoate States with a right of immediate accession to full participation in the international community',[214] while Sanborn has talked of 'quasi-States' in the sense of entities with international rights and duties but lacking one or more of the criteria of statehood.[211] Clearly, such entities are not entitled to the same rights as States nor are they subject to the obligations.[216] One must not confuse personality and capacity. However, it is felt that such peoples may acquire title to the territory in question pending statehood. It could be argued that this title may be acquired and held on their behalf by national liberation movements, by virtue of a process of delegation, in relation to which effectiveness and recognition are crucial, but State practice is not sufficiently developed to be able to accept this proposition. Indeed, it is noticeable that no such claim has apparently been put forward by any State.[217]

5

Territorial Integrity

I. THE CONCEPT OF TERRITORIAL INTEGRITY

(a) *Generally*

In any system of international law founded upon sovereign and independent States, the principle of the protection of the integrity of the territorial expression of such States is bound to assume major importance.[1] Together with the concept of non-intervention, territorial integrity is crucial with respect to the evolution of the principles associated with the maintenance of international peace and security.[2] It also underlines the decentralized State-orientated character of the international political system and reflects the sovereign equality of States as a legal principle.

It is, however, with regard to the rules relating to the use of force in international law that the principle of the territorial integrity of States has been most intensively examined. This is apparent both in the sphere of customary law[3] and in relation to conventional formulations. Article 10 of the Covenant of the League of Nations declared that 'the Members of the League undertake to respect and preserve as against external aggression the territorial integrity and existing political independence of all the Members of the League'.[4] Article 11 of the Montevideo Convention on Rights and Duties of States, 1933, provided that 'the territory of a State is inviolate and may not be the object of military occupation nor of other measures of force imposed by another State directly or indirectly or for any motive whatever even temporary'. Article 2(4) of the United Nations Charter emphasized that 'all Members shall refrain in their international relations from the threat or use of force against the territorial integrity or political independence of any State'. Such views have also been reflected in other documents. Article 17 of the Charter of the Organization of American States in 1948 proclaimed that 'the territory of a State is inviolate',[5] while Article 9 of the Draft Declaration on Rights and Duties of States noted that 'every State has the duty to refrain from resorting to war as an instrument of national policy and to refrain from the threat or use of force against the territorial integrity or political independence of another State'.[6]

However, one must distinguish between the concepts of territorial integrity and inviolability of frontiers. Although they are clearly connected in that a violation of a frontier, for example, could also involve a violation of the territorial integrity of a State, there is a basic conceptual difference in that not every border violation constitutes a violation of territorial integrity. The incursion across the frontiers of another State might occur as a result of the right of self-defence in which case the territorial integrity of the State is not offended in international law. There are fundamental differences between the notions of territory and frontier, since the former operates to express the physical basis of the State and manifests its identity within the international community, while the latter marks the extent of the physical expression of the State. The concept of territorial integrity is therefore broader and more fundamental than that of the inviolability of frontiers. It may indeed be that the latter is but one aspect of the former, since in many ways the inviolability of frontiers constitutes a concretization of the concept of territorial integrity. However, the two principles have been on occasions separately treated. This was particularly so in the Final Act of the Conference on Security and Co-operation in Europe, 1975.[7] The seminal resolution 1514 (XV) declared in paragraph 6 that 'any attempt aimed at the partial or total disruption of the national unity and the territorial integrity of a country is incompatible with the purposes and principles of the Charter of the United Nations' and this was echoed in the 1970 Declaration on Principles of International Law. It was noted in the section on the principle of equal rights and self-determination of peoples that every State 'shall refrain from any action aimed at the partial or total destruction of the national unity and territorial integrity of any other State or country'. The point was also included under the principle of the sovereign equality of States, which was deemed to include the proposition that 'the territorial integrity and political independence of the State are inviolable'. The 1974 Consensus Definition of Aggression noted in the preamble that States were under a duty not to use armed force to deprive peoples of their right to self-determination, freedom, and independence, or to disrupt territorial integrity, and additionally that the territory of a State was not to be violated by being the object of military occupation or of other measures of force taken in contravention of the Charter. In Article 1, aggression was defined as the use of armed force by a State against the sovereignty, territorial integrity, or political independence of another State.

Thus, it is abundantly clear that the concept of territorial integrity in international law protects the State from unlawful interference by other

States with regard to its territory. It is not, however, an absolute concept since the doctrine of self-defence permits States in certain circumstances to resort to the use of force against the territorial integrity of other States. In addition, of course, a State may voluntarily alter its territorial composition by acquiring territory or ceding or exchanging territory.[8] What is not permissible in the light of the principle would be changes in territorial extent by force. The concept of territorial integrity, however, stretches beyond this. It constitutes an important element within the context of the legal right of self-determination since it provides the rule for identifying the people or unit entitled under international law to exercise the right to self-determination, freedom, and independence. As previously noted,[9] this right accrues to the inhabitants of the colonially defined non-self-governing territory so that the people concerned have the right to choose their political status within the framework of the territorial integrity of the colonially established unit. Two questions arise at this stage. The first would concern the issue of the territorial integrity of pre-colonial entities and whether this may be projected forward to influence either the decolonization process or post-independence dispositions. The second centres on the application of the concept of territorial integrity and its relationship with self-determination in post-independence situations. In other words, can the notion of territorial integrity be extended from its involvement with the protection of the territorial composition of the States to cover the threat of territorial reduction from within, that is, the menace of secessionism? It can indeed be contended that the newly sovereign States have laid great store by the principle of territorial integrity in order to protect themselves from the dangers of internal secessionist movements. Thus, the principle under consideration has undergone or is undergoing a subtle change in meaning in order to create a presumption against the claim of secessionists in already independent States. It could be argued that, far from its traditional posture of neutrality in such situations, international law is now adopting an adverse position. These propositions will be examined in this Chapter.

(*b*) *African Practice*

Prior to independence, African attitudes to the territorial integrity of independent States were somewhat ambiguous and reflected a general dissatisfaction with the colonial boundaries that had created a variety of European-delimited territories. It appeared that a general campaign of frontier rearrangement was under consideration.[10] In 1945 the Pan-

African Congress held in Manchester adopted a resolution proclaiming that 'the artificial divisions and territorial boundaries created by the imperialist powers are deliberate steps to obstruct the political unity of the West African peoples'.[11] This resolution did not, however, demand the revision of frontiers.

Many factors combined to produce African discontent with the colonial territorial arrangements, ranging from the artificial nature of such entities in geographical, ethnic, and economic terms to the psychological effect of the European division of Africa. This encouraged the pre-independence African political parties to think in terms of the readjustment of borders once sovereignty had been achieved. The high point of this approach occurred in the All-Africa People's Conference at Accra in 1958 which approved a resolution in four parts entitled 'Frontiers, Boundaries, and Federations'. The third part of the resolution denounced the artificial frontiers drawn by the imperialist powers, particularly those which cut across ethnic lines and divided peoples of the same stock, and called for the abolition or adjustment of such frontiers at an early date. The guiding principle by which this was to be effected was to be 'the true wishes of the people'.[12] President Nkrumah of Ghana was particularly active in seeking the realignment of colonial borders. He called on the Sanniquellic Conference of 1959 to examine methods of 'eradicating the artificial divisions and boundaries which are responsible for the Balkanisation of our continent'.[13] This kind of approach was underlined by the resolutions adopted at the conferences of the radical parties and States which supported Somalia's attempts to unify all the areas containing Somali inhabitants under its flag,[14] and mirrored the approach earlier adopted as to Morocco's irredentist claims.[15]

However, within a few years the atmosphere changed and more and more African States, upon obtaining independence, sanctioned the boundaries imposed by the colonial powers. This was already evident at the debates at the UN General Assembly concerning the Mauritanian question. Morocco claimed that Mauritania was an artificial State and that its territory rightly belonged to Morocco. While such claims received some backing from the Arab and Communist States, the majority of African States rejected Morocco's demands.[16] The territorial unit as determined by the colonial powers began to be accepted as the framework for the newly independent entity. This was reflected in resolution 1514 (xv), with its expressed concern with the preservation of the national unity and territorial integrity of a country.[17]

The Congo crisis precipitated in 1960[18] was an important landmark as

Katanga sought to secede. African States decided to uphold the territorial integrity of the Congo. At the Leopoldville Conference in August 1960 the secession was condemned,[19] and at the Monrovia Conference in 1961 African States were called upon 'to desist from such activities as the hasty recognition of breakaway regimes'.[20] At the Lagos Conference in 1962 of the Monrovia bloc, the principle of respect for existing borders was proclaimed[21] and the Conference adopted the Charter of the Inter-African and Malagasy Organization, Article 3 of which stressed 'respect for the sovereignty and territorial integrity of each State' and Article 5 of which underlined that 'each State has the right of defence of its territorial integrity'. Although the majority of African States by the early 1960s had accepted the validity of the colonial frontiers and the preservation of the territorial status quo, expressed in terms of the overwhelming adoption of the doctrine of the territorial integrity of States, a few did dissent. Morocco pressed its claims to Mauritania and Spanish Sahara as well as parts of Algeria and Mali on historical grounds, while Somalia pursued its object of reuniting all Somali tribesmen. The Somali president expressed the view that other principles of international law could override the concept of the territorial integrity of States, which was described as an 'outmoded concept . . . [which] must vanish from our habitual thinking because its roots are embedded in colonialism and it is incompatible with Pan-Africanism'.[22] The vast majority of African States, however, disagreed with such an approach and endorsed the supremacy of the principle of territorial integrity when faced with territorial claims either from within by secessionist pressures or from without by irredentist forces. This has emerged clearly from the attitudes adopted in the Conference of the Organization of African Unity during 1963 and 1964.

At the inaugural conference of the OAU in Addis Ababa in May 1963, delegates stressed the necessity of working within the framework of the territorial integrity of States and of respecting the colonial boundaries. Ethiopia in particular pointed out that many African States would cease to exist if boundaries were redrawn on religious, racial, and linguistic grounds.[23] The Mali representative noted that

> we must take Africa as it is and we must renounce any territorial claims if we do not wish to introduce what we might call black imperialism in Africa . . . African unity demands of each one of us complete respect for the legacy that we have received from the colonial system, that is to say, maintenance of the present frontiers of our respective States.[24]

Other African States adopted the same approach.[25]

Although the Charter of the Organization of African Unity does not specifically refer to the sanctity of the colonial borders its provisions are unambiguous. The preamble refers to the determination to safeguard and consolidate the hard-won independence as well as the sovereignty and territorial integrity of member-States. In Article 2(1)c, the Charter notes that one of the purposes of the Organization is to defend the sovereignty, territorial integrity, and independence of African States, while in Article 3(3) respect for the sovereignty and territorial integrity of each State and for its inalienable right to independent existence is formulated as one of the principles of the OAU.[26] Emerson concluded that 'the net effect of such pronouncements as of the relevant sections of the 1960 UN Declaration is for all purposes to deny the legitimacy of any further disintegration or reshaping which impairs the integrity of the colonially defined States'.[27] This view was overwhelmingly supported by the discussions at the First Ordinary Session of the Assembly of Heads of State and Government of the Organization at Cairo in July 1964. Emperor Haile Selassie of Ethiopia declared that the acceptance of imperialist borders was necessary for Africa's safety and that the provisions of the OAU Charter regarding the preservation of territorial integrity must be supported.[28] The representative of the Ivory Coast noted that the conference 'should decide as one of the surest means of achieving unity on absolute respect for the frontiers of member States of our Organisation'.[29] President Nkrumah of Ghana in a decidedly minority stand emphasized that the artificial divisions of African States were too numerous and irrational for permanent and harmonious settlement save within the framework of continental union.[30] Kenya, however, called for a Charter to be drawn up with the object of preserving the territorial status quo and making impossible any frontier realignment except by mutual consent.[31] In the event, a specific resolution was adopted by the Assembly in the issue. The preamble of resolution AHG/Res.16(I) noted that the borders of African States on independence constituted a 'tangible reality' and recalled Articles 3(3) and 4 of the Charter of the OAU. The essence of the resolution was contained in the second operative paragraph, which 'solemnly declares that all member States pledge themselves to respect the borders existing on their achievement of national independence'.

The resolution was not, however, unanimously accepted. Both Somali and Morocco refused to be bound by it.[32] The question also arose as to the meaning of the phrase 'achievement of national independence' since it could be construed as validating the pre-colonial borders of such independent entities as Morocco, Ethiopia, and Liberia, and therefore used as a basis for reclaiming lost territories.[33] In addition, the resolution did not cover the problems caused by the different interpretations of documents defining boundaries, a situation a number of African States found themselves concerned with.[34] It is also interesting to note that the principle of self-determination was not referred to, nor was the difficulty of reconciling it with the acceptance of the territorial status quo alluded to. Nevertheless, the border resolution can be said to have marked the acceptance by Africa as a whole of a new territorial regime, one based on the legal validity of the colonial frontiers of independent States.[35] It is no longer possible to deny the impact of this rule as a binding practice of African States.[36]

There are a number of reasons for this approach to the problem. Apart from the fear of anarchy and chaos if the map were to be redrawn on ethnic lines, the need is felt for a source of legitimation of statehood. In European countries this is found in the identity of the nation-State, but African territories with only a few exceptions contain considerable numbers of different tribal groups. The vast majority of African countries do not consist of a defined 'nation' as such in the Western sense, and accordingly have sought the root of their legitimacy in the territorial unit rather than in the ethnic characteristics of the State. As Zartman has pointed out (as regards West Africa, but it is true for the continent as a whole), 'it is not the boundary but the nation that is artificial'.[37]

If ethnic unity does not exist in any given country, the question of self-determination of peoples in its sociological meaning of identifiable cultural groups becomes highly controversial. This is especially so since the end result could well be the creation of large numbers of competing and often hostile States each based upon a different ethnic or cultural unit. Accordingly, the legal and political emphasis has been not upon the characteristics of the population of the State but upon the territorial definition of that State, and not unnaturally the doctrine of territorial integrity has been elevated to a principle of prime importance for the African continent. Save for those States like Morocco or Somalia that have founded their *raison d'être* upon historical or ethnic factors, the overwhelming majority of African countries see their existence in terms of their territorial integrity and identify their 'nations' in strict territorial terms. In Africa, therefore, the notion of the nation-State has been replaced by the concept of the territorial State. In so linking the principle of territorial integrity with the preservation of the inviolability of the colonial frontiers and thus establishing a legal basis for the rejection of both irredentist and secessionist demands,[38] African States have laid down the basic thesis relating to questions regarding territory on the continent. This approach has been characterized as constituting the creation of an African *uti possidetis*.[39] This concept, derived from Roman Law,[40] is related to State succession and was an idea adopted by the newly independent States of Latin America whereby the administrative divisions of the Spanish empire as they existed in South America in 1820 and in Central America in 1821 were deemed to constitute the basis for the frontiers of the new States. It was intended to end boundary conflicts in Southern America and forestall any attempts at European colonization by preventing any part of the subcontinent from being regarded as *terra nullius*.[41] The transfer of the concept to Africa has been criticized, particularly in view of the different circumstances pertaining to the two continents.[42] Touval preferred to see the process of the acceptance of the colonial frontier as a 'common law of successor States'.[43] Whichever phrase is used, the essence of the proposition remains, namely that the doctrine of territorial integrity has been adopted specifically in Africa as a rule operating as a blocking mechanism to any post-independence territorial rearrangement except where attained by mutual consent.[44]

(*c*) *The Temporal Definition of Territorial Integrity*

The claim has been made that the critical date at which the unit of territory is to be defined should not be restricted to the post-colonial stage. This argument has been used particularly by Morocco, and to a lesser extent by Mauritania, to justify territorial claims. Morocco has declared that the territory which has to be considered as the relevant unit in international law today for the purposes of the rule of territorial integrity may also include the pre-colonial definition of the State. In Morocco's case the implication could well be that this might comprise all of Mauritania and Western Sahara as well as parts of Algeria, Mali, and even arguably Senegal. This argument was used with respect to Morocco's claim to Mauritania in the period leading up to and immediately after the independence of the latter[45] and with regard to the Saharan question. In its assertions the Moroccan government emphasized that it was seeking the integrity of its territory, by which it meant all those areas, including Morocco as constituted in the post-colonial era, which could be regarded as having been under Moroccan sovereignty prior to the colonial period.[46] Morocco maintained that the concept of territorial integrity proclaimed in paragraph 6 of resolution 1514 (xv)[47] referred to the integrity of a country already in existence and already constituted as a State and that this had been re-emphasized in the 1970

Declaration on Principles of International Law.[48] However, by that Morocco meant that the concept of territorial integrity was available to any independent State in order to recover all of its territory as defined according to pre-colonial history. As far as Sahara was concerned, Morocco's sole concern 'was the liberation of Western Sahara and its reintegration into the Moroccan State'.[49] Mauritania, during the course of the hearings before the International Court in the Sahara case, added the point that the principle of African *uti possidetis* only concerned States which had obtained independence and did not ban regroupings before accession to independence.[50]

Algeria's stated view was that a claim to territorial integrity was more than lawful, it was sacred.[51] It distinguished three varieties of territorial integrity. The territorial integrity of a colony with respect to the territory of the administering power was now well established and enshrined in the 1970 Declaration on Principles of International Law. The territorial integrity of the non-self-governing territory *vis-à-vis* a neighbouring State was an issue governed by the principle of *uti possidetis juris* or respect for the frontiers bequeathed by colonization. It amounted to a general and valid rule and not a mere *de facto* practice and it constituted the basis upon which African States were achieving independence. More than that, Algeria emphasized that the principle of the inviolability of frontiers was one of the pillars of international law.[52] The third type of territorial integrity derived from the concern to preserve the territorial integrity of the neighbouring State in relation to the non-self-governing territory. It concerned the question of decolonization by integration and this, it was stressed, could take place only on the basis of the free choice of the population of the dependent territory and not by virtue of the territorial integrity of the neighbouring State.[53] The view that paragraph 6 of resolution 1514 (XV) could refer to territories formerly detached from a State and now the subject of a claim on the grounds of the principle of integrity was strongly rejected. Paragraph 6 related only to future attempts to impair the territorial integrity of a State and could not be used to give territorial claims priority over the principle of self-determination.[54]

A variation in the temporal-shift approach to the concept of territorial integrity is afforded by Alexandrowicz's views on 'reversion to sovereignty'.[55] This was based on the claim by Ceylon in the General Assembly Sixth Committee discussions on the report of the International Law Commission on Succession of States and Governments in respect of Treaties that, in view of its existence as an independent kingdom prior to the nineteenth century, it should be classified not as a new State but as an original State in the Family of Nations.[56] Judge Moreno Quintana appeared to take the view that such reversion to sovereignty was essentially of a procedural character and did not therefore affect the acts of the colonial power resulting from the legitimate exercise of its right of sovereignty in the colonial period.[57] Brownlie, however, has pointed to the dangers of accepting this theory as valid in international law. The logical consequence of such a doctrine of reversion may create a threat to the security of legal relations, it is noted, for 'it would follow that the successor would not be bound by territorial grants or recognition of territorial changes by the previous holder'.[58] This, of course, would introduce a serious element of instability in the international system as well as challenging the dominant interpretation of self-determination.[59]

The court in the *Western Sahara* case did not directly discuss whether the concept of territorial integrity could refer to pre-colonial States, but it did emphasize that the right to self-determination, predicated upon 'the need to pay regard to the freely expressed will of peoples', was one of the basic principles governing the decolonization process.[60] The presumption was clearly against upsetting the wishes of the inhabitants of the territory to be decolonized and, should they be against integration or reintegration with an independent State, their views would prevail.[61] The legal basis for any merger would thus be the freely expressed wishes of the people of the territory and not any principle of territorial integrity accruing to another State.

Judge Dillard unambiguously made the point that 'any claim to what has been called automatic retrocession is not applicable to the Western Sahara and therefore it was unnecessary for the court to pronounce upon the principle of territorial integrity embodied in paragraph 6 of resolution 1514 (XV)'.[62] It was suggested that the court might have discussed the matter further had it decided that the Moroccan claim had been established, but in any event Dillard's own view of paragraph 6 'makes it unlikely that [it] could justifiably be applied to the decolonisation of Western Sahara as a principle of territorial integrity overriding the right of the people to self-determination'.[63] Judge Nagendra Singh was of a similar opinion with respect to Western Sahara. He noted that there was no evidence of a single State comprising Morocco and Western Sahara or Mauritania and Western Sahara at the time of Spanish colonization 'which would have been dismembered by the coloniser and thus justified reunion on decolonisation at the present time',[64] and therefore paragraph 6 of resolution 1514 (XV) was not applicable. The legal ties which did exist at the time of Spanish colonization between the claimants and Western

Sahara 'were not of such a character as to justify today the reintegration or retrocession of the territory without consulting the people'.[65]

The Judge appeared to leave open the possibility that if legal ties of territorial sovereignty were deemed to exist between the territory in question and a claimant State prior to colonization, then the concept of territorial integrity might conceivably be utilized to justify a retrocession.[66] In a sense, a gap exists in the court's advisory opinion on Western Sahara. However, two things ought to be noted. Firstly, that the principle of territorial integrity in this sense is relevant in cases of colonial enclaves, where in essence the right of self-determination exists only in an extremely attenuated form,[67] and secondly, in usual decolonization situations, the applicability of this principle may be of relevance only in a procedural context. The court noted in the *Western Sahara* case that 'the right of self-determination leaves the General Assembly a measure of discretion with respect to the forms and procedures by which that right is to be realised'.[68]

The court went on to say that as far as the future action of the General Assembly was concerned, 'various possibilities exist, for instance with regard to consultations between the interested States, and the procedures and guarantees required for ensuring a full and genuine expression of the will of the people'.[69] Accordingly, the existence of ties might affect the form in which any plebiscite questions may be phrased, the extent of any consultations with interested parties, and indeed the manner in which the inhabitants of the particular territory may be consulted. Such consultation may be, for instance, by plebiscite or by simple consent of institutions deemed representative. There is thus some scope for the expression in international practice of such ties, although care would be needed to prevent the procedural aspects from having a serious impact upon the fundamental substantive provision. One may also note with interest how the court discussed the issue of self-determination before turning to the two questions asked of it, thus emphasizing the crucial role of the concept. The court stressed in particular that neither the request for the advisory opinion nor the terms of resolution 3292 (XXIX) affected the right to self-determination of the people of Sahara.[70]

If the temporal-shift interpretation of territorial integrity is not to be applied as regards a pre-colonial State, the question arises as to its applicability to pre-colonial non-State entities. The court, while accepting the variation in forms of States, nevertheless identified personality in terms of a legal entity in the light of the essential test as to whether the entity was in such a position as to possess in regard to its members rights which it is entitled to ask them to respect.[71] The 'Mauritanian entity' at the date of decolonization was not such an entity.[72] Therefore, the notion of territory and territorial integrity in international law was of no direct relevance as far as it was concerned. It would also be logical to suggest that the concept of territorial integrity can have no applicability in the law as far as pre-colonial non-State entities are concerned.

Accordingly, one may conclude that the correct temporal context for the definition of territorial integrity is the period of decolonization. The territorial configuration of any given entity at an earlier historical period would of itself have no legal importance, although when allied to strong historical and cultural ties, for example, existing between the successor State and the territory in question, it might at the discretion of the United Nations have some procedural relevance.[73]

(*d*) *Territorial Integrity and Self-Determination*

The link between the two concepts in the period of decolonization is, therefore, crucial, for the right of the people to self-determination takes place only within the framework of the colonially defined territory. In post-independence situations, the link is twofold. Firstly, it reinforces the norm of non-intervention in the internal affairs of any State, for all States have the right to choose their own political, economic, and social systems. Secondly, the two principles together will operate to render unlawful any territorial diminution of an independent State which takes place in conditions where a legal right to self-determination might exist and where the effect of such action would be counter to any right of the people concerned to self-determination. To date, this proposition relates specifically and uniquely to South Africa and its Bantustan policy.[74] In resolution 2775E (XXVI), the UN General Assembly stated that the Bantustan policy was in pursuance of apartheid and it condemned the policy as violating the right to self-determination and as prejudicial to territorial integrity. This was repeated in resolution 3411D (XXX), which also reaffirmed that the establishment of Bantustans was a measure 'essentially designed to destroy the territorial integrity of the country in violation of the principles enshrined in the Charter of the United Nations'. In June 1976, the OAU Council of Ministers reaffirmed 'the OAU's sacred commitment to the principles of territorial and national integrity of all territories under foreign domination and fighting for liberation and self-determination' and called on all States not to recognize any of the Bantustans, in particular the Transkei.[75] The Chairman of the Special Committee against Apartheid declared that the agreements signed between South Africa and the proposed Transkei Chief Minister[76] were of no validity and were not agreements for the granting of self-determination or independence to the African people, but a fraud. An appeal was made to all governments and organizations for solidarity with the people of Namibia and South Africa in their struggle against the Bantustan policy and for the territorial integrity of their nations.[77]

On 26 October 1976 the Transkei was declared independent by South Africa,[78] and on the same day the General Assembly, in resolution 36/6A, condemned the change in status of the Transkei and referred to its 'sham independence'. The establishment of Bantustans was strongly attacked as designed to consolidate apartheid and destroy the territorial integrity of the country. All governments were called upon to deny recognition to the Transkei or any other Bantustan.[79] In June 1977 the Security Council unanimously endorsed Assembly resolution 31/6A.[80] The principles behind these resolutions may be stated as follows. The right of self-determination applies to the people of South Africa as a single unit. An integral part of this right is the right to territorial integrity. Any activity involving territorial diminution not in accordance with the right of all the people to determine their political status contravenes not only the right to self-determination but also the interconnected principle of territorial integrity. Thus, until the right of the people as a whole to exercise self-determination is granted in accordance with UN resolutions, there appears to be a duty not to reduce or adversely affect the territorial integrity of the nation. To this extent, paragraph 6 of resolution 1514 (xv) is relevant.

II. THE NATURE OF CLAIMS AGAINST TERRITORIAL INTEGRITY

Once a State has become independent and thereby exercised the right to self-determination as spatially defined, the question of the temporal application of self-determination arises. In other words, does the right of self-determination in international law subsist beyond the achievement of independence to challenge the territorial integrity of the new State or is it temporally restricted to the period of decolonization? If the latter is the case, as is contended—although the potential for change exists, as the South African situation demonstrates—one may posit a fundamental harmony between self-determination and territorial integrity on a number of planes. As we have seen, the colonial borders delimited the territories in Africa and gave them thereby a certain national, linguistic, and cultural framework. Additionally, the territory so delimited became a unit both externally in relation to other such territories and the international community in general and internally as regards a particular self-image. However, a number of claims have been made against the territorial integrity of States, although one must distinguish between irredentist and secessionist claims since the situation in law is distinct. Such claims have revolved primarily around ethnic and historical factors, although economic and geographic contentions have also been pressed. In most situations a variety of assertions are made at the same time in order to demonstrate the strength of a particular claim, while it is interesting to note just how many are actually expressed in terms of the right of self-determination, although interpreting it in ways inconsistent with accepted formulations. This use of the concept is presumably an attempt to derive some benefit from the charisma of the principle itself.[81] We shall note some of the types of claims made against the territorial integrity of States before proceeding in subsequent sections to an examination of practice.

(*a*) *Historical Claims*[82]

These are propounded upon the basis that what has been ought now to be and that the existence (usually before colonization) of a sovereign State should entitle it in the post-colonial era to claim the extent of its previous territorial limits. In the context of African affairs, there has been only one major such claimant and that is Morocco. Morocco has claimed all of Mauritania and Western Sahara and parts of Mali, Algeria, and possibly Senegal on the basis of historical connection, since it was argued that from the eleventh century to the establishment of the French protectorate in 1912, the Kingdom of Morocco had extended from the Mediterranean to the Senegal River.[83] This historical connection was expressed in terms of personal and religious allegiance to the Sultan of Morocco rather than in the light of the European concept of territorial jurisdiction within a State.[84] Although the International Court accepted the specific character of the late nineteenth-century Moroccan State, the test of extent of sovereignty was still based upon evidence of actual exercise of authority.[85] Using this test, it was concluded that although a legal tie of allegiance had existed between the Sultan and some of the peoples of the territory at the time of colonization, Morocco's claim of immemorial possession based on the public display of sovereignty uninterrupted and uncontested for centuries was not accepted.[86] Judge De Castro in particular emphasized that the doctrine of inter-temporal law, expressed in the rule *tempus regit factum*, was relevant in such cases. Whatever the ties between Morocco and Western Sahara in the 1880s, the fact of colonization had created a new situation with sociological and legal implications which had to be assessed in accordance with the law in force at that time. In addition, the decolonization process based on the UN Charter and resolutions had created a new legal context for the non-self-governing territories and, as the court had declared in the *Namibia* case,[87] the principle of self-determination had become applicable to them all.[88] Judge De Castro noted that whatever the existing ties with Western Sahara at the time of colonization by Spain, '*legally* those ties remain subject to intertemporal law and that as a consequence they cannot stand in the way of application of the principle of self-determination'.[89]

Morocco's claims regarding Mauritania and Algeria,[90] similarly based on historically oriented factors, failed to arouse much international support and ultimately Morocco accepted the reality of the colonial frontiers.[91] In the Sahara, Morocco first compromised its claim by its arrangement with Mauritania and then proceeded to enforce it in defiance of the opinion of the International Court. A number of other historical claims in Africa have also been made. Liberia claimed the Mount Nimba region of Guinea and the land between the Cavally and Cess river in the Ivory Coast on historical grounds, but renounced these claims upon the independence of the two States.[92] In 1975 Lesotho asserted a claim before the United Nations for 'conquered territory' in South Africa's Orange Free State and Cape, which had originally belonged to Basutoland before being added to the South African areas over one hundred years earlier.[93] Uganda claimed large areas of territory taken from it in colonial times and transferred to Sudan and Kenya,[94] while Malawi in 1968 claimed districts in Zambia and Tanzania which it asserted belonged to it on historical and other grounds and which had been detached in colonial times.[95] None of these claims succeeded, while historical claims in general have not been accepted as valid legal claims to territory in international law.[96]

(*b*) *Ethnic Claims*[97]

Since claims are closely linked with the political definition of self-determination and consist of the assertion that either a particular ethnic group is entitled to secede from an existing State or that an existing State may extend its territorial limits to include all members of a particular ethnic group.[98] The ethnic secessionist claim has manifested itself in a number of instances, the most prominent being the Biafra case, while the ethnic irredentist claim is most clearly instanced by the Somali case. In a number of cases the two claims have merged, so that a secessionist claim will be subsumed under an irredentist assertion by a neighbouring State.[99] The use of the ethnic argument to found title to territory has been singularly unsuccessful in this purist form, because once granted it could lead to widespread disruption and destroy the territorialist conception of the State maintained by African States.

(*c*) *Geographic Claims*[100]

Allied with strategic claims or demands for a natural frontier,[101] the concept of geographic claims could have been used to a far larger extent than has in fact occurred in a continent of such arbitrary borders as Africa. The fact that it has not (apart from indirectly in the special case of colonial enclaves) reinforces the acceptance of colonial borders. Morocco attempted to use the geographic contiguity of Western Sahara as an additional reason for the foundation of its title upon an analogy with the *Eastern Greenland* case.[102] However, the International Court, after noting that the geographic unity of Western Sahara with Morocco was in any case debatable, declared that even if the 'geographic contiguity of Western Sahara with Morocco could be taken into account in the present connection it would only make paucity of evidence of unambiguous display of authority with respect to Western Sahara more difficult to reconcile with Morocco's claim to immemorial possession'.[103] On 1 November 1978 Uganda announced that it was annexing a 710 sq. mile area of Tanzania up to the Kagera river. Part of the reason for this was that Uganda saw the river as its 'natural frontier' with Tanzania rather than the arbitrary land boundary fixed between Britain and Germany before the First World War. A week later, under OAU pressure, Uganda proclaimed its intention to evacuate the salient.[104] It is clear that under international law geographic claims are insufficient to found title[105] and African practice has underlined this.

(*d*) *Economic Claims*[106]

Although economic reasons have underlain a number of territorial claims, direct economic claims have been very rare. However, Tunisia did claim a 'prolongation' of its territory into Algerian Sahara up to marker 233 or an agreement that beyond a certain limit in the Sahara 'the door opens on an area undivided and shared by all, where communications, water points, pasturage and underground wealth are at the disposal of all',[107] upon an analogy of the desert with the sea. Tunisia did seem to be seeking economic rights rather than actual territorial acquisition, in the event, and this was expressed in the theory of *dépassement*, according to which border disputes would be left behind by a higher level of co-operation agreements. Ultimately, Tunisia formally renounced any territorial claims and recognized the territorial status quo in a series of agreements with Algeria.[108]

III. STATE PRACTICE

In this section, African State practice regarding irredentist and secessionist claims against independent States will be examined. Such claims have been made in the light of primarily historical and ethnic factors, although cultural elements were necessarily involved.

(*a*) *Irredentist Claims*

1. *Moroccan Claims to Algerian Territory*

In pursuit of its pre-colonial borders, Morocco has also claimed areas of Algeria on the basis of respect for the territorial integrity of its pre-colonial territorial extent. However, large parts of the border were never demarcated in view of the nature of the territory.[109] Prior to its independence, the provisional Algerian government recognized the existence of a 'territorial problem' with Morocco in an agreement signed at Rabat on 6 July 1961,[110] and negotiations were promised. However, upon the achievement of independence a year later, Algerian attitudes changed, and when French troops were withdrawn, both Morocco and Algeria sent in soldiers to occupy positions in the disputed areas. An agreement was signed in April 1963, but it proved a failure. In September, Morocco occupied border posts claimed by both sides, but they were captured the next month by Algeria. This precipitated a wider conflict and on 15 October King Hassan of Morocco declared that his country was determined 'to impose respect for our national territory and the integrity of its authentic frontiers'.[111] After a series of unsuccessful mediation attempts,[112] a meeting was held at Bamako at the end of October with the president of Mali and the emperor of Ethiopia as mediators. This resulted in an agreement which comprised a cease-fire, a commission to determine a demilitarization zone composed of the parties and the mediators, and a proposed meeting of OAU Foreign Ministers at Addis Ababa to establish an arbitration commission.[113] This arbitration commission was set up in November with representatives of Ethiopia,

Mali, Ivory Coast, Nigeria, Senegal, Sudan, and Tanganyika, and the following February an agreement regarding a demilitarized zone, troop withdrawals, the establishment of a no man's land, and an exchange of prisoners, was signed.[114] In January 1969 Morocco and Algeria signed a Treaty of Solidarity and Cooperation valid for twenty years according to which all questions at issue were to go to joint commissions.[115] On 27 May 1970 the two parties met at Tlemcen in Algeria and agreed upon a final settlement of the frontier dispute with a joint commission to map out the delimitation. The frontier was to be the same as during the colonial period, while Morocco was to have a share in mineral exploitation in the Gara-Djebilet area.[116] In June 1972, at the Rabat Conference of the OAU, the leaders of the two countries met again and declared that the border issue was resolved. Two conventions were signed, a border agreement declaring that the disputed area of Tindouf would remain part of independent Algeria and an economic co-operation agreement regarding the mining of iron ore deposits south-east of Tindouf.[117] King Hassan declared that 'frontiers have nowadays lost their former importance'.[118] Moroccan claims to Algerian territory were never recognized by any other country and ultimately Morocco itself felt compelled to accept the existing frontier as colonially defined, with some delimitation of areas that had been left undelimited. A major territorial dispute therefore resolved itself into an exercise of delimitation. It is interesting to note that when the issue was discussed at the Extraordinary Session of the OAU Council of Ministers in November 1963, a resolution was adopted proclaiming that African States must seek solutions to disputes 'within the framework of the principles and the institutions prescribed by the Charter of the Organisation of African Unity',[119] and Article 3(3) of the OAU Charter emphasizes the principle of 'respect for the sovereignty and territorial integrity of each State'.

2. *Somali Claims to Ethiopian and Kenyan Territory*

Somalia is unique among African States in being a homogeneous nation-State on European lines. It therefore has had no need for the territorial principle of State legitimacy since it possesses its own ethnic *raison d'être*. However, there are a substantial number of Somali tribesmen inhabiting areas of Ethiopia, Kenya, and Djibouti and in its claims to extend its boundaries it has demonstrated the classic ethnic assertion.[120] Somalia has consistently opposed the status quo approach to African borders and has argued instead for the right of self-determination, by which it means not the legal doctrine as defined in international practice, but rather the political concept founded as it is upon ethnic or national factors. Having no fear of secessionist movements itself since it is ethnically united,[121] Somalia has failed to perceive African apprehensions of tribal conflict in the event of a rearrangement of borders on ethnic lines. It itself is a merger of the former British and Italian Somalilands and its constitution and five-star flag[122] reflect its aim of promoting the political unification of the Somali nation. Somalia opposed the important OAU resolution on respect for colonial borders, as did Morocco. In its wishes to unite all Somalia, Somalia received some initial sympathy from the more radical gatherings of African and other States, but support has since waned appreciably.

The First Afro-Asian Peoples' Solidarity Conference at Cairo in December 1957 approved a resolution regarding the right of self-determination of the people of Somaliland,[123] while the All-Africa Peoples' Conference at Tunis in 1960 supported the struggle of the Somalis 'for independence and unity in order to give birth to a bigger Somaliland'.[124] The Conakry Conference of 1960 of the Afro-Asian Peoples' Solidarity Organization adopted a resolution in favour of the 'glorious struggle of the Somali people for their freedom, independence and unification'.[125] The Somali case was discussed at a preparatory meeting of Foreign Ministers at Addis Ababa dealing with the creation of the OAU in 1963. Somalia requested an item on the agenda dealing with territorial disputes between neighbouring African States and the establishment of machinery to resolve them.[126] It was included under item VII, dealing with the creation of a Permanent Conciliation Commission, but never actually dealt with as the establishment of a conciliation commission was subsumed under the discussion on the setting up of an organization of African States.[127] At the first OAU Summit Conference, the Somali president put forward his case but was faced with arguments supporting the territorial integrity of States based upon colonial borders put forward by Ethiopia and the representatives of the pre-independent Kenya-African National Union.[128]

In July 1963 Ethiopia and Kenya signed a mutual defence agreement and in January and February 1964 incidents in the Haud and Ogaden regions of Ethiopia claimed by Somalia led to fighting between the Ethiopian and Somali regular armies.[129] Somalia informed the OAU Secretariat of the fighting and requested a meeting of the Security Council.[130] On the same day, Ethiopia asked the OAU to consider its complaint against Somalia. The UN Secretary-General preferred an African framework to be used for the discussion of the problem[131] and the issue was accordingly placed before an Extraordinary Session of the OAU Council of Ministers at Dar es Salaam.[132] Somalia informed the UN Secretary-General that it would not raise the matter with the Security Council while the problem was in the hands of the OAU.[133] At the conference, Somalia restricted its demands to a cease-fire and disengagement of the armies, while Kenya and Ethiopia broadened out the discussion into matters of principle. Kenya suggested that a further charter should be established which would prohibit territorial claims. Ultimately a resolution was adopted calling for a cease-fire, cessation of hostile propaganda, and negotiations for a peaceful settlement of the dispute between Somalia and Ethiopia.[134] A resolution dealing with the Somali–Kenyan dispute was limited to calling for steps to be taken to settle the dispute without actually requesting negotiations between the parties.[135] The issue was further discussed at the Second Ordinary Session of the OAU Council of Ministers at Lagos. In spite of Somali objections that a territorial dispute was involved, the Ethiopian–Somali dispute was listed as a border one. Ethiopia and Kenya called on Somalia to renounce its territorial claims. A resolution was eventually adopted on the Ethiopian–Somali dispute which confirmed the Dar es Salaam resolution and called on the parties to respect the cease-fire. The resolution also requested Ethiopia and Somalia to open direct negotiations and significantly referred to Article 3(3) of the OAU Charter, which specifically mentions respect for the sovereignty and territorial integrity of States.[136] The resolution on the Somali–Kenyan dispute similarly called for negotiations and referred to Article 3(3).[137] It thus appeared that African States accepted the territorial positions of Ethiopia and Kenya and were prepared only to seek means to defuse the crisis. A cease-fire was in fact agreed through Sudanese mediation in March and the joint Ethiopian–Somali communiqué issued at the end of the meeting noted that the talks had taken place in accordance with the OAU's recommendations.[138]

The Somali disputes were to be discussed at the first OAU Assembly of Heads of State and Governments in Cairo in July 1964, but this was postponed in view of a Somali government crisis.[139] However, at this conference the OAU resolution was adopted which called on member-States to respect the colonial borders.[140] At the Second OAU Assembly at Accra in October 1965, an agreement was signed between Ethiopia and Somalia against using hostile propaganda, but the tension continued.[141] During December 1965, President Nyerere of Tanzania arranged a Somali–Kenyan meeting at Arusha, but this had no positive results.

Kenya refused to negotiate about its territorial integrity, while Somalia demanded the right of self-determination for its kin in northern Kenya.[142] The next year, Sudan attempted to mediate between the two, but it was not until after a change in government in Somalia in June 1967 that progress could be effected. During the Fourth OAU Assembly in Kinshasa in September 1967, the Zambian President encouraged Somalia and Kenya to meet and a joint declaration emerged in which both parties agreed to negotiate in accordance with the OAU Charter and this was endorsed by the Assembly.[143] The Kinshasa Declaration noted that 'both sides have expressed their desire to respect each other's sovereignty and territorial integrity in the spirit of paragraph 3 of Article 3 of the OAU Charter'.[144] Thus, Somalia had appeared to accept the principle of territorial integrity in practice although its hopes for eventual unification remained.[145] In October 1967 a conference was convened between the parties at Arusha under Zambian mediation and an agreement was signed relating to the easing of tensions and the ending of the propaganda war.[146]

The Ethiopian–Somali situation remained quiescent for a number of years. However, in 1973 the issue was revived owing to a number of factors, ranging from the growing tension between the two over the French Territory of the Afars and Issas to the discovery of oil and gas in the Ogaden region claimed by Somalia. At the OAU Council of Ministers in May 1973, Somalia accused Ethiopia of massing troops in the area and insisted on placing the issue on the agenda of the OAU Assembly in terms of a territorial dispute. Ethiopia maintained that it was merely a border dispute involving the demarcation of part of the boundary in accordance with existing agreements. In the event, the Council decided upon a compromise and a five-man commission was appointed.[147] The following month, an OAU Good Offices Committee was established at the OAU Assembly with a Sudanese mediator.[148] Both Ethiopia and Somalia maintained their positions. At the OAU Assembly of June 1974, Ethiopia declared that the Somali dispute was only a question of demarcating an unmarked border, while Somalia pursued its territorial claim.[149] Throughout 1976 violence increased in the Ogaden region as the Somali-backed Western Somali Liberation Front (WSLF) forces infiltrated into the area, and by summer 1977 it was clear that the WSLF effectively controlled the whole of the Ogaden plain.[150] On 2 August 1977 the Ethiopians failed to secure the necessary two-thirds vote when they tried to convene an emergency session of the OAU Council of Ministers to consider the alleged Somali aggression.[151] The eight-nation OAU

Committee established in 1973 attempted to mediate but the WSLF was refused a hearing and Somalia boycotted the closing session of the meetings. A resolution was adopted by the commission which reaffirmed the inviolability of African frontiers as at the date of independence and condemned political subversion.[152] Somalia argued against this that the principle of the respect for borders as at the grant of independence did not apply in this case, since Somali territory had been colonized by Ethiopia in the past. It was stated that Ethiopia was a colonial State which had taken part in the partition of Africa at the 1884–5 Berlin Conference and this meant that the population of the Ogaden retained the right to self-determination.[153] In other words, the WSLF were merely exercising the accepted right with regard to the recolonization of a colonial territory. On 11 February 1978 Somalia officially announced that its regular army was being sent into Ogaden, but the Cuban and Soviet aid to Ethiopia proved decisive and on 9 March Somalia declared that its forces were being withdrawn. Somalia received no international support for its irredentist activities,[154] and it was made clear that military aid would only be sent to Somalia to defend its recognized borders.[155] The degree of Somalia's isolation with regard to its 1976–8 Ogaden adventure is compelling evidence as to the unacceptability of the active pursuit of irredentist aims. The Fifteenth OAU summit in 1978 stressed the absolute need to respect the principles of territorial integrity, inviolability of State frontiers, non-use of force, and non-interference in the internal affairs of States,[156] while the August 1980 session of the OAU eight-nation committee concluded with the adoption of resolutions including 'the recognition, affirmation, implementation and application' of the principle of the inviolability of frontiers of member-States as attained at the time of independence.[157] Nevertheless, sporadic fighting continued in succeeding years[158] and the basic problem is far from being resolved.[159]

3. *Ghana's Claims to the Ivory Coast*

Before the independence of the Ivory Coast, a delegation of Sanwi leaders went to France to request autonomy under the terms of an 1834 treaty, and after failing to receive a positive response a Sanwi independence movement was established early in 1959. This was set up in neighbouring Ghana, which supplied it with arms. In 1960 Ghana claimed the south-east corner of the Ivory Coast, which was inhabited by the Sanwis, on grounds of tribal unity, since the Sanwis were related to the Nzima tribe of the President of Ghana. However, the claim was soon dropped and aid to the Sanwi movement ceased.[160]

4. *Ghana, Togo, and the Ewe Question*

The problem of the Ewe people, split between Ghana and Togo, caused severe tensions between the two countries and stimulated irredentist claims by both. The unification of British Togoland with the Gold Coast following a plebiscite in May 1956 resulted in some 100,000 Ewes being divided between Ghana and Togo. President Nkrumah of Ghana called for the integration of Togo (then French Togoland) into Ghana as its seventh region in order to unify the Ewes, while the newly independent Togo favoured the reunification of the two Togos, i.e. claiming the former British Togoland for the same reason.[161] Personal factors played a large role and the antagonism abated somewhat after the assassination of the Togo President in January 1963, although it recurred on a number of occasions in subsequent years. The Togo President in April 1966 called for a reunion of ex-British Togoland with the Republic of Togo, declaring that it was necessary to satisfy the legitimate aspirations of the people. In that month, the Ghana–Togo border was formally reopened after a three-year closure.[162] The secessionist element which is often involved in irredentist situations came to prominence when in 1964 a call was made for the secession of Ghana's Volta region and its merger with Togo. The Ghana government declared that it had no intention of betraying the confidence reposed in it by the people of the former British Togoland in the UN plebiscite of 1956.[163] In February 1975, however, a delegation from the Volta region presented a letter together with resolutions, a petition, and a memorandum to the Ghanaian ambassador in Togo calling for negotiations between Ghana and a national liberation movement committee to solve the reunification question concerning the two Togos. It was proclaimed that 'Western Togo' could no longer be a region or a part of a region of Ghana.[164] The Togo government for its part ceased to call publicly for the cession of the former British Togoland.[165]

(*b*) *Secessionist Claims*

1. *Katanga*

At a round-table conference in Brussels in early 1960, it was agreed that the Belgian colony of the Congo would become independent on 30 June 1960. The Congo, comprising an area of some 2,345,525 sq. km. and a population at the time of about 14,000,000 persons, possessed 'one of the most complex tribal structures in Africa'.[166] Tribal fighting broke out in the spring of 1960,[167] while upon independence separatist strains became evident.[168] On 5 June the Force Publique mutinied near Leopoldville and disorder spread.[169] On 10 July Belgian troops, stationed in military bases in the country by virtue of the Treaty of Friendship and Cooperation (which was never in fact ratified), intervened in Katanga and Kasai provinces and later throughout the country.[170] The Belgian government represented its action as a form of humanitarian intervention designed to protect its nationals and the interests of the Congo and the international community.[171]

On 11 July Tshombe announced the independence of Katanga and its secession from the Congo. Belgian aid was requested and a Belgian officer appointed by Tshombe to command his forces.[172] The Central Government immediately appealed to the United Nations 'not to restore the internal situation in the Congo but rather to protect the national territory against acts of aggression committed by Belgian metropolitan troops'.[173] This request of 12 July followed upon a request for technical assistance to the Congo security forces made on 10 July. Belgium was accused of engineering the secession and the urgency of the appeal was emphasized[174] Ghana announced that a mission offering all aid, including military aid, was being sent to the Congo and stressed its recognition of Katanga as an integral part of the Congo and condemned any attempt to detach it as a 'flagrant violation of the Congo's territorial integrity'.[175] On 13 July the UN Secretary-General, acting under Article 99 of the Charter, called for an urgent meeting of the Security Council,[176] and strongly recommended sending military aid to the Congo government. The UN force would not include personnel from the permanent members of the Security Council and would not be authorized to take action beyond self-defence or action which would make it a party to internal disputes.[177] The Council adopted a resolution by 8 votes to 0 with 3 abstentions, on 14 July calling on Belgium to withdraw its troops from the Congo and authorizing the Secretary-General 'to take the necessary steps in consultation with the government of the Republic of the Congo to provide the government with such military assistance as may be necessary'.[178] The same day, the Congo broke off diplomatic relations with Belgium and Katanga declared that it would not permit the entry of UN troops.[179] Offers of troops from Ghana, Guinea, Morocco, and Tunisia were accepted and as a first stage it was agreed that seven battalions from Ethiopia, Ghana, Guinea, Morocco, and Tunisia would be sent to the Congo.[180]

African reaction to the Katanga secession was strongly hostile. Guinea declared it was contrary to the interests of the Congo while Ghana noted that Katanga was 'a natural, integral part of the Congo Republic'.[181] The UN Secretary-General emphasized that the Security Council resolution of 14 July applied to the whole of the territory of the Congo, although UN forces would not intervene in domestic conflicts.[182] The Security Council adopted a resolution on 22 July recognizing that it had itself called for the admission of the Congo to membership of the United Nations as a unit,[183] and calling on Belgium to withdraw its troops. All States were requested to refrain from any action which might impede the restoration of law and order and undermine the territorial integrity and political independence of the Republic of the Congo.[184] By the end of July, the UN force in the Congo numbered over 11,000[185] but had not yet entered Katanga in view of Katangan hostility and the belief that violence would be involved.[186] The Security Council adopted a resolution on 8 August calling on Belgium to withdraw its troops from Katanga under speedy modalities determined by the UN Secretary-General and declared that the entry of UN troops into that province was necessary for the full implementation of the resolution. It was reaffirmed that the UN force in the Congo would not be involved in any internal disputes.[187] Ghana, Guinea, and the UAR, offered to send troops to end the secession if the United Nations was not able or willing,[188] while a number of other countries indicated their support for the territorial integrity of the Congo, but preferred action to be taken through the United Nations.[189] The Secretary-General of the United Nations was accused by the Congo Prime Minister of tacitly recognizing Katanga's secession by refusing to supply military assistance to enable government forces to enter the province.[190] The Secretary-General noted that he was primarily concerned with the international peace and security aspect of the problem, i.e. the withdrawal of the Belgian troops, and, although he criticized the Katangan secession and stressed the need to respect the territorial integrity of the Congo, he did not regard the ending of the secession as a function of the UN force. On the other hand, the Congo government and most African States were primarily concerned about reintegrating the province into the territory of the Congo.[191]

A conference of African States with representatives from Cameroon, Congo (Brazzaville), Ethiopia, Ghana, Guinea, Liberia, Libya, Mali, Morocco, Sudan, Togo, Tunisia, and the UAR was held in the Congo capital of Leopoldville at the end of August and it concluded with a declaration of total support for the territorial integrity of the Congo and condemnation of the secession.[192] During this period, the Central Government's intentions to attack Katanga became known and there was some criticism of this at the conference.[193] In the event, this operation foundered in Kasai province. A meeting of the Security Council in early September resulted in deadlock[194] and the suggestion of the US delegation to remit the whole matter to the General Assembly under the Uniting for Peace machinery was accepted.[195]

The Fourth Emergency Special Session of the General Assembly opened on 17 September with a dispute between the USA and USSR over the supply of Soviet technicians, transport planes, and trucks to the Congo. Despite differences over the interpretation and implementation of the Security Council resolutions, delegates supported the territorial integrity of the Congo and condemned the Katangan secession. Libya proclaimed the need to maintain the territorial integrity of the Congo,[196] while Ethiopia emphasized that at the start of the crisis African States had tacitly agreed on a number of fundamental principles. These were that the Congolese people were one and that the territory of the Congo must be maintained as a unit and that collective action should be taken through the United Nations in order to maintain the unity, integrity, and complete independence of the Congo.[197] On 18 September resolution 1474 ES-IV was adopted, by 70 votes to 0, with 11 abstentions. This supported the Security Council resolutions of 14 and 22 July and 9 August and declared that it was essential for the United Nations to continue to assist the Central Government, 'with a view to preserving the unity, territorial integrity and political independence' of the Congo. The Secretary-General was requested to continue to take vigorous action to safeguard the unity, territorial integrity, and political independence of the Congo in the interests of international peace and security and the resolution appealed to all States to refrain from any action that might undermine that unity, territorial integrity, and political independence.[198]

In February 1961 the Security Council adopted a resolution by 9 votes to 0, with 2 abstentions, expressing regret at the killing of Lumumba and urging the United Nations to take all appropriate measures to prevent civil war in the Congo, including, in the last resort, the use of force. It expressed grave concern at the prevalence of conditions which seriously imperilled peace and order and the unity and territorial integrity of the Congo and called for the reconvening of the Parliament and the reorganization of the Congolese armed units.[199] In order to implement this resolution, the UN Force was substantially increased.[200] In April the General Assembly adopted three resolutions, calling *inter alia* for the withdrawal of Belgian and other foreign personnel,[201] and by the summer a government of national unity and political reconcilation was established in the Congo, one of whose aims would be to annul the secession of Katanga.[202] Since the February resolution of the Security Council had urged that measures be taken for the immediate withdrawal and evacuation of all Belgian and other foreign military and paramilitary personnel and political advisers not under UN command, and mercenaries, and since Katanga depended to a large extent upon such personnel,[203] it became apparent that a ready weapon was at hand for the United Nations to involve itself in the Katanga situation. On 24 August the Congo President issued an ordinance for the immediate expulsion of all non-Congolese officers and mercenaries in Katanga that had not entered into contractual arrangements with the Central Government, and UN assistance to achieve this was requested.[204] This was clearly designed to provide the United Nations with the legal authority to act within the Congo to implement the February Security Council resolution. The resulting operation by the United Nations in Katanga had some initial success, but fighting broke out in September.[205] A truce was arranged and a number of agreements signed, but the United Nations soon alleged that they were being broken by the Katangans who had retained the foreign mercenaries.[206] It is clear that during this period the Secretary-General felt that nothing in the UN Charter or resolutions justified UN moves to end the Katangan secession and that action was to be limited to removing foreign personnel in accordance with the Security Council resolution of February.[207] The Security Council was reconvened on 13 November[208] and a resolution adopted on 24 November by 9 votes to 0, with 2 abstentions.[209] This set out the policies and purposes of the United Nations with respect to the Congo. These included the maintenance of the territorial integrity and political independence of the Congo and the prevention of civil war. The resolution completely rejected the claim that Katanga was a sovereign, independent nation and strongly deprecated the secessionist activities carried out by the provincial administration of Katanga with the aid of external resources and foreign mercenaries. It also declared that all secessionist activities were contrary to the Loi Fondamentale of the Congo and Security Council decisions, and it demanded that such activities in Katanga should cease forthwith. It underlined UN support for the national unity and territorial integrity of the Congo and requested all member-States to refrain from any action which might directly or indirectly impede the policies and purposes of the United Nations in the Congo. This resolution clearly changed the basis of the UN actions in the Congo. On 24 November the acting Secretary-General declared that action was necessary to avert civil war and this action implied not neutrality but a sympathetic attitude to the efforts of the Central Government to suppress all secessionist activities.[210] After more fighting,[211] the position of the Katangan authorities became untenable. On 19 December Tshombe entered into negotiations with the Central Government at Kitona and two days later he made a declaration accepting the application of the Loi Fondamentale of the Congo, the indissoluble unity of the Republic, and the authority of the Central Government over all parts of the country. President Kasavubu was also recognized as Head of State and Tshombe agreed to carry out all UN resolutions and place the Katangan gendarmerie under the President's authority.[212] The end of the secession was formally accepted in a declaration by Tshombe on 14 January 1963 from Kolwezi.[213]

It would be inaccurate to regard the Katangan issue as demonstrating the intention of the United Nations to maintain the status quo and become involved against all secessionist attempts. Although Tshombe claimed the right of self-determination,[214] this was clearly not accepted by the international community. But to assert from this the validity of UN actions to suppress such activities would be incorrect. There was present in the Katanga situation one factor which clearly distinguished it from other secessionist attempts and that was the extent to which the secession was seen by the international community as a foreign-inspired move.[215] The Belgian intervention against the Congolese mutiny of the Force Publique was the original cause of recourse to the United Nations, while the crucial Belgian presence in Katanga deemed indispensable to the survival of the secessionist regime was considered to be the single most important factor governing the relations between the United Nations and Katanga. The representative of the Secretary-General of the United Nations in the Congo in 1960 submitted a report stating that 'in Katanga, Belgian influence is omnipresent. Virtually all key civilian and security posts are either held directly by officials of Belgian nationality or controlled by advisers to recently appointed and often inexperienced Congolese officials.'[216] The element of Belgian control of the secessionist move was regarded by the United Nations as justifying actions to counter the secession. Paragraph 1 of Security Council resolution S/5002 'strongly deprecates the secessionist activities illegally carried out by the provincial administration of Katanga, with the aid of external resources and manned by foreign mercenaries', and thus demonstrated that the fact of foreign intervention was considered to be the crucial relevant point concerning the secession. Indeed, force was to be used by the United Nations not to end the secession itself but to apprehend and/or deport all foreign military and paramilitary personnel and political advisers not under the UN command and mercenaries. Although that amounted to the same thing as ending the secession in practice, the difference is crucial, for the United Nations was not using force to end a secession. Nevertheless, it was always recognized by the United Nations that the territorial integrity and national unity of the Congo should be maintained. There was strong African hostility to the secession, which was never recognized by any State and the impact of African views was marked. Hoskyns noted that this case provided the first experiment in pan-Africanism in a practical sense and demonstrated the influence of joint African action. As soon as the United Nations and the USA decided to take active steps against Katanga, however, the African role diminished in importance.[217]

2. *Biafra*[218]

The Eastern Region of Nigeria declared its independence on 30 May 1967 as the sovereign State of Biafra. This followed two coups in 1966 and widespread disturbance in the north of the country which resulted in massacres of Ibos and the fleeing of the rest to the Ibo heartlands in the Eastern Region. As a result, the military government of the Eastern Region led by Colonel Ojukwu boycotted constitutional talks until the security of Ibos was guaranteed. An agreement was ultimately signed at Aburi in Ghana between the military governors of Nigeria in an attempt to resolve differences between the Eastern Region and the rest of the country, but it broke down over questions of interpretation.

In March 1967 Ojukwu announced the cessation of revenue payments to the federal treasury and the federal government responded with an economic boycott. At the end of May a decree was issued decentralizing Nigeria and creating twelve new States and this provoked the secession of the Eastern Region. Fighting commenced on 6 July 1967, and continued until the Biafran surrender on 12 January 1970.[219]

In spite of some Nigerian misgivings, the situation was discussed by the Organization of African Unity at the Kinshasa Conference of the Assembly of Heads of State and Government in September 1967. The resolution that emerged reaffirmed the adherence of the African Heads of State and Government to the principle of respect for the sovereignty and territorial integrity of member-States and reiterated their 'condemnation of secession in any member-State'. The Nigerian situation was recognized as an internal one, the solution of which was a Nigerian responsibility, and it was resolved to send a consultative mission of six

Heads of State to the Head of the Nigerian Federal Government 'to assure him of the Assembly's desire for the territorial integrity, unity and peace of Nigeria'.[220] The situation was therefore seen as a matter of legitimate concern to African States, while the support of the principles of territorial integrity and non-intervention in internal affairs and the consequent condemnation of secession were crucial in the diplomatic field. This was so, not only because any support for Biafra was at best postponed but because the UN Secretary-General emphasized that regional organizations should deal with local conflicts and accordingly the United Nations did not become involved.[221] The mission, consisting of the Heads of State of Cameroon, Congo (Kinshasa), Ethiopia, Ghana, Liberia, and Niger, arrived in Lagos after initial Nigerian reservations on 23 November.[222] The communiqué issued afterwards condemned all secessionist attempts in Africa and reaffirmed that any solution to the crisis had to be in the context of Nigeria's unity and territorial integrity.[223]

Between 15 April and 20 May four African States (Tanzania, Gabon, the Ivory Coast, and Zambia) recognized Biafra as a sovereign State. The first was Tanzania, which declared that the need for African unity was superseded by the need of the Ibo people, who could not be protected in Nigeria. President Nyerere stated that 'where borders were drawn up without African consent they need not be respected'.[224] The Foreign Minister of Burundi took the view that if the war continued many African States would recognize Biafra. He noted that the civil war issue was non-political and 'should be viewed from humanitarian grounds', while the Information Minister of Congo (Brazzaville) declared that the war had become a human problem 'and it is that aspect which concerns the Congo government'.[225] However, a number of African States feared that recognition of Biafra would, far from helping the Ibos, encourage further disintegration and warfare on the continent.[226] The following month three African States recognized Biafra. Gabon emphasized the pogrom against the Ibos,[227] the Ivory Coast declared its indignation against the 'inexplicable guilty indifference of the whole world towards the massacres',[228] while Zambia, although wanting African unity, emphasized the belief that 'it would be morally wrong to force anyone into unity founded on bloodshed'.[229] Accordingly, it is within a humanitarian context that one ought to view the four African recognitions.[230] Such recognitions did not result in the establishment of normal diplomatic relations and were apparently an effort to moderate Nigeria's declared aim of total victory and facilitate negotiations.[231] The comments made by the four States at the time bear out this view.

The worsening conditions in the battle areas impelled a renewal of the activities of the OAU mission in July 1968 and the leaders of both sides went for talks to the Niger capital of Niamey, at which it was decided to continue negotiations at Addis Ababa in August.[232] These negotiations eventually petered out at the beginning of August, following the Nigerian declaration of a final offensive.[233] In September the fifth Assembly of the OAU met at Algiers and adopted a resolution calling on member-States of the OAU and United Nations to refrain from any action detrimental to the peace, unity, and territorial integrity of Nigeria and appealing for the restoration of peace and unity in Nigeria.[234] However, Uganda announced the next month that it was considering recognizing Biafra,[235] while Sierra Leone hinted in September 1969 that it might soon recognize the secessionist State.[236] Very little mention was made of the Nigerian crisis at the 1968 session of the UN General Assembly. Only a few States raised the issue of possible UN discussion of the crisis and no State sought to have the question inscribed on the agenda.[237]

The last meeting of the OAU mission was held in Monrovia, Liberia, in April 1969 and ended with no progress towards reconciling Nigeria and Biafra. The mission proposed that the 'two parties of the civil war accept, in the supreme interest of Africa, a united Nigeria, which ensures all forms of security to all citizens'. While Nigeria accepted this, Biafra did not.[238] In September 1969, at the sixth Assembly of the OAU at Addis Ababa, a resolution was adopted which called on both sides 'to agree to preserve in the overriding interests of Africa the unity of Nigeria', although the four African States that had recognized Biafra, plus Sierra Leone, abstained.[239] On 12 January 1970 Biafra surrendered, both sides referring to the acceptance of the 'OAU resolution'.[240]

The overwhelming majority of African States clearly accepted the need to maintain Nigeria's territorial integrity and wished to achieve an African solution to the conflict that would uphold that territorial integrity. The concept of self-determination was not regarded as applicable.[241] The four African recognitions of Biafra appeared to have been motivated primarily by humanitarian considerations rather than being an assessment of the fulfilment by Biafra of the criteria of statehood in international law. The Biafran experience can be seen as a crucial piece of State practice in Africa with regard to post-independence secessions, and the high level of consensus reached by African States on this basic issue of territorial integrity demonstrates a strongly held belief militating against secessionist attempts. The viability of the colonial territorial frontiers was underlined both militarily and diplomatically.

3. *Southern Sudan*[242]

The three southern provinces of the Sudan, Bahr el Ghazal, Equatoria, and Upper Nile, differ radically from the northern part of the country in that they are populated by black Africans, Christian and pagan, rather than by Muslim Arabs and consequently a different cultural identity has developed. They were treated as a distinct entity under the Anglo-Egyptian condominium of 1899–1956,[243] and were far less advanced. In 1953 the Sudan was granted self-government, and one year prior to independence in 1956 a mutiny had taken place in the south which greatly embittered relations between north and south and precipitated a seventeen-year war.[244] Sudanese independence was declared on 1 January 1956, and, contrary to pledges made, considerations of federation as the basis of the proposed constitution was rejected. The military take-over of 1958 and the banning of political parties exacerbated the situation. In 1962 the Anya-Nya guerrilla organization was formed and the fighting entered a new phase.[245] In March 1965, after the overthrow of the military regime, a round-table conference was held in Khartoum attended by representatives from the south, delegates from six northern parties, and observers from Algeria, the UAR, Uganda, Kenya, Nigeria, and Ghana.[246] However, it ended indecisively with the north offering some form of regional government and the south demanding self-government or federation. This led to severe action against the south and southern calls for secession or merger with neighbouring African States. Ultimately, in 1971, the new Numeiry regime in the Sudan began negotiations with representatives of the Anya-Nya[247] which led to a peace agreement the following year after a conference in Addis Ababa.[248] This called for a cease-fire and amnesty, return and resettlement of refugees, and regional autonomy for the south.[249] Although some African States were sympathetic to the struggle of the Anya-Nya[250] and Uganda appeared to tolerate the existence of its bases on its territory, there was never any support at governmental level for the proposed secession. Uganda and other concerned African States directed their influence primarily at an attempt to convince the separatists to compromise with the Sudanese authorities. Touval concludes with regard to these States that

> concern over possible reprisals by the Sudanese army, fear of possible Sudanese aid to separatist movements or subversive groups in their own territories and commitment to the principle of the territorial status quo, resulted in a fluctuation of policy between assistance to the rebels and pressure on them to cease their activities and accept the Sudan government's terms.[251]

4. *Eritrea*

This area was placed under Ethiopian administration in 1952 as an autonomous unit[252] in a federal structure, but in 1955 Ethiopia became a unitary State.[253] In November 1962 Eritrea was officially annexed as Ethiopia's fourteenth province,[254] following a period during which all signs of Eritrean separatism were abolished.[255] The Eritrean armed struggle began in 1961 and received intermittent aid from Arab States, particularly Sudan, Syria, Iraq, and Libya.[256] In many respects, a curious parallel developed between Eritrea and Southern Sudan, the former an Arab-backed insurgency against an African State and the latter an African rising against an Arab State.[257] By 1970 violence had substantially increased in the area and the declared aim of the Eritrean Liberation Front (ELF) was a UN-held referendum for an independent Eritrea.[258] The headquarters of the movement was established in Damascus, and Ethiopia accused certain Arab States of causing the disorders.[259] The Second Conference of Foreign Ministers of Islamic Countries held at Karachi in 1970 adopted a resolution pledging support for the struggle of the people of Eritrea for freedom and independence,[260] while the Fourth Conference of this organization in 1973 strongly backed the ELF.[261] Arab support of the Eritrean movement was limited and sporadic at times, however.[262] Ethiopia refused to concede the principle of its national unity and territorial integrity, as the Ten-point Plan of 1974,[263] and the Nine-Point Plan of 1976[264] demonstrated. By Spring 1977 it was estimated that some two-thirds of the coastline and some 80 per cent of the countryside of Eritrea were in Eritrean rebel hands.[265] Sudan pledged open support for the separatists in early 1977[266] and was condemned by Ethiopia for breaking the OAU Charter.[267] With Soviet and Cuban aid, Ethiopia launched a counter-attack in Eritrea in early 1978 that met with considerable success.[268] African attitudes towards the Eritrea issue reflected the concern for the territorial integrity of the independent African States that had proved so potent on the continent.[269] It is also worthy of note that the headquarters of the Organization of African Unity is situated in Ethiopia's capital. The OAU itself has been noticeably reluctant to criticize Ethiopia and the overall African position remains that of support for the territorial integrity of that country.[270] This has also been true of the United Nations, although it could be suggested that as a result of the binding power of disposal granted the General Assembly by the Big Four Powers and the consequent Assembly resolution on the status of Eritrea,[271] the Assembly retains a special interest in this matter in the light of the unilateral incorporation of Eritrea into a unitary Ethiopia.

5. *The Dissolution of the Mali Federation*

One interesting example so far of a successful secession from a recognized independent State is afforded by the break-up of the Mali Federation, but there are grounds for regarding the case as exceptional.

On 19 January 1959 a federal constituent assembly drawn from the Republics of Senegal, Soudan, Dahomey, and Upper Volta met at Dakar and unanimously adopted a draft constitution for the Federation of Mali consisting of sixty-two articles and a preamble adhering to the constitution of the Fifth French Republic and the fundamental rights of man.[272] The Federation of Mali came into official existence on 4 April, minus Dahomey and Upper Volta, and at the end of the year Mali requested full independence within the French community.[273] The French National Assembly ratified the agreement for Mali's independence in June and the agreement was subsequently ratified by the Assemblies of Senegal and Soudan. Mali was proclaimed an independent State on 20 June and was immediately recognized by seventeen States, including the USA, United Kingdom and USSR.[274] Mali's membership of the United Nations was unanimously approved by the Security Council on 29 June.[275] However, after increasing discord between the leaders of the two components of the Federation, the Senegal Legislative Assembly unanimously proclaimed its independence and secession from the Federation in August.[276]

The acting Premier of Soudan declared that the Federation was indissoluble and asked for French troops to ensure Mali's territorial integrity. An appeal was also made for UN intervention.[277] Further requests for UN military assistance and appeals for a Security Council meeting were also made, while Senegal asked to be admitted to the Organization.[278] On 11 September France formally recognized Senegal, which was soon recognized by a number of other countries, including the United Kingdom, and the General Assembly agreed to defer a decision on the Mali Federation's application for membership. Ultimately, the Soudanese Assembly decided to proclaim Soudan independent as the Republic of Mali, declaring that the Federation had ceased to exist and that the new State was to be free of all ties with France.[279] A few days later, France recognized the Republic of Mali and the General Assembly recommended UN membership for both Senegal and Mali.[280] Senegal justified its secession by declaring that the component parts of the Federation remained fully sovereign States with an inherent right of withdrawal. It was argued that the Federation was a *sui generis* union emanating from the application of international law to African needs and that the component States therefore retained their sovereign status.[281] The tripartite thesis of sovereign status for Senegal, Soudan, and the Federation of Mali was difficult to sustain absolutely in view of the provision in the Federal Constitution that 'la souveraineté nationale appartient au peuple du Mali',[282] the recognition of the Federation by a substantial number of countries, and its acceptance by the Security Council for membership in the United Nations. According to the Federal Constitution, it was the Federation itself which was to make treaties, although the component States had to pass laws to enact them. Indeed treaties were made with France. This would all appear to suggest that the Federation was itself not only a legal person, but actually a State from which Senegal seceded.[283]

However, to treat the matter as straightforward secession from an independent State would be to misinterpret the situation. The two component States retained considerable powers and many of the attributes and characteristics of States and the traditional international law specification of federations and unions is not particularly helpful in trying to determine the legal position in this case.[284] Senegal and Soudan, as autonomous States within the French Community, agreed to form a federation and became independent in that form, after which Senegal seceded. To compare this situation with that of a particular group seceding from an independent State would not be accurate in view of the solidity of the identity of the two component elements. Of particular importance was the acquiescence in and acceptance of the situation by Soudan (later Mali), while international reaction also accepted the break-up of the Federation and the emergence of two separate sovereign States.

(*c*) *Conclusions*

Unlike cession, which is accomplished by virtue of the attribute of sovereignty possessed by States, secession constitutes an act contrary to the will of the State. Like cession, secession necessarily impinges upon the territorial integrity of States and the inviolability of frontiers. One must distinguish, however, between territorial diminution occurring as a result of external forces or irredentism and that occurring as a result of internal revolt or secession proper. In the former instance, two or more States are included, in the latter case only one. International law is accordingly deeply concerned with territorial aggrandizement by States or attempts to achieve the dissolution of another State's territorial integrity and this has been noted on a number of occasions and particularly in the

UN Charter, resolution 1514 (XV), and the 1970 Declaration on Principles of International Law, as well as in the 1974 Consensus Definition of Aggression. Thus, irredentist claims by States against other independent States are clearly not justifiable under international law and the use of force to accomplish such aims is unlawful. These propositions are true despite the existence of strong ethnic, historic, cultural, and other ties that link the claimant State with the object of its irredentist assertion. As Judge De Castro noted in the *Western Sahara* case, 'to deduce, from the existence of ethnic, cultural and geographic analogies, the existence of legal ties is like leaping into an abyss',[285] and such a leap has proved particularly unsuccessful in Africa. Notwithstanding one or two exceptions, what is surprising with regard to African States is not the presence but the absence of territorial claims, despite the existence of ethnic and other ties across State borders. In other words, it is clearly accepted that such ties cannot found title to territory and irredentist claims offend against the principle of the territorial integrity of States.

In a rather different category lies the problem of secessions. The international instruments relating to territorial integrity that are binding bind States and not particular inhabitants within particular States. Thus, as a general proposition, it can be stated that the principle of territorial integrity does not constitute an obligation under international law upon individual members or groups within State communities. Secession, therefore, is not contrary to international law. Where such a secession succeeds in the light of the principle of effectiveness in establishing a viable State and one that is recognized by other States, international law will recognize this situation. As a corollary to this, international law does not recognize that parts of sovereign States possess the right of secession. International law is neutral. However, what is clear from State practice, and particularly African State practice, is that the legal right of self-determination does not incorporate the right of peoples in independent States to form new States. Self-determination does not extend to secession. It may indeed be possible to go further than this and say that, although international law neither permits nor prohibits secessions, the presumption of the maintenance and continuity of the concept of territorial integrity of States means that the question of the establishment of secessionist States is weighted in favour of the original State and against the secessionist endeavour. This in turn will influence the level of proof of effectiveness relative to the creation of such a new State. State practice shows that there exists a bias in the international community against secessions, although this bias will not extend to the use of international force to suppress them in the absence of other factors. The UN Secretary-General noted that when a State joined the United Nations there was an implied acceptance by the entire membership of its territorial integrity and sovereignty. In addition, 'as an international organisation, the United Nations has never accepted and does not accept and I do not believe it will ever accept the principle of secession of a part of its member-State'.[286] This, together with specific State practice, would appear to point not to an underlining of the classic international law relating to secessions, but to a subtle modification of it to strengthen the presumption against secession.

The rule that the appropriate unit for decolonization is the territorial entity as defined by the colonial power is thus established, as is the rule that the principle of self-determination in international law is applicable only in pre-independent entities within the colonial framework. One possible exception may appear to be South Africa and its apartheid policies. The United Nations began considering 'the question of race conflict in South Africa resulting from the policies of apartheid of the government of the Union of South Africa' in 1952. Apartheid was alleged to be creating a situation which constituted both a threat to international peace and security and a violation of the basic principles of the UN Charter.[287] In a number of resolutions, the Assembly declared that 'it is in the higher interests of humanity to put an immediate end to religious and so-called racial persecution and discrimination'.[288] A new phase in the relations of the United Nations and South Africa with respect to the apartheid issue opened in 1960, as a result of the increasing number of African member-States of the United Nations following decolonization and a series of disturbances in South Africa, such as the Sharpeville shootings. The Security Council discussed the issue for the first time and called on South Africa to abandon its apartheid policies.[289] The situation in South Africa was termed one that, if continued, might endanger international peace and security.[290] In 1962 the General Assembly adopted resolution 1761 (XVIII) in which it criticized South Africa for refusing to abandon its racial policies and called on States to initiate a diplomatic, economic, and arms boycott of South Africa. A Special Committee on Apartheid was also established. In July 1963 the Security Council again discussed the situation in South Africa resulting from apartheid[291] and declared that it was 'seriously disturbing international peace and security'. South Africa was again called on to abandon apartheid and all States were requested to cease the sale and shipment of arms and ammunition to it.[292] In resolution 191 (1964), the Council in addition termed the policies of apartheid 'contrary to the principles and purposes of the Charter of the United Nations and inconsistent with the provisions of the Universal Declaration of Human Rights as well as South Africa's obligations under the Charter'.[293] The General Assembly began to adopt resolutions condemning apartheid in even stronger language from this point, stating that the situation constituted a threat to international peace and security, calling for arms and economic boycotts of South Africa, and appealing for assistance to be granted to the opponents of apartheid.[294] In resolution 2396 (XXIII), the Assembly referred to apartheid as a 'crime against humanity' and reaffirmed 'the urgent necessity of eliminating the policies of apartheid so that the people of South Africa as a whole can exercise their right to self-determination and attain majority rule based on universal suffrage'.[295] In 1970 the Security Council resumed its discussions on apartheid and in resolution 282 (1970) recognized the 'legitimacy of the struggle of the oppressed people of South Africa in pursuance of their human and political rights as set forth in the Charter of the United Nations and in the Universal Declaration of Human Rights'. The situation resulting from the continued application of apartheid and the South African arms build-up constituted a 'potential threat to international peace and security' and the Council called on all States to strengthen the arms embargo against South Africa. In resolution 311 (1972), the Council reiterated its total opposition to apartheid, which was contrary to South Africa's obligations under the Charter. The Assembly termed apartheid a negation of the UN Charter and a crime against humanity in resolution 2671 (XXV) and reaffirmed its recognition of 'the legitimacy of the struggle of the people of South Africa to eliminate by all means at their disposal, apartheid and racial discrimination and to attain majority rule in the country as a whole based on universal suffrage'. The establishment by South Africa of Bantustans was termed 'a violation of the principle of self-determination and prejudicial to the territorial integrity of the State and the unity of its people'.[296] In 1976 the General Assembly took an additional step by declaring that 'the racist regime of South Africa is illegitimate and has no right to represent the people of South Africa'. It reaffirmed that the authentic representatives of the overwhelming majority of the South African people were the national liberation movements recognized by the OAU.[297]

The World Conference for Action against Apartheid held in Lagos in 1977 issued a declaration condemning apartheid as a flagrant violation of the UN Charter and the Universal Declaration of Human Rights and a crime against the conscience and dignity of mankind.[298] In November 1977 the Security Council voted unanimously to impose a mandatory arms embargo against South Africa under Chapter VII of the Charter, having determined that the policies and actions of South Africa made its acquisition of arms and related material a threat to international peace and security. Specifically cited in resolution 418 (1977) were South Africa's acts of repression, its defiant continuance of the system of apartheid, and its attacks against neighbouring independent States.[299] Thus, the weight of the UN practice clearly demonstrates the unacceptability of apartheid as a lawful ideology in international law. As the International Law Commission noted in its report of 1976, 'the international community now appears to recognise that such acts as the forcible maintenance of colonial domination or the forcible pursuit of a policy of apartheid constitute internationally wrongful acts of a particularly serious character.[300]

The question arises therefore of the legal status of apartheid. The numerous resolutions in the United Nations are clearly crucial here.[301] The basic approach stressed in such resolutions is that apartheid is contrary to the principles and purposes of the UN Charter, and two provisions are particularly relevant here. Article 1(3) calls for 'promoting and encouraging respect for human rights and for fundamental freedoms for all without distinction as to race, sex, language or religion', while Article 1(2) stresses that the purposes of the United Nations include the development of 'friendly relations among nations based on respect for the principle of equal rights and self-determination'.[302] In other words, in view of the number and contents of the appropriate Assembly and Security Council resolutions, a rule of UN law has emerged via a process of Charter interpretation prohibiting the practice of apartheid. The International Court declared that

> to establish ... and to enforce distinctions, exclusions, restrictions, and limitations exclusively based on grounds of race, colour, descent or national or ethnic origin which constitute a denial of fundamental human rights is a flagrant violation of the purposes and principles of the Charter.[303]

Apartheid is also unlawful under conventional international law. In the International Convention on the Elimination of All Forms of Racial Discrimination, 1965 (which entered into force in 1969), racial discrimination is defined as 'any distinction, exclusion, restriction or preference based on race, colour, descent, or national or ethnic origin' and Article 3 provides that States parties 'particularly condemn racial segregation and apartheid and undertake to prevent, prohibit and eradicate all practices of this nature in territories under their jurisdiction'. The International Convention on the Suppression and Punishment of the Crime of Apartheid 1973[304] (which came into effect in 1976), provides in Article 1 that the States parties declare that apartheid is a crime against humanity and that inhuman acts resulting from the policies and practices of apartheid are crimes violating the principles of international law, in particular the purposes and principles of the UN Charter. A comprehensive definition of apartheid is contained in Article 2. Apartheid is also contrary to customary international law, having regard in particular to the Universal Declaration of Human Rights, which was stated to be an obligation for members of the international community by the UN Conference on Human Rights in Tehran in 1968,[305] and relevant State practice.

The question thus arises as to the repercussions of this with regard to territorial integrity and with regard to self-determination. It would appear that the establishment of new States by a State based on enshrined racial discrimination clearly in pursuit of such illegal policies under international law must affect the competence of that State. In such a situation, it is suggested, a presumption arises of unlawfulness which the State must seek to rebut. In other words, there is an onus of proof upon the State to demonstrate the legality of the proposed creation of new States out of parts of its territory. If that cannot be discharged—and third-party recognition would be a critical evidential element here—then one could well be faced with an illegal and invalid act. Accordingly, the proposed new States in question might not have fulfilled the necessary conditions of statehood.

It could be argued that, in addition to the State's territorial competence being affected, the principle of self-determination may also be relevant since the principle imposes a duty on all States to promote its realization. This argument would be based on an analogy with the Rhodesian situation in the light of that aspect of self-determination that deals with the right of the inhabitants of an existing State to participate in the political life of that State. While international law does not impose a particular model upon States in such a situation, it could well be argued that States are restrained under this doctrine from ceding territory contrary to the wishes of the population and with the primary expressed intention to exclude people from the State altogether and in particular its political life. This approach, however, remains tentative.

Even more tentative is the suggestion that the principle of self-determination applies generally with regard to South Africa, outside the Bantustan factor, as has been mooted by a number of General Assembly resolutions.[306] This exception to the generally accepted definition of self-determination must be regarded, at least at this stage, as *de lege ferenda* and as illustrating primarily a claim that may or may not become concretized within the normative structure of international law.

6

Boundaries

I. THE NATURE OF BOUNDARIES

Closely connected with the concepts of territory and territorial sovereignty is the notion of a boundary. Huber noted in the *Island of Palmas* case that

> territorial sovereignty is, in general, a situation recognized and delimited in space, either by so-called natural frontiers as recognized by international law or by outward signs of delimitation that are undisputed or else by legal engagements entered into between interested neighbours, such as frontier conventions, or by acts of recognition of States within fixed boundaries.[1]

Thus boundaries mark the limitation of State sovereignties and are themselves marked by acceptance by members of the international community. Unrecognized unilateral determinations of where boundaries lie would therefore remain without international effect in the absence of acquiescence or recognition. The importance of boundaries[2] is that they demarcate State jurisdictions,[3] and thus profoundly influence the regime, nationality, and cultural milieu of the inhabitants of such areas. Accordingly, the notion and existence of boundaries is closely allied with the concept of territorial integrity and plays a symbolic as well as a practical role. Actions relating to the establishment of boundaries by States are acts of sovereignty, while the boundaries themselves constitute the limit of the exercise of sovereignty by States concerned. The existence of a boundary, therefore, between two or more States would be conclusive of effective sovereignty and its limits as between such States.[4] Huber stated in the *Island of Palmas* case that 'sovereignty in relation to a portion of the surface of the globe is the legal condition necessary for the inclusion of such portion in the territory of any particular State'.[5]

The protection of the inviolability of boundaries has assumed an important role in the international system,[6] while in the field of boundary determination the need for the harmonious interaction of at least the interested States is pronounced. Indeed, for a boundary to be effective, it has to be accepted by the States concerned. Judge Bebler, in his dissenting opinion in the *Indo-Pakistan Western Boundary (Rann of Kutch)* case, delcared that

there is no doubt that an international boundary ranks high among matters which cannot be settled otherwise than by agreement between neighbouring States concerned. One could, in good logic, go so far as to suggest the axiom that a boundary is there where the neighbouring States have agreed it to be. The agreement may have been entered into with more or less of freedom of will, it may have been forced on one side by force of arms, in a war and through the victory of one neighbour over the other, but it must have been accepted, when peace was restored, by both sides, the victorious and the defeated, to be looked upon as the boundary by the community of nations.[7]

The legal force of a boundary may derive, therefore, either from a treaty or by virtue of acquiescence or recognition by the parties concerned.

Since the concept of boundaries is of such crucial importance to the international community, the element of stability in the determination and maintenance of boundaries has been consistently emphasized. The International Court noted in the *Temple* case that 'in general, when two countries establish a frontier between them, one of the primary objects is to achieve stability and finality. This is impossible if the line so established can, at any moment, and on the basis of a continuously available protest, be called in question and its rectification claimed'.[8] Jennings has written that

the bias of existing law is toward stability, the status quo, and the present effective possession; the tendency of the International Court is to let sleeping dogs lie. This is right, for the stability of territorial boundaries must always be the ultimate aim. Some other kinds of legal ordering need to be capable of constant change to meet new needs of developing society; but in a properly ordered society, territorial boundaries will be among the most stable institutions.[9]

This aim of 'stability and finality' appears clearly with regard to the expressed purposes of boundary treaties in particular cases[10] and agreements providing for arbitration.[11] The Permanent Court in the *Iraq-Turkey Boundary* case noted that 'the very nature of a frontier and of any convention designed to establish frontiers between two countries imports that a frontier must constitute a definite boundary line throughout its length',[12] while the court in the *Beagle Channel* Arbitration award affirmed that it was common ground between the parties (Argentine and Chile) that the Boundary Treaty of 1881 'was intended to provide, and must be taken as constituting, a complete, definitive and final settlement of all territorial questions still outstanding at that time, so that nothing thereafter remained intentionally unallocated'.[13] Further consequences of the supremacy of the stability factor with regard to boundaries may be seen in the treatment of boundary treaties in the context of the *rebus sic stantibus* rule and State succession to treaties.[14]

The tenor, therefore, of the discussion of boundaries in international law is characterized by the perceived requirement for certainty. This militates against boundary changes and underlines the role played by acts of sovereignty by the parties with respect to the disputed areas. In other words, the criterion of effectiveness is of crucial importance. The notion of stability, which implies a state of affairs conducive to peaceful enjoyment, may also affect the content of any delimitation whether by joint discussions or by a third party. The Chairman of the tribunal in the *Indo-Pakistan Western Boundary (Rann of Kutch)* case, in referring to two deep inlets in dispute, noted that

> it would be inequitable to recognize these inlets as foreign[15] territory. It would be conducive to friction and conflict. The paramount consideration of promoting peace and stability in this region compels the recognition and confirmation that this territory, which is wholly surrounded by Pakistan territory, also be regarded as such.[16]

An important distinction is usually made between boundaries and frontiers. A boundary is a line separating States, whereas a frontier connotes a zone, having therefore width as well as length.[17] De Lapradelle regards a frontier as a zone of communication bound to a special legal, political, and economic regime in municipal and international law,[18] while Holdich noted that 'a frontier is but a vague and indefinite term until the boundary sets a hedge between it and the frontier of a neighbouring State'.[19] Kristoff pointed out that while a boundary is defined and regulated by international and municipal law, the frontier was a phenomenon of history and always unique. It was difficult to pin-point essential features of the frontier which are universally valid.[20] Historically, the earliest boundaries were in the form of separate zones, which Cukwurah has described as 'the extreme limit of the areas from which the people living within them obtained their necessary supplies of food at any given time'.[21] With the decline of nomadism and the rise of agricultural settlements, partition zones evolved, usually following natural barriers, as they were 'conspicuous, easily identifiable and physically unmistakable by any potential trespasser'.[22] In ancient Greece, imperial Rome, and during the Middle Ages, the concept of border zones predominated over fixed-line boundaries.[23] The notion of a strict, linear boundary is a relatively modern conception, the need for defined boundaries arising as States developed in the post-Westphalian era and populations expanded into border areas and communicated across boundary lines. Exact boundaries, however, could only develop when map-making and geographic techniques were sufficiently advanced to facilitate delimitations and demarcation.[24] To some extent, the doctrine of natural frontiers was an attempt to achieve precise boundaries in earlier centuries and was founded upon the assertion that certain natural features such as mountain ranges, forests, water, and deserts were preferable to artificial boundaries, which denoted 'such signs as have been purposely put up to indicate the way of the imaginary boundary line' and which consisted of 'posts, stones, bars, walls, trenches, roads, canals, buoys in the water and the like'.[25] However, as Boggs pointed out, a line marked by nature did not always imply that it constituted the best line to separate neighbouring peoples. The crest of a mountain range may not be a natural frontier where people of the same language and tradition inhabit both sides of the mountain.[26] Fenwick wrote that 'if by *natural* should be meant "desirable from an economic or social point of view", many present boundaries of States are admittedly unnatural whatever natural landmarks there may be to designate them'.[27] In other words, what constitutes a natural boundary is a complex of different factors of varying importance depending upon the circumstance of the case.[28] In reality, all boundaries are artificial in that they are established by persons—it is just that some coincide with geographic or ethnic divisions and others do not.

A distinction may also be drawn between boundary disputes and territorial disputes.[29] Boundaries are lines defining a territory, marking the limits of territorial sovereignty and jurisdiction, whereas territories are those areas over which such rights are exercised. Boundaries are part of the territory in that sense, of course, but they separate territories of different jurisdictions. While boundary disputes are concerned with either written or verbal or geographic uncertainties, territorial disputes involve large areas of land relatively and claims to title. The latter involve such rules of international law as relate to the acquisition of territorial sovereignty, for instance occupation, prescription, cession and conquest, while assertions of self-determination and historial continuity are frequently made. In the case of boundary disputes, the usual situation relates to ambiguities in the instruments creating the boundaries or to problems in fixing the borderline on the ground. Boundary problems in general concern disputes between adjacent States over the line to be drawn between their areas of sovereignty, whereas territorial disputes involve one State claiming to dislodge another from an area of its sovereignty on the ground of better title. However, there are a number of common elements that render it unwise to pursue this distinction too rigidly. Both boundary and territorial disputes ultimately involve the question of sovereignty over a defined piece of land, while many of the same types of State activity are relevant both to the question of title to territory and to the correct determination of a boundary. Examples would include manifestations of sovereign authority in various ways and geographical and historical factors, as well as any appropriate reactions or views adopted by the other party and third States. Treaties would be relevant in both cases, although more likely to be involved in disputes over boundaries. The best approach, therefore, would be to regard boundary disputes as a particular kind of territorial dispute, one that has evolved some special rules of its own.[30] Prescott distinguishes between territorial disputes, which emerge as a result of some quality of the borderland making it attractive to the claimant State, and positional disputes, which concern the actual location of the boundary.[31] While territorial disputes generally arise out of the superimposition of the border upon the cultural or physical landscape, as for example in many cases in the colonial partition of Africa or the granting of German-speaking areas south of the Brenner Pass to Italy,[32] positional disputes arise, according to Prescott, because of incomplete boundary evolution.[33] Such defects in the boundaries become a source of contention when the borderlands become utilized or developed, as for example the boundary delimitation between northern Nigeria and Niger, at the beginning of the century, unquestioned by France until it was discovered that an important communication route between Niger towns lay partially within British territory.[34]

Accordingly, although boundary, or positional, disputes may involve recourse to particular rules, such as the principle, for example, of the thalweg, the fact remains that such disputes concern, as do territorial disputes, both specific, or relatively specific, areas, and the display of sovereignty. Judge Huber, it should be noted, declares that the fact of peaceful and continuous display was one of the most important considerations in establishing boundaries between States[35] and that if no conventional line of sufficient topographical precision exists or if there are gaps in frontiers otherwise established or if a conventional line leaves room for doubt, 'the actual continuous and peaceful display of State functions is, in case of dispute, the sound and natural criterion of territorial sovereignty'.[36] This common reliance on display of sovereignty, depending always on the circumstances of the case, means that the two types of dispute are closer than some analyses would suggest.[37]

A number of views have been expressed concerning the nature and functions of boundaries. Ratzel regarded the boundary itself as an abstraction and the border area as the reality. The latter zone intimately reflected the power of the State itself and consisted of three zones, two of which were the periphery of the adjoining States and the third a central zone where there was a mingling of the two States. Ratzel held that one could not analyse a boundary separately from the State, since it was an integral element of it and one could not maintain the greater importance of the centre. He also believed that as the relationship between States altered so the boundary would change, as it was an indication of power.[38] Curzon talked in terms of natural and artificial boundaries, but distinguished between natural boundaries based on some physical feature and so-called natural boundaries, claimed by nations on grounds of ambition, expediency, or sentiment.[39] Artificial boundaries were divided into astronomical, mathematical, and referential types. Astronomical boundaries followed a parallel of latitude or a meridian, mathematical boundaries connected two specified points, and referential boundaries were defined with regard to some point or points and included arcs of circles and straight lines.[40] Curzon also emphasized the strategic role of boundaries, as did Holdich, who remarked that 'boundaries must be barriers—if not geographical and natural they must be artificial and strong as military device can make them'.[41] Fawcett criticized the division into natural and artificial boundaries and held that frontiers were distinct regions of transition, whose function was to protect the State.[42] De Lapradelle noted that 'le caractère marquant de la notion de frontière est son universalité d'acception'.[43] While peripheral flanking areas between States, i.e. frontiers, were governed by municipal law, a central zone or *territoire limitrophe* was subject to international law. This led into a twofold division of the whole problem of frontiers into delimitation and *voisinage*. Delimitation concerned the limits and method of establishment of frontier and *voisinage* concerned the effects of delimitation on the regime of the territory in question.[44] Rousseau, in fact, defined the concept of *voisinage* in international law as 'l'ensemble des problèms juridiques que pose la proximité existant entre États limitrophes et les rapports juridiques d'ordre divers qui en résultent tant pour ces États que pour leurs ressortissants'.[45] De Lapradelle held that only artificial frontiers existed. While boundaries drawn with reference to a natural feature, such as a river or a mountain, were 'derived artificial boundaries', boundaries astronomically, mathematically, or referentially calculated were 'artificial boundaries properly speaking'.[46] By this classification, it could be seen that all boundary delimitations were accomplished by persons in the light of perceived national interests.[47] De Lapradelle also referred to three stages in the evolution of a boundary. The preparation stage consists in formulating the principles applicable to the actual delimitation, the decision stage concerns the delimitation itself, and the execution stage consists of transcribing the delimitation on to the territory in question.[48] Boggs emphasized the changing role of boundaries and listed the various functions of boundaries in the light of persons and things.[49] His belief that one of the principal reasons for studying boundaries was the desire to determine what kinds of boundaries are 'good' and what kinds have been found to be bad[50] was criticized by Jones, who noted that 'each boundary is almost unique and therefore many generalizations are of doubtful validity'.[51] Prescott concludes that a review of the ideas regarding boundaries suggests that boundaries are of interest to many types of scholars and that most of the studies reflect the preoccupations of the period when written. It has also been generally accepted that one must consider the boundary in its overall territorial context and the dangers of generalizing about boundaries are being appreciated.[52] One clear distinction that Prescott, following Jones, does draw is between internal and international boundaries, since 'the presence or absence of overriding sovereignty is the crucial basis of classifying boundaries'.[53]

It is possible to classify boundaries in a number of ways in addition to the rather simplistic and discredited division into natural and artificial boundaries. Boggs elaborated a fourfold classification. Physical boundaries were those following a natural feature; geometric boundaries involved the use of straight lines, arcs, meridians, and so forth; anthropogeographic boundaries were closely related to human settlement factors; while compounded boundaries comprised elements of the preceding types.[54] Pounds, on the other hand, approached the problem historically and categorized boundaries in terms of the cultural development of the area. Boundaries could be antecedent, that is prior to the development of the 'cultural landscape'; subsequent, or drawn after such a development; superimposed, that is subsequent to cultural development but without regard to it; or relict, that is boundaries visible in the cultural landscape without any present political function.[55]

Pre-colonial Africa knew frontiers or zones rather than strict linear boundaries,[56] while colonial boundaries were in many cases originally established on basically geometric lines radiating from the coasts into the interior, generally paralleling European power relationships in the nineteenth century. Kapil writes that African international boundaries are irrelevant to the historical-cultural patterns of African development and that except for Ethiopia none of them delimits the outcome of traditional, historical processes. Ethnic factors were generally ignored in boundary-making.[57] Such boundaries therefore were superimposed on established cultural patterns, it was argued, and thus were inherently conflict-generating.

Two stages are particularly important in establishing a boundary.[58] Delimitation is the determination of the boundary line by treaty or otherwise and its expression in verbal terms, while demarcation is the physical demonstration of the delimitation on the ground by means of boundary posts and the like.[59] Tribunals have generally followed this distinction[60] but occasionally the terminology has been confused.[61] Usually the delimitation is political and established by diplomats, while the demarcation is a technical operation. Delimitation problems are more rare than demarcation disputes, since the latter often reflect the dangers of delimitation without precise geographic knowledge of the areas involved. The vast majority of Africa's borders were delimited by agreement between European powers at the end of the nineteenth and beginning of the twentieth centuries when knowledge of the geographic and ethnic conditions of the interior of the continent was limited. This was one reason for the heavy reliance upon geometric lines. Barbour calculated 'very approximately' that at the end of the 1950s something like 44 per cent of the boundary mileage in Africa was defined according to parallels and meridians, 30 per cent by straight lines, arcs of circles, and so on, and the remaining 26 per cent by reference to topographical features such as rivers, streams, watersheds, mountains, and valleys.[62] Demarcation commissions were in general severely restricted in their discretions when marking out the actual border, often with absurd results. For instance, the Anglo-German agreement of 1910 dealing with the Uganda–Ruanda border allowed the demarcation commission to depart from some of the delimited straight lines in order to make the boundary coincide with natural features, provided the deviations 'shall not, however, exceed five kilometres on either side of the straight lines and neither the total area of British territory nor the total area of German territory shall be altered thereby'.[63]

This has meant that, while there are relatively few delimitation disputes in Africa, there are a number of demarcation problems resulting from the difficulties in translating often ambiguous treaty provisions and administrative diversions into geographic reality.

The causes of territorial and boundary disputes are many and range from ethnic or historic irredentism, as in the Moroccan and Somali cases, to the attraction of natural resources, a factor which has stimulated a number of boundary and territorial disputes, and to the need for a diversion from internal pressures. Other elements may also be involved, such as ideological and personal antagonisms, as well as political manœuvrings to gain advantages often unrelated to the border issue itself.[64] A large number of African boundary disputes are quiescent and only erupt as a result of some kind of specific stimulus, whether economic or ideological. Occasionally such claims may stimulate a counter-claim as a reaction. This occurred, for instance, in the Algerian–Moroccan dispute when Algeria declared that it too could assert claims. However, African border disputes are in general characterized more by moderation than by excess, particularly when one considers the non-African establishment of many of the borders involved.

Africa possesses the greatest total length of land boundaries of any continent, because relative to its area it is the most politically divided continent. Most African States have borders with at least four or five other States, while Niger has borders with seven other States, Sudan with eight, and Zaïre with nine. On the other hand, Africa has the shortest coastline relative to area and the highest number of landlocked States of the continents. Zaïre, it should be noted, has an area of over 905,000 sq. miles and a sea front of some 30 miles.[65] However, the very instability inherent in the domestic and international environment of African boundary and territorial conflicts is a constraining factor, since it ensures that radical change in this area could have widespread and unpredictable consequences.

II. BOUNDARY TREATIES

Judge Bebler in the *Indo-Pakistan Western Boundary (Rann of Kutch)* case remarked as to the general origins of international boundaries that they

> have usually emerged by custom. They have become gradually well determined by mutual acquiescence and/or recognition by the neighbours concerned . . . Mutual

acquiescence and mutual recognition are therefore the most general origin of existing international boundaries. Very many of them still nowadays have no other legal foundation for their validity'.[66]

In the case of Africa, however, it would seem that the role of the international boundary treaty has been somewhat more prominent than Bebler's views would allow. The vast majority of African borders were laid down not as a result of prescription over a period of time, but by European treaties. The question of the validity and determination of such boundaries is therefore connected with the status in law of the particular treaties specifying such boundaries. This has raised two particular questions. Firstly, whether it could be argued that the demise of colonialism and the establishment of the principle of self-determination have resulted in a fundamental change in circumstances as regards particular boundary treaties, thus terminating the treaty or enabling a party or a successor to a party to the treaty to terminate it, and secondly, whether, in view of the dominant 'clean slate' principle governing new States and State succession to the treaties of its predecessor, such boundary treaties lapse upon independence.

(a) The rebus sic stantibus *Rule*

This rule states that a party to a treaty may unilaterally invoke as a ground for terminating or suspending the operation of the treaty the fact that there has been a fundamental change of circumstances from those which existed at the time of the conclusion of the treaty.[67] Fitzmaurice noted that few questions of treaty law were more controversial than the place of this doctrine. One could detect a marked reluctance by international and municipal courts actually to apply it, while not rejecting it in principle and professing to view it with sympathy. Although attractive in theory and possibly necessary in practice within limits, the rule could prove dangerous and could reduce the concept of *pacta sunt servanda* to a mere form of words.[68] Elias, indeed, referred to the view that the doctrine was somewhat frivolously invoked in the period between the World Wars.[69] The doctrine has been raised before international courts. In the *Nationality Decrees in Tunis and Morocco* case,[70] France argued that the establishment of the French protectorate over Morocco had *ipso facto* extinguished certain Anglo-French treaties.[71] France also raised the question of *rebus sic stantibus* in the *Free Zones of Upper Savoy and the District of Gex* case, stating that the provisions of 1815 establishing the customs-free zones had lapsed in view of the alteration of the particular factual situation.[72] Switzerland, however, argued *inter alia* that the doctrine did not apply to treaties creating territorial rights.[73] The court held that, in the light of the particular facts, it was unnecessary to consider the doctrine.[74] The rule has not been extensively examined in any other international cases,[75] although the International Court in the *Fisheries Jurisdiction* cases noted the existence of the doctrine in customary law.[76] Its basis may be seen in the desire to prevent an unnecessary burden on one of the parties to a treaty in the event of a fundamental change of circumstances and thus avoid the possibility of unlawful termination. The doctrine has also been seen by the new Afro-Asian States in particular as embodying a rule of crucial concern to them.[77]

In article 44 of the draft articles on the Law of Treaties prepared in 1963, it was provided that the doctrine did not apply 'to a treaty fixing a boundary'.[78] This formulation was retained in the 1966 draft articles. Australia suggested that the provision be slightly extended to cover all other determinations of territorial sovereignty in a treaty, while the Netherlands suggested that the exception to the *rebus sic stantibus* rule should apply 'to stipulations of a treaty which effect a transfer of territory or the settlement of a boundary, since such treaties often covered other issues as well'.[79] Waldock, the Special Rapporteur, agreed with these comments and felt that the provision should be revised to cover transfers of territories.[80] Canada proposed adding to the provision the phrase 'except if such a boundary is based directly on a thalweg or other natural phenomenon the physical location of which subsequently significantly altered as a result of a natural occurrence'.[81] The Special Rapporteur, however, correctly felt that the Canadian suggestion raised questions regarding the correct interpretation and application of the treaty in the light of changed geographical facts[82] and no more was heard of this proposal. Draft article 44 became draft article 59, paragraph 2 of which provided that: 'A fundamental change of circumstances may not be invoked: (*a*) as a ground for terminating or withdrawing from a treaty establishing a boundary'. The ILC commentary to this provision noted that some members of the Commission had suggested that the total exclusion of treaties establishing boundaries might be going too far and might indeed be inconsistent with the principle of self-determination, recognized in the Charter. The Commission, however, concluded that treaties establishing a boundary should be accepted as an exception to the rule, because otherwise the rule, instead of being an instrument of peaceful change, might become a source of dangerous frictions. With regard to self-determination, the Commission felt that it was, as envisaged in the Charter, an independent principle and that it might lead to confusion if in the context of the law of treaties it were presented as an application of the rule regarding *rebus sic stantibus*. This view must be seen as accurate. To have permitted the revision of nineteenth-century territorial arrangements, or those of any other era, on the grounds of the post-1945 principle of self-determination would have had the effect not only of ignoring inter-temporal law but of opening the door to a large number of territorial claims, particularly in Africa. The ILC also made the point by altering the phrase 'treaty fixing a boundary' to 'treaty establishing a boundary', so that not only delimitation treaties but also treaties of cession were to be covered.[83]

In the UN Conference on the Law of Treaties in 1968, the United States argued that the proposed article 59(2) was too restrictive and failed to cover important groups of treaties, such as those establishing territorial status or settling territorial disputes, while not establishing boundaries. Examples were given of the US–UK condominium agreement over Canton and Enderbury islands, agreements where parties agreed not to press claims in the light of mutual concessions and treaties dealing with the aim of settling boundary disputes in the spirit of co-operation, such as US–Mexican treaties. If the *rebus sic stantibus* rule were to apply, it was argued, the object of such treaties would be defeated.[84] It was suggested that the phrase 'or otherwise establishing territorial status' be added to article 59(2)a.[85] However, this was rejected by the Committee of the Whole by 43 votes to 14, with 28 abstentions.[86] It was felt that the American formulation was far too broad. Cuba argued that it would be incompatible with self-determination.[87] The ILC provision regarding *rebus sic stantibus* and boundary treaties was generally supported at the UN Conference,[88] the need to preserve peace being particularly noted in this context.[89] Afghanistan, however, stated that boundary treaties should not be exempted from the general rule as it might be contrary to self-determination and treaties imposed during the colonial era for colonial or military reasons should be subject to the *rebuc sic stantibus* doctrine.[90] Morocco declared that draft article 59(2)a was open to objection and particularly criticized the view of the ILC that treaties of cession were to be included in the provison.[91] Syria expressed a similar criticism and noted that stability and finality could not be expected if they were to be achieved at the expense of justice and self-determination or by upholding colonial treaties, under which territory was ceded contrary to the wishes of the inhabitants.[92] Poland argued against this that unequal colonial treaties were void *ab initio* as they conflicted with norms of *jus cogens* and they had thus no relevance to draft article 59. Paragraph (2)a was essential to the maintenance of international peace and security as provided in the UN Charter and was a direct consequence in the law of treaties of the rule in article 2 of the Charter regarding the territorial integrity of States.[93] In the event, a proposal to delete paragraph (2)a was not put to the vote[94] and article 62(2) of the Convention on the Law of Treaties provides that 'A fundamental change of circumstances may not be invoked as a ground for terminating or withdrawing from a treaty: (*a*) if the treaty establishes a boundary'.

(*b*) *State Succession*

The question of State succession to treaties has been the subject of much debate, particularly in the light of the decolonization process.[95] Ultimately, the Vienna Convention on Succession of States in Respect of Treaties declared in article 16 that 'a newly independent State is not bound to maintain in force or to become a party to, any treaty by reason only of the fact that at the date of the succession of States the treaty was in force in respect of the territory to which the succession of States relates'.[96] This marked the victory of the 'clean slate' theory as against the view that 'succession rather than non-succession should be the rule'.[97] Accordingly, the question is raised as to boundary treaties.[98] An acceptance of the clean slate principle here would mean that new States, upon gaining independence, would be able to denounce treaties establishing boundaries and thus legitimately claim not to be bound by the former borders. It would open the way to claims for further territory. Of relevance also in this discussion are the principles of sovereign equality of States and self-determination of peoples.

Waldock, in his first report on Succession of States and Governments in Respect of Treaties, declared that

> the weight both of opinion and practice seems clearly to be in favour of the view that boundaries established by treaties remain untouched by the mere fact of a succession. The opinion of jurists seems, indeed, to be unanimous on the point even if their reasoning may not always be exactly the same. In State practice the unanimity may not be quite so absolute; but the State practice in favour of the continuance in force of boundaries established by treaty appears to be such as to justify the conclusion that a general rule of international law exists to that effect.[99]

1. *The Opinion of Jurists*

Most writers emphasize that boundary treaties devolve upon successor States despite the change of sovereignty.[100] The basic reason for the rule is accepted as that of the necessity to maintain the stability and continuity of boundaries as an essential condition of international life as emphasized in the recognized principle of respect for the territorial integrity of States.[101] A number of authors express the process by which this is accomplished in terms of a transmutation of the provisions of the boundary treaty into a territorial settlement subsisting in its own right. Lester writes that upon ratification the boundary agreement is deemed to be executed and thereafter operates as a kind of conveyance. The successor State thus succeeds 'not to the treaty but to the frontiers of its territory as it does to the other facts of its new international life'.[102] Therefore, upon execution, the boundary terms lose their contractual character and may be severed from non-boundary provisions. This will not prevent, however, the parties from referring to the terms of the treaty in any subsequent dispute as to title.[103] The result is that the boundary terms take on a life of their own, distinct from their conventional origin.[104] Keith, in discussing the continuity of boundary provisions, emphasized that 'the real fact is, of course, that a treaty of this sort is no longer a contract; the contract has passed into a conveyance, and the transaction cannot, therefore, be affected by the fact that one of the parties to the original conveyance has changed'.[105] Another possible explanation put forward is that the principle of *nemo dat quod non habet* applies in such cases. In other words, the predecessor State may transfer to the successor State only the territorial extent of its own competence. O'Connell notes that 'since a State can acquire from another only so much territory as that other possessed, the latter's boundary treaties with neighbouring States delimit the extent of the territory absorbed'.[106] However, this is linked with the territorial theory, for 'if a boundary treaty merely defines a frontier, then it is instantly executed, and what is inherited is not the treaty but the territorial extent of sovereignty'.[107] The International Law Association adopted a series of eight resolutions on State succession to treaties in 1968, and the final one provided that 'when a treaty which provides for the delimitation of a national boundary between two States has been executed in the sense that the boundary has been delimited and no further action needs to be taken, the treaty has spent its force and what is succeeded to is not the treaty but the extent of national territory so delimited'.[108] Where, however, a boundary treaty provides for future action to delimit it, or provides for future reciprocal rights in relation to the boundary, it is considered that the question whether the treaty is or is not succeeded to should be governed by the general presumptions of continuity envisaged by it for all treaties of the predecessor State.[109] Thus, in a sense, one is not considering a question of succession to boundary treaties, but rather succession to the existing and delimited territorial dimensions of the predecessor State.[110]

Although this exception to the clean slate rule has been virtually universally accepted in doctrine, some authors have tended to be rather cautious. Mochi Onory writes that boundary disputes often concern the maintenance or otherwise of rights guaranteed in connection with, and as a condition of, the settlement of the boundary and that the dispute over these rights tends to provoke the reopening of the boundary itself,[111] while Udina notes that succession occurs only through the tacit agreement of the neighbouring State.[112] The latter proposition would appear not to be supported by either international doctrine or State practice. One should also note at this stage that both the ILC and the UN Conference on the Law of Treaties held that boundary treaties constituted a special category forming an exception to the general rule that a fundamental change of circumstances may be invoked as a ground for terminating, withdrawing from, or suspending the operation of a treaty.

2. *State Practice*

The Special Rapporteur of the ILC felt that the attitudes adopted by States with regard to article 62(2)a of the Convention on the Law of Treaties were extremely pertinent in the context of succession to treaties[113] and that the weight of the evidence of State practice and of legal opinion in favour of the view that in principle a boundary settlement is unaffected by the occurrence of a succession of States was 'powerfully reinforced' by the decision to exempt treaties establishing boundaries from the *rebus sic stantibus* rule.[114] Although certain differences are evident between the expression of the exception to the *rebus sic stantibus* rule and the provision relating to succession to boundary treaties,[115] the connection between the two reinforces the characterization of boundary treaties as *sui generis* when compared with other treaties.[116]

It is also to be noted that in the *Temple* case,[117] the International Court did not appear to doubt that the 1904 treaty between France and Siam (Thailand) establishing the boundary between Cambodia and Thailand was binding as between these two. Indeed, both Cambodia and Thailand seemed to assume that in the case of a newly independent State, there would be a succession not only in respect of a boundary settlement but also treaty provisions ancillary to such settlement. Thailand felt that succession would be limited to stipulations forming part of the boundary settlement itself, while Cambodia considered that it would extend to provisions in a subsequent treaty directly linked to it.[118]

Practice reveals that, in general, States have accepted the principle of succession to boundary settlements embodied in treaties. The United States, while not accepting that it was bound by United Kingdom treaties after independence,[119] did accept the previously established boundaries. In 1856 the United State's Secretary of State wrote that

> the United States regard it as an established principle of the public law and of international right that when a European colony in America becomes independent it succeeds to the territorial limits of the colony as it stood in the hands of the present country. That is the doctrine which Great Britain and the United States concurred in adopting in the negotiations of Paris, which terminated this country's war of independence.[120]

This was followed in *US* v *Texas*, where it was held that the Texan boundary with the United States was that established in a treaty of 1828 between the United States and Mexico.[121]

As far as African practice is concerned, the OAU has adopted a policy of succession to boundaries. Resolution 16 (I) of 1964 proclaimed that 'all member States pledge themselves to respect the borders existing on their achievement of national independence'.[122] Only Somalia and Morocco did not accept this. Although Tanzania declared in 1961 that bilateral treaties, concluded by the United Kingdom on behalf of the territory of Tanganyika, were to remain in force for a period of two years and thereafter it would regard 'such of those treaties which could not, by the application of the rules of customary international law, be considered as otherwise surviving as having terminated',[123] as regards boundary treaties it has adopted a different attitude. Such boundary agreements were deemed to have survived independence, for example those defining the Kenya–Tanzania border, and those regarding the boundaries with Rwanda and Burundi.[124] TheTanzania–Malawi border is, however, subject to dispute.[125]

(i) *The Somali Disputes.* Somalia has two boundary disputes with Ethiopia and one with Kenya. Its claims to Ethiopian and Kenyan territory are based primarily on self-determination[126] and are not strictly claims that as a successor State it is able to denounce treaties concluded by its predecessor States. However, it did denounce the 1897 treaty between Great Britain and Ethiopia and has stated that it 'does not recognize the legal validity of treaties concluded between foreign colonial powers without the consent or knowledge and against the interests of the

Somali people'.[127] Such unrecognized treaties included, in addition to the 1897 one, the 1908 Ethiopian–Italian treaty and the 1924 Anglo-Italian treaty.[128] The boundary between Ethiopia and the former British Somaliland was defined in the 1897 agreement between the Ethiopian emperor and the United Kingdom. By this treaty, Ethiopia acquired territory inhabited by Somali nomads. An exchange of letters annexed to this treaty provided that tribes on either side of the frontier would be permitted to cross for grazing purposes.[129] However, these grazing rights were not put into effect until 1954 when a new agreement was concluded between Ethiopia and Britain.[130] In April 1960 the British government announced that, upon the independence of British Somaliland, the provisions of the 1897 treaty should be regarded as remaining in force between Ethiopia and the successor State while the terms of the 1954 agreement relating to grazing rights and certain facilities accorded to British Somaliland with regard to Ethiopian territory would lapse.[131] On 5 June 1960 Ethiopia declared that upon British Somaliland's independence the grazing rights permitted under the 1954 agreement would be regarded as 'automatically invalid';[132] this was followed after Somalia's independence by a statement that Somalia would not acknowledge the validity of the 1897 treaty.[133]

The boundary between Ethiopia and the former Italian Somaliland was less clear. By the 1896 treaty between Italy and Ethiopia, following the Italian defeat at Adowa, Italy was obliged to cede Somalia-inhabited territory to Ethiopia. The definition of the boundary was left to the 1908 treaty between Italy and Ethiopia, but the failure to demarcate it contributed to the Italian attack on Ethiopia in 1936.[134] In 1941 Britain established a military administration in the area and defined a provisional administrative line. This became the *de facto* boundary during the trusteeship of Somalia[135] and constituted the border upon independence. It is Somalia's assertion that its borders with Ethiopia are 'provisional administrative boundaries pending final demarcation and solution of the dispute'.[136]

The boundary between Kenya and Somalia was defined in the Anglo-Italian treaty of 1924,[137] by which Jubaland was transferred to Italian Somaliland in pursuance of the Treaty of London, 1915. The Treaty of London had offered Italy territorial gains in Africa if it joined the war against Germany.[138] This boundary was also disputed by Somalia.[139] Somalia's view has been that Ethiopia and Kenya are 'unlawfully exercising sovereignty over Somali territories to which they are not entitled'.[140] This is because 'the *de facto* Somali–Ethiopian and Somali–

Kenyan boundaries are based on the provision of illegal treaties which are in conflict with prior treaties of protection signed between protecting colonial powers and the Somali people'.[141] Ethiopia and Kenya argue, on the other hand, that the treaties defining the respective boundaries are valid and binding as determining the limits of sovereignty of the States concerned.[142] Although it was open to Somalia to argue, at least, on the basis of the non-succession of new States to boundary treaties, it does not appear to have actually done so. Its basic argument has related to the supremacy of the principle of self-determination, which it has defined to refer to the free choice of inhabitants of both colonial and independent States. It declared that 'the Charter recognition of the right to self-determination therefore prevails over rights which Somalia's neighbours claim under earlier treaties'.[143] The fact that Somalia seems to have refrained from expressing the view that as a successor State it is not bound by the boundary agreements entered into by its predecessor States of British Somaliland and Italian Somaliland is particularly interesting. It appears not to have wished to establish such a precedent. On the other hand, to have accepted unreservedly the opposite proposition, namely that boundary agreements constitute an exception to the clean slate doctrine of succession to treaties, would have had the effect of undermining its own position. Accordingly, it declared that 'no rigid universal principle could be laid down to govern all treaties on boundaries and territorial regimes unless saving clauses were incorporated to provide for special situations'.[144] Somalia proposed that the draft articles relating to boundaries and territorial regimes should be deleted as 'international boundaries and territorial arrangements were matters which fell essentially within the domain of bilateral negotiations, conciliation and arbitration'.[145] Needless to say, Ethiopia and Kenya took the position that boundary treaties were an exception to the clean slate rule and therefore bound successor States.[146]

(ii) *The Algerian–Moroccan Boundary.*[147] In 1845 France and Morocco signed the treaty of Lalla-Marnia, which defined in detail the Moroccan–Algerian[148] boundary from the coast to some 80 miles inland. Article IV provided, however, that in the Sahara 'there is no territorial limit to establish between the two countries as the land cannot be ploughed but is used only as grazing land'. Each sovereign was to exercise full rights over their respective subjects in the Sahara. It was also provided that a number of named villages were accepted as belonging to the parties, but that 'the territory which is located south of the villages in uninhabitable and delimitation thereof would be superfluous'. These grazing grounds could be used by a list of nomad cattle-herding groups, including those from

Morocco and Algeria.[149] French forces, however, gradually moved into the area. Although an official French map of 1848 placed the oases of Tuat in Morocco, France claimed in the 1880s they were in Algeria and militarily occupied them in 1899–1900.[150] The treaty of 1901 included the Colomb-Bechar area as part of Algeria and in 1912 the frontier was demarcated by the so-called Varnier line between Colomb-Bechar and Morocco, which was recognized by the Sultan of Morocco in 1928 as an administrative and fiscal frontier.[151] In 1912 Morocco became a French protectorate. French maps throughout the administration period conflicted as to whether particular areas were in Algeria or Morocco and the precise outline of the Varnier line was subject to various interpretations. In 1938 Colonel Trinquet, a French administrator in Morocco, proposed a new boundary which would have placed most of the desert region in Morocco, but it was rejected by the French government. However, the Tindouf area (placed within Algeria) remained under Franco-Moroccan administration until 1952.[152]

Morroco recognized the treaty of Lalla-Marnia, but not subsequent agreements, and contended that French encroachments upon her territory had violated her sovereignty and could not therefore act as a ground for claims by Algeria as successor to France.[153] In its comments on the draft articles dealing with succession to treaties, Morocco declared that to take account only of treaties, many of which had been concluded to the disadvantage of the decolonized States, was tantamount to perpetuating the effects of colonization.[154] It could be argued that Morocco, in accepting the 1845 treaty as the starting-point for the definition of its frontier line with Algeria, is merely disputing the interpretation of that agreement.[155] However, the Sahara area in question was not even delimited in this treaty and subsequent agreements contain an element of ambiguity, unless one considers them in the light of the actual boundary in the sense of *de facto* possession at the time of Algerian and Moroccan independence.[156] Therefore, the principle of territorial integrity in the light of *de facto* possession pending independence becomes crucial with regard to the definition of the boundary, while the narrower question of succession to boundary treaties does assume in the circumstances of the case a lesser role. Again, it is interesting to note that Morocco does not appear to have argued that as a successor State it may repudiate the boundary agreements of the predecessor State; it has argued rather that issues of historical rights and territorial integrity of its pre-colonial empire override the general principle of the inviolability of the colonial borders.[157]

(iii) *Other Cases*. A number of other cases may be cited with regard to the practice of States relating to succession to boundary treaties. In the convention of 1930 between the United States and Great Britain for the delimitation of the boundary between the Philippine archipelago and the State of North Borneo, certain rights and obligations were assumed by the United States. Upon the independence of the Philippines in 1946, the United Kingdom recognized that the former had succeeded to the United States rights and obligations under the 1930 agreement.[158] Following the independence of India and Pakistan, the United Kingdom made a statement with regard to the continuing in force of the treaty of Kabul of 1921 defining the boundary between British India and Afghanistan. The United Kingdom noted that, whereas certain provisions, being political in nature or relating to continuous exchange of diplomatic missions, did not devolve to the successor State (Pakistan), 'any executed clauses such as those providing for the establishment of an international boundary or, rather, what had been done already under executed clauses of the treaty, could not be affected whatever the position about the treaty itself might be'.[159] Other cases of disputed borders really appear to concern treaties not fully delimiting boundaries or where the validity of such treaties is questioned. The issue of succession therefore merely provides an opportunity for the raising of the problems.[160] The conclusion, therefore, that State practice has recognized that boundary treaties constitute an exception to the clean slate principle of succession to treaties appears incontestable.[161]

3. *The International Law Commission and the Vienna Convention on Succession of States in Respect of Treaties*

Article 4 of Waldock's draft articles on succession to treaties declared that 'nothing in the present articles shall be understood as affecting the continuance in force of a boundary established by or in conformity with a treaty prior to the occurrence of a succession'.[162] The point was made that the provision meant only that the other articles dealing with the application or cessation of treaties did not affect established boundaries.[163] In the draft articles prepared by the Special Rapporteur in 1972, two alternatives were posited with regard to the question of succession to boundary treaties. Alternative A noted that:

> 1. The continuance in force of a treaty which established a boundary is not affected by reason only of the occurrence of a succession of States in respect of a party.
>
> 2. In such a case the treaty is considered as in force in respect of the successor State from the date of the succession of States, with the exception of any

provisions which by reason of their object and purpose are to be considered as relating only to the predecessor State.

Alternative B stated that:

1. A Succession of States shall not by reason only of its occurrence affect the continuance in force of a boundary settlement which has been established by a treaty.
2. In such a case the boundary settlement is to be considered as comprising any provisions of the treaty relating to the boundary.[164]

The difference between the two formulations relates essentially as to whether it is the treaty itself or the boundary situation established by a treaty which devolves upon the successor State. In favour of the former, it could be said that treaty interpretation may be required in order to define the boundary properly and that certain ancillary provisions may be stipulated as part of the boundary regime created by the treaty which, if held not to devolve on a succession of States, might be said to change materially the boundary settlement. To support the latter, it could be argued that a boundary treaty has constitutive effects and it is the legal and factual situation thus created which passes to the successor State rather than the treaty.[165] In the event, the latter approach was adopted.[166] Draft article 29 on boundary regimes provided thus that 'A Succession of States shall not as such affect: (*a*) a boundary established by a treaty; or (*b*) obligations and rights established by a treaty and relating to the regime of a boundary.'[167] This is in accordance with practice and doctrine, it is believed, since the succession *ipso facto* of a boundary treaty might involve the continuance of provisions not directly related to the creation of the boundary that might prove unacceptable to the successor State. More importantly, it is believed that the essence of the exception to the clean slate rule of succession is due to the centrality of the concept and consequences of territorial sovereignty in international law, with regard to stability and certainty in international relations and the maintenance of international peace and security. It is, of course, also true that international society in its present form is firmly based upon the notion of State sovereignty, territorially defined; therefore, one can accept that boundary treaties in establishing a particular regime give birth to an objective situation which constitutes a legal fact for the international community.[168]

Draft article 29 as finally adopted[169] was accepted by the Vienna Conference on Succession of States In Respect of Treaties as article 11. It was approved by the Committee of the Whole without a vote,[170] and the

Convention on Succession of States in Respect of Treaties was adopted on 23 August 1978 by 82 votes to 0, with 2 abstentions (France and Switzerland).[171] A few further points remain to be considered, however, regarding the doctrine of the boundary exception to the general rule, embodied in article 16 of the Convention.

(*a*) The basis of the exception to the clean slate rule was generally accepted to lie in the requirements of the international community with regard to the maintenance of international peace and security. The Special Rapporteur in 1974, Sir Francis Vallat, declared that acceptance of the idea that a bilateral boundary treaty could be swept aside by a succession of States 'would result in chaos. It was unthinkable that it should become necessary to renegotiate a boundary whenever a succession of States occurred.'[172] It was pointed out that 'the disturbance of existing boundaries is much more likely to create chaos than their maintenance'.[173] This view was also put by a number of the members of the ILC,[174] and by a number of governments.[175] A number of members[176] and governments[177] expressed the view that the exception was already part of customary international law. Zambia was gratified that the ILC was giving effect to the OAU border resolution of 1964.[178]

(*b*) The limits of the exception to the general rule were fairly clearly expressed. The Special Rapporteur noted that the article was a saving clause of limited character, dealing only with the effects of succession *qua* succession and not touching upon questions pertaining to the international law of treaties. The article was (as indeed was the article concerning other territorial regimes) concerned with the results of certain treaties and not with the treaties themselves. The words 'established by a treaty' meant, therefore, 'validly established by a valid treaty'. The intention was to refer to situations lawfully and validly created.[179] In other words, the article could not operate to legalize a boundary founded upon an unlawful treaty.[180] Nor was the provision concerned with a situation created otherwise than by a treaty.[181] Hambro, as a member of the ILC, made the point that draft article 29 did not state or imply that boundary treaties were sacrosanct and would last for ever, it simply stated that succession of States as such would not affect those treaties.[182] The article did not prevent the settlement of boundary disputes by accepted methods, such as negotiation and arbitration.[183] Nor could it affect boundary situations, which could be lawfully challenged. Thus, where a boundary treaty failed to delimit adequately and clearly the proposed boundary or where it validity could be challenged on any of a series of grounds, the article was of little influence one way or the other. The article would be of no direct value where the boundary was contested in the light of other principles, such as territorial integrity or self-determination. The Special Rapporteur stressed that 'the mere occurrence of a succession of States would be considered neither to consecrate the existing boundary if it is open to challenge nor deprive it of its character as a legally established boundary, if such it was at the date of the succession of States'.[184]

(*c*) The principle of self-determination was clearly of concern with regard to the topic of State succession in general and the question of boundary agreements in particular. The Special Rapporteur noted in 1969 that the traditional principle of State succession whereby a new State begins its treaty relations with a clean slate was certainly consistent with self-determination, while the approach of the International Law Association,[185] formulated in terms of a presumption in favour of the transmission of the treaties of the predecessor State to the successor State, may raise questions with regard to self-determination.[186] The comments made by governments in 1974 demonstrated 'overwhelming support for the clean slate doctrine',[187] which, it was felt, was the main implication of the principle of self-determination.[188] The clean slate principle was chosen by the ILC as the basic provision of the draft articles relating to newly independent States and incorporated in article 16 of the Vienna Convention. With regard to the exception to the rule in that case of boundary treaties, it was possible to argue that self-determination was being overriden by the continuity principle. Zambia, in particular, stated that in its draft articles relating to boundary and other territorial regimes, the ILC had appeared to cut across the principles of self-determination, equal rights, and the sovereign equality of States. Under both the Vienna Convention on Treaties and customary law, a State could only be bound by a treaty through an act of will establishing consent to be bound and this also applied to boundary regimes.[189] The Special Rapporteur, however, correctly pointed out that in the case of a newly independent State, which has acquired independence by the exercise of self-determination, 'it may well be said that it can only acquire the territory in respect of which self-determination has been exercised and not part of the territory of a neighbouring State'. Reference was also made to the need to consider the principle of respect for the territorial integrity of States.[190]

This approach, which is consistent with the accepted definition of the right to self-determination, was to some extent endorsed by Kenya, which stressed that 'in the event of a succession, the successor State replaced the predecessor State as far as boundaries were concerned not because of the boundary treaty, but because of the mere fact of the existence of such boundaries. In such a case it was irrelevant and confusing to raise the issue of self-determination.'[191] It may also be noted that the treatment of the principle of self-determination as an independent principle, which should not be imported ambiguously into other branches of the law, was adopted also with regard to the law of treaties.[192]

(c) Conclusions

The accepted approach that neither the *rebus sic stantibus* rule nor the clean slate doctrine is based in law upon the principle of self-determination,[193] in addition to preventing some confusion, obviated the need to posit exceptions to the legal right of self-determination with regard to treaties establishing boundaries and boundary regimes. The centrality of the concept of territory in international law, coupled with the need to ensure the stability and finality of boundaries in the interests of international peace and security, has produced a situation in which the delimitation of sovereignty by an international agreement remains binding despite State succession or a fundamental change of circumstances. Such an approach refers only to boundary treaties. Whether or not a legitimate territorial claim on other grounds may or may not be made is another question, as is the challenging of the validity of the treaty itself. But the fact that a treaty is the most convenient and most utilized method of resolving territorial and boundary issues means that the exceptions to the *rebus sic stantibus* and clean slate rules are of considerable importance. Their acceptance by African States, despite some reservations by a couple of African countries, reinforces the legal validity of colonial territorial adjustments and thus underlines the requirement to respect the colonial borders as at the date of independence. It is also noteworthy that the opposition by, for example, Somalia and Morocco to the principles examined above has been carefully formulated and has by no means consisted of outright hostility. It is Afghanistan that has appeared to reject most strongly the relevance and applicability of such principles. These principles may also be seen as reinforcing the accepted definition of the right to self-determination in international law, that is in terms of the pre-independent entity territorially defined by the administering power exercising its right to sovereignty so delimited in space.

The fact that boundary agreements may establish objective legal circumstances which may subsist independently of the particular treaty itself means that provisions in such agreements are severable when dealing with the creation of a boundary. This was the view adopted by the United Kingdom with regard to the Ethiopia–British Somaliland boundary and is to be regarded as correct.[194]

III. OTHER TERRITORIAL REGIMES

More controversial than the question of treaties establishing boundaries is the problem of treaties creating other territorial regimes. Such treaties have been termed 'dispositive', or 'real' or 'localized'.[195] Agreements may be 'localized' if they: '(*a*) are in the nature of objective territorial regimes created in the interests of one nation or the community of nations; (*b*) are applied locally in virtue of territorial application clauses; (*c*) touch or concern a particular area of land.'[196] In such cases, it is argued, these territorial provisions devolve upon a successor State.[197] Boundary treaties have been treated as a species of such dispositive treaties.[198] However, there is an important difference. As Waldock noted, in the case of a boundary established by a treaty one is concerned with a legal situation resulting from the execution of the treaty, whereas localized treaty stipulations involve executory obligations and therefore may appear to raise a question of succession in respect of treaty obligation as well as one of the continuance of a legal situation.[199] In addition, of course, whereas a State may accept that it must exercise its sovereignty within territorial limits established by its predecessor, it may be reluctant to accept the limitations upon its sovereignty by restrictions imposed by a previous authority which continue in an open and apparent fashion. In a sense, the principles of self-determination and the sovereign equality of States may appear more offended in the instances of dispositive treaties than with regard to boundary agreements.[200]

The International Court in the *Free Zones* case appeared to endorse the principle that certain treaties of a territorial character are binding *ipso jure* upon a successor State,[201] although the extent of the principle was in doubt.[202] The Committee of Jurists dealing with the *Aaland Islands* question felt that Finland was bound to respect the provisons of the 1856 treaty between France, the United Kingdom, and Russia, according to which the latter agreed to the demilitarization of the Aaland Islands. These provisions 'constituted a special international status relating to military considerations, for the Aaland Islands'. Finland, by declaring itself independent and claiming recognition, could not escape from 'the obligations imposed on it by such a settlement of European interests'.[203]

(a) African Practice

(i) *US Military Bases in Morocco*. In 1950 France and the United States signed an agreement providing for five US military bases in Morocco.[204] This was deemed to be pursuant to the treaty of Fez of 1912 by which Morocco became a French protectorate, permitting it 'to proceed to such military occupation of the Moroccan territory as it might deem necessary for the maintenance of good order and the security of commercial transactions'.[205] Upon Moroccan independence in 1956, the government declared that it did not recognize the 1950 agreement, which constituted a violation of its sovereignty.[206] The Franco-Moroccan Declaration of 1956 terminated the treaty of Fez, while the protocol annexed to it provided that pending the conclusion of new agreements the 'present status of the French army in Morocco shall remain unchanged'.[207] It was accepted that the continued rights of the US forces were dependent upon the status of the French army.[208] In the Franco-Moroccan accord of May 1956, it was suggested that Morocco would not maintain those treaties concluded by France on its behalf which had been the subject of Moroccan comment,[209] while in a note to France, Morocco reserved its position with regard to the 1950 agreement.[210] The United States recognized Moroccan sovereignty over the US bases in 1957 and 1959[211] and agreed to withdraw all its forces by the end of 1963.[212] The United States did not seek to recover the $410 million invested in the base.[213] However, as Udokang rightly notes, neither France, Morocco, nor the United States seemed to hold that the 1950 agreement had created a 'real' or 'localized' right on Moroccan territory in favour of the United States which would be binding upon Morocco.[214] It may be suggested that the personal and political nature of military agreements is such as to override any territorial aspects and thus prevent the operation of any principle of devolution to a successor State.[215]

(ii) *The Belbase Agreements of 1921 and 1951.* Following the First World War, the former German East African territories were given to Britain and Belgium as mandated territories. The fact that the eastern region, Tanganyika, was awarded to Britain meant that the Belgian-administered territories of Ruanda and Urundi, as well as the Congo, were cut off from their natural port of Dar es Salaam. In 1921 Britain and Belgium concluded an agreement whereby the latter was granted a lease in perpetuity of port sites in Dar es Salaam and Kigoma (on Lake Tanganyika). Various transit facilities and customs exemptions were also provided for.[216] In 1951 a further agreement was entered into which provided for a change in the site at Dar es Salaam, but otherwise the 1921 treaty was continued.[217] Belgium spent a considerable sum in developing the port facilities at the leased sites. Nine days before independence, the Prime Minister of Tanganyika declared that it intended to treat both agreements as void and to resume possession of the sites.[218] However, Tanganyika's objection was not with regard to all pre-independence agreements dealing with territorial rights. It noted that it had no objection to the enjoyment by foreign States of special facilities in its territory, if such facilities 'had been granted in a manner fully compatible with our sovereign rights and our new status of complete independence'.[219] The problem with regard to the Belbase agreements was that they had been granted 'in perpetuity' by a mandatory authority that did not have the competence to bind the territory in perpetuity. The Prime Minster stated that 'in appearing to bind the territory of Tanganyika for all time, the United Kingdom was trying to do something which it did not have the power to do'.[220] In 1962 Tanganyika gave notice of its request for the evacuation of the sites, but the now independent States of Congo (Leopoldville), Rwanda, and Burundi claimed to have succeeded to Belgium's rights under the 1921 and 1951 agreements.[221] Discussions were held between the parties as regards the use of the port facilities, but it does not appear that new arrangements have been concluded and *de facto* the port facilities are being operated as before.[222] In the event, the fact that Tanganyika rested its argument on the limited competence of the mandatory power to bind the territory might appear to mean that it accepted that binding territorial provisions could devolve upon successor States in other circumstances.

(iii) *The Nile Waters Agreement of 1929*. This agreement between Britain and Egypt provided that, save with the previous agreement of the Egyptian government, no works were to be undertaken by Britain in its territories which would affect adversely the quantity of water arriving in Egypt from the Nile.[223] Egypt was given the right to construct in the Sudan works on the Nile, subject to prior agreements with the local authorities to safeguard local interests. Such works would, however, remain under the direct control of the Egyptian government. Upon independence, the Sudan denied the continued validity of the 1929 agreement.[224] Sudan did not dispute Egypt's rights in the Nile waters, but denied that it was bound after independence with regard to the burdensome incidences of the agreement.[225] In 1959 Sudan and Egypt concluded an agreement providing for additional regulation of the Nile waters on the basis of existing rights.[226]

(b) The Vienna Convention on Succession of States in Respect of Treaties, 1978

Practice would appear to accept that territorial treaties may devolve upon successor States, although the precise definition of such treaties remains the problem.[227] The ILC took the view that such treaties constituted another exception to the clean slate rule. Despite some reservations by ILC members[228] and by some governments,[229] the Vienna Convention accepted the concept. Article 12 provides that:

1. A succession of States does not as such affect:
(*a*) obligations relating to the use of any territory, or to restrictions upon its use, established by a treaty for the benefit of any territory of a foreign State and considered as attaching to the territories in question;
(*b*) rights established by a treaty for the benefit of any territory and relating to the use, or to restrictions upon the use, of any territory of a foreign State and considered as attaching to the territories in question.

2. A succession of States does not as such affect:
(*a*) obligations relating to the use of any territory, or to restrictions upon its use, established by a treaty for the benefit of a group of States or of all States and considered as attaching to that territory;
(*b*) rights established by a treaty for the benefit of a group of States or of all States and relating to the use of any territory, or to restrictions upon its use, and considered as attaching to that territory.

3. The provisions of the present article do not apply to treaty obligations of the predecessor State providing for the establishment of foreign military bases on the territory to which the succession of States relates.

IV. THE DELIMITATION AND DEMARCATION OF AFRICAN BOUNDARIES[230]

In the definition and recognition of international boundaries in the interests of stability and finality, a number of factors are or may be crucial. Where a boundary has been delimited by treaty and demarcated on the ground, a State may yet seek to maintain that it is not bound by that arrangement on the grounds of, for example, ethnic or historical claims. Where a boundary has been delimited but not demarcated, problems may arise as to the application in practice of the treaty provisions. Thus issues of treaty interpretation, acquiescence, and estoppel, and the role of particular administrative acts will be of relevance. But where a boundary has not been delimited, the question of its positioning will basically depend upon either mutual agreement or actual practice on the ground. In all cases, the value of acts of sovereignty is high, although the role played by such acts will depend upon all the circumstances of the case in question.

(a) Delimitation Disputes

In some cases, there may be no delimitation of the boundary at all or a disputed delimitation.

(i) *The Ethiopian–Somali Dispute.* In 1884 and 1886 the British government concluded a series of agreements with the leaders of the five tribes inhabiting the Somali coast region. One group of agreements involved a pledge by the Somalis not to cede or otherwise alienate any portion of the tribal lands to anyone accept the British government,[231] while a second group of agreements provided for the protection of such tribes by the British Crown. The tribes also pledged not to enter into relations with foreign powers without the knowledge and approval of the British government.[232] However, the extent of the land owned by the Somali tribes was unclear since written records of tribal limits apparently did not exist.[233] This resulted in border disputes with Ethiopia. Certain of the claims made by the parties overlapped. Accordingly, the UK–Ethiopia treaty of 1897 was concluded, and the boundary delimited by notes exchanged between a British representative and an Ethiopian representative in accordance with article 2 of the treaty.[234] The Haud, one of the main grazing areas of the Somali tribes, was divided between the protectorate and Ethiopia, and the so-called 'reserved area' to the north-west, also incorporating grazing grounds, was given to Ethiopia.[235]

Somalia declared that the 1897 treaty was invalid as it was *inter alia* inconsistent with the earlier agreements. It was contended that the United Kingdom could not cede in 1897 what by the 1884–6 agreements it did not have.[236] However, the United Kingdom had general authority under the protectorate agreements to determine borders, it would appear, and it may be possible to infer Somali consent from those earlier agreements. In addition, the status of the 1884–6 agreements is subject to doubt. Sharma declares that they were of a lower status than international agreements,[237] but one has to be careful of this type of approach of grading treaties. Certainly the type and level of control exercised by the United Kingdom over the area subsequent to the 1884–6 agreements would appear to suggest quite strongly that the United Kingdom did possess the competence to define the boundaries of the region. The 1897 treaty was a binding and valid treaty in law and was acted upon by the parties in the decades that followed. Subsequent conduct may be taken as confirmation of the treaty.

In 1935, as a consequence of the Italian invasion of Ethiopia, the Haud was incorporated into Italian Somaliland. An agreement between the

Italian government and the authorities of British Somaliland provided for the protection of grazing and watering rights 'on either side of the frontier of British Somaliland'.[238] This presupposed that the 1897 delimitation was both valid and operative. An Ethiopian–UK agreement in 1942 provided that those parts of Ethiopia included in the Italian Somaliland region would be temporarily administered as part of British Somaliland, following the defeat of the Italian forces.[239] By the 1944 Ethiopian–UK agreement, this arrangement was confirmed 'without prejudice to their [i.e. the Ethiopians] underlying sovereignty'.[240] Negotiations for the return of the areas commenced in 1946 and the treat concluded in 1954 provided for the resumption of Ethiopian control and the legal regime created by the 1897 agreement was officially acknowledged.[241] The Secretary of State for the Colonies declared that 'although these areas are used predominantly by members of British protected tribes from the Somaliland protectorate they have been Ethiopian territory in international law since the Anglo-Ethiopian treaty of 1897'.[242]

A difference in the interpretation of the 1908 Ethiopian–Italian treaty concerning the delimitation of the Ethiopian–Italian Somaliland boundary has also manifested itself. The treaty delimited the boundary in the light of the territorial extent of particular tribes.[243] However, the extent of such tribal areas was in doubt. Accordingly, an Italian–Ethiopian demarcation commission in 1910 was unable to complete its task.[244] The details of the 1897 Ethiopian–Italian agreement were ambiguous and thus of no help.[245] The conclusion with relation to this boundary must be that no clear delimitation was laid down.

Article 1 of the trusteeship agreement for the former Italian Somaliland stated that its boundaries were to be those fixed by international agreement and 'in so far as they are not already delimited shall be delimited in accordance with a procedure approved by the General Assembly'. Such a procedure has never been established and the result is that the *de facto* boundary line remains the 'provisional line' suggested by a British proposal accepted by the Trusteeship Council in 1950.

The line set out in the British letter dated 1 March 1950 was stated to be provisional only and without prejudice to the final settlement of the question.[246] It cannot therefore be described as the agreed boundary between the States in question, but it remains operative pending a final settlement.

(ii) *The Algerian–Moroccan Dispute.* As noted above,[247] the 1845 treaty between France and Morocco did not delimit the area beyond Teniet-El-Sassi, some 80 miles from the coast, since the delimitation of uninhabited territory was deemed to be superfluous.[248] In 1901 a protocol signed in Paris extended the border between Algeria and Morocco from Teniet-El-Sassi (or Teniet-ess-Assi) to the Hammada du Guir. The delimitation in this area was by tribal lands rather than geographical features. Provision was made for military and customs posts along the border to be controlled by both powers.[249] In 1902, by the agreement of Algiers, the 1901 provisions regarding these posts were abrogated except at Figuig, and instead areas of joint authority were created along the border.[250] France occupied further areas, but these were returned to Morocco by an arrangement in 1910. Varnier, a French High Commissioner, was deputed to execute this arrangement and his line (the Varnier line) coincided with the 1901 Protocol boundary between Teniet-El-Sassi and Figuig; however, to the south-west of Figuig the line running north and west of the former boundary enlarged Algeria by several hundred square miles. The Varnier line was adopted by a French ministerial decree of 1912.[251] In 1912 Morocco became a French protectorate. In 1938 the Trinquet line was proposed, which would have enlarged Morocco, but it was not accepted. It became, however, the basis of Moroccan claims over Algerian territory in the 1960s.[252] French maps were inconsistent throughout this period and the precise outline of the Varnier line was subject to various interpretations. Since the Varnier line was based on the 1910 agreement, it must be accepted as the correct delimitation of the boundary in the region in question. But since there were different French views as to the placement of this line,[253] the presumption must lie in favour of the line deemed by France to constitute the boundary on Algeria's independence. This would appear to be in accord with French acts of administration during the period pending independence. In the event, Morocco accepted the boundary as colonially defined (i.e. during the latter stages).[254]

(iii) *The Sudanese–Egyptian Dispute.* In the agreement of 1899 between Egypt and the United Kingdom, it was provided that Sudan included all territories to the south of the 22nd parallel of latitude which had never been evacuated by Egyptian troops, which had been lost as a result of the Sudan rebellion and reconquered, or 'which may hereafter be conquered by the two governments acting in concert'.[255] It was also provided that Wadi Halfa and Suakin could be most effectively administered in conjunction with the reconquered provinces (of Egypt) to which they were respectively adjacent. Suakin was later excepted from the regime of martial law proclaimed over Sudan.[256] The distinction here between the establishment of a political boundary and adminstrative control is particularly to be noted. In the years that followed, a number of other administrative arrangements were entered into which resulted in Sudanese administration of Egyptian areas to the north of the 22nd parallel and Egyptian administration of some Sudan territory to the south of this latitude.[257] On 1 February 1958 Egypt sent a note to Sudan requesting the return of all territory north of the 22nd parallel being administered by Sudan. In return, Egypt would transfer the territory it was administering south of the parallel to Sudan.[258]

Egypt claimed that the territories north of the parallel were under its sovereignty, being merely administered by Sudan under a bilateral arrangement 'on a strictly local level, confined to administrative agents on either side of the frontier'[259] or through unilateral Egyptian acts, such as the *arrêtés* of 1899 and 1902.[260] Sovereignty could not be transferred either by such local acts or by unilateral actions.[261] It was also noted that no actual delimitation had taken place to give effect to the administrative arrangements, and that the outcome of discussions between the Survey Administration of Egypt and the Sudanese authorities in 1909 was a line on the map showing the political international boundary based on the 22nd parallel and a separate line showing the administrative boundaries.[262]

The Sudanese argument was based on effective possession, and Egyptian acquiescence in it for some fifty years, of the areas it was administering. The sovereign acts it had performed in the territory had gone unchallenged by Egypt until 1958, while Egypt had denounced the 1899 agreement and recognized the independence of Sudan without comment. In addition, Egypt had received a note from Sudan in January 1956 dealing with the Sudanese position relative to existing agreements and had not formally protested.[263] It does seem as if Egypt had clearly acquiesced in Sudanese control of the area in question and that this administrative line had altered the international boundary, having ripened into sovereignty. Sudan's case is also strengthened by the border principle adopted by the OAU, whereby all States in the Organization were to accept and respect the colonial borders. Sudan, which had existed as a distinct entity prior to independence, thus inherited the borders from its Anglo-Egyptian predecessor, including the administered area.

Egypt sent in troops to the area in February 1958 and Sudan complained to the UN Security Council. However, Egypt declared its readiness to postpone the settlement of the issue until after Sudan's elections at the end of February.[264] The boundary issue had really been precipitated as a result of a deadlock in the negotiations on Sudanese claims resulting from the construction of the Aswan Dam (which particularly affected the Wadi Halfa area). Touval regards the raising of the border issue at that time as an attempt to pressure Sudan into accepting Egyptian proposals for a settlement.[265] In the event, the countries agreed in 1959 on questions related to the Nile waters and Aswan Dam issues[266] and the boundary problem does not appear to have been raised again. In the light of all these factors, it is clear that Sudan has title to the disputed territory on the basis of the modification of the delimitation line by the accepted administrative arrangements and Egypt's acquiescence in the same,[267] coupled with the succession of Sudan and Egypt to the borders as colonially administered.

(iv) *The Libya–Chad Dispute.*[268] As from June 1973, Libya began occupying a strip of Chad, called the Aozou strip, parallel to the Libyan border. The area occupied was within a short time some 800 km. long by 100 km. wide.[269] In September 1976 Libya issued new official maps showing *inter alia* that it included some 37,000 sq. miles of Chadian territory.[270] Libya claimed that the correct boundary between it and Chad was that as delimited by the Italian–French (Mussolini–Laval) treaty of January 1935.[271] However, this treaty, although in fact ratified by France on 26 March 1935, was never ratified by Italy and indeed the instruments of ratification were never exchanged.[272] In other words, the agreement never came into force. France maintained that it recognized only those borders existing upon Chad's independence in 1960 which were not challenged upon the latter's entry into the United Nations.[273] Chad points to the OAU border principle as supporting its case. The Libyan claim to an alternative delimitation of the boundary with Chad based upon an agreement that never came into force is clearly untenable in law and the colonial border as at 1960 is the valid one.

(v) *The Tanzanian–Malawi Dispute over Lake Malawi.* The lake forms about three-quarters of the length of the boundary between the two States and extends some 180 miles. The Anglo-German agreement of July 1890 defined the British and German spheres of influence in East Africa and clearly placed the lake within the British protectorate of Nyasaland, by describing the border as running along 'the eastern, northern and western shores of the lake to the northern bank of the River Songwe'.[274] McEwen notes that the shoreline boundary was due to a number of factors, including Britain's determination to control the lake as a means of protecting its missionary and commercial interests and to eliminate the slave trade, and Germany's concentration upon the Indian

Ocean coast. It is also to be noted that Germany was given access to and right of transit upon the lake.[275]

The border was not modified by any subsequent agreement but in later years official maps and documents demonstrated considerable uncertainty as to whether the boundary line was in fact on the eastern shoreline or a median line. The British Central Africa Order in Council of 1902 described the Protectorate of Central Africa (renamed the Nyasaland Protectorate in 1907) as bounded by German East Africa and, although no boundary was defined, taken in conjunction with the 1890 treaty, it would appear to refer to the shoreline boundary. However, as Brownlie notes, in the years before 1914 'the British authorities appeared to have acquiesced in a continuing pattern of public and official German activity on the waters of the lake'.[276] British assistance was given to transport German steamers to the lake, which were used for administrative purposes and travel between the German and British ports on the lake. German activity occasioned no British protest until the outbreak of war in 1914.[277] It is to be noted, however, that the 1890 treaty provided for freedom of trade and navigation with respect *inter alia* to the lake.

German maps prior to 1920, the date at which Britain established civil government in Tanganyika, showed either a shoreline boundary or a middle line, while British maps of the period demonstrated a similar uncertainty.[278] German East Africa was occupied towards the end of the First World War, and until 1922, when the mandates were created, annual reports on the territory were published. The first report, covering the period from the conclusion of the armistice to the end of 1920, was ambiguous as to the placement of the boundary.[279] A map appended to the report seemed to show a middle line.[280] The reports for 1921 and 1922 are similarly ambiguous. On 20 July 1922 the mandate agreement was concluded. Article 1 of the British mandate defined the territory in terms of German East Africa east of the line dividing Tanganyika from Ruanda-Urundi, but contained no detailed description of the borders.[281] With the establishment of the mandate, the boundary crystallized, for no alteration of the limits could occur without the consent of the League of Nations.[282] The vital period is, therefore, from 1890 to 1922. The Tanganyika annual reports to the League from 1924 to 1934 all refer to a middle-line boundary in the lake and accompanying maps illustrate this. However, from 1935 onwards a shoreline boundary was presented.[283] On 13 December 1946 the UN General Assembly approved the trusteeship agreement for Tanganyika within the bounds of the former British mandate.[284] United Kingdom reports to the General Assembly, submitted annually from 1947 to 1961, all included maps showing the boundary on the eastern shoreline. The texts of the reports for 1947 to 1952 specifically noted a shoreline boundary, while later reports omitted such textual references.[285]

In 1959 the Minister of Lands and Surveys reported to the Tanganyikan Legislative Council that the opinion of legal advisers was that no part of the lake was within the bounds of Tanganyika.[286] Six months after independence, the Tanganyikan Prime Minister declared that no part of the lake was within the boundaries of German East Africa and accordingly no part of the lake was within Tanganyika. He noted that there was no question of any change in the boundaries by agreement after the assumption of the mandate by the United Kingdom in 1922.[287]

With increasing tension between Malawi (formerly Nyasaland) and Tanzania (i.e. the union of Tanganyika and Zanzibar), particularly over South Africa, the lake issue was raised.[288] The period of maximum Tanzanian agitation occurred between May 1967 and September 1968 after which time the issue became relatively quiescent.[289] Tanzanian arguments centred around British acquiescence in German use of the lake before 1914 and the consequent modification of the boundary as delimited by the 1890 agreement. It was also noted that in the absence of treaty provisions, and presumably in cases of ambiguity, the principles of customary international law would apply and these would provide for a middle-line boundary.[290]

Brownlie's view is that by the time the mandate came into being, the boundary was the middle line of the lake by virtue of British acquiescence in German use of the lake and in the light of those publications which before and after the establishment of the mandate referred to a middle line. Since this was so, Britain could not unilaterally modify the boundary and, accordingly, Tanzania was entitled to a median-line boundary on the lake.[291] However, it is to be doubted whether the issue is this clear. The 1890 treaty provided for freedom of trade, navigation, and passage of goods within the free zone area as defined by the Berlin Act of 1885, which included Lake Nyasa/Malawi. The ensuing confusion as to the border on the lake may be attributed to a number of causes, ranging from genuine uncertainty resulting from growing German usage to the fact that the treaty was only dealing with spheres of interest. Other factors such as colonial unconcern and paucity of geographic knowledge may also have been of relevance. German activity on the lake and the British attitude thereto may be explained in law in terms of a comprehensive and growing exploitation of the freedom of navigation and trade clauses in the 1890 agreement. As far as the maps are concerned, the long list of equivocal maps should militate against a definitive judgement either way. Wartime maps in particular should be treated with great circumspection. Excluding these from consideration, the weight of evidence would appear to veer towards the shoreline boundary, although many inconsistencies remain. British maps showing a middle line up to July 1922 are especially important since they are evidence against interest.[292] The maps published in the Nyasaland and Tanganyikan annual reports of the inter-war years showing a middle-line boundary are particularly to be noted.

The statements of the Tanganyikan Prime Minister in 1962, coupled with the fact that until 1965 Tanzanian maps showed a shoreline boundary, might be treated as creating an estoppel since they marked acceptance of a particular boundary.[293] Brownlie's argument that independent States should be treated differently in the early years of their independence in respect of such statements[294] must be regarded with some caution. Statements against interest are particularly important as evidence and should not be minimized on the grounds that the State in question has only recently acquired its sovereignty. It is believed that in the light of the ambiguity that clearly exists in relation to the lake boundary, the presumption in favour of the delimitation of 1890 is to be supported and that British acquiescence in German activities on the lake cannot be unequivocally seen as altering that boundary. The Tanganyikan government statements of 1962 are of especial importance in this context. The fact that the Tanzanian claim has been suspended since 1968 would appear to support the proposition put forward.[295]

(vi) *The Dahomey*[296]*–Niger Dispute.* This dispute over the interpretation of the administrative delimitation by France concerned the island of Lété in the river Niger, with both sides claiming exclusive jurisdiction over it. On 1 January 1964 the Head of the provisional Dahomey government cabled the UN Secretary-General over the 'inhuman treatment' of its nationals in Niger and the occupation by the latter of the island of Lété, 'an integral part of Dahomeian territory'.[297] The problem was exacerbated by the overthrow of the previous Dahomey president, with whom the Niger authorities had established warm relations. Suspicions of Niger's involvement in a suspect counter-coup led to the killing and arrest of Niger nationals living in northern Dahomey.[298] Each side accused the other of preparing to seize the island of Lété and mobilized. The problem was discussed at a conference of Heads of State of the Union Africaine et Malgache in Dakar and a reconciliation agreement was initialled. This provided for the protection of the nationals of the parties and for the reference of the Lété dispute to a commission for re-examination.[299] Following the growth of internal political instability, talks were suspended, with Dahomey complaining of the expulsion of its nationals and Niger emphasizing the Lété issue.[300] A settlement of the dispute, however, was proclaimed at a joint meeting of the parties in June 1965,[301] following a meeting of the Conseil de l'Entente at Cotonou the previous January,[302] which included a provision for dual citizenship for the inhabitants of Lété.[303] The problem of sovereignty over the island was not settled but the *de facto* situation was, as it were, formalized.[304]

(vii) *The Ghana–Upper Volta Dispute.* This issue also turned on the interpretation of documents from the colonial era, compounded by the fact that Upper Volta's border had never been demarcated. Political antagonisms exacerbated this relatively minor dispute, which concerned an area regarded by Upper Volta as within its territory, in which Ghana had built a school in 1963 and a road leading to it.[305] After a number of meetings over the problem, Ghana proceeded to raise its flag in the area and establish a police post. At Upper Volta's request, the issue came before the OAU Council of Ministers. Ghana expressed its willingness to withdraw and called for the border to be demarcated,[306] and this was duly noted by the Assembly of Heads of State and Government.[307] However, subsequent meetings of Ghanaian and Upper Voltan commissioners, appointed in 1963 to study the problem, failed to reach agreement on the demarcation of the border.[308] At the Fifth Extraordinary Session of the OAU Council of Ministers in 1965, Ghana noted that its nationals had lived for many years in the disputed area, but reaffirmed its willingness to withdraw after criticizing the methods of demarcation adopted by Upper Volta.[309] Ghana, in fact, withdrew, but challenged the interpetation of the Anglo-French treaty of 1893 delimiting the border. In June 1966, following the overthrow of President Nkrumah of Ghana, agreement was reached on the 1893 delimitation[310] and in 1970 the final report of the border demarcation commission was signed by both States.[311] In April 1977 a treaty was signed formally demarcating 135 miles of the joint border. By 1981 the physical demarcation of the whole borderline had been completed.[312] The 1893 delimitation was therefore accepted by the parties, once the political antagonisms between them had died down, and speedy progress made on actually demarcating the border.

(viii) *The Mali–Upper Volta Dispute.* This dispute concerned the Oudalen region, some 150 km. long and 15–0 km. wide, claimed by Mali. The issue had been in existence, though quiescent, since the independence of the two countries, but reports of the presence of minerals, oil, and gas caused the problem to become acute. Upper Volta had first been created by France from the Sudan territory in 1919, divided between Mali, Niger, and the Ivory Coast in 1932, and re-established in 1947.[313] Mali's claim was based on an *arrêté* of the governor of Sudan in 1935 putting the disputed area in Mali, but Upper Volta argued that the French National Assembly law of 1949 reconstituting the territory of Upper Volta put the region within its borders.[314] A series of clashes on the border occurred at the end of 1974,[315] followed by talks in Lomé with the Presidents of Niger and Togo as mediators. A mediation commission was established consisting of Togo, Niger, Guinea, and Senegal, and it was agreed that the dispute was to be resolved on the basis of existing documents, the withdrawal of troops from the border zone, and the guaranteeing of the safety of the nationals of both parties.[316] A series of documents were sent from France[317] and a military disengagement agreement was announced.[318] In June 1975 a neutral technical committee was set up, consisting of cartographers, an ethnologist, an army officer, and a jurist, to determine the nationality of five border villages and define the border,[319] and a peace agreement was signed at Conakry on 1 July 1975.[320] However, the issue was not finally resolved. A meeting between delegations from the two States took place in November 1979, at which it was decided that a joint commission should seek a solution to the disputed area, that a policy of consultation should be followed, and that the local authorities should meet regularly to settle border incidents.[321] In September 1983 the two parties agreed to submit the issue to the International Court of Justice.[322]

(ix) *The Gabon–Equatorial Guinea Dispute.* In August 1972 Gabon extended its territorial waters to 100 nautical miles distance from its coasts and occupied a series of islands off the Equatorial Guinea coast. Equatorial Guinea sent a series of messages to countries participating at the Dar es Salaam meeting of Eastern and Central African States, declaring that it had been invaded by Gabon, while Gabon sent a letter to the UN Secretary-General on 8 September stating that fishing camps on the uninhabited islands of Mbanie and Cocotiers had been attacked by a force from Equatorial Guinea.[323] The dispute was concerned with conflicting interpretations of the Franco-Spanish treaty of June 1900 delimiting the boundary between Gabon and Spanish Guinea. According to Equatorial Guinea, this implicitly recognized Spanish sovereignty over the coastal islands, while Gabon declared that it had referred only to the islands of Corisco and Eloby as Spanish and that it had therefore recognized French sovereignty over the uninhabited islands of Mbanie and Cocotiers. France and Spain were asked to help clarify the treaty.[34]

At a meeting in Kinshasa between the parties, with Congo and Zaïre, an agreement was reached on the establishment of a commission of representatives of the four States to draw up a set of measures to ease the situation.[325] However, Equatorial Guinea declared that it would not accept the unilateral extension of Gabonese territorial waters to 100 miles[326] and delivered an ultimatum that Gabon was to be removed from the islands by 17 October. Another meeting was thereupon arranged by representatives of the Congo and the OAU assistant secretary-general at Brazzaville, at which neutralization of the Bay of Corisco was agreed upon as well as the establishment of an OAU commission to delimit the boundary between the two States.[327] In April 1974 Gabon declared Mbanie island a Gabonese military zone[328] and in July the President of Equatorial Guinea announced that he accepted the present boundaries as legitimate and the dispute subsided.[329]

Conclusions Where a boundary has been delimited[330] by the colonial powers by international treaty, the doctrine of State succession, coupled with the African *uti possidetis* principle as laid down in the OAU border resolution of 1964, will ensure that this boundary will be binding upon the post-colonial independent African successor States.[331] The only exception to this is where the colonial power has acquiesced in a modification of the delimited boundary. This is shown in the Egypt–Sudan border case and was argued with regard to Lake Malawi where the evidence would not appear to have supported the claim. Assertions by, for example, Libya and Mali of sovereignty over areas beyond the former colonial borders, and thus in neighbouring States, supported only by ethnic affiliation or inferior documentary material, such as an unratified treaty or a governor's ordinance, faced with clear delimitations by the colonial powers concerned, are clearly not valid in law and are extremely hazardous and destabilizing in practice. However, where there has either been no delimitation of the area in question or it is ambiguous and thus disputed, other factors necessarily intrude in an attempt to achieve that stability and finality of boundaries that is of such significance in international law and relations. Of importance will be any acts of sovereignty, governmental activities, or administrative actions in the disputed area.[332] Should these be proved and accompanied by the absence of protests from the other party, this should suffice to establish a boundary on a disputed territory. Where the other party has objected to the activities in the area, the issue will not be resolved, but in such cases a presumption will be in favour of the limits of *de facto* possession transmitted by the colonial power to the successor State. This is demonstrated by the Algerian–Moroccan dispute. The intentions, if ascertainable, of the colonial parties to the treaty in dispute will provide valuable evidence as to the interpretation of the problematic delimitation, as will any subsequent practice of the parties relative to it, while in the absence of any delimitation the issue will rest upon sovereign activities and acquiescence.[333] In these instances, the principles of recognition and estoppel will also be relevant in attempting to define an acceptable boundary line.[334] In the absence of any clear indications as to the placement of the boundary in colonial times, the issue will fall to be resolved by the States concerned, for the consent of the parties is the most important element in the achievement of a stable and final boundary.[335]

A number of the cases surveyed briefly in this section also demonstrate that territorial issues are a keen indicator of political relations. A boundary dispute may be seized upon or may provide the opportunity for the expression of personal, political, or ideological hostility by the parties concerned, and may just as easily be resolved or suspended in the face of reconciliation, however brought about. It is also clear that a number of quiescent boundary differences have become acute as a result of a re-evaluation of the disputed region itself. Discoveries of, or indications of the existence of, minerals, oil, gas, water, and so forth will stimulate a desire to resolve the border issue and settle the question of the sovereignty of the territories involved, one way or the other.

The fact that the initial delimitation of many of Africa's present-day borders took place upon the background of poor geographical knowledge has meant that the task of interpreting such delimitation provisions is that much more difficult and renders the demarcation of the agreed boundary both crucial and complex.

(b) Demarcation Problems

Cukwurah has called demarcation, the physical marking out of the delimited boundary line, the 'crux of all boundary making',[336] and while this is perhaps something of an exaggeration within the context of title to territory in African States, it is clear that it is during the process of transcribing the boundary onto the ground that many issues not apparent during delimitation arise. A number of African boundaries were not demarcated for reasons of expense or lack of trained pesonnel, while in the case of boundaries between two colonies (or two parts of one colony) belonging to the same State, demarcation was often deemed unnecessary.[337]

Another problem has been that once a boundary is demarcated, usually by means of posts, poor maintenance has led to uncertainty as to where the line runs. This occurred with regard to the Kenya–Somali border demarcation referred to in the 1927 agreement. The demarcation was accomplished by means of principal boundary beacons supplemented by a number of secondary cairns. After only a short time, it was noticed that of the twenty-nine beacons only four were in good condition, while the cairns had disappeared, and that lines cut through vegetation were no longer traceable owing to new growth.[338] The problem also arose in the case of the Nigerian–Dahomey demarcation of 1911-12, following an agreement in 1906. The line was marked by a series of low concrete pillars, which, as Anene has noted, were to be found being used by the local inhabitants for the sharpening of cutlasses.[339]

An ambiguous delimitation can cause great problems when it comes to executing the demarcation process. This was illustrated in the Kenya–Sudan border situation. By an order of 1914, following a boundary commission report two years earlier, the Uganda–Sudan border was delimited. The delimitation defined the eastern limit of the boundary by utilizing an imaginary line drawn 'due east of the northernmost point of the northernmost crest of the long spur running north from Mount Lubur'.[340] However, that description could be interpreted in a number of different ways, while the boundary continued by reference to what proved to be a false assumption as to the relative position of certain grazing lands. Problems arose after the transfer of land from Uganda to Kenya in 1926 and this boundary formed the Kenya–Sudan border. In 1931 agreement was reached between the provincial commission of Kenya's Turkana province and the district commissioner of the eastern district of Mongolla province of Sudan on the basis of the northern limits of the relevant grazing area, and this became known as the Red Line. The delimitation was altered northwards a number of times in subsequent years. In 1938 the demarcation of the line was commenced. To this day, there is no finally agreed line, but Kenya has maintained police posts up to and beyond the Red Line with Sudanese consent. The 1914 order contains the only valid delimitation, but the two States have apparently accepted the Red Line *de facto* as the basis of the boundary.[341]

Many of the demarcations took place in Africa many years after the original delimitation agreements. The Ethiopian–British Somaliland boundary was delimited in 1897, but demarcated only in the years between 1933 and 1935, while the Kenyan–Ethiopian border was delimited in 1907 and demarcated in the 1950s. In the latter case, what occurred was that the 1907 delimitation was not demarcated for a number of decades, until a new delimitation was proposed in 1947.[342] A mixed demarcation commission was established in 1950[343] and it finally reported in 1955. However, the Ethiopian government refused to ratify the work of the commission and the agreement failed to come into operation. Further discussions followed after Kenya's independence and the dispute, centring upon the Gaddaduma and Godama wells, was resolved in 1970, with the former being allocated to Ethiopia and the latter to Kenya. The agreement also provided for the nationals of both parties to use the wells and the surrounding areas for watering and grazing.[344]

(i) *The Ethiopian–Sudan Dispute.* The Sudan–Eritrea border was defined by a series of Anglo-Italian agreements in December 1898, June 1899, April 1901, and November 1901 and by the Anglo-Italian–Ethiopian agreement of May 1902. The Ethiopia–Sudan border was delimited in the Anglo-Ethiopian treaty of May 1902, which declared that a red line drawn on two maps was to constitute the boundary. This was to run from Khot Um Hagar to Galbar, to the Blue Nile, and thence, via the Baro, Pibar, and Akoho rivers, to Melile. From there, the border was to reach to the point where 6° north crosses 35° east. Persons were appointed to demarcate the border; however, no Ethiopian boundary commission was appointed, nor was the treaty ratified by either side. A Major Gwynne was sent by the British to survey the border and his line has operated as the boundary.

A series of issues led to strained relations between the two States[345] and a number of meetings were held in the 1960s, during which the Eritrea–Sudan borderline was reaffirmed, and it was agreed to accept the 1902 treaty as the basis of the boundary further inland, particularly with regard to the 6° north, 35° east point.[346] In July 1972 the border dispute regarding the undemarcated areas was declared resolved and Major Gwynne's demarcation line was in fact to be followed. North of Mount Takle the border was to be redemarcated in order to pass along the peaks of certain mountains. A joint special committee was also to be set up to deal with settlement and agricultural questions.[347] Thus, agreement confirmed a previous unilateral demarcation, with certain minor alterations, and provided for the cases where the populations of the two States intermingled.[348]

(ii) *The Mali–Mauritania Dispute.* In this case, the mixture of nomadic and semi-nomadic populations in the desert and savannah border region caused problems as to the exact line of the boundary between the two States. In 1944 France transferred the Hodh region from Mali (then known as Sudan) to Mauritania, but the demarcation was haphazard. Between 1958 and 1960 representatives of the two autonomous territories sought to demarcate the boundary, but unsuccessfully. From the date of independence until 1962, a series of minor incidents occurred, while until 1963 official maps showed the border in two different places. In 1963, however, the two sides came to an agreement and an exchange of territory took place. The new border was purely political, being based on no natural geographic or ethnic line.[349]

The usual method of demarcating a boundary is by means of a joint commission and in most cases the degree of discretion possessed by those marking out the delimited line is restricted. Demarcation involves a number of specific techniques that will be employed in the process of transferring a line from a map onto the ground. Where no agreed demarcation takes place, the parties may acquiesce in a *de facto* line pending final agreement. If they fail to do so, incidents are likely to occur, depending always on the value of the land concerned and the state of relations between the parties.

Notes

INTRODUCTION

1. *The Law of Nations or the Principles of Natural Law*, vol. ii (1758), p. 3.
2. *International Law*, vol. i, (8th edn., 1955), p. 451.
3. See Delbez, 'Du territoire dans ses rapports avec l'état', 39 *Revue générale de droit international public*, (1932), 46.
4. *Claims to Territory in International Law and Relations* (1945), p. 3.
5. See Plato's *Laws*, iv. 704–10 and v. 737, and Aristotle's *Politics*, book 7 chaps. iv and v. See also Gottmann, *The Significance of Territory*, (1973), pp. 17–26.
6. Op. cit., p. 27.
7. Ibid., pp. 36–44.
8. See Nussbaum, *A Concise History of the Law of Nations* (1954), p. 115.
9. Gross, 'The Peace of Westphalia, 1648–1948' in *International Law in the Twentieth Century*, ed. Gross (1969), p. 25.
10. See, e.g., Schoenborn, 'La Nature juridique du territoire', 30 *HR* (1929 V), 85, 97–8.
11. *International Law*, vol. i, (2nd edn., 1970), p. 403.
12. Jennings, *The Acquisition of Territory in International Law* (1963), p. 87. See also Judge Huber in the *Island of Palmas* case, 2 *RIAA* (1928), 829, 838.
13. Op. cit., p. 14.
14. See, e.g., Schoenborn, cit., pp. 92–4.
15. *Introduction à l'étude du droit*, vol. i, pt. 1, (1951), p. 87, quoted in Gottmann, op. cit., p. 14.
16. Op. cit., p. 15.
17. See the *Nuclear Tests* case, *ICJ Reports*, 1974, p. 253.
18. House Comm. on Foreign Affairs, 93rd Cong. 2nd Sess., Rep. of Official Visit to Congress by a Delegation of the European Parliament 40 (Comm. Print. 1973), cited in Falk, 'A New Paradigm for International Legal Studies: Prospects and Proposals', 84 *Yale Law Journal* (1975), 969, 1006.
19. *Theory and Reality in Public International Law* (1968), p. 405.
20. Op. cit., pp. 126–7. See also Delbez, loc. cit., pp. 705–6 for an early view.
21. 'Le Territoire et le développement du droit international', *Annuaire suisse de droit international* (1975), pp. 121, 145.
22. Ibid., p. 123.
23. Ibid., p. 121. See also Schou, 'Le Rôle du territoire dans le droit international', *Nordisk Tidsskrift for International Ret* (Acta Scandinavica Juris Gentium 10,) (1939), 17, 23.

24. Loc. cit., p. 973.
25. Ibid., p. 1020. See also ibid., p. 969.
26. See, e.g., Lauterpacht, *International Law and Human Rights* (1950); Jenks, *The Common Law of Mankind* (1958).
27. e.g. Friedmann, *The Changing Structure of International Law* (1964).
28. See generally Sohn and Buergenthal, *The International Protection of Human Rights* (1973).
29. See further Articles 55–91.
30. See, e.g., Article 1 of the International Covenants on Human Rights, 1966, and the Declaration on Principles of International Law concerning Friendly Relations and Co-operation among States in accordance with the Charter of the United Nations, 1970.
31. See, generally, Bowett, *The Law of International Institutions* (3rd edn., 1975).
32. Entered into force on 10 October 1967. See also General Assembly resolutions 1721 (XVI), 1962 (XVIII), and 1884 (XVIII).
33. See, on the law of space, Fawcett, *International Law and the Uses of Outer Space* (1968); Jenks, *Space Law*, (1965); and McDougal, Lasswell and Vlasic, *Law and Public Order in Space* (1963).
34. Adopted on 17 December 1970 in resolution 2749 (XXV) by 108 votes to 0, with 14 abstentions. See also Assembly resolutions 2340 (XXII), 2467 (XXIII), and 2574 (XXIV).
35. Those principles were reaffirmed in Articles 3 and 4 of Part I, Informal Single Negotiating Text, produced in 1975 by the Chairmen of the three main committees of the Third UN Conference on the Law of the Sea, A/Conf.62/WP.10. See also Articles 136 and 137 of the Convention on the Law of the Sea, 1982, A/Conf.62/121.
36. Article 56 of the 1982 Convention specified the rights, jurisdiction, and duties of the coastal State, and Article 58 sets out the rights and duties of other States in the exclusive economic zone.
37. Op. cit., p. 461.
38. Note that the International Law Commission in its commentary on the Draft Articles relating to Diplomatic Immunity declared that it was guided by the theory of functional necessity justifying diplomatic privileges and immunities while bearing in mind the representative character of the mission and head of mission. It clearly rejected the extraterritoriality theory; see *Yearbook of the ILC* (1958), ii, 94–5. See also Sahovic and Bishop, 'The Authority of the State: Its Range With Respect to Persons and Places' in *Manual of Public International Law*, ed. Sørensen (1968), pp. 331, 313–4.
39. *Principles of Public International Law* (2nd edn., 1973), p. 280.
40. Brownlie expresses the principal corollaries of the sovereignty and equality of States as '(1) a jurisdiction, *prima facie* exclusive, over a territory and the permanent population living there; (2) a duty of non-intervention in the area of exclusive jurisdiction of other States; and (3) the dependence of obligations arising from customary law and treaties on the consent of the

obliger', op. cit., p. 280 (footnotes omitted). Article 2(1) of the UN Charter states that 'the Organisation is based on the principle of the sovereign equality of all its Members'.

41. Note that Article 51 of the Charter refers to the 'inherent right of individual or collective self-defence'.
42. Without a vote, in General Assembly resolution 3314 (XXIX).
43. Article 3 specifies that the invasion or attack by the armed forces of a State on the territory of another State, or any military occupation, however temporary, resulting from such invasion or attack, or any annexation by the use of force of the territory of another State or part thereof would qualify as aggression. Article 5 emphasizes that no territorial acquisition or special advantage resulting from aggression are or shall be recognized as lawful. See, generally, Stone, *Conflict Through Consensus* (1977).
44. *The Corfu Channel* case, *ICJ Reports*, 1949, pp. 6, 22. The Court noted that the exclusivity of control of the territorial State might affect the proof obtainable by the other State in the former's territory and thus require a more liberal recourse to inferences of fact and circumstantial evidence, ibid., p. 19. See also the *Trail Smelter* arbitration, 3 *RIAA*, p. 1905, and Eagleton, *Responsibility of States in International Law* (1928) and the Draft Articles of the International Law Commission, *Yearbook of the ILC* (1976), vol. i, pp. 19–91, and vol. ii, pt. 2, pp. 69–122.
45. See also Sohn, 'The Stockholm Declaration on the Human Environment', 14 *Harvard International Law Journal* (1973), 423, and Teclaff and Utton (eds.), *International Environmental Law* (1974), covering the extension of the principle to areas under a State's jurisdiction and control for certain purposes.
46. *PCIJ* Series A, no. 10, p. 18.
47. See *U.S. Nationals in Morocco*, *ICJ Reports*, 1952, p. 176. The right of a State to apply social legislation to strangers on its territory was affirmed in the *Case Concerning the Application of the Convention of 1902 Governing the Guardianship of Infants*, *ICJ Reports*, 1958, p. 55.
48. *ICJ Reports* 1950, pp. 266, 275.
49. *ICJ Reports*, 1960, pp. 6, 45. Cf. the declaration of Judge Basdevant, ibid., p. 49, the separate opinion of Judge Wellington Koo, ibid., p. 68, and the dissenting opinion of Judge Spender, ibid., p. 114.
50. See Dembinski, loc. cit., p. 127.
51. See Bowett, op. cit., pp. 15–20; Stone, *Legal Controls of International Conflict* (1959), chap. 4; and Scott, *The Rise and Fall of the League of Nations* (1973).
52. Note also that each Member has one vote in the General Assembly and that the jurisdiction of the International Court of Justice in contentious matters is based on the consent of the parties (see Article 36 of the Statute of the ICJ), while in the case of advisory matters a State cannot be compelled to submit a dispute to a tribunal without its consent, *Eastern Carelia* case, *PCIJ* Series B, no. 5 (1923). But see, as regards the modification of this rule, the

Peace Treaties case, *ICJ Reports*, 1971, pp. 16, 24, and the *Western Sahara case, ICJ Reports*, 1975, pp. 12, 22–7.

53. The customary rule to this effect developed rapidly in the early years of this century, see Oppenheim, op. cit., pp. 517–19, and Article 1 of the Chicago Convention on International Civil Aviation, 1944.

54. See, e.g., Article 2 of the Geneva Convention on the Continental Shelf, 1958, Article 24 of the Convention on the Territorial Sea and the Contiguous Zone, 1958 (which talks of controls to be exercised by Coastal States in the Contiguous Zone), and Article 56 of the Informal Composite Negotiating Text, 1977 (and the Draft Convention of 1980) of the Third UN Conference on the Law of the Sea. By way of a contrast, Article 1 of the Chicago Convention (see previous note) specifies that 'every State has *complete and exclusive sovereignty* over the airspace above its territory' (emphasis added).

55. See, e.g., Phillips 'The Exclusive Economic Zone as a Concept in International Law', 26 *ICLQ* (1977), 585.

56. See in general Umozurike, *Self-Determination: International Law* (1972); Rigo Sureda, *The Evolution of the Right of Self-Determination* (1973); Shukri, *The Concept of Self-Determination in the United Nations* (1965); Calogeropoulos-Stratis, *Le Droit des peuples à disposer d'eux-mêmes* (1973); Cobban, *The Nation-State and National Self-Determination* (1969); and Johnson, *Self-Determination Within the Community of Nations* (1967). See also Emerson, 'Self-Determination', 65 *AJIL* (1971), 461; Gross, 'The Right of Self-Determination in International Law' in *New States in the Modern World*, ed. Kilson (1975), p. 136; Kaur, 'Self-Determination in International Law', 10 *IJIL* (1970), 479; and Suzuki, 'Self-Determination and World Public Order: Community Response to Territorial Separation', 16 *Virginia Journal of International Law* (1976), 779.

57. The Declaration on Principles of International Law, 1970, contained in General Assembly resolution 2625 (XXV).

58. See, for a discussion of this, Higgins, *The Development of International Law Through the Political Organs of the UN* (1963), p. 130, and El Erian, 'The Legal Organisation of International Society' in *Manual of Public International Law*, ed. Sørensen (1968), p. 95. For examples of cases, see *UN Repertory of Practice* (1955), vol. i, pp. 55–156. See also Judge Ammoun, *ICJ Reports*, 1970, pp. 313–4.

59. *Nationality Decrees Issued in Tunis and Morocco, PCIJ* Series B, no. 4, p. 24.

60. See, e.g., the separate opinion of Judge Bustamente, *South-West Africa* case, *ICJ Reports*, 1962, pp. 6, 357, and the dissenting opinion of Judge Nervo, ibid., p. 458. See also Wright, *Mandates under the League of Nations* (1930).

61. See Article 22 of the League of Nations Covenant and Chapter XII of the UN Charter.

62. Chapter XI of the Charter.

63. The *Namibia* case, *ICJ Reports*, 1971, pp. 11, 31. See also the *Western Sahara case, ICJ Reports* 1975, pp. 12, 31.

64. In the case of the Belgian trust territory of Ruanda-Urundi, the Trusteeship Council and the General Assembly of the United Nations recommended the evolution of a single, united, and composite State, see T/L 985 and Add.1, and T/L 1004 and T/L 1005 and resolutions 1579 (XV) and 1605 (XV); however, a UN Commission for the territory called for the partition of the territory on the grounds of the 'psychosis of mutual distrust' affecting the rival Tutsi and Hutu tribes, GAOR, 16th Session, 4th Committee, 1205 meeting, para. 14. This was accepted by the General Assembly, which noted the desires of the constituent territories of Rwanda and Burundi to become separate States, resolution 1746 (XV). In the case of Palestine, General Assembly resolution 181 (II) emphasized that 'the present situation . . . is likely to impair the general welfare and friendly relations among nations and called for the partition of the territory into a Jewish and an Arab State. It should also be noted that the Palestine mandate incorporated the Balfour Declaration regarding the establishment of a Jewish national home in Palestine and there is nothing comparable in any other mandate or trust agreement. Additionally, while self-determination may have become a customary right in the early 1960s it was clearly not so in the late 1940s.
65. Although not, of course, upon the citizens of that State.
66. Adopted in resolution 3281 (XXIX) by the General Assembly by 120 votes to 6, with 10 abstentions. The UK and USA voted against, while Canada, Japan, and the Netherlands abstained.
67. See also Articles 4, 5, 10, 12, 13, and 27, and the Declaration on the Establishment of a New International Economic Order, General Assembly resolution 3201 (S-VI).
68. See, e.g., Dembinski, loc. cit., and Gottmann, op. cit.
69. As, for example, economic development law: note the growing importance of UN Conferences on Trade and Development and the work of the UN Commission on International Trade Law.
70. Maine wrote that 'if sovereignty had not been associated with the proprietorship of a limited portion of the earth, had not, in other words, become territorial, three parts of the Grotian theory would have been incapable of application', *Ancient Law* (1861), p. 66.
71. 2 *RIAA*, 829, 838. See The Report of the Commission of Jurists in the *Aaland Islands* case, *LNOJ* Suppl. no. 3, p. 6.
72. Op. cit., p. 2.
73. 2 *RIAA* (1928), 829, 838.
74. 'That much abused word' according to Brierly, *The Law of Nations* (6th edn., 1963), p. 162.
75. Ibid.
76. 2 *RIAA* (1928), 829, 838.
77. Ibid. 839.
78. See the separate opinion of Judge Alvarez in the *Corfu Channel* case, *ICJ Reports*, 1949, pp. 4, 43. Bastid notes that 'sur son territoire, l'État est en

droit d'exclure l'action des autres États. Mais, par contre, la souveraineté territoriale est source d'obligations internationales'; see 'Les Problèmes territoriaux dans la jurisprudence de la Cour Internationale de Justice', 107 *HR* (1962 III), 360, 367.

79. See Schoenborn, loc. cit., p. 96.
80. Westlake, *International Law*, pt. i (1904), p. 86. See also Cavaglieri, 'Règles générales du droit de la paix', 26 *HR* (1929 I), 305, 385.
81. Op. cit., pp. 403–4.
82. Op. cit., p. 84. See also Grotius, *De Jure Belli ac Pacis*, vol. ii, (1625), chapter iii, s. 42.
83. Vattel, op. cit., p. 84.
84. *ICJ Reports*, 1975, pp. 12, 48, 64, and 68.
85. Ibid., p. 47.
86. Ibid., p. 63.
87. Ibid., pp. 93–4.
88. *LNOJ* Suppl. no. 3, 1920, p. 6.
89. *ICJ Reports*, 1975, pp. 12, 164.
90. Ibid., p. 68.
91. Ibid., p. 64.
92. See Schoenborn, loc. cit., pp. 100–2, and Rousseau, *Droit international public*, vol. ii (1974), pp. 48–50.
93. Cavaglieri noted that 'le droit de l'État sur son territoire est un droit de nature réelle, un *dominium*, dont la nature et les effets appartiennent au droit public', loc. cit., p. 385. See also Donati, *Stato e Territorio* (1924).
94. Schoenborn, loc. cit., p. 112, and see as regards servitudes ibid., pp. 108–12.
95. See Hall, *A Treatise on International Law* (8th edn., 1924), pp. 125 ff.; Lawrence, *The Principles of International Law* (7th edn., 1929), pp. 136ff.; and O'Connell, *State Succession in Municipal Law and International Law*, vol. i (1967), pp. 22.
96. See Delbez, loc. cit., p. 711, and Rousseau, op. cit., pp. 45–8.
97. See Schoenborn, loc. cit., p. 114, and O'Connell, op. cit, (n. 95), pp. 22–3.
98. See Delbez, loc. cit., p. 712, and Rousseau, op. cit., pp. 50–2.
99. Schoenborn, loc. cit., p. 117, and O'Connell, op. cit, (n. 95), pp. 22–3.
100. See Kelsen, *General Theory of Law and State* (1949).
101. *Principles of International Law* (2nd edn., 1966), p. 307.
102. Ibid., p. 308.
103. See, e.g., Delbez, loc. cit., p. 712; Schoenborn, loc. cit., p. 124; and Verzijl, *International Law in Historical Perspective*, vol. iii (1970), pp. 12–13, who notes that territorial sovereignty may be adequately defined as 'the plenitude of exclusive competencies [*sic*] appertaining to a State under public international law within the boundaries of a definite portion of the globe'.
104. Op. cit., p. 452.
105. *International Law*, vol. i (1970), pp. 367–9.

106. e.g. *Lighthouses in Crete and Samos* case, *PCIJ* Series A/B, no. 71 (1937), p. 103, and O'Connell, op. cit. (n. 95) chap. 10. Instances of divided sovereignty include mandated and trust territories, condominiums, servitudes, etc.
107. *International Law*, vol. i (1970), p. 377.
108. See O'Connell, op. cit. (n. 95), p. 27.
109. See, on sovereignty, Schwarzenberger, *International Law and Order*, (1971), chap. 5; Larson, *Sovereignty Within the Law* (1965); and Stankiewicz (ed.), *In Defence of Sovereignty* (1969).
110. Anzilotti, *Cours de droit international* (3rd edn., 1929; trans. by Gidel), p. 51, cited in De Visscher, op. cit., p. 205.
111. De Visscher, op. cit., p. 206. The international argument is seen as minimizing the full human and national significance of territory, ibid. Judge Alvarez in the *Corfu Channel* case declared that sovereignty 'has its foundation in national sentiment and in the psychology of the peoples', *ICJ Reports*, 1949, pp. 4, 43.
112. *PCIJ* Series A, no. 10 (1927), p. 18.
113. 'The Plea of Domestic Jurisdiction before International Legal Tribunals', 31 *BYBIL* (1954), 96, 142.
114. See, e.g. *Nationality Decrees Issued in Tunis and Morocco*, *PCIJ* Series B, no. 4, p. 24. C.f. *Free Zones of Upper Savoy and the District of Gex*, *PCIJ* Series A/B, no. 46, p. 167, and Judge Read dissenting in the *Anglo-Iranian Oil Co.* case, *ICJ Reports*, 1952, p. 143.
115. Op. cit., p. 308.
116. Kelsen, 'Sovereignty and International Law' in Stankiewicz (ed.), op. cit., p. 120.
117. But cf. Wheaton who notes that 'every State has certain sovereign rights, to which it is entitled as an independent moral being; in other words because it is a State', *Elements of International Law*, vol. i (6th edn., 1929), p. 150.
118. *Corfu Channel* case, *ICJ Reports*, 1949, pp. 4, 43.
119. Op. cit., p. 4. See also *Salmond on Jurisprudence* (12th edn., 1966), p. 331, where it is noted that 'the title is the *de facto* antecedent, of which the right is the *de jure* consequent'. The *Dictionnaire de la terminologie de droit international* (1960), s.v. *titre*, defines 'title', as 'terme qui, pris dans le sens de titre juridique, désigne tout fait, acte ou situation qui est la cause et le fondement d'un droit'. See also Brownlie, op. cit., pp. 126–7.
120. See, e.g., the *Eastern Greenland* case, *PCIJ* Series A/B, no. 53, p. 46.
121. See, e.g., *The Island of Palmas* case, 2 *RIAA*, p. 829.
122. e.g. in the case of belligerent occupation.
123. To this some would add adjudication; see, e.g., Starke, *Introduction to International Law* (8th edn., 1977), p. 184, but cf. Akehurst, *A Modern Introduction to International Law* (3rd edn., 1977), p. 144. See also Shaw, *International Law* (1977), pp. 211–29.
124. See Oppenheim, op. cit., p. 546; Brownlie, op. cit., pp. 134–5; and

Jennings, op. cit., pp. 6ff. A number of writers have stated that such a distinction is of little importance; see, e.g., De Louter, *Le droit international public positif*, vol. i (1920), p. 340; Verzijl, op. cit., p. 347; and Johnson, 'Consolidation as a Root of Title in International Law', *CLJ* (1955), 215, 217.

125. See O'Connell, op. cit., (n. 11), p. 405.
126. See, e.g., the *Island of Palmas* case, 2 *RIAA*, p. 829; *The Eastern Greenland* case, *PCIJ* Series A/B, no. 53; and the *Minquiers and Ecrehos case, ICJ Reports*, 1953, p. 47.
127. See Oppenheim, op. cit., p. 575; Blum, *Historic Titles in International Law* (1965), chap. 2; and Brownlie, op. cit., pp. 156–63.
128. 'The increase of land through new formations', Oppenheim, op. cit., p. 563.
129. Ibid., p. 547.
130. This flows from Article 2(4) of the UN Charter prohibiting the threat or use of force against the territorial integrity or political independence of any State and from the doctrine of *injuria jus non oritur*, see Lauterpacht, op. cit., p. 420. Security Council resolution 242 (1967) on the Middle East emphasized the 'inadmissibility of the acquisition of territory by war', while the 1970 Declaration on Principles of International Law stated that 'the territory of a State shall not be the object of acquisition by another State resulting from the threat or use of force. No territorial acquisition resulting from the threat or use of force shall be recognised as legal'; note also Article 5, para. 3 of the Definition of Aggression adopted in 1974 by the General Assembly. See Ferencz, *Defining International Aggression* (1975), p. 45.
131. See Article 52 of the Vienna Convention on the Law of Treaties, 1969. See also *Yearbook of the ILC* (1963), ii. 197, and ibid. (1969), ii. 246–7.
132. See Johnson, loc. cit., p. 215.
133. Jennings notes that the case of the emergence of a new State is 'by far the most important case of territorial change at the present time' and that international law here is 'singularly undeveloped, uncertain and . . . comparatively unstudied', *The Acquisition of Territory in International Law* (1963), p. 12. See also Starke, 'The Acquisition of Title to Territory by Newly Emerged States', 41 *BYBIL* (1965–6), 411.
134. See especially the article by Schwarzenberger, 'Title to Territory: Response to a Challenge' in *International Law in the Twentieth Century*, ed. Gross (1969), p. 287.
135. However, see, e.g., as regards the 'independent' Bantustans of South Africa, General Assembly resolutions 2775E (XXVI), 3411d (XXX) 31/69 and 32/14, Security Council resolution 407 (1977) and OAU resolution CM/Res. 493 (XXVII). See also Richardson, 'Self-Determination, International Law and the South African Bantustan Policy', 17 *Columbia Journal of Transnational Law* (1978), 185.
136. Cavaglieri notes the doctrine which declares that sovereignty is not transmissible between States. The cessionary State will exercise its power

and sovereignty over the region rendered *terra nullius* by withdrawal of the ceding State's sovereign power, loc. cit., p. 403.

137. See *Reparation Commission* v. *German Government*, *AD*, 1923–4, no. 199. Huber stated in the *Island of Palmas* case that 'it is evident that Spain could not transfer more rights than she herself possessed', 2 *RIAA*, p. 829.
138. Op. cit., p. 292. Huber declared that the new land accrued to a 'portion of territory where there exists an actual sovereignty capable of extending to a spot which falls within its sphere of activity', 2 *RIAA*, pp. 829, 839.
139. See in particular Kelsen, op. cit., pp. 420–32, and De Visscher, op. cit., pp. 3, 8, and 32.
140. It should, however, be noted that acquisition by prescription may be harder than acquisition by occupation, since there is a presumption against loss of title by the former sovereign, and since acquiescence by the former sovereign is required.
141. Op. cit., p. 209. See also the *Anglo-Norwegian Fisheries* case, *ICJ Reports*, 1951, pp. 116, 138.
142. Ibid. Prescription depends upon the possession by one State of the territory of another and relies upon the passage of time and the acquiescence of the displaced sovereign; see Johnson, 'Acquisitive Prescription in International Law', 27 *BYBIL* (1950), 332, 349 and 353. See also Becket, 'Les Questions d'intérêt général au point de vue juridique dans la jurisprudence de la Cour Permanente de Justice Internationale', 50 *HR* (1939 IV), 189, 218–55. Occupation does not apply to maritime areas; see De Visscher, op. cit., p. 209.
143. Op. cit. (n. 124), p. 223.
144. Op. cit., p. 26.
145. *ICJ Reports*, 1951, pp. 116, 138–9, and see also ibid., p. 130.
146. See MacGibbon, 'The Scope of Acquiescence in International Law', 31 *BYBIL* (1954), 143, 160.
147. Jennings, op. cit., pp. 25–6. Emphasis added.
148. See O'Connell, op. cit. (no. 11), p. 407. Note also Jennings's criticism that the notion of consolidation is based upon 'the merest hint in the case reports', op. cit., p. 27.
149. *Island of Palmas* case, 2 *RIAA*, pp. 829, 839.
150. 2 *RIAA*, pp. 829, 840.
151. *PCIJ* Series A/B, no. 53.
152. 2 *RIAA*, p. 1105.
153. *ICJ Reports*, 1953, p. 47.
154. See the *Island of Palmas* case, 2 *RIAA*, pp. 829, 840. See also Von der Heydte, 'Discovery, Symbolic Annexation and Virtual Effectiveness in International Law', 29 *AJIL* (1935), 462–3.
155. 2 *RIAA*, p. 846. See also Von der Heydte, op. cit., pp. 448ff.
156. 2 *RIAA*, p. 869. See also the *Beagle Channel* award, HMSO (1977), and Jennings, op. cit., pp. 74–6.

157. Hill, *Claims to Territory in International Law and Relations* (1945), p. 152. See also Westlake, op. cit., pp. 114–15.
158. See Corbett, *Law and Society in the Relations of States* (1951), pp. 95–6.
159. The *Island of Palmas* case, 2 *RIAA* pp. 829, 839.
160. Ibid.; presumably a State.
161. See, e.g., Jennings, op. cit., pp. 28–31, and Jessup, 22 *AJIL* (1928), 735, 739–40. See also *Minquiers and Ecrehos* case, *ICJ Reports*, 1953, pp. 47, 56.
162. Note also the strong tendency not to change a 'state of things which actually exists and has existed for a long time', the *Grisbadarna* case, 1 Scott, *Hague Court Reports*, pp. 121, 130.
163. See *Island of Palmas* case 2 *RIAA*, pp. 829 and 870.
164. The reference here is not to consent or acquiescence as regards the creation of rules of international law.
165. See generally McDougal and Feliciano, *Law and Minimum World Public Order* (1961), pp. 733–6 and 739–44; Stone, op. cit., pp. 744–51; and Oppenheim, op. cit., vol. ii, p. 618.
166. *SCOR*, 16th year, 987th meeting, especially paras. 46, 60, and 74.
167. See also the case of Ifni: Mathy, 'L'Autodétermination de petits territoires revendiqués par États tiers (deuxième partie)', *Revue belge de droit international* (1975), 129, and the comments of the International Court in the *Western Sahara* case, *ICJ Reports*, 1975, pp. 12, 35.
168. S/5033.
169. See Elliott, 'The East Timor Dispute', 27 *ICLQ* (1978), 238; Guillhaudis, 'La Question de Timor' *AFDI* (1977), 307; and Crawford and Dayanidhi, 'East Timor: A Study in Decolonisation', 33 *India Quarterly* (1977), 419.
170. See also Security Council resolution 389.
171. S/12133.
172. See, e.g., Assembly resolutions 32/53, 32/34, 35/27, and 36/50.
173. See, e.g., *UNC* Jan. 1982, p. 19.
174. See, e.g., *GAOR* 9th Session, 1st Committee, 726th meeting, paras. 10–11 and 26 and A/4944. See also Rigo Sureda, *The Evolution of the Right of Self-Determination* (1973), pp. 143–51 and 228–33.
175. *Yearbook of the United Nations* (1962), 124–7.
176. A/7723 and *Yearbook of the UN* (1969), 175–7.
177. Ibid., pp. 177–8.
178. Not all such acts would operate within the context of title creation; see the *Frontier Lands* case, *ICJ Reports*, 1959, pp. 209, 229, and the *Western Sahara* case, *ICJ Reports*, 1975, p. 12.
179. See the *Eastern Greenland* case, *PCIJ* Series A/B, no. 43, pp. 51–2. See also Jennings, op. cit., pp. 38–45; Schwarzenberger, op. cit., pp. 295–6; and Blum, op. cit., pp. 49–52.
180. Blum states that recognition 'is one of the main means of expressing consent in international relations', op. cit., p. 49. Schwarzenberger refers to its 'wide actual, and a still greater potential, scope', 'Fundamental Principles

of International Law', 87 *HR* (1955 II), 195, 228.

181. See Akehurst, op. cit., p. 147, but cf. Brownlie, op. cit., p. 173.

182. See in particular General Assembly resolutions 2145 (XXI), 2248 (XXII), 2372 (XXII), 2403 (XXIII), 3031 (XXVII), and 3111 (XXVIII); Security Council resolutions 264 (1969), 269 (1969), 276 (1970), 301 (1971), 323 (1972), and 385 (1976), and the *Namibia* case, *ICJ Reports*, 1971, p. 16. See, generally, Dugard, *The South-West Africa/Namibia Dispute* (1973) and Slonim, *South-West Africa and the UN: An International Mandate in Dispute* (1973).

183. For example, the Bantustans situation; see no. 135 above.

184. See Jennings, op. cit., p. 85, and Brownlie, op. cit., p. 164. Brownlie notes that the 'strength of institutionalised and general recognition is obvious', ibid.

185. In addition to the Bantustans situation, one may note the case of Rhodesia; see General Assembly resolutions 2024 (XX) and 2151 (XXI) and Security Council resolutions 216 (1965) and 217 (1965). See also, e.g., Fawcett, 'Security Council Resolutions on Rhodesia', 41 *BYBIL* (1965–6), 103, and Higgins, 'International Law, Rhodesia and the United Nations' in *The World Today* (March 1967), p. 94. Note that non-recognition does not invalidate a valid title. It withholds validation from a title which is invalid for some other reason.

186. See Oppenheim, op. cit., p. 551, and Corbett, *Law and Society in the Relations of States* (1951), pp. 104–5. The situation with regard to trusteeship territories where there are conflicting options as to the end result of an act of self-determination is rather different. See as to the Cameroons plebiscite T/1556 and A/4684/Add.1 and as to the Togoland plebiscite T/1270 and T/1301.

187. There may, of course, exist constitutional provisions which call for the consent of the inhabitants in such a cession; see, e.g., Article 27 of the 1946 French Constitution which provided that 'no cession, no exchange, and no additions of territory shall be valid without the consent of the populations concerned', Peaslee, *Constitutions of Nations*, vol. ii (2nd edn., 1956), pp. 6, 10.

188. See Articles 17–26 of the 1982 Convention on the Law of the Sea.

189. Ibid., Articles 55–6, 60, 77–8, and 80.

190. Ibid., Article 76. See also the *North Sea Continental Shelf* cases, *ICJ Reports*, 1969, p. 3; the *Anglo-French Continental Shelf* case, Cmnd. 7438 (1978), and the *Tunisian–Libyan Continental Shelf* case, *ICJ Reports*, 1982, p. 18.

191. Articles 60 and 80 of the 1982 Convention on the Law of the Sea. This Convention was adopted on 30 April 1982 by 130 votes to 4 with 17 abstentions. As of February 1984, there were 132 signatories and 8 ratifications, see *The Times*, 16 February 1984, p. 4.

192. *Yearbook of the ILC* (1964), ii. 12–15. See also McNair, *Law of Treaties* (1961), pp. 116–9, and Verzijl, *International Law in Historical Perspective*, vol.

vi (1973), pp. 284–5. When it is desired that the particular treaty in question should cover also territories for which the UK is internationally responsible this will usually appear clearly. For example, the 1972 UK–USA extradition treaty was extended to cover twenty-one territories for which the former was internationally responsible by an Exchange of Notes in 1976; see Cmnd. 6723. Note also that Article 63 of the European Convention on Human Rights, 1950, provides that the Convention may be extended to territories for which the contracting parties are internationally responsible by notification to the Secretary-General of the Council of Europe. On 19 August 1981 the UK renewed the acceptance of Articles 25 and 46 of the Convention on behalf of Belize, Bermuda, the Cayman Islands, the Falkland Islands, Gibralta, the Turks and Caicos Islands, the Bailiwick of Guernsey, and St Helena under this provision; see Minutes of the 150th Session of the European Commission of Human Rights, November 1981, p. 9. As for practice relating to the Channel Islands and the Isle of Man, see McNair, op. cit., p. 118 n. 2, and Waldock's Commentary on Article 58 of the ILC Draft on the Law of Treaties, *Yearbook of the ILC* (1964), ii. 13. See also, generally, Sinclair, *The Vienna Convention on the Law of Treaties* (1973), pp. 56–62.

193. *Yearbook of the ILC* (1964), i. 49. See also Yasseen, ibid., p. 50.

194. For example, El Erian, ibid., p. 46, and Payedes, ibid., p. 233. It is interesting to note here that the International Labour Organization adopted in 1964 an amendment to its constitution stating that 'members ratifying conventions shall accept their provisions so far as practicable in respect of all territories for whose international relations they are responsible', ibid., p. 233, and Johnston, *The International Labour Organization* (1970), chap. 20. See also the comments of Algeria, *Yearbook of the ILC* (1966), ii. 65.

195. *Yearbook of the ILC* (1964), i. 233, and ibid. (1966), i. 46. In its commentary to the article in question, the Commission noted that the phrase 'the entire territory of each party' was a comprehensive term designed to embrace all the land and appurtenant territorial waters and airspace which constitute the territory of the State; UN Conference on the Law of Treaties, Official Records, First Session, p. 33.

196. There were arguments over the extraterritorial application of treaties but reference to this particular issue in the draft article was not accepted by the Commission. See *Yearbook of the ICL* (1966), i. 46–8 and ii. 64–6.

197. See *UN Conference on the Law of Treaties, Official Records*, 1st Session, 30th meeting, paras. 49–51 and 61.

198. Although our purpose here has been to discuss the nature and concept of territory as a phenomenon of international law, it should also be noted in passing that, within the sphere of municipal law, municipal courts may in the course of treaty or statute interpretation analyse the notion of territory in a slightly different fashion. In particular, territory may for these specific purposes often be assimilated to the concept of jurisdiction. For example,

the House of Lords in *Schtraks* v *Government of Israel* had to determine whether 'territory' within the context of an Israel–UK extradition arrangement also included Jerusalem, recognized *de facto* and not *de jure* by the UK as part of the State of Israel. It was held that for these purposes 'territory' included areas over which *de facto* authority was being exercised. [1962] 3 All ER 526, especially at pp. 532 (Lord Reid), 537 (Viscount Radcliffe), 541 (Lord Evershed), and 548 (Lord Hodson). See also *R.* v. *Governor of Brixton Prison, ex parte Minervini* [1959] 1 QB 155.

CHAPTER 1

1. See generally Oliver and Fage, *A Short History of Africa* (3rd edn., 1970); Mair, *Primitive Government* (1962); id. *African Kingdoms* (1977); and Fortes and Evans-Pritchard (eds.), *African Political Systems* (1940).
2. The arbitrator in the *Barotse* award of 1905 referred to the 'notorious instability of the tribes and their frequent intermingling' making a precise boundary delimitation between the UK and Portugal on the basis of the territorial extent of the Barotse kingdom impossible; see Hertslet, *Map of Africa by Treaty*, vo. iii (3rd edn., 1909), p. 1076.
3. Anene, *The International Boundaries of Nigeria* (1970), pp. 5–6. See also Yakemtchouk, *L'Afrique en droit international* (1971), pp. 67–9.
4. Colson has written that 'political and ethnic boundaries rarely coincided in pre-colonial Africa'; 'African Society at the Time of the Scramble' in Gann and Duignan (eds.), *Colonialism in Africa 1870–1960*, vol. i (1969), p. 31. Anene has referred to the endemic warfare between neighbouring groups at this time, op. cit., p. 7. The nature of African societies and their political structure and history are beyond the scope of this work.
5. See generally Oliver and Fage, op. cit., and Davidson, *Africa in History* (1974).
6. Op. cit., p. 5.
7. Ibid., pp. 10–11. Maine writes that the political tie of kinship marks the start of the history of political ideas, and the change to an alternative basis of common political action, such as 'local contiguity', amounts to a startling and complete revolution: op. cit. p. 76.
8. *Conflict in Africa* (1976), p. 122.
9. Ibid.
10. Ibid., pp. 131–2. Examples are given of the Ghana, Mali, and Gao empires in West Africa, Bantu States in Southern Africa, and Congolese kingdoms in Central Africa, ibid., pp. 132–3. Anene notes that between most African traditional communities 'boundaries, as lines separating States, did not exist'; op. cit. p. 5.
11. 'La Notion de territoire arabe et son application au problème du Sahara' *AFDI* (1957), 73, 76.
12. Ibid.

13. Ibid., pp. 78–81.
14. *ICJ Reports*, 1975, p. 12.
15. Ibid., pp. 43–4.
16. Ibid., p. 44. The 'Mauritanian Entity' was not a legal entity since it was not an entity capable of availing itself of obligations incumbent upon its constituent elements, although they did possess certain rights, including rights over the lands through which they migrated; ibid., pp. 63–5. But cf. Judge Ammoun, ibid., p. 102.
17. See Allott, 'Boundaries and the Law in Africa' in *African Boundary Problems*, ed. Widstrand (1969), p. 10.
18. See Coleman, 'Tradition and Nationalism in Tropical Africa' in *New States in the Modern World*, ed. Kilson (1975), pp. 12–15.
19. Hargreaves, *West Africa Partitioned*, Vol. 1: *The Loaded Pause, 1885–1889* (1974), p. 5.
20. Ibid. Note also the increasing influence in this period of Islam: see Oliver and Fage, *A Short History of Africa* (3rd edn. 1970), p. 180.
21. Op. cit., p. 1.
22. See generally Robinson and Gallagher, *Africa and the Victorians* (1961), and Hargreaves, *Prelude to the Partition of West Africa* (1963).
23. Alexandrowicz, 'The Role of Treaties in the European–African Confrontation in the Nineteenth Century' in *African International Legal History*, ed. Mensah-Brown (1975), pp. 27, 28.
24. For example, the British claim to 'Mount Mfumbiro' as falling within the British sphere of influence by virtue of the 1890 Anglo-German agreement was based on alleged treaties concluded by Stanley. In the event the claim was not contested and it was not until much later that it was discovered that no mountain of that name existed, but rather that Mfumbiro was the name of a plain near the imaginary mountain. See Hertslet, *The Map of Africa by Treaty*, vol. iii (3rd edn., 1909), p. 124, and Jentgen, *Les Frontières du Ruanda-Urundi et le régime international de tutelle* (1957), pp. 22–3.
25. For example, the ultimately successful challenge to a British treaty made by Lugard with Nikki on the present Nigeria–Dahomey (Benin) border on the grounds *inter alia* that the African signing the treaty had no power whatsoever to sign; see Touval, 'Treaties, Borders and the Partition of Africa', 7 *Journal of African History* (1966), 279, 281–2.
26. See, e.g., the Gabon–Equatorial Guinea dispute and the Ethiopian–Sudan dispute, Chapter 6 below.
27. Anene, *The International Boundaries of Nigeria* (1970), pp. 5–12. See also Lloyd, *Yoruba Land Law* (1962), p. 62, as regards the definite boundaries possessed by the Yoruba ethnic group.
28. See *Western Sahara* case, *ICJ Reports*, 1975, pp. 12, 39. See also Brownlie, *Principles of Public International Law* (3rd edn., 1979), pp. 142 and 180; the *Island of Palmas* arbitration, 2 *RIAA*, p. 829; and Crawford, *The Creation of States in International Law* (1979), pt. ii.

29. *De l'occupation des territoires sans maîtres* (1889), p. 200.
30. Abandonment involves the relinquishment of actual possession by the former sovereign and the intention not to resume possession; see Oppenheim, *International Law*, vol. i (8th edn., 1955), pp. 579–80.
31. See Lindley, *The Acquisition and Government of Backward Territory in International Law* (1926), pp. 11–20; Fauchille, *Traité de droit international public*, vol. i (1925), pp. 697ff.; and Jèze, *Étude théorique et pratique sur l'occupation comme mode d'acquérir les territoires en droit international* (1896).
32. Lindley, op. cit., pp. 12–14. But cf. Westlake's view that Vitoria, Soto, and other theorists were not so much inpugning the titles of Spain and Portugal as trying to influence their conduct; *Collected Papers on Public International Law* (1914), p. 139. Blackstone declared that only deserts and uncultivated lands could be obtained by means of occupation, cultivated lands being acquired by means of conquest or cession: *Commentaries on the Laws of England*, vol. i, (1765), pp. 106–7.
33. Lindley, op. cit., p. 17. See also Vattel, *The Law of Nations or the Principles of Natural Law* (1916 edn.), pp. 37–8 and 85–6.
34. Op. cit., pp. 143–5. See also Lawrence, *The Principles of International Law* (7th edn., 1929).
35. Westlake perceived such a government partly in terms of the preservation of security, but 'when people of European race come into contact with American or African tribes, the prime necessity is a government under the protection of which the former may carry on the complex life to which they have been accustomed in their homes', op. cit., p. 143. See also Jennings, 'The Progress of International Law', 34 *BYBIL* (1958), 334.
36. See Alexandrowicz, *The European–African Confrontation* (1973), p. 6. Lorimer declared that recognition of State-existence depends on the intent of the receiving party to reciprocate and non-Christian States could not be expected to provide this, *The Institutes of the Law of Nations*, vol. i (1883), pp. 113–25. He also noted that States' relative value depended on a number of factors, including 'moral and intellectual qualities', ibid., pp. 182–8. Wheaton wrote that 'the public law, with slight exceptions, has always been, and still is, limited to the civilised and Christian people of Europe or to those of European origin', *Elements of International Law* (8th edn., 1866), pp. 17–18. See also Kent, *Commentary on International Law* (2nd edn., 1978, p. 8), and Phillimore, *Commentaries upon International Law*, vol. i (3rd edn., 1879), pp. 23–4.
37. Op. cit., p. 555. See also Brierly, *The Law of Nations* (6th edn., 1963), p. 163.
38. *The Acquisition of Territory in International Law* (1963), p. 20.
39. *ICJ Reports*, 1975, p. 12.
40. General Assembly resolution 32933 (XXIXX).
41. Pleadings, CR.75/18, p. 29.
42. Ibid., pp. 36–55. See also Pleadings, CR.75/19, pp. 2–23.

43. Pleadings, CR.75/18, pp. 33–4.
44. Pleadings, CR.75/19, pp. 4–5.
45. Ibid., p. 39.
46. Ibid., p. 36.
47. Ibid., p. 17.
48. Lindley, op. cit., p. 34. See Alexandrowicz, op. cit. (n. 23), p. 64. See also O'Connell, *International Law* vol. i (2nd edn., 1970), pp. 408–9 and sources therein cited.
49. Lindley, op. cit., p. 34. Judge Ammoun was guilty of the same misinterpretation. See *ICJ Reports*, 1975, pp. 12, 86, and *ICJ Reports*, 1971, pp. 16, 86.
50. *ICJ Reports*, 1975, pp. 12, 39.
51. Pleadings, CR.75/19, p. 40.
52. The request stated that 'if the answer to the first question is in the negative, (2) what were the legal ties between this territory and the Kingdom of Morocco and the Mauritanian entity?'
53. These solutions will be examined below, pp. 55–8.
54. Pleadings, CR.75/6, p. 23.
55. A/C.4/SR.2130, p. 24. See also Judge Dillard, *ICJ Reports*, 1975, pp. 12, 123.
56. Spanish Written Statement, paras. 264 and 265.
57. Except for a peripheral reference to the concept in discussing the development of spheres of influence and protectorates, Pleadings CR.75/23, p. 58.
58. A/C.4/SR.2130, p. 24. During this discussion in the 4th Committee, Spain appeared to be suggesting at one point that the territory was not *terra nullius* since 'the Sahara was populated by Saharans', but this view of *terra nullius* as purely uninhabited areas was dropped, ibid.
59. Pleadings, CR.75/26, p. 45.
60. Pleadings, CR.75/29, pp. 31–2.
61. Moroccan Written Statement, Introduction, pp. 6ff.; Part I p. 9; and Part II, pp. 99–100. See also Pleadings, CR.75/12, pp. 2–4.
62. Morocco declared that 'the court will ascertain that the Sahara was not *terra nullius* at the time of Spanish colonisation, and that it was, without any geographical void, an aggregation of Moroccan and Mauritanian lands, where Moroccans and Mauritanians exercised political authority in different forms and places', Pleadings, CR.75/6, p. 8.
63. Pleadings, CR.75/17, p. 17. Mauritania noted that there was no problem of *res nullius* in the part of the territory linked with Morocco since the latter was an entity recognized as a State at the time, ibid.
64. *ICJ Reports*, 1975, pp. 12, 74. His contention that States at the time spoke only of zones of influence is not strictly accurate, ibid.
65. Ibid., p. 75.
66. Ibid., pp. 113 and 114.
67. Ibid., p. 123. See also ibid., p. 75.
68. Ibid., p. 124.

69. See Judges De Castro, ibid., p. 171; Dillard, ibid., p. 124; Gros, ibid., p. 74; and Ignacio-Pinto, ibid., p. 78.
70. Ibid., p. 37.
71. Ibid.
72. Ibid. This, however, does raise a problem not considered by the court, and that is the extent of the *terra* in question. In the case of a sparsely inhabited area, such as parts of Southern Africa and Patagonia in the early nineteenth century, one might be faced with an area which is partly *terra nullius* and partly occupied in such a fashion as to render classification of the territory as a whole a complicated matter.
73. See, for example, Pleadings, CR.75/19, p. 17 (Algeria).
74. *ICJ Reports*, 1975, pp. 12, 39. Cf. Judge Huber in the *Island of Palmas* case, 2 *RIAA*, pp. 829, 858.
75. Pleadings, CR.75/19, p. 18 (Algeria).
76. Pleadings, CR.75/29, p. 32 (Mauritania).
77. For examples of such State practice see Lindley, op. cit., pp. 34–44, and Alexandrowicz, op. cit. (n. 36). See also the succeeding section.
78. *ICJ Reports*, 1978, pp. 12, 124.
79. 2 *RIAA*, pp. 829, 858.
80. For example, Australia; see Evatt, 'The Acquisition of Territory in Australia and New Zealand', *Grotian Society Papers* (1968), pp. 16, 18.
81. Op. cit., p. 45.
82. Alexandrowicz, op. cit. (n. 23), p. 64. It should be noted that what was acquired was the title to the land of the entity, or territorial sovereignty, not private law rights over land in that territory. This was expressly proclaimed in a number of treaties, e.g. those with the Kafir Bulloms, 1827, and the King of Combo, 1840. See Hertslet, op. cit., vol. i, pp. 12, 34, 125, 137ff. The Judicial Committee of the Privy Council declared that 'a mere change in sovereignty is not to be presumed as meant to disturb rights of private owners', *Amodu Tijani* v. *Secretary of the Southern Provinces* (1921) 2 2 AC 299. See also Alexandrowicz, op. cit. (n. 23), p. 52.
83. See Lindley, op. cit., pp. 32–3. This proviso was inserted in view of the claims of the Sultan of Zanzibar, ibid. A report presented to the Conference by the Commission noted that 'with regard to the native Princes, the majority have already alientated their rights of sovereignty and with the others it will be right and possible to arrive at equitable arrangements', ibid., p. 33.
84. Ibid., p. 144, and Hertslet, op. cit., vol. ii, p. 468. See also Annex I to Protocol no. 8 of the Conference, Report of the Commission charged with the examination of the Project of Declaration respecting the New Occupations on the Coasts of Africa, C.4361.
85. Op. cit., p. 417.
86. See generally Crowe, *The Berlin West Africa Conference 1884–5* (1942), and Ward, *The Great International Share-Out* (1958).

87. Alexandrowicz, op. cit. (n. 36), p. 6.
88. Hargreaves, 'Towards a History of the Partition of Africa', 1 *Journal of African History* (1960), 97, 99.
89. Op. cit. (n. 36), p. 7.
90. Lindley, op. cit., pp. 34–5.
91. Ibid., pp. 35–6. Further examples provided by Lindley as to the acceptance of the acquisition of title by means of treaties of cession signed with tribal chiefs include Bechuanaland, South-West Africa, East African territories, and the Congo: ibid., pp. 36–9.
92. Ibid., p. 34.
93. Ibid., p. 166.
94. 110 *BFSP* 843.
95. Lindley, op. cit., p. 167.
96. Hertslet, op. cit., vol. i, p. 12.
97. Ibid., pp. 92–3. See also Alexandrowicz, op. cit. (n. 23), pp. 38–43.
98. Hertslet, op. cit., vol. i, pp. 137ff.
99. Ibid., vol. iii, p. 988.
100. Ibid., p. 996.
101. Ibid., p. 1074.
102. Lindley, op. cit., p. 170.
103. Ibid., pp. 170–1.
104. Hertslet, op. cit., vol. i, p. 105.
105. Ibid., p. 106. See also similar statements with regard to the Ibu towns, the Kingdom of Ibaro, and the Kingdom of Ondo, also in southern Nigeria, ibid., pp. 107–8.
106. See Alexandrowicz, op. cit. (n. 36), pp. 34–5. Further examples of this kind of statement are also cited ibid., pp. 35–6.
107. See n. 99. See also Lindley, op. cit., p. 172.
108. See the treaty between France and the King of Comendo, 1687; the agreement by the King and Chiefs of Sierra Leone to the cession of land to King George III of Britain in 1788; the treaty between Britain and the King of North Bulloms in 1821; and the treaty between Britain and the King of Brekama in 1827: Alexandrowicz, op. cit. (n. 36), pp. 39–40.
109. *UK Parliamentary Papers*, 1899, vol. 60, p. 15 (C.9388).
110. Hertslet, op. cit., vol. iii, p. 894.
111. Op. cit., p. 172.
112. *The Rise of an East African Empire*, vol. ii (1893), pp. 33, 579ff.
113. 81 *BFSP* 995–7. Emphasis added.
114. 85 *BFSP* 680.
115. 47 *BFSP* 540.
116. Hertslet, op. cit., vol. i, pp. 137ff.
117. Ibid., p. 142.
118. Ibid., p. vi.
119. Op. cit. (n. 36), p. 47. The practical question of the extent to which consent

was actually forthcoming in particular situations is beyond the scope of this work.

120. See Articles 51 and 52 of the Vienna Convention on the Law of Treaties, 1969.
121. Lindley, op. cit., pp. 189–90.
122. Ibid., p. 175.
123. Ibid., p. 176.
124. O'Connell points out that the cessions made by Indian and South-East Asian protectorates to the British Crown were the bases of title and that it would be profitless to speculate on the degree of civilization which would qualify a ruler for international personality, op. cit., p. 440.
125. See Jenks, *The Common Law of Mankind* (1958), pp. 62–89, and Jennings, 'The Progress of International Law', 34 *BYBIL*, (1958), 334, 350–4.
126. *International Law*, pt. i, *Peace* (1904), pp. 40–1.
127. *International Law* (5th edn., 1918), p. 53. See also Westlake, *Collected Papers on Public International Law* (1914), pp. 143–5.
128. Op. cit., p. 50.
129. *Principes du droit des gens*, vol. i (1896), pp. 45–51.
130. Andrews, 'The Concept of Statehood and the Acquisition of Territory in the Nineteenth Century', 94 *LQR*, pp. 408, 413. For examples of such pre-nineteenth-century relations see Alexandrowicz, op. cit. (n. 36), pp. 9–28.
131. 165 ER 515.
132. 165 ER 480.
133. Smith, *Great Britain and the Law of Nations*, vol. i (1932), p. 12.
134. *ICJ Reports*, 1975, pp. 12, 43–4.
135. Ibid., p. 44.
136. Oppenheim, op. cit., p. 566.
137. See Article 2(4) of the UN Charter and e.g. Langer, *Seizure of Territory* (1946), and Jennings, *The Acquisition of Territory in International Law* (1963), pp. 52–68.
138. Lindley, op. cit., p. 160.
139. (1919) AC 211.
140. Ibid. 221.
141. Lindley, op. cit., p. 160.
142. Westlake, op. cit., p. 65. But see Oppenheim, op. cit., p. 571, who regards this as an example of premature annexation.
143. Lindley, op. cit., pp. 161–4.
144. *In Re Southern Rhodesia* (1919) AC 211.
145. Lindley, op. cit., p. 164.
146. Ibid., pp. 190–1.
147. *In Re Southern Rhodesia* (1919) AC 211. See also Alexandrowicz, op. cit. (n. 36), pp. 76–7.
148. Lindley, op. cit., pp. 190–1.

149. It appears that there were no cases of territory being acquired by prescription in Africa during the period of colonization.
150. Op. cit., p. 342.
151. See Lindley, op. cit., pp. 181–2.
152. *PCIJ* Series B, no. 4, p. 27.
153. *US Nationals in Morocco, ICJ Reports*, 1952, pp. 176, 188.
154. See Vattel, *The Law of Nations*, vol. i (1758), para. 16. This view was cited by Lord Salisbury with regard to the dispute with the French over the latter's declaration of a protectorate of Madagascar; see Alexandrowicz, op. cit. (n. 36), p. 62.
155. [1910] 2 KB 576 at 620. See also the Foreign Office view that a protectorate involves not the direct assumption of territorial sovereignty but is 'the recognition of the right of the aborigines, or other actual inhabitants to their own country, with no further assumption of territorial rights than is necessary to maintain the paramount authority and discharge the duties of the protecting Power', FO 403/9, no. 92 (14 January 1885). See also Gavin and Betley, *The Scramble for Africa* (1973).
156. Op. cit., p. 183.
157. For example the 1827 treaty between Britain and the King of Brekoma: Alexandrowicz, op. cit. (n. 23), p. 55; the 1837 treaty between France and Adb-el Kader; Hertslet, op. cit., vol. i, pp. ii; and the 1884 treaty between Britain and the ruler of Opobo; 89 *BFSP* 1089. See also Lindley, op. cit., pp. 183–4.
158. Alexandrowicz, op. cit. (n. 23), p. 55.
159. See Lindley, op. cit., p. 187.
160. [1910] 2 KB 576, 619.
161. Ibid. 603–4.
162. A distinction may be drawn here between the 'traditional' protectorates of North Africa, i.e. Tunis and Morocco, and the 'revisionist' protectorates of black Africa; see Okoye, *International Law and the New African States* (1972), p. 8. The difference lies in the acceptance of the objects of the former protectorates as States (if not within the European family of nations) but not in the case of the latter.
163. Above, p. 43.
164. See Lindley, op. cit., pp. 189–93. Treaties of protection were also signed with rulers in the Gambia, Gold Coast, and in Nigeria by the British, and in West Africa generally and in the Congo by France; see Hertslet, op. cit., vol. i, pp. 19–20, 64–120, and 137. See also McNair, *International Law Opinions*, vol. i (1956), pp. 41–55, and Lewis, *The Modern History of Somaliland* (1965), pp. 40–62.
165. See Lindley, op. cit., pp. 148–9.
166. Westlake defined a colonial protectorate as 'a region in which there is no state of international law to be protected, but which the power that has assumed it does not yet claim to be internationally its territory, although that

power claims to exclude all other States from any action within it', op. cit., pp. 123–4. Note that Oppenheim declared that the protectorates over African tribes acquired through treaty possessed no international status whatsoever, op. cit., p. 196. This would emphasize the distinction between protectorates over States and over other entities; see n. 162 above.

167. The term 'sphere of interest' was also used, but was of less significance than the other expressions; see Curzon, Frontiers (1907), p. 42.
168. Holdich declared that it was a way of setting up a 'warning to trespassers', *Political Frontiers and Boundary Making* (1916), pp. 96–7.
169. Op. cit., p. 128.
170. See Uzoigwe, 'Spheres of Influence and the Doctrine of the Hinterland in the Partition of Africa', 3 *Journal of African Studies* (1976), 183, 186.
171. 76 *BFSP* 772.
172. See Lindley, op. cit., p. 210, and Uzoigwe, op. cit., pp. 186–7.
173. When the Sultan of Zanzibar protested that territory recognised as belonging to him was allotted under a German–Portuguese treaty of 1886 to the latter State, Germany pointed out the treaty did not affect the Sultan's rights but merely provided that Germany would not interfere with any arrangements that Portugal might wish to make regarding the territory whether with the Sultan or with others: 78 *BFSP* 1254–5.
175. Uzoigwe, op. cit., 194–5. See also Westlake, op. cit., pp. 114–6.
175. Uzoigwe, op. cit., pp. 195.
176. McEwen, *International Boundaries of East Africa* (1971), p. 172.
177. Cd. 5857 (1911), p. 32, cited in Lindley, op. cit., p. 235.
178. Lindley, op. cit., pp. 229–30.
179. Ibid., p. 235.
180. Ibid., p. 212.
181. Yakemtchouk, *L'Afrique en droit international* (1971), pp. 70–3.
182. Touval, op. cit., p. 291. See also Boggs, *International Boundaries* (1940), pp. 156–8.
183. Mangongo-Nzamb, 'La Délimitation des frontières du Gabon (1885–1911)', 9 *Cahiers d'études africaines* (1969), 5.
184. Apparently in order to ease the construction of British railway communications; Permanent Mandates Commission, Minutes of the 2nd Session, 9 August 1922, p. 72.
185. Cmnd. 1974. See also McEwen, op. cit., pp. 154–5, and Touval, *The Boundary Politics of Independent Africa* (1972), p. 10.
186. Lindley, op. cit., p. 282. See also Murty, 'Evidence on Traditional Boundaries and some Problems in its Interpretation', 8 *IJIL* (1968), 487–8 n. 14.
187. Hertslet, op. cit., vol. ii, p. 229. See also Anene, op. cit., p. 13.
188. Touval, op. cit. (n. 25), p. 289.
189. Ibid.
190. Ibid.
191. Lindley, op. cit., pp. 282–3, and Murty, op. cit., pp. 487–8 n. 18.

192. Lindley, op. cit., pp. 289–90. See also Touval, op. cit. (n. 185), p. 10.
193. Lindley, op. cit., p. 290. See also Jones, *Boundary Making* (1945), p. 42.
194. McEwen, op. cit., p. 129.
195. Hertslet, op. cit., vol. iii, pp. 899–906.
196. Touval, op. cit. (n. 185), p. 14.
197. *ICJ Reports*, 1975, pp. 12, 14.
198. Pleadings, CR.75/12, p. 29.
199. Ibid., p. 6.
200. Pleadings, CR.75/11, pp. 18–19.
201. Ibid., p. 6. The court, in fact, accepted this analysis; *ICJ Reports*, 1975, pp. 12, 44–5.
202. Pleadings, CR.75/12, pp. 36–7.
203. Ibid., pp. 6–29.
204. Ibid., p. 38. See also A/C.4/SR.2004.
205. Allegedly from the river Senegal to the Wadi Sakiet El Hamra, with the proviso that to the south of the latter there was a zone of overlap with the Tekna nomads of the Moroccan Bled Siba; Pleadings, CR.75/17, p. 24.
206. Ibid., p. 28.
207. Dealing *inter alia* with agricultural and water issues, rules relating to area, and methods for the peaceful settlement of disputes: ibid., p. 29.
208. Ibid., p. 28.
209. Ibid., p. 25.
210. Ibid., pp. 32, 33, and 37.
211. Ibid., p. 41. See also Pleadings, CR.75/30, pp. 38–40.
212. See Pleadings, CR.75/22, pp. 12–25 and 42–51, and Pleadings CR.75/23, pp. 2–33 and 44.
213. Pleadings, CR.75/24, pp. 9–43. The term 'Mauritanian entity' was first used during the General Assembly debates of 1974; *ICJ Reports*, 1975, pp. 12, 57.
214. Pleadings, CR.75/24, pp. 44–9. Spain emphasized that this approach was adopted by the Saharan political movements, including Polisario; ibid., pp. 49–51. The Algerian approach to the issue of legal ties as of the date of colonization was to assert the primacy of the principle of self-determination and the will of the people; Pleadings, CR.75/31, p. 121.
215. *ICJ Reports*, 1975, pp. 12, 43.
216. The court regarded the historical material presented to it as ambiguous, while the factor of geographical contiguity (even if it could be considered, which was doubtful) only emphasized the paucity of evidence of unambiguous display of Moroccan authority regarding Western Sahara; ibid., pp. 42–4.
217. *PCIJ* Series A/B, no. 53, p. 45.
218. *ICJ Reports*, 1975, pp. 12, 43–4.
219. But see Judges Ammoun and Forster who declared that the court had erred in not recognizing that in the circumstances ties of allegiance amounted to

ties of sovereignty; ibid., pp. 102 and 103. But cf. Judge De Castro, ibid., p. 136.

220. In essence the court adopted the Spanish interpretation of the facts regarding the internal aspects of Morocco's claim to immemorial possession; ibid., pp. 47–8, and above, n. 212.
221. Ibid., p. 49.
222. Evidence was adduced showing a certain influence upon the Tekna tribes by the Sultan; ibid., pp. 48 and 56.
223. The court also appeared to give a broader interpretation to the question of legal ties than was justified in the case. The question was centred on legal ties between the *territory* of Sahara and the claimants; it did not go further and call for a discussion of ties with sections of the population of the territory. The court's opinion, therefore, fell between the Moroccan position that personal ties of allegiance amounted to ties of sovereignty over the territory and the terms of resolution 3292 (XXIX) which clearly concerned only territorial ties in Morocco's case. As far as the various international acts invoked by Morocco were concerned, the court felt that although they did not show that the international community did recognize Moroccan territorial sovereignty in Sahara at the relevant time, they did provide indications of the Sultan's authority or influence over some nomads in the territory; ibid., p. 56.
224. Morocco declared that the court's opinion meant that Western Sahara was part of Moroccan territory and that 'Moroccan claims have been recognised by the legal advisory organ of the United Nations', S/PV.1849, p. 11 (16 October 1975).
225. *ICJ Reports*, 1975, pp. 12, 43 and 63. See also the Reparations case, *ICJ Reports*, 1949, pp. 174, 178.
226. *ICJ Reports*, 1975, p. 63. Thus, no ties of sovereignty or allegiance existed; ibid., p. 64. See also Judges Petren, ibid., p. 115; De Castro, ibid., p. 165; and Ruda, ibid., p. 175.
227. Ibid., p. 64–5. See also the analysis by Judge Dillard, ibid., pp. 155–6.
228. Ibid., p. 64. Cf. Judge de Castro, ibid., p. 165.
229. Note, however, that the court accepted that there existed a certain overlapping of Moroccan and Mauritanian ties: ibid., pp. 65–7.
230. See below, Chapters 2 and 3.
231. Legal ties were defined in terms of their impact upon the decolonization of the territory: *ICJ Reports*, 1974, pp. 12, 68.
232. See ibid., pp. 36 and 37. Cf. Judge Petren, ibid., p. 112.
233. Pleadings, CR.75/19, pp. 43–5. Algeria actually rejected such an approach since it was argued that one had to presume the predominance of European international law in the circumstances of the nineteenth century: ibid. Cf. Pleadings, CR.75/26, p. 50 (Morocco).
234. Pleadings, CR.75/30, pp. 38–9.
235. Pleadings, CR.75/25, p. 13.

236. Pleadings, CR.75/22, p. 16. See also Pleadings, CR.75/23, p. 57.
237. Pleadings, CR.75/11, pp. 15 and 18.
238. Ibid., p. 11.
239. Pleadings, CR.75/27, pp. 9–11. See also Pleadings, CR.75/26, p. 52.
240. *ICJ Reports*, 1975, pp. 12, 41.
241. Ibid., p. 42.
242. Ibid., p. 44. See also Judges Ammoun, ibid., p. 83, and Forster, ibid., p. 103.
243. Ibid.
244. Ibid., p. 49.
245. Ibid., p. 63.
246. Ibid. See also the *Reparations* case, *ICJ Reports*, 1949, pp. 174, 178.
247. Ibid., p. 64.
248. See *Island of Palmas* case, 2 *RIAA*, pp. 829 and 845, and *ICJ Pleadings, Minquiers and Ecrehos* case, vol. ii, p. 375. See also Jennings, op. cit., pp. 28–31.
249. Pleadings, CR.75/26, p. 54. The terra nullius question was to be interpreted, the court held, by reference to the law in force at the time of Spanish colonization of the territory, *ICJ Reports*, 1975, pp. 12, 38–9, but the legal ties question had to be interpreted in the light of the decolonization process, ibid., pp. 40–1. This posed some awkward problems as to time.
250. Pleadings, CR.75/31, p. 15.
251. For example, see *ICJ Reports*, 1975, pp. 12, 36, and 68.
252. Ibid., pp. 12, 167–71.

CHAPTER 2

1. See in general Umozurike, *Self-determination in International Law* (1972); Rigo Sureda, *The Evolution of the Right of Self-determination* (1973); Shukri, *The Concept of Self-determination in the United Nations* (1965); Calogeropoulos-Stratis, *Le Droit des peuples à disposer d'eux-mêmes* (1973); Cobban, *The Nation-State and National Self-determination* (1969); Johnson, *Self-determination Within the Community of Nations* (1967); Pomerance, *Self-determination in Law and Practice* (1982). See also Introduction, n. 56.
2. *International Law in Historical Perspective*, vol. i (1968), p. 321.
3. Cobban, op. cit., pp. 33–6. The word 'self-determination' is derived from the German *Selbstbestimmungsrecht*, used by the radical philosophers of the mid nineteenth century; see Umozurike, op. cit., p. 3.
4. See Emerson, *From Empire to Nation* (1960), p. 297.
5. Tunkin, *Droit international public* (1965), p. 43. Note that although self-determination and the principle of nationalities were often used synonymously, there is a theoretical difference in that the unit of self-determination may well

make a decision which runs counter to the attraction of the nation and leads not to greater unity but greater fragmentation of the nation; see Redslob, 'Le Principe des nationalités', 37 *HR* (1931), 5. See also Carr, *The Conditions of Peace* (1942), p. 60.

6. Cobban declared that 'the individual did not determine his nation, rather the nation determined the individual', op. cit., p. 115. See also Macartney, *National States and National Minorities* (1934), p. 100. It is suggested that the idea should be phrased in terms of the individual not being able to choose his State, that function being performed by the nation. Judge Dillard commented that the 'cardinal restraint which the legal right of self-determination imposes' is that it is 'for the people to determine the destiny of the territory, and not the territory the destiny of the people', *ICJ Reports*, 1975, pp. 12, 122.
7. Zimmern wrote that 'English people when they invoke the principle of nationality mean the principle of democracy', *Nationality and Government* (1918), p. 50, quoted in Cobban, op. cit., p. 114. See also De Visscher, *Theory and Reality in Public International Law* (3rd edn. (trans.), 1968), pp. 33–7.
8. The nationalist school of international lawyers following Mazzini did indeed propose that national self-determination was a legal right, but their position was an extreme one in the period; see Wright, *Mandates under the League of Nations* (1930), p. 11.
9. Self-determination was included in a resolution in the London International Socialist Congress in 1969; see Lenin, *The Right of Nations to Self-determination* (1951), p. 42.
10. *US Congressional Record*, L. III part 9, 8854, 27 June 1916. This principle was his 'favourite panacea' according to Minogue, *Nationalism* (1967), p. 137.
11. The last of the four points put to Congress. *US Congressional Record*, L. VI part 2, 1952, 11 February 1918. The 1919 border adjustments were to follow 'clearly recognised lines of nationality'; Secretary Lansing proclaimed 'what misery it will cause', *The Peace Negotiations: A Personal Narrative* (1921), pp. 97–8. Wambaugh, *Plebiscites Since the World War*, vol. i (1933), p. 4. Temperly wrote that Wilson's ideas 'in themselves were few and simple but their consequences when developed by the war were such as to produce the most far-reaching results', *A History of the Peace Conference of Paris* (1920–4), vol. i, p. 173. See also Pomerance, 'The United States and Self-determination: Perspectives on the Wilsonian Conception', 70 AJIL (1976), 1.
12. Wilson put forward a suggestion in the first and second drafts of the Covenant that territorial adjustments between States should be pursuant to the principle of self-determination, but this was not accepted; Miller, *The Drafting of the Covenant*, vol. ii (1928), pp. 12–13.
13. Dupuis, 'Règles générales du droit de la paix', 32 *HR* (1931), 37. Cobban

noted that the more the work of the peace conference was studied, the less it seemed to have been under the control of this principle, op. cit., p. 32. Schuman wrote that self-determination was appealed to when there was a possibility of reducing the territory and power of the defeated States, *International Politics* (5th edn., 1953), p. 492. See also Wambaugh, op. cit., p. 42, and Calogeropoulos-Stratis, op. cit., pp. 49–52.

14. See, e.g., De Azcarate, *The League of Nations and National Minorities: An Experiment* (1945); Claude, *National Minorities—An International Problem* (1955); Lador-Lederer, *International Group Protection* (1968). Kunz writes that the international law for the protection of minorities was a substitute in cases where the principle of self-determination could not be applied and can be regarded as a 'strict and logical corollary of the principle of self-determination of nations': 'The Present Status of International Law for the Protection of Minorities', 48 *AJIL* (1954), 282. See also Robinson, 'From Protection of Minorities to Promotion of Human Rights', *Jewish Yearbook of International Law* (1949), 115.
15. The Aaland Islands Dispute, Council Doc. B7/21/68/106.
16. Hall, *Mandates, Dependencies and Trusteeship* (1948); Wright, op. cit.; Haas, 'The Reconciliation of Conflicting Colonial Policy Aims: The Acceptance of the League of Nations Mandate System', 6 *International Organisation* (1952), 521.
17. Article 22 of the Covenant of the League. The International Court emphasized that the mandate was created in the interests of the territory's inhabitants and of humanity in general as an international institution with an international object, i.e. the sacred trust of civilization; *ICJ Reports*, 1950, p. 132. ICJ noted that there was 'little doubt that the ultimate objective of the sacred trust was the self-determination and independence of the peoples concerned', *ICJ Reports*, 1971, p. 31.
18. It was, however, proclaimed by the USSR in her peace treaties with the Baltic States in 1920. See Martens, *Recueil général de traités*, 3rd Series, xi, pp. 864, 877, and 888; Cobban, op. cit., pp. 187–218. The Treaty of Brest-Litovsk in 1917 imposed on Russia by Germany was declared to be founded on the cardinal principles of the renunciation of war and self-determination; see Shapiro (ed.), *Soviet Treaty Series*, vol. i (1950), p. 1. The communist theory subordinated self-determination to the interests of the working class; see Lenin, *Marx, Engels, Marxism* (1934), p. 147. Stalin emphasized that the border territories of Russia and the nations therein 'like all other nations have an inalienable right to secede from Russia . . . but the interest of the popular masses tells us that the demand of secession . . . is deeply counter-revolutionary at the present stage of the Revolution'. See Whiteman, *Digest of International Law* vol. iv (1965), p. 56.
19. The Aaland Islands Question, *LNOJ* Sp. Suppl. no. 3, Report of the Commission of Jurists, 1920, pp. 5–6. See also Barros, *The Aaland Islands Question: Its Settlement by the League of Nations* (1968); Verzijl, op. cit., pp.

328–32; and Modeen, 'The International Protection of the National Identity of the Aaland Islands' in *Scandinavian Studies in Law* (1973), p. 177.

20. Op. cit., p. 329.
21. 'History of the Principle of Self-Determination', *Grotian Society Papers* (1968), p. 96.
22. *Decade of American Foreign Policy, Docs. 1941–9* (1950), p. 1. These and other principles were reaffirmed in the Declaration by the United Nations in January 1942, ibid., pp. 2–3, and in the Declaration on Liberated Europe in February 1945, ibid., pp. 27, 29. Churchill later noted that the Atlantic Charter was only intended to apply to conquered Europe; see Huber, 'National Self-determination', *Social Research*, (1943), p. 1.
23. *Docs. of the UN Conference on International Organisation*, iii (1945), p. 622.
24. Lachs, however, regarded self-determination as a pre-existing legal norm, 'Law In and Of the UN', *IJIL* (1960), 432; Brown, 'Self-determination in Central Europe', 14 *AJIL* (1920), 235; Starushenko, 'Principle of National Self-determination', in *Soviet Foreign Policy* (1963), p. 162; and Rousseau, *Droit international public* (1953), p. 82; cf. Briggs, *The Law of Nations* (1953), p. 65.
25. Article 73 of the Charter proclaimed the paramountcy of the interests of the inhabitants of non-self-governing territories and noted that the administering powers were pledged to develop self-government. Article 76 emphasized the promotion of progressive development towards self-government or independence, having regard to the wishes of the people concerned as one of the basic objectives of the trusteeship system.
26. E/CN.4/SR.505, p. 5. See also the views of the British delegate that self-determination was purely a political principle, E/CN.4/SR.503, p. 7. See also O'Connell, *International Law*, vol. i (2nd edn., 1970), p. 312.
27. Bentwich and Martin, *Commentary on the Charter of the UN* (1950), p. 7. See also Giraud, 'Le Droit international public et la politique', 110 *HR* (1966), 744; cf. Nincic, *The Problem of Sovereignty in the Charter and in the Practice of States* (1970), p. 221, and Wright, 'Recognition and Self-determination', *PASIL* (1954), 23–7, and id., *HR* (1959 III), 182.
28. However, Bokor-Szego regards this not as detracting from its legality but as constituting it as a *lex imperfecta* which has been perfected by later regulation and application, *New States and International Law* (1970), pp. 16–27, but see Schwarzenberger, *Dynamics of International Law* (1976), p. 10.
29. Op. cit., p. 7.
30. 'The Role of the United Nations in Relation to Human Rights—Is it Misconceived?', *Nobel Symposium*, 7 (1968), 95–101.
31. See the Views of Ethiopia, Liberia, and Egypt, African Original Members of the UN, that the Charter provisions regarding self-determination have given rise to international legal rights and obligations, *GAOR* 6th Session, 3rd Committee, 361st, 363rd, 366th, 371st meetings, E/CN.4/SR.252–9; *GAOR* 7th Session, 3rd Committee, 286th, 400th–47th, 465th, and 438th

meetings; *GAOR* 9th Session, 3rd Committee, 562nd–73rd, 575th, and 580th–582nd meetings.

32. *Law of the United Nations* (1950), pp. 51–3. See also pp. 29–32. See, generally, Schwelb, 'The International Court of Justice and the Human Rights Clauses of the Charter', 66 *AJIL* (1972), 337. In his report to Commission I, the Rapporteur noted that it was understood that the 'principle of equal rights of peoples and that of self-determination are two component elements of one norm'. Summary Reports of Committee I/I Doc.1/1/1 of 16 May 1945, 6 *UNCIO Docs*., p. 296.
33. 'Recognition and Self-determination', *PASIL* (1954), 23–37, and id., 'National Courts and Human Rights—the Fujii Case', 45 *AJIL* (1951), 73. Lauterpacht stated that 'there is a distinct element of legal duty in the undertaking expressed in Article 56 . . . any construction of the Charter according to which members of the United Nations are in law entitled to disregard—and violate—human rights and fundamental freedoms is destructive of both the legal and moral authority of the Charter as a whole', *International Law and Human Rights* (1950), pp. 147–9. Sloan noted that the provisions on human rights, Articles 55 and 56, embodied a definite and positive legal obligation; 'Human Rights, the United Nations and International Law', *Nordisk Tidsskrift for International Ret* (Acta Scandinavica Juris Gentium 20) (1950), 30–1. See Judge Tanaka, *ICJ Reports*, 1966, pp. 288–9. Cf. Hudson's view that the human rights provisions in the Charter are purely a programme of action and no more—'A frame for a picture must not be mistaken for the picture itself'—'Integrity of International Instruments', 42 *AJIL* (1948), 105–8, and *Yearbook of the ILC* (1949), 178. See also Akehurst, *A Modern Introduction to International Law* (3rd edn., 1977), p. 77.
34. 'Problems of Self-determination and Political Rights in Developing Countries', *PASIL* (1966), 134.
35. *Transactions of the Grotius Society* (1953), 5, 23.
36. See, e.g. Kaeckenbeeck, 'La Charte de San Francisco dans ses rapports avec le droit international', 70 *HR* (1947), 113, 266.
37. Schwarzenberger notes that 'when the Charter of the United Nations came into existence, neither the principle of national self-determination nor that of the self-determination of peoples was a principle of customary international law, a general principle of law recognised by civilised nations or in the framework of the Charter of the United Nations more than a constituent element of Purpose Two of the United Nations', *International Constitutional Law* (1976), p. 153.
38. See Robinson, *Human Rights and Fundamental Freedoms in the Charter of the United Nations—A Commentary* (1946), p. 105.
39. Schwarzenberger, op. cit., pp. 158–67.
40. Judge Tanaka noted that 'the accumulation of authoritative pronouncements such as resolutions, declarations, decisions, etc. concerning the

interpretation of the Charter by the component organs of the international community can be characterised as evidence of the *international custom* referred to in Article 38(1)b', *ICJ Reports*, 1966, p. 292 (emphasis added). Judge Nervo declared that 'included among the international rules which are binding on the administration of the international territory of Namibia are declarations formally adopted by the principal organs of the United Nations which represent generally accepted interpretations and applications of the provisions in the United Nations Charter', *ICJ Reports*, 1971, p. 119.

41. See, e.g., Kelsen, op. cit.; Schwarzenberger, op. cit.; Higgins, *The Development of International Law Through the Political Organs of the UN* (1963); Asamoah, *The Legal Significance of the Declarations of the General Assembly of the United Nations* (1966); Castaneda, *The Legal Effects of United Nations Resolutions* (1969), and other works cited.
42. Article 38(1) of the Statute of the ICJ.
43. Kelsen emphasized that the act of choice by the political bodies of the UN has a law-creating character which may result in replacing a legal norm by another norm of totally different content, op. cit., p. xv. Schachter has noted that when an organ applies a principle or rule of law to a particular set of facts, it is asserting a new rule of a more specific character and 'this is a law-creating act' so that 'once a decision is rendered by an authoritative body it has entered into the stream of decisions that will normally be looked to as a source of law': 'The Quasi-Judicial Role of the Security Council and General Assembly, 58 *AJIL* (1964), 964.
44. 'The Development of International Law by the Political Organs of the UN', *PASIL* (1965), 116–8. Schwelb notes that after the 1960 Colonial Declaration 'there are international documents which, although not concluded or ratified as treaties, are not "non-binding". One can say that they comprise a third category': 'Neue Etappen der Fortentwicklung des Völkerrechts durch die Vereinten Nationen', 13 *Archiv des Völkerrechts* (1966), 25–6. He declared that the difference between treaties and resolutions of international organizations is disappearing, ibid., p. 44.
45. See D'Amato, 'On Consensus', 8 *Canadian Yearbook of International Law* (1970), 104; ib., *The Concept of Custom in International Law* (1971), pp. 33–41, 187–99. Cf. Thirlway, *International Customary Law and Codification* (1972), pp. 76–9.
46. e.g. Elias, *Africa and the Development of International Law* (1972), p. 82. See also Judge Tanaka, *ICK Reports*, 1966, pp. 292, 294. Hevener writes, regarding the discussions of the ICJ in the South-West Africa case, 1966, and Namibia case, 1971, on the subject of human rights and international law that 'the general obligation is based on convention; its interpreted definition has developed as custom. The custom aspect of the court's opinion derives from a combination of custom reflected in the Charter and subsequent United Nations resolutions and action which interprets the Charter and gives evidence of the practice of States and *their* recognition of

the present binding nature of rules protective of human rights': 'The 1971 South-West Africa Opinion. A New International Juridical Philosophy', 24 *ICLQ* (1975), 794–5 (emphasis in original).

47. See Kelsen, op. cit., pp. xiiiff., and Oppenheim, *International Law*, vol. i (7th edn.), p. 857.
48. This is 'without prejudice to any relevant rules of the organisation'. This may provide a way around the literal-interpretation approach of Article 31 of the Vienna Convention, since it could be argued that rules permitting a more teleological and practice-oriented approach to Charter interpretation have been adopted. Such rules may be derived from practice as well as from the constituent documents of the organization concerned; see *UN Conference on the Law of Treaties, Official Records*, 1st Session, p. 147, para. 15. But cf. Judge De Castro's view that the Charter would not appear to fall within the framework of the Vienna Convention, *ICJ Reports*, 1971, pp. 16, 184.
49. Tunkin refers to the Charters of international institutions as treaties *sui generis*, *Theory of International Law* (1974), p. 325. Rosenne notes that by origin such charters are international treaties but by operation they are of a different genus and are in practice governed by fundamentally different principles; 'Is the Constitution of an International Organisation an International Treaty?', *Communicazioni e Studi* (1966), 21, 86, 66. See also *ICJ Reports*, 1962, p. 157.
50. See El Erian, 'The Legal Organisation of International Society' in *Manual of Public International Law*, ed. Sørensen (1968), p. 92.
51. Op. cit. (n. 44), p. 119.
52. *International Status of South-West Africa* case, *ICJ Reports*, 1050.
53. But see Judge Gros's dissenting opinion in the *Namibia* case, *ICJ Reports*, 1971, pp. 16, 341.
54. See, e.g., the Advisory Opinions on *Admission to the United Nations*, *ICJ Reports*, 1948, p. 63, and *Reparations for Injuries Suffered in the Service of the United Nations*, *ICJ Reports*, 1949, pp. 178–9. See also *Competence of the General Assembly for the Admission of a State to the United Nations*, *ICJ Reports*, 1950, p. 8. Fitzmaurice notes that the International Court in the years succeeding 1945 favoured a general approach to treaty interpretation based primarily on an elucidation of the text; 'The Law and Procedure of the International Court of Justice, 1951–4', 33 *BYBIL* (1957), 209.
55. See the joint dissenting opinion of Judges Basdevant, Winiarski, McNair, and Reed, *ICJ Reports*, 1948, p. 92.
56. See Fitzmaurice, 'The Law and Procedure of the International Court of Justice', 28 *BYBIL* (1951), 1–2.
57. Ibid. They, of course, will be of greater importance regarding the interpretation of ordinary treaties. See the Opinion of the Court in the *Interpretation of Peace Treaties* case (2nd Phase) to the effect that 'the Principle of Interpretation expressed in the maxim: *ut res magis valeat quam pereat* often referred to as the rule of effectiveness cannot justify the court in

attributing to the provisions for the settlement of disputes in the Peace Treaties a meaning . . . contrary to their letter and spirit', *ICJ Reports*, 1950, p. 221. See also *The Iranian Oil* case, *ICJ Reports*, 1952, p. 105, and the *Rights of US Nationals in Morocco* case, *ICJ Reports*, 1952, p. 196.

58. See e.g., the delegates of Afghanistan, *GAOR* 17th Session, 6th Committee, 142–4-A/C.6/SR.762; Algeria, ibid., 138–9-A/C.6/SR.761; Argentina, ibid., 119–20-A/C.6/SR.758; Ceylon, ibid., 149–50-A/C.6/SR.762; Hungary, ibid., 112-A/C.6/SR.756; Syria, ibid., 156-A/C.6/SR.764; UAR, ibid., 18th Session, 6th Committee, 164-A/C.6/SR.811. See also McDougal, 'International Law, Power and Policy', 82 *HR* (1953), 143–57.

59. See Judge Azevedo, *ICJ Reports*, 1950, pp. 23–4. See also Judge Alvarez, who noted that 'an instrument . . . must develop not in accordance with the views of those who created it, but in accordance with the requirements of international life', *ICJ Reports*, 1948, p. 68. See also Schwarzenberger, op. cit., p. 137.

60. *ICJ Reports*, 1971, pp. 16, 31. Judge Alvarez went further than this in his dissenting opinion in the *Competence* case when he declared that 'a treaty or a text . . . acquires a life of its own. Consequently in interpreting it one must have regard to the exigencies of contemporary life rather than to the intentions of those who framed it', *ICJ Reports*, 1950, p. 18. This has been especially true with regard to the interpretation of the European Convention on Human Rights. In a number of cases the European Court of Human Rights has stressed that the Convention is a living instrument that must be interpreted 'in the light of present-day conditions'; see, e.g., *Tyrer* case, Series A, no. 26 (1978) at p. 15; the *Marckx* case, Series A, no. 32 (1979) at p. 14. See also Waldock, 'The Evolution of Human Rights Concepts and the Application of the European Convention on Human Rights' in *Mélanges offerts à Paul Reuter* (1981), p. 535.

61. *ICJ Reports*, 1971, pp. 16, 31.

62. See Higgins, who noted that 'in interpreting the constitutions of dynamic international organisations the primary canon should not be the intention of the original parties but rather the evidence which can be adduced of the obligations which the present members feel are incumbent upon them': 'The Development of International Law by the Political Organs of the United Nations', *PASIL* (1965), 119. This approach is characterized by Fitzmaurice as the theory of 'emergent purpose', whereby the teleological school is extended so that the objects become liable to change through time. He notes that 'whatever the attractions of this idea, it is clear that the process in question is a legislative rather than an interpretative one and must involve the assumption of a quasi-legislative function': 'The Law and Procedure of the International Court of Justice 1951–4' 33 *BYBIL* (1957), 203, 208.

63. *ICJ Reports*, 1971, pp. 16, 185. References were made here to *ICJ Reports*, 1949, p. 182, and *ICJ Reports*, 1962, pp. 208–15. See also the court's view

that 'when the Organisation takes action which . . . [is] appropriate for the fulfilment of one of the stated purposes of the United Nations, the presumption is that such action is not ultra vires the Organisation', *ICJ Reports*, 1962, p. 168. Judge Spender noted that 'the meaning of the text will be illuminated by the stated purposes to achieve which the terms of the Charter were drafted', ibid., p. 187. This last proposition is quoted by Judge De Castro as 'an authoritative criterion', *ICJ Reports*, 1971, pp. 16, 185.

64. *ICJ Reports*, 1971, p. 184. See also Judge Alvarez, *ICJ Reports*, 1950, p. 18, and ibid., 1951, p. 53. Judge Spender noted that 'the Charter must accordingly be interpreted, whilst in no way deforming or dislocating its language, so that the authority conferred upon the Organisation and its various organs may attach itself to new and unanticipated situations and events', *ICJ Reports*, *1962*, p. 187. The court had already declared that 'the rights and duties of an entity such as the Organisation must depend upon its purposes and functions as specified or implied in its constituent documents and developed in practice', *ICJ Reports*, 1949, p. 180. See also Fitzmaurice, loc. cit., p. 211; Gross, 'The International Court of Justice and the United Nations', 120 *HR* (1967), 370, 385; and Lauterpacht, *The Development of International Law by the International Court*, p. 280. See, for other examples of a teleological approach by the court, the *International Status of South-West Africa*, *ICJ Reports*, 1950, pp. 136–7; *South-West Africa Voting Procedure*, *ICJ Reports*, 1955, pp. 99, 104–5; *The Admissibility of Hearings of Petitioners by the Committee on South-West Africa*, *ICJ Reports*, 1956, p. 22; and *South-West Africa Preliminary Objections*, *ICJ Reports*, 1962, pp. 329 and 326.

65. Higgins has made the point that the treatment of treaties by the political organs of the UN has involved the prevalence of the teleological rather than the literal approach. She notes that 'given the fact that the advent of the general multi-lateral convention with its large participation and provisions for subsequent accession makes it hard to ascertain precisely the intention of the parties, it is understandable that the mushrooming of such instruments under United Nations auspices should encourage the view of interpretation which rests on the presumed objects of the treaty', *The Development of International Law Through the Political Organs of the UN* (1963), pp. 308–9. This is, of course, a manifestation of the general approach adopted with regard to the interpretation of the UN Charter itself.

66. 13 *UNCIO Docs.*, pp. 709–10. See also Higgins, op. cit., p. 304, and Brugiero, *Les Pouvoirs de l'Assemblée Générale des Nations Unies en matière politique et de sécurité* (1955), p. 25. As regards the doctrine of implied powers, see the view of the International Court, *ICJ Reports*, 1949, pp. 179 and 198. See Judge Fitzmaurice, *ICJ Reports*, 1971, pp. 281–2, and Judge Gros, ibid., p. 339. See also Bowett, *The Law of International Institutions* (3rd edn., 1975), p. 301; Seyersted, 'International Personality of Intergovernmental Organisations', 4 *IJIL* (1964), 55; and Tunkin, op. cit. (n. 49), pp. 334–5.

67. 'The General Assembly and the Security Council of the United Nations', 29 *BYBIL* (1952), 66–7. See also El Erian, op. cit., p. 92.
68. See, e.g., Lachs, 'Law In and Of the United Nations', 1 *IJIL* (1960–1), 429, 439.
69. See Schachter, 'The Relation of Law, Politics and Action in the United Nations', 109 *HR* (1963), 169, 187.
70. *ICJ Reports*, 1971, pp. 16, 111. See also Judge Ammoun, *ICJ Reports*, 1970, pp. 302–4. However, Virally notes that the absence of an organ of final competence weakens the argument that Assembly resolutions and declarations can be regarded as authoritative interpretations of the Charter; 'Droit international et décolonisation', (1963), 563.
71. 'Any such question relating to the maintenance of international peace and security on which action is necessary shall be referred to the Security Council by the General Assembly either before or after discussion.'
72. *ICJ Reports*, 1962, pp. 151, 164.
73. Ibid., p. 165.
74. 'The expenses of the Organisation shall be borne by the members as apportioned by the General Assembly.'
75. *ICJ Reports*, 1962, p. 168. This case contrasts with the *Competence* case, *ICJ Reports*, 1950, p. 4, where the court stressed that the Assembly could not decide upon an application for admission in the absence of a Security Council recommendation and that 'it is in the nature of things that the recommendation should come before the decision', ibid., p. 7. The court rejected the argument that no recommendation was equivalent to an unfavourable recommendation on which the Assembly could then decide positively, ibid., p. 9. Greig differentiates the cases on the basis of the more generally framed provisions in the former which permitted a more dynamic approach by the court, *International Law* (2nd edn., 1976), p. 486. In addition one must point out that the purposes of the Organization include the maintenance of international peace and security and that according to Article 24 the Council possesses only the primary responsibility for this, whereas universality of membership is not a stated purpose of the Organization, though highly desirable.
76. A similar process of interpretation and application has taken place with respect to Article 2(7), which declares that nothing in the Charter is to authorize the UN to intervene in matters essentially within the domestic jurisdiction of States. Matters concerning colonial affairs have in practice been excluded from this provision. Higgins notes that a narrow interpretation of the Article has taken place in the UN practice, and that 'the actions of the Organisation have been in conformity with the principle that an area covered by international law changes and develops—not in an arbitrary manner, but in accordance with interpretation made in good faith and in the hope of making the Charter effective', op. cit., p. 130. El Erian stresses that 'wherever possible a flexible interpretation has been maintained by the concept of domestic jurisdiction, the main criterion being the attainment of

the aims and purposes of the Organisation', loc. cit., p. 95. See, for example of cases, *UN Repertory of Practice* (1955), vol. i, pp. 55–156. See also Judge Ammoun, *ICJ Reports*, 1970, pp. 313–14.

77. *ICJ Reports*, 1962, p. 168. See also *ICJ Reports*, 1971, p. 45.

78. The competence of the political organs of the UN may to a large extent depend upon commonly accepted practices. For example, the right of the Assembly to determine which territories fell within the scope of Article 73 of the Charter has now been recognized. See Higgins, op. cit., pp. 110–13. Resolution 1747 (XVI), for example, affirmed that Southern Rhodesia was a non-self-governing territory within the meaning of Chapter XI of the Charter. Note also the statement of the Philippines delegate that if there was a lacuna in Chapter XI, it 'could be remedied by a reasonable interpretation in keeping with the principle that any restrictive construction of an international agreement which would nullify or circumvent its manifest purpose should be rejected', *GAOR* 1st Session, part 2, 4th Committee, part 3, pp. 34–55.

79. e.g. Security Council resolution 301 (1971) accepting the *Namibia* opinion of the ICJ.

80. The court has, however, noted that 'the political character of an organ cannot release it from the observance of the treaty provisions established by the Charter when they constitute limitations on its powers or criteria for its judgement', *ICJ Reports*, 1948, p. 64; cf. Judge Morelli, *ICJ Reports*, 1962, pp. 960–1. See also Judges Fitzmaurice, ibid., p. 200, and Winiarski, ibid., p. 230.

81. Asamoah, however, writes that the danger of arbitrariness has been overestimated and this is because when 'protests of irregularity have been raised and overruled expressly or impliedly, and practice proceeds on the assumption that the interpretation is valid, the interpretation will become unimpeachable and the practice built upon it will attain the status of law', op. cit., p. 39. It is suggested nevertheless that one does not follow from the other.

82. Verdross notes that 'any authentic interpretation of a legal norm may proceed only from the authority which created it, or from a superior authority, or perhaps as a result of a procedure which has been determined by these authorities. We find such a procedure for the present case in Articles 108 and 109 of the United Nations Charter', *Kann die Generalversammlung der Vereiten Nationen das Völkerrecht weiterbilden?* p. 695, quoted in Tunkin, op. cit. (n. 49), p. 171; see, generally, Kelsen, op. cit., pp. 816ff., and Goodrich, Hambro, and Simons, *The Charter of the United Nations, Commentary and Documents* (3rd edn., 1969), p. 641ff.

83. See Rousseau, *Droit international public* vol. i (1970), para. 283, and the *Air Transport Services Agreement Arbitration*, 38 ILR 182.

84. 'The Law and Procedure of the International Court of Justice, 1951–4', 33 *BYBIL* (1951), 20–1.

85. See the *Competence of the ILO with Respect to Agricultural Labour*, *PCIJ* Series

B, no. 2; *The Rights of US Nationals in Morocco*, *ICJ Reports*, 1952, p. 185; *The Anglo-Iranian Oil* case, *ICJ Reports*, 1952, p. 92. In the latter case the court, in interpreting an Iranian unilateral declaration accepting its compulsory jurisdiction, referred to an Iranian law passed after the date of the signature of the declaration, and before its ratification, and noted with respect to a particular clause in the law that 'this clause . . . is in the opinion of the court a decisive confirmation of the intention of the government of Iran at the time when it accepted the compulsory jurisdiction of the court', ibid., p. 107. See also Waldock's 3rd Report to the ILC, *Yearbook of the ILC* (1964), ii, 198.

86. Article 38 of the International Law Commission's Draft Articles on the Law of Treaties provided that 'a treaty may be modified by subsequent practice in the application of the treaty establishing the agreement of the parties to modify its provisions'; see *Yearbook of the ILC* (1966), ii, 236. This provision was deleted at the Vienna Conference by 53 votes to 15, with 26 abstentions; UN Conference on the Law of Treaties, Official Records, First Session, pp. 207–15. After a consideration of the views expressed by States voting in favour of the proposal to delete, Akehurst concludes that 'it is thus difficult to interpret the deletion of Article 38 as a clear rejection of the view that existing law allowed a treaty to be amended by subsequent practice'; 'The Hierarchy of the Sources of International Law', 47 *BYBIL* (1974–5), 273, 277.
87. Akehurst notes that 'subsequent practice often modifies the constituent treaties of international organisations', ibid.
88. Fitzmaurice emphasizes that 'it is, of course, axiomatic that the conduct in question must have been . . . in the case of general multilateral conventions, of the great majority of the parties', loc. cit., p. 223. Rajan writes that a majority is sufficient, *United Nations and Domestic Jurisdiction* (2nd edn., 1961), p. 405.
89. But cf. Tunkin, op. cit. (n. 49), p. 339. See also Judge Spender, *ICJ Reports*, 1962, pp. 151, 191. There is much to commend Akehurst's view that one ought to apply by analogy any amendment clause that exists in the constituent treaty so that, in the case of the UN, the Charter may be amended by a practice supported by two-thirds of the members States, including the permanent members of the Security Council; loc. cit., p. 278.
90. Op. cit. (n. 49), p. 339.
91. Ibid., pp. 124, 146.
92. Ibid., pp. 171–2, 339. See Schachter, op. cit., p. 186. See also id., 'Interpretation of the Charter in the Political Organs of the United Nations' in *Law, State and International Order; Essays in Honour of Hans Kelsen* (1964), p. 269.
93. Fitzmaurice notes that 'it is difficult to deny that the meaning of a treaty, or some part of it (particularly in the case of certain kinds of treaties and conventions) may undergo a process of change or development in the

course of time. Where this occurs it is the practice of the parties in relation to the treaty that effects and indeed *is* that change or development', loc. cit., p. 225.

94. Judge Spender has argued that one cannot equate a principle of subsequent practice of parties to a treaty with the practice of international organizations themselves, *ICJ Reports*, 1962, pp. 192, 195. However, the subsequent conduct of international organizations is based upon the practice of States; for example, voting and statements and the actions of the former are predicated upon the practice of the latter. See also Tunkin, op. cit., p. 339.
95. *ICJ Reports*, 1962, pp. 196–7. Judge Spender notes that changes in treaty-charters may be accomplished only in accordance with the revision clauses in such instruments; they 'cannot be altered at the will of the majority of the member States no matter how often that will is expressed . . . and no matter how large be the majority of member States which asserts its will in this matter', ibid. See also Vallat, 'The Competence of the United Nations General Assembly', 97 *HR* (1959), 211, and Bokor-Szego, op. cit., pp. 29–30.
96. See generally Cross, *Statutory Interpretation* (1976), and Dias, *Jurisdiction* (4th edn., 1976), chap. 7.
97. Loc. cit., p. 212.
98. Op. cit. (n. 49), p. 339. He notes that to allow custom to modify any treaty provisions would be inadvisable and dangerous for the stability of international treaties, ibid., p. 146. Lachs suggests that there may be no need to amend the Charter where the interpretation confirms a general principle defined in the Charter, 'Law In and Of the United Nations', 1 *IJIL* (1960), 429, 440.
99. See *ICJ Reports*, 1971, p. 22, and p. 117 (Judge Nervo) and 186 (Judge De Castro).
100. Op. cit. (n. 49), pp. 339–43. Cf. Goodrich, who treats resolution 377 (v) as a 'liberal interpretation' of the UN Charter: *The United Nations* (1959), p. 168.
101. See Tunkin, op. cit. (n. 49), p. 160, and Akehurst, loc. cit., pp. 277–8, n. 7.
102. Op. cit., pp. 186–7. See also Lachs, loc. cit., p. 439, and Judge Winiarski, *ICJ Reports*, 1962, pp. 227–34. Asamoah adopts this approach as well, op. cit., p. 35. Schachter also appears to suggest that only recommendations associated with the assertion of legal rights and obligations may constitute authoritative precepts derived from the Charter; 'Interpretation of the Charter in the Political Organs of the UN', *Law, State and International Order: Essays in Honour of Hans Kelsen* (1964), pp. 269, 271.
103. Schachter makes the point that such an authoritative interpretation can just as easily be contained in actions and statements made within or outside the UN as in General Assembly resolutions: 'The Relation of Law, Politics and Action in the United Nations', 109 *HR* (1963), 169, 186. Schwarzenberger writes that UN practice in the field of colonialism has departed from the

text of the Charter and indeed 'amounts to a *de facto* revision of the Charter which on the basis of acquiescence or ineffective opposition on the part of a diminishing number of colonial powers tends to harden into a *de jure* revision of the constitution of the United Nations', *A Manual of International Law* (5th edn., 1976), pp. 226–7.

104. A/811, resolution 217 (III).

105. Note here that resolution 637 (XVII) in 1952 declared that the right to self-determination was a prerequisite to the enjoyment of other human rights, and called for the inclusion of the right to self-determination in the International Covenants on Human Rights.

106. See Lauterpacht, *International Law and Human Rights* (1950), pp. 397–408, and Ganji, *International Protection of Human Rights* (1962), p. 161.

107. This view is taken by Brownlie, *Principles of Public International Law* (3rd edn., 1979), p. 571; id. *Basic Documents in International Law* (2nd edn., 1972), p. 144; and Judge Tanaka, *ICJ Reports*, 1966, p. 293. See Waldock, 106 *HR* (1962) 198–9, but cf. Oppenheim, op. cit., p. 745. See also 9 *Journal of the International Commission of Jurists* (1968), 94–5. The International Conference on Human Rights at Teheran in 1968 declared that the Universal Declaration 'states a common understanding of the peoples of the world concerning the inalienable and inviolable rights of all members of the human family and constitutes an obligation for the members of the international community', A/Conf.32/41. The Teheran Declaration was proclaimed by the General Assembly to be 'an important and timely reaffirmation of the principles embodied in the Universal Declaration of Human Rights', see resolution 2442 (XXIII). See also, with regard to the Teheran approach, the *Annual Report of the Secretary-General on the Work of the Organisation*, Sept. 1968, A/7201/Add.1 at 13; see Sohn and Buergenthal, *International Protection of Human Rights* (1973), p. 519. In a confusing phrase, Asamoah writes that the Universal Declaration is 'of quasi-legal significance as distinct from being the *fons et origo* of legal rights and duties', op. cit., p. 190. Waldock noted that 'the Declaration has acquired a status inside and outside the United Nation which gives it high authority as the accepted formulation of the common standard of human rights', *Human Rights in Contemporary International Law and the Significance of the European Convention* (1963), p. 15.

108. e.g. the need to maintain peace and security, as in Palestine in 1947–8 and Ruanda-Urandi in 1961.

109. e.g. the Tunisian and Algerian cases before the General Assembly; see Higgins, op. cit., pp. 94–7.

110. Below, pp. 83–6ff.

111. *ICJ Reports*, 1971, p. 22; the case here also reinforces the view that a practice, to constitute interpretation, does not necessarily have to amount to a custom. The court referred to a practice 'consistently and uniformly' followed, thus recalling the discussion in the *Asylum* case, *ICJ Reports*, 1950,

p. 266, but omitting any mention of *opinio juris*. Nevertheless the practice became a general practice of the Organization and thus an authoritative interpretation of the relevant Charter provisions.

112. See Judge Ammoun, *ICJ Reports*, 1970, pp. 313–14, and Higgins, op. cit., pp. 58–130.
113. Ibid., pp. 113–16, and Schwarzenberger, op. cit., p. 167.
114. See Rigo Sureda, *The Evolution of the Right of Self-Determination* (1973), pp. 48–53, and *ICJ Reports*, 1975, pp. 12, 36.
115. The voting on the part of the resolution concerning self-determination as a human right was 38 to 13 with 9 abstentions (with France, UK, and USA opposing); see A/C.3/SR.642. See also Calogeropoulos-Stratis, op. cit., p. 139. The proclamation of self-determination as a human right tended to confuse the issue since it was really only intended to stress decolonization as a fundamental norm in international relations. The conclusion that self-determination as a human right was therefore applicable beyond the colonial situation and with reference to minority situations in particular was strongly rejected; see, e.g. A/C.31SR.671, A/C.3/SR.888, and A/C.3/SR.642. The right to self-determination was also stressed in resolution 742 (VIII), which set out a list of factors to be considered regarding the readiness of a people for self-government. See also resolution 648 (VIII).
116. See the preceding discussions in the 8th Session of the Commission on Human Rights, *ECOSOC OR*, 14th Session, suppl. 4, paras. 75–91, E/2256 and E/2256 annexe 1. See also ECOSOC resolution 472(XV).
117. See, e.g., E/1371, E/1681, E/1992, E/2256, E/2447. See in general on the Commission on Human Rights, A/Conf.36/6 at pp. 33–47.
118. E/2573.
119. ECOSOC resolution 545G(XVIII).
120. By ECOSOC resolution 586 D (XX). See for the text of the recommendation E/2731 and Corr. 1. See also for the discussion E/CN.4/SR.500, p. 15, E/CN.4/SR.503, p. 8, and E/CN.4/SR.505, p. 5.
121. Resolution 738 (VIII).
122. *ECOSOC OR* 18th Session suppl. 7, annexes I, II, III and ECOSOC resolution 545B (XVIII). By resolution 833 (IX) the Assembly recommended that the 3rd Committee should give priority to an article-by-article consideration of the draft Covenants.
123. Commission on Human Rights, report of 10th Session, ECOSOC OR 18th Session, suppl. 7, pp. 62, 65, 66.
124. A/3077. Para. 2 referred to the right to dispose freely of natural wealth and resources. Certain members of the 3rd Committee felt that the inclusion of an article on the right to self-determination would be incompatible with Article 2(7) of the Charter, A/2910/Add.2. The text which was to appear in both International Covenants was adopted by 33 votes to 12 with 13 abstentions.
125. The fact that a resolution is adopted as a declaration rather than a

recommendation is not significant as far as straight legal principle is concerned, although it is more formal and the level of expectation regarding its implementation is higher. See the reply of the UN Secretariat, E/CN.4/L.610, quoted in Asamoah, op. cit., p. 24, and Sohn and Buergenthal, op. cit., pp. 519–20.

126. *GAOR* 18th Session, 1169th meeting, para. 5 (Nov. 1962). Rosenstock described it as 'a document only slightly less sacred than the Charter' for the Afro-Asian States; 'The Declaration of Principles of International Law Concerning Friendly Relations: A Survey', 65 *AJIL* (1971), 713, 730.
127. *The Sources and Evidence of International Law* (1965), p. 22.
128. A/4501, A/BUR/SR.130, A/L.312/Rev.1, and *GAOR* 15th Session, 902nd, 903rd, 925th–939th, 944th–947th meetings. See *UN Repertory of Practice* (1972, vol. iii, suppl. no. 3, pp. 44–52.
129. See *Yearbook of the UN* (1960), 44–50.
130. e.g. Liberia, *GAOR* 15th Session, 931st meeting; Madagascar, ibid., 944th meeting; Peru, ibid., 930th meeting; Tunisia, ibid., 929th meeting; Yugoslavia, ibid., 928th meeting; and UAR, ibid., 18th Session, 6th Committee, 164.
131. e.g. Brownlie, op. cit., p. 576; Lachs, op. cit., p. 439; Asamoah, op. cit., pp. 177–85; cf. Arangio-Ruiz, 'The Normative Role of the General Assembly of the United Nations and the Declaration on Principles of Friendly Relations', 137 *HR* (1972, 517.
132. e.g. the Swedish delegate, *GOAR* 15th Session, 946th meeting. See also the Australian delegate, ibid., 18th Session, 6th Committee, 205, A/C.6/SR.817.
133. It has also been possible for the mandate relationship to continue unconverted to the trusteeship system. Article 77(1) of the Charter noted this; see also *International Status of South-West Africa, ICJ Reports*, 1950, p. 128.
134. A/4502 and Corr. 1, *GAOR* 15th Session, 947th meeting. See also *Yearbook of the UN* (1960), 44–50.
135. Resolution 748 (VIII). The changed status of the island was later declared to be 'a new political formula which respected the right of peoples to self-determination', A/C.4/SR.1007, p. 32.
136. Resolution 2064 (XX).
137. Resolution 3155 (XXVIII), resolution 3285 (XXIX). See *UNMC* Oct. 1974, pp. 50–1, and ibid., Jan. 1975, pp. 56–7. See also resolution 849 (IX) regarding Greenland's association with Denmark, resolution 945 (X) regarding Netherlands and Antilles and Surinam, and resolution 1469 (XIV) regarding the integration of Alaska and Hawaii with the USA. However, by resolution 742 (VII) a non-self-governing territory choosing self-government only must be free to change its status in the future if so desired. See Rigo Sureda, op. cit., p. 63, Whiteman's *Digest*, vol. v, pp. 61–6, vol. vi, pp. 392ff. In the case of Puerto Rico an attempt in the Special Committee on Decolonization to reopen the question of its status in 1967 was

adjourned *sine die*, *Yearbook of the UN* (1967), 622–3. However, in 1972 a resolution was adopted by the Special Committee recognizing the 'inalienable right of the people of Puerto Rico to self-determination and independence'. See 'The Applicability of the Principle of Self-determination to Unintegrated Territories of the United States—The Cases of Puerto Rico and the Trust Territory of the Pacific Islands', *PASIL* (1973), pp. 1–27. In 1974 and 1975 the question was adjourned, but in October 1976 the Special Committee reaffirmed the right of the people of Puerto Rico to self-determination and independence, and agreed to resume consideration of the question at its next session in September 1977, *UNMC* Oct. 1976, p. 17.

138. Report of the UN Secretary-General, UN Special Release SPL/84. See generally resolutions 742 (VII) and 2625 (XXV), which accept statuses other than independence as legitimate exercises of self-determination.

139. Op. cit., pp. 29–30.

140. 'Le Comité de Décolonisation et le droit international', Revue générale de droit international public (1970), 402. See also Virally, 'Droit international et décolonisation', *AFDI* (1963), 536.

141. Castaneda refers to the Declaration as the 'modern interpretation of the principle of self-determination rendered by the most representative organ of the international community, on the basis of political trends and events since the Charter was signed', op. cit., p. 175. He stresses that the Declaration 'not only reflects the change that has been wrought; it also symbolises and concretises a new politico-juridical conception: the definite repudiation and end of colonialism', ibid. Lachs stresses that the Declaration bridges the gap regarding self-determination between the state of affairs at the time of the adoption of the Charter and the situation at the time of the Declaration; quoted in Bokor-Szego, op. cit., p. 29. Tunkin notes that the principle of self-determination in the Charter found 'authoritative confirmation and concretisation . . . in the Declaration of the General Assembly on the Granting of Independence to Colonial Countries and Peoples', op. cit., p. 65.

142. See also resolution 1541(XV). The ICJ referred to self-determination as 'the need to pay regard to the freely expressed will of peoples', *ICJ Reports*, 1975, pp. 12, 32, 33. See also Judge Dillard, ibid., p. 123.

143. The International Court has stressed that the Declaration 'provided the basis for the process of decolonisation' without explaining whether this is to be understood as a legal or political basis, *ICJ Reports*, 1975, pp. 19, 32. See also *ICJ Reports*, 1971, pp. 16, 31. Sukovic regarded the Declaration as 'an intermediate between the Charter which is an international treaty . . . and . . . resolutions of the General Assembly which have no binding force': 'The Colonial Question in the Charter and in the Practice of the UN', *International Problems of the Institute of Political Economy* (1966), p. 73. The Declaration was cited by no fewer than 95 subsequent resolutions in the 6

sessions following its passage: Anand, *New States and International Law* (1972), p. 82.

144. Op. cit., p. 101.

145. Ibid., p. 100. See also Feinberg, *The Arab–Israel Conflict in International Law* (1970), p. 47.

146. Assembly resolution 1654 (XVI) adopted by 97 votes to 0 with 4 abstentions. States administering trust and non-self-governing territories were called upon to 'take action without further delay with a view to the faithful application and implementation of the Declaration'. Higgins wrote that in the light of the lack of opposition to the Declaration and resolution 1654 (XVI) 'it seems academic to argue that as Assembly resolutions are not binding nothing has changed and that "self-determination" remains a mere "principle"' op. cit., p. 101.

147. Resolution 1890 (XVII). See also resolutions 1810 (XVII) and 2105 (XX).

148. See, e.g. *Contemporary Practice of the UK*, ed. Lauterpacht (1962), ii, pp. 280–2; Martine, op. cit., p. 357; and Mittelman 'Collective Decolonisation and the UN Committee of 24', 14 *JMAS* (1976), 41–64.

149. For example, resolutions 1064 (XI), 1568 (XV), 1579 (XV), 1596 (XV), 1065 (XV), 1626 (XVI), 1650 (XVI), 1724 (XVI), 1742 (XVI), 1746 (XVI), 1747 (XVI), 1807 (XVII), 1819 (XVII), 1897 (XVIII), 1913 (XVIII), 1949 (XVIII), 1954 (XVIII), 2063 (XX), 2107 (XX), 2184 (XX), 2183 (XXI), 2185 (XXI), 2226 (XXI), 2354 (XXII), 2379 (XXIII), 2383 (XXIII), 2428 (XXIII), 2983 (XXVII), 3162 (XXVIII), and 3292 (XXIX).

150. *ICJ Reports*, 1975, pp. 12, 136n.

151. *ICJ Reports*, 1971, pp. 16, 31.

152. *ICJ Reports*, 1975, pp. 12, 32.

153. The International Covenants had been under consideration since the 6th Session of the UN, and a draft prepared by the Commission on Human Rights was transmitted to the General Assembly by the Economic and Social Council on 29 July 1954, by resolution 545B (XVIII). See Ganji, op. cit., pp. 167–227; *Contemporary Practice of the UK*, ed. Lauterpacht (1963), ii, p. 223; Sohn and Buergenthal, op. cit., pp. 535–9. The movement to include self-determination in human rights was led by the USSR and the Afro-Asian States; see, e.g., A/C.3/SR.671.

154. See *UNMC* Apr. 1976, pp. 50–2.

155. Rao declared that once the Covenants came into force, self-determination would become 'a legal right beyond doubt, but its contours can only become clear through the medium of State practice', 'Right of Self-determination: Its Status and Role in International Law', *Internationales Recht und Diplomatie* (1968), p. 28; cf. Nincic's view that the Covenants 'reaffirm the legally binding nature of self-determination as a norm of international law for all States, whilst at the same time defining the concept and the contents of self-determination with considerable precision', *Problem of Sovereignty in the Charter and in the Practice of States* (1970), p. 221.

156. See, e.g., A/7326 (1968) p. 58 for a general view of the value of the Covenants. Mustafa has referred to the apparent anomaly of inserting an identical article on self-determination into two differing Covenants, since the Covenant on Civil and Political Rights recognizes certain rights as already in existence, while the Covenant on Social, Economic and Cultural Rights may be defined as a promotional instrument binding its signatories to take steps to achieve progressively the specified rights. This incompatibility argues Mustafa, makes self-determination ambiguous, especially since the parties are called upon to 'promote and respect' self-determination only, while they must 'respect and ensure' other civil and political rights: 'The Principle of Self-determination in International Law', 5 *International Lawyer* (1971), 482. Schwelb argues that the implementation rules of the Covenants are not applicable to self-determination: 'Some Aspects of the International Covenants on Human Rights of December 1966', *International Protection of Human Rights, Proceedings of the 7th Nobel Symposium* (1967), p. 111.
157. Emphasis added. See also Judge Nervo, *ICJ Reports*, 1971, p. 117, and *ICJ Reports*, 1975, p. 33.
158. Loc. cit., p. 522.
159. Ibid., p. 523. Arangio-Ruiz stresses later that the Declaration *per se* is neither part of customary international law nor an authoritative determination or interpretation of custom or treaty: ibid., p. 525.
160. See *UN Juridical Yearbook* (1966), 124–5; ibid. (1967), 198–201; ibid. (1968), 123–6; and ibid. (1969), 96–8. See also the various reports of the 6th Committee, e.g. A/6547, A/6955, A/7429, A/7809—discussing the reports of the Special Committee on Principles of International Law—A/6230, A/6799, A/7326, A/7619. See also Witten, 'The Friendly Relations Declaration', 12 *Harvard International Law Journal* (1971), 517–9, and Judge Nervo, *ICJ Reports*, 1971, pp. 16, 111, 115.
161. Judge Nervo has said that 'among the international rules which are binding on the administration of the international territory of Namibia are declarations and resolutions formally adopted by the principal organs of the United Nations which represent generally accepted interpretations and applications of the provisions of the United Nations Charter and which either are of general application or are stated to have specific reference to the situation of Namibia', *ICJ Reports*, 1971, pp. 16, 119.
162. See Akehurst, 'Custom as a Source of International Law', 47 *BYBIL* (1974–5), 1, 7, and Schwarzenberger, op. cit., pp. 28–9, 156, 299.
163. See Rigo Sureda, op. cit., pp. 54–67; Higgins, op. cit., pp. 110–16; Rajan, *United Nations and Domestic Jurisdiction* (1961). An analysis of how the Assembly's competence was established is beyond the scope of this work, but see in particular the letter of the Secretary-General inviting the views of member States on the definition of non-self-governing territories, A/74 under resolution 9 (I), 'Non-self-governing territories, A/74 under

resolution 9 (I), 'Non-self-governing territories: Summaries of Information transmitted to the Secretary-General during 1946' (1947), pp. 132–7, and resolutions 66 (I), 222 (III), 334 (IV), 567 (VI), 648 (VII), 742 (VIII), 1467 (XIV), 1541 (XV), 1542 (XV), 1747 (XVI). See also Higgins, op. cit., pp. 113–16.

164. See, e.g., resolutions 748 (VIII), 849 (IX), 945 (X), 1469 (XIV), 1747 (XVI).

165. Similarly with regard to the determination of a territory as a non-self-governing territory; above, p. 75, and see Wright, op. cit., 32–3, 69; Schachter, op. cit., 187–8; and *ICJ Reports*, 1962, p. 163.

166. Cf. Castaneda, op. cit., pp. 127–8, and Sloan, op. cit., p. 29.

167. Earlier draft resolutions proclaiming the right of the Moroccan and Tunisian peoples to self-determination narrowly failed to obtain the necessary two-thirds majority, see A/2526 and A/2530.

168. A/2924 and Add. 1.

169. General Assembly resolution 909 (X).

170. S/3609.

171. See the resolution before the 1st Committee in the 11th Session, A/C.1/L.167, and the two moderate resolutions which went before the Assembly, A/C.1/L.166 and A/C.1/L.167. Resolution 1012 (XI), which was adopted after the two resolutions were defeated, merely called for a peaceful, democratic, and just solution to the problem. In the 12th Session there was no agreement in the 1st Committee as to a resolution to be presented to the Assembly, A/C.1/L.194. Resolution 1184 (XII) merely stresses the need for a solution to the problem. In 1958, a draft resolution was adopted by the 1st Committee calling for the right of the Algerian people to independence, but it failed by one vote to be adopted by the Assembly, A/C.1/L.232. In 1959 a similar solution was similarly defeated, A/C.1/L.276. Higgins remarks that despite such failures support for the concept of a legal right to self-determination in such situations was growing, op. cit., p. 96.

172. Resolution 1573 (XV).

173. Above, p. 79.

174. See A/AC.109/L.9, A/5124, and General Assembly resolution 1747 (XVI) (opposed only by South Africa). The Special Committee had established a subcommittee on Southern Rhodesia, comprising India, Mali, Syria, Tanganyika, Tunisia, and Venezuela.

175. See Higgins, op. cit., pp. 102–3, and id., 'International Law, Rhodesia and the UN', *The World Today*, March 1967, pp. 94–106; McDougal and Reisman, 'Rhodesia and the UN: The Lawfulness of International Concern', 62 *AJIL* (1968), 1; and Fawcett, 'Security Council Resolutions on Rhodesia', 41 *BYBIL* (1965–6), 103.

176. See also A/5127 and Add. 1 and 2, A/5124, and *SCOR* 18th Year, 1066th meeting, para. 51, and ibid., 20th Year, 1202nd meeting, para. 90.

177. Resolution 2138 (XXI). See also resolutions 2151 (XXI), 2379 (XXIII), and 2383 (XXIII).

178. Kay, op. cit., p. 54.
179. Mittelman, op. cit., pp. 41–2.
180. *Per* Judge Ammoun, *ICJ Reports*, 1971, pp. 16, 75.
181. Schwarzenberger has listed a number of ways in which the purposes of the UN may be enlarged or transformed into legal duties of member States. Of these, three may be attained under the Charter itself, viz. treaty, practice accepted as law by the preponderant number of UN members, and general principles of law recognized by civilized nations: op. cit., pp. 156–7. These rules are based upon Article 38 of the ICJ Statute and it is suggested that this categorization is unduly restricting in requiring a practice to be accepted as law before it can operate within the framework of binding Charter interpretation.
182. One should note also Skubiszewski's view that 'law made by international organisations' is to be placed alongside treaty, custom, and general principles as sources of law, 'Enactment of Law by International Organisations', 41 *BYBIL* (1965–6), 198. See also Friedman, 'General Course in Public International Law', 127 *HR* (1969), 142–6.
183. *Law of Nations* (6th ed., 1963), p. 59.
184. Op. cit., p. 27 See also *ICJ Reports*, 1950, pp. 276, 277.
185. Gény regarded usage as the 'material and detectable element' in custom and *opinio juris* as the 'immaterial and psychological element', *Méthode d'interprétation et sources en droit privé positif*, (1899), para. 118. Different schools have arisen emphasizing one or other of these elements, e.g. Strupp, '*Les Règles générales du droit de la paix*', 47 *HR* (1934), 263, 304; Tunkin, 'Remarks on the Juridical Nature of Customary Norms of International Law', 49 *California Law Review* (1961), 419, 420–1, and op. cit. (n. 49), pp. 113–33; Cheng, 'UN Resolutions on Outer Space: "Instant" International Customary Law?' 5 *IJIL* (1965), 23, 35, 36, tend to stress the need for *opinio juris* while Kelsen, 'Théorie du droit international coutumier', *Revue international de la théorie du droit* (new series) (1939), 253, 264–6, and Guggenheim, *Traité de droit international public* (1953), pp. 46–8, appear to dispute this. See also D'Amato, *The Concept of Custom in International Law* (1971); Thirlway, *International Customary Law and Codification* (1972); and Akehurst, 'Custom as a Source of International Law', 47 *BYBIL* (1974–5), 1.
186. *The New Nations in the United Nations* (1970), p. 45. Kay notes that there were 511 speeches devoted to decolonization (in plenary and main committee meeting) in the 15th Session, 928 in the 16th Session, 661 in the 17th Session, 554 in the 18th Session, 153 in the 19th Session, 624 in the 20th Session, and 896 in the 21st Session: ibid., pp. 46–8.
187. *GOAR* 16th Session, 1015th meeting, para. 54. Henkin has written that 'the struggle to end colonialism also swallowed up the original purpose of cooperation for promotion of human rights', 'The United Nations and Human Rights' 19 *International Organisation* (1965), 512. Self-determination, he declared, was 'added to the roster of human rights as an

additional weapon against colonialism', ibid. 513.

188. Resolutions could constitute statements of general principles of law recognized by civilized nations. Precisely what amounts to such general principles of law is a matter of controversy; see Asamoah, op. cit., pp. 61–6. O'Connell notes that there are three approaches to this problem: one, that it incorporates natural law into positive international law; two, that the general principles are only sources of positive international law and must be embodied in treaty or custom before they become legally operative; and three, that the court may utilize general principles embodied in the municipal laws of States: op. cit., p. 9. As far as self-determination is concerned, it is clear that points two and three are not relevant, while if point one is to be of use it has to be shown that the right is part of natural law, and that would be difficult.

189. See Thirlway, op. cit., 63–4.

190. General Assembly resolution 1962 (XVIII). Resolution 1721 (XVI), also unanimously adopted by the Assembly, proclaimed certain principles of law relating to outer space. The US representative in the Legal Sub-Committee of the Committee on the Peaceful Uses of Outer Space noted that 'when a General Assembly resolution proclaimed principles of international law—as resolution 1721 (XVI) had done—and was adopted unamimously, it represents the law as generally accepted in the international community', A/AC.105/C.2/SR.20, pp. 10–11. See also A/AC.105/C.2/SR.20, p. 7.

191. e.g. by the US and USSR, the only space powers at that time, A/C.1/PV.1342 at pp. 6–27 and ibid., pp. 27–46. These statements are reproduced in 58 *AJIL* (1964), 720–1.

192. e.g. Schwelb, 'The Nuclear Test Ban Treaty and International Law', 58 *AJIL* (1964), 645–6; Jenks wrote that the Declaration, while somewhat less than a treaty, must be regarded as rather more than a statement of custom: *Space Law* (1965), p. 185. But cf. Thirlway, op. cit., pp. 70–1; Darwin, 'The Outer Space Treaty', 42 *BYBIL* (1967), 280; and Cheng, loc. cit.

193. Akehurst proposes that one should accept as State practice 'any act or statement by a State from which views about customary law can be inferred', op. cit., p. 53. This would include physical acts, claims, declaration *in abstracto* (e.g. General Assembly resolutions), national laws and judgements, and omissions: ibid. But cf. D'Amato, op. cit., p. 88, and Thirlway, op. cit., pp. 58–9.

194. The necessity for *opinio juris* is accepted by virtually all writers in one form or another and by the International Court; see, e.g. *North Sea Continental Shelf* cases, *ICJ Reports*, 1969, pp. 3, 44; the *Asylum* case, *ICJ Reports*, 1950, pp. 266, 277; and Akehurst, op. cit., pp. 31–42.

195. Op. cit., p. 68. He notes that it is doubtful to regard the 1963 Declaration as an expression of existing law because it appears to lack sufficient State practice: ibid., p. 71.

196. The acceptance of UN resolutions as reflecting and strengthening

customary rules is widespread; see, e.g., *Anglo-Iranian Oil Co. Ltd* v *Supor*, 22 ILR (1955), 23, 40–1, and Assembly resolution 96 (I) on genocide. Akehurst argues that to constitute authority for the content of customary law, such resolutions must actually claim to be declaratory of existing law: 'Custom as a Source of International Law', 47 *BYBIL* (1974–5), 1, 6. Judge Ammoun has suggested that a number of similar Assembly resolutions might *per se* constitute a custom: *ICJ Reports*, 1975, pp. 12, 99.

197. See Briggs, *The Law of Nations*, p. 65, and Nussbaum, *Concise History of International Law* (1954), p. 186.
198. Higgins writes: 'The practice of the United Nations in this complex area of international affairs is very revealing and its importance can hardly be exaggerated', op. cit., p. 91.
199. *ICJ Reports*, 1975, pp. 12, 121.
200. See also the *Aaland Islands* question, p. 60 above. In the *Rights of Passage* case, India referred to the principle of self-determination as regards the population of the Portuguese enclaves. Portugal replied by asking the court to dismiss this line of argument, but the court held that it was no part of its judicial function to declare in the operative part of its judgement that such arguments were or were not well founded: *ICJ Reports* 1960, pp. 16–19, 32. Judge Nervo rhetorically declared that concepts of equality and freedom 'will inspire the vision and conduct of peoples the world over until the goal of self-determination and independence is reached', *ICJ Reports*, 1966, p. 457.
201. *ICJ Reports*, 1971, pp. 16, 31.
202. Judge Ammoun picked this up by declaring that 'although the Opinion does not lack persuasive force, it would be more persuasive if it traced the path by which this right of peoples has made its entry into positive international law', ibid., p. 74.
203. Ibid., p. 31.
204. Ibid. The court stressed that 'these developments leave little doubt that the ultimate objective of the sacred trust was that self-determination and independence of the peoples concerned', ibid.
205. *ICJ Reports*, 1975, p. 12, 32.
206. Ibid., p. 33.
207. Ibid., p. 34. Judge Petren emphasized that the law of decolonization does not yet constitute a complete body of doctrine and practice although its guiding principles have emerged inspired by a series of General Assembly resolutions and in particular the Colonial Declaration; ibid., p. 110.
208. Ibid., p. 121. He makes it clear that the court is thereby stating the law, not creating it: ibid., p. 122.
209. Ibid., p. 121. See further on this case below, p. 93.
210. But cf. Verzijl, op. cit., pp. 557–8; Kaur, 'Self-Determination in International Law' *IJIL* (1970), 479; Gross, 'The Right of Self-Determination in International Law' in *New States in the Modern World* (ed.

Kitson), quoted by Emerson, 'Self-Determination', 65 *AJIL* (1971), 461; Jennings, op. cit., p. 78; Emerson, *Self-Determination Revisited in the Era of Decolonisation*, (1964), pp. 63–4.

211. However, the discussions by the court, as distinct from individual judges, would appear to suggest that the binding quality of the rule lies in its character as an interpretation of the Charter.

212. See, e.g., Suy, *The Concept of Jus Cogens in International Law* (1967), pp. 17–77; Riesenfeld, 'Jus Dispositivum and Jus Cogens in International Law: in the Light of a Recent Decision of the German Supreme Constitutional Court', 60 AJIL (1966), 511; Schwarzenberger, 'International Jus Cogens', 43 *Texas Law Review* (1965), 455.

213. See Verdross, 'Jus Dispositivum and Jus Cogens in International Law', 60 *AJIL* (1966), 55, 56; Bokor-Szego, op. cit., p. 66; Tunkin, op. cit., (n. 49), p. 147.

214. Quadri, 'Cours général de droit international public', 113 *HR* (1964), 335; Lauterpacht, *Yearbook of the ILC* (1953), ii. 155; cf. Rousseau, *Principles généraux de droit international public*, vol. i, pp. 340–1. Note that the International Court has distinguished between obligations of a State vis-à-vis another State and obligations towards 'the international community as a whole', *ICJ Reports*, 1970, p. 32. Tunkin speaks of the growing internationalization of aspects of the life of society as the reason for jus cogens: op. cit. (n. 49), p. 157. See also Thirlway, op. cit., p. 29.

215. See *GOAR* 20th Session, 6th Committee, p. 40. Suy writes that 'the most surprising feature of the Commission's [i.e. ILC] debates is the unanimity with which members of the Commission approved the idea of *jus cogens*', op. cit., p. 50. Schwarzenberger writes that since *jus cogens* presupposes the existence of an effective *de jure* order, with legislative, judicial, and enforcement machinery, no such rules exist in customary law (op. cit., p. 24), although they do exist in relation to the Charter and organization of the UN (ibid., p. 206).

216. *Yearbook of the ILC* (1963), ii. 187, at pp. 198, 211, 216.

217. Ibid. (1966), ii. 247–9, as Article 50.

218. Op. cit., p. 244.

219. See Tunkin, op. cit. (n. 49), pp. 158–9. See also Bokor-Szego, op. cit., pp. 69–70; Verzijl, *International Law in Historical Perspective*, vol. i, (1968), p. 85; and Akehurst, 'The Hierarchy of the Sources of International Law', 47 *BYBIL* (1974–5), 273, 282–5, and the sources therein cited.

220. See Tunkin, op. cit. (n. 49), p. 158. He denies the automatic binding force of *jus cogens* upon new States: ibid., p. 159n.; cf. Bokor-Szego, op. cit., p. 70. See also Akehurst, loc. cit., p. 283.

221. The ILC left the full content of *jus cogens* 'to be worked out in State Practice and in the jurisprudence of international tribunals', *Report of the ILC*, A/6309/Rev.1, pp. 76–7. D'Amato falls between the two stools of the

existence or not of *jus cogens* by noting that it could be argued that a rule of *jus cogens* meant simply 'a *very strong* rule of customary international law' that might be changed by a number of treaties with contrary provisions, but is unlikely to be changed: op. cit., p. 132 (emphasis in original). It is submitted that this is a poor compromise since it possesses the disadvantages of the concept without the advantages.

222. The ILC refrained from providing such examples in its work since the inclusion of some examples might lead to misunderstanding as to the position of other cases not specifically mentioned and since any attempt to draw up examples of *jus cogens* would involve it in a prolonged study of matters falling outside the scope of the draft articles, see *Report of the ILC*, A/6309/Rev.1. pp. 76–7; but, for the views of some members, *Yearbook of the ILC* (1963), ii. 199.
223. See McNair, *Law of Treaties* (1961), pp. 214–15.
224. Brownlie, op. cit., p. 561, and Tunkin, op. cit. (n. 49), p. 160. Note that resolution 2074 (XX) condemned apartheid and racial discrimination as crimes against humanity. This was reaffirmed in resolution 2145 (XXI) and Security Council resolution 276 (1970).
225. Brownlie, op. cit., p. 500.
226. See *ICJ Reports*, 1970, p. 32, and Judge Ammoun, ibid., p. 304. See also Judge Tanaka, *ICJ Reports*, 1966, p. 298, and Judge Ammoun, *ICJ Reports*, 1971, pp. 78–81.
227. See Judge Ammoun, *ICJ Reports*, 1970, p. 304, and Brownlie, op. cit., pp. 512–5.
228. See *Yearbook of the ILC* (1963), ii. 199. See also Gros-Espiell, 'Self-Determination and Jus Cogens' in *United Nations Law/Fundamental Rights*, ed. Cassese (1979), p. 167.

CHAPTER 3

1. *ICJ Reports*, 1971, pp. 16, 31, and 73–5.
2. Ibid., 1975, pp. 12, 29–36.
3. See Deutsch, *Nationalism and Social Communication* (1952), p. 78; Scelle, *Précis de droit des gens, principes et systématique*, pt. 2, chap. 1, p. 259, cited by the Egyptian delegate, A/C3/SR.43 para. 34, and Cobban, *The Nation-State and National Self-Determination* (1969), p. 107. See also the *Greco-Bulgarian Communities* case, *PCIJ*, Series B, no. 17, p. 21.
4. Rejai and Enloe, 'Nation-States and State-Nations', 13 *International Studies Quarterly* (1969), 143. Hoffman refers to 'governments still in search of their nation' in 'International Systems and International Law', 14 *World Politics* (1961), 230.
5. See further below, Chapter 5, p. 180.

6. Article 1 of the International Covenant on Human Rights, 1966. See also the 1970 Declaration on Principles of International Law. Below, p. 102.
7. See Luard, 'The Origins of International Concern Over Human Rights' in *The International Protection of Human Rights*, ed. Luard (1967), p. 10. See also Thomas and Thomas, *Non-Intervention* (1956), p. 369, and Umozurike, *Self-Determination in International Law* (1972), p. 192. Note also A/C.3/SR.447, paras. 4–10.
8. Calogeropoulos-Stratis called this the principle of total sovereignty. Espoused particularly by Third World States, it treats self-determination as protecting the independence and integrity of the newly independent State: *Le Droit des peuples à disposer d'eux-mêmes* (1973), pp. 162–4.
9. See General Assembly resolutions 523 (VI), 626 (VII), 1514 (XV), and 1803 (XVII). See also the Declaration on the Establishment of a New International Economic Order, *UNMC* May 1974, pp. 66–84, and the Charter of Economic Rights and Duties of States, 1974, (resolution 3881 (XXIX)). See in addition the study by Cristescu on *The Historical and Current Development of the Right to Self-Determination*, E/CN.4/Sub.2/404.
10. In the *Namibia* case, the court declared that 'the subsequent development of international law in regard to non-self-governing territories . . . made the principle of self-determination applicable to all of them', *ICJ Reports*, 1971, pp. 16, 31.
11. See above Chapter 1, p. 32, and below, p. 123.
12. *ICJ Reports*, 1975, pp. 12, 30. The court declared that its opinion would provide the UN General Assembly with legal factors relevant to the decolonization of the territory: ibid., p. 37.
13. Ibid., p. 36.
14. Morocco had voted in favour of all such resolutions except resolution 2983 (XXVII), while Mauritania had voted in favour of all of them; see resolutions 2229 (XXI), 2354 (XXII), 2591 (XXIV), 2711 (XXV), 2983 (XXVII), 3162 (XXVIII), and 3292 (XXIX).
15. Spain had voted for resolution 2354 (XXII), against resolutions 2072 (XX), and 2229 (XXI), and abstained in the rest.
16. Algeria had voted in favour of all such resolutions.
17. See A/10023/Add.5, Annexe, paras. 269 (Spain), 305 (Morocco), 348 (Algeria), and 104 (Mauritania). See also the Agadir meeting of July 1973 at which the latter three reaffirmed the right as regards Sahara. A/9623/Add.4, pt. 11 at p. 23 and A/10023/Add.5, Annexe, Appendix IIID.
18. Pleadings, CR.75/26, p. 60.
19. Pleadings, CR.75/8, pp. 11–16.
20. Pleadings, CR.75/12, p. 38.
21. Ibid., p. 44. See also Pleadings, CR.75/17, p. 27.
22. Pleadings CR.75/13, pp. 9–13. The return of French and Portuguese territories to India was referred to, as was the Gibraltar situation, ibid. See also resolution 2429 (XXII).

23. Pleadings CR.75/31, p. 34. It was declared that decolonization was clearly only a species of a larger genus, viz. self-determination, which was the right of peoples to independence, to set up their own political and economic system and non-interference in the internal affairs of States: ibid.
24. See above, Chapter 1, p. 31.
25. Pleadings, CR.75/20, pp. 10–12 and 26.
26. This stated that any attempt to disrupt the 'national unity and the territorial integrity of a country is incompatible with the . . . principles of the Charter'.
27. Pleadings, CR.75/31, pp. 36–8.
28. A/10023/Add.5, Annexe, para. 351.
29. Pleadings, CR.75/20, pp. 18–23.
30. Pleadings, CR.75/21, pp. 14–19. Spain also regarded the right of self-determination as a rule of *jus cogens*; Spanish Written Statement, para. 344.
31. *ICJ Reports*, 1975, pp. 12, 32. See also *ICJ Reports*, 1971, pp. 16, 31.
32. See also Pleadings, CR.75/8, pp. 17ff. (Morocco); Pleadings, CR.75/13, pp. 7–9 (Mauritania); and Pleadings, CR.75/20, pp. 38–9 (Algeria).
33. *ICJ Reports*, 1975, pp. 12, 32–3. See also resolution 2625 (XXV), the 1970 Declaration on Principles of International Law.
34. *ICJ Reports*, 1971, pp. 16, 31.
35. Ibid., 1975, pp. 12, 34–6.
36. Ibid., p. 36.
37. Ibid., p. 121.
38. Ibid., p. 110.
39. Ibid., p. 68.
40. Ibid., p. 37.
41. One should note in this context the claims of Spain to Gibraltar, Argentina to the Falkland Islands, and Guatemala to Belize.
42. Ibid., p. 174.
43. Below, p. 105. See also Chapter 5, p. 180.
44. See Pleadings, CR.75/31, pp. 25–32 and 36–9.
45. See Judge Dillard, *ICJ Reports*, 1975, pp. 12, 120.
46. Judge Nagendra Singh declared that 'even if integration of territory was demanded by an interested State, as in this case, it could not be had without ascertaining the freely expressed will of the people—the very *sine qua non* of all decolonisation', ibid., p. 81. See also Judge Boni, ibid., pp. 173–4. Note, in particular, the court's approach, ibid., pp. 34–7. See further, below, p. 190.
47. *ICJ Reports*, 1975, p. 33. See also ibid., p. 68.
48. But cf. Judge Amoun, ibid., pp. 99–100.
49. Ibid., p. 81.
50. Ibid., p. 122. The same phrase was in fact used by Ambassador Bedjoaui, Pleadings, CR.75/31, p. 15. However, since the people of a non-self-governing territory must make the determination as to its future political

status within the confines of the territory as colonially defined, there is an argument for saying that in a sense it is the territory which determines the destiny of the people.

51. Op. cit., p. 78. See also Wright, *A Study of War* (1954), pp. 998–9.
52. Op. cit., p. 259.
53. Op. cit., p. 107. Emphasis in original. Claude writes that 'nationality is in essence a subjective phenomenon . . . a group of people constitute a nation where they feel that they do . . . there is no uniform or necessary pattern of objective factors whence national feeling is derived or in which it manifests itself', *National Minorities: An International Problem* (1953), p. 2. See also *Greco-Bulgarian Communities* case, *PCIJ*, Series B, no. 17, p. 21.
54. See, e.g., the Haiti delegate, A/C.3/SR.444 para. 40. See also Cristescu's study (above, n. 9), paras. 260–87.
55. e.g. the UK delegate, A/C.3/SR.444, paras. 24 and 25.
56. See A/7326, p. 61.
57. *Self-Determination Within the Community of Nations* (1967), p. 55. The Indian delegate to the Commission on Human Rights declared that if an ethnic group claiming to be a minority was actually a people, it would succeed in obtaining its independence whether or not its right to do so was recognized; A/C.3/SR.651, para. 4. Emerson noted that all too frequently the determination as to whether a people was involved was made after the fact; *From Empire to Nation* (1960), p. 90.
58. Op. cit., pp. 42–3.
59. Zartman, *International Relations in the New Africa* (1966), p. 108.
60. Yakemtchouk, *L'Afrique en droit international* (1971), pp. 70–2.
61. *Towards a Pax Africana: A Study of Ideology and Ambition* (1967), pp. 14, 33–4, and 'Consent, Colonialism and Sovereignty', 11 *Political Studies* (1963), 48. Cf. Kamanu, 'Secession and the Right of Self-Determination: An OAU Dilemma', 12 *JMAS* (1974), 355.
62. See below, Chapter 5, p. 211.
63. *Self-Determination in International Law* (1972), p. 195.
64. Ibid.
65. Ibid., pp. 3, 192.
66. Ibid., p. 196.
67. Ibid. The quotation is from the *Aaland Islands* case, *LNOJ* Suppl. no. 3, 1920, p. 5.
68. *ICJ Reports*, 1975, pp. 12, 33. See also Judge Dillard, ibid., p. 121.
69. See, e.g., para. 6 of resolution 1514 (XV); the 1970 Declaration on Principles (2625 (XXV)); and Article III(3) of the OAU Charter.
70. Judge Quintana characterized the mood of the present period as 'the age of national independence', *ICJ Reports*, 1960, p. 95.
71. UN Charter, Article 73. See *The Sacred Mission of Civilisation: The Belgian Thesis* (1953): Toussaint, 'The Colonian Controversy in the United Nations', 10 *YBWA* (1956), 177–9; Kunz, 'Chapter XI of the United

Nations Charter in Action', 48 *AJIL* (1954), 109; and Nawaz, 'Colonies, Self-government and the United Nations', 1 *Indian Yearbook of World Affairs* (1962), 3. See also A/AC.58/1, pp. 3–14, and A/AC.67/2, pp. 3–31.

72. See, e.g., *GAOR* 7th Session, 4th Committee, 254th meeting, paras. 5, 7, and 8; ibid., 258th meeting, paras. 24, 40, and 41; ibid., 255th meeting, paras. 31, 39, and 40; ibid., 257th meeting, paras. 5 and 58; ibid., Plenary, 402nd meeting, para. 134; and ibid., 8th Session, 4th Committee, 327th meeting, para. 2. Note that Article 74 of the Charter distinguishes between 'the Territories to which this Chapter applies' and 'their metropolitan areas', whereas Article 73 envisages the possibility of future assumption of responsibilities respecting non-self-governing territories; see Crawford, *The Creation of States in International Law* (1979), p. 360 n. 14. See also *Yearbook of the ILC* (1949), 73.
73. Note that this apparently makes 1945 the critical date.
74. The USA argued unsuccessfully in 1961 for the Colonial Declaration to be used in non-colonial situations; see *GAOR* 16th Session, 4th Committee, 1175th meeting, para. 35.
75. *GAOR* 7th Session, 3rd Committee, 451st meeting, para. 11.
76. Cristescu, op. cit., para. 279.
77. E/CN.4/Sub.2/384/Rev.1, especially at p. 96.
78. See, e.g., resolutions 2189 (XXI), 2621 (XXV), 2625 (XXV), 2649 (XXV), 2708 (XXV), 2787 (XXVI), and 2878 (XXVI). See also Article 1(4) of the 1977 Protocol I to the 1949 Geneva Conventions and the Gros-Espiell Report on the *Implementation of UN Resolutions Relating to the Right of Peoples under Colonial and Alien Domination to Self-Determination*, E/CN.4/Sub.2/390 (1977) and E/CN.4/Sub.2/405 (1978).
79. Ibid., vol. i., p. 28.
80. See Cassese, 'The Self-Determination of Peoples' in *The International Bill of Rights*, ed. Henkin (1981), p. 92.
81. Originally the determination of the classification of non-self-governing territories was left to those States which accepted that they administered such territories. A list was made under resolution 66 (I) of seventy-four territories with respect to which States were willing to transmit information under Article 73(e) of the Charter. Over the years, however, the General Assembly began to assert its own competence to decide whether or not a territory was non-self-governing and this process culminated in the principles enunciated in resolution 1541 (XV) noted above. See, for example, resolutions 334 (IV), 567 (VI), 648 (VI), 742 (VII), and 1467 (XIV). See also Crawford, op. cit., pp. 93–4 and 360–3, and Rigo Sureda, *The Evolution of the Right of Self-Determination* (1973), pp. 54–8.
82. See, in particular, Dugard, *The South-West Africa/Namibia Dispute* (1973); Slonim, *South-West Africa and the UN: An International Mandate in Dispute* (1973); and Wellington, *South-West Africa and its Human Issues* (1967). For details of the mandate agreement see Dugard, op. cit., pp. 72–4. See also

Alexandrowicz, 'The Juridical Expression of the Sacred Trust of Civilisation', 65 *AJIL* (1971), 149. South Africa tried to incorporate South-West Africa as the fifth province of the Union with the support of the all-white South-West Africa Assembly; see League of Nations Doc. C.489M.214 (1934) 50, but this was declared contrary to the principles of the mandate and rejected by the Permanent Mandates Commission; see *PMC Minutes*, 1925, pp. 59, 60, and 61.

83. 21st Ordinary Session, Report of the 1st Committee, pp. 5–6. See also Umozurike, 'International Law and Self-Determination in Namibia', 8 *JMAS* (1970), 585–603.
84. *ICJ Reports*, 1950, p. 128.
85. See resolutions 1143A (XII) and 1361 (XIV), in which the General Assembly pointed out the legal action provided for in a joint reading of Article 7 of the mandate agreement and Article 37 of the ICJ Statute. The action to take legal proceedings was commended in resolution 1565 (XV). See Falk, 'The South-West Africa Cases: An Appraisal', 21 *International Organisation* (1967), 7; Higgins, 'The International Court of Justice and South-West Africa', 42 *International Affairs* (1966), 573; and Green, 'The United Nations, South-West Africa and the World Court', 7 *IJIL* (1967), 491.
86. *ICJ Reports*, 1962, p. 318, and ibid., 1966, p. 6.
87. A/3900.
88. Resolution 1243 (XIII), para. 2, emphasis added. Since South Africa was not prepared to consider UN supervision of the territory nor the UN to accept partition, there was no basis for an agreement; see Report of the Good Offices Committee, 1959, A/4224, para. 16.
89. Resolution 1702 (XVI). See also resolution 1596 (XV).
90. *Report of the Commission of Enquiry into South-West African Affairs, 1962–3* (1964), Pretoria. See D'Amato, 'The Bantustan Proposals for South-West Africa', 4 *JMAS* (1966), 177. See also A/AC.109/L.108. The allocations were as follows: 312, 433 sq. km. for 424,047 black africans, 14,785 sq. km. for 23,965 coloureds, and 495,927 sq. km. for 73,464 whites (including government lands) (1960 population figures). See Odendaal Report, tables, A, B, and C, pp. 109, 111, tables XI, XVIII, and XIX at pp. 29, 39, and 41. See also D'Amato, loc. cit., p. 181, and *ARB* Feb. 1964, p. 27.
91. *ARB* Mar. 1964, p. 42.
92. See Kahn, *Annual Survey of South African Law* (1964), pp. 41–3.
93. *UNMC* June 1964, pp. 33ff.
94. Resolution 2074 (XX).
95. Resolution 2145 (XXI). Adopted by 114 votes to 2 (South Africa and Portugal), with 3 abstentions (France, Malawi, and UK). See, as to the legality of the resolution and the question of the Assembly's competence, e.g. Crawford, 'South-West Africa: Mandate Termination in Historical Perspective', 6 *Columbia Journal of Transnational Law* (1967), 91; Higgins, 'The International Court and South-West Africa: the Implications of the

Judgements', 8 *Journal of the International Commission of Jurists* (1967), 3; and Dugard, 'The Revocation of the Mandate for South-West Africa', 62 *AJIL* (1968), 78.

96. *UNMC* July 1967, p. 87; ibid., Aug.–Sept. 1967, pp. 39–40; and ibid., Nov. 1967, pp. 28–30. See A/6640. See also Herman, 'The Legal Status of Namibia and of the United Nations Council for Namibia', 13 *Canadian Yearbook of International Law* (1975), 306.
97. See Dugard, op. cit., pp. 431–3.
98. Ovamboland Legislative Council Proclamation no. R.291, GGE no. 2177 (Reg. Gaz. no. 1025); Kavango Legislative Council Proclamation R196, GG 2770 (Reg. Gaz. no. 1313); and Eastern Caprivi Legislative Council Proclamation R6, GG 3373 (Reg. Gaz. no. 1566). See Dugard, op. cit., pp. 434–5. See also the Caprivi Constitution Proclamation, *ARB* Mar. 1976, p. 3975.
99. See also resolution 276 (1970).
100. *ICJ Reports*, 1971, pp. 16, 31. See also ibid., 1975, pp. 12, 31–3.
101. Ibid., 1971, pp. 16, 58. The court declared that the decisions of the Security Council declaring South Africa's presence in Namibia illegal (i.e. resolution 264 (1969), 269 (1969), and 276 (1970)) were in accordance with Articles 24 and 25 of the Charter and 'consequently binding on all States members of the United Nations', ibid., p. 53. See Higgins, 'The Advisory Opinion on Namibia: Which United Nations Resolutions are Binding Under Article 25 of the Charter?' 21 *ICLQ* (1972), 27.
102. See the proposals of the Commissioner General for Indigenous Peoples of South-West Africa, *ARB* Oct. 1974, p. 3406. The possibility was also suggested of the Ovambos of Angola and Namibia uniting to form a State; ibid. See also *ARB* Jan. 1975, p. 3511.
103. See *UNMC* May 1973, pp. 39–40 and 59–60.
104. See, e.g., Security Council resolutions 323 (1972) and 385 (1976) and Assembly resolutions 3031 (XXVII) and 3111 (XXVIII).
105. Sept. 1975, p. 3769. See also ibid., Mar. 1976, pp. 3973–4.
106. Ibid., Aug. 1976, p. 4136. This was rejected by the UN Council for Namibia and by SWAPO, ibid., pp. 4136–7.
107. Ibid., Jan. 1977, p. 4301, and ibid., Mar. 1977, pp. 4370–1. Of the 60-seat proposed Assembly, 12 would go to Ovambos, 6 to whites, and 4 or 5 proportionately to 9 other groups; ibid., Feb. 1977, p. 4336. See also S/12180.
108. *UNMC* Aug.–Sept. 1976, pp. 26–7. See also S/12185. The EEC stated that these Turnhalle talks held at Windhoek were not representative without the participation of SWAPO; *ARB* Feb. 1977, pp. 4336–7. SWAPO was effectively barred by the ban on non-white political parties; *UNMC* Aug.–Sept. 1976, p. 27.
109. Ibid., June 1977, pp. 41–8. See also *ARB* May 1977, pp. 4418–21.
110. Ibid., June 1977, pp. 4471–2, and ibid., July, 1977, p. 4516.

111. See also resolution 32/42, and the Declaration of Lusaka by the UN Council for Namibia, A/S–9/2–S/12631.

112. The Western proposals may be seen in *ILM* May 1978, pp. 762–9. They involved a reduction in the number of South African troops in the territory, the entry of SWAPO personnel, and a UN-supervised election for a consistuent assembly. See also *ARB* Apr. 1978, p. 4829. SWAPO accepted the proposals, ibid., July 1978, p. 4935.

113. See the report of the debates in *UNMC* June 1978, pp. 49–106.

114. The major episodes in this series of negotiations may be found in *ARB* Oct. 1978, pp. 5038–40; ibid., Mar. 1979, pp. 5203–4; ibid., May 1979, pp. 5279–81; ibid., Aug. 1979, pp. 5386–7; ibid., Oct. 1979, pp. 5448–9; ibid., Apr. 1980, pp. 5655–6; ibid., May 1980, pp. 5688–90; ibid., July 1980, pp. 5750–2; ibid., Oct. 1980, pp. 5838–9; ibid., Jan. 1981, pp. 5940–4; ibid., May 1981, pp. 6052–4; ibid., June 1981, pp. 6069–70 and 6090–3. See also *UNC* Sept.–Oct. 1980, pp. 18–21; ibid., Nov. 1980, pp. 13–14; ibid., Jan. 1981, pp. 5–7; ibid., Mar. 1981, pp. 5–10; ibid., May 1981, pp. 5–8; ibid., July 1981, pp. 5–8; and ibid., Nov. 1981, pp. 13–20. See in addition *KCA*, pp. 30861–6 and 31205–10.

115. See S/14459, S/14460/Rev.1, S/14461, and S/14462.

116. *UNC* Aug. 1981, pp. 50–4. See also Security Council resolutions 435 (1978) and 532 (1983) and Assembly resolutions 35/227A, 36/121A, 37/233A, and E5–8/2; *UNC* July 1982, pp. 33–6; ibid., Feb. 1983, pp. 37–43; ibid., Mar. 1983, pp. 17–32; and *KCA*, pp. 31996–32004. See also S/15776, S/15943, and the Paris Declaration on Namibia adopted on 29 April 1983 at the conclusion of the International Conference in Support of the Struggle of the Namibian People for Independence, *UNC* June 1983, pp. 55–8. See for Walvis Bay below, p. 137.

117. See generally McEwan, *International Boundaries of East Africa* (1971); Drysdale, *The Somali Dispute* (1964); Touval, *Somali Nationalism* (1963); Castagno, 'The Somali–Kenyan Controversy', 2 *JMAS* (1964), 165; and Lewis, 'The Problem of the Northern Frontier District of Kenya', 5 *Race* (1963), 48.

118. This was mitigated to some extent by the cession of the Jubaland province to Italy from Kenya by the Anglo-Italian Treaty of 1924 as a reward for Italian participation in the First World War in accordance with the 1912 Treaty of London; see McEwan, op. cit., pp. 117–19. However, it is argued that the critical period is the period prior to independence, thus excluding territorial changes made decades before independence from our thesis.

119. See the Report of the NFD Commission, Cmnd. 1900 (1962), Appendix D; Lewis, 'The Somali Conquest of the Horn of Africa', 1 *Journal of African History* (1960), 213; and Castagno, loc. cit., pp. 173–6.

120. 621 HC Debates 55, Written Answers, cols. 104–5.

121. Report of the Kenyan Constitutional Conference, Cmnd. 1700, p. 11. It was claimed that as well as being historically, ethnically, and culturally

distinct, the NFD had always been governed as a separate entity, with its own laws and courts and with special passes needed to enter the rest of Kenya; see *The Issue of the NFD*, White Paper issued by the Government of Somalia (1963), pp. 15–16.

122. Report of the NFD Commission, Cmnd. 1900. The split was basically on Muslim/non-Muslim lines. The Commission consisted of a Nigerian lawyer and a Canadian major.
123. Drysdale, op. cit., pp. 145 and 157–8. See also Castagno, loc. cit., p. 180.
124. In a Somali press communiqué of 29 August 1963, after the abortive Rome conference with Britain, quoted in Drysdale, op. cit., p. 133.
125. *Pan-African Unity and the NFD Question in Kenya*, May 1963, quoted in Emerson, *Self-Determination Revisited in the Era of Decolonisation* (1964), pp. 35–6. Note also the Report of the Commission on the Problem of the Kenya Coastal Strip, which recommended integration with Kenya because *inter alia* it would provide no precedent for the disintegration of Kenya and would avoid the creation of boundary problems; *KCA*, pp. 19403 and 19741.
126. Note that prior to the independence of Kenya and Tanganyika, a delegation from the Masai tribe split between the two territories requested the UK to remain in Masailand after Kenyan independence. The petitioners were also seeking the unification and independence of the Masai lands; see McEwan, op. cit., p. 149.
127. See Coleman, *Togoland* (International Conciliation, 1956, no. 509), and Rigo Sureda, op. cit., pp. 151–63.
128. By resolution 441 (V), the General Assembly stressed the importance of the problem and requested a solution by the administering authorities in accordance with the wishes of the people concerned. The All-Ewe Conference had petitioned the UN Trusteeship Council in 1947 over the division of the Ewe people; see Rigo Sureda, op. cit., p. 15.
129. See resolution 860 (IX) and T/1218, pp. 16 and 62, essentially dividing the territory into Ewe and non-Ewe areas. See also Rigo Sureda, op. cit., p. 157.
130. *GAOR* 10th Session, 4th Committee, 539th meeting, para. 17 (Venezuela), and ibid., 544th meeting, para. 46 (Togoland Congress).
131. Ibid., 536th meeting, para. 39; ibid., 537th meeting, para. 18; ibid., 538th meeting, para. 16; ibid., 537th meeting, paras. 49 and 82; and ibid., 540th meeting, para. 54.
132. Resolution 1044 (XI). See also *Yearbook of the UN* (1956), 368–70.
133. *GAOR* 9th Session, 4th Committee, 562nd meeting, para. 1.
134. A/3173.
135. Zartman, *International Relations in the New Africa* (1966), p. 14.
136. See generally Ardener, 'The Nature of the Reunification of Cameroon', *African Integration and Disintegration*, ed. Hazlewood (1967), p. 285. Note that 'Cameroun' is the correct spelling of the independent French-speaking

republic of 1960–1, while 'the Cameroons' applies to the pre-independent divisions of the territory, and either 'Cameroun' or 'Cameroon' to the unified, independent State: ibid. See also T/1440, para. 10.

137. Report of the Visiting Mission, 1958, T/1446 and Add. 1, para. 16.
138. Ibid., para. 170. The problem had arisen because of the British announcement that Nigeria was to become independent on 1 October 1960; see *GAOR* 12th Session, 4th Committee, 803rd meeting.
139. Resolution 1350 (XIII). However, some countries had argued, unsuccessfully, that the differences between north and south Cameroons were no greater than those existing in Nigeria, Togoland, and the Gold Coast and that therefore one plebiscite unit was sufficient. See *GAOR* 13th Session, 4th Committee, 860th meeting, para. 31, and ibid., 862nd meeting, paras. 13–15. See also ibid., 865th meeting, para. 2, and ibid., 878th meeting, para. 5.
140. Resolutions 1350 (XIII) and 1352 (XIV). See also *KCA*, p. 16821. The French Cameroons was proclaimed independent on 1 January 1960: ibid., p. 17226.
141. The actual votes were 70,546 favouring a later decision, 42,788 in favour of joining Nigeria, and 526 rejected votes. Voting was by universal male suffrage; see Umozurike, *Self-Determination in International Law* (1972), p. 106, and Rigo Sureda, op. cit., pp. 166–7.
142. A/4314 and Add. 1. See also *GAOR* 14th Session, 4th Committee, 989th meeting, para. 13.
143. By 233,571 votes to 97,751; see Umozurike, op. cit., p. 106, and Rigo Sureda, op. cit., pp. 166–7.
144. Resolution 1473 (XIV). The result was 146,296 votes to 97,659; see Umozurike, op. cit., p. 106, and Rigo Sureda, op. cit., pp. 106–7. See also *KCA*, pp. 17179 and 17484.
145. Cameroun was dissatisfied with the preparations and conduct of the plebiscite in the northern part of British Cameroons and instituted proceedings before the International Court, which, however, dismissed the case; *ICJ Reports*, 1963, p. 15.
146. But see Rigo Sureda, op. cit., pp. 167–8.
147. See generally Lemarchand, *Rwanda and Burundi* (1970). See also Lemarchand and Martin, *Selective Genocide in Burundi* (Minority Rights Group, 1974), p. 3.
148. T/1551 and T/1538.
149. T/L.985 and Add. 1, and T/L.1004 and T/L.1005.
150. See the Report of the UN Commission for Ruanda-Urundi, A/4706 and Add. 1.
151. A/C.4/518.
152. *GAOR* 15th Session, 4th Committee, e.g. 1080th meeting, para. 10 (Ghana); ibid., 1086th meeting, para. 12 (Ivory Coast); ibid., 1091st meeting, paras. 4 (Somalia) and 53 (Pakistan); and ibid., 1093rd meeting, para. 19 (Guinea).

153. A/4929 and Add. 1. See also resolution 1743 (XVI).
154. A/5126 and Add. 1.
155. See *GAOR* 16th Session, 4th Committee, 1305th meeting, para. 14 and ibid., 1307th–1327th meetings. Note also that the units had been separate kingdoms and continued this way under both German and Belgian rule.
156. Note also Assembly resolution 181 (II) on Palestine, which emphasized that 'the present situation . . . is likely to impair the general welfare and friendly relations among nations'. Two other points need to be noted with regard to the Palestine issue. Firstly, that the Mandate for Palestine incorporated the Balfour Declaration with regard to the establishment of a Jewish national home in Palestine, and there is nothing similar in any other mandate, and secondly, that the principle of self-determination was not a legal right as of 1947–8. See generally *The Arab–Israel Conflict*, ed. Moore (1974), 3 vols.
157. See 'Notes sur Cabinda, partie intégrante de l'Angola', an anonymous text sent by anti-separatist Cabindese to African States and published in 121 *Revue française d'études politiques africaines* (1976), 58–69. See also Brownlie, *African Boundaries* (1979), pp. 484–8.
158. Article 1(e) of the resolution referred to 'Angola, including the enclave of Cabinda'.
159. *ARB* July 1975, p. 3706. The Congolese Foreign Minister declared that 'Cabinda exists as a reality and is historically and geographically different from Angola'. ibid. But cf. 'Notes sur Cabinda' (n. 157 above), pp. 59–63. Zaïre called for a referendum in the enclave: *ARB* May 1975, p. 3632.
160. See the terms of the Mombasa agreement of January 1975, in Legum and Hodges, *After Angola* (1976), p. 67.
161. The UN adopted a number of resolutions calling for the independence and self-determination of such territories, as well as reaffirming their territorial integrity; see, e.g., resolutions 1542 (XV), 1807 (XVII), 1819 (XVII), 1913 (XVIII), 2107 (XX), 2184 (XXI), 2395 (XXIII), and 2918 (XXVII). By resolution 3294 (XXIX), the Assembly welcomed Portugal's acceptance of self-determination and stressed the need for preserving the territorial integrity and national unity of the territories.
162. See *ARB* Oct. 1977, p. 4601 (regarding also a split in the separatist forces) and ibid., Apr. 1978, p. 4820. The separatist argument included not only geographic and ethnic factors, but also a claim based on the treaty of Simulambuco, 1895, between Portugal and the Cabinda princes: ibid. See also *KCA* p. 31419.
163. Resolution 2067 (XX).
164. Resolutions 2230 (XXI) and 2355 (XXII). See *ARB* Dec. 1966, p. 686.
165. See Rigo Sureda, op. cit., p. 200.
166. Resolution 3161 (XXVIII). See also *UNMC* Jan. 1974, p. 51.
167. *ARB* Dec. 1974, p. 3466.
168. Ibid., June 1975, p. 3666.

169. Ibid., July 1975, pp. 3707–8.
170. Ibid., Oct. 1975, p. 3802.
171. See *UNMC* 1976, p. 6. The Comoros joined the UN on 12 November 1975; see *ARB* Nov. 1975, p. 3833. See also resolutions 3291 (XXIX) and 3385 (XXX), reaffirming the need to respect the unity and territorial integrity of the new State, composed of the four islands, including Mayotte.
172. *ARB* May 1976, p. 4019.
173. Ibid., Dec. 1976, pp. 4252–3. At the OAU Summit Conference in July 1976, a resolution was adopted rejecting all French laws intended to legalize the French presence on Mayotte: ibid., July 1976, p. 4080. See also ibid., Sept. 1977, p. 4554.
174. A Security Council resolution calling on France not to jeopardize the independence, unity, and territorial integrity of the Comoros was vetoed by France; see S/11967 and *UNMC* Mar. 1976, p. 5. See also Assembly resolution 31/34.
175. *ARB* July 1978, p. 4914.
176. See *UNC* 1980, pp. 45 and 100; ibid., Jan. 1981, pp. 26–7; ibid., Feb. 1982, p. 81; and ibid., Feb. 1983, pp. 30–1. See also A/34/467, and A/37/147.
177. See also the cases of Aden, Anguilla, and the British Indian Ocean Territory: Rigo Sureda, op. cit., pp. 199–202.
178. See generally Trevaskis, *Eritrea, A Colony in Transition:* 1941–52 (1960); Henderson, *The Making of the Modern Sudan* (1953); Longrigg, *A Short History of Eritrea* (1945); Cumming, 'The Disposal of Eritrea', 7 *Middle East Journal* (1953), 18; and Abuetan, 'Eritrea: United Nations Problem and Solution', 2 *Middle Eastern Affairs* (1951), 35.
179. Trevaskis, op. cit., p. 4.
180. The Christians were concentrated around Asmara on the plateau bordering Ethiopia and the Muslims on the coastal strip and in the western province: ibid., pp. 132–3.
181. Primarily through the medium of the Coptic Church, encouraged by Ethiopia: ibid., pp. 59–60.
182. See Henderson, op. cit., p. 335, and Longrigg, op. cit., pp. 174–5.
183. Trevaskis, op. cit., p. 84.
184. See Castaneda, *Legal Effects of United Nations Resolutions* (1969), pp. 141–2.
185. *Report of the Four Power Commission of Investigation*, vol. i, *Eritrea* (1948), pp. 88–9 and 96.
186. In May 1949. See *GAOR* 3rd Session, 1st Committee, Annexes, A/C.1/466.
187. By 14 to 37 against, with 7 abstentions, even though the part dealing with Eritrea had in fact been approved by 37 votes to 11, with 10 abstentions; see Trevaskis, op. cit., p. 93. See also Rivlin, 'The Italian Colonies at the General Assembly', 3 *International Organisation* (1949), 469.
188. Resolution 289C (IV).
189. Report of the UN Commission for Eritrea, *GAOR* 5th Session, Suppl. No.

8, A/1285. In its subsequent comments, the UK supported the partition of the territory between Ethiopia and Sudan: ibid.

190. Resolution 390A (v).
191. Final Report of the UN Commissioner for Eritrea, appointed to draft the constitution, A/2188.
192. A/1959.
193. Resolution 390 (v).
194. See A/2188, para. 44.
195. See *Yearbook of the UN* (1948–9), 257.
196. Formerly known as French Somaliland. The change in terminology was made in the law of 3 July 1967 and recognized by the UN on 15 April 1968; see *Yearbook of the UN* (1970), pp. 717–8.
197. See *ARB* June 1974, p. 3272. An OAU fact-finding mission estimated the population of the territory in 1976 at 220,000, 120,000–150,000 inside the barbed-wire enclosed area around the port of Djibouti and the rest nomads. The number of French troops was put at 6,000: ibid., May 1976, p. 4031. The Afars are related to the Ethiopians, while the Issas are akin to the Somalis. Djibouti handled some 75 per cent of Ethiopia's foreign trade: ibid.
198. *GAOR* 14th Session, annexes, agenda item 36, p. 2.
199. Lewis, 'The Referendum in French Somaliland: Aftermath and Prospects in the Somali Dispute', *The World Today*, July 1967, p. 308.
200. See, e.g., the statements of the French Minister of State for Overseas Territories and Departments, *ARB* Feb. 1972, p. 2385, and by the French President, ibid., Nov. 1974, p. 3437.
201. A/6300/Rev.1, pp. 637–42 and 647.
202. Resolution 2228 (xxi).
203. A/AC.109/121, paras. 37–40. Somalia appeared to be hoping for a merger of the territory with the Somali republic.
204. *ARB* Jan. 1973, p. 2726. See also *Yearbook of the UN* (1966) 58ff., and A/6300/Rev.1.
205. *ARB* Aug. 1975, p. 3720. Ethiopia had been backing the Djibouti Liberation Movement (MLD), while Somalia was supporting the Somali Coast Liberation Front (FLCS): ibid.
206. These views were reaffirmed before a UN Special Mission on Djibouti that held talks with Somali officials in Mogadishu; ibid., Apr. 1976, pp. 4000–1.
207. In a French–Somali communiqué in January 1977, the Somalis agreed to respect the independence and territorial integrity of the territory: ibid., Jan. 1977, p. 4294.
208. Ibid., Mar. 1977, pp. 4367–8; ibid., May 1977, pp. 4436–7; and ibid., June 1977, pp. 4458–60.
209. Ashford, 'The Irredentist Appeal in Morocco and Mauritania', 15 *Western Political Quarterly* (1962), 641. See also Gallagher, *Morocco and its Neighbours*, Part 3: *Morocco and Mauritania* (1967).

210. *GAOR* 15th Session, 1st Committee, 1109th meeting, para. 3, A/4445 and Add. 1; ibid., General Committee, 128th meeting, para. 16; ibid., Plenary, 898th meeting, para. 134; and ibid., 904th meeting, para. 96.
211. Ibid., 1st Committee, 1109th meeting, paras. 1, 3, and 4.
212. Ibid., para. 6. Morocco noted that the 'attributes of sovereignty were exercised in accordance with the conditions of the time, but the whole population had recognised the authority of the Sultan of Morocco unreservedly until 1912', ibid. See also ibid., paras. 7–8. It was stated that France was seeking to 'shatter a geographic, political, ethnic, linguistic, and religious entity', ibid., para. 16.
213. Ibid. See also Ashford, loc. cit., p. 647.
214. See also Zartman, *International Relations in the New Africa* (1966), pp. 27 and 34.
215. *GAOR* 15th Session, 1st Committee, 1109th meeting, paras. 21–3.
216. Ibid., paras. 23–5.
217. Ibid., 1111th meeting, para. 2. See also Thiam, *La Politique étrangère des États africains* (1963), pp. 101–2.
218. *GAOR* 15th Session, 1st Committee, 1111th meeting, para. 3.
219. Ibid., para. 17.
220. Ibid., 1113th meeting, para. 22. See also Central African Republic, ibid., para. 12; Upper Volta, ibid., 1114th meeting, para. 2; and Nigeria, ibid., Plenary, 893rd meeting, para. 196. Note also Senegal, *SCOR* 16th Year, 971st meeting, para. 163, and Ivory Coast, ibid., para. 183.
221. *ARB* June 1970, p. 1776. See also Brownlie, op. cit., p. 147.
222. See generally Rezette, *The Western Sahara and the Frontiers of Morocco* (1975); Gretton, *Western Sahara: the Fight for Self-Determination* (1976); Mercer, 'Confrontation in the Western Sahara', *The World Today*, June 1976, p. 230; and Hodges, 'The Western Sahara File', 6 *Third World Quarterly* (1984), 74. See also Brownlie, op. cit., pp. 149–58.
223. *GAOR* 19th Session, annexes no. 8, pt. 1., chap. XI, para. 112. Spain maintained for a number of years that its African territories were Spanish provinces, but in November 1960 agreed to transmit information regarding them to the UN Secretary-General under Chapter XI of the Charter, *GAOR* 15th Session, 4th Committee, 1048th meeting. This was noted with satisfaction in Assembly resolution 1542 (XV).
224. See, e.g., resolutions 2354 (XXII), 2428 (XXIII), 2591 (XXIV), 2711 (XXV), 2983 (XXVII), 3162 (XXVIII), and 3292 (XXIX).
225. The Sahara has an area of some 266,000 sq. km., with a population of about 95,000, according to a Spanish census of 1974; see Report of the UN Visiting Mission to Spanish Sahara, 1975, A/10023/Add.5, Annex, pp. 26–7. See also Gretton, op. cit., pp. 9–14.
226. A/10023/Add.5, annex, paras. 89–91 and 93–100.
227. *Western Sahara* case, Pleadings, CR.75/12, p. 2.
228. Pleadings, CR.75/9, pp. 29–31, and *ICJ Reports*, 1975, pp. 12, 45.

229. Ibid. See also Pleadings, CR.75/12, pp. 6–29.
230. A/10023/Add.5, annex, para. 91.
231. Pleadings, CR.75/12, pp. 36–7.
232. Ibid., pp. 6 and 29.
233. Ibid., pp. 34–5. It was also claimed that Sheikh Ma ul-'Aineen, who in the 1890s controlled Sakiet-El Hamra and neighbouring areas, was an agent of the Sultan; Pleadings, CR.75/11, pp. 58–68.
234. Pleadings, CR.75/12, p. 31. See also, as regards the importance of contiguity, ibid., p. 32. See also Pleadings, CR.75/9, pp. 8–12 and 26–54.
235. At the time, Morocco was divided into the Bled Makhzen, the area fully under the control of the Sultan, and the Bled Siba, the area where the inhabitants possessed a great deal of power, but nevertheless acknowledged the spiritual authority, of the Sultan; see Pleadings, CR.75/11, p. 6, and *ICJ Reports*, 1975, pp. 12, 44–5.
236. Pleadings, CR.75/8, pp. 3–4.
237. Pleadings, CR.75/13, pp. 47–9.
238. A/10023/Add.5, annex, paras. 378–9, and Pleadings, CR.75/12, p. 38.
239. Pleadings, CR.75/17, pp. 24, 29, and 41.
240. Both Spain and Algeria disagreed with the Moroccan and Mauritanian contentions; see, e.g., Pleadings, CR.75/22, pp. 12–25, 41–51; Pleadings, CR.75/23, pp. 2–33 and 44; Pleadings, CR.75/24, pp. 9–43; and Pleadings, CR.75/31, p. 121. See also above, p. 95.
241. A/10023/Add.5, annex, para. 298. The Moroccan king declared that he would accept the will of the Saharan population only if it was faced with a referendum choice between continued Spanish rule or merger with Morocco: ibid., Appendix II, para. 24. Mauritania noted that 'by rejoining Mauritania the people of that area would achieve self-determination and independence', A/10023/Add.5, annex, para. 387.
242. A/6300/Rev.1.
243. A/9176, annex iv.
244. A/9655. See also A/10023/Add.5, annex, paras. 84, 143–50.
245. A/9714.
246. A/9771, annex. Mauritania did not at this stage associate itself with the Moroccan initiative, A/9715, annex.
247. A/C.4/SR.2130 and A/C.4/SR.2131.
248. A/C.4/SR.2125. The proposed resolution was adopted by the Fourth Committee by 81 voltes to 0, with 43 abstentions, and resolution 3292 (XXIX) was adopted by the General Assembly by 87 votes to 0, with 43 abstentions.
249. p. 96.
250. *ICJ Reports*, 1975, pp. 12, 36.
251. Ibid., p. 68.
252. Ibid., p. 33. See also Judge Nagendra Singh, ibid., p. 81, and Judge Dillard, ibid., pp. 120–1.

253. Ibid., p. 68. As regards the relationship between the Moroccan and Mauritanian claims themselves, see A/10023/Add.5, annex, paras. 14, 15, 66–7, and 381. See also *ICJ Reports*, 1975, pp. 12, 65, and 67, and Judge De Castro, ibid., p. 131.
254. A/10023/Add.1, annex, para. 202. See also ibid., paras. 201–64.
255. Ibid., para. 229. The mission was itself set up pursuant to resolution 3292 (XXIX) by the Special Committee on Decolonisation.
256. Press release of the Permanent Mission of Morocco to the UN, 16 October 1975, quoted in S/PV, 1849, p. 11.
257. S/11852. This was the so-called Green March. See also S/11874.
258. *ARB* Nov. 1975, pp. 3836–8.
259. Security Council resolutions 377 (1975) and 379 (1975). See also the Reports of the UN Secretary-General, S/11863 and S/11874.
260. S/PV, 1852, p. 76.
261. S/11876, S/11880, para. 2, and ibid., annex I and annex II. Algeria regarded the declaration as null and void, refusing to recognize the right of Spain, Morocco, and Mauritania to dispose of the territory: ibid., annex IV.
262. See Franck, 'The Stealing of the Sahara', 70 *AJIL* (1976), 694, 715–7. It was reported that by this agreement Spain retained a 35 per cent interest in the Bou-Craa phospate mines and secured both fishing rights for the Canary Islanders and a period of Moroccan toleration for its enclaves on the southern Mediterranean shore: Mercer, 'Confrontation in the Western Sahara', *The World Today*, June 1976, pp. 230, 232–3.
263. *ARB* Dec. 1975, pp. 3872–4 and 3910–12.
264. Ibid., Feb. 1976, pp. 3942–3. In March, Morocco and Mauritania broke off diplomatic relations with Algeria: ibid., Mar. 1976, p. 3952.
265. Ibid., Apr. 1976, p. 3985. See also *West Africa*, 3 May 1976, p. 622.
266. *The Diplomatic World Bulletin* (no. 5), pp. 1237 and 1242 (8 Mar. 1976).
267. The Yema'a consisted of 103 members, including 40 sheikhs elected by tribal councils, 40 representatives elected by male Saharans over 21 from the family units and 16 representatives of corporate groups; see A/10023/Add.5, annex, para. 136. It was created by Spain in May 1967 as the highest representative body of the local administration with certain limited powers: ibid., para. 127.
268. S/11874, annex III.
269. *ARB* Feb. 1976, pp. 3942–3. The figure of 60 was a UPI one; according to the *New York Times* of 28 Feb. 1976, p. 6, the figure was 65.
270. According to the Algerian representative at the UN, 57 members of the Yema'a left, A/PV.2435 at p. 92.
271. *UNMC* Mar. 1976, pp. 41–2. Zambia noted that 'policies of annexation and expansion were being pursued in total disregard of the aspirations of the inhabitants of the territories concerned and the United Nations was being asked to bless these unjust designs', A/C.4/SR.2175, p. 32.
272. *ARB* June 1976, p. 4047, and ibid., July 1976, pp. 4078 and 4081.

273. Ibid., July 1977, pp. 4486–7; ibid., Aug. 1977, p. 4523; ibid., Sept. 1977, p. 4554; and ibid., Mar. 1978, pp. 4770–1.
274. Ibid., July 1978, p. 4914. See also ibid., Sept. 1978, pp. 4979–80. The UN General Assembly in resolution 32/22 reaffirmed its commitment to the principle of self-determination with regard to the Western Saharan case and expressed the hope that a just and lasting solution to the problem could be found in accordance with UN principles at the proposed OAU summit meeting devoted to the question.
275. Ibid., July 1978, p. 4928; ibid., Aug. 1978, p. 4960; ibid., Apr. 1979, p. 5230; and ibid., Aug. 1979, p. 5379. Morocco occupied the area left by Mauritania; ibid., p. 5380. Mauritania recognized the Saharan Arab Democratic Republic in early 1984, see *West Africa*, 5 Mar. 1984, p. 530.
276. *ARB* July 1978, p. 4914; ibid., Nov. 1978, p. 5052; and ibid., Dec. 1978, p. 5088.
277. Ibid., Jan. 1979, p. 5144, and ibid., June 1979, pp. 5290–1.
278. Ibid., July 1979, pp. 5330–1.
279. Ibid., Dec. 1979, p. 5498.
280. Ibid., July 1980, pp. 5731–2.
281. Ibid., Sept. 1980, p. 5794. General Assembly resolution 35/19 reaffirmed the right of the people of Western Sahara to self-determination and independence in accordance with the UN and OAU Charters and resolution 1514 (xv). It also welcomed the efforts of the OAU and its *ad hoc* committee and reaffirmed the determination of the UN to co-operate fully with the OAU. See also General Assembly resolution 34/37.
282. *ARB* June 1981, p. 6068. See also *KCA*, pp. 31053–5. The efforts of the OAU and the implementation committee were welcomed. See General Assembly resolutions 36/46 and 37/28. See also *UNC* Jan. 1983, pp. 82–3.
283. See *KCA*, pp. 31487–90. Both the Council of Ministers and the Assembly of Heads of State and Government meetings failed to achieve the necessary two thirds quorum in July–August 1982 because of this issue, see ibid., pp. 31935–6. The Assembly of Heads of State and Government eventually met in June 1983, once the Saharan Arab Democratic Republic had agreed to withdraw, ibid., p. 32419. The resolution adopted at this meeting called for direct negotiations between Morocco and Polisario for a cease-fire and referendum to be supervised by the UN and the OAU, ibid., p. 32420. See also *West Africa*, 23 May 1983, pp. 1229–30.
284. Cmnd. 3231. See also the written answer of the Secretary of State for the Colonies, HC Debates, 1965–6, vol. 720, Written Answers, cols. 1–2, 10 Nov. 1965. The UK–USA agreement emphasizes that the territory is to remain under UK sovereignty and that the islands shall remain available to meet the possible defence needs of the two governments for 'an indefinitely long period'.
285. See Madeley, *Diego Garcia: a Contrast to the Falklands* (Minority Rights Group Report no. 54, 1982); Houbert, 'Mauritius: Independence and

Dependence', 19 *JMAS* (1981), p. 75; Latham-Koenig, 'Mauritius After the June Elections', *The World Today*, July–Aug. 1982, p. 253; and Ogunbadejo, 'Diego Garcia and Africa's Security', 4 *Third World Quarterly*, Jan. 1982, p. 104.

286. The islands of Aldabra, Farquhar, and Desroches were returned to the Seychelles in 1976 on the occasion of the territory's independence as unnecessary for UK–USA defence purposes; see HC Debates, 1976, vol. 912, cols. 169–70.

287. See *GAOR* 20th Session, 4th Committee, meetings 1549–51, 1557, 1558, 1566, and 1570. See also *Yearbook of the UN* (1965), 585–7.

288. Madeley notes, in fact, that the islands were not uninhabited at the date of British acquisition, but rather that their peopling began in 1776, albeit primarily by leprosy sufferers from Mauritius: op. cit., p. 4.

289. See resolutions 2232 (XI), 2357 (XXII), and 2430 (XXIII), all adopted without opposition.

290. *ARB* June 1980, pp. 5723–4. See also *KCA*, p. 31764.

291. *ARB* July 1980, p. 5732.

292. See the statement of the Prime Minister, HC Debates, 11 July 1980, Written Answers, col. 314.

293. HC Debates, 13 July 1982, Written Answers, cols. 356–7. See also *KCA*, p. 31764. The Agreement provided for a sum of £4 million to be paid to the persons concerned (the Ilois) by the UK government in full and final settlement of all claims, while Mauritius would provide land to the value of £1 million.

294. Op. cit., p. 4.

295. Cited in Houbert, op. cit., pp. 84–5 n. 7.

296. *ARB* July 1980, p. 5754.

297. See, as regards estoppel, Brownlie, *Principles of Public International Law* (3rd edn., 1979), pp. 637–9; the *Arbitral Award by the King of Spain*, *ICJ Reports*, 1960, pp. 192, 213; and the *Temple* case, *ICJ Reports*, 1962, pp. 6, 32.

298. See Oraison, 'A propos du différend franco-malgache sur les îles éparses du canal de Mozambique', 85 *Revue générale de droit international Public* (1981), 465.

299. See *Journal officiel de la République française*, 10 July 1897, p. 3893; ibid., 13 Sept. 1899, p. 6144; ibid., 10 Apr. 1908, p. 250; ibid., 3 Aug. 1912, p. 6961; ibid., 26 Feb. 1914, p. 1807; and ibid., 10 May 1946, p. 3973. See also Oraison, loc. cit., p. 499.

300. Ibid., pp. 499–500.

301. This island is in fact claimed by Mauritius: see Miclo and Oraison, 'A qui appartient le récif de Tromelin?' *Annuaire des pays de l'océan Indien* (1978), 263. See also *KCA*, p. 31764.

302. Decree no. 60-555, *Journal officiel de la République française*, 13–14 June 1960, p. 5343. See text in Oraison, loc. cit., p. 507.

303. Ibid., pp. 485–7. See also *Journal officiel de la République française*, June 1980, p. 1558.

304. *La Succession d'États à Madagascar* (1970), p. 342 n. 94. See also Oraison, loc. cit., pp. 489–90.
305. Ibid., pp. 468–9. See also CM/Res.732 (XXXIII) and *ARB* July 1979, p. 5327.
306. See *UNC* Jan. 1980, p. 47, and ibid., Feb. 1981, pp. 26–7. The question of the islands was deferred in December 1981 for a further session: ibid., Feb. 1982, p. 78. See also A/34/245; A/34/784; A/36/718, and A/SPC/34/SR.37–9.
307. See. e.g., the *Oxford English Dictionary*. See also Krenz, *International Enclaves and Rights of Passage* (1961), pp. 19–22, and Raton, 'Les Enclaves' *AFDI* (1958), 186.
308. See practice with regard to small islands, *UNMC* Apr. 1973, pp. 64–70. Assembly resolutions 3427 (XXX) and 3433 (XXX), for example, relating to Pacific and West Indian small island territories, emphasized that the question of the territorial size, geographical isolation, and limited resources should not be used to delay the implementation of resolution 1514 (XV).
309. Claims to the maintenance of colonial enclaves appeared to reach their ultimate absurdity in the case of the Portuguese enclave of São João Baptista de Ajude (St John the Baptist of Ajouda) taken over by Dahomey (now Benin) on 31 July 1961. It consisted of one two-storey house on 11½ acres of land demarcated by eight boundary pillars in the former slave port of Ouidah. The enclave had two governors and no population. Portugal continued to lay claim to the enclave for a while after its seizure; see Harrison, *Environment and Policies in West Africa* (1963), p. 77.
310. Mathy, 'L'Autodétermination de petits territoires revendiqués par États tiers (deuxième partie)', *Revue belge de droit international* (1975), 129–31, and *ARB* Jan. 1969, pp. 103–4. See also Reyner, 'Morocco's International Boundaries: A Factual Background', 1 *JMAS* (1963), 324.
311. A/5800 Rev. 1.
312. Mathy, loc. cit., p. 132. The transfer took place on 30 June 1969 and was duly noted by the General Assembly, ibid. and A/7630, p. 80. The International Court noted that 'since 1969, Ifni, having been decolonized by transfer to Morocco, has no longer appeared in the resolutions of the Assembly', *ICJ Reports*, 1975, pp. 12, 35. There are a number of other Spanish enclaves surrounded by Morocco. These include Ceuta, Melilla, Peñón de Vélez, Peñón de Alhucemas, Islote del Mar and Isla de Tierra and Islas Chafarinas; see Reyner loc. cit., pp. 324–5.
313. Op. cit., p. 214.
314. Note that in the instance of the French Territory of the Afars and Issas, no special standing was claimed by or accorded to Ethiopia or Somalia in the decolonization process.
315. Rigo Sureda, op. cit., pp. 78–9, 183–99, and 282–8. See also A/AC.109 SR.291 and resolutions 2070 (XX) and 2231 (XXI).
316. See A/AC.109/PV p. 284.

317. See resolutions 2353 (XXII) and 2429 (XXIII).
318. For example the Western Sahara situation and the Falkland Islands cases: see resolution 2065 (XX); *Yearbook of the UN* (1964), 432; ibid. (1966), 659; *UNMC* Jan. 1970, p. 124; and A/AC.109/PET.1132. See, as regards other enclave situations, Mathy, loc. cit., and id., 'L'Autodétermination de petits territoires revendiqués par des États tiers (première partie)', *Revue belge de droit international* (1974), p. 167.
319. See Prinsloo, *Walvis Bay and the Penguin Islands: Background and Status* (South African Foreign Affairs Association Study Report no. 8, 1977) and Brooks, 'The Legal Status of Walvis Bay', 2 *South African Yearbook of International Law* (1976), 187.
320. See Prinsloo, op. cit., pp. 11–12, and Marshall, 'Namibia and Walvis Bay', 27 *ICLQ* (1978), 683. See also 69 *BFSP* 1177, 70 *BFSP* 495–6, and 75 *BFSP* 407.
321. 104 *BFSP* 50.
322. Article 1 of the Mandate Agreement; see Dugard, *The South-West Africa/Namibia Dispute* (1973), pp. 72–4.
323. The Penguin Islands were not administered as part of South-West Africa: Prinsloo, op. cit., p. 20.
324. *ARB* Apr. 1976, p. 4007.
325. Prinsloo, op. cit., p. 17.
326. *UNMC* June 1977, pp. 41, 43, and 46.
327. *UNMC* Oct. 1977, p. 23, and A/AC 131/67. The South African decision was termed illegal and an act of racist and colonialist expansion, ibid. See also the UN Council for Namibia's Panama Declaration of 5 June 1981, *UNC* Aug. 1981, pp. 50–4.
328. Walvis Bay was stated to be 'an integral part of Namibia with which it is inextricably linked by geographical, historical, economic, cultural and ethnic bonds'. This resolution was adopted by 117 votes to 0, with 24 abstentions. See also resolution 35/227A.
329. *ARB* Feb. 1978, p. 4736. SWAPO declared that Walvis Bay was an inviolable and non-negotiable part of Namibia; see *UNMC* Mar. 1978, p. 12. The UN Council for Namibia at its Lusaka session in 1978 repeated its earlier statements on Walvis Bay: ibid., Apr. 1978, p. 45. See also the final resolution of the 1981 OAU Assembly, *ARB* June 1981, p. 6069.
330. Ibid., May 1978, p. 20.
331. Especially Security Council resolution 385 (1976) which stressed the need to maintain the territorial integrity of Namibia.
332. See *UNMC* June 1978, pp. 49–106.
333. S/12636. See also *ILM* May 1978, p. 762.
334. *UNMC* June 1978, p. 6.
335. *ARB* July 1978, p. 4936. This was supported by the five 'front-line' States of Zambia, Tanzania, Botswana, Angola, and Mozambique: ibid., June 1978, p. 4900.

336. Ibid., July 1978, p. 4936. The fear was that the Security Council might impose sanctions on South Africa because of the Walvis Bay issue: ibid., p. 4937. According to reports in Pretoria, the Western powers gave an assurance to South Africa that they recognized its legal right to Walvis Bay: ibid.
337. *ILM* Sept. 1978, pp. 1307–8. See the South African restatement of its views on Walvis Bay, ibid., pp. 1309–10. See also General Assembly resolution 37/233A and the Paris Declaration on Namibia (n. 116 above), *UNC* June 1983, p. 56.
338. See Higgins, *The Development of International Law Through the Political Organs of the United Nations* (1963), p. 105. Note particularly resolution 2012 (xx) which declared that the perpetuation of minority rule in Southern Rhodesia would be incompatible with the principle of equal rights and self-determination.
339. The UK Minister of State stated in the constitutional conference held in London in 1978 regarding the Gilbert Islands, that the key principle in leading colonial territories to independence is 'the importance now widely attached to the principle of territorial integrity'. Successive governments had always believed that 'the wishes of the people as a whole within the existing boundaries should be the main guide': quoted in a letter to the *Guardian*, 9 Jan. 1979, p. 8, by Sir Bernard Braine. See also 'Report of the Gilbert Islands Constitutional Conference', Cmnd. 7445.
340. 'The Scope of Acquiescence in International Law', 31 *BYBIL* (1954), 143, 171. See also Bowett, 'Estoppel before International Tribunal and its Relation to Acquiescence', 33 *BYBIL* (1957), 176; Lauterpacht, 'sovereignty over Submarine Areas', 27 *BYBIL* (1950), 376; MacGibbon, 'Some Observations on the Role of Protest in International Law', 3 *BYBIL* (1953), 293; id., 'Customary International Law at Acquiescence', 33 *BYBIL* (1957), 115; Blum, *Historic Titles in International Law* (1965); and Jennings, *The Acquisition of Territory in International Law* (1963).
341 See, e.g., Alaskan Boundary Tribunal Award, 1903, Cmnd. 1877; Great Britain–Brazil dispute re British Guiana Boundary, 1904, Cmnd. 2166; *Guatemala–Honduras Boundary* arbitration, 1933, 7 *RIAA*, p. 1309; the *Temple* case, *ICJ Reports*, 1962, p. 5; and the *Eastern Greenland* case, 1933, *PCIJ* Series A/B, no. 53.
342. In August 1975 a civil war broke out in the Portuguese colony, which appeared to have ended in September. The following month, clashes were reported on the Indonesian–Timor border, and in December Indonesia intervened and took over the territory. See 'Issue on East Timor', 7 *Decolonisation* (1976), 19–32. See also S/12011.
343. See resolutions 31/53, 32/34, 33/39, 35/27, 36/50 and 37/30. See also Security Council resolutions 384 (1975) and 389 (1976), *UNC* Jan. 1983, pp. 81–2 and *KCA*, pp. 32258–9.
344. See resolutions 3422 (xxx), 31/50, 32/32, 33/36, and 35/20. Belize became independent on 21 September 1981.

345. See resolution 1514 (XV), resolution 2625 (XXV) and *ICJ Reports*, 1975, pp. 12, 33, 66, 81, and 123. See also Article 76(b) of the UN Charter and Summary Report of Committee 1/1, doc. 1/1/1, 16 May 1945, 6 *UNCIO Docs.*, p. 296.
346. See Brownlie, *Principles of Public International Law* (3rd edn., 1979), p. 181.
347. Lindley, *The Acquisition and Government of Backward Territory in International Law* (1926), p. 168. See also the Anglo-Portuguese agreement of February 1884 by which the UK obtained a right of pre-emption regarding the Portuguese fort of St John the Baptist of Ajouda on the Gold Coast; see Yakemtchouk, *L'Afrique en droit international* (1971), p. 304.
348. Lindley, op. cit., pp. 168–9.
349. *KCA*, p. 17318. Belguim also noted that even if such a right existed it could not be exercised in the instant case since the transfer of power to the people of the Congo could not be regarded as an alienation of the territory by Belgium: ibid.
350. The fact that Algeria was intended by this phrase is clear; see Pleadings, CR.75/3, pp. 3–4. Note also that in one of the preambular paragraphs of resolution 3292 (XXIX) Algeria, as well as Spain, Morocco, and Mauritania, is specifically named.
351. This may be assimilated with the view expressed by the International Court that 'the right of self-determination leaves the General Assembly a measure of discretion with respect to the forms and procedures by which that right is to be realised', *ICJ Reports*, 1975, pp. 12, 36.
352. See Rigo Sureda, op. cit., pp. 294–323; Umozurike, *Self-Determination in International Law* (1972), pp. 105–8; and Merle, 'Plébiscites organisés par les Nations Unies', *AFDI* (1961), 425.
353. Resolution 289 (IV).
354. Trusteeship Council resolution 1907 (XXII).
355. Resolution 860 (IX). Commissions of Enquiry were also sent *inter alia* to Western Samoa in 1959 and Sabah and Sarawak in 1963.
356. Resolution 3292 (XXIX).
357. Regarding the question of the monarchy, or Mwami, of Rwanda.
358. A/1285 and resolution 390 (V).
359. T/1440. *GAOR* 13th Session, 4th Committee, 844th–880th meetings, and resolution 1350 (XIII).
360. T/1218 and resolution 944 (X).
361. Note that the French *loi cadre* of 23 June 1956 and subsequent elections in French West Africa developed the territorial framework of the eight States that subsequently became independent. Plebiscites were held in 1958 in French territories, offering the choice between autonomous status in the French community, retention of existing status with representation in the French Parliament, or full integration with France. Only Guinea voted to reject the new constitution and thereby attain full independence at that time; see *KCA*, pp. 16544 and 16529.

362. The case of Namibia is a special one. Following the termination of the Mandate by the General Assembly in 1966 in resolution 2145 (XXI), a UN Council for South-West Africa (later Namibia) was established by resolution 2248 (S-V). This Council was empowered 'to administer South-West Africa until independence' and 'to promulgate such laws, decrees and administrative regulations as are necessary for the administration of the territory until a legislative assembly is established'. In 1974 a Decree on the Natural Resources of Namibia was adopted by the Council requiring the Council's consent for any exploration, mining, or extraction of natural resources found in Namibia; see A/C.131/33.

CHAPTER 4

1. See, e.g., Higgins, *The Development of International Law Through the Political Organs of the United Nations* (1963), p. 11, and Crawford, 'The Criteria for Statehood in International Law', 48 *BYBIL* (1976–7), 93.
2. See, as regards Antarctica, O'Connell, *International Law* vol. i (2nd edn., 1970), p. 451.
3. e.g. Rhodesia, Transkei, Taiwan. Note also the problem of the divided States such as Korea, Germany, and pre-1975 Vietnam. See, e.g., Caty, *Le Statut juridique des États divisés* (1969).
4. See Higgins, op. cit., p. 11.
5. See Brownlie, *Principles of Public International Law* (3rd edn., 1979), p. 75; cf. Higgins, op. cit., p. 13.
6. Any reasonable number of inhabitants may suffice; see the cases of Nauru and Tuvalu. However, the limits of reasonableness may be tested in the light of the Falkland Islands situation. As regards nationality, see O'Connell, *State Succession in Municipal Law and International Law*, vol. i (1976), pp. 479ff., and Brownlie, op. cit., p. 638.
7. 5 *AD*, 1929, no. 5, p. 15.
8. *SCOR* 3rd Year, 383rd meeting, p. 41. Jessup was speaking on behalf of the US with regard to the admission of Israel to the UN.
9. Brownlie, op. cit., p. 75. See *LNOJ* 1st Ass. 651 and the *Monastery at St Naoum* case, *PCIJ* Series B, no. 9 (1924) pp. 9–10. See also Lauterpacht, *Recognition in International Law* (1948), p. 30.
10. By Arab States, e.g. *SCOR* 3rd Year, 385th meeting, pp. 3–4, and ibid., 386th meeting, pp. 19–20, and by the UK, ibid., 383rd meeting, pp. 15–16.
11. See General Assembly resolution 273 (III) and Security Council resolution 70 (1949). By that time, all members of the Security Council bar Egypt had recognized Israel, as had over two-thirds of the members of the General Assembly: Higgins, op. cit., p. 18.
12. *ICJ Reports*, 1969, pp. 3, 32. It does not appear necessary that there should

be a minimum size of territory; see Oppenheim, *International Law*, vol. i (8th edn., 1955), p. 415.

13. See A/4445 and Add. 1, above, p. 120.
14. S/4969 and General Assembly resolution 1631 (XVI). See also the case of Kuwait, Higgins, op. cit., p. 19.
15. Op. cit., p. 28.
16. Ibid.
17. *LNOJ* Sp. Suppl. no. 4, 1920, pp. 8–9. But cf. the view of the Commission of Rapporteurs in this case, League of Nations Council Doc. B7 21/68/106 (1921), p. 22.
18. Op. cit., p. 21. Emphasis in original. See, with regard to Vietnam, *SCOR* 7th Year, 603rd meeting, p. 12, and Israel, *SCOR* 3rd Year 385th meeting pp. 4–5. See also Okeke, *Controversial Subjects of Contemporary International Law* (1974), p. 159.
19. See, e.g., Crawford, loc. cit., p. 119, and Brownlie, op. cit., p. 76.
20. The *Austro-German Customs Union* case, *PCIJ* Series A/B, no. 41 (1931), pp. 57–8. See Marek, *The Identity and Continuity of States in Public International Law* (1954), pp. 166–80.
21. See Rousseau, *Droit international public*, vol. ii (1974), pp. 55–93.
22. See Higgins, op. cit., p. 26; Lauterpacht, op. cit., pp. 46–51; and Crawford loc. cit., p. 126. See also *Lighthouses in Crete and Samos* case *PCIJ* Series A/B (1937), pp. 71, 127 *per* Judge Hudson, and the Commission of Jurist's Report on the *Aaland Islands* case, *LNOJ* Sp. Suppl. no. 4, 1920, pp. 8–9.
23. 6 *UNTS* 143.
24. *SCOR* 1st Year, 2nd ser. suppl. 4 at p. 136, and *GAOR* 2nd Session, 117th meeting, pp. 1044–53. See also Higgins, op. cit., p. 31, and Okoye, *International Law and the New African States* (1972), p. 16.
25. *SCOR* 3rd Year, 351st meeting, pp. 11–12.
26. *Commonwealth Survey* (1960), 501; Higgins, op. cit., pp. 31–2; and Okoye, op. cit., p. 17.
27. Higgins, op. cit., pp. 32–3.
28. *ARB* May 1978, p. 4859.
29. France was accused of trying to restore colonialism in Africa by the Algerian President (ibid.), while Libya stated that French 'colonial' forces were used in Chad to repress a popular uprising using 'genocidal' methods: ibid., July 1978, p. 4924.
30. One is talking here of entities becoming new States rather than existing States losing their statehood. There is a presumption in international law against loss of statehood; see, e.g., Crawford, loc. cit., p. 139.
31. *ARB* Oct. 1976, p. 4189.
32. But geographical unity is not essential for statehood, as the case of pre-1971 Pakistan shows.
33. *ARB* Dec. 1977, pp. 4666–8.
34. Ibid., Sept. 1979, pp. 5401–2.

35. *KCA*, pp. 31469–70. It is interesting to note that the Transkei government opposed the independence of Ciskei on the grounds that it divided the Xhosa people: *ARB* Feb. 1981, p. 5963.
36. *UNC*, Feb. 1982, p. 42.
37. Below, p. 161.
38. Above, p. 59.
39. *Yearbook of the ILC* (1975) 49. See also Rigo Sureda, *The Evolution of the Right of Self-Determination* (1973), p. 353, and Calogeropoulos-Stratis, *Le Droit des peuples à disposer d'eux-mêmes* (1973), p. 113.
40. See, e.g., The *Wimbledon* case, *PCIJ* Series A, no. 1 (1923), p. 25.
41. *SCOR* 16th Year, 987th meeting, paras. 46 and 47.
42. Above, p. 57. See also Akehurst, *A Modern Introduction to International Law* (4th edn., 1982), p. 256, and *The Rights of Passage* case, *ICJ Reports*, 1960, pp. 6, 39.
43. Above, pp. 120 ff.
44. Above, p. 120.
45. Loc. cit., p. 117. See also Crawford, *The Creation of States in International Law* (1979), pp. 42–7.
46. *UN Economic Bulletin for Africa*, June 1961, p. 72. The proportion in Katanga province was even higher: ibid.
47. *KCA*, pp. 17594–5.
48. Ibid., pp. 17639–40.
49. See Hoskyns, *The Congo Since Independence* (1965), pp. 96–9.
50. Ibid., p. 99.
51. See Security Council resolution 142 (1960) and General Assembly resolution 1480 (XV). At the time of the Assembly resolution in September 1960, two different factions of the Congolese government sought to be accepted by the UN as the legitimate representative of the Congo. The Assembly postponed a choice, referring the question to the Credentials Committee. Ultimately, the delegation authorized by the Head of State was accepted and that of the Prime Minister rejected; see Higgins, op. cit., pp. 162–4. In any event, it underlines the doubt as to the existence of a stable and effective government at the time.
52. S/4387.
53. Below, p. 202.
54. Above, p. 113.
55. A/5126 and Add. 1.
56. Ibid., cited in Higgins, op. cit., p. 23.
57. Security Council resolutions S/5149 and S/5150 and General Assembly resolutions 1748 (XVII) and 1749 (XVII).
58. See *Yearbook of the UN* (1971), 566–7.
59. Resolution 2795 (XXVI). The Special Mission consisted of representatives from Ecuador, Sweden, and Tunisia and visited the area between 2 and 8 April 1972.

60. A/AC.109/L.804, p. 19.
61. Ibid.
62. A/8723/Rev.1. The General Assembly commended the Mission for its work and also affirmed that the PAIGC was the authentic representative of the true aspirations of the people of the territory; see resolution 2918 (XXVII).
63. *ARB* Sept. 1973, p. 2992. See also *Revue générale de droit international public* (1974), 1168.
64. Ibid.
65. *West Africa*, 8 Oct. 1973, p. 1403.
66. *ARB* Oct. 1973, p. 3008.
67. Ibid., p. 3018.
68. Proposed by fifty-eight States, A/9196 and Add. 1 and 2.
69. *GAOR* 28th Session, General Committee, 213th meeting, pp. 25–6, 28 and 30.
70. Ibid., pp. 28, 30, and 31.
71. *GAOR* 28th Session, Plenary, 2156th meeting, p. 12.
72. Ibid., p. 8.
73. Ibid., p. 16. See also Venter, *Portugal's War in Guinea-Bissau* (1973) and Bruce, *Portugal: The Last Empire* (1975).
74. See the comments of the Portuguese Foreign Minister, *GAOR* 28th Session, Plenary, 2138th meeting, p. 76.
75. A/L.702.
76. *GAOR* 28th Session, Plenary, 2163rd meeting, pp. 27 and 36. See also the statement of the US Department of State on 10 October 1973, *Digest of US Practice in International Law 1973*, (1974), p. 17.
77. *GAOR* 28th Session, Plenary, 2163rd meeting, p. 56. See also the South African view, ibid., p. 62. Portugal, Greece, the United Kingdom, USA, South Africa, Brazil, and Spain cast the seven negative votes to resolution 3061 (XXVIII).
78. e.g. Bolivia, *GAOR* 28th Session, Plenary, 2156th meeting, p. 51; Chile, ibid., 2163rd meeting, p. 31; Belgium, ibid., p. 37; Australia, ibid., p. 41; Netherlands, ibid., p. 52; Ireland, ibid., p. 57; France, ibid., p. 61; and West Germany, ibid., p. 66. See also the joint declaration of Denmark, Norway, Sweden, Finland, and Iceland, *Revue générale de droit international public* (1974), 1169.
79. The resolution also demanded that Portugal desist from further violation of the sovereignty and territorial integrity of Guinea-Bissau, drew the attention of the Security Council to the critical situation resulting from the illegal presence of Portugal in Guinea-Bissau, and invited all member-States of the UN and all organizations within the UN system to render all assistance to the government of Guinea-Bissau.
80. *GAOR* 28th Session, Plenary, 2157th meeting, pp. 22–5.
81. Ibid., pp. 65–7. See also Uganda, ibid., 2159th meeting, pp. 82–3; Ethiopia, ibid., 2160th meeting, pp. 21–2; Rwanda, ibid., 2162nd meeting, pp. 3–6 (speaking on behalf of the eighteen Arab UN members); and Tanzania, ibid., pp. 116–18.

82. Ibid., p. 36.
83. Ibid., 2158th meeting, p. 26. See also Ghana, ibid., 2157th meeting, p. 62; Hungary, ibid., 2158th meeting, p. 7; and Poland, ibid., pp. 33–5.
84. Ibid., 2159th meeting, p. 86. Note that in February 1974 the Diplomatic Conference on the Reaffirmation and Development of International Humanitarian Law adopted a resolution by consensus (from which Portugal dissociated itself) calling for the participation in the Conference of the Republic of Guinea-Bissau with the same rights as all other participating States; see CDDH/SR.4, pp. 33–7.
85. See further below, p. 168.
86. *ARB* Nov. 1975, p. 3819.
87. See Legum and Hodges, *After Angola*, (1976), p. 58.
88. *ARB* Feb. 1976, pp. 3942–3. See also above, p. 127.
89. *KCA*, pp. 31487–90.
90. Ibid., p. 31935.
91. Ibid., pp. 31003 and 31490. See also ibid., p. 32102, and *West Africa* 5 Nov. 1984, p. 530.
91*a*. In November 1984, while this book was in the press, the OAU Assembly of Heads of State and Government agreed to admit SADR to membership, thus precipitating Moroccan withdrawal from the Organization. This clearly adds to the burden of evidence in favour of SADR's statehood, without being decisive of itself.
92. As to the importance of the recognition of Guinea-Bissau, see below, p. 163.
93. See also Higgins, op. cit., pp. 23–4, and Brownlie, op. cit., p. 75.
94. Op. cit., p. 165; cf. Higgins, 'International Law and Civil Conflict' in *The International Regulation of Civil War* ed. Luard (1972), pp. 169, 175.
95. Secession itself, of course, is not contrary to international law; see Lauterpacht, op. cit., p. 409.
96. Above, pp. 98 ff.
97. See Fawcett, 'Security Council Resolutions on Rhodesia', 41 *BYBIL* (1965–6), 103, 107.
98. Op. cit., p. 26.
99. Op. cit., p. 112.
100. See the statement by the UN Secretary-General, *SCOR* 21st Year, 1280th meeting, p. 23.
101. See, e.g., Security Council resolutions 217 (1965), 221 (1966), 232 (1966), 253 (1968), 277 (1970), 288 (1970), and 328 (1973), and Assembly resolution 2024 (XX).
102. But cf. Okeke, op. cit., pp. 104–5.
103. See also Higgins, 'International Law, Rhodesia and the United Nations', *The World Today* (1967), pp. 94, 98; Brownlie, op. cit., p. 101; and Crawford, op. cit. (n. 45), pp. 103–6.
104. See further below, p. 162.
105. See Fawcett, op. cit., pp. 112–13, and id., *The Law of Nations* (2nd edn.,

1971), p. 46. Cf. Devine, 'The Requirements of Statehood Re-examined', 34 *MLR* (1971), 410. See also Crawford, op. cit. (n. 45), pp. 104–5.

106. See, e.g., Obozuwa, 'Some Legal Aspects of the Rhodesian Situation', 5 *Nigerian Journal of Contemporary Law* (1974), 1, 19. Starke defines 'government' as it appears in Article 1 of the Montevideo Convention as 'a government to which the population renders habitual obedience', *Introduction to International Law* (8th edn., 1977), p. 107.

107. In December 1979 the Zimbabwe Act was adopted in the UK Parliament whereby Rhodesia was to be granted 'fully responsible status as a republic'. This followed the successful conclusion of the London constitutional conference by which the civil war in Rhodesia was brought to an end. During February 1980 an election monitored by Commonwealth observers was held in the territory, which brought the Mugabe government to power in an internationally recognized Zimbabwe. UN sanctions were lifted. See *ARB* Nov. 1979, pp. 5485–93; ibid., Dec. 1979, pp. 5511–18; and ibid., Feb. 1980, 5586–91. See also *KCA*, pp. 30165–77 and 30365–78, and *ILM* Mar. 1980, pp. 387–408. Note Security Council resolutions 460 (1979) and 463 (1980) and General Assembly resolution 34/192.

108. *ILM* Sept. 1976, p. 1175.

109. The Status of the Transkei Act 1976 also included as Transkei citizens every South African citizen who is not a citizen of a territory within the Republic and who speaks a language used by the Xhosa- or Sotho-speaking section of the population of the Transkei or who is related to any such person who has identified himself with any part of such population or is culturally or otherwise associated with any member as part of such population; see paras. (*f*) and (*g*) of schedule B, *ILM* Sept. 1976, p. 1177.

110. *ARB* Oct. 1976, p. 4189.

111. p. 149.

112. e.g. Assembly resolution 2775E (XXVI).

113. Self-determination is however, relevant with regard to independent States, for example in the sense that it reinforces the sovereignty of those States and underlines the doctrine of non-interference in internal affairs.

114. Below, p. 216.

115. See Crawford, op. cit., (n. 45), pp. 222–7.

116. Blum notes that recognition is one of the main means of expressing consent in international relations, *Historic Titles in International Law* (1965), p. 49. Schwarzenberger writes that recognition is of a general character and has a 'wide actual, and a still greater potential, scope', 'The Fundamental Principles of International Law', 87 *HR* (1955), 195, 228.

117. Lauterpacht, op. cit., p. 38.

118. Oppenheim, op. cit., p. 125. See also generally Kelsen, 'Recognition in International Law', 35 *AJIL* (1941), 605; Kunz, 'Critical Remarks on

Lauterpacht's "Recognition in International Law"', 44 *AJIL* (1950), 713; and Wright, 'Some Thoughts about Recognition', ibid., p. 549.

119. See Chen, *The International Law of Recognition* (1951); Charpentier, *La Reconnaissance internationale et l'évolution du droit des gens* (1956); and Lauterpacht, op. cit., pp. 41–2.

120. See, e.g., *Deutsche Continental Gas Gesellschaft* v. *Polish State* 5 *AD*, 1929, no. 5, p. 15; The Report of the Commission of Jurists on the *Aaland Islands* case *LNOJ* Sp. Suppl. no. 4, 1920, p. 8; The *Tinoco Concessions* arbitration, 1 *RIAA* (1923), 369; and Article 3 of the Montevideo Convention on Rights and Duties of States, 1933. See also Brownlie, op. cit., p. 94; O'Connell, op. cit., pp. 123–4; and Akehurst, *A Modern Introduction to International Law* (4th edn., 1982), pp. 57–61.

121. States not recognizing other States do not regard the latter as free from the obligations of international law, e.g. with regard to the law relating to the use of force; see Brownlie, op. cit., p. 92 n. 1.

122. Op. cit., pp. 73–7.

123. See Brownlie, op. cit., pp. 94–5, and Kunz, op. cit., pp. 713–19.

124. Op. cit., p. 94.

125. Above, p. 153.

126. See 78 *Revue générale de droit international public* (1974), 1170.

127. Op. cit., p. 128. See also Hyde, *International Law Chiefly as Interpreted and Applied by the US*, vol. i (2nd rev. edn., 1947), pp. 152–3.

128. Oppenheim, op. cit., p. 129. See also Lauterpacht, op. cit., p. 283, and Hall, *International Law* (8th edn., 1924), para. 26.

129. *GAOR* 28th Session, Plenary, 2156th meeting, pp. 12–13.

130. Ibid., 2157th meeting, p. 26 (Guinea), and ibid., 2158th meeting, pp. 77–81 (Uganda).

131. Oppenheim, op. cit., p. 129 n. 2.

132. Lauterpacht, op. cit., p. 8.

133. Oppenheim, op. cit., p. 129 nn. 1 and 2.

134. *GAOR* 28th Session, Plenary, 2161st meeting, p. 92.

135. Ibid., 2162nd meeting, p. 107.

136. See generally Fall, 'La Reconnaissance de la Guinée-Bissau et le droit international', *Annales Africaines* (1973), p. 153.

137. As, for example, in the Biafra case; see Ijalaye, 'Was "Biafra" at any time a State in International Law?' 65 *AJIL* (1971), 551.

138. See also Akehurst, op. cit., pp. 59–61, and Higgins, op. cit., p. 41.

139. Noted in a letter circulated on 20 November 1973 by Morocco in the UN, A/9332 and S/11125.

140. See also Assembly resolution 3181 (XXVIII), adopted by 108 votes to 0, with 9 abstentions, which approved the credentials of the Portuguese representatives 'on the clear understanding that they represent Portugal as it exists within its frontiers in Europe and that they do not represent the Portuguese-

dominated territories of Angola and Mozambique nor could they represent Guinea-Bissau, which is an independent State'.

141. Note also Guinea-Bissau's membership of the World Health Organization on 16 May 1974, see 78 *Revue générale de droit international public*, (1974), 1171, and its admission to the Conference on International Humanitarian Law as a participating State by consensus, see CDDH/SR.4, p. 34 (28 Feb. 1974).
142. Experience to date relating to the Saharan Arab Democratic Republic bears out these general comments: above, p. 158.
143. Below, p. 202.
144. Resolution 31/6A. See further above, p. 149.
145. See generally Fischer, 'La Non-Reconnaissance du Transkei', *AFDI* (1976), 63.
146. See generally Lauterpacht, op. cit., chap. xxi; Langer, *Seizure of Territory* (1947); and Sagay, 'Non-Recognition of the Illegal Occupation of Territory', 16 *IJIL* (1976), 219.
147. See, e.g., Article 2(4) of the UN Charter, the 1970 Declaration on Rights, and Article 5(3) of the 1974 Definition of Aggression. See also Security Council resolution 242 (1967).
148. *ICJ Reports*, 1971, p. 16.
149. Ibid., pp. 55–6. Cf. Judges Petren, ibid., p. 134, and Onyeama, ibid., p. 149.
150. See, e.g., *Madzimbamuto* v. *Lardner-Burke* [1969] 1 AC 645, and *Re James* [1977] Ch. 41.
151. See, e.g. Security Council resolutions 403 (1977), 406 (1977), 411 (1977), and 428 (1978).
152. Such an entity would not, however, be able to benefit from the whole range of international rules; for example, it could not maintain full diplomatic and consular relations with existing States, while the scope for the conclusion of treaties is necessarily limited.
153. 'La Naissance des États en droit international public', 66 *Revue générale de droit international public* (1962), 469, 472. See also Charpentier, op. cit., pp. 127–8, and the comments of the Israeli delegate to the UN, Briggs, *The Law of Nations* (2nd edn., 1953), p. 66.
154. See also the case of Taiwan.
155. The Western Sahara situation provides evidence that this approach is not absolute and must be treated carefully; see above, p. 156.
156. Op. cit., p. 409.
157. Jennings has written that the case of the emergence of a new State is 'by far the most important case of territorial change at the present time' and that international law respecting this problem is 'singularly undeveloped, uncertain and . . . comparatively unstudied', *The Acquisition of Territory in International Law* (1963), p. 12. See also ibid., p. 8.
158. Starke, 'The Acquisition of Title to Territory by Newly Emerged States', 41 *BYBIL* (1965–6), 411. See, for example, the manner in which the French African territories became independent: *KCA*, pp. 17513 and 17569. See also Crawford, op. cit., (n. 45), pp. 396–9.

159. Op. cit., p. 544.
160. Ibid.
161. Op. cit., p. 413.
162. Op. cit., p. 37.
163. Ibid.
164. Ibid.
165. A further problem with the constitutive approach to a new State's title to territory is that the boundaries of that State might thus be left uncertain, since it is rare for a recognizing State to specify the extent of the recognized State's territory.
166. Greig, *International Law* (2nd edn., 1976), p. 156. Greig believes that where the territory establishes its independence by force, however, 'the international status and the creation of the new title to the territory depend upon recognition', ibid.
167. Akehurst, op. cit., p. 142, but cf. Starke, op. cit., p. 415.
168. Akehurst, op. cit., p. 145. But prescription is founded upon an adverse or at the least uncertain title which is then validated through the process of time and acquiescence; see Greig, op. cit., p. 163.
169. *ICJ Reports*, 1950, pp. 128, 150.
170. Ibid., 1962, pp. 319, 329.
171. Ibid., 1971, pp. 16, 31.
172. Ibid., p. 115 Judge Ammoun declared that Namibia was a subject of law lacking only the *exercise* of its national sovereignty which 'did not cease to belong to the people subject to mandate', ibid., p. 68. See also Brownlie, 'A Provisional View of the Dispute Concerning Sovereignty over Lake Malawi/ Nyasa', *East Africa Law Review* (1968), 258, 271.
173. *ICJ Reports*, 1971, p. 31. See also the *Western Sahara* case, ibid., 1975, pp. 12, 31.
174. See further above, pp. 50 ff.
175. As for example in the mandated territory of Palestine, 1948, and the trust territory of Rwanda-Urundi, 1961–2.
176. 'The Subjects of International Law in *International Law* vol. ii, pt. 1 (1975), p. 489. See also Anzilotti, *Cours de droit international* (1929), p. 134; Schwarzenberger, *International Law* (3rd edn., 1957), pp. 140, 155; Kelsen, *Principles of International Law* (2nd edn., 1966), p. 180; Briggs, *The Law of Nations* (1948), p. 16.
177. *ICJ Reports*, 1949, pp. 178, 179.
178. See Lauterpacht, *International Law and Human Rights* (1950), and Brownlie, *Principles of Public International Law*, chap. xiv.
179. See, e.g., Falk, 'A New Paradigm for International Legal Studies: Prospects and Proposals', 84 *Yale Law Journal* (1975), 969; 'US Positions at 29th UN General Assembly', US Department of State, Special Report no. 13 (1975), p. 4; and Verzijl, *International Law in Historical Perspective*, vol. ii (1969), p. 205.

180. However, in the cases of a number of international organizations non-independent territories were permitted separate representation; see Kovar, 'La Participation des territoires non-autonomes aux organisations internationales', *AFDI* (1969), 522.
181. Lazarus, 'Le Statut des mouvements de libération nationale à l'Organisation des Nations Unies', *AFDI* (1974), 173, 177. See also Beauté, *Le Droit de pétition dans les territoires sous tutelle* (1958).
182. A/C.4/744 and A/C.4/SR.1975, p. 20. An Irish proposal to seek the opinion of UN Legal Counsel was rejected, ibid.
183. A/C.4/759 and A/9174.
184. This was extended to the Arab League; see, e.g., resolution 3102 (XXVII). Only the Palestine Liberation Organization has been so recognized.
185. See Boutros-Ghali, *L'Organisation de l'Unité Africaine* (1968), pp. 70–4, and Cervenka, *The Unfinished Quest for Unity* (1977), p. 47. The recognition awarded to the FNLA in 1963 was withdrawn the following year for failing to meet the criteria: ibid.
186. Ibid., p. 48.
187. See generally Andemicael, *The OAU and the UN* (1976), and especially pp. 29–30. See also Lazarus, loc. cit., p. 181. A slightly different situation operates with regard to the UN-administered territory of Namibia, where the UN Council for Namibia acts as *inter alia* the recognizing agent; see A/8024 paras. 28–36, resolution 2248 (S-V) and A/AC.131/SR.77, p. 6.
188. The Two South African liberation movements recognized by the OAU.
189. Lazarus, loc. cit., p. 189.
190. See also resolution 3280 (XXIX).
191. A/C.4/SR.1978, p. 23.
192. Resolution 3237 (XXIX). A strong argument may be made criticizing this move by the Assembly and the recognition of the PLO as a liberation movement relating to a non-colonial situation; see, e.g., Lazarus, loc. cit., pp. 193–4, and Silverburg, 'The Palestine Liberation Organisation in the United Nations: Some Implications for International Law and Relations' 12 *Israel Law Review* (1977), 365.
193. See, e.g., resolutions 3280 (XXIX) and 3412 (XXX).
194. ECOSOC resolution 1949 (LVIII), 8 May 1975, rule 73.
195. CHR resolution 19 (XXIX).
196. See, e.g., General Assembly resolutions 33/41 and 35/29.
197. *Yearbook of the UN* (1978), 633.
198. A/Conf.62/SR.38. The voting was 88 to 2, with 35 abstentions.
199. CDDH/SR.7, p. 1.
200. Cmnd. 6927, p. 16. See, e.g., the Israeli reaction in London, *UN Weekly Summary*, 11 May 1982, pp. 2–3.
201. See Resulovic, 'Ten Years of the Organisation of African Unity', 24 *Review of International Affairs* (1973), 34.
202. But without reference to Guinea (Bissau), which had declared independence.

A number of UN resolutions have stated that the views of particular movements have been taken into account, e.g. resolutions 2707 (XXV), 2795 (XXVI), 2871 (XXVI), 2652 (XXV), 2796 (XXVI), and 31/30, while many resolutions have called specifically for moral and material assistance to be given to national liberation movements generally and particularly: see, e.g., resolutions 2105 (XX), 2189 (XXI), 2704 (XXV), 2874 (XXVI), 3118 (XXVIII), 3300 (XXIX), and 3421 (XXX). Prisoner-of-war status for captured members of such movements has been called for: see resolutions 2674 (XXV), 2621 (XXV), 2795 (XXVI), and 3103 (XXVIII); see also Article 44, Protocol I, additional to the General Conventions of 1949. The use of mercenaries against such movements has been declared to be criminal: see, e.g., resolutions 2548 (XXIV), 2708 (XXV), and 3103 (XXVIII).

203. But note that while in resolution 3297 (XXIX) it was reaffirmed that the national liberation movements of Zimbabwe were the sole and authentic representatives of the true aspirations of the people, no attempt was made to designate which of the competing movements was to be treated as *the* representative.
204. Fourth Report of the Special Rapporteur on State Responsibility, *Yearbook of the ILC* (1972), ii. 129.
205. Ibid.
206. Ibid., p. 131.
207. He was criticized on this point, rightly, it is suggested, by Reuter, *Yearbook of the ILC* (1975), i. 45.
208. Op. cit., p. 131.
209. Brownlie, *Principles of Public International Law* (3rd edn., 1979), p. 82.
210. Insurrectional movements in general may possess personality in the light of rules relating to insurgency and belligerency; see Lauterpacht, *Recognition in International Law* (1948), pt. iii. It is here suggested that movements relating to people accepted as entitled in law to exercise the right of self-determination form a distinct category subject to special rules. See also *Yearbook of the ILC* (1975), i. 59.
211. See to this effect, e.g., the Moroccan delegate to the 1974 session of the conference on International Humanitarian Law, CDDH/I/SR.2, p. 6, and the Senegalese delegate, CDDH/I/SR.6, p. 3. See also Article 1(4) of Protocol I additional to the Geneva Conventions of 1949.
212. But cf. Blishchenko and Solntseva, 'The Struggle Against Portuguese Colonialism in the Light of International Law', 8 *International Affairs* (Moscow, 1971), 60.
213. The *Reparations* case, *ICJ Reports*, 1949, pp. 174, 178. See also the *Western Sahara* case, *ICJ Reports*, 1975, pp. 12, 63.
214. 'The Regulation of Foreign Intervention in Civil Armed Conflict', 142 *HR* (1974), 291, 369.
215. 'Standing Before the International Court of Justice: The Question of Palestinian Statehood Exemplifies the Inconsistencies of the Requirement of State-

hood', 7 *California Western International Law Journal* (1977), 454, 456.

216. Abi-Saab has argued that common Article 2 of the Geneva Conventions of 1949 could cover both States and non-State entities, in particular belligerent entities, 'Wars of National Liberation and the Laws of War', 3 *Annals of International Studies* (1972), 102, 107. See also Sagay, 'The Legal Status of Freedom Fighters in Africa', 6 *East Africa Law Review* (1975), 15, 27. But cf. letter by Draper in *The Times*, 22 Sept. 1978, p. 15.

217. Note that in the case of Namibia, UN resolutions have characterized the armed conflict as between South Africa and the people of Namibia; see, e.g., resolutions 264 (1969) and 301 (1971).

CHAPTER 5

1. Oppenheim notes that 'independence and territorial as well as personal supremacy are not rights but recognised and therefore protected qualities of States as International Persons', *International Law*, vol. i (8th edn., 1955), p. 286. Bowett regards this principle as fundamental in international law and an essential foundation of the legal relations between States, *Self-Defence in International Law* (1958), p. 29.
2. Suzuki, 'Self-Determination and World Public Order: Community Response to Territorial Separation', 16 *Virginia Journal of International Law* (1976), 779, 783.
3. Bowett writes that 'the most obvious substantive right for which the right of self-defence serves as a means of protection is the right of territorial integrity', op. cit., p. 29.
4. See Langer, *Seizure of Territory* (1947), pp. 40–5.
5. See Whiteman's *Digest of International Law*, vol. v (1965), p. 186.
6. *Yearbook of the ILC* (1949), 277, 288.
7. Cmnd. 6198. Principle III, on the inviolability of frontiers, noted that 'the participating States regard as inviolable all one another's frontiers as well as the frontiers of all States in Europe and therefore they will refrain now or in the future from assaulting these frontiers. Accordingly, they will also refrain from any demand for, or act of, seizure and usurpation of part or all of the territory of any participating State.' Principle IV, on the territorial integrity of States, provided that 'the participating States will respect the territorial integrity of each of the participating States. Accordingly, they will refrain from any action inconsistent with the purposes and principles of the Charter of the United Nations against the territorial integrity, political independence or the unity of any participating State, and in particular from any such action constituting a threat or use of force. The participating States will likewise refrain from making each other's territory the object of military occupation or other direct or indirect measure of force in contravention of international law, or the object of acquisition by means of such measures or

the threat of them. No such occupation or acquisition will be recognised as legal', ibid., pp. 3–4.

8. See generally Minh, 'Remarques sur le principe de l'intangibilité des frontières', *Peuples et États du Tiers monde à l'ordre international* ed. Fenet (1978), p. 51.
9. Above, p. 92.
10. See generally Yakemtchouk, *L'Afrique en droit international* (1971), pp. 63–97; Touval, *The Boundary Politics of Independent Africa* (1972); and id., 'African Frontiers', 42 *International Affairs* (1966), 641. See also M'buyinga, *Pan-Africanism or Neo-Colonialism: The Bankruptucy of the OAU* (1982).
11. See *History of the Pan-African Congress*, ed. Padmore (1963), p. 55.
12. Legum, *Pan-Africanism* (1962), pp. 229–32, and Touval, op. cit., pp. 58–60.
13. See Barden, *Awakening Africa: The Conference of Independent African States* (1962), pp. 149–50. See also the joint communiqué of the Presidents of Ghana and Somalia in October 1961 stressing 'the imperative need to call upon the principle of self-determination as a means of removing the artificial colonial frontiers', quoted by Emerson, 'Pan-Africanism', 16 *International Organisation* (1962), 278.
14. For example, the resolution adopted at the All-Africa Peoples' Conference, Tunis, 1960, see Legum, op. cit., p. 246, and the resolution adopted by the Afro-Asian Peoples' Solidarity Conference, 1960, see Touval, op. cit., p. 63.
15. For example, the First Afro-Asian Peoples' Solidarity Conference at Cairo, 1957; see Touval, op. cit., pp. 51–3.
16. See above, p. 120.
17. Above, p. 101.
18. Below, p. 202.
19. Legum, op. cit., p. 48.
20. This Conference involved a number of African States seeking to bridge the gap between the radical Casablanca bloc and the French-dominated Brazzaville grouping; see Zartman, *International Relations to the New Africa* (1966), pp. 26–34. The conferences of the more radical States at Casablanca and Cairo in early 1961 gave strong support to the territorial integrity of the Congo; see Touval, op. cit., p. 72.
21. Ibid., p. 78
22. *The Somali Republic and African Unity* (1962), p. 7 (a Somali government publication). See also Emerson, *Self-Determination Revisited in the Era of Decolonisation* (1964), p. 53.
23. Proceedings of the Summit Conference of Independent African States, I, Section 2, Documents, CIAS/GEN/INF/43.
24. Ibid., CIAS/GEN/INF/33. This countered Ghana's view that only continental unity could solve border disputes: ibid., CIAS/GEN/INF/36.
25. See, for example, the speeches of the delegates from the Malagasy Republic, ibid., CIAS/GEN/INF/14, and Nigeria, ibid., CIAS/GEN/

INF/35. Morocco refused to attend the conference as it might have been interpreted as recognition of Mauritania; see *KCA*, p. 19463.

26. In Article 6, member States pledged themselves to observe scrupulously the principles enumerated in Article 3. See also Krishnan, 'African State Practice Relating to Certain Issues of International Law', 14 *Indian Journal of International Affairs* (1965), 196, 207–8, and Cervenka, *The Organisation of African Unity and its Charter* (1968).
27. Op. cit., p. 35.
28. *ARB*, July 1964, p. 122.
29. Ibid., p. 123.
30. Ibid.
31. Ibid., pp. 123–4. See also the speech of the delegate from Sierra Leone, ibid., p. 125.
32. Ibid., p. 108.
33. See Touval, 'The Organisation of African Unity and African Borders', 21 *International Organisation* (1967), 102, 124–5. See also below, p. 193.
34. See below, pp. 229 ff.
35. See also the resolutions of the Cairo Conference of Non-Aligned Countries, 1964, which declared that 'the established frontiers of States shall be inviolate' and pledged the States 'to respect frontiers as they existed when [they] gained independence'. See *ARB* Oct. 1964, p. 164.
36. The Assistant Secretary-General of the OAU noted in 1967 that ideally the Organization should be an instrument of solidarity and defence of the territorial integrity of all African States', *ARB* Sept. 1967, p. 854. But note the attitudes adopted by Somalia and Morocco, below, pp. 196–201.
37. Op. cit., p. 109. Yakemtchouk writes that 'en Afrique, l'État précède la nation, il la crée, il lui imprègne ses modes d'expression et d'existence... ce processus est diamétralement opposé à celui qui se manifeste en Europe a partir du XVIe mais surtout au XIXe siècle', op. cit., p. 88.
38. See Petkovic, 'Intégrité territoriale et droit à l'autodétermination en Afrique', *Revue de la politique internationale* 20 Feb. 1969, p. 20.
39. See Yakemtchouk, op. cit., pp. 83–7. See generally Boggs, *International Boundaries*, (1940), pp. 79–80, and Cukworth, *The Settlement of Boundary Disputes in International Law* (1967), pp. 112–16.
40. Jolowicz, *Historic Introduction to Roman Law* (1954), p. 273. See also Schwarzenberger, *International Law*, vol. i (1957), p. 289.
41. See *Columbia-Venezuela* arbitral award, 1 *RIAA*, pp. 223, 228. See also Cukwurah, op. cit., p. 114, and De Lapradelle, *La Frontière* (1928), pp. 86–7.
42. McEwen, *International Boundaries of East Africa* (1971), pp. 30–1.
43. 'Africa's Frontiers', 42 *International Affairs* (1966), 642, 644. Touval described the concept as 'the right of undisturbed possession of the inheritance; existing borders are not to be challenged', ibid.
44. The concept was re-emphasized in a seminar on International Law and

Africa organized in Ghana by UNITAR in 1971, *ARB* 1971, p. 1983. Note also the comment by the Upper Volta Minister of the Interior that there could be no place in Africa without scrupulous respect for the colonial borders, no matter how imperfect they may be: ibid., Sept. 1974, p. 3258.

45. A/4445 and Add. 1.
46. A/10023/Add.5, annex, para. 294. See also *Western Sahara* case, ICJ, Pleadings CR.75/8, pp. 11–16.
47. Above, p. 181.
48. A/10023/Add.5, annex, para. 295.
49. Ibid., para. 298. See also ibid., appendix II, para. 16.
50. *Western Sahara* case, ICJ, Pleadings, CR.75/13, p. 48.
51. Pleadings, CR.75/31, p. 25.
52. Ibid., pp. 25–31.
53. Ibid., p. 36.
54. Ibid., pp. 37–8.
55. See 'New and Original States', 45 *International Affairs* (1969), 465, and 'The New States and International Law', 3 *Millennium Journal of International Studies* (1974–5), 226.
56. A/C.6/SR.1036. See also *ICJ Reports*, 1960, p. 6.
57. Ibid., pp. 93–6.
58. *Principles of Public International Law* (3rd edn., 1979), pp. 672–3.
59. Alexandrowicz made the point that the doctrine would generally not apply in Africa, except for Algeria; see 'New and Original States', 45 *International Affairs* (1969), 465, 473 and 478.
60. *ICJ Reports*, 1975, pp. 12, 33, and 34.
61. Ibid., p. 68. See also Judges Dillard, ibid., p. 123, and Nagendra Singh, ibid., p. 81.
62. Ibid., p. 120.
63. Ibid., footnote.
64. Ibid., pp. 79–80.
65. Ibid., p. 79. The effect of recognition of legal ties by the court between the claimants and Sahara was to point out the possible options open to the inhabitants of the territory: ibid., p. 80. But see resolution 1514 (XV) and the 1970 Declaration on Principles of International Law. Judge Petren noted that the question of the role of past legal ties in the decolonization process fell within an, as yet, inadequately explored area of contemporary international law: ibid., p. 112.
66. Ibid., p. 80. See also Judge Petren, ibid., p. 114.
67. See above, p. 134.
68. *ICJ Reports*, 1975, pp. 12, 36.
69. Ibid., p. 37.
70. Ibid., p. 36.
71. Ibid., p. 63. Note also the definition of State sovereignty in terms of genuine display or exercise of the State authority: ibid., p. 44.

72. Ibid., pp. 63–4.
73. See n. 68, above.
74. See also above, p. 161.
75. CM/Res.493 (XXVII).
76. Such agreements were a prelude to independence, *ARB* Sept. 1976, p. 5153.
77. *UNMC* Oct. 1976, p. 15.
78. See the Status of the Transkei Act 1976, *ILM* Sept. 1976, p. 1175. See also the Republic of Transkei Constitution Act, 1976, *ILM* Sept. 1976, p. 1136.
79. The resolution was sponsored by 67 States and adopted by 134 votes to 0. The USA, the sole abstaining State, declared that it was prepared to support a resolution calling on all States not to recognize the Transkei and not to have official contacts with the Transkei government, but it had certain reservations about the clause prohibiting individuals from dealing with the Bantustans; *UNMC* Nov. 1976, p. 14. See also the statement by the UN Secretary-General, ibid.
80. Resolution 407 (1977). See also Assembly resolution 32/14. On 6 December 1977 the independent State of Bophuthatswana was proclaimed amidst condemnation from the OAU and the EEC: *ARB* Nov. 1977, p. 4631, and ibid., Dec. 1977, pp. 4666–8. See generally Richardson, 'Self-Determination, International Law and the South African Bantustan Policy' 17 *Columbia Journal of Transnational Law* (1978), 185. See further above, p. 149.
81. This emphasizes the point made by Hill that the 'types of claims made by a State to territory reflect the doctrines and conditions dominant in international relations at the time', *Claims to Territory in International Law and Relations* (1945), p. 35.
82. See ibid., pp. 81–91, and Jennings, *The Acquisition of Territory in International Law* (1963), pp. 76–8.
83. A/4445 and Add. 1. See also Rezette, *The Western Sahara and the Frontiers of Morocco* (1975), pp. 35–50; Wild, 'The Organisation of African Unity and the Algeria–Morocco Border Conflict', 20 *International Organisation* (1966), 18; and Zartman, 'The Politics of Boundaries in North and West Africa', 3 *JMAS* (1965), 155.
84. Above, p. 52.
85. *ICJ Reports*, 1975, pp. 12, 43–4.
86. Ibid., pp. 48–9.
87. *ICJ Reports*, 1971, pp. 16, 31.
88. *ICJ Reports*, 1975, pp. 12, 168–71.
89. Ibid., p. 171. Emphasis in original. See also Judge Dillard, ibid., p. 118.
90. In this case there was also uncertainty as to the precise location of the borders; see below, p. 196.
91. Algeria did note at one time that, although it had no claims of its own, there

were historical rights it could assert over territory Morocco claimed and occupied; see *ARB* Mar. 1967, p. 734.

92. Zartman, 'The Politics of Boundaries in North and West Africa', 3 *JMAS* (1965), 155, 172.
93. *ARB* Jan. 1975, pp. 3485–6, and ibid., Oct. 1975, pp. 3783–4.
94. Ibid., Feb. 1976, pp. 3919–20. Note also the historical claims by Ethiopia in 1945–8 to Eritrea and Somaliland; see A/C.1/8 and Mariam, 'The Background of the Ethio-Somalian Boundary Dispute', 2 *JMAS* (1964), 189ff.
95. *ARB* Sept. 1968, pp. 11, 78–9. See also the claims by Togo, below n. 161.
96. See Hill, op. cit., p. 171, and Jennings, op. cit., pp. 76–8.
97. See, for example, Hill, op. cit., 115–30, and Yakemtchouk, *L'Afrique en droit international* (1971), pp. 88–90.
98. Not all ethnic groups always wish to live in the same State. See for example the case of Bugulfi, which was included in Tanganyika in the mandate agreements of 1922. In 1948 the ruler of Urundi petitioned the Trusteeship Council for the return of the area. A UN Visiting Mission in July of that year declared that Bugulfi was geographically clearly part of Urundi and its people were Barundi; T/217/Add.1, p. 101. The matter was further discussed between the British and Belgian authorities, but a resolution of the Trusteeship Council in February 1950 recognized that the evidence showed that an overwhelming majority of the people of Bugulfi wished to retain the status quo and accordingly no action was taken: T/635 and resolution 116 (VI).
99. See below, p. 197.
100. See, for example, Hill, op. cit., pp. 71–80, and Jennings, op. cit., p. 74.
101. See Blum, *Secure Boundaries and Middle East Peace* (1971).
102. *PCIJ* Series A/B, no. 53.
103. *ICJ Reports*, 1975, pp. 12, 42–3.
104. *ARB* Nov. 1978, pp. 5052–5. Madagascar has claimed with regard to the Malagasy Islands that international law provided that geographical proximity gave a neighbouring State a natural right of sovereignty, *UNC* Jan. 1980, p. 47. See also above, p. 132.
105. See, for example, the *Island of Palmas* case, 2 *RIAA*, p. 829, and Waldock, 'Disputed Sovereignty in the Falkland Island Dependencies', 25 *BYBIL* (1948), 342.
106. Hill, op. cit., pp. 92–113 and 172.
107. Speech by President Bourguiba of Tunisia on 5 February 1959 quoted in Zartman, loc. cit., p. 113. See also Touval, *The Boundary Politics of Independent Africa* (1972), pp. 251–4.
108. See *ARB* Jan. 1970, p. 1633, and ibid., May 1970, p. 1748.
109. See the Treaty of Lalla-Marnia, 1845, *KCA*, p. 19939, and below, p. 238.
110. *KCA*, p. 19940, and *ARB* Oct. 1966, p. 632. Algeria declared that any Franco-Algerian agreement regarding territorial delimitation between it

and Morocco would not be binding on Morocco, *KCA*, p. 19940. See also Brownlie, *African Boundaries* (1979), p. 55.
111. *KCA*, p. 19940.
112. By Ghana, Syria, Tunisia, Iraq and Egypt and also by the Council of the Arab League: ibid., p. 19941.
113. Ibid., p. 19942.
114. Ibid.
115. Ibid., p. 24125.
116. Ibid. See also *ARB* May 1970, p. 1748.
117. The signing of the conventions was witnessed by the representatives of the forty States attending the conference: *KCA*, p. 25372, and *ARB* June 1972, p. 2502. However, it appears that the 1972 conventions were not ratified by Morocco; see, e.g., ibid., Aug. 1979, p. 5381.
118. Ibid., June 1972, p. 2502.
119. ECM/Res.1(I).
120. See Hill, op. cit., p. 115. This is what Zartman calls 'national overhang', 'The Foreign and Military Politics of African Boundary Problems', *African Boundary Problems*, ed. Widstrand (1969), p. 81. See also Hoskyns, *The Ethiopia–Somali–Kenya Dispute 1960–7* (1969) and Brownlie, op. cit., pp. 767–74, 826–51, and 888–916.
121. Touval, *Somali Nationalism* (1963), pp. 16–25 and 29.
122. Representing British Somaliland, Italian Somaliland, Djibouti, and the Somali-inhabited parts of Kenya and Ethiopia.
123. Touval, *The Boundary Politics of Independent Africa* (1972), pp. 51–3.
124. Legum, *Pan-Africanism* (1962), p. 246.
125. Touval, op. cit. (n. 123), p. 63.
126. Procs. I, Sec. I, Doc. Agenda/Conf./5, 15 May 1963.
127. CIAS/Plenary/3, 22 May 1963.
128. CIAS/GEN/INF/25 and 43. See also Wolfers, *Politics in the Organisation of African Unity* (1976), pp. 132–3.
129. *ARB* Feb. 1964, pp. 22–3.
130. S/5536.
131. See Wolfers, op. cit., p. 134.
132. The Extraordinary Session had been called to discuss the army mutinies in East Africa, but the dangers of renewed fighting between Ethiopia and Somalia convinced the representatives to consider the issue. Kenya's request that its dispute with Somalia be placed on the agenda was subsequently accepted by the Council; see Touval, 'The Organisation of African Unity and African Borders', 21 *International Organisation* (1967), 102, 112.
133. S/5542. See also S/5557 and S/5558.
134. ECM/Res.3 (II).
135. ECM/Res.4 (II), and in accordance with Article 3(4) of the Charter of the OAU. See Touval, *The Boundary Politics of Independent Africa* (1972), pp. 212–6, and Hoskyns, op. cit., pp. 50–60.

136. CM/Res.16 (II).
137. CM/Res.17 (II).
138. *OAU Review*, May 1964, vol. i, no. 1, pp. 40–1.
139. *The Somali Republic and the Organisation of African Unity* (Mogadishu, 1964), pp. 39–40.
140. AHG/Res.16 (I). At the conference, Somalia objected to the Ethiopia–Kenyan defence pact and requested the OAU to denounce such agreements, but this item was dropped from the agenda following a note proposed by Tanzania; see Touval, 'The Organisation of African Unity and African Borders', 21 *International Organisation* (1967), 102, 116–17.
141. *ARB* Oct. 1965, p. 381.
142. Hoskyns, op. cit., pp. 73–4.
143. AHG/St.1 (IV).
144. Brownlie, *Basic Documents on African Affairs* (1971), pp. 362–3.
145. See the speech by the Somali premier quoted in Hoskyns, op. cit., p. 80.
146. Ibid., pp. 82–3. See also *ARB* Oct. 1967, pp. 880–2.
147. Ibid., May 1973, p. 2845.
148. Ibid., June 1973, pp. 2883–4 and 2850.
149. Ibid., June 1974, p. 3257.
150. See Mayall, 'The Battle for the Horn: Somali Irredentism and International Diplomacy', *The World Today*, Sept. 1978, p. 336.
151. Mayall, loc. cit., p. 337.
152. Ibid.
153. See *Revue générale de droit international public* (1978), 664–5, and *UNMC* Nov. 1977, pp. 52–3 and 108–9.
154. The majority of African States, Western countries, and the USSR condemned the Somali violations of its inherited borders: *Revue générale de droit international public* (1978), 664.
155. Mayall, loc. cit., p. 336.
156. *ARB* July 1978, p. 4914. See also the resolution of the 18th OAU summit affirming that the Ogaden was part of Ethiopia: *KCA*, p. 31055.
157. *ARB*, Aug. 1980, p. 5764.
158. See, e.g., ibid., Nov. 1980, pp. 5851–2; ibid., June 1981, p. 6074; and *KCA*, pp. 31058 and 31689–90.
159. A dispute between Gabon and Congo (Brazzaville) over the latter's claims to territory on ethnic grounds was apparently resolved by an agreement on 1 December 1962 at Dorala, Cameroon, on the basis of respect for the sovereignty and territorial integrity of each State; see Touval, *The Boundary Politics of Independent Africa* (1972), pp. 196–7.
160. See Zartman, *International Relations in the New Africa* (1966), pp. 24 and 113, and Touval, 'The Sources of Status Quo and Irredentist Policies', *African Boundary Problems*, ed. Widstrand (1969), p. 111. Personal and political antagonism between the Ghanaian and Ivory Coast Presidents exacerbated the problem: ibid.

161. Togo also claimed the territory on historical grounds in an attempt to reconstitute the borders of the former German colony; see Touval, loc. cit. (n. 160), p. 110, and Zartman, op. cit., p. 112. See also Austin, 'The Uncertain Frontier: Ghana–Togo', 1 *JMAS* (1963), 139. Austin noted that there had never been an Ewe State, but rather a series of autonomous Ewe communities along the coast and in the Togo Hills: ibid., p. 141. See also Pedler, *Main Currents of West African History 1940–1978* (1979), chap. 8, and Brownlie, op. cit. (n. 110), p. 250.
162. *ARB* Apr. 1966, pp. 509–10.
163. Ibid., Mar. 1974, p. 3162.
164. Ibid., Feb. 1975, p. 3525.
165. But see ibid., Sept. 1977, p. 4555.
166. Hoskyns, *The Congo Since Independence* (1965), pp. 2–5. According to the UN Economic Commission for Africa, some 80 per cent of commercialized production was in European hands in the private sector, while this proportion was even higher in Katanga, one of the provinces of the Congo; see *UN Economic Bulletin for Africa* June 1961, p. 72. See also Higgins, *United Nations Peacekeeping, 1946–1967*, Vol. III: *Africa* (1980).
167. Particularly between the Baluba and Lulua tribes, which spread from Kasai province to Leopoldville, the capital; see *KCA*, pp. 17594–5.
168. The Abako party of the Bakongo tribe threatened to create a separate government for the Bakongo areas and hinted at a merger with the French Congo, while President Tshombe of Katanga was unhappy at the exclusion of his party from discussions as to the composition of the national government: ibid., pp. 17595–6. See also Hoskyns, op. cit. (n. 166), p. 81.
169. *KCA*, pp. 17639–40. See also Legum, *Congo Disaster* (1961).
170. Hoskyns, op. cit. (n. 166), pp. 96–9. Tshombe had reportedly made a request for Rhodesian troops to restore order: ibid., p. 97. See also Abi-Saab, *The United Nations Operation in the Congo 1960–4* (1978), pp. 7–8.
171. Hoskyns, op. cit. (n. 166), p. 96. See also *SCOR* 15th Year, 873rd meeting, para. 196. The action could not have been justified by the Treaty of Friendship and Cooperation with the Congo as Belgium was not granted any right of intervention without the express request of the Congo government: Abi-Saab, op. cit., p. 8.
172. Hoskyns, op. cit. (n. 166), p. 99, and *KCA*, p. 17641. The UK, Central African Federation, and Southern Rhodesia all refused to send police and military aid to Katanga, while Belgium adopted a sympathetic attitude: ibid., pp. 17641–2.
173. S/4382. The Central Government had requested 3,000 American troops, but the US had advised recourse to the UN: *KCA*, pp. 17641–2.
174. S/4382. See also A/4390 and Add. 1, and Auma-Osolo, 'A Retrospective Analysis of United Nations Activity in the Congo and its Significance for

Contemporary Africa', 8 *Vanderbilt Journal of Transnational Law* (1975), 458.

175. *KCA*, p. 17642.
176. S/4381.
177. *SCOR* 15th Year, 873rd meeting, pp. 3–5. See also A/3943.
178. S/4387. See Miller, 'Legal Aspects of the United Nations Action in the Congo', 55 *AJIL* (1961), 10.
179. *KCA*, pp. 17644–5.
180. Hoskyns, op. cit. (n. 166), p. 131. Ghanaian and Tunisian troops started arriving on 15 July, while on that date Tshombe cabled UN members asking for recognition: *KCA*, p. 17645.
181. Ibid., p. 17646.
182. *SCOR* 15th Year, 877th meeting, pp. 1–4. See also A/4389 and Adds. 1–6.
183. By resolution S/4377, adopted unanimously on 7 July 1960.
184. S/4405.
185. *Yearbook of the UN* (1960), 54.
186. S/4414. This was the subject of criticism by Ghana, Guinea, and the USSR, S/4415 and S/4416. See also S/4417 and Adds. 1–10 and *KCA*, pp. 17754–6. On 7 August the Prime Minister of the Congo demanded the entry of UN troops into Katanga without delay, S/4421.
187. S/4426. The Secretary-General declared that the UN was concerned with the attitude of the Katanga authorities to the extent that it might be founded on the presence of Belgian troops; apart from this the dispute between the Congo and Katanga was one in which the UN was not a party and could not involve itself, S/4417/Add.6. The Premier of the Congo contested this view, S/4417/Add.7.
188. See *Congo*, vol. ii (1960), p. 630, published by the Belgian Centre de Recherche et d'Information Socio-Politiques.
189. *KCA*, p. 17758. These included Togo, Morocco, and Tunisia.
190. S/4448. The situation in the Congo grew worse with the declaration of independence by Kalonji of the 'État Minier' in South Kasai; see *KCA*, p. 17759. The Central Government sent forces and by the end of August claimed to have ended the rebellion: ibid., pp. 17781–3.
191. *SCOR* 15th Year, 887th–889th meetings. A Soviet draft resolution criticizing UN actions was put to the vote for lack of support, S/4453.
192. Hoskyns, op. cit. (n. 166), pp. 170–4. The Conference of African States at Monrovia in 1961 called on African States not to recognize breakaway regimes, while the Casablanca Conference and the Cairo Conference of 1961 strongly supported the territorial integrity of the Congo; see Legum, *Pan-Africanism* (1962), pp. 192, 195 and 199.
193. Hoskyns, op. cit. (n. 166), pp. 192–3.
194. This was partly the result of an internal crisis in the Congo, as the President and Prime Minister sought to dismiss each other and sent rival delegations

to the UN, and partly the result of a more activist policy pursued by the USSR; see S/4531, S/4523, S/4482 and Adds. 1–4, and S/4519.

195. S/4526.

196. GAOR 4th Emergency Special Session, A/PV, paras. 16–18 and 23. See also the delegates of Ghana, ibid., A/PV.868, paras. 151–9; the UAR, ibid., para. 221; and Liberia, ibid., A/PV.862, para. 149.

197. Ibid., A/PV.863, paras. 103–7.

198. The issue was further discussed during the 15th Session of the General Assembly, centring on the constitutional crisis in Leopoldville; see *GAOR* 15th Session, Plenary, 911th–913th and 917th–924th meetings, and A/4578. Further unrest took place in the Congo with Lumumba supporters taking power in Stanleyville, the capital of Orientale province: A/4557 and Add. 1, and *KCA*, pp. 18202–3. The Security Council discussed the situation in early December, particularly the move by Colonel Mobutu against Lumumba, see Hoskyns, op. cit. (n. 166), pp. 266–74, but no resolution was adopted, S/4578 and Res. 1 and S/4579. The Assembly resolved to keep the matter on its agenda, resolution 1592 (xv).

199. S/4741.

200. S/4752 and Corr. 1, and Adds. 1–4.

201. Resolutions 1599 (xv), 1600 (xv) and 1601 (xv). See also A/4711 and Corr. 1 and Adds. 1–2, and S/4721.

202. *Yearbook of the UN* (1961), 60.

203. See Hoskyns, op. cit. (n. 166), pp. 384–9.

204. S/4940, Annex 1.

205. Hoskyns, op. cit. (n. 166), pp. 404–8. See also Abi-Saab, op. cit., pp. 129–33, and *KCA*, p. 19342.

206. S/4940 and Adds. 1–12. Fighting broke out in October between Central Government and Katanga forces on the borders of Kasai and Katanga provinces; S/4940 and Add. 13.

207. See Abi-Saab, op. cit., pp. 129–48. Dr Hammarskjöld, the Secretary-General, was killed in an aircraft in September on his way to meet Tshombe to arrange a cease-fire: *Yearbook of the UN* (1961), 63.

208. Following a request by Ethiopia, Nigeria, and Sudan, S/4973.

209. S/5002.

210. S/PV.982. See also Auma-Osolo, 'A Retrospective Analysis of United Nations Activity in the Congo and its Significance for Contemporary Africa', 8 *Vanderbilt Journal of Transnational Law* (1975), 458, 468–70, for a discussion of the different attitudes to the secession adopted by Hammarskjöld and his sucessor, U Thant.

211. S/4940, Adds. 14–19.

212. S/5038. The 'État Minier' of South Kasai was ended in autumn 1962 with Kalonji's arrest; see *KCA*, pp. 19349–50.

213. S/5053, Add. 15, Annex V, and S/5240.

214. S/4988. On 17 November 1961, in a message to the Security Council.

215. It could also be argued that the controlling élite in Katanga was not representative of the province at all. The Baluba of North Katanga were hostile to Tshombe's regime, while the southern intelligentsia, composed primarily of Kasai Baluba, had been largely reduced to refugee status in UN camps; see Abi-Saab, op. cit., pp. 133 n. 36 and 167. The US delegate stated before the Security Council that the present Katangan authorities had no claim to speak for the entire province, the parliament was merely a rump organization of the original Assembly, and the ethnic groupings supporting the regime were a minority of the province's inhabitants; see 42 *Department of State Bulletin*, 1061 and 1062 (1961).
216. A/4557, para. 38. See also Higgins, op. cit., pp. 48–53.
217. Op. cit. (n. 166), p. 471.
218. See generally Stremlau, *The International Politics of the Nigerian Civil War 1967–70* (1977); Wodie, 'La Sécession du Biafra et le droit international public', 73 *Revue générale de droit international public* (1969), 1021; Panter-Brick, 'The Right of Self-Determination: Its Application to Nigeria', 44 *International Affairs* (1968), 254; and Post, 'Is There a Case for Biafra?' 44 *International Affairs* (1968), 28.
219. Stremlau, op. cit., pp. 59–60, and *ARB* Jan. 1970, pp. 1642–54.
220. See Stremlau, op. cit., p. 93; Kirk-Greene, *Crisis and Conflict in Nigeria: A Documentary Sourcebook 1966–70* vol. ii (1971), pp. 172–3; and *ARB* Sept. 1967, p. 856. The Assembly also reaffirmed the principle of territorial integrity in a resolution dealing with the Israel–Arab conflict: ibid.
221. See *UNMC* Aug.–Sept. 1968, p. 104, and ibid., Feb. 1969, p. 39.
222. In fact, the Presidents of Congo (Kinshasa) and Liberia declared that they were unable to attend owing to internal duties; see Chime, 'The Organisation of African Unity and African Boundaries', *African Boundary Problems*, ed. Widstrand (1969), pp. 74, 75. It was reported that the Nigerian Head of State only agreed to receive the mission after being reassured of OAU support for Nigerian unity and condemnation of secession; see Cervenka, *The Organisation of African Unity and its Charter* (1968), p. 197, and *ARB* Nov. 1967, p. 901.
223. Ibid.
224. *ARB* Apr. 1968, pp. 1031–2 and 1041. This was ironic in view of the fact that it was Tanzania that had proposed the famous border resolution at the OAU in 1964.
225. Ibid., p. 1044.
226. See, for example, the comments of the governments of Congo (Kinshasa), Guinea, Madagascar, and Mali, ibid.
227. Ibid., May 1968, p. 1072. Gabon declared later that its recognition had been because of humanitarian reasons: ibid., Jan. 1970, p. 1647.
228. Ibid., May 1968, p. 1073.
229. Ibid. Nigeria broke off diplomatic relations with Tanzania, the Ivory Coast, and Zambia, but not with Gabon, as they did not maintain embassies in each

other's countries: ibid. The Kampala peace talks the same month broke down upon Nigeria's insistence on the renunciation of secession and Biafra's refusal to accept this; see Cervenka, op. cit., pp. 199–204.

230. Haiti recognized Biafra in March 1969 for reasons that remain unclear; see Stremlau, op. cit., p. 141.
231. Ibid., pp. 127–8.
232. Cervenka, op. cit., pp. 206–10.
233. Ibid., pp. 210–16.
234. Ibid., p. 217. See also ARB Sept. 1968, p. 1174.
235. Ibid., Oct. 1968, p. 1214.
236. Ibid., Sept. 1969, p. 1531.
237. Stremlau, op. cit., p. 279.
238. Cervenka, *The Unfinished Quest for Unity* (1977), p. 105.
239. *ARB* Sept. 1968, p. 1531.
240. Ibid., Jan. 1970, pp. 1643–4.
241. See Panter-Brick, loc. cit., p. 256. Cf. Kamanu, 'Secession and the Right of Self-Determination: An OAU Dilemma', 12 *JMAS* (1974), 361. See also Nayar, 'Self-Determination Beyond the Colonial Context: Biafra in Retrospect', 10 *Texas International Law Journal* (1975), 321.
242. See Eprile, *War and Peace in the Sudan 1955–72* (1974); Kyle, 'The Southern Problem in the Sudan', *The World Today*, Dec. 1966, p. 512; Shepherd, 'National Integration and the Southern Sudan', 4 *JMAS* (1966), 193; Gray, 'The Southern Sudan', 6 *Journal of Contemporary History* (1971), 108; and Oded, 'The Southern Sudan Civil War' in *Case Studies on Human Rights and Fundamental Freedoms*, ed. Veenhoven, vol. iv, (1976), p. 227.
243. See *The Basic Facts about the Southern Provinces of the Sudan* (Central Office of Information, Khartoum), 1964.
244. Eprile, op. cit., pp. 39–48. Oded notes that the 1955 disturbances were the product of a century-old tension and traditional violence between northerners and southerners: op. cit., p. 229.
245. Eprile, op. cit., pp. 90–102.
246. Ibid., p. 21; Shepherd, loc. cit., p. 204; and Kyle, loc. cit., p. 516. See also *ARB* Dec. 1964, p. 203; ibid., Jan. 1965, p. 222; and ibid., Feb. 1965, p. 241.
247. Eprile, op. cit., p. 147.
248. Ibid., p. 151. See also *ARB* Feb. 1972, pp. 2381–4, and Oded, loc. cit., pp. 254–5.
249. Eprile, op. cit., pp. 151–2.
250. However, the Fourth Afro-Asian Peoples' Solidarity Organisation Conference in Ghana in 1965 criticized the Southern Sudan revolt as an imperialist conspiracy. See *Resolutions of the Fourth Afro-Asian Peoples' Solidarity Organisation Conference* (Cairo, 1965), p. 52. See also Touval, *The Boundary Politics of Independent Africa* (1972), p. 118. Oded emphasizes the bitterness felt by the Africans as a result of the struggle: loc. cit., pp. 257–8.

251. Op. cit. (n. 250), p. 154.
252. Above, p. 117.
253. *KCA*, p. 14598.
254. See Cervenka, 'Eritrea: Struggle for Self-Determination or Secession', 12 *Afrika Spectrum* (1977), 37, 40. See also Johnson and Johnson 'Eritrea: The National Question and the Logic of Protracted Struggle', 80 *African Affairs* (1981), p. 181.
255. For example, political parties, labour unions, and the Eritrean flag. The authorized languages of Tigrinya and Arabic were replaced by Amharic as the official language in 1959; see Bell, 'Endemic Insurgency and International Order: The Eritrean Experience', 18 *Orbis* (1974), 427, 431. Boyce notes that the federation of Ethiopia and Eritrea was 'a fiasco', 'The Internationalising of Internal War: Ethiopia, the Arabs and the Case of Eritrea', 5 *Journal of International and Comparative Studies* (1972), 51, 56.
256. Ibid., pp. 58–60; *KCA*, pp. 21611 and 24507. See also Legum and Lee, *Conflict in the Horn of Africa* (1977), pp. 25–6.
257. See Bell, loc. cit., p. 433.
258. *KCA*, pp. 23306, 23606, 24400, and 24507.
259. Ibid., p. 24507. See also ARB Dec. 1970, pp. 1056–7.
260. *KCA*, p. 24482.
261. *ARB* Mar. 1973, 2778. This movement, however, has split into two major factions, the ELF and the EPLF.
262. See the comments of Osman Salih Sabbe, one of the Eritrean leaders, quoted in Cervenka, loc. cit., p. 43.
263. *KCA*, p. 27029. Point I stated that 'Ethiopia would remain a united country without ethnic, religious, linguistic or cultural differences', ibid.
264. *ARB* May 1976, p. 4025. This called for an Eritrean Administrative Region.
265. Ibid., Apr. 1977, pp. 4393–5. See also ibid., Dec. 1977, p. 4675.
266. Ibid., Jan. 1977, p. 4282, and ibid., Oct. 1977, p. 4603.
267. Ibid., p. 4603.
268. Ibid., May 1978, p. 4840; ibid., June 1978, pp. 4886–7; and ibid., July 1978, p. 4925. See also ibid., Oct. 1978, pp. 5027–8. Since that date, however, guerrilla fighting has continued, although with greater Ethiopian control over the major population centres of Eritrea. It should also be noted that the two major Eritrean liberation movements, ELF and EPLF, have clashed violently on many occasions; see *KCA*, pp. 30592, 31057, 31685–7 and 32237–9.
269. This was recognized by a spokesman for the ELF in 1973; see Cervenka, loc. cit., p. 45. Note also the impact of the Arab–Israel dispute, ibid. p. 46.
270. See Cervenka, *The Unfinished Quest for Unity* (1977), pp. 70 and 83.
271. Above, p. 117.
272. *KCA*, p. 16618. See also the 1958 French Constitution, Articles 76 and 86. These Republics were not independent States, but 'autonomous': ibid., Articles 77 and 78.

273. *KCA*, p. 17207.
274. Ibid., p. 17513.
275. Ibid., p. 17535.
276. Ibid., p. 17685.
277. Ibid., p. 17686.
278. Ibid., p. 17687.
279. Ibid.
280. Ibid., p. 17688. See Security Council resolutions S/4543 and S/4544.
281. See Cohen, 'Legal Problems Arising out of the Dissolution of the Mali Federation', 36 *BYBIL* (1960), 375.
282. Loi Constitutionelle no. 60-11, 18 June 1960, *Journal officiel de la République Soudanaise*, 2nd yr., no. 59, 15 July 1960.
283. Zemanek, 'State Succession After Decolonisation', 116 *HR* (1965), 210–11.
284. See O'Connell, 'State Succession and the Effect upon Treaties of Entry into a Composite Relationship', 39 *BYBIL* (1963), 54, and Gandolfi, 'Naissance et mort sur le plan international d'un État éphémère: la Fédération du Mali', *AFDI* (1960), 904.
285. *ICJ Reports*, 1975, pp. 12, 165.
286. *UNMC* Feb. 1970, p. 36.
287. A/2183. For the issue of the treatment of Indians in South Africa see Sohn and Buergenthal, *International Protection of Human Rights* (1973), pp. 556–87. As regards apartheid see, e.g., ibid., pp. 634–739; Pierson-Mathy, 'L'Action des Nations unies contre l'apartheid', 6 *Revue belge de droit international* (1970), 203; *Apartheid and United Nations Collective Measures*, ed. Leiss (1965); and Tolen, 'Les Implications internationales de la politique d'apartheid', 69 *Présence Africaine* (1969), 164.
288. For example resolutions 616 (VII) and 721 (VIII). See also resolutions 820 (IX), 917 (X), 1016 (XI), 1178 (XII), 1278 (XII), and 1375 (XIV).
289. S/4729.
290. S/4300.
291. S/5802.
292. Resolution 181 (1963). See also resolutions 182 (1963) and 190 (1964).
293. The Security Council did not discuss the apartheid issue again until 1970. For African views relating to apartheid, see Andemicael, *The OAU and the UN* (1976), pp. 133–9, and Cervenka, op. cit. (n. 238), pp. 110–22.
294. See, for example, resolutions 2054 (XX), 2202 (XXI), and 2307 (XXII).
295. See also resolutions 2506 (XXIV). In resolution 2636 (XXV), the Assembly refused to accept the credentials of the South African representatives on the grounds that they only represented the white minority. See also resolutions 2862 (XXVI) and 2948 (XXVII) and A/9179.
296. See also resolutions 2775E (XXVI), 2923E (XXVII), 3151G (XXVIII), 3324E (XXIX), and 3411G (XXX).
297. Resolution 31/61. The legitimacy of the struggle of the oppressed people of

South Africa by all possible means for the seizure of power and the exercise of the right of self-determination was also stressed. It was recognized that the people had no alternative but to resort to armed struggle to achieve their legitimate rights. See also resolutions 31/77 and 31/33.

298. Apartheid was defined as the policy of institutionalized racist domination and exploitation, *UNMC* Aug.–Sept. 1977, pp. 6–10 at p. 7. See also A/Conf.91/9.

299. See also Council resolutions 417 (1977) and 473 (1980). Further Assembly resolutions include resolutions 32/10, 32/14, 32/35, 32/42, 35/206A–R, 36/172A-M and 37/69 A-J. In September 1978 the Special Committee against Apartheid called upon the Security Council to impose a petroleum embargo against South Africa, *UNMC* Oct. 1978, p. 39.

300. *Yearbook of the ILC* (1976), vol. ii, pt. 2, p. 108. This conclusion was reached in the light of 'an objective examination of State practice in the United Nations', ibid.

301. Judge Jessup noted that 'the accumulation of expressions of condemnation of apartheid . . . especially as recorded in the resolutions of the General Assembly of the United Nations are proof of the pertinent contemporary international community standard' *ICJ Reports*, 1966, pp. 6, 441. McDougal, Lasswell, and Chen stated that 'the thrust of all these authoritative condemnations, repeated again and again with only minor variations, is clearly towards the cystallisation of shared community expectations that apartheid as an aggregate net of practice is unlawful', 'The Protection of Respect and Human Rights', 24 *American University Law Review* (1974), 919, 1010.

302. Article 55 states that the UN shall promote universal respect for and observance of human rights and fundamental freedoms for all without distinction as to race, sex, language, or religion, while Article 56 notes that all members 'pledge themselves' to take action to achieve the purposes set out in Article 55. See above, pp. 61–4.

303. *ICJ Reports*, 1971, pp. 16, 57. The court emphasized that in such circumstances the question of intent or governmental discretion was not relevant, nor was it necessary to investigate or determine the effects of these measures upon the welfare of the inhabitants in question: ibid. The specific reference to Namibia as a territory with 'an international status' should not detract from the general conclusion: ibid.

304. South Africa is not a party to either of these conventions.

305. A/Conf.32/41. For a list detailing South Africa's violations of the Universal Declaration see E/CN.4/949 and Adds. 1–5 and E/CN.4/979 and Adds. 1–8. See Farah, 'South Africa's Apartheid Policy: An Assessment' in *Africa and International Organisation*, ed. El–Ayouty and Brooks (1974), p. 71. See also Article 19(3)C and commentary thereon of the International Law Commission's draft Articles on State Responsibility stating that an international crime may result *inter alia* from 'a serious breach on a

widespread scale of an international obligation of essential importance for safeguarding the human being, such as those prohibiting slavery, genocide and apartheid', *Yearbook of the ILC* (1976), vol. ii, pt. 2, pp. 95, 107–8.

306. Above, p. 162. Similar claims have been made with regard to the 'people of Palestine'; see, e.g., resolutions 2649 (XXV), 2672 (XXV), 2787 (XXVI), 3070 (XXVII), 3376 (XXX), 31/20, and 32/20. The problem really arises here if one includes within 'Palestine' the territory of Israel proper in addition to the territories of the West Bank and Gaza occupied in the 1967 war, since the elimination of a member-State of the UN contrary to the wishes of its population would be required. Indeed, in view of the Assembly partition resolution of 1947 and resolution 273 (III) and the acceptance of Israel by the UN as a member-State in 1949, it could be strongly argued that the UN is itself estopped from denying its existence and continuity as an independent State. Note also Security Council resolution 242 (1967) which emphasized the 'sovereignty, territorial integrity and political independence of every State in the area', reaffirmed in Security Council resolution 338 (1973).

CHAPTER 6

1. 2 *RIAA*, pp. 829, 838.
2. We are here concerned with international boundaries, i.e. 'all the boundaries between any two national States', Cukwurah, *The Settlement of Boundary Disputes in International Law* (1967), p. 9, excluding sea coasts; see Boggs; *International Boundaries* (1940), p. 22. See also Sharma, *International Boundary Disputes and International Law* (1976), p. 1.
3. Verzijl, *International Law in Historical Perspective*, vol. iii (1970), p. 513 and Adami, *National Frontiers in Relation to International Law* (1927), p. 3. Although, of course, a State may in certain instances under international law exercise jurisdiction beyond its territorial extent; see, e.g., article 56 of the 1982 Convention on the Law of the Sea.
4. Sharma, op. cit., p. 2.
5. 2 *RIAA*, pp. 829, 838. Huber also noted that 'the fact of peaceful and continuous display is still one of the most important considerations in establishing boundaries between States', ibid., p. 839.
6. See above, Chapter 5, p. 180.
7. 50 ILR 406.
8. *ICJ Reports*, 1962, pp. 6, 34.
9. *The Acquisition of Territory in International Law* (1963), p. 70.
10. See, for example, the 1929 Treaty between the Dominican Republic and Haiti, in which the preamble stressed that the parties 'must find a final solution of the controversies which have divided them in the past in

connection with the delimitation of the frontier separating the respective territories'.

11. See, for example, the preamble to the 1925 agreement between the USA and Holland leading to the *Island of Palmas* arbitration, 2 *RIAA*, p. 829; and the Guatemala–Honduras treaty of arbitration of 1930, ibid., p. 1309.
12. *PCIJ* Series B, no. 12, pp. 19, 20.
13. The Award, HMSO (1977), p. 4.
14. Below, pp. 230 ff.
15. i.e. non-Pakistan in this context.
16. 50 ILR 520.
17. Boggs, op. cit., p. 22, and Cukwurah, op. cit., p. 11.
18. *La Frontière* (1928), p. 14.
19. 'Political Boundaries', 32 *Scottish Geographical Magazine* (1916), 497, 501, cited in Cukwurah, op. cit., p. 11.
20. 'The Nature of Frontiers and Boundaries', 49 *Annals of the Association of American Geographers* (1959), 269, 273.
21. Op. cit., p. 13.
22. Ibid., p. 14.
23. Ibid. See also Reeves, 'International Boundaries', 38 *AJIL* (1944), 533.
24. Hill, *Claims to Territory in International Law and Relations* (1945), p. 23.
25. Oppenheim, *International Law* vol. i (8th edn., 1955), pp. 531–2.
26. Op. cit., p. 23.
27. *International Law* (4th edn., 1965), p. 438. Emphasis in original.
28. Verzijl notes that the concept of natural frontiers is highly political; op. cit., p. 516. See also generally Schoenborn, 'La Nature juridique du territoire', 30 *HR* (1929), 85, 126–35.
29. A dispute was defined in the Mavrommatis case as a 'disagreement on a point of law or fact, a conflict of legal views or of interests between two persons', *PCIJ* Series A, no. 2, p. 11.
30. See Jennings, op. cit., pp. 12–13, and Sharma, op. cit., pp. 4–7.
31. *The Geography of Frontiers and Boundaries* (1965), p. 109. Prescott also notes the existence of functional disputes and disputes over resource development, which do not involve claims for changes in boundary location: ibid.
32. Ibid., p. 113.
33. Ibid., p. 122.
34. Ibid., p. 123.
35. 2 *RIAA*, pp. 829, 838.
36. Ibid., p. 840. Huber also noted that 'international arbitral jurisprudence in disputes on territorial sovereignty ... would seem to attribute greater weight to—even isolated—acts of display of sovereignty than to contiguity of territory, even if such contiguity is combined with the existence of natural boundaries', ibid., p. 855.
37. But note that whereas a State must possess territory, it need not possess defined borders as a condition of existence; see above, Chapter 4, p. 146.

38. *Politische Geographie* (1895), as cited in Prescott, op. cit., pp. 10–11.
39. *Frontiers* (1907), p. 54. Curzon did not distinguish between boundaries and frontiers.
40. See also Prescott, op. cit., pp. 12–14. Rousseau distinguishes between natural and artificial boundaries and subdivides the latter into astronomical and geometric types, *Droit international public*, vol. iii, (1977), pp. 241–6.
41. *Political Frontiers and Boundary Making* (1916), p. 46.
42. *Frontiers, a study in Political Geography* (1918). See also Prescott, op. cit., pp. 15–16.
43. *La Frontiére* (1928), p. 9.
44. Ibid., p. 17.
45. Op. cit., p. 273–88.
46. Op. cit., p. 175.
47. Prescott points out that it is strange that boundaries related to cultural factors were not considered in this scheme: op. cit., p. 18.
48. Op. cit., p. 73.
49. *International Boundaries* (1940), pp. 9–12.
50. Ibid., p. 21.
51. *Boundary-Making* (1945), p. vi. He declared that the process of boundary-making is smoothed by considering each boundary as a special case with individuality more pronounced than resemblance to a theoretical type, ibid., p. 11.
52. Op. cit., pp. 26–8.
53. Ibid., p. 30.
54. Op. cit., pp. 25–6. This scheme is followed by Cukwurah, op. cit., p. 18.
55. *Political Geography* (1963), pp. 61–5. Prescott defines a relict boundary as one which, although abandoned, is still marked by differences in the landscape which developed during its lifetime: op. cit., pp. 30–1. See also Tagil, 'The Study of Boundaries and Boundary Disputes', *African Boundary Disputes*, ed. Widstrand (1969), p. 22, and Kapil, 'On the Conflict Potential of Inherited Boundaries in Africa', 4 *World Politics* (1966), 656, 657–8.
56. See Anene, *The International Boundaries of Nigeria* (1970), pp. 5–6, and Person, 'L'Afrique noire et ses Frontières', 80 *Revue française d'études politiques africaines* (1972), 18, 22–3. See above, Chapter 1, p. 27.
57. Loc. cit., p. 662. See also Brownlie, *African Boundaries* (1979), pp. 5–9.
58. Jones also refers to allocation, being the political decision on the distribution of territory, and administration, which is concerned with the regulation of activities in relation to the demarcated boundary: op. cit., p. 5.
59. See McMahon, 'International Boundaries', 84 *Journal of the Royal Society of Arts* (1935), 4. Curzon wrote that delimitation 'signifies all the earlier processes for determining the boundary down to and including its embodiment in a treaty or convention. But when the local commissions get to work it is not delimitation but demarcation on which they are engaged', op. cit., p. 51.

60. For example, the *Argentine–Chile* award of 1966, 38 ILR 10.
61. For example, see Judge Spender, *ICJ Reports*, 1962, pp. 6, 103.
62. 'A Geographical Analysis of Boundaries in Inter-Tropical Africa', *Essays in African Populations*, ed. Barbour and Prothero (1961), p. 305.
63. 107 *BFSP* 394, 395. A similar provision existed in the Anglo-Belgian agreement of 1910, except that the permitted deviation was restricted to 3 km.: ibid., p. 348.
64. See Zartman, 'The Foreign and Military Politics of African Boundary Problems', *African Boundary Problems*, ed. Widstrand (1969), pp. 86–9, and Cukwurah, op. cit., pp. 89–116. Another cause in many cases in simple confusion as to the correct alignment; see Brownlie, op. cit., pp. 14–15.
65. Hamdan, 'The Political Map of the New Africa', 53 *The Geographical Review* (1963), 418.
66. 50 ILR 2, 466.
67. Elias, *The Modern Law of Treaties* (1874), p. 119. See also McNair, *The Law of Treaties* (1961), pp. 681–91; Lissitzyn, 'Treaties and Changed Circumstances (Rebus Sic Stantibus)', 61 *AJIL* (1967), 895; Garner, 'The Doctrine of Rebus Sic Stantibus and the Termination of Treaties', 21 *AJIL* (1927), 509; De Caviedes, 'De la clause "Rebus Sic Stantibus" à la clause de révision dans les conventions internationales', 118 *HR* (1966), 109; and Haraszti, *Some Fundamental Problems of the Law of Treaties* (1973), pp. 327–420.
68. Second Report on the Law of Treaties, *Yearbook of the ILC* (1957), ii. 56.
69. Op. cit., p. 119.
70. *PCIJ* Series B, no. 4.
71. *PCIJ* Series C, no. 2, pp. 187–8 and 208 and 209. The court did not examine the doctrine, because, on the facts as found by the court, it was unnecessary to do so. See also the *Case Concerning the Denunciation of the Sino-Belgian Treaty of 1865*, *PCIJ* Series C, no. 16, vol. i, p. 52.
72. *PCIJ* Series A/B, no. 46, pp. 155–8, and ibid., Series, C, no. 58, pp. 463–76.
73. Ibid., pp. 109–46, 405–15, and 578–9. Note that France admitted that one had to distinguish between territorial rights and 'personal' rights created on the occasion of a territorial settlement: ibid., pp. 463–76. Waldock regarded these Swiss and French views as correct, Second Report on the Law of Treaties, *Yearbook of the ILC* (1963), ii. 85.
74. *PCIJ* Series A/B, no. 46, p. 158.
75. McNair refers to a number of municipal law cases which make reference to *rebus sic stantibus*: op. cit., pp. 690–1. See also Haraszti, op. cit., pp. 368–72.
76. *ICJ Reports*, 1973, pp. 3, 18.
77. See *Yearbook of the ILC* (1963), i. 139.
78. Ibid. ii. 207. This was contained in draft article 44(3)a.
79. *Yearbook of the ILC* (1966), ii. 39.
80. Ibid. 44.

81. Ibid. 39.
82. Ibid. 44.
83. Ibid. 259.
84. *UN Conference on the Law of Treaties, Official Records*, First Session, p. 367.
85. A/Conf.39/C.1/L.335.
86. *UN Conference on the Law of Treaties, Official Records*, Documents of the Conference, p. 184.
87. *UN Conference on the Law of Treaties, Official Records*, First Session, p. 371.
88. Article 59 was adopted by the Committee of the Whole without formal vote: *UN Conference on the Law of Treaties, Official Records*, Documents of the Conference, p. 184. It had already been decided with regard to the organization of the work of the Conference that the Committee of the Whole might adopt draft articles without a formal vote where 'there appeared to be very substantial or overwhelming support for the text . . . on the understanding that the summary records would reflect statements and reservations expressed', ibid., p. 108.
89. See, for example, the comments of Poland, *UN Conference on the Law of Treaties, Official Records*, First Session, pp. 371–2, and the USSR, ibid., p. 374. Kenya noted that territorial boundaries were so inextricably interwoven with the sovereignty and territorial integrity of States that the ILC was wholly justified in excluding treaties establishing boundaries from the *rebus sic stantibus* rule: ibid., p. 381.
90. Ibid., p. 373, and ibid., Second Session, pp. 118 and 121.
91. Ibid., First Session, pp. 379–80, and ibid., Second Session, pp. 120–1.
92. Ibid., p. 117. Sinclair notes that Syria entered a specific reservation not accepting the non-applicability of *rebus sic stantibus* to boundary treaties: *The Vienna Convention on the Law of Treaties* (1973), pp. 46–9.
93. *UN Conference on the Law of Treaties, Official Records*, Second Session, p. 118.
94. Sinclair, op. cit., p. 107.
95. See, for example, O'Connell, *State Succession in Municipal Law and International Law*, 2 vols. (1967); Udokang, *Succession of New States to International Treaties* (1972); Castren, 'Aspects récents de la succession d'États', 78 *HR* (1951), 385; Lester, 'State Succession to Treaties in the Commonwealth', 12 *ICLQ* (1963), 475; and Lekocha, 'The Problem of Succession of African States in Respect of Post-Colonial Boundaries in the Light of Practice', 1 *Studies in the Developing Countries* (1971), 131. See also *The Effect of Independence on Treaties*, published under the auspices of the International Law Association, 1965, and the many discussions in the International Law Commission, the relevant elements of which are noted during the course of this subsection.
96. 'Newly independent States' are defined in article 2(1)f as former dependent territories for the international relations of which the predecessor State was responsible. Note that, by article 7, the Convention provides that it is to

apply only as regards a succession of States occurring after the entry into force of the Convention, without prejudice to the application of customary rules which coincide with the Convention.

97. O'Connell, 'Independence and Problems of State Succession', *The New Nations in International Law and Diplomacy*, ed. O'Brien (1965), pp. 7, 21, 25. See Udokang, op. cit., pp. 132–66.
98. As regards treaties dealing with other territorial regimes, see the following section, below, p. 245.
99. *Yearbook of the ILC* (1968), ii. 92–3 (footnotes omitted). Bedjaoui noted that 'in principle the territory devolves upon the successor State on the basis of the pre-existent boundaries. These boundaries will have been established by a treaty, an instrument issuing from an international conference, a Statute or regulation of the predecessor State, or a *de facto* situation sanctioned by the passage of time', ibid. 112.
100. See, for example, Guggenheim, *Traité de droit international public*, vol. i. (1953–4), p. 465; Ross, *A Textbook of international law* (1947), p. 127; and McNair, *Law of Treaties* (1961), pp. 656–7.
101. Pereira, *La Succession d'États en matière de traités* (1969), p. 111.
102. Loc. cit., p. 492.
103. Cukwurah, op. cit., p. 106.
104. Castren notes that 'Les traités concernant les frontières ayant été mis en exécution et établissant une situation juridique déterminée, celle-ci doit être respectée par le nouveau souverain du territoire au même titre que tout pouvoir territorial étranger', loc. cit., p. 437. See also McNair, op. cit., p. 256.
105. *Theory of State Succession* (1907), p. 22.
106. *State Succession in Municipal Law and International Law*, vol. ii (1967), p. 273.
107. Ibid.
108. International Law Association, Report of the 53rd Conference, 1968, pp. 603 and 605. Quoted in *Yearbook of the ILC* (1969) ii. 48.
109. Ibid.
110. This approach may be expanded to explain why servitudes are also exempt from the clean slate rule. See further below, p. 240.
111. *La Succession d'États aux traités* (1968), pp. 128–31.
112. 'La Succession des États quant aux obligations internationales autres que les dettes publique', 44 *HR* (1933), 704, 748–9.
113. *Yearbook of the ILC* (1972), ii. 52.
114. Ibid. 54.
115. Below, p. 240.
116. As regards other territorial treaties, see below, p. 245.
117. *ICJ Reports, 1962*, p. 6.
118. *ICJ, Pleadings*, 1959, vol. i, pp. 145–6 (Thailand) and 165 (Cambodia). See also *Yearbook of the ILC* (1972), ii. 51. Note that in the *Right of Passage* case, the court held that India had succeeded to the legal situation created by a

UK–Portuguese custom 'unaffected by the change of regime in respect of the intervening territory which occurred when India became independent', *ICJ Reports*, 1960, pp. 6, 40.

119. McNair, op. cit., p. 601.
120. Manning's *Diplomatic Correspondence*, vol. iii (Great Britain), doc. 2767. Cited in Cukwurah, op. cit., p. 106.
121. 143 US 621, 633. See also McNair, op. cit., p. 603, with regard to Belgian independence from the Netherlands in 1830.
122. See also article 3(3) of the OAU Charter.
123. *UN Materials on Succession of States*, ST/LEG/SER.B/14, p. 177.
124. Seaton and Maliti, 'Treaties and Succession of States and Governments in Tanzania', *African Conference on International Law and African Problems* (1967), pp. 76, 81–2.
125. Ibid. See further below, p. 253. As regards other African practice relating to devolution agreements with the colonial power, see Okoye, *International Law and the New African States* (1972), pp. 62–8, and Cukwurah, op. cit., pp. 107–8.
126. Above, Chapter 3, p. 110, and Chapter 5, p. 197. See, for detailed survey, Brownlie, op. cit., pp. 826–51.
127. See *Yearbook of the ILC* (1974), vol. ii, pt. 1, p. 79.
128. Ibid., p. 77.
129. 537 HC Debates, 1954–5, cols. 1683–4. See also Latham-Brown, 'The Ethiopia–Somaliland Frontier Dispute', 5 *ICLQ* (1956), 245, 249.
130. See Udokang, op. cit., p. 384.
131. 621 HC Debates, 1960, 5th series, p. 105. See also Cmnd. 9348 and *UN Materials on Succession of States*, p. 185.
132. Latham-Brown, 'Recent Developments in the Ethiopia–Somaliland Frontier Dispute', 10 *ICLQ* (1961), 167, 169.
133. Ibid., p. 171.
134. See O'Connell, op. cit., p. 284. A joint boundary commission delimited and demarcated the frontier in 1910–11 in pursuance of the 1908 agreement for a mere 30 km. north and east of Dolo, at the extreme western end of the alignment. The two sides could not continue further as they disagreed on the interpretation of the 1908 agreement; see Brownlie, op. cit., p. 829.
135. O'Connell, op. cit., p. 284.
136. *Yearbook of the ILC* (1974), vol. ii, pt. 1, p. 80.
137. Notes defining a section of the boundary were exchanged in June 1925; see 36 *LNTS* p. 379. See also Brownlie, op. cit., pp. 888–915.
138. See, in particular, article 13 of the treaty. See also McEwen, *International Boundaries of East Africa* (1971), pp. 113–20.
139. See further above, Chapter 3, p. 110.
140. *Yearbook of the ILC* (1974), vol. ii, pt. 1, p. 80.
141. Ibid. See also the 1884 and 1885 agreements giving British access to Somali territories and providing that Somalis would not alienate territory except to

Britain, 76 *BFSP* 99–106, and the 1886 agreements by which the UK government extended protection to the Somali tribes and their territories, 77 *BFSP* 1263–9. However, the exact area of the territories covered by the agreements was never defined; see 537 HC Debates, 5th series, 1954–5, col. 1683. See also O'Connell, op. cit., p. 284.

142. *Yearbook of the ILC* (1974), vol. ii, pt. 1, p. 78.
143. Ibid., p. 80.
144. *UN Conference on Succession of States in Respect of Treaties, 1977*, Comments of Governments (A/Conf.80/5), p. 168.
145. Ibid., p. 169. Somalia argued that 'problems arising from boundary treaties could not be satisfactorily solved by universal rigid rules which were in contradiction with the right of self-determination and independence', ibid.
146. Ibid., pp. 148–9 and 156.
147. See above, Chapter 5, p. 194. See also Brownlie, op. cit., pp. 55–83.
148. France acquired sovereignty over Algeria in 1830; see Cukwurah, 'The Organisation of African Unity and African Territorial and Boundary Problem: 1963–1973', 13 *IJIL* (1973), 176, 184.
149. *KCA*, p. 19939; Cukwurah, loc. cit., p. 185, and Udokang, op. cit., pp. 395–6.
150. O'Connell, op. cit., p. 290. The Tindouf area was occupied by France in 1934; see *KCA*, p. 19939.
151. O'Connell, op. cit., p. 290.
152. Ibid.
153. Ibid. Cukwurah, loc. cit., pp. 186–7; Okoye, op. cit., p. 100; and Wild, 'The OAU and the Algerian–Moroccan Border Conflict', 20 *International Organisation* (1966), 19–22. See also Boutros-Ghali, *Les Conflits de frontière en Afrique* (1972), pp. 33–45, and *ARB* Oct. 1966, pp. 631–3.
154. *UN Conference on Succession of States in Respect of Treaties, 1977*, Comments of Governments (A/Conf.80/5), p. 163.
155. O'Connell, op. cit., p. 291.
156. See Journal Officiel, Débats CR, p. 2025, 3 Oct. 1956.
157. See, for example, *UN Conference on Succession of States in Respect of Treaties, 1977*, Comments of Governments (A/Conf.80/5), pp. 162–3.
158. *UN Materials on Succession of States*, p. 190.
159. Ibid., p. 187. Afghanistan argues that the treaty itself was illegal and that Pakistan as a new State does not succeed to the agreements of the predecessor State: ibid., pp. 2–3. Afghanistan in general strongly argued that the clean slate principle applied to boundary treaties: see ibid. and *UN Conference on Succession of States in Respect of Treaties, 1977*, Comments of Governments (A/Conf.80/5), pp. 139–42.
160. *Yearbook of the ILC* (1972), ii. 54. Examples would include the Surinam–Guyana and Venezuela–Guyana borders and Chinese claims with regard to Burma, India, and Pakistan; see O'Connell, op. cit., pp. 274–5 and 277–82.
161. *Yearbook of the ILC* (1972), ii. 54.

162. Ibid. (1968), ii. 92.
163. Ibid. 93.
164. Ibid. (1972), ii. 44.
165. Ibid. 54–5.
161. In accordance also with Waldock's formulation, ibid. (1968), ii. 92, and the views of the International Law Association, ibid. (1969), ii. 48.
167. Ibid. (1974), i. 203. See also A/CN.4/L.183/Add.6.
168. The Egyptian representative in the 6th Committee asked how in legal theory the rights and obligations of parties under a treaty could be separated from the international instrument creating them, A/CN.4/278/Add.6, para. 417. The Special Rapporteur noted that, as a matter of principle, it is the nature of the effects of the treaty which gives rise to the element of permanence rather than the general character of the treaty as such. The formulation of the ILC would also avoid providing a ground for saying that an unlawful treaty would be perpetuated by the articles: *Yearbook of the ILC* (1974), vol. ii, pt. 1, p. 85.
169. The Drafting Committee substituted 'shall' for 'does' in the first line of the text in order to emphasize that the article 'was in the nature of what the French called *une constatation de fait*', ibid. (1974), i. 261.
170. *Report of the UN Conference on Succession of States in Respect of Treaties, 1977* (A/Conf.80/15), Annex. II, p. 21.
171. A/Conf.80/31.
172. *Yearbook of the ILC* (1974), i. 204. The first Special Rapporteur, Sir Humphrey Waldock, referred to the Commentary of the ILC with regard to the exception to the *rebus sic stantibus* rule constituted by treaties establishing a boundary, which pointed to the need to avoid the rule becoming a source of dangerous frictions: ibid. (1968), ii. 92.
173. Ibid. (1974), vol. ii, pt. 1, p. 83.
174. For example, Moreno, ibid. (1974), i. 210; Ago, ibid. 213; Tsuruoka, ibid. 216; Yasseen, ibid. 219; Ustor, ibid. 221.
175. For example, Australia, *UN Conference on Succession of States in Respect of Treaties, 1977*, Comments of Governments (A/Conf.8/5), pp. 143–4; the German Democratic Republic, ibid., p. 150; Indonesia, ibid., pp. 152–3; and the Philippines, ibid., p. 166.
176. For example, Sette Camara, *Yearbook of the ILC* (1974), i. 206; Ushakov, ibid. 210; Ago, ibid. 213. The Special Rapporteur stressed that the basis of his proposal was to be found in long-established customary law, ibid. 222. Cf. Tabibi, ibid. 206–8.
177. For example, the German Democratic Republic, *UN Conference on Succession of States in Respect of Treaties, 1977*, Comments of Governments (A/Conf.80/5), p. 150; USSR, ibid., p. 172; and USA, ibid., p. 175.
178. Ibid., p. 176.
179. This point was emphasized in article 14 of the Convention, which provides that 'nothing in the present Convention shall be considered as prejudging in

any respect any question relating to the validity of a treaty'.

180. *Yearbook of the ILC* (1974), i. 204.
181. Ibid. 222.
182. Ibid. 213.
183. Ibid. 204.
184. Ibid. (1972), ii. 54.
185. International Law Association, Report of the 53rd Conference, 1968, pp. 603–5.
186. *Yearbook of the ILC* (1969), ii. 50.
187. Ibid. (1974), vol. ii, pt. 1, p. 9.
188. Ibid. p. 7. See, for example, the comments of Denmark, ibid. Sweden and the UK expressed some reservations over this: ibid., pp. 8 and 9.
189. Ibid., p. 76. See also the comments of Romania, ibid., p. 75. Afghanistan, Swaziland, and Syria made similar criticisms: *UN Conference on Succession of States in Respect of Treaties*, 1977, Comments of Governments (A/Conf.80/5), pp. 139, 170, and 171.
190. *Yearbook of the ILC* (1974), vol. ii, pt. 1, p. 84. Guyana noted that the principle of self-determination could not be extended to the point of removing the very foundation of the existence of the new State from the moment of its creation, otherwise 'the old colonial world would become an unbounded chaos', ibid., p. 76. See also the comments of Algeria and Ethiopia, *UN Conference on Succession of States in Respect of Treaties, 1977*, Comments of Governments (A/Conf.80/5), pp. 143 and 149.
191. Ibid., p. 157.
192. *Yearbook of the ILC* (1966), ii. 259. Waldock pointed out that 'by excepting from succession in respect of treaties boundaries established through treaties, the present article in no way excludes the independent operation of the principle of self-determination in any case where the conditions for its application exist', ibid. (1968), ii. 93.
193. As distinct from being merely 'confirmed' by it; see *Yearbook of the ILC* (1974), vol. ii, pt. 1, p. 8.
194. See Cukwurah, op. cit., p. 111, and O'Connell, op. cit., pp. 302–4.
195. See ibid., p. 231; Udokang, op. cit., p. 327; McNair, op. cit., p. 656; and Lester, loc. cit., p. 498. Sometimes the term 'servitude' has been used, but this can cause confusion; see O'Connell, op. cit., p. 231, and International Law Association, *The Effect of Independence on Treaties* (1965), p. 352.
196. O'Connell, op. cit., p. 231.
197. See Oppenheim, *International Law* (8th edn., 1955), p. 159. Brownlie argues that 'there is insufficient evidence in either principle or practice for the existence of this exception to the general rule', *Principles of Public International Law* (3rd edn., 1979), p. 667. See also Castren, loc. cit., pp. 448–9, and Brierly, *The Law of Nations* (6th edn., 1963), p. 154.
198. Udokang, op. cit., pp. 328–9, and *The Effect of Independence on Treaties*, p. 361.

199. *Yearbook of the ILC* (1968), ii. 93.
200. It is also to be noted that the exception in article 62(2) of the Vienna Convention on the Law of Treaties applies only with regard to treaties establishing boundaries and not to other territorial treaties.
201. *PCIJ* Series A, no. 24, p. 17, and ibid., Series A/B, no. 46, p. 145.
202. See *Yearbook of the ILC* (1972), ii. 50. See also Brownlie, op. cit., p. 646.
203. *LNOJ*, Sp. Suppl. no. 3, 1920, p. 18. The Committee of Jurists also held that 'the recognition of any State must always be subject to the reservation that the States recognised will respect the obligations imposed upon it either by general international law or by definite international settlements relating to territory', ibid. See also the *Temple* case, *ICJ Reports*, 1962, p. 6, and the *Right to Passage* case, ibid., 1960, p. 6. The latter case, however, dealt with the succession of customary rights over territory.
204. This agreement was not published; see Udokang, op. cit., p. 353; O'Connell, op. cit., p. 257; and Esgain, 'Military Servitudes and the New Nations', *The New Nations in International Law and Diplomacy*, ed. O'Brien, (1965), pp. 72–6.
205. Article II.
206. Udokang, op. cit., p. 355, and O'Connell, op. cit., 257.
207. See 51 *AJIL* (1957), 676.
208. O'Connell, op. cit., p. 258.
209. 51 *AJIL* (1957), 679–81.
210. Ibid., p. 682. The French admitted that the 1950 agreement was made on behalf of France and not in the name of Morocco: O'Connell, op. cit., p. 258.
211. 37 *Department of State Bulletin* (1957), 956, and 41 *Department of State Bulletin*, (1959), 723.
212. 45 *Department of State Bulletin* (1961), 973.
213. O'Connell, op. cit., p. 258.
214. Op. cit., p. 357. As regards the US military bases in the West Indies acquired under an agreement in 1941 with the UK, both the US and the West Indies appeared to accept that their future status on independence would depend upon an agreement by the parties; see Esgain, op. cit., pp. 78–9, and O'Connell, op. cit., pp. 259–62.
215. See *Yearbook of the ILC* (1972), ii. 56.
216. O'Connell, op. cit., pp. 241–2; Udokang, op. cit., pp. 357–60; and Seaton and Maliti, loc. cit., pp. 93–4. See also 5 *LNTS* 319–27.
217. 110 *UNTS* 3.
218. *UN Materials on Succession of States*, pp. 187–8.
219. Seaton and Maliti, loc. cit., p. 93.
220. Ibid.
221. O'Connell, op. cit., p. 243, and *Yearbook of the ILC* (1972), ii. 56.
222. O'Connell, op. cit., p. 243.
223. 93 *LNTS* 43, 46.

224. *The Nile Waters Question* (Ministry of Irrigation, Sudan, 1955), pp. 2–3, and 596 HC Debates, 5th Series, col. 342. Egypt upheld the validity of the 1929 agreement, ibid.
225. O'Connell, op. cit., p. 246. In 1958 Sudan formally repudiated the agreement, ibid.
226. Udokang, op. cit., pp. 365–6. See, as regards neighbouring States' attitudes, O'Connell, op. cit., pp. 246–7, and with regard to Tanzania, Seaton and Maliti, loc. cit., p. 95.
227. See, for example, Zemanek, 'State Succession After Decolonisation', 116 *HR* (1965), 180, 242–3.
228. Particularly by Tabibi, who felt the draft article was politically orientated and insufficiently supported by State practice: *Yearbook of the ILC* (1974), i. 206–7. But cf. Sette Camara, ibid., pp. 205–6.
229. For example, Botswana, *UN Conference on Succession of States in Respect of Treaties, 1977*, Comments of Governments (A/Conf.80/5), p. 145; Iran, ibid., p. 153; Mexico, ibid., p. 161; Romania, ibid., p. 167; Swaziland, ibid., p. 170; Syria, ibid., p. 171; and Cameroon, ibid., p. 173. Kenya declared that in cases of localized treaties, a newly independent State did not inherit the territorial regime created, but it did inherit an obligation where necessary to renegotiate the provisions of such a treaty so as to achieve the protection of the vital interests of a beneficiary State while not jeopardizing the successor State's independence, ibid., p. 157.
230. Above, p. 228. See Brownlie, *African Boundaries* (1979), p. 4.
231. These agreements also provided for free access for British shipping to the Somali coast and the suppression of the slave trade; see, e.g., 76 *BFSP* 99–107 for a series of such agreements. See also 537 HC Debates, 5th Series, 1954–5, col. 1683, and Sharma, op. cit., p. 97.
232. See, e.g., 77 *BFSP* 1263–7.
233. But tribal tradition defined such areas reasonably clearly; see Latham-Brown, 'The Ethiopia–Somaliland Frontier Dispute', 5 *ICLQ* (1956), 245, 249. See also 537 HC Debates, 5th Series, 1954–5, col. 1683.
234. 89 *BFSP* 31 and 36–7.
235. Britain was negotiating under a military disadvantage in the light of the situation at that time in the Sudan; see Sharma, op. cit., p. 98.
236. See 537 HC Debates, 5th Series, 1954–5, col. 1679, and Latham-Brown, loc. cit., p. 255. See also Somalia's comments to the ILC to this effect. *Yearbook of the ILC* (1974), vol. ii, pt. 1, p. 77. This raises the question of the nature of colonial protectorates and the powers of the colonial State. It is clear that the concept of the colonial protectorates was substantially different from protectorates in general; see above, Chapter 1, and Crawford, *The Creation of States in International Law* (1979), pp. 198–201.
237. Op. cit., p. 101.
238. Cmd. 5775.
239. Cmd. 6334.

240. 145 *BFSP* 460, 462.
241. Cmd. 9348. See also Latham-Brown, loc. cit., p. 259, and Brownlie, op. cit., pp. 843–5.
242. 537 HC Debates, 1955, col. 1281.
243. See Mariam, 'The Background of the Ethio-Somalian Boundary Dispute', 2 *JMAS* (1964), 189, 203–6. See also *ARB* May 1966. Article 1 of the Treaty, for example, provides that the frontier line starts at Dolo and continues as far as the Uebi Scebeli 'following the territorial boundaries between the tribe of Rahanuin, which remains dependent on Italy, and all the tribes to the north, which remain dependent on Abyssinia', 101 *BFSP* 1000.
244. Sharma, op. cit., p. 105, and above, p. 237.
245. Mariam, loc. cit., p. 200. See also Sharma, op. cit., pp. 106–9.
246. Brownlie, op. cit., pp. 846 and 849.
247. p. 238. See also Brownlie, op. cit., pp. 55–83.
248. See Reyner, 'Morocco's International Boundaries: A Factual Background', 1 *JMAS* (1963), 315. See also Trout, *Morocco's Saharan Frontiers* (1969).
249. Sharma, op. cit., p. 110, and Reyner, loc. cit., p. 317.
250. Ibid.
251. Ibid.
252. Ibid., p. 318.
253. See Sharma, op. cit., p. 112.
254. Above, p. 197.
255. See Abdalla, 'The Sudanese Boundary Conflict', 14 *Revue égyptienne de droit international* (1958), 1, 3. See also Brownlie, op. cit., pp. 55–83.
256. Abdalla, loc. cit. This area was kept for some time under the jurisdiction of the Egyptian courts: ibid., p. 4.
257. For example, the *arrêté* of the Egyptian Ministry of the Interior of 1902 implemented by a decree that year aimed at facilitating the administration of nomadic tribes along the boundary and retaining the continuity of certain tribal areas; see Sharma, op. cit., p. 192, and Abdalla, loc. cit., pp. 13–14. See also the *arrêté* of 1899, ibid., p. 11.
258. Sharma, op. cit., p. 192, and Touval, *The Boundary Politics of Independent Africa* (1972), p. 194. Egypt wished the inhabitants of the area it was claiming to vote in the plebiscite scheduled for 21 February 1958: ibid.
259. Abdalla, loc. cit., p. 4.
260. Ibid.
261. Abdalla notes that 'the renunciation of any right must be so manifest as to exclude any other interpretation', ibid., p. 5.
262. Ibid., pp. 4 and 17–18. The map demonstrating these lines appears ibid., p. 8.
263. Sharma, op. cit., p. 193.
264. Touval, op. cit., p. 194. See also 12 *International Organisation* (1958), 333–5.

265. Op. cit., p. 195.
266. Ibid.
267. See the *Temple of Preah Vihear* case, *ICJ Reports*, 1962, p. 6. See also the *Venezuelan Preferential Claims* case (1904), 9 *RIAA*, p. 100; the *Anglo-Norwegian Fisheries* case, *ICJ Reports*, 1951, p. 116, and the *Indo-Pakistan Western Boundary (Rann of Kutch)* case, 50 ILR 2.
268. See Brownlie, op. cit., pp. 121–6; Lanne, 'Les Frontières du Tchad et de la Libye', 3 *Revue juridique et politique. Indépendance et coopération* (1977), 953; and id., *Tchad–Libye: La Querelle des frontières* (1982).
269. Rousseau, *Revue générale de droit international public* (1978), p. 298. See also *Africa Contemporary Record 1975/6* (1976), pp. B70 and B465–6.
270. *Africa Contemporary Record 1976/7* (1977), p. B75, and Rousseau, *Revue générale de droit international public* (1977), p. 564.
271. Ibid. (1978), p. 298; *Africa Contemporary Record 1975/6* (1976), pp. B465–6; and *ARB* Oct. 1975, p. 3784, and ibid., Aug. 1977, pp. 4524–5.
272. Rousseau, *Revue générale de droit international public* (1978), pp. 299–300. See also Brownlie, op. cit., pp. 110–20.
273. *ARB* Aug. 1977, pp. 4524–5. See also ibid., Oct. 1975, p. 3784.
274. Hertslet, *Map of Africa by Treaty*, vol. ii (3rd edn., 1909), p. 899. The shoreline part of the boundary was not the subject of a further agreement, but 'this fact may have little significance since a shoreline may not have been considered susceptible to further delimitation', Brownlie, 'A Provisional View of the Dispute Concerning Sovereignty over Lake Malawi/Nyasa', 1 *East Africa Law Review* (1968), 258, 259. See also Brownlie, op. cit., pp. 956–67.
275. *International Boundaries of East Africa* (1971), p. 179.
276. Loc. cit., p. 261.
277. Ibid.
278. Ibid., p. 262, and McEwen, op. cit., pp. 184–9. The Handbook of German East Africa produced by the Admiralty War Staff Intelligence Division, 1916, contained a map showing a middle-line boundary, ibid., p. 185, while a British War Office map of 1918 showed a shoreline boundary, Brownlie, loc. cit. (n. 274), p. 262.
279. It noted that the western boundary of the former German territory ran 'south-east to the northern end of Lake Nyasa. Rather less than halfway down the lake it turns east and joins the Ruvuma river, whose course it follows to the sea', Cmnd. 1428. See also Brownlie, loc. cit. (n. 274), p. 263.
280. However, McEwen's view is that the map appears to show an eastern shoreline boundary on the lake. He also notes that the eastern shore of Lake Tanganyika is incorrectly shown as the international boundary, op. cit., pp. 187–8.
281. See Hudson, *International Legislation*, vol. i (1931), pp. 84–99. That line was in fact amended; see 54 *LNTS* 239 and 190 *LNTS* 95. The Tanganyika Order in Council, 1920, was similarly imprecise as to the boundary.

282. Article 12 of the mandate agreements.
283. Nyasaland sources during this period were ambiguous, but a number of reports and handbooks did refer to a middle line; see Brownlie, loc. cit., p. 265.
284. 8 *UNTS* 116.
285. Nyasaland sources during the 1940s and 1950s show a shoreline boundary; see Brownlie, loc. cit., pp. 267–71.
286. McEwen, op. cit., p. 189. See also Mayall, 'The Malawi–Tanzanian Boundary Dispute', 11 *JMAS* (1973), 611, 612.
287. Tanganyikan Parliamentary Debates, National Assembly, Official Report, 1st Session, 11 June 1962, col. 264.
288. See Mayall, loc. cit., p. 611.
289. Ibid., p. 612.
290. Seaton and Maliti, loc. cit., p. 82.
291. Loc. cit., p. 267. See also Okoye, *International Law and the New African States* (1972), pp. 102–3.
292. See Huber in *Island of Palmas* case, 2 *RIAA*, pp. 829, 852. See also the *Labrador Boundary* (1927) 43 TLR 289, 298–9.
293. See the *Temple* case, *ICJ Reports*, 1962, p. 6.
294. The OAU border resolution of 1964 is not really of any help in circumstances of genuine doubt as to the existence of a boundary, but in this case it could indeed be argued that the resolution supports the shoreline boundary, since the Tanganyikan government soon after independence made its view known as to the placement of the colonial border, which it was bound to accept upon independence.
295. In the case of the Tanzanian–Zambian boundary on Lake Tanganyika some doubt has existed as to its exact position. Only the boundary terminal points were defined by agreement and the point at which Zaïre reaches the western shore of the lake is open to dispute. In the event, a median-line boundary between Tanzania and Zambia on the lake has been accepted, it appears, *de facto* by the parties and this is shown on maps. The line takes the form of a curve down the centre of the lake from the Kalambo river to the Zaïre tripoint; see McEwen, op. cit., pp. 225–7. See also Brownlie, op. cit., pp. 1017–22.
296. Later renamed Benin. See Brownlie, op. cit., pp. 160–3.
297. *ARB* Jan. 1964, p. 4.
298. Zartman, *International Relations in the New Africa* (1966), p. 114. See also Touval, op. cit., pp. 198–9.
299. *ARB* Mar. 1964, pp. 36–7, and ibid., Apr. 1964, p. 53.
300. Ibid., July 1964, p. 110.
301. Ibid., June 1965, p. 313.
302. Rousseau, *Revue générale de droit international public* (1965), pp. 465–6.
303. Zartman, op. cit., p. 115.
304. Touval, op. cit., p. 201. According to a communiqué of 19 January 1965,

the two states agreed that the island 'leur appartiendrait en commun', Brownlie, op. cit., p. 163. The exact meaning of this is unclear. The island dispute was never important in itself: it was a symptom of the crisis in relations between the States generated by internal political instability rather than its cause, Touval, op. cit., p. 198.

305. Touval, 'The Organisation of African Unity and African Borders', 21 *International Organisation* (1967), 102, 120. See also Brownlie, op. cit., pp. 280–95.
306. Touval, loc. cit. (n. 305), p. 121.
307. AMG/Res.19 (I).
308. Touval, loc. cit., p. 121.
309. Ibid., pp. 121–2.
310. *ARB* June 1966, p. 549.
311. Ibid., Feb. 1970, p. 1665.
312. Ibid., Apr. 1977, p. 4384, and ibid., May 1981, p. 6039. All that remained was to plant trees along the line and resolve the question of compensation for property affected by the exercise.
313. Rousseau, *Revue générale de droit international public* (1975), p. 835. See also Brownlie, op. cit., pp. 427–30.
314. Rousseau, *Revue générale de droit international public* (1975), pp. 835–6. A series of maps in 1923, 1925, 1926, and 1960 by the French National Geographical Institute supported the Upper Voltan case, ibid.
315. *ARB* Dec. 1964, pp. 3452–4.
316. Ibid., p. 3454.
317. Ibid., Jan. 1975, p. 3487.
318. Ibid., Feb. 1975, p. 3525.
319. Ibid., June 1975, p. 3650.
320. Ibid., July 1975, p. 3687. See also *KCA*, p. 27268.
321. Ibid., Dec. 1979, p. 5500.
322. *KCA* p. 32484 and communiqué of the International Court of Justice no. 85/5, 15 Oct. 1983.
323. *ARB* Sept. 1972, p. 2596. See also Cukwurah, 'The Organisation of African Unity and African Territorial and Boundary Problems: 1963–73' 13 *IJIL* (1973), 176, 201–2. See also Brownlie, op. cit., pp. 670–3.
324. *ARB* Sept. 1972, p. 2597.
325. *West Africa*, 29 Sept. 1972, p. 1302, and ibid., 13 Nov. 1972, p. 1542.
326. Ibid., 29 Sept. 1972, p. 1302.
327. *ARB* Nov. 1972, p. 2658. See also Cukwurah, loc. cit., p. 204.
328. *ARB* Apr. 1974, p. 3193.
329. Ibid., July 1974, p. 3294. Nigeria and Cameroon were involved in a dispute over territorial waters in the Calabar estuary, see ibid., July 1970, p. 1805; ibid., Feb. 1971, p. 2070; and ibid., June 1975, p. 3650. Parts of the land boundary between the two were also in dispute because of incomplete maps; see ibid., May 1972, p. 2467; ibid., July 1973, p. 2916; and ibid., Aug. 1973,

p. 2951. See also Brownlie, op. cit., pp. 553–87 and *KCA* pp. 31132 and 32058.

330. As de Visscher notes, delimitation is a juridical and political operation, *Problèmes de confins en droit international public* (1969), p. 28. A series of delimitation techniques have been developed; see Cukwurah, *The Settlement of Boundary Disputes in International Law* (1967), pp. 40–78.
331. It should be noted that many African boundaries do not derive from international treaties but represent the former administrative divisions of French West Africa and French Equatorial Africa. The above principles will apply, but on the basis of colonial legislation, official maps, and administrative practices; see Brownlie, op. cit., p. 16.
332. Brownlie notes with regard to the Algerian–Moroccan disputes that much of the relevant evidence 'took the form of a mass of pieces of circumstancial evidence concerning French administrative acts in the region', op. cit., p. 55.
333. Brownlie discusses the issue here in terms of 'acquiescence by conduct', ibid., p. 16.
334. See, as regards the value of maps in such cases, Weissberg, 'Maps as Evidence in International Boundary Disputes: A Reappraisal', 57 *AJIL*, p. 781, and Hyde, 'Maps as Evidence in International Boundary Disputes', 27 *AJIL*, p. 311. See also the *Island of Palmas* case, 2 *RIAA*, pp. 829, 853; the *Guatemala–Honduras* case, 2 *RIAA*, p. 1307; the *Temple* case, *ICJ Reports*, 1962, p. 6; the *Argentine–Chile* case, 38 ILR 10, 94–5, the *Indo-Pakistan Western Boundary (Rann of Kutch)* case, 50 ILR 2, 423, and 514–15; the *Frontier Lands* case, *ICJ Reports*, 1959, pp. 209, 220, 216 and 225–6; and the *Beagle Channel* case, HMSO (1977), pp. 81–100.
335. There are a variety of means available by which disputes may be peacefully settled; see Shaw, 'Dispute Settlement in Africa', *Yearbook of World Affairs* (1983), 149.
336. Op. cit., p. 78.
337. This was particularly so with regard to the former French possessions in west and equatorial Africa. The boundaries of Upper Volta, for example, were never demarcated; see Zartman, op. cit., p. 115.
338. McEwen, op. cit., pp. 121–2.
339. *The International Boundaries of Nigeria*, (1970), p. 189. The final report of the Ghana–Upper Volta demarcation commission noted in 1970 that many of the border pillars were frequently removed: *ARB* Feb. 1970, p. 1665.
340. *The Uganda Official Gazette*, 30 May 1914, p. 256.
341. See McEwen, op. cit., pp. 132–4.
342. 82 *UNTS* 191.
343. 99 *UNTS* 338, 348.
344. *ARB* June 1970, p. 1775.
345. Primarily the Eritrean and Southern Sudanese rebellions.
346. *ARB* Feb. 1968, pp. 975–7, and ibid., Mar. 1971, p. 2036.

347. Ibid., July 1972, p. 2530.
348. A joint Sudan–Chad committee was established in 1962 to demarcate the border, but problems arose because of disputes among the tribes over water, pasture, and cultivation issues; see *ARB* 1964, p. 38. There was agreement regarding the demarcation of the Sudan–Uganda border following a series of incidents in the undemarcated border areas; see McEwen, op. cit., pp. 257–64.
349. Zartman, op. cit., p. 115, and id., 'A Disputed Frontier is Settled', 8 *Africa Report* (1963), 13–14. See also Touval, op. cit., pp. 249–51, and *ARB* June 1969, p. 1434.

Bibliography

BOOKS

ABI-SAAB, G., *The United Nations Operation in the Congo 1960–4* (1978).

ADAMI, N., *National Frontiers in Relation to International Law* (1927).

AKEHURST, M. B., *A Modern Introduction to International Law* (4th edn., 1982).

ALEXANDER, Y. and FRIEDLANDER R. (eds.) *Self-Determination: National, Regional and Global Dimensions* (1980).

ALEXANDROWICZ, C. H., *The European–African Confrontation* (1973).

ANAND, R. P., *New States and International Law* (1972).

ANDEMICAEL, B., *The OAU and the UN* (1976).

ANENE, J. C., *The International Boundaries of Nigeria* (1970).

ANZILOTTI, D., *Cours de droit international* (3rd edn., 1929).

ARNOLD, G., *The Last Bunker* (1976).

ASAMOAH, O. Y., *The Legal Significance of the Declarations of the General Assembly of the United Nations* (1966).

BARDEN, A. K., *Awakening Africa: The Conference of Independent African States* (1962).

BARDONNET, D., *La Succession d'États à Madagascar* (1970).

BARNET., R. J., *Intervention and Revolution* (1968).

BARROS, J., *The Aaland Islands Question: Its Settlement by the League of Nations* (1968).

BEAUTÉ, J., *Le Droit de Pétition dans les territoires sous tutelle* (1958).

BENTWICH, N. and MARTIN, A., *Commentary on the Charter of the United Nations* (1950).

BERNSTEIN, I., *Delimitation of International Boundaries* (1974).

BLACKSTONE, W., *Commentaries on the Laws of England*, vol i (1765).

BLUM, Y. Z., *Historic Titles in International Law* (1965).

—— *Secure Boundaries and Middle East Peace* (1971).

BOGGS, S. W., *International Boundaries* (1940).

BOKOR-SZEGO, H., *New States and International Law* (1970).

BOUTROS-GHALI, B., *Les Conflits de frontière en Afriques* (1972).

—— *L'Organisation de l'Unité Africaine* (1968).

BOWETT, D. W., *The Law of International Institutions* (3rd edn., 1975).

—— *Self-Defence in International Law* (1958)

BOZEMAN, A., *Conflict in Africa* (1976)

BRIERLY, J. L., *The Law of Nations* (6th edn., 1963).

BRIGGS, H. W., *The Law of Nations* (1953).

BROWNLIE, I., *African Boundaries: A Legal and Diplomatic Encyclopaedia* (1979).

—— *Basic Documents In International Law* (2nd edn., 1972).
—— *Basic Documents on African Affairs* (1971).
—— *International Law and the Use of Force by States* (1963).
—— *Principles of Public International Law* (3rd edn., 1979).
BRUCE, N., *Portugal: The Last Empire* (1975).
BRUGIERO, P. F., *Les Pouvoirs de l'Assemblée Générale des Nations Unies en matière politique et de sécurité* (1955).
CALOGEROPOULOS-STRATIS, S., *Le Droit des peuples à disposer d'eux-mêmes* (1973).
CAPOTORTI, F., *The Rights of Persons Belonging to Ethnic, Religious and Linguistic Minorities* (E/CN.4/Sub.2/384/Rev.1, 1979).
CARR, E. H., *The Conditions of Peace* (1942).
CASTANEDA, J., *The Legal Effects of United Nations Resolutions* (1969).
CASTREN, E., *Civil War* (1966).
CATY, F., *Le Status juridique des états divisés* (1969).
CERVENKA, Z., *The Organisation of African Unity and its Charter* (1968).
—— *The Unfinished Quest for Unity* (1977).
CHARPENTIER, J., *La Reconnaissance internationale et l'évolution du droit des gens* (1956).
CHEN, T. C., *The International Law of Recognition* (1951).
CHURCH, R. J. HARRISON *Environment and Policies in West Africa* (1963).
CLAUDE, I., *National Minorities: An International Problem* (1955).
COBBAN, A., *The Nation-State and National Self-Determination* (1969).
COLEMAN, J. S., *Togoland* (1956).
COLLINS, J. F., *The United Nations and Indonesia* (1950).
CORBETT, P., *Law and Society in the Relations of States* (1951).
CRAWFORD, J., *The Creation of States in International Law* (1979).
CRISTESCU, A., *The Historical and Current Development of the Right to Self-Determination* (E/CN.4/Sub.2/404, 1978).
CROSS, R., *Statutory Interpretation* (1976).
CROWE, S. E., *The Berlin West Africa Conference 1884–5* (1942).
CUKWARAH, A. O., *The Settlement of Boundary Disputes in International Law* (1967).
CURZON, Lord G. N., *Frontiers* (1907).
D'AMATO, A. A., *The Concept of Custom in International Law* (1971).
DAVIDSON, B., *Africa in History* (1974).
DE AZCARATE, P., *The League of Nations and National Minorities: An Experiment* (1945).
DE LAPRADELLE, P., *La Frontière* (1928).
DE LOUTER, J., *Le Droit international public positif* (1920).
DEUTSCH, K. W., *Nationalism and Social Communication* (1952).
DE VISSCHER, C., *Problèmes de confins en droit international public* (1969).
—— *Theory and Reality in Public International Law* (3rd edn., 1968).
DIAS, R., *Jurisprudence* (4th edn. 1976).
DONATI, C., *Stato e Territorio* (1924).

DRAPER, G. I. A., *The Red Cross Conventions of 1949* (1958).
DRYSDALE, J., *The Somali Dispute* (1964).
DUGARD, J. R., *The South West Africa/Namibia Dispute* (1973).
EAGLETON, C., *Responsibility of States in International Law* (1928).
ELIAS, T. O., *Africa and the Development of International Law* (1972).
—— *The Modern Law of Treaties* (1974).
EMERSON, R., *From Empire to Nation* (1960).
EPRILE, C., *War and Peace in the Sudan 1955–72* (1974).
FALK, R. A., *Legal Order in a Violent World* (1968).
—— (ed.) *The International Law of Civil War* (1971).
FAUCHILLE, P., *Traité de droit international public*, vol. i (1925).
FAWCETT, C. B., *Frontiers, a Study in Political Geography* (1918).
FAWCETT, J. E. S., *International Law and the Use of Outer Space* (1968).
—— *The Law of Nations* (2nd edn. 1971).
FEINBERG, N., *The Arab–Israel Conflict in International Law* (1970).
FENWICK, C. G., *International Law* (4th edn., 1965).
FERENCZ, B., *Defining International Aggression*, 2 vols. (1975).
FORTES, M., and EVANS-PRITCHARD, E. E., (eds.) *African Political Systems* (1940).
FRIEDMANN, W. G., *The Changing Structure of International Law* (1964).
GALLAGHER, C. F., *Morocco and its Neighbours*, Part 3; *Morocco and Mauritania* (1967).
GANJI, M., *International Protection of Human Rights* (1962).
GAVIN, R. J., and BETLEY, J. A., *The Scramble for Africa* (1973).
GÉNY, F., *Méthode d'interprétation et sources en droit privé positif* (1899).
GIBSON, R., *African Liberation Movements* (1972).
GOEBEL, J., *The Struggle for the Falkland Islands* (1927).
—— HAMBRO, E., and SIMONS, A. P., *The Charter of the United Nations: Commentary and Documents* (3rd edn., 1969).
GOTTMANN, J., *The Significance of Territory* (1973).
GREIG, D. W., *International Law* (2nd edn., 1976).
GRETTON, J., *Western Sahara: The Fight for Self-Determination* (1976).
GROS-ESPIEL, L. H., *The Implementation of United Nations Resolutions Relating to the of Peoples under Colonial and Alien Domination to Self-Determination* (E/CN.4/Sub.2/390, 1977, and E/CN.4/Sub.2/405, 1987).
GROTIUS, H., *De Jure Belli ac Pacis* (1625).
GUGGENHEIM, P., *Traité de droit international public* 2 vols., (1953–4).
HALL, H. D., *Mandates, Dependencies and Trusteeship* (1948).
HALL, W. G., *A Treatise on International Law* (8th edn., 1924).
HARASZTI, G., *Some Fundamental Problems of the Law of Treaties* (1973).
HARGREAVES, J., *Prelude to the Partition of Africa* (1963).
—— *West Africa Partitioned*, Vol. I: *The Loaded Pause, 1885–1889* (1974).
HENDERSON, K. D. D., *The Making of the Modern Sudan* (1953).
HENKIN, L. (ed.) *The International Bill of Rights* (1981).
HERTSLET, L., *Map of Africa by Treaty*, 3 vols. (3rd edn., 1909).

HIGGINS, R., *The Development of International Law Through the Political Organs of the United Nations* (1963).
—— *United Nations Peacekeeping, 1946–1967*, Vol. III: *Africa* (1980).
HILL, N., *Claims to Territory in International Law and Relations* (1945).
HOLDICH, T. H., *Political Frontiers and Boundary Making* (1916).
HOSKYNS, C., *The Congo Since Independence* (1965).
—— *The Ethiopia–Somali–Kenya Dispute 1960–7* (1969).
HUDSON, M. O., *International Legislation* (1931).
HYDE, C. C., *International Law Chiefly as Interpreted and Applied by the United States* (2nd revised edn. 1947).
INTERNATIONAL LAW ASSOCIATION, *The Effect of Independence on Treaties* (1965).
JENKS, C. W., *Space Law* (1965).
—— *The Common Law of Mankind* (1958).
JENNINGS, R. Y., *The Acquisition of Territory in International Law* (1963).
JENTGEN, P., *Les Frontières du Ruanda-Urundi et le régime international de tutelle* (1957).
JESSUP, P. C., *A Modern Law of Nations* (1948).
JÈZE, G. P. A., *Étude théorique et pratique sur l'occupation comme mode d'acquérir les territoires en droit international* (1896).
JOHNSON, H. S., *Self-Determination Within the Community of Nations* (1967).
JOHNSTON, G. W., *The International Labour Organization* (1970).
JOLOWICZ, J. A., *Historical Introduction to Roman Law* (1954).
JONES, S. B., *Boundary-Making* (1945).
KAY, D. A., *The New Nations in the United Nations* (1970).
KEITH, A. B., *Theory of State Succession* (1907).
KELLER, A. S., LISSITZYN, O. J., and MANN, F. J., *Creation of Rights of Sovereignty through Symbolic Acts 1400–1800* (1938).
KELSEN, H., *General Theory of Law and State* (1949).
—— *Law of the United Nations* (1950).
—— *Principles of International Law* (2nd edn., 1966).
KENT, J., *Commentary on International Law* (2nd edn. 1878).
KIRK-GREENE A. H. M., *Crisis and Conflict in Nigeria: A Documentary Sourcebook 1966–70*, 2 vols. (1971).
KOTZSCH, L., *The Concept of War in Contemporary History and International Law* (1956).
KRENZ, F. E., *International Enclaves and Rights of Passage* (1961).
LADOR-LEDERER, J. J., *International Group Protection* (1968).
LANGER, R., *Seizure of Territory* (1947).
LANNE, B., *Tchad–Libye: La Querelle des frontières* (1982).
LANSING, R., *The Peace Negotiations: A Personal Narrative* (1921).
LARSON, A. (ed.), *Sovereignty Within the Law* (1965).
LAUTERPACHT, E. (ed.), *Contemporary Practice in the UK* (1962 and 1963).
—— *Jerusalem and the Holy Places* (1968).
—— *International Law (Collected Papers)*, vol. i (1970).

—— *International Law and Human Rights* (1950).
——*The Development of International Law by the International Court* (1958).
—— *Recognition in International Law* (1948).
LAWRENCE, T., *The Principles of International Law* (7th edn., 1929).
LEGUM, C., *Congo Disaster* (1961).
—— *Pan-Africanism* (1962).
—— *Southern Africa—The Year of the Whirlwind* (1977).
—— and HODGES, T., *After Angola* (1976).
—— and LEE, B., *Conflict in the Horn of Africa* (1977).
LEISS, A. C., (ed.), *Apartheid and United Nations Collective Measures* (1965).
LEMARCHAND, R., *Rwanda and Burundi* (1970).
—— and MARTIN, D., *Selective Genocide in Burundi* (1974).
LENIN, V. I., *Marx, Engels, Marxism* (1934).
—— *The Right of Nations to Self-Determination* (1951).
LEWIS, I. M., *The Modern History of Somaliland.* (1965).
LILLICH, R. (ed.), *Humanitarian Intervention and the United Nations* (1973).
LINDLEY, M. F., *The Acquisition and Government of Backward Territory in International Law* (1926).
LLOYD, P. C., *Yoruba Land Law* (1962).
LONGRIGG, S. H., *A Short History of Eritrea* (1945).
LORIMER, J., *The Institutes of the Law of Nations*, vol. i. (1883).
LUGARD, F. J. D., *The Rise of an East African Empire*, vol. ii (1893).
MACARTNEY, C. S., *National States and National Minorities* (1934).
MCDOUGAL, M. S., and FELICIANO, F. P., *Law and Minimum World Public Order* (1961).
—— LASSWELL, H., and VLASIC, I. A., *Law and Public Order in Space* (1963).
MCEWEN, A. C., *International Boundaries of East Africa* (1971).
MCNAIR, A. D., *International Law Opinions* (1956).
—— *The Law of Treaties* (1961).
MADELEY, J., *Diego Garcia: A Contrast to the Falklands* (Minority Rights Group Report no. 54, 1982).
MAINE, H., *Ancient Law* (1861).
MAIR, L., *African Kingdoms* (1977).
—— *Primitive Government*, (1962).
MARTENS, G. F. DE, *Nouveau recueil général de traités*, 3rd Series, 41 vols. (1908–44).
MAZRUI, A. A., *Towards a Pax Africana: A Study of Ideology and Ambition* (1967).
M'BUYINGA, E., *Pan-Africanism or Neo-Colonialism: The Bankruptcy of the OAU* (1982).
MILLER, D. H., *The Drafting of the Covenant* (1928).
MINOGUE, K., *Nationalism* (1967).
MOCHI ONORY, A. G., *La Succession d'États aux traités* (1968).
MOORE, J. N., (ed.) *Law and Civil War in the Modern World* (1974).
—— (ed.), *The Arab–Israeli Conflict*, 3 vols. (1974).

NINCIC, D., *The Problem of Sovereignty in the Charter and in the Practice of States* (1970).
NOGUEIRA, A. F., *The United Nations and Portugal* (1963).
NUSSBAUM, A., *The Concise History of the Law of Nations* (1954).
O'CONNELL, D. P., *International Law*, 2 vols. (2nd edn., 1970).
—— *State Succession in Municipal Law and International Law*, 2 vols. (1967).
OKEKE, C. N., *Controversial Subjects of Contemporary International Law* (1974).
OKOYE, F. C., *International Law and the New African States* (1972).
OLIVER, R., and FAGE, J. D., *A Short History of Africa* (3rd edn., 1970).
OPPENHEIM, L., *International Law* (8th edn., 1955).
PADMORE, G., (ed.), *History of the Pan-African Congress* (1963).
PARRY, C., *The Sources and Evidences of International Law* (1965).
PEASLEE, A. J., *Constitutions of Nations, vol. ii* (2nd edn., 1956).
PEDLER, F. J., *Main Currents of West African History 1940–1978* (1979).
PEREIRA, A. G., *La Succession d'États en matière de traité* (1969).
PHILLIMORE, R., *Commentaries Upon International Law*, vol. i. (3rd edn., 1879).
PICTET, J. (ed.), *Commentary on the Geneva Conventions of 1949*, vol. iii (1960).
POMERANCE, M., *Self-Determination in Law and Practice* (1982).
POUNDS, N. J. G., *Political Geography* (1963).
PRESCOTT, J. R. V., *The Geography of Frontiers and Boundaries* (1965).
—— *Boundaries and Frontiers* (1978).
PRINSLOO, D. S., *Walvis Bay and the Penguin Islands: Background and Status* (South African Foreign Affairs Association Study Report No. 8, 1977).
RAJAN, M. S., *United Nations and Domestic Jursidiction* (2nd edn., 1961).
REZETTE, R., *The Western Sahara and the Frontiers of Morocco* (1975).
RIGO SUREDA, A., *The Evolution of the Right of Self-Determination* (1973).
RIVIER, A. P. O., *Principes du droit des gens*. vol. i (1896).
ROBINSON, N., *Human Rights and Fundamental Freedoms in the Charter of the United Nations: A Commentary* (1946).
ROBINSON, R., and GALLAGHER, J., *Africa and the Victorians* (1961).
ROSS, A., *A Textbook of International Law* (1947).
ROUSSEAU, C., *Droit international public*. vol. i (1953), vol. ii (1974), and vol. iii (1977).
SALMOND, J., *On Jurisprudence* (12th edn., 1966).
SALOMON, C., *De l'occupation des territoires sans maîtres* (1889).
SCELLE, G., *Introduction à l'étude du droit* (1951).
SCHUMAN, F. L., *International Politics* (5th edn., 1953).
SCHWARZENBERGER, G., *Dynamics of International Law* (1976).
—— *International Constitutional Law* (1976).
—— *International Law* (3rd edn. 1957).
—— *International Law and Order* (1971).
—— and BROWN, E. D., *Manual of International Law* (6th edn., 1976).
SCOTT, G., *The Rise and Fall of the League of Nations* (1973).
SHAPIRO, L. (ed.), *Soviet Treaty Series*, vol. i (1950).

SHARMA, S. P., *International Boundary Disputes and International Law* (1976).
SHAW, M. N., *International Law* (1977).
SHUKRI, M. A., *The Concept of Self-Determination in the United Nations* (1965).
SINCLAIR, I., *The Vienna Convention on the Law of Treaties* (1973).
SIOTIS, J., *Le Droit de la guerre et les conflits armés d'un caractère non-international* (1958).
SLONIM, S., *South West Africa and the United Nations: An International Mandate in Dispute* (1973).
SMITH, F. E., *International Law* (5th edn. 1918).
SMITH, H. A., *Great Britain and the Law of Nations*, vol. i (1932).
SOHN, L., and BUERGENTHAL, T., *The International Protection of Human Rights* (1973).
SØRENSEN, M. (ed.) *Manual of Public International Law* (1968).
STANKIEWICZ, W. J., (ed.), *In Defence of Sovereignty* (1969).
STARKE, J. G., *Introduction to International Law* (8th edn. 1977).
STONE, J. *Aggression and World Order* (1958).
—— *Conflict Through Consensus* (1977).
—— *Legal Controls of International Conflict* (1959).
STREMLAU, J. J., *The International Politics of the Nigerian Civil War 1967–70* (1977).
SUY, E., *The Concept of Jus Cogens In International Law* (1967).
TECLAFF, L. A., and UTTON, A. E., (eds.), *International Environmental Law* (1974).
TEMPERLY, H. W. D., *A History of the Peace Conference of Paris* (1920–4).
THIAM, D., *La Politique étrangère des états africains* (1963).
THIRLWAY, H. W. D., *International Customary Law and Codification* (1972).
THOMAS, A., VAN, W., and THOMAS A. J. JR., *Non-intervention* (1956).
TOUVAL, S., *Somali Nationalism* (1963).
—— *The Boundary Politics of Independent Africa* 1972).
TREVASKIS, G. K. N., *Eritrea, A Colony in Transition: 1941–52* (1960).
TROUT, F. E., *Morocco's Saharan Frontiers* (1969).
TUNKIN, G. I., *Droit international public* (1965).
—— *Theory of International Law* (1974).
UDOKANG, O., *Succession of New States to International Treaties* (1972).
UMOZURIKE, U. O., *Self-Determination in Internation Law* (1972).
United Nations, *Materials on Succession of States* (1967).
VATTEL, E. DE., *The Law of Nations or the Principles of Natural Law* (1758; repub. 1916).
VENTER, A. J., *Portugal's War in Guinea-Bissau* (1973).
VERZIJL, J. H. W., *International Law in Historical Perspective*, vol. i (1968), vol. ii (1969), vol. iii (1970), and vol. vi (1973).
WALDOCK, C. H. M., *Human Rights in Contemporary International Law and the Significance of the European Convention* (1963).
WAMBAUGH, S., *Plebiscites Since the World War* (1933).
WARD, B., *The Great International Share-Out* (1958).

WELLINGTON, J. H., *South West Africa and Its Human Issues* (1967).
WESTLAKE, J., *Collected Papers on Public International Law* (1914).
—— *International Law*, Part I: *Peace* (1904).
WHEATON, H., *Elements of International Law*, ed. Dara (1866).
—— *Elements of International Law*, ed. Keith (1929).
WHITEMAN, M. M., *Digest of International Law*, 15 vols. (1963–73).
WIDSTRAND, C. G. (ed.), *African Boundary Problems* (1969).
WOLFERS, M., *Politics in the Organisation of African Unity* (1976).
WRIGHT, Q., *A Study of War* (1942).
—— *Mandates Under the League of Nations* (1930).
YAKEMTCHOUK, R., *L'Afrique en droit international* (1971).
ZARTMAN, W., *International Relations in the New Africa* (1966).
ZIMMERN, A. E., *Nationality and Government* (1918).

ARTICLES

ABDALLA, M. M., 'The Sudanese Boundary Conflict', 14 *Revue égyptienne de droit international* (1958), 1.
ABI-SAAB, G., 'Wars of National Liberation and the Development of Humanitarian Law', *Declaration on Principles*, ed. Akkerman, Van Kreiken, and Pannenborg (1977), p. 43.
—— 'Wars of National Liberation and the Laws of War', 3 *Annals of International Studies* (1972), 93.
ABUETAN, B., 'Eritrea: United Nations Problem and Solution', 2 *Middle Eastern Affairs* (1951), 35.
AKEHURST, M. B., 'Custom as a Source of International Law', 47 *BYBIL* (1974–5), 1.
—— 'Enforcement Action by Regional Agencies', 42 *BYBIL* (1967), 175.
—— 'The Hierarchy of the Sources of International Law', 47 *BYBIL* (1974–5), 273.
—— 'The Use of Force to Protect Nationals Abroad', 5 *International Relations* (1977), 3.
ALEXANDROWICZ, C. H., 'New and Original States', 45 *International Affairs* (1969), 465.
—— 'The Juridical Expression of the Sacred Trust of Civilisation', 65 *AJIL* (1971), 149.
—— 'The New States and International Law', 3 *Millennium—Journal of International Studies* (1974–5), 226.
—— 'The Role of Treaties in the European–African Confrontation in the Nineteenth Century', *African International Legal History*, ed. Mensah-Brown (1975), 27.
ALLOTT, A. N., 'Boundaries and the Law in Africa', *African Boundary Problems*, ed. Widstrand C. G. (1969), p. 10.

ANDREWS, J., 'The Concept of Statehood and the Acquisition of Territory in the Nineteenth Century', 94 *LQR* (1978), 408.

ARANGIO-RUIZ, G., 'The Normative Role of the General Assembly of The United Nations and the Declaration on Principles of Friendly Relations', 137 *HR* (1972), 517.

ARDENER, E., 'The Nature of the Reunification of Cameroon', *African Integration and Disintegration*, ed. Hazlewood (1967), p. 285.

ASHFORD, D. E., 'The Irredentist Appeal in Morocco and Mauritania', 15 *Western Political Quarterly* (1962), 641.

AUMO-OSOLO, A., 'Retrospective Analysis of United Nations Activity in the Congo and its Significance for Contemporary Africa', 8 *Vanderbilt Journal of Transnational Law* (1975), 458.

AUSTIN, D., 'The Uncertain Frontier: Ghana–Togo', 1 *JMAS* (1963), 139.

BARBOUR, K. M., 'A Geographical Analysis of Boundaries in Inter-Tropical Africa', *Essays on African Populations*, ed. Barbour and Prothero (1961), p. 305.

BASTID, S., 'Les Problèmes territoriaux dans la jurisprudence de la Cour Internationale de Justice', 107 *HR* (1962), 360.

BECKET, E., 'Les Questions d'intérêt général au point de vue juridique dans la jurisprudence da la Cour Permanente de Justice Internationale', 50 *HR* (1934), 189.

BELL, J. B., 'Endemic Insurgency and International Order: The Eritrean Experience', 18 *Orbis* (1974), 427.

BLISHCHENKO, I., and SOLNTSEVA, M., 'The Struggle Against Portuguese Colonialism in the Light of International Law', 8 *International Affairs* (Moscow, 1971), 60.

BOALS, K., 'The Relevance of International Law to the Internal War in Yemen', *The International Law of Civil War*, ed. Falk (1971), p. 303.

BOWETT, D. W., 'Problems of Self-Determination and Political Rights in Developing Countries', *PASIL* (1966), 134.

—— 'The Inter-Relation of Theories of Intervention and Self-Defence', *Law and Civil War in the Modern World*, ed. Moore (1974), p. 38.

—— 'Estoppel before International Tribunals and its Relation to Acquiescence', 33 *BYBIL* (1957), 176.

BOYCE, F., 'The Internationalising of Internal War: Ethiopia, the Arabs and the Case of Eritrea', 5 *Journal of International and Comparative Studies* (1972), 51.

BRIGGS, H. W., 'Non-Recognition of Title by Conquest Limitations on the Doctrine', *PASIL* (1940), 72.

BROOKS, P., 'The Legal Status of Walvis Bay', 2 *South African Yearbook of International Law* (1976), 187.

BROWN, ?, 'Self-Determination in Central Europe', 14 *AJIL* (1920). 235.

BROWNLIE, I., 'A Provisional View of the Dispute Concerning Sovereignty over Lake Malawi/Nyasa', *East Africa Law Review* (1968), 258.

—— 'History of the Principle of Self-Determination', *Grotian Society Papers* (1968), 96.

—— Humanitarian Intervention', *Law and Civil War in the Modern World*, ed. Moore (1974), p. 217.

CASSESE, A., 'The Self-Determination of Peoples', *The International Bill of Rights*, ed. Henkin (1981), p. 92.

CASTAGNO, A. A., 'The Somali–Kenyan Controversy', 2 *JMAS* (1964), 165.

CASTREN, E., 'Aspects récents de la succession d'états', 78 *HR* (1951), 385.

CAVAGLIERI, A., 'Règles générales du droit de la paix', 26 *HR* (1929), 315.

CERVENKA, Z., 'Eritrea: Struggle for Self-Determination or Secession', 12 *Afrika Spectrum* (1977), 37.

—— 'Major Policy Shifts in the Organisation of African Unity 1963–73', *Foreign Relations of African States*, ed. Ingham (1974), p. 323.

CHENG, B., 'United Nations Resolutions on Outer Space: "Instant" International Astronomy Law' 5 *IJIL* (1965), 23.

CHILSTROM, R. M., 'Humanitarian Intervention Under Contemporary International Law: A Policy-Oriented Approach', 1 *Yale Studies in World Public Order* (1974), 93.

CHIME, S. C., 'The Organisation of African Unity and African Boundaries', *African Boundary Problems*, ed. Widstrand (1969), p. 74.

COHEN, R., 'Legal Problems Arising out of the Dissolution of the Mali Federation', 36 *BYBIL* (1960), 375.

COLEMAN, J. S., 'Tradition and Nationalism in Tropical Africa', *New States in the Modern World* ed. Kilson (1975), p. 12.

COLSON, E., 'African Society at the Time of the Scramble', *Colonialism in Africa 1870–1960*, ed. Gann and Duignan, vol. i (1969), p. 31.

CRAWFORD, J. F., 'South West Africa: Mandate Termination in Historical Perspective', 6 *Columbia Journal of Transnational Law* (1967), 91.

CRAWFORD, J., 'The Criteria for Statehood in International Law', 48 *BYBIL* (1976–7), 93.

CRAWFORD, R., and DAYANIDHI, P., 'East Timor: A Study in Decolonisation', 33 *India Quarterly* (1977), 419.

CUKWURAH, A. O., 'The Organisation of African Unity and African Territorial and Boundary Problems: 1963–1973', 13 *IJIL* (1973), 176.

CUMMING, D., 'The Disposal of Eritrea', 7 *Middle East Journal* (1953), 18.

D'AMATO, A., 'On Consensus', 8 *Canadian Yearbook of International Law* (1970), 104.

—— 'The Bantustan Proposals for South West Africa', 4 *JMAS* (1966), 177.

DARWIN, H., 'The Outer Space Treaty', 42 *BYBIL* (1967), 280

DE CAVIEDES, A. P., 'De La Clause "rebus sic stantibus" à la clause de révision dans les conventions internationales', 118 *HR* (1966), 109.

DELBEZ, L., 'Du territoire dans ses rapports avec l'état', 39 *Revue générale de droit international public* (1932), 46.

DEMBINSKI, L., 'Le Territoire et la développement du droit international public', *Annuaire suisse de droit international* (1975), 121.

DEVINE, D. J., 'The Requirements of Statehood Re-examined', 34 *MLR* (1971), 410.

DUGARD, J. R., 'The Organisation of African Unity and Colonialism: An Enquiry into the Plea of Self-Defence as a Justification for the Use of Force in the Eradication of Colonialism', 16 *ICLQ* (1967), 157.

—— 'The Revocation of the Mandate for South West Africa', 62 *AJIL*, (1968), 78.

DUPUIS, R., 'Règales générales du droit de la paix', 32 *HR* (1931), 37.

EL ERIAN, A., 'The Legal Order of International Society', *Manual of Public International Law*, ed. Sørensen (1968), p. 55.

ELLIOTT, P. D., 'The East Timor Dispute', 27 *ICLQ* (1978), 238.

EMERSON, R., 'Pan-Africanism', 16 *International Organisation* (1962), 278.

—— 'Self-Determination', 65 *AJIL* (1971), 461.

ESGAIN, A. J., 'Military Servitudes and the New Nations', *The New Nations in International Law and Diplomacy* ed. O'Brien (1965), p. 42.

EVATT, E., 'The Acquisition of Territory in Australia and New Zealand', *Grotian Society Papers* (1968), 16.

FALK, R. A., A New Paradigm for International Legal Studies: Prospects and Proposals', 84 *Yale Law Journal* (1975), 969.

—— 'Janus Tormented: The International Law of Internal War', *International Aspects of Civil Strife*, ed. Rosenau, (1964), p. 185.

—— 'The South West Africa Cases: An Appraisal', 21 *International Organisation* (1967), 7.

FALL, I., 'La Reconnaissance de la Guinée-Bissau et le droit international', *Annales Africains* (1973), 153.

FARAH, T. E., 'South Africa's Apartheid Policy: An Assessment', *Africa and International Organisation*, ed. El-Ayouty and Brooks (1974), p. 71.

FARER, T., 'Intervention in Civil Wars: A Modest Proposal', 67 *Columbia Law Review* (1967), 266.

—— 'The Regulation of Foreign Intervention in Civil Armed Conflict', 142 *HR* (1974), 291.

FAWCETT, J. E. S., 'Security Council Resolutions on Rhodesia', 41 *BYBIL* (1965–6), 103.

—— 'The Role of the United Nations in Relation to Human Rights—Is it Misconceived?' *Proceedings of the Nobel Symposium* 7 (1968), 95.

FISCHER, G., 'La Non-Reconnaissance du Transkei' *AFDI* (1976), 63.

FITZMAURICE, G. G., 'The Law and Procedure of the International Court of Justice', 28 *BYBIL* (1951), 1.

—— 'The Law and Procedure of the International Court of Justice, 1951–4', 33 *BYBIL* (1957), 209.

FLORY, M., 'La Notion de Territoire arabe et son application au problèmes du Sahara', *AFDI* (1957), 73.

FONTEYNE, J. P., 'The Customary International Law Doctrine of Humanitarian

Intervention: Its Current Validity under the United Nations Charter', 4 *California Western International Law Journal* (1974), 203.

FRALEIGH, A., 'The Algerian Revolution as a Case Study in International Law', *The International Law of Civil War* ed. Falk (1971), p. 179.

FRANCK, T. M., 'The Stealing of the Sahara', 70 *AJIL* (1976), 694.

—— and HOFFMAN, P., 'The Right of Self-Determination in Very Small Places', 8 *New York Journal of International Law and Politics* (1976), 331.

—— and RODLEY, N. S., 'After Bangladesh: The Law of Humanitarian Intervention by Military Force', 67 *AJIL* (1973), 275.

FRIEDMANN, W. G., 'General Course in Public International Law', 127 *HR* (1969), 142.

—— 'Intervention, Civil War and the Rule of International Law', *PASIL* (1965), 67.

GANDOLFI, A., 'Naissance et mort sur le plan international d'un état éphémère: la Fédération du Mali', *AFDI* (1960). 881.

GARNER, J. W., The Doctrine of Rebus Sic Stantibus and the Termination of Treaties', 21 *AJIL* (1927), p. 509.

GINSBURGS, G., 'Wars of National Liberation and the Modern Law of Nations—The Soviet Thesis', *The Soviet Impact on International Law*, ed. Baade (1965), p. 66.

GIRAUD, E., 'Le Droit international public et la politique', 110 *HR* (1966), 744.

GRAY, R., 'The Southern Sudan', 6 *Journal of Contemporary History* (1971), 108.

GREEN, L. C., 'The United Nations, South West Africa and the World Court', 7 *IJIL* (1967), 491.

GROS-ESPIELL, H., 'Self-Determination and Jus Cogens', *United Nations Law-Fundamental Rights*, ed. Cassese (1979), p. 167.

GROSS, L., 'The Peace of Westphalia, 1648–1948', *International Law in the Twentieth Century*, ed. Gross (1969), p. 25.

—— 'The International Court of Justice and the United Nations', 120 *HR* (1967), 313.

—— 'The Right of Self-Determination in International Law', *New States in the Modern World*, ed. Kilson (1975), p. 136.

GUILHAUDIS, J.-F., 'La Question de Timor', *AFDI* (1977), 307.

HAAS, E. B., 'The Reconciliation of Conflicting Policy Aims: The Acceptance of the League of Nations Mandate System', 6 *International Organisation* (1952), 521.

HAMDAN, G., 'The Political Map of the New Africa', 53 *The Geographical Review* (1963), 418.

HARGREAVES, J., 'Towards a History of the Partition of Africa', 1 *Journal of African History* (1960), 97.

HARKABI, Y., 'The Position of the Palestinians in the Israel–Arab Conflict and their National Covenant (1968)', 3 *New York University Journal of International Law and Politics* (1970), 209.

HENKIN, L., 'The United Nations and Human Rights', 19 *International Organisation* (1965), 512.

HERMAN, L. J., 'The Legal Status of Namibia and of the United Nations Council for Namibia', 13 *Canadian Yearbook of International Law* (1975), 306.

HEVENER, N. K., 'The 1971 South West Africa Opinion: A New International Judicial Philosophy', 24 *ICLQ* (1975), 791.

HIGGINS, R., 'Internal War and International Law', *The Future of the International Legal Order* ed. Black and Falk; vol. 3, 1971, p. 81.

—— 'International Law and Civil Conflict', *The International Regulation of Civil Wars* ed. Luard (1972), p. 169.

—— 'International Law, Rhodesia and the United Nations', *The World Today*, Mar. 1967, p. 94.

—— 'The Advisory Opinion on Namibia: Which United Nations Resolutions are Binding under Article 25 of the Charter?' 21 *ICLQ*, (1972), 27.

—— 'The Development of International Law By the Political Organs of the United Nations', *PASIL* (1965), 116.

—— 'The International Court of Justice and South West Africa', 42 *International Affairs*, (1966), 573.

—— 'The International Court and South West Africa: The Implications of the Judgement', *Journal of the Commission of Jurists* (1967), 3.

—— 'The Place of International Law in the Settlement of Disputes by the Security Council', 64 *AJIL* (1970), 7.

HODGES, T., 'The Western Sahara File', 6 *Third World Quarterly* (1984), 74.

HOFFMAN, S., 'International Systems and International Law', 14 *World Politics* (1961), 230.

HOLDICH, T. H., 'Political Boundaries', 32 *Scottish Geographical Magazine* (1916), 497.

HOLLICK, J. C., 'French Intervention in Africa in 1978', *The World Today*, Feb. 1979. p. 71.

HOUBEN, P-H., 'Principles of International Law Concerning Friendly Relations and Co-operation Among States', 61 *AJIL* (1967), 703.

HOUBERT, J., 'Mauritius: Independence and Dependence, 19 *JMAS* (1981), 75.

HUBER, M., 'National Self-Determination', *Social Research*, x (1943), 1.

HUDSON, M. O., 'Integrity of International Instruments', 42 *AJIL* (1948), 105.

HYDE, C. C., 'Maps as Evidence in International Boundary Disputes', 27 *AJIL* (1933), 311.

IJALAYE, D. A., 'Was "Biafra" at Any Time a State in International Law?' 65 *AJIL* (1971), 551.

JENNINGS, R. Y., 'The Progress of International Law', 34 *BYBIL* (1958), 334.

JESSUP, P. C., 'The Palmas Island Arbitration', 22 *AJIL* (1928), 735.

JOHNSON, D. H. N., 'Acquisitive Prescription in International Law', 27 *BYBIL* (1950), 332.

—— 'Consolidation as a Root of Title in International Law', *CLJ* (1955), 215.

JOHNSON, M., and JOHNSON, T., 'Eritrea: The National Question and the Logic of Protracted Struggle', 80 *African Affairs* (1981), 181.

KAECKENBEECK, G., 'La Charte de San Francisco dans ses rapports avec le droit international', 70 *HR* (1947), 113.
KAMANU, O. S., 'Secession and the Right of the Self-Determination: An OAU Dilemma', 12 *JMAS* (1974), 355.
KAPIL, R. L., 'On the Conflict Potential of Inherited Boundaries in Africa', 4 *World Politics* (1966), 656.
KAUR, S., 'Self-Determination In International Law', 10 *IJIL* (1970), 479.
KELSEN, H., 'Recognition in International Law', 35 *AJIL* (1941), 405.
—— 'Sovereignty and International Law', *In Defence of Sovereignty*, ed. Stankiewicz (1969), p. 115.
—— 'The Quasi-Judicial Role of the Security Council and the General Assembly', 58 *AJIL* (1964), 964.
——'Théorie du droit international coutumier', *Revue internationale de la théorie du droit* (1939), 253.
KOVAR, R., 'La Participation des territoires non-autonomes aux organisations internationales', *AFDI* (1969), 522.
KRISHNAN, V. M., 'African State Practice Relating to Certain Issues of International Law', 14 *Indian Journal of International Affairs* (1965), 196.
KRISTOFF, L. A. D., 'The Nature of Frontiers and Boundaries', 49 *Annals of the Association of American Geographers* (1959), 269.
KUNZ, J. L., 'Chapter XI of the United Nations Charter in Action', 48 *AJIL* (1954), 109.
—— 'Critical Remarks on Lauterpacht's "Recognition in International Law" ', 44 *AJIL* (1950), 713.
—— 'The Present Status of International Law for the Protection of Minorities', 48 *AJIL* (1954), 282.
KYLE, K., 'The Southern Problem in the Sudan', *The World Today*, Dec. 1966, p. 512.
LACHS, M., 'Law in and of the UN', 1 *IJIL* (1960), 432.
LANNE, B., 'Les Frontières du Tchad et de la Libye', 3 *Revue Juridique et politique. Indépendance et coopération* (1977), 953.
LATHAM-BROWN, D. J., 'Recent Developments in the Ethiopia-Somaliland Frontier Dispute', 10 *ICLQ* (1961), 167.
—— 'The Ethiopia–Somaliland Frontier Dispute', 5 *ICLQ* (1956), 245.
LATHAM-LOENIG, A. L., 'Mauritius after the June Elections', *The World Today*, July-Aug. 1982, p. 253.
LAUTERPACHT, H., 'The Subjects of International Law', *International Law (Collected Papers)*, vol. ii, pt. 1 (1975), p. 489.
—— 'Sovereignty over Submarine Areas', 27 *BYBIL* (1950), 376.
LAZARUS, C., 'Le Status des mouvements de libération nationale à l'Organisation des Nations Unies', *AFDI* (1974), 173.
LEE, L. T., 'The Mexico City Conference of the UN Special Committee on Principles of International Law Concerning Friendly Relations and Co-operation Among States', 14 *ICLQ* (1965), 1296.

LESTER, A. P., 'State Succession to Treaties in the Commonwealth', 12 *ICLQ* (1963), 475.

LETOCHA, T., 'The Problem of Succession of African in Respect of Post-Colonial Boundaries in the Light of Practice', 1 *Studies in the Developing Countries* (1971), 131.

LEWIS, I. M., 'The Problem of the Northern Frontier District of Kenya', 5 *Race* (1963), 48.

—— 'The Referendum in French Somaliland: Aftermath and Propects in the Somali Dispute', *The World Today*, July 1967, p. 308.

—— 'The Somali Conquest of the Horn of Africa', 1 *Journal of African History* (1960), 213.

LILLICH, R., 'Forcible Self-Help by States to Protect Human Rights', 53 *Iowa Law Review* (1967), 325.

—— 'Intervention to Protect Human Rights', 15 *McGill Law Journal* (1969), 205.

LISSITZEN, O. J., 'Treaties and Changed Circumstances (Rebus Sic Stantibus), 61 *AJIL* (1967), 895.

LUARD, E., 'The Origins of International Concern over Human Rights', *The International Protection of Human Rights*, ed. Luard (1967), p. 10.

MCDOUGAL, M. S., LASSWELL, H., and CHEN, L. C., 'The Protection of Respect and Human Rights', 24 *American University Law Review* (1974), 919.

—— and REISMAN, W. M., 'Rhodesia and the UN: The Lawfulness of International Concern', 62 *AJIL* (1968), 1.

MACGIBBON, I., 'The Scope of Acquiescence in International Law', 31 *BYBIL* (1954), 143.

—— 'Customary International Law and Acquiescence', 33 *BYBIL* (1957), 115.

—— 'Some Observations on the Role of Protest in International Law', 30 *BYBIL* (1953), 293.

MCMAHON, M. M., 'International Boundaries', 84 *Journal of the Royal Society of Arts* (1935), 4.

MCWHINNEY, E., 'The "New" Countries and the "New" International Law: The UN Special Conference on Friendly Relations and Co-Operation among States', 60 *AJIL* (1966), 1.

MANGONGO-NZAMBI, A., 'La Délimitation des frontières du Gabon (1885–1911)', 9 *Cahiers d'études africaines* (1969), 5.

MARIAM, M. W., 'The Background of the Ethio-Somalian Boundary Dispute', 2 *JMAS* (1964), 189.

MARSHALL, H. H., 'Namibia and Walvis Bay', 27 *ICLQ* (1978), 683.

MARTINE, F., 'Le Comité de Decolonisation et le droit international', *Revue générale de Droit international public* (1970), 402.

MATHY, D., 'L'Autodétermination de petits territoires revendiqués par États tiers (première partie)', *Revue belge de droit international* (1974), 167.

—— 'L'Autodétermination de petits territoires revendiqués par États tiers (Deuxième partie)', *Revue belge de droit international* (1975), 129.

MAYALL, J., 'The Battle for the Horn: Somali Irredentism and International Diplomacy', *The World Today*, Sept. 1978, p. 336.
—— 'The Malawi–Tanzanian Boundary Dispute', 11 *JMAS* (1973), 611.
MAZRUI, A., 'Consent, Colonialism and Sovereignty', 11 *Political Studies* (1963), 48.
MENDELSON, M. H., 'Diminutive States in the United Nations', 21 *ICLQ*(1972), 609.
MERCER, J., 'Confrontation in the Western Sahara', *The World Today*, June 1976, p. 230.
MERLE, M., 'Plébiscites organisés par les Nations Unies', *AFDI* (1961), 425.
MICLO, F., and ORAISON, A., 'A qui appartient le Récif de Tromelin?', *Annuaire des pays de l'ocean Indien* (1978), 263.
MILLER, E. M., 'Legal Aspects of the United Nations Action in the Congo', 55 *AJIL* (1961), 10.
MINH, 'Remarques sur le principe de l'intangibilité des frontières', *Peuples et États du Tiers monde face à l'ordre international*, ed. Fenet (1978), p. 51.
MITTLEMAN, J., 'Collective Decolonisation and the United Nations Committee of 24', 14 *JMAS* (1976), 41.
MODEEN, T., 'The International Protection of the National Identity of the Aaland Islands', *Scandinavian Studies in Law* (1973), 177.
MOORE, J. N., 'The Control of Foreign Intervention in Internal Conflict', *Law and the Indo-China War*, ed. Moore (1972), p. 115.
MOUSHKELY, M., 'La Naissance des États en droit international public', 66 *Revue générale de droit international public* (1962), 469.
MURTY, T. S., 'Evidence on Traditional Boundaries and Some Problems in its Interpretation', 8 *IJIL* (1968), 479.
MUSTAFA. Z., 'The Principle of Self-Determination in International Law', 5 *International Lawyer* (1971), 482.
NANDA, V. P., 'The United States' Action in the 1965 Dominican Crisis: Impact on World Order—Part I', 43 *Denver Law Journal*, p. 437.
NAWAZ, M. K., 'Colonies, Self-Government and the United Nations', 1 *Indian Yearbook of World Affairs* (1962), 3.
NAYAR, M. C. K., 'Self-Determination Beyond the Colonial Context: Biafra In Retrospect', 10 *Texas International Law Journal* (1975), 321.
OBOZUWA, A. U., 'Some Legal Aspects of the Rhodesian Situation', 5 *Nigerian Journal of Contemporary Law* (1974), 1.
O'CONNELL, D. P., 'Independence and Problems of State Succession', *The New Nations in International Law and Diplomacy*, ed. O'Brien (1965), p. 7.
—— 'State Succession and the Effect upon Treaties of Entry into a Composite Relationship', 39 *BYBIL* (1963), 54.
ODED, A., 'The Southern Sudan Civil Way', *Case Studies on Human Rights and Fundamental Freedoms*, ed. Veenhoven, vol. iv (1976), p. 227.
OGUNDADEJO, O., 'Diego Garcia and Africa's Security', 4 *Third World Quarterly*, Jan. 1982, p. 104.

ORAISON, A., 'A propos du différend franco-malgache sur les îles éparses du canal de Mozambique', 85 *Revue générale de droit international public* (1981), 465.

PANTER-BRICK, S. K, 'The Right of Self-Determination: Its Application to Nigeria', 44 *International Affairs* (1968), 254.

PERSON, Y., 'L'Afrique noire et ses frontières', 80 *Revue française d'études politiques africaines*. (1972), 18.

PETKOVIC, R., 'Intégrité territoriale et droit à l'autodétermination en Afrique', *Revue de la politique internationale* (1969), 20.

PHILLIPS, J. C., 'The Exclusive Economic Zone as a Concept in International Law', 26 *ICLQ* (1977), 585.

PIERSON-MATHY, P., 'L'Action des Nations unies contre l'apartheid', 6 *Revue belge de droit international* (1970), 203.

POMERANCE, M., 'The United States and Self-Determination: Perspectives on the Wilsonian Conception', 70 *AJIL* (1976), 1.

POST, K. W. J., 'Is There a Case for Biafra?' 44 *International Affairs* (1968), 26.

RAO, T. S. RAMA, 'Right of Self-Determination: Its Status and Role in International Law', *Internationales Recht und Diplomatie* (1968), 19.

RATON, P., 'Les Enclaves', *AFDI* (1958), 186.

REDSLOB, R., 'Le Principe des Nationalités', 37 *HR* (1931), 5.

REEVES, J. S., 'International Boundaries' 38 *AJIL* (1944), 533.

REJAI, M., and ENLOE, C. H., 'Nation-States and States-Nations', 13 *International Studies Quarterly* (1969), 140.

RESULOVIC, 'Ten Years of the Organisation of African Unity'. 24 *Review of International Affairs* (1973), 34.

REYNER, A. S., 'Morocco's International Boundaries: A Factual Background', 7 *JMAS* (1963), 324.

RICHARDSON, H. J., III, 'Self-Determination, International Law and the South African Bantustan Policy', 17 *Colombia Journal of Transnational Law* (1978), 185.

RIESENFELD, S. A., 'Jus Dispositivum and Jus Cogens In International Law in the Light of a Recent Decision of the German Supreme Constitutional Court', 60 *AJIL* (1966), 511.

RIVLIN, B., 'The Italian Colonies at the General Assembly', 3 *International Organisation* (1949), 459.

ROBINSON, N., 'From Protection of Minorities to Promotion of Human Rights', *Jewish Yearbook of International Law* (1949), 115.

ROHLIK, J., 'Some Remarks on Self-Defence and Intervention', 6 *Georgian Journal of International and Comparative Law* (1976), 395.

RONZITTI, N., 'Resort to Force in Wars of National Liberation', *Current Problems of International Law*, ed. Cassese (1975), p. 319.

—— 'Wars of National Liberation—A Legal Definition', 1 *Italian Yearbook of International Law* (1975), 192.

ROSENNE, S., 'Directions for a Middle East Settlement—Some Underlying Problems', *The Middle East Crisis: Test of International Law*, ed. Halderman (1969), p. 59.

—— 'Is the Constitution of an International Organisation an International Treaty?' *Comunicazioni e Studie*, 12 (1966), 21.

ROSENSTOCK., R., 'The Declaration of Principles of International Law Concerning Friendly Relations: A Survey', 65 *AJIL* (1971), 713.

SAGAY, I., 'Non-Recognition of the Illegal Occupation of Territory', 16 *IJIL* (1976), 219.

—— 'The Legal Status of Freedom Fighters in Africa', 6 *East Africa Law Review* (1975), 15.

SAHOVIC, M., and BISHOP, W. W., 'The Authority of the State: Its Range with Respect to Persons and Places', *Manual of Public International Law* ed. Sørensen (1968), p. 31.

SALMON, J. J. A., 'La Conférence diplomatique sur le réaffirmation et le développement du droit international humanitaire et les guerres de liberation nationale', 12 *Revue belge de droit international* (1976), 27.

SANBORN, M. H., 'Standing Before the International Court of Justice: The Question of Palestinian Statehood Exemplifies the Inconsistencies of the Requirement of Statehood', 7 *California Western International Law Journal*, (1977), 454.

SCHACHTER, 'Interpretation of the Charter in the Political Organs of the United Nations', *Law, State and International Order: Essays In Honour of Hans Kelsen* (1964), p. 269.

—— 'The Relation of Law, Politics and Action in the United Nations', 109 *HR* (1063), 169.

SCHOENBORN, W., 'La Nature juridique du territoire', 30 *HR* (1929), 85.

SCHOU, P., 'Le Rôle du territoire dans le droit international', *Nordisk Tidsskrift for International Ret* (Acta Scandinavica Juris Gentium 10, 1939), 17.

SCHWARZENBERGER, G., 'Fundamental Principles of International Law', 87 *HR* (1955), 195.

—— 'International Jus Cogens', 43 *Texas Law Review* (1965) 455.

—— 'Title to Territory: Response to a Challenge', *International Law in the Twentieth Century*, ed. Gross (1969), p. 287.

SCHWEBEL, S., 'Aggression, Intervention and Self-Defence in Modern International Law', 136 *HR* (1972), 411.

—— 'Wars of Liberation as Fought in UN Organs', *Law and Civil War in the Modern World*, ed. Moore (1974), p. 446.

SCHWELB, E., 'Neue Etappen der Fortentwicklung des Völkerrechts durch die Vereinten Nationen', *Archiv des Völkerrechts*, 13 (1966) 25.

—— 'Some Aspects of the International Covenants on Human Rights of December 1966', *Proceedings of the Nobel Symposium*, 7 (1968), 111.

—— 'The International Court of Justice and Human Rights Clauses of the Charter', 66 *AJIL* (1972), 337.

— 'The Nuclear Test Ban Treaty and International Law', 58 *AJIL* (1964), 654.

SEATON, E. E., and MALITI, S. T. M., 'Treaties and Succession of States and Governments in Tanzania', *African Conference on International Law and African Problems* (1967), p. 76.

SEYERSTED, F., 'International Personality of Inter-Governmental Organisations', 4 *IJIL* (1964), 55.

SHAW, M. N., 'Dispute-Settlement in Africa', *Year Book of World Affairs* (1983), 149.

—— 'International Status of National Liberation Movements, *Liverpool Law Review* (1983), 19.

—— 'Territory in International Law', 13 *Netherlands Yearbook of International Law* (1982), 61.

—— 'Western Sahara Case', 49 *BYBIL* (1978), 119.

SHEPHERD, G. W., 'National Integration and the Southern Sudan' 4 *JMAS* (1966), 193.

SILVERBURG, S. R., 'The Palestine Liberation Organisation in the United Nations: Some Implications for International Law and Relations', 12 *Israel Law Review* (1977), 365.

SINCLAIR, I., 'Principles of International Law Concerning Friendly Relations and Co-operation among States', *Essays on International Law in Honour of Krishna Rao* (1976), p. 107.

SKUBISZEWSKI, K., 'Enactment of Law by International Organisations', 41 *BYBIL* (1965–6), 198.

—— 'Use of Force by States', *Manual of Public International Law*, ed. Sørensen (1968), p. 739.

SLOAN, B., 'Human Rights, and United Nations and International Law', *Nordisk Tidsskrift for International Ret* (Acta Scandinavica Juris Gentium 20, 1950), 30.

SOHN, L., 'The Stockholm Declaration on the Human Environment', 14 *Harvard International Law Journal* (1973), 423.

STARUSHENKO, G. B., 'Principle of National Self-Determination', *Soviet Foreign Policy* (1963), p. 162.

STARKE, J. G., 'The Acquisition of Title to Territory by Newly Emerged States', 41 *BYBIL* (1965–6), 411.

STRUPP, K., 'Les Règles générales du droit de la paix', 47 *HR* (1934), 264.

SUKOVIC, O., 'The Colonial Question in the Charter and in the Practice of the UN', *International Problems of the Institute of Political Economy* (1966), p. 73.

SUZUKI, E., 'Self-Determination and World Public Order: Community Response to Territorial Separation', 16 *Virginia Journal of International Law* (1976), 779.

TAGIL, L S., 'The Study of Boundaries and Boundary Disputes', *African Boundary Disputes*, ed. Widstrand (1969), p. 22.

TOLEN, A., 'Les Implications internationales de la politique d'apartheid', 69 *Présence africaine* (1969), 164.

TOUSSAINT, C. E., 'The Colonial Controversy in the United Nations, 10 *YBWA* (1956), 177.

TOUVAL, S., 'African Frontiers', 42 *International Affairs*, (1966), 641.
—— 'The Organisation of African Unity and African Borders', 21 *International Affairs*, (1967), 102.
—— 'The Sources of Status Quo and Irredentist Policies', *African Boundary Problems, ed. Widstrand* (1969), p. 111.
—— 'Treaties, Borders and the Partition of Africa', 7 *Journal of African History* (1966), 279.
TUNKIN, G. I., 'Remarks on the Juridical Nature of Customary Norms of International Law, 49 *California Law Review* (1961), 419.
UDINA, M., 'La Succession des États quant aux obligations inter nationales autres que les dettes publiques', 44 *HR* (1933), 704.
UMOZURIKE, U. O., 'International Law and Self-Determination in Namibia, 8 *JMAS* (1970), 585.
UZOIGWE, G. N., 'Spheres of Influence and the Doctrine of the Hinterland in the Partition of Africa', 3 *Journal of African Studies*, (1976), 183.
VALLAT, F. A., 'The Competence of the United Nations General Assembly', 97 *HR* (1959), 211.
—— 'The General Assembly and the Security Council of the United Nations', 29 *BYBIL* (1952), 63.
VAN ASBECK, F. M., 'International Law and Colonial Administration', *Transactions of the Grotius society* (1953), 5.
VERDROSS, A., 'Jus Dispositivum and Jus Cogens in International Law', 60 *AJIL* (1966), 55.
VIRALLY, M., 'Droit international et décolonisation', *AFDI* (1963), 563.
VON DER HEYDTE, F. A. F., 'Discovery, Symbolic Annexation and Virtual Effectiveness in International Law', 29 *AJIL* (1935), 448.
WALDOCK, C. H. M., 'Disputed Sovereignty in the Falkland Island Dependencies', 25 *BYBIL* (1948), 342.
—— 'The Plea of Domestic Jurisdiction before International Legal Tribunals', 31 BYBIL (1954),96.
—— 'The Evolution of Human Rights Concepts and the Application of the European Convention on Human Rights', *Mélanges offerts à Paul Reuter* (1981), p. 535.
—— 'The Regulation of the Use of Force by Individual States in International Law', 81 *HR* (1952), 455.
WEISSBERG, G., 'Maps as Evidence in International Boundary Disputes: A Reappraisal', 57 *AJIL* (1963), 781.
WENGLER, W., 'L'Interdiction de recourir à la force', *Revue belge de droit international* (1971), 401.
WILD, P. B., 'The Organisation of African Unity and the Algerian–Moroccan Border Conflict', 20 *International Organisation* (1966), 18.
WITTEN, R. M., 'The Friendly Relations Declaration', 12 *Harvard International Law Journal* (1971), 509.
WODIE, F., 'La Sécession du Biafra et le doit international public', 73 *Revue générale de droit internationale public* (1969), 1021.

WRIGHT, Q., 'National Courts and Human Rights—The Fujii Case', 45 *AJIL* (1951), 73.
—— 'Recognition and Self-Determination', *PASIL* (1954), 23.
—— 'Some Thoughts about Recognition', 44 *AJIL*(1950), 549.
—— 'The Goa Incident', 56 *AJIL* (1962), 617.
—— 'The Middle East Crisis', 64 *AJIL* (1970), 74.
—— 'The Strengthening of International Law', 98 *HR* (1959), 182.
—— 'United States Intervention in the Lebanon', 53 *AJIL* (1959), 112.
ZARTMAN, I. W., 'A Disputed Frontier is Settled', 8 *Africa Report* (1963), 13.
—— 'The Foreign and Military Politics of African Boundary Problems', *African Boundary Problems*, ed. Widstrand (1969), p. 81.
—— 'The Politics of Boundaries in North and West Africa', 3 *JMAS* (1965), 155.
ZEMANEK, K., 'State Succession After Decolonisation', 116 *HR* (1965), 180.

Table of Cases

Index

The manufacturer's authorised representative in the EU for product safety is Oxford University Press España S.A. of El Parque Empresarial San Fernando de Henares, Avenida de Castilla, 2 - 28830 Madrid (www.oup.es/en or product.safety@oup.com). OUP España S.A. also acts as importer into Spain of products made by the manufacturer.
Printed and bound by CPI Group (UK) Ltd, Croydon, CR0 4YY
14/09/2026
02216290-0003